Baedeker's

ITALY

P9-DHP-519

Hints for using the Guide

Following the tradition established by Karl Baedeker in 1846, sights of particular interest, outstanding buildings, works of art, etc., as well as good hotels and restaurants are distinguished by stars as follows: especially worth attention★, outstanding★★.

To make it easier to locate the various places listed in the "A to Z" section of the Guide, their co-ordinates on the large map of Italy are shown in red at the head of each entry: e.g., Rome G12.

Coloured lines down the right-hand side of the page are an aid to finding the main heading in the Guide: blue stands for the Introduction (Nature, Culture, History, etc.), red for the "A to Z" section, and yellow indicates Practical Information.

Only a selection of hotels and restaurants can be given; no reflection is implied therefore on establishments not included.

In a time of rapid change it is difficult to ensure that all the information given is entirely accurate and up-to-date, and the possibility of error can never be entirely eliminated.

Although the publishers can accept no responsibility for inaccuracies and omissions, they are constantly endeavouring to improve the quality of their Guides and are therefore always grateful for criticisms, corrections and suggestions for improvement.

Preface

This guide to Italy is one of the new generation of Baedeker guides.

These guides, illustrated throughout in colour, are designed to meet the needs of the modern traveller. They are quick and easy to consult, with the principal places of interest described in alphabetical order, and the information is presented in a way that is both attractive and easy to follow.

The subject of this guide is Italy, including the Italian islands and archipelagoes, also the Republic of San Marino and Vatican City with St Peter's Basilica.

The guide is in three parts. The first gives a general account of the country, its population, economy, history, art and culture and a number of suggested routes. The second part describes the places and features of tourist interest – cities and towns, the different regions and islands. The third part contains a variety of practical information. Both the sights and the practical information are listed in alphabetical order.

The Isle of Capri in the Gulf of Naples

The new Baedeker guides are noted for their concentration on essentials and their convenience of use. They contain numerous specially drawn plans and colour illustrations; and at the end of the book is a large map making it easy to locate the various places described in the "A to Z" section of the guide with the help of the co-ordinates given at the head of each entry.

Contents

Baedeker Specials

Benvenut

The tourist's yearning to visit Italy goes back over many years. "The lan where the lemon trees blossom" enjoyed a marked rise in popularity in th eighteenth and nineteenth centuries, when famous writers such as Dan Defoe, Horace Walpole, Lord Byron, Shelley, Keats and Wordsworth all wax lyrical about the country's many delights. At that time the main reaso behind this new-found surge of interest were an eagerness to improve th mind coupled with a romantic enthusiasm, but these soon changed as mo and more people began to travel abroad. As well as cultural and scenic attra tions visitors also came simply to enjoy the "dolce far niente", idle bliss under the southern sun.

However, the charm and attraction of the Appenine peninsula did not come about just by chance; for many centuries Italy had played a major role in the development of the western world. Its early civilisation began with the emergence of the mysterious Etruscans. Where they came from nobody really knows; what is clear is that it was they who inspired the Romans in the fields of culture and art. By the second century AD the latter had established a vast empire from which great wealth flowed back to the mother country. The legacy of those times can still be seen today in some of the country's classical sights and monuments.

Then, for a time, there was compara-

A land
where the lemon trees blossom

Taormina
An ancient theatre near Etna

Venice
The Italian dream destination

amici!

...ve quiet in this land between the Alps and Sicily, until it produced the flowering of the Renaissance in about 1350. New forms of cultural expression were demanded by the citizens of northern Italy, and the architect, sculptor and artist, usually dependent on support from a rich patron, now proudly and personally submitted their work to a critical public. Cities such as Venice, Pisa or Siena remain glittering highlights of a journey through an Italy reborn.

As well as wishing to improve the mind and enjoy the history and romance of the country, later visitors began to seek the natural and scenic pleasures

that Italy has to offer. So, from about 1850 onwards, a tourist trade developed, initially along the romantic lakes and coasts of northern Italy where visitors from Europe in particular could spend the winter in a pleasant climate and surroundings.

Finally, Italy is the home of Bacchus, the Roman god of wine and fruitfulness, and this is evident in every province in the country. It is this exciting mix of art, culture and the culinary arts that makes this Mediterranean peninsula so attractive. The abundance of places to visit and things to savour is so vast that no tourist can ever hope to do more than touch on the vast riches that Italy has to offer. Not for nothing do Italians say "arriverderci" when taking their leave of you – come back again to beautiful Italy.

Volterra
Relief on the cathedral façade

Augustus
One of the important Caesars of Rome

Siena
The Torre del Mangia in the Palazzo Pubblico

**Nature, Culture
History**

Facts and Figures

General

Italy, the central of three south European land masses, in the shape of a boot, stretches like a giant breakwater 1000 km (629 mi.) long into the Mediterranean, linking the Alpine chain with Africa. The Apennine Peninsula together with Sicily and Sardinia surrounds the Tyrrhenian Sea to the west of the Mediterranean. Its central location at the intersection of several European and African regions makes Italy an important link between the various geographical areas.

At the Strait of Otranto (the entrance from the Ionian Sea to the Adriatic Sea) near the south-eastern "heel" Italy lies only 73 km (45 mi.) from the Balkan Peninsula. In the Strait of Tunis a mere 70 km (43 mi.) separates the island of Pantelleria from North Africa.

The land border of some 1000 km (620 mi.) mainly follows the natural line, namely, the main ridge of the Alps. The Italian coasts on the Ariatic and Ionian Seas, together with those of the Tyrrhenian and Ligurian Seas, link the country to its Mediterranean neighbours along a length of over 8600 km (5300 mi.).

The national territory of Italy extends over nearly eleven degrees of latitude from 47° 5'N at its northernmost point in the Ahm Valley, to Cape Passeno, 1200 km (750 mi.) south of Sicily, at 35° 29' 24". From west to east the peninsula covers over twelve degrees of longitude, from the Alpi Cozie at 6° 32' 59" to Cape Otranto on its "heel" at 18° 31' 18"E.

Anyone wishing to drive from the Brenner Pass to the "toe" of the boot at Reggio di Calabria must cover some 1500 km (930 mi.) in total. It is nearly 700 km (435 mi.) from the French border to Trieste.

Italy has a total area of 301,302 sq. km (116,333 sq. mi.).

San Marino

In northern central Italy is the tiny independent republic of San Marino, an enclave that has a treaty of friendship with Italy.

Regions and provinces

The Republic of Italy is divided into 20 regions (regioni) and 95 provinces (province). The autonomous regions of Trentino–Alto Adige, Valle d'Aosta, Friuli–Venezia Giulia, Sardinia and Sicily have a special status (statuto speciale). These are predominantly regions inhabited by other ethnic groups with their own language as well as by Italians (Alto Adige, Valle d'Aosta), or by Italians with their own local dialect (Friuli–Venezia Giulia, Sardinia).

Lombardia (Lombardy)
Bergamo (BG), Brescia (BS), Como (CO), Cremona (CR), Milano (Milan; MI), Mantova (Mantua; MA), Pavia (PV), Sondrio (SO), Varese (VA)

Trentino–Alto Adige
Bolzano (BZ), Trento (TN)

◄ *San Gimignano, one of the most attractive little towns in Tuscany*

General

Italy
Repubblica
Italiana

(I)

- Boundaries of regions
- ● Capitals of regions

Veneto (Venezia Euganea)
Belluno (BL), Padova (Padua; PD), Rovigo (RO), Treviso (TV), Venezia (Venice; VE), Verona (VR), Vicenza (VI)

Friuli–Venezia Giulia
Gorizia (GO), Pordenone (PN), Trieste (TS), Udine (UD)

Piemonte (Piedmont)
Alessandria (AL), Asti (AT), Cuneo (CU), Novara (NO), Torino (Turin; TO), Vercelli (VC)

Valle d'Aosta/Val d'Aoste
Aosta (AO)

Liguria
Genova (Genoa; GE), Imperia (IM), La Spezia (SP), Savona (SV)

Emilia–Romagna
Bologna (BO), Ferrara (FE), Forlé (FO), Modena (MO), Parma (PR),
Piacenza (PC), Ravenna (RA), Reggio nell'Emilia (RE)

Toscana (Tuscany)
Arezzo (AR), Firenze (Florence; FI), Grosseto (GR), Livorno (LI), Lucca
(LU), Massa-Carrara (MS), Pisa (PI), Pistoia (PT), Siena (SI)

Marche (Marches)
Ancona (AN), Ascoli Piceno (AP), Macerata (MC), Pesaro e Urbino (PS)

Umbria
Perugia (PG), Terni (TR)

Lazio (Latium)
Frosinone (FR), Latina (LT), Rieti (RI), Roma (Rome; ROMA), Viterbo
(VT)

Abruzzo (Abruzzi)
Chieti (CH), L'Aquila (AQ), Pescara (PE), Teramo (TE)

Molise
Campobasso (CB), Isernia (IS)

Campania
Avellino (AV), Benevento (BN), Caserta (CE), Napoli (Naples; NA),
Salerno (SA)

Puglia (Apulia)
Bari (BA), Brindisi (BR), Foggia (FG), Lecce (LE), Taranto (TA)

Basilicata
Matera (MT), Potenza (PZ)

Calabria
Catanzaro (CZ), Cosenza (CS), Reggio di Calabria (RC)

Note: since 1992 there have been changes in administrative divisions; some provinces have been added.

Sicilia (Sicily)
Agrigento (AG), Caltanissetta (CL), Catania (CT), Enna (EN), Messina
(ME), Palermo (PA), Ragusa (RG), Siracusa (Syracuse; SR), Trapani
(TR)

Sardegna (Sardinia)
Cagliari (CA), Nuoro (NU), Oristano (OR), Sassari (SS)

State and government

Since the national referendum of June 2nd 1946, which put an end to
the monarchy (the House of Savoy), Italy has been a democratic and
parliamentary republic, the Repubblica Italiana. The Italian Parliament
(Parlamento) consists of two chambers, the House of Representatives
(Camera dei Deputati) and the Senate (Senato). The 630 members of
the House of Representatives are elected in a general election held
every five years; the 320 members of the Senate are elected on a
regional basis, also for five years. The Parliament is a legislative body
which is also responsible for controlling the executive.

The President of the Republic, whose functions are mainly of a
representative nature, is elected for a seven-year term by both houses

of Parliament together with three additional delegates from each region.

The government consists of the Prime Minister (Presidente del Consiglio) and other ministers, who together form the Cabinet (Consiglio dei Ministri). There is a Constitutional Court (Corte Costituzionale) responsible for ensuring that the requirements of the constitution are observed.

The capital of Italy is Rome, situated in Central Italy some 20 km (12 mi.) inland from the coast of the Tyrrhenian Sea. It is the seat of the President (in the Palazzo del Quirinale), the government and both houses of Parliament (the Senate in the Palazzo Madama, the House of Representatives in the Palazzo di Montecitorio).

Capital

Within the territory of Rome is the tiny state of Vatican City (Stato della Città del Vaticano), of which the Pope is sovereign.

Vatican City

Italy is a member of the United Nations (UN) and its subsidiary organisations, a founder member of the European Community (EC) and a member of the Council of Europe, Western European Union (WEU), the Organisation of Economic Cooperation and Development (OECD), the North Atlantic Treaty Organisation (NATO) and many other international organisations. It has a military assistance agreement with Malta.

International commitments

Population

Italy has a population of 57 million and a population density of around 189 inhabitants per sq. km (490 per sq. mi.). Densities, apart from the concentrations of population round Rome and the Bay of Naples, are higher in the industrial north than in the south, although the birth rate is higher in the south. The most thinly populated areas are the Alpine regions, Umbria, the Basilica, parts of Calabria, and Sardinia. The balance is maintained as a result of immigration and emigration, and the trend to urbanisation is still discernible.

Almost all Italians belong to the Roman Catholic church, and the (sometimes naïve) religious faith of the population is reflected in the social structure. However, Catholicism has not been the State religion since 1984 and attending religious instruction classes in schools is now a matter of personal decision. The family bond is generally stronger in Italy than in other European countries, though the position of women is now increasingly in process of radical change (divorce having been possible since 1970).

Religion

In addition to Italians in the narrower sense the population includes many people belonging to other ethnic groups. They are found mainly in border regions or on islands, and they speak the language of the neighbouring country or a local dialect as well as Italian. The largest group is the 1.5 million Sardinians, who speak Sard; and Sardinia also has numbers of Catalan-speakers, particularly in and around the town of Alghero (L'Alguer in Catalan). Another minority is the Rhaeto-Romanic group (750,000), to which the Friulians and Ladins belong; Friulian, a Rhaeto-Romanic dialect, is spoken in the Friuli–Venezia Giulia region. There are 300,000 German-speakers in the Alto Adige (in German called Südtirol, Southern Tirol), where German is now recognised as an official language, after many years of repression. The Alto Adige also has a number of Ladins, speaking their own dialect. In the Aosta valley, which has changed its political allegiance several times in the course of its history, and in Piedmont there are 200,000 Franco-Provençals, who speak French or a Franco-Provençal dialect. In the

Ethnic groups

13

Valle d'Aosta region, by law, French has equal status with Italian. In Trieste, near the Italian–Yugoslav frontier, there are over 50,000 Slovenes. There are an Albanian minority in Calabria and a Greek minority in Apulia.

The inhabitants of areas in which another language as well as Italian is spoken have long been concerned to secure the right of self-government, and a number of regions have been granted a special status giving them autonomy in domestic affairs.

Economy

In the later Middle Ages Italy enjoyed great economic prosperity. Its port towns, in particular Venice and Genoa, achieved economic predominance in the Mediterranean through their commercial participation in the Crusades, and Italian merchants established trading companies *(commendie)* to carry on their extensive foreign business. Double-entry book-keeping was an Italian invention, and many financial terms come from Italian. Italy retained its leading place in commerce and finance into the 16th century.

Modern Italy

After the Second World War Italy enjoyed a sharp economic upswing, developing from an agricultural into an industrial state. This development was promoted by various forms of government assistance, particularly in the field of heavy industry.

Italy is now one of the world's leading industrial nations. Only about 8 per cent of the working population is engaged in agriculture, producing only about 3 per cent of the gross domestic product, while around a third is employed in industry, contributing 32 per cent of the gross domestic product. 60 per cent of the working population is engaged in commerce and the service industries contributing 65 per cent of the gross domestic product.

The unemployment rate is around 11–12 per cent.

In 1992–3 Italy entered a period of economic crisis. Although the economy appears to be recovering since 1994, many problems remain, such as the high national debt, the annual budget deficit of some 10 per cent of the gross national product, excessive demands on the social system, an inflated bureaucracy, loss-making nationalised industries, privatisation, the black market and tax evasion which is well in excess of the EU average.

History

Prehistory and early historical times (*c.* 2000 to 400 BC)

The name of Italia (from Latin *vituli,* "bull calves", sons of the bull god) was first applied by the Greeks to the south-western tip of the peninsula; it was extended only in Roman Imperial times to mean the whole territory as far as the Alps. The names of the original inhabitants have sometimes been preserved in modern place-names. Italy was occupied by man in the palaeolithic period.

Early Metal Age in northern Italy: Remedello culture (copper daggers), named after the find-spot near Brescia.	1800–1600
Bronze Age: Terramare culture (Italian *terramara* = "earth mound") in northern Italy, with fortified villages of pile dwellings.	1600–1200
Migrations of Indo-European peoples coming from the north. The Italic peoples break up into the Latin group, to which the Romans belong, and the Umbro-Sabellian group, to the main branch of which, the Oscans, the Samnites of Campania belong. Other Oscan tribes later move into southern Italy and Sicily.	from 1200
An Illyrian people, the Veneti, move into the Veneto.	from 1000
The Iron Age Villanovan culture, developed by an Indo-European people (named after the type site near Bologna).	1000–500
The Etruscans, apparently coming from Asia Minor, move into Etruria (Tuscia, Tuscany), Campania and the Po plain. Confederation of twelve cities on the Ionian model; active trade, centred on Felsina (Bologna), with central and northern Europe; highly developed cult of the dead (cemeteries). The Etruscans bring to Italy the culture and art of Greece and Asia Minor, technology and administrative skills.	900–500
Establishment of naval bases in western Sicily and Sardinia by the Phoenicians in order to protect their sea trading routes in the western Mediterranean.	from 800
The Greeks establish colonies in southern Italy and Sicily (Magna Graecia): Kyme (Cumae), Neapolis (Naples), Kroton (Crotone), Taras (Taranto), Akragas (Agrigento), Rhegion (Reggio di Calabria), Syracuse and many more. Conflicting commercial interests lead to wars with the Carthaginians and Etruscans. Development of the Latin alphabet from the Greek alphabet.	750–550
Building of temples in Magna Graecia (remains at Segesta, Selinunte, Agrigento, Paestum, etc.).	600–400
Tyranny (absolute rule) of Gelo and Hiero I in Syracuse, now the dominant power in the western Greek territories. Aeschylus and Pindar at Hiero's court.	485–467

Roman rule (753 BC–AD 476)

Rome, at first merely a city state, wins control, in spite of the resistance of the Italic peoples, of the whole of the Italian mainland, then of the islands, and finally of western Europe and the East. Under Roman generals and later under the Emperors, ruling with absolute power, the Roman Empire is held together and defended for centuries against attacks by neighbouring peoples. The spread of Christianity and urban life provide the basis for the cultural development of western Europe.

753	Legendary foundation of Rome (probably from Etruscan *Rumlua*) by Romulus, a descendant of the Trojan Aeneas. (Settlement on Palatine as early as *c.* 900).
600–510	Rome is ruled by the Etruscan Tarquins until the establishment of the Republic in 510.
c. 400	The Celts invade northern Italy. The Romans are defeated in the battle of the River Allia (387/386).
396–280	Rome conquers central Italy and ensures control of its territory by the building of military roads and the foundation of military colonies. Latinisation of the Italic peoples.
c. 378	Rebuilding of Rome after its destruction by the Gauls and erection of walls round the seven hills.
312	Construction of the Via Appia, a military road to Capua, later extended to Brundisium (Brindisi).
c. 300–146	Extension of Roman rule to northern Italy, southern Italy and Sicily. In the three Punic Wars Carthage is defeated and its dominant role in the western Mediterranean is taken over by Rome.
229–64	By conquering Macedonia, Greece and Asia Minor Rome gains control of the eastern Mediterranean. Exploitation of the provinces, use of slave labour, development of a monetary economy, increased Hellenistic influence (assimilation of Greek and Oriental culture), increasing luxury.
220	Construction of the Via Flaminia to Rimini; extended in 187 to Placentia (Piacenza).
133–30	Civil wars, caused by increasing impoverishment of the peasants, and slave risings reveal grave shortcomings in the state.
113–101	Wars with Cimbri and Teutons.
58–51	Caesar conquers Gaul.
45 BC	Caesar becomes sole ruler (murdered March 14th 44); end of Republic.
30 BC–AD 14	Augustus establishes the Empire (Principate) and maintains peace both internally and externally (the Pax Augusta). Cultural flowering (Virgil, Horace, Ovid) and much building activity in Rome. The Empire is romanised.
AD 14–195	The Roman Empire reaches its greatest extent.
64	Burning of Rome. Nero initiates the first persecution of Christians.
79	Pompeii and Herculaneum are destroyed in a great eruption of Vesuvius.
from 220	Arabs, Germans, Persians and others attack the frontiers of the Empire.
303	Last and greatest persecution of Christians in the reign of Diocletian.

Constantine the Great grants freedom of worship to Christians (Edict of Milan).	313
Constantine makes Byzantium capital of the Roman Empire under the name of Constantinople.	330
The Huns thrust into Europe: beginning of the great migrations.	*c.* 375
Theodosius makes Christianity the state religion.	391
Division of the Empire by Theodosius into the Western Empire (capital Ravenna) and the Eastern Empire.	395
The Visigoths, led by Alaric, take Rome.	410
Devastation by the Huns in the Po plain.	452
Sack of Rome by the Vandals, led by Gaiseric.	455
Romulus Augustulus, the last Western Roman Emperor, is deposed by the Germanic general Odoacer.	476

Early Middle Ages and the German emperors (493–1268)

The Great Migrations of the Germanic peoples have a profound effect on the development of western and southern Europe. In spite of the Great Schism (1045) Byzantium remains in contact with the West, on which it exerts a strong influence, through its possessions in southern Italy. The attempts by German kings and emperors to re-establish the unity of Italy founder mainly on the resistance of the Papacy: the Investiture conflict.

Theodoric the Great, with the authority of the Eastern Roman Emperor, founds an Ostrogothic kingdom in Italy, with Ravenna, Pavia and Verona as capitals.	493–526
Justinian makes Italy a province (exarchate) of the Eastern Roman Empire.	535–553
Lombard kingdom in northern Italy (Lombardy: capital Pavia). Tuscia, Spoleto and Benevento become Lombard duchies.	568–774
The Carolingian King Pepin defeats the Lombards and compels them to recognise Frankish suzerainty. The Exarchate of Ravenna and the Pentapolis (Ancona, Rimini, Pesaro, Fano and Senigallia) are handed over to the Pope.	754–756
Charlemagne conquers the Lombard kingdom and unites it with his Frankish kingdom; the duchies, with the exception of Benevento, become Frankish marquisates.	773–774
Charlemagne is crowned Emperor in Rome.	800
The Magyars move into the Po plain for the first time.	827
The Saracens, coming from Tunisia, conquer Sicily, which becomes an independent emirate in 948 and enjoys a great cultural flowering (capital Palermo).	827–901
Fighting between native and Frankish nobles for the Lombard crown.	887–1013

History

899	The Magyars plunder northern Italy.
951	The German Emperor, Otto the Great, is appealed to for help by Adelheid, widow of the Lombard king, and gains control of northern Italy. Beginning of German intervention in Italian affairs.
962	Otto I is crowned Emperor in Rome.
951–1268	Italy ruled by the German Emperors. Perpetual conflicts with the Popes, native rulers and the towns. Formation of two parties – the Ghibellines, who support the Emperor, and the Guelfs, who support the Pope.
982	The Arabs inflict an annihilating defeat on Otto II at Cotrone.
1000–1200	Southern Italy and Sicily are united by the Normans in a new kingdom. Although this puts an end to Byzantine and Arab rule their cultural influence continues.
1059	The Pope invests the Norman Duke Robert Guiscard with southern Italy and Sicily (not yet conquered).
1076–1122	In the Investiture conflict, the decisive confrontation between the Empire and the Papacy, the Pope breaks free of the influence of the Emperor and turns to the rising Latin states.
1077	The excommunicated Emperor Henry IV travels to Canossa as a penitent and humbles himself before the Pope.
c. 1110	Foundation of a medical school at Salerno.
1119	Foundation of the first university in Europe at Bologna.
1130	After the union of southern Italy and Sicily Roger II is crowned king in Palermo. Heyday of the Norman/Saracen culture.
1154–77	Frederick I Barbarossa tries to secure recognition of his suzerainty from the Lombard towns, but after a defeat at Legnano in 1176 is compelled to recognise their privileges. He becomes reconciled with Pope Alexander III in 1177.
1186	Henry VI marries Constance, heiress of the Norman kingdom. The struggle between the Emperor and the Pope is exacerbated by the encirclement of the Papal possessions by the Hohenstaufens.
1194–1268	Southern Italy and Sicily under Hohenstaufen rule.
1212–50	Frederick II, crowned Emperor in Rome in 1220, makes the Norman kingdom a rigidly organised absolutist state and a base of imperial power; conflicts with the Papal and Lombard party. Art and learning are fostered.
1222	Foundation of Padua University, followed by Naples University in 1224.

Rise of the city states to the Congress of Vienna (1250–1815)

In a politically fragmented country city states are established, and later also princely states, which rise to great intellectual, cultural and economic importance in Europe and come into conflict with the neighbouring great powers.

Rise of independent states in Italy. The republican constitutions of the towns give place, following internal party strife, to rule by *signorie*. Through the conquest of neighbouring towns a number of larger units are formed:

from 1250

In Milan the Viscontis come to power, and Giangaleazzo Visconti purchases the ducal title. From 1450 the city is ruled by the Sforzas.

Verona is ruled by the Della Scala (Scaliger) family. Dante Alighieri, after his banishment from Florence, lives at their court. In 1387 the Scaligers lose the whole territory to the Viscontis of Milan.

Mantua is ruled by the Gonzaga family.

Venice achieves naval superiority over Genoa and a commanding position in the Levantine trade. In the 13th century it establishes trading posts in the Peloponnese, Crete, Cyprus and elsewhere, and in 1339 begins to expand on to the Italian mainland. Venice has a strictly aristocratic constitution; the Doge is elected for life.

From 1050 Piedmont is ruled by the Counts (from 1416 Dukes) of Savoy.

The aristocratic republic of Genoa develops into an important commercial city, and in 1284 gains possession of Sardinia, Corsica and Elba.

From 1264 Ferrara is ruled by the Este family.

Florence, an important commercial city and the home of large banking houses, gains a democratic constitution in 1282. Around 1400 the Medici rise to prominence and, as ruling princes, to great political influence.

Humanism and the Renaissance. Italian humanists (Dante, Petrarch, Boccaccio, etc.) rediscover ancient literature, which becomes a stimulus to literature and learning.

c. 1250–1600

The Renaissance, concerned with this world rather than the next, finds its principal expression in painting and architecture, but also in science and learning.

Increasing wealth of the cities and princely rulers; luxurious and often unprincipled life of both lay and ecclesiastical rulers; patronage of the arts (Florence, Rome).

From the end of the 16th century the Renaissance spreads to all the courts and great commercial cities of Europe (painters, sculptors and architects, among them Giotto, Raphael, Michelangelo and Leonardo da Vinci).

Naples is ruled by the House of Anjou.

1268–1442

The "Sicilian Vespers": murder or expulsion of all the French in Palermo, and later in the whole of Sicily. The kingdom of Charles of Anjou (1265–85) is reduced to Naples.

1282

Sicily is ruled by the House of Aragon.

1282–1442

Last campaigns of the German Emperors in Sicily.

1310–1452

Unsuccessful attempt by Cola di Rienzo to re-establish the Roman Republic.

1347

Milan becomes the most powerful state in northern Italy.

c. 1350

War of Chioggia, a naval war between Genoa and Venice for supremacy in the Mediterranean. Venice is victorious, and further extends its influence in the East. Genoa turns towards the West.

1378–81

The Aragonese rulers of Sicily succeed in reuniting it with the kingdom of Naples.

1442–1504

In Florence, after the temporary expulsion of the Medici, the Dominican prior Savonarola establishes a republic. In 1498 he is burned at the stake as a heretic.

1494

History

1494–1556	The French attempt, without success, to assert their supremacy in Italy.
1504–1713	Sicily is ruled by the Spanish Habsburgs. A number of risings are repressed by the Spanish viceroys.
1515	Francis I of France takes Milan.
1521–44	The Emperor Charles V fights four wars with Francis I, who is taken prisoner at Pavia in 1515.
1527	Rome is plundered by Charles V's troops (the "Sacco di Roma").
1540	Charles V gives his son Philip II the duchy of Milan, which remains a possession of the Spanish crown until 1700 and together with the kingdom of Naples and Sicily maintains Spanish influence in Italy.
1569	Cosimo de' Medici, Duke of Florence, becomes Grand Duke of Tuscany.
1633	Galileo is compelled by the Roman Inquisition to retract his acceptance of the Copernican picture of the universe.
1703–37	Mantua (1703), Lombardy (1714) and Tuscany (1737) fall into the hands of the Austrian Habsburgs.
1718	After the Turkish War (1714–18) Venice loses its possessions in the Levant and with them its leading position in trade with the East.
1718–20	Victor Amadeus II, Duke of Savoy, receives Sardinia, and with it the title of king.
1719	Herculaneum, buried by the eruption of Vesuvius in AD 79, is rediscovered. Excavations at Herculaneum in 1737, at Pompeii in 1748.
1735–1806	The Bourbons in Naples and Sicily. From 1735 Charles of Bourbon carries through reforms based on the principles of the Enlightenment.
c. 1750	A new national consciousness comes into being in Italy, preparing the way for the liberation and unification movement of the 19th century.
1768	Genoa sells Corsica to France.
1783	Severe earthquake in Messina.
1796	Bonaparte's Italian campaign.
1797	Establishment of the Cisalpine Republic (Milan, Modena, Ferrara, Bologna, Romagna) and the Ligurian Republic (Genoa).
1798	Tiberine Republic (Rome).
1800	Napoleon defeats the Austrians at Marengo.
1805	Napoleon King of Italy; the Ligurian Republic is incorporated in France.
1806	Napoleon's brother Joseph becomes King of Naples, followed in 1808 by his brother-in-law Murat.
1814–15	Congress of Vienna, presided over by Prince Metternich (Austria). The former petty states are re-established.

The Risorgimento to the end of the First World War (1815–1919)

The Napoleonic era had strengthened the newly awakened national consciousness, but it is left to Cavour to bring the idea of an independent national state within sight of realisation. After achieving reunification Italy, like other national states, seeks to promote its imperialistic interests.

Ferdinand IV unites Naples and Sicily in the Kingdom of the Two Sicilies and henceforth styles himself Ferdinand I. 1816

Austrian troops suppress several risings against reactionary governments. The secret society of the Carbonari ("Charcoal-Burners") and the underground republican movement of Giovine Italia (Young Italy) founded by Mazzini in Marseilles lead the fight for unification and liberation. 1820–32

The newspaper which gives its name to the whole unification movement, "Il Risorgimento", appears in Turin. 1847

Revolution in Italy and Sicily, of which King Charles Albert of Sardinia puts himself at the head. After the victory of the Austrian Field-Marshal Radetzky at Custozza and Novara he abdicates in favour of his son Victor Emmanuel II. 1848–49

The process of reunification begins with a rapprochement with France initiated by Count Cavour. 1859–60

The allied army of Sardinia and France defeats Austrian forces at Magenta and Solferino. Austria loses Lombardy to Napoleon III, who cedes it to Sardinia in exchange for Nice and Savoy. 1859

Expulsion of the ruling princes from the states of central and northern Italy. Garibaldi and his irregular forces defeat the Bourbons and occupy the States of the Church. Plebiscites all over the country declare for union with Sardinia. 1860

Victor Emmanuel II becomes king. The first capital of the Kingdom of Italy is Florence. 1861

War with Austria. In spite of defeats at Custozza and Lissa Italy acquires Venice by negotiation. 1866
  Mazzini puts forward Italian claims to Istria, Friuli and South Tirol ("Italia irredenta", "unrecovered Italy").

Rome is occupied by Italian troops and becomes capital of Italy. The Pope retains sovereignty over Vatican City. 1870

Under Umberto I Italy develops into a great power. 1878–1900

Italy forms the Triple Alliance with Germany and Austria–Hungary. 1882

Foundation of the Italian Socialist Party. 1882–83

War with Abyssinia. Italy gains the colonies of Eritrea and Italian Somaliland. 1887–89

Treaty defining Italian and French spheres of influence in Morocco and Tripoli. 1900

War with Turkey. Italy annexes Cyrenaica, Tripoli and the Dodecanese, including Rhodes. 1911–12

Introduction of universal suffrage. 1912

On the outbreak of the First World War Italy declares its neutrality (Aug. 3rd). 1914

History

1915–18	Italy in the First World War.
1915	Secret treaty of London: Italy's colonial and irredentist claims are guaranteed by Britain and France (Apr. 26th). Italy declares war on Austria–Hungary (May 23rd) and Germany (Aug. 28th 1916).
1915–17	Austrian and German troops hold the Isonzo line in eleven battles, and in the twelfth battle of the Isonzo (Oct.–Dec. 1917) break through at Caporetto and reach the Piave.
1918	Italian counter-offensive: collapse of the Austro–Hungarian front at Vittorio Veneto.
1919	Treaty of St-Germain-en-Laye (Sept. 10th): Italy receives South Tirol as far as the Brenner, Istria (apart from Fiume) and a number of Dalmatian islands.

End of the First World War to the present

After the First World War Italy seeks to acquire further territory by an expansionist policy and to overcome the "crisis of democracy" by a new ideology, Fascism. Although during the Second World War it fights on the side of the Allies from 1943 onwards, it has to bear the consequences of the power politics of the Fascist period. After the war the new Republic of Italy is rent by ideological conflict and faced with grave social and economic problems. Internal political developments are influenced by the numerous separate parties with their changing relationships and alliances.

1919–21	Mussolini forms "fighting groups" *(fasci di combattimento)*; growing influence of the Fascists; attacks on Communists, with open violence.
1922	The "March on Rome": Mussolini is granted dictatorial powers by Parliament; the Fascists gradually take over the government.
1923	Beginning of a rigorous policy of assimilation in Alto Adige (South Tirol).
1924	Fiume becomes Italian.
1926	British–Italian agreement on Abyssinia, which is divided into economic spheres of interest. Treaty of Friendship with Spain.
1931	Measures of state control to deal with the economic crisis.
1933	Treaty of Friendship with the Soviet Union.
1934	"Economic Protocol of Rome" between Italy, Austria and Hungary. First meeting between Mussolini and Hitler in Venice.
1935–36	Invasion and annexation of Abyssinia.
1936	Establishment of the "Rome–Berlin Axis" in a treaty with Germany. Italian troops support Franco in the Spanish civil war.
1937	Italy leaves the League of Nations (of which it had been a founder member).
1939	Occupation of Albania (April). Military alliance with Germany.
1939–45	Second World War. Mussolini attempts to mediate, without success. Italy at first remains neutral.

Italy declares war on France and Britain (June 10th). Italian–French armistice signed in Rome (June 24th). Three-power pact with Germany and Japan (Sept. 27th).	1940
Military failures in North Africa; Abyssinia is lost.	1941
Surrender of Italian forces in North Africa (May 13th). Allied landings in Sicily (July 10th). Fall of the Fascist regime; Mussolini is arrested (July 24th). Formation of a new government under Badoglio, who signs an armistice with the Allies (Sep. 3rd) and declares war on Germany (Oct. 13th). Rival government established by Mussolini (freed by a German commando group), who continues the war against the Allies.	1943
Surrender of German forces in Italy (Apr. 28th). Mussolini is shot by partisans. The Christian Democrat party (Democrazia Cristiana, DC) forms a government, led by de Gasperi (until 1953).	1945
King Victor Emmanuel III abdicates. Plebiscite in favour of a Republic (June 18th).	1946
Treaty of Paris: Italy cedes the Dodecanese to Greece and Istria to Yugoslavia; Trieste becomes a free state. Italy renounces its colonies.	1947
A new democratic constitution comes into force. Economic and social disparities between the well developed North of Italy and the under-developed South. After the economic difficulties of the immediate post-war period (Marshall Aid) there is an economic resurgence. Italy joins the Western powers, becoming a founder member of NATO (1949), the European Coal and Steel Community (1951), the European Economic Community (1957), etc.	1948
Partial expropriation of large landowners, with compensation, under the Sila Law.	1950
The Christian Democrats lose their absolute parliamentary majority; thereafter frequent changes of government.	1953
The free state of Trieste is divided between Italy and Yugoslavia.	1954
Rapid increase in emigration from southern Italy to the industrial North and to other countries.	from 1957
Summer Olympic Games in Rome.	1960
Moro (DC) forms the first Centre-Left government. The latent governmental crisis remains unresolved.	1963
Catastrophic floods in northern and central Italy.	1966
Self-government for the Alto Adige (recognition by Austria of the package in June 1992).	1969
Increased contacts with East European and Balkan states.	from 1970
Government of the Centre.	1972
Centre-Left government. Domestic political crisis: balance of payments deficit, inflation, economic crisis.	1973
The world-wide energy crisis and the economic recession hit Italy particularly hard: increasing unemployment, high inflation, foreign debts, etc. New economic programme, frustrated by increasingly	from 1974

acute domestic political crisis, party strife, numerous strikes and acts of terrorism, corruption scandals and kidnappings accompanied by ransom demands.

1975   Final settlement of the Trieste problem.
     Great gains by the Communist party (PCI) in regional, provincial and municipal elections.

1976   Severe earthquake in the provinces of Udine and Pordenone (Friuli; May 6th).
     Minority DC government, dependent on Communist support (June).
     Escape of poisonous gas at Seveso, near Milan (July 10th).

1977   Heavy destruction in street fighting with demonstrating students (Mar. 13th).
     Parliament approves a programme of economic reform, stepping-up of internal security, educational and press policy and regionalisation (July 16th).
     Violent political reactions after a former SS officer named Kappler escapes from the military prison in Rome (Aug. 15th).

1978   Moro, chairman of the Christian Democrats and a former prime minister, is kidnapped on Mar. 13th by members of the "Red Brigades" and found murdered 54 days later. Tightening-up of the laws against terrorism (March).
     Political crisis following the resignation of President Leone (June 15th); the 81-year-old Socialist Pertini is elected to succeed him (July 8th).

1979   Parliamentary elections in June confirm the DC as the strongest party, while the Communists suffer losses. Cossiga forms a new cabinet (minority government of Christian Democrats, Liberals and other parties), the fortieth since the Second World War. The Communists go into opposition. Large increases in the cost of energy.

1980   Death of the Socialist leader Nenni (Jan. 1st).
     Renewed terrorist attacks on judges, politicians and the police.
     A new fiscal regulation requires hotels and restaurants to give all customers receipted bills.
     Since the Socialists and Republicans are no longer willing to support the government by abstaining from voting, Cossiga resigns (Mar. 19th), but at the beginning of April forms a new government composed of Christian Democrats, Socialists and Republicans.
     Economic summit of the leading western industrial nations in Venice (June 22nd–23rd).
     Bomb attack in Bologna railway station kills over 80 people (Aug. 2nd).
     After a vote of no confidence in Parliament Cossiga finally resigns (Sep. 27th).
     The Christian Democrat Arnoldo Forlani forms a new government (Oct. 18th) of Christian Democrats, Socialists, Social Democrats and Republicans, and introduces a programme of economies.
     Severe earthquake in southern Italy, with almost 3000 dead (Nov. 23rd).

1981   The Forlani government wins a vote of confidence.
     The Italian Parliament ratifies a treaty of neutrality with Malta (Apr.).
     Pope John Paul II is dangerously wounded in an attempt on his life in front of St Peter's (May 13th).
     The most important result of referendums on domestic political questions is the retention of the liberal laws on abortion, the anti-terrorist laws and the sentence of life imprisonment (May 17th–18th).

The affair of the P2 freemasonry lodge, whose members are accused of currency frauds and of forming secret quasi-military organisations, leads to the resignation of the Forlani government (May 27th).

The Republican Giovanni Spadolini forms a coalition government of Christian Democrats, Socialists, Republicans, Social Democrats and Liberals (June 28th).

The Italian government give the United States bases for their cruise missiles.

Kidnapping of the American General J.L. Dozier, deputy head of NATO forces in southern Europe, by the Red Brigades (Dec. 17th).

General Dozier is freed by the anti-terrorist police (Jan. 28th).   1982

After two firms terminate a 1975 agreement on the index-linking of wages (the *scala mobile*) there are numerous strikes.

A government decree introduces measures for bringing the budget under control (end July).

Tensions between Socialists and Christian Democrats lead to the res-ignation of the Spadolini government (Aug. 7th).

Spadolini forms a new government (end August).

Resignation of the new Spadolini government (mid November).

Amintore Fanfani (CD) forms Italy's 43rd post-war government, a coalition of Christian Democrats, Socialists, Social Democrats and Liberals (Dec. 1st).

Signature of a "Social Pact" to combat the recession (partial reform of   1983
the *scala mobile*; end Jan.).

The Socialists' withdrawal from the government leads to prime minister Fanfani's resignation (Apr. 29th). President Pertini dissolves Parliament (May 4th).

Socialist gains in parliamentary elections (June 26th–27th). A new government of Socialists, Christian Democrats, Social Democrats, Republicans and Liberals, with the Socialist Bettino Craxi as prime minister, is sworn in (Aug. 4th).

On the basis of a new concordat between the Italian government and   1984
the Vatican Catholicism ceases to be the state religion of Italy, and Rome ceases to be the "holy city" (Feb. 18th).

Francesco Cossiga (DC) is elected President in succession to Sandro   1985
Pertini (June 24th).

Resignation of the Cossiga government following the "Achille Lauro" affair (hijacking of the cruise liner "Achille Lauro" by Palestinians, leading to disagreement with the United States); the five-party coalition government continues in office with Bettino Craxi as prime minister (Oct.).

Italy signs the anti-terrorism convention of the Council of Europe in   1986
Strasbourg (spring).

Following a government defeat in a vote on municipal budgets Craxi resigns (June 27th).

The hijackers of the "Achille Lauro" are sentenced to long terms of imprisonment.

Agreement is reached on the continuation of the five-party govern-ment under Bettino Craxi (July 29th).

Resignation of Craxi (Mar. 3rd); formation of an interim government   1987
(Apr.). In parliamentary elections in June the Christian Democrats gain and the Communists lose votes. Giovanni Goria (DC) becomes prime minister, leading a five-party coalition of Christian Democrats, Socialists, Social Democrats, Republicans and Liberals (July 19th).

Goria resigns (Mar. 11th) and is succeeded by Ciriaco De Mita (DC);   1988
continuation of the five-party coalition.

The government promulgates regulations on autonomy for the Alto Adige (South Tirol), including provision for the use of German in court proceedings (May 13th).

1989

At the beginning of the holiday season large stretches of the Adriatic coast suffer from a plague of algae.

Resignation of the Christian Democrat prime minister, De Mita, since the Socialists have announced that they have joined the five-party coalition (May). On July 23rd Giulio Andreotti forms a new government to which the five parties of the previous coalition belong.

In north Italy the protest movement "Lega Lombarda" (Lombardian League) demands a solution from the central government; at the same time the aim of joining Europe beyond the Alps is declared.

1990

In September Italy joins the Schengen agreement, an association of several West European countries, with the aim of removing all frontier controls within Europe.

1991

In late February large numbers of Albanian refugees flee by ship and arrive at the Italian ports of Brindisi and Otranto; subsequently several thousand are forced to return to their own country.

Resignation of Andreotti's government for politico-financial reasons (end of March). In mid-April Andreotti forms a new cabinet to which the Republicans do not belong (four-party coalition).

In April an oil-tanker explodes and sinks off the Ligurian coast; in a second disaster two ships collide off the Tuscan coast and over 140 people lose their lives.

1992

In parliamentary elections at the beginning of April the ruling coalition (Christian Democrats, Socialists, Social Democrats and Liberals) gain majorities in both the House of Representatives and the Senate. The "Liga Nord" (an amalgamation of the political movements of the north Italian regions of Lombary, Liguria, Piedmont, Friuli-Giulia, Venetia) gain almost 10% of the votes cast; the Christian Democrats, however, lose heavily. At the end of April President Cossiga regigns.

On May 25th, at the 16th ballot, Oscar Luigi Scalfaro (DC), a politician from Piedmont, is elected as the new president of Italy. Giuliano Amato (PS) becomes prime minister (end of July); he forms a four-party coalition government of Christian Democrats (DC), Socialists (PSI), Social Democrats (PSDI) and Liberals (PLI).

Abolition of the "Scala Mobile", the automatic gearing of wages and salaries to the rate of inflation (July 7th).

Start of the greatest ever wave of arrests of Mafia members (Nov. 16th).

1993

Bettino Craxi, leader of the Socialist party, resigns from office following allegations of illegal use of party funds (February). Other politicians are also in the news.

Former prime minister Giuilio Andreotti is investigated on suspicion of complicity with the Mafia. Links between politicians and the Camorra (Naples) are also uncovered.

On April 22nd prime minister Amato resigns from office. He is succeeded by the independent Carlo Azeglio Ciampi, who leads a transitional government. In addition to the conventional parties the cabinet includes for the first time members of the Democratic Party of the Left (PDS) and the "Greens".

In a bomb attack in the centre of Florence six people are killed and government offices damaged (end of May).

Parliament passes an electoral reform bill. More than 100,000 people join in a demonstration in Rome against the government's economic and social policies (September).

On Nov. 1st the Maastrict Treaty comes into force (EU).

In the middle of January Ciampi resigns and President Scalfaro dissolves the Italian parliament. 1994

The former Democrazia Cristiana (DC) party is dissolved and reformed as the Partito Popolare Italiano (PPI: Italian Popular Party).

Formation of the right-wing Alleanza Nazionale and the Alleanza Progressista, a merger of left-wing parties. Pact between the Lega Nord and the Forza Italia movement of Silvio Berlusconi (Feb.)

The parliamentary elections in March are a victory for the right; the coalition of Forza Italia, Lega Nord and Alleanza Nazionale wins a majority of the seats in the lower house, but fails do so in the Senate. The three parties join to form the "Polo della Libertà". Silvio Berlusconi is the new prime minister.

The heads of the seven Western industrial nations (the G7 Group) meet in Naples: politicians from the USA, Japan, Germany, France, Great Britain, Italy and Canada, as well as a Russian delegation led by President Yeltsin.

At the end of July an order is issued for the arrest of Paolo Berlusconi, brother of the prime minister and a member of the family firm of Fininvest Holdings, on bribery and corruption charges. Silvio Berlusconi is under increasing pressure and resigns on Dec. 22nd after seven months in office.

In the middle of January President Scalfaro asks the financial expert Lamberto Dini to form a government, to be composed mainly of "experts". The government under Dini starts work on Jan. 18th. On Jan. 24th the lower house passes a vote of confidence in the new government by a narrow majority; the parties of the right abstain. 1995

In the regional elections (15 of the 20 regions) the centre-left led by the left-wing democrats is victorious. The centre-left parties are also the winners in the final ballot in the provinces.

The position of the "Czar of the media" Berlusconi is strengthened by a referendum held in June in which the majority of the citizens do not wish for any restriction on private television by the state.

At the end of July the CDU (Cristiani Democratici Uniti) party is formed in Rome, as the successor to the right-wing of the PPI (formerly DC) formed in 1994.

Prime minister Dini resigns on Jan. 11th. The left win the parliamentary election of April 21st. The designated prime minister Romani Prodi forms a cabinet in which ministers of the centre-left "Ulivo" (olive tree) alliance form the majority. At numerous political meetings Umberto Bossi, head of the Lega Nord, demands self-government for northern Italy to be known as "Padania". 1996

On Sept. 26th a heavy earthquake shakes Umbria and Marche, causing serious damage. Aftershocks follow. 1997

On April 1st Italy becomes a full member of the Shengen Agreement: the Italian borders now also form the external borders of the EU while the border with Austria becomes virtually extinct. Resignation of prime minister Rodi (October); the new prime minister will be Massimo D'Alema, head of the "Democratic Party of the Left". 1998

Culture

Art

The Italian peninsula, like the rest of the Mediterranean world, has been occupied by man since the remotest times, and over this long period Italy has accumulated an almost incalculable wealth of art treasures. In spite of serious difficulties the Italian authorities have considerable achievements to their credit in the preservation, study and presentation of these treasures.

Prehistory

Remains of the Stone Age are to be found particularly in Sicily and northern Italy, and the museums of Florence, Bologna, Turin, Milan and many smaller towns have much valuable material dating from this period, including domestic utensils, weapons and articles buried in graves from the settlements of pile-dwellings on the North Italian lakes.

Stone Age

Remains of buildings, chambered tombs and standing stones belonging to the Megalithic culture can be seen at Taranto and on the islands of Lampedusa and Pantelleria. On Sardinia there are the curious round towers known as *nuraghi*, and on both Sardinia and Sicily there are remains of the Iberian Beaker culture.

During the Bronze Age Italy appears to have had links with the Creto-Mycenaean culture, as is shown, for example, by finds from Ascoli Piceno. The Terramare culture which came to Italy from Illyria can be ascribed with reasonable certainty to the original Italic population (urn burials).

Bronze Age

The Villanovan culture (Umbrians, Latins), an Iron Age culture which developed out of the Terramare culture in the Po plain and Central Italy (900–400 BC), produced the characteristic situla, a kind of bucket with rich figured decoration which attained its finest form about 500 BC.

Iron Age

The best place to study the cultures of the prehistoric and early historical periods is the Museo Preistorico Etnografico Luigi Pigorini in Rome.

Early civilisations

From the 8th to the 5th century BC the Etruscans (Latin Tusci or Etrusci) occupied a dominant position in central and northern Italy. In addition to numerous local centres there was a confederation of twelve cities to which Velathri (Volterra), Arretium (Arezzo), Curtuns (Cortona), Perusia (Perugia), Camars/Clevsin/Clusium (Chiusi), Rusellae (Roselle), Vatluna (Vetulonia), Volsinii (Orvieto), Vulci, Tarchuna/Tarquinii (Tarquinia), Caere (Cerveteri) and Veii (Veio) belonged. The Etruscans appear to have been a non-Indo-European people of advanced culture who came to Italy from the East. The magnificent works of art they produced are mostly known to us from their tombs (sarcophagi with life-size recumbent terracotta figures from the Banditaccia cemetery, Cerveteri; wall paintings, in a realistic style showing Greek influence, in chamber tombs at Tarquinia and elsewhere). The famous She-Wolf in

Etruscans

◄ *Details of the façade of Ferrara cathedral*

the Capitoline Museum in Rome is also Etruscan work. In architecture the Etruscans had mastered the structure of the true arch and the technique of the barrel vault. Their arts and crafts are represented by an abundance of objects of high quality to be seen in the Archaeological Museum in Florence, the Villa Giulia in Rome and museums in Cerveteri, Chiusi, Tarquinia, Veii, Volterra and many other towns.

Greek colonies

Between the 8th and 5th centuries BC more than forty Greek colonies were founded in Sicily and southern Italy (Greek Megale Hellas, Latin Magna Graecia, "Greater Greece"), including Neapolis (Naples), Poseidonia (Paestum), Metapontion (Metaponto), Taras (Taranto), Kroton (Crotone), Rhegion (Reggio di Calabria), Zankle (Messina), Tauromenion (Taormina), Katana (Catania), Syrakousai (Syracuse), Akragas (Agrigento), Selinus (Selinunte) and Segesta. Unlike the Etruscans, who used wood and terracotta, the Greeks constructed their monumental buildings in marble. The most impressive demonstration of their skill is provided by the temple precinct of Paestum. The Paestum temples, magnificent examples of Doric architecture (metopes from the Temple of Hera in the Paestum Museum), together with the temples of Selinunte and Segesta and the theatres of Syracuse, Catania, Segesta and above all Taormina, give a powerful impression of the beauty, power and nobility of ancient Greek architecture.

Only a few examples of Greek sculpture from southern Italy have been preserved, among them the metopes from Selinunte (in the National Museum, Palermo), a bronze statue of Apollo from Pompeii (in the National Archaeological Museum, Naples), a Medusa head (in the Museo delle Terme, Rome) and the famous Laocoön group (in the Museo Pio-Clementino in the Vatican). Examples of Greek sculpture can also be seen in the National Museum in Reggio di Calabria. Terracotta sculpture is better represented, with numerous examples in various museums in southern Italy.

Etruscan funerary casket (4th c. BC)

Etruscans and Greeks in Italy

● Etruscan Centres

1 Arretium (Arezzo)
2 Velathri (Volterra)
3 Curtuns (Cortona)
4 Perusia (Perugia)
5 Camars/Clevsin/Clusium (Chiusi)
6 Rusellae (Roselle)
7 Vatluna (Vetulonia)
8 Velsna/Volsinii (Orvieto)
9 Velch/Vulci (Vulci)
10 Tarchuna/Tarquinii (Tarquinia)
11 Cisra/Caere (Cerveteri)
12 Veii (Veio)

● Greek Foundations

13 Neapolis (Naples)
14 Poseidonia (Paestum)
15 Metapontion (Metaponto)
16 Taras (Taranto)
17 Kroton (Crotone)
18 Rhegion (Reggio di Calabria)
19 Zankle (Messina)
20 Tauromenion (Taormina)
21 Katana (Catania)
22 Syrakousai (Syracuse)
23 Akragas (Agrigento)
24 Selinus (Selinunte)
25 Segesta

Greek painting is known only from the work of the vase-painters (particularly the black-figure type) and the Hellenistic wall paintings of Pompeii in a later period.

Roman period

Between 400 and 200 BC the Romans became masters of Italy. Originally a people of farmers and warriors, they assimilated the art and culture of the territories they conquered – first of the Etruscans, later of the Greeks and finally of the East.

Buildings

The remains of Roman buildings are to be found all over Europe, in western Asia and North Africa. A vivid impression of Roman life is provided by the remains, excavated from the 18th century onwards, of the towns of Pompeii and Herculaneum, which were buried under layers of lava, ash and cinders by an eruption of Vesuvius in AD 79. Imposing examples of Roman architecture can also be seen in Rome itself (Forum Romanum, etc.), in spite of later destruction and new buildings. Perhaps the main Roman contribution to Western architecture was the development of the method of vaulted construction which the Romans took over from the Etruscans. Roman industrial and commercial buildings can be seen in the excavations of Ostia, the port of ancient Rome.

Forum

The centre of any Roman town was the forum, which served as a market square, a meeting-place and a political arena. In and around the forum were the principal public buildings.

Temple

The Roman temple, which like its Etruscan counterpart is built on a platform, differs from the Greek temple in having only a single

The Roman forum, centre of Roman life

entrance; the cella is usually preceded by an open hall (as in the temple of Fortuna Virilis in Rome).

Another important feature of a Roman town was the basilica (lawcourt), a long pillared hall with the entrance on one of the side walls: a structure which developed into the early Christian churches of basilican type.

Basilica

Roman baths (*thermae*) had cold, warm and hot rooms and were often large and extravagantly luxurious. The church of Santa Maria degli Angeli in Rome, built by Michelangelo, incorporates the tepidarium (warm bath) of the Baths of Diocletian.

Baths

The palaces of the Roman Emperors were large architectural complexes with barrel vaulting and domes, richly decorated with frescoes, mosaics and festoons and articulated by columns.

Palaces

The Roman theatre developed out of its Greek forerunner. The auditorium was semicircular, and the stage wall became an elaborate architectural structure. Alongside the theatre there developed the amphitheatre, oval in plan, with seating for many thousands of spectators (Colosseum, Rome; Arena, Verona).

Theatres

The triumphal arch was originally a gateway erected for the ceremonial entrance of victorious troops, but developed into an elaborate structure, richly decorated with sculpture, commemorating the victories of Roman emperors (Arches of Constantine, Septimius Severus and Titus in Rome). Triumphal columns served a similar purpose (Trajan's Column, Rome).

Triumphal arches

Roman aqueducts were masterpieces of engineering which carried water into the towns from many miles away, often on a long series of towering arches. The roads and bridges are also impressive demonstrations of Roman technical skill.

Aqueducts

The houses of wealthy Romans were built around an open inner courtyard, the *atrium*, and entered through a hall or *vestibulum*. Along the sides of the houses were private apartments, and to the rear were a pillared courtyard, a dining room and a garden. The interior was richly decorated with frescoes, mosaics and sculpture (often copies of Greek originals); good examples can be seen in Pompeii.

Houses

Roman sculpture was largely based on Greek models, but in the portrait sculpture of the Republican period achieved a remarkable degree of realism. Under the Empire the most imposing form of portrait sculpture, the equestrian statue, came to the fore; the only surviving example is the figure of Marcus Aurelius (AD 179) on the Capitol in Rome.
   Sculptured reliefs were also used to depict great historical events (Trajan's Column and the Ara Pacis in Rome).

Sculpture

Roman painting shows Hellenistic influence. The fine wall paintings of which numerous examples can be seen in Pompeii show great diversity of style; realistic and almost impressionistic grotesques alternate with *trompe-l'oeil* architecture, classical Greek themes, gay bucolic scenes and heroic legends. Mosaics were also used for the decoration of walls and floors (pavement mosaics of "Alexander's Battle" in Pompeii, AD 50).

Painting

Early Christian period

In the Early Christian period the basilican church developed out of the Roman law-court *(basilica)*. The nave, which probably had a flat roof,

Churches

was usually divided into three or five aisles, the central aisle being as a rule higher than the others; the west end faced on to the street, and there was a semi-circular apse at the east end. Externally the basilicas were plain brick buildings, but the interiors were usually sumptuously decorated, showing Byzantine influence. From the 7th century onwards there was usually a separate bell-tower. A small circular baptistery served for adult baptism.

In the reign of Justinian (527–565) churches began to be built also on a circular plan, the model for this new type being the Great Church (Hagia Sophia) in Constantinople. The central feature was the space under the dome, with four barrel-vaulted wings opening off it in the form of a cross. These might also be domed, as in St Mark's in Venice (begun in 830).

Ravenna

Ravenna now became an important political and religious centre, and it still preserves magnificent examples of early Christian and Byzantine art, such as the basilicas of Sant'Apollinare in Classe and Sant'Apollinare Nuovo, the Mausoleum of Galla Placidia and the Baptistery of the Orthodox (both on a centralised plan), and the church of San Vitale, an octagonal structure with a central dome supported on piers. The rows of columns are now spanned by arcades in the Byzantine fashion.

Mosaics

The great achievement of this period in the artistic field was the mosaic decoration of the churches. Byzantine art, subject to strict hierarchical rules, evolved a series of formal prototypes, with no sense of space or perspective, which were set on a golden ground, the symbol of heaven (San Vitale, Sant'Apollinare Nuovo, Mausoleum of Galla Placidia, all in Ravenna).

Catacombs

Mention should also be made of the Roman catacombs; underground burial places constructed on several levels with an extensive system of corridors and passages and frequently decorated with painting on Christian themes.

Sculpture

Christian sculpture began by following pagan models – sarcophagi with carved decoration, figures of Christ depicted as a young man (e.g. the "Good Shepherd", a marble statuette of the 3rd century AD in the Vatican Museum, Rome).

Tomb of Theodoric

The Great Migrations from 400 AD onwards brought a succession of Germanic peoples into Italy – Goths, Vandals, Lombards. The tomb of the Ostrogothic King Theodoric the Great (c. 456–526) in Ravenna, a circular structure roofed with a single massive slab of stone, is one of the few surviving examples of Germanic architecture in stone, though it was undoubtedly based on Roman and Eastern models.

Romanesque

Romanesque architecture developed out of early Christian architecture in the 11th century, with variations in style in different regions. At first Rome remained backward in this field, while the cities of Tuscany vied with one another in building churches in the new style. An early example is San Frediano in Lucca (1112–47), a basilica of rather old-fashioned stamp. About 1050 a new type of façade, with inlaid marble decoration, came into vogue (San Miniato, Florence; pillared arcades of Pisa and Lucca cathedrals). Pisa Cathedral (begun 1063), with its massive transepts, is the most imposing building of this period.

Churches

The Lombard churches of northern Italy show German and Burgundian influence. They are mostly basilicas, with groined vaulting and richly articulated façades (Sant'Ambrogio, Milan; San Zeno, Perugia; cathedrals of Piacenza, Modena, Parma and Ferrara).

In Apulia many fine churches (Barletta and Trani cathedrals; pilgrimage church of San Nicola and Cathedral, Bari; Bitonto Cathedral) were built in Apulian Romanesque, which shows a mingling of Byzantine, Lombard, Norman and even Saracen influences.

In Sicily the Norman influence was less strongly felt than in Apulia, but there are a number of notable buildings of this period in Palermo – the church of San Giovanni degli Eremiti, a building of rather Oriental aspect with its five tall red domes; the Martorana, a beautiful church with fine Byzantine mosaics; San Cataldo, a domed Byzantine church of 1161; and the Cappella Palatina, built by Roger II in 1132–40, with superb mosaic decoration which makes it surely one of the finest of all royal chapels. Monreale Cathedral (c. 1180) is the largest Norman building in Sicily, with a magnificent choir; adjoining it is the largest and most beautiful cloister in the Italian Romanesque style. | Sicily

The secular architecture of this period also has some fine buildings to its credit. In northern Italy, for example, the castles in the Dora Baltea valley and at Canossa, Cannero and Prato, and the defensive towers built by noble families in the towns (e.g. in Bologna). The thirteen towers of San Gimignano and its picturesque town walls are particularly impressive. In central and southern Italy there are also elegant palaces (Palazzo dei Normanni, Palermo; the Cuba and Zisa, showing Saracen influence) and town halls (Orvieto). | Secular buildings

Romanesque sculpture long remained under strong Byzantine influence. From the end of the 11th century the casting of bronze doors with relief decoration reached a consummate degree of skill (San Zeno, Verona; door by Barisanus, Trani Cathedral; doors of Amalfi, Atrani and Salerno cathedrals; door by Bonanus, Pisa Cathedral, 1180). | Sculpture

Sculpture in stone enjoyed a great flowering along with architecture, and Lombard sculptors in particular produced work of the highest quality. The first to undertake large figures was Wiligelmus, who carved the scenes from Genesis on the façade of Modena Cathedral about 1100. Around 1135 Master Niccolò was working on the doorways of Ferrara and Verona cathedrals. | Lombard sculptors

The leading sculptor of the high Romanesque period in northern Italy was Benedetto Antelami, among whose principal works are the "Descent from the Cross" in Parma Cathedral, the bishop's throne in the choir and the outer walls and doorway of the baptistery. French and above all Provençal influences can be detected in his work. | Antelami

There were also notable sculptors in Tuscany, like Guidetto and Guido Begarelli of Como (font in Baptistery, Pisa). In Rome the group known as the Cosmati (from the name Cosmas borne by some of its members), worked on the decoration of churches and religious houses, evolving the distinctive style known as Cosmatesque. | Cosmati

In southern Italy the busts from the Volturno Gate of Capua (now in the Campanian Provincial Museum, Capua) are particularly notable. The Apulian churches also have rich sculptural decoration (episcopal thrones at Canossa and Bari; pulpit, Bitonto). | Southern Italy

Romanesque sculpture reached its final culmination in the work of Nicola Pisano (1225–78), the first artistic personality of the Middle Ages with whom we have any real acquaintance, who bases himself on ancient models (marble pulpits in the Baptistery, Pisa, 1260, and in Siena Cathedral, 1268; fountain outside Perugia Cathedral). | Pisano

The painting of the Romanesque period is dominated by Byzantine influence (the *maniera greca*); and the mosaics of Venice and those | Painting produced in Sicily in the 12th century are still wholly within the Byzantine tradition. The leading master of Romanesque painting, who towards the end of the 13th century sought to break away from the old rigid tradition and thus prepared the way for Giotto, was Giovanni Cimabue (mentioned in 1272 and 1301–02; "Madonna Enthroned with Angels", Uffizi, Florence).

Gothic

Italy entered its Gothic period at a time when French Gothic had already passed its peak. But the older traditions were never entirely forgotten; reflected in countless buildings which still survive, the inheritance from the East (*maniera greca* or *maniera bizantina*) made its way into Europe by way of Italy. Alongside all these various influences, however, there now began to emerge new and distinctively Italian creative forces which were to extend their influence over the whole of Europe.

Italian art first begins to show distinctive national characteristics in the age of Dante, at the end of the 13th century. Thereafter the centuries are known by the following names:

Duecento = 13th century
Trecento = 14th century
Quattrocento = 15th century
Cinquecento = 16th century
Seicento = 17th century
Settecento = 18th century
Ottocento = 19th century
Novecento = 20th century

Trecento

The art of the late Middle Ages (Trecento, 14th century), the *stile gotico*, was introduced into Italy mainly by the mendicant orders; but the

The Palazzo Communale in Pistoia

Italian sense of form soon displaced the Burgundian influence (Santa Croce, Florence, begun by Arnolfo di Cambio in 1295, still without vaulting). Particularly notable are the double church in Assisi (upper church completed 1253, the earliest Gothic church in Italy), Sant'Anastasia in Verona and, in Venice, the Dominican church of Santi Giovanni e Paolo (1330–90) and the Franciscan church of Santa Maria Gloriosa dei Frari (1330–1470). Italian taste, however, was against the excessive reduction of the wall surfaces; the horizontals were still stressed, as they had been in Romanesque architecture, and the façades of cathedrals were lavishly encrusted with decoration.

The cathedrals built at municipal expense became steadily more sumptuous as each town sought to outdo the other (Siena, Florence, Bologna). The Duomo in Florence, a three-aisled church with a triple-apsed choir which was probably begun by Arnolfo di Cambio in 1296, the dome being added later by Brunelleschi, is the most impressive of these cathedrals, exceeded in size and massiveness only by Milan Cathedral, a cruciform church begun in 1386. The radiant exterior, with its 135 pinnacles and 2300 marble statues *(giganti)*, is in striking contrast to the rather dark interior with its 52 massive piers and its huge windows.

Cathedrals

Gothic secular architecture continues the tradition of Romanesque with a strict sense of form. Huge Gothic public buildings and palaces were now built in towns (Palazzo Vecchio, Florence; Palazzo Pubblico, Siena; Scaliger castles in Verona and Sirmione; Gonzaga palace, Mantua; Este palace, Ferrara; Doges' Palace and Ca' d'Oro, Venice), and the houses of patrician families steadily increased in comfort and luxury.

Secular buildings

Romanesque and Gothic features are combined in the Hohenstaufen castles in Apulia. Castel del Monte, near Foggia (built about 1240), a polygonal structure crowning an isolated hill, is particularly impressive; it is said to have been designed by the Emperor Frederick II himself, who paid frequent visits to the region for relaxation or for hunting. Other important Hohenstaufen buildings are the castles of Gioia del Colle and Lagopesole and Frederick II's castle at Lucera, of which only fragments survive, though sufficient to show the monumental character of the original palace.

Hohenstaufen castles

Gothic sculpture established itself only towards the end of the 13th century. Its greatest master was Giovanni Pisano, son of Nicola (pulpits in Sant'Andrea, Pistoia, and Pisa Cathedral; Madonna in Scrovegni Chapel, Padua). Andrea Pisano continued Giovanni's rhythmically flowing style (oldest of the three bronze doors of the Baptistery, Florence). Other sculptors of the period were Andrea di Cione, known as Orcagna (d. about 1368 in Florence), who was also active as an architect and a painter (tabernacle in Or San Michele, Florence, 1348–59), and Tino di Camaino (Gothic tombs of the Anjou family in Santa Chiara, Naples).

Sculpture

In the 14th century the practice of erecting huge monuments to the dead came into vogue (equestrian figures of Paolo Savelli, 1305, in the Frari church, Venice; Scaliger tombs in San Francesco cemetery, Verona).

Funerary monuments

In the field of Gothic painting the work of Giotto (Giotto di Bondone, *c.* 1266–1337) marked a great advance. Although influenced by Cimabue and Duccio di Buoninsegna ("Maestà", the Madonna enthroned with angels, 1308–11; now in Cathedral Museum, Siena), in whom reminiscences of the *maniera greca* can still be detected, Giotto took the decisive step which provided the basis for the whole of modern painting. Painting now acquired, as sculpture had done at an earlier

Giotto

stage, the ability to depict spiritual events; and Giotto, breaking away from the constraints of Byzantine iconography, was able to give his Biblical subjects a new form and a new content. His principal works are the overwhelming cycle of scenes in the Scrovegni Chapel in Padua, freed only a few years ago from later overpaintings, and the frescoes in the two choir chapels in Santa Croce, Florence (unfortunately much repainted). In Florence the school of Giotto remained active throughout the whole of the 14th century (series of frescoes in Santa Croce, Santa Maria Novella and the Cappella degli Spagnoli by Andrea da Firenze; frescoes in Campo Santo, Pisa).

A distinctive school also developed at the Visconti court in Milan around 1500 (Zavattari and Giovannino de' Grassi, Casa Borromeo, Milan; representations of the Months in the Torre dell'Aquila, Castello, Trento).

Renaissance

In this period the separate discussion of painting, sculpture and architecture is no longer appropriate, since many Renaissance artists worked in more than one of these fields.

The Renaissance (Italian *Rinascimento*) was literally a rebirth of the spirit of antiquity. While the Middle Ages had seen the purpose of life in overcoming the terrestrial world and preparing for the world beyond, men now began, in a return to the attitudes of antiquity, to discover themselves and the world as independent entities in their own right and to seek their tasks in the world here below. The metaphysical orientation of Gothic, concerned only with the world to come, was no longer adequate: the new conception of the beauty of the world, the joys of life and the freedom of the spirit demanded quite new forms of expression. There was no smooth transition as there had been between Romanesque and Gothic, but a sudden break. The master craftsman of the past now became an artist, who was no longer content to take second place to his work. He was now an individual artistic personality putting his work before a critical public, not a devout community of believers.

Rebirth

The architects of the Quattrocento (15th century) were the first to adopt the new style modelled on the architectural forms of antiquity. Filippo Brunelleschi (1377–1446) was the pioneer of the early Renaissance, using new techniques in building the dome of Florence Cathedral, the churches of San Lorenzo and the Santo Spirito, and the Pazzi Chapel.

Quattrocento Filippo Brunelleschi

Leon Battista Alberti (1404–72), an artistic personality of universal scope and author of an interesting treatise on architecture, began the church of Sant'Andrea in Mantua in the last year of his life: forward-looking in its conception of space, it ranks with the church of San Francesco in Rimini as his finest achievement.

Leon Battista Alberti

The indebtedness of the new period to classical art is particularly evident in the field of sculpture. The range of subject matter was now extended to take in secular themes, and mythology and contemporary history alike supplied subjects for artistic treatment. The study of anatomy enabled artists to depict the human body in a new way. Portrait sculpture now also developed, producing realistic representations of the sitters who commissioned them. Medieval symbolism gave place to delineations of actual people, the world of spiritual forces to visible down-to-earth reality.

Sculpture

Lorenzo Ghiberti (1378–1455), painter and sculptor, created the second and the famous third door (the Porta del Paradiso) of the Baptistery in

Lorenzo Ghiberti

◀ *Interior of San Lorenzo church, Florence*

Florence. Other major works by Alberti are the reliefs on the font in San Giovanni, Siena, and the bronze figures of Or San Michele, Florence.

Donatello

Donatello (Donato de' Bardi, 1368–1466) is generally regarded as the leading figure of the early Renaissance. A pupil of Ghiberti, he produced both marble sculpture (Duomo, Florence) and bronze statues ("David", c. 1430; in the Bargello, Florence). One of his most powerful works is the equestrian statue of the condottiere Gattamelata in Padua; other major works are "Judith and Holofernes" (in front of the Palazzo Vecchio in Florence), the first free-standing sculptured group of modern times, and "St George", also in Florence.

Andrea del Verrocchio

Andrea del Verrocchio (1436–88) worked mainly for the Medici in Florence ("David", 1465; bronze group, "Christ and Thomas", Or San Michele), but also created the equestrian statue of the condottiere Bartolommeo Colleoni in Venice – less massive than Donatello's Gattamelata but livelier and tauter.

Luca della Robbia

Luca della Robbia (1399–1482) was the third of the great masters of the early Renaissance in Florence. He applied the techniques of faience to larger works of sculpture and produced a whole series of works in majolica (Madonna figures).

Masaccio

Early Renaissance painting began with the work of Masaccio (Tommaso di Giovanni di Simone Guidi), who died young (1401–28). He painted the frescoes in the Brancacci Chapel of Santa Maria del Carmine and the "Virgin with St Anne" in the Uffizi.

Andrea Mantegna

Andrea Mantegna (1431–1506) was the leading North Italian painter of the Quattrocento. His pictures, works of high seriousness and rigour, depict plastic bodily forms with almost exaggerated clarity, achieving a very characteristic effect of depth by the use of perspective, with drastic foreshortening (altarpiece, San Zeno, Verona; "St Sebastian", Museo Nazionale, Florence; Camera degli Sposi in the Castello, Mantua, with the first group portrait and the first *trompe-l'oeil* ceiling painting in the history of art; "Madonna della Vittoria", Louvre, Paris).

Fra Angelico

Fra Angelico (Fra Giovanni da Fiesole, 1387–1455) created works of an exclusively religious character, deeply devout and peopled with graceful angel figures (frescoes in the monastery of San Marco, Florence).

Piero della Francesca

Piero della Francesca (c. 1420–92) was the Quattrocento's great master and teacher of perspective. Among his principal works are the votive picture of Sigismondo Malatesta (in San Francesco, Rimini), the portrait of Federigo da Montefeltro (Uffizi, Florence), the "Resurrection" in Urbino, and the "Adoration of the Child" in the National Gallery, London.

Sandro Botticelli

Sandro Botticelli (1444–1510), a Florentine, worked during the most brilliant period of the Medici. A kind of dreamy melancholy hangs over his graceful youths and maidens, and there is a touch of the same feeling even in his pagan mythological pictures ("Spring" and "Birth of Venus", both in the Uffizi, Florence).

Fra Filippo Lippi

Fra Filippo Lippi (1406–69), a Carmelite friar working in Florence, painted pictures transfiguring Biblical scenes by the depiction of secular and terrestrial beauty. His work radiates fresh sincerity and love of nature ("Coronation of the Virgin", Uffizi; "Annunciation", San Lorenzo, Florence; frescoes in Spoleto Cathedral).

Domenico Veneziano

Domenico Veneziano (c. 1400–61) worked in Venice, where painting was concerned primarily with brilliance of colour and delicacy of sentiment. In his "Sacra Conversazione" the Virgin is surrounded by a group of saints.

Piero della Francesca: "Battista Sforza"   *Rafael: "Pope Leo X"*

The High Renaissance falls into the first half of the Cinquecento (16th century). One of its great masters was Donato Bramante (1444–1514), the clarity and harmonious beauty of whose buildings is best seen in his plan for the new St Peter's in Rome, a centralised structure in the form of a Greek cross. He did not live to complete the building, which was continued by Michelangelo and crowned with a mighty dome.

Cinquecento
Donato Bramante

Michelangelo Buonarroti (1475–1564), a universal genius and one of the greatest artistic personalities in a period rich in geniuses, was the leading master of the High Renaissance. A pupil of Ghirlandaio, he worked as an architect, painter and sculptor, and in addition made a name for himself as a poet with his sonnets. Among the works he produced in Florence were his "David" (Accademia), the Medici mausoleum in San Lorenzo (Sagrestia Nuova) and the staircase of the Biblioteca Lauren-ziana. Summoned to Rome by Pope Julius II, he worked on Julius's tomb (figure of Moses, "Fettered Slave" and "Dying Slave"), which remained unfinished, completed the building of St Peter's and painted the magnificent frescoes in the Sistine Chapel. With the "harmony" and "power" (Michelangelo's watchwords) of his work he moved beyond the High Renaissance and prepared the way for the Baroque.

Michelangelo

The second universal genius (*"uomo universale"*) of the High Renaissance was Leonardo da Vinci (1452–1519), sculptor, architect, painter, scientist and engineer. Working at the Sforza court in Milan, in Florence, in Rome and finally for Francis I in France, he was the richest incarnation of the universal man of the Renaissance. In him art and science were fused into a unity, and his achievements in the field of natural science alone would entitle him to a leading place in the history of human intellectual development. Among his greatest works are the "Virgin of the Rocks", the "Virgin and Child with St Anne and the Infant St John" and "Mona Lisa" ("La Gioconda"), all in the Louvre, and his

Leonardo da Vinci

"Last Supper", a mural (unfortunately much damaged) in the monastery of Santa Maria delle Grazie in Milan. A unique insight into his methods of working is given by his drawings and studies, in a great variety of techniques.

Raphael

The name of Raphael (Raffaello Santi, 1483–1520) calls up the image of a serene artist, beloved of gods and men, the painter of charming Madonnas ("Madonna della Sedia", Madonna Tempi, Sistine Madonna). In Rome he decorated the Stanze di Raffaello in the Vatican with wall and ceiling paintings, worked as an architect and directed excavations of ancient Rome.

Giovanni Bellini

Another important painter of the High Renaisance was Giovanni Bellini (1430–1516), who sought to achieve simplicity, clarity and grandeur. His paintings of Madonnas are built up symmetrically, in the form of a pyramid (*figura piramidale*). One of his principal works is an altarpiece, "Madonna Enthroned with Saints", in San Zaccaria in Venice. Among his pupils were Giorgio, Palma Vecchio and Titian.

Vittore Carpaccio

Vittore Carpaccio (*c.* 1460–*c.* 1526) was a master of the narrative picture and a vivid portrayer of the Venice of his day ("Miracle of the Cross"; scenes from the life of St Ursula, Accademia, Venice).

Giorgione

In Venice Giorgione (Giorgio da Castelfranco, 1478–1510) continued the tradition of Bellini and became the founder of the Venetian school of High Renaissance painting ("Three Philosophers", "Tempesta", "Sleeping Venus").

Andrea Palladio

The Neo-Classical architecture of the Late Renaissance, exemplified by the work of Andrea Palladio (1508–80), provided models for the whole of Europe. Palladio was both a practical architect and an architectural theorist, author of "Quattro libri dell'architettura", and his return to the styles of ancient Rome was of major importance to the development of architecture. His principal works were the Basilica and the Palazzo Chiericati in Vicenza and the churches of San Giorgio Maggiore and the Redentore in Venice. A new type of building now developed in Italy, the *palazzo*, successor to the old castles built in towns in the Middle Ages (Palazzo Pitti and Palazzo Rucellai, Florence; Cancelleria and Palazzo dei Conservatori, Rome).

Titian

The great master of Venetian painting, already belonging to the Late Renaissance, is Titian (Tiziano Vecellio, 1477–1576), whose work in many ways looks forward to the Baroque ("Assunta" in the Frari church, Venice; "Worship of Venus" and "Bacchanal", both in the Prado, Madrid; portraits of the Emperor Charles V, seated and on horseback; "Danaë", "Nymph and Shepherd", "Jacopo da Strada").

Palma Vecchio

Palma Vecchio (1480–1528) also worked in Venice. His favourite theme was the "Sacra Conversazione" (altarpiece in Santa Maria Formosa).

Tintoretto

Tintoretto (Jacopo Robusti, 1518–94), all of whose work was done in Venice, stood at the point of transition to the Mannerist and Baroque style (wall and ceiling paintings in Scuola di San Rocco, Venice; "Paradise", Sala del Maggior Consiglio, Doges' Palace, Venice).

Mannerism

Mannerism, the style which flourished in the second half of the 16th century, between the late Renaissance and the early Baroque period, was characterised by its delight in the unusual and bizarre: it loved allegory and metaphor and the extravagantly complex, corkscrew-like movement of the *figura serpentina*.

Leading representatives of this period were the painters Parmigianino (Francesco Mazzola, 1503–40) and Giuseppe Arcimboldo (1527–93), who worked in Prague as court painter to Rudolf II, and Giovanni Bologna (Giambologna, 1529–1608), the most notable sculptor of the late Mannerist period. Mannerism achieved some of its most remarkable effects in the field of landscape gardening, in which natural scenery, architecture and grotesque sculpture in classical style combined to produce startling results (e.g. in the Parco dei Mostri at Bomarzo, between Terni and Viterbo).

Baroque

The age of Baroque was marked in architecture by the emergence of a new type of church. The rectangular nave now increasingly gave place to a centralised plan, crowned by a dome.

    Architecture

    An intermediate example is the Jesuit church of the Gesù in Rome, built by Giacomo Vignola (1507–73). Carlo Maderna (1556–1629) lengthened St Peter's by the addition of a basilican nave (c. 1610).

In the Seicento (17th century) the most influential Baroque architect and sculptor was Giovanni Lorenzo Bernini (1598–1680), who was responsible for the semicircular colonnades in St Peter's Square in Rome and the magnificent fountains in the Piazza Barberini (Triton Fountain) and Piazza Navona (Four Rivers Fountain). Among his other works of sculpture are his "Apollo and Daphne" (Villa Borghese, Rome), the tomb of Pope Urban VIII in St Peter's and "Santa Teresa" (Santa Maria della Vittoria, Milan).

Seicento
Giovanni Lorenzo
Bernini

Contemporary with Bernini was Francesco Borromini (1599–1667), a master of the flowing lines and curves characteristic of the High

Francesco
Borromini

Bernini: "St Teresa of Avila"   *Caravaggio: "Conversion of St Paul"*

Art

Baroque, whose work at first encountered violent opposition (San Carlo alle Quattro Fontane, Rome).

Guarino Guarini

Guarino Guarini (1624–83) worked in a similar style, mainly in Turin. Baldassare Longhena (1604–82) worked in Venice (Palazzo Pesaro, Palazzo Rezzonico).

Painting
Paolo Veronese

An early representative of Baroque painting was Paolo Veronese (P. Caliari, 1528–88), a master of illusionist painting who marshals large numbers of figures in lively attitudes of rather theatrical effect.

Caravaggio

Michelangelo da Caravaggio (M. Meristi, 1573–1610) was the initiator of the realistic chiaroscuro painting which was to be so influential in the whole of European painting; his concern was to achieve a plastic modelling of his figures in a setting which was often merely hinted at.

Annibale Carracci

Annibale Carracci (1560–1609) painted frescoes on themes from ancient mythology in the Palazzo Farnese in Rome, and was also a considerable landscape painter (ideal landscapes, often with mythological figures). Domenichino (Domenico Zampieri, 1581–1641) and Guido Reni (1575–1642) were two of Carracci's principal pupils. Other painters of this period were Guercino (Giovanni Francesco Barbieri, 1591–1666) and Pietro da Cortona (1596–1669), the great master of illusionist ceiling painting (Palazzo Barberini and Palazzo Pamphili, Rome; Palazzo Pitti, Florence). Two later exponents of this art were Andrea del Pozzo (ceiling paintings in Sant'Ignazio, Rome, 1685) and Giovanni Battista Tiepolo (1696–1770), both of whom also worked outside Italy. Two artists of the period who worked in Naples were the Spanish painter Jusepe de Ribera, known as Lo Spagnoletto (1599–1652), and Salvatore Rosa (1615–73), a painter of very distinctive style who specialised in wild and rugged landscapes and battle scenes teeming with life and activity.

Rococo

Settecento

In the Settecento the leading place in Italian painting was taken by Venice. The principal masters of the Rococo period, in addition to Tiepolo (frescoes in the Villa Vilmarana, Vicenza; numerous altars and frescoes in Venice) and Giovanni Battista Piazzetta (1682–1754), were the two Canalettos, Antonio Canale (1697–1768) and Bernardo Bellotto (1720–80), who painted views *(vedute)* of great architectural exact-ness (Canale of Venice, Bellotto of Vienna, Warsaw and Dresden). Francesco Guardi (1712–93) depicted Venetian life and festivals in lively scenes with numerous figures. The woman painter Rosalba Carriera (1675–1757) specialised in charming pastel portraits and miniatures.

In parallel with the characteristic painting of the Rococo period there was a Neo-Classical school of artists who devoted themselves to depicting the excavated sites of Pompeii and Herculaneum (which began to be revealed in the first half of the 18th century) and to romantically idealised pictures of the ruins of ancient Rome. The leading member of this group was Giovanni Battista Piranesi (1720–78), an architect and engraver working in Rome, who also produced eerie and grotesque architectural fantasies ("Prisons", 1745).

In this period the architect Filippo Juvara (1678–1736) built some notable palaces and churches in Piedmont.

Neo-Classicism

The 18th century also saw the emergence in Italy of Neo-Classicism, the principal exponent of which was Antonio Canova (1757–1822). His tomb of Pope Clement XIV in Rome (1783–87) was a work of epoch-making significance, but perhaps his best known work is the statue of Pauline Borghese (1807; Villa Borghese, Rome).

Historicism

In the 19th century Italian architecture lived on the traditions of a great past, with various brands of Historicism (a return to the styles of the past). Giuseppe Piermarini (1734–1808) was a typical representative of the Neo-Classical school of architecture, which looked to antiquity for its models. Among the buildings he designed was Milan's great opera-house, La Scala. A master of Neo-Classical town planning was Giuseppe Valadier, who laid out the Piazza del Popolo in Rome. These trends appealed to the Fascist regime which came to power after the First World War, and it was only with the formation in 1927 of the group of architects known as Gruppo 7 that Italian architecture began to break out of this eclectic fossilisation.

Ottocento

The painting of the 19th century was of purely local importance; and, as in the rest of Europe, it was committed to the ideas of Historicism. Only Giovanni Segantini (1858–99) achieved international reputation as a Neo-Impressionist and Symbolist. The graphic artist Alberto Martini (1876–1954) also merits mention.

Painting

Modernism

In the early years of the 20th century the Futurists (a movement which came into being in 1909) called for a break with tradition. Leading members of this school were Carlo Carrà (1881–1966), Umberto Boccioni (1882–1916), Gino Severini (1883–1966) and Luigi Russolo (1885–1947).

Novecento
Futurism

Afro Basaldella: "Angelica" (1964)

Giorgio de Chirico (1880–1978), regarded by many as the leading painter of his day, founded the school of *pittura metafisica*, which came to an end about 1920. Thereafter its objectives were pursued by the Surrealists.

Cubism

Giorgio Morandi (1890–1964) came under the influence of Cubism at an early stage, and was then associated with de Chirico for a time before evolving a very individual style of great clarity and purity. Mario Sironi (1885–1961) sought to find common ground between *pittura metafisica* and Cubism/Futurism. The painter and sculptor Amedeo Modigliani (1884–1920) worked principally in Paris, where he came under the influence of Cézanne and the Cubists.

Guttuso

Renato Guttuso (1912–87), a painter with socialist leanings, was aware of modern artistic trends but for the most part followed the realist line prescribed by the party. In his pictures he gave expression to his sympathy with the suffering and the oppressed.

Architecture

After the Second World War there was a great industrial building boom (Olivetti building, Ivrea, 1948–50), and the Neo-Liberty architectural style, using Art Nouveau detailing, came into vogue (R. Gabetti, A. d'Isola). Leading industrial firms like Olivetti, Pirelli and Fiat promoted the development of architecture and industrial design (Pirelli building, 1955–58, and Torre Velasca, 1957, in Milan; car design, office machinery, furniture, lamps).

Nervi

Pier Luigi Nervi (1891–1979), one of the leading architects of the 20th century, was a representative of "rationalist" architecture and has had great influence on whole generations of artists. He was one of the first architects to use reinforced concrete. He built exhibition halls (Turin, 1950 and 1961), sports stadia (stadium, Florence, 1930–32; large and

Aldo Rossi: Administration Centre in Perugia

small sports palaces and stadium for the Summer Olympics in Rome, 1956–59), airport terminals and office blocks (UNESCO, Paris, 1953–57).

In our own day Italian sculpture has at last produced successors to Canova in the persons of Marino Marini (1901–80), famed for his horses and riders, and Giacomo Manzù (1908–91), who returned to an older genre with his bronze doors decorated in relief (docr of Salzburg Cathedral, 1959; Porta della Morte, St Peter's, Rome, 1964).

Sculpture

After 1945 abstract painting and sculpture came to the fore in Italy as in other Western countries, in a great range of variations (Tachism, Montage, "Lyrical Abstraction"). Leading exponents of non-representational painting are Giuseppe Santomaso (b. 1907), Afro Basaldella (1912–76) and Emilio Vedova (b. 1919).

Abstract painting and sculpture

In the field of sculpture there are a variety of trends, represented by Fausto Melotti (1901–86), Carmelo Cappello (b. 1912), Pietro Consagra (b. 1920) and the brothers Arnoldo Pomodore (b. 1926) and Giò Pomodore (b. 1930). The ingenious Piero Manzoni (1934–63) finally declared the whole earth to be a work of art and set himself up on a pedestal to become a forerunner of Concept Art (1962).

A central figure, at the intersection of the most varied artistic trends, was the painter and sculptor Lucio Fontana (1899–1968), who developed the theory of "Spatialism". Antonio Corpora (b. 1909) and other Italian artists became associated with the Ecole de Paris. Among painters of the younger generation are Enrico Castellani (b. 1930), Lucio del Pezzo (b. 1933), Michelangelo Pistoletto (b. 1933), Agostino Bonalumi (b. 1935), Gino Marotta (b. 1935), Giuseppe Spagnulo (b. 1936), Mario Ceroli (b. 1938), Ugo La Pietra (b. 1938), Giulio Paolini (b. 1940) and Gianni Piacentino (b. 1945).

Other artists

As "objective artists" of the Arte Povera school Mario Merz (b. 1925), Giovanni Anselmo (b. 1934), Alighiero Boetti (b. 1940), Piero Gilardi (b. 1942) and Gilberto Zorio (b. 1944) have made a name for themselves.

Finally mention should be made of the Italian school of Photo-Realism, represented by Gianni Bertini (b.1922), Vincenzo Agnetti (b.1926), Carlo Massimo Asnaghi (b. 1927), Luca Patella (b. 1934), Mario Schifano (b.1934), Antonio Paradiso (b.1926), Mirko Tagliaferro (b.1936), Franco Vaccari (b.1936), Bruno di Bello (b.1938), Ketty La Rocca (b.1938), Luigi Ontani (b.1943), Elio Mariani (b.1943) and Claudio Parmiggiani (b.1943).

Photo-Realism

Music

Among all the countries of the West the Italian peninsula has the richest heritage of vocal music from the early Christian period, with much early liturgical music (Milan, Rome, Benevento). The medieval neums (an early form of musical notation) have not yet been satisfactorily deciphered, but nevertheless reflect, in their short-paced melodic structure, a national characteristic, and probably also the influence of the folk music of southern Italy. This early music was supported by the theoretical writings of St Augustine ("De musica", 387–389) and Boethius ("De institutione musicae", c. 500). The father of Western church singing was St Ambrose, Bishop of Milan in the 4th century, who introduced the Ambrosian Liturgy still used in parts of northern Italy. This was the foundation on which Pope Gregory the Great developed Gregorian chant at the end of the 6th century.

Early Christian period

In the 11th century Guido of Arezzo (992–1050) devised a new form of musical notation, the origin of the system still used today.

The origins of unison liturgical singing (plainsong) are closely bound up with folk music, Greco-Roman and Jewish traditions. The folk

11th–13th centuries

music, which was for long repressed by the Church, enjoyed a revival between the 11th and 13th centuries in the form of *laudi* and *ballati*.

Renaissance

At the beginning of the 14th century the stylistically more refined art of the Renaissance developed in Italy, facilitated by the increasing importance of Italian as a literary language (Dante, Petrarch, Boccaccio). Forms like the *caccia*, the ballade and the madrigal sought to give expression to the new spirit, the most notable figures in this field being Jacopo da Bologna (14th c.), Batilinus of Padua (*c.* 1400) and above all the poet and organist Francesco Landino (1325–97), the leading representative of the Florentine "Ars Nova".

Dutch and Flemish composers, among them Johannes Ciconia (1335–1411), Guillaume Dufay (*c.* 1400–74) and Heinrich Isaac (1450–1517), dominated musical life at the Italian princely courts in the 15th and early 16th centuries. In addition to the madrigal, the main form of secular music, and the motet and mass in sacred music, a number of forms derived from folk music also came into vogue – the *frottola*, the villanelle, the *villota*, the laud and, from the end of the 15th century, the *canti carnascialeschi*.

In the 16th century differences began to arise between the musical centres of Venice and Naples on the one hand and Rome on the other. In the Papal chapel in Rome there grew up a Roman school, the most celebrated representative of which was Giovanni Pierluigi Palestrina (1525–94). In his contrapuntally perfect masses, motets and other works he brought a *cappella* polyphony to a pitch of perfection which marked one of the peaks of the Roman Catholic church music of the Renaissance. In Venice Andrea Gabriele (1515–86) and his nephew Giovanni Gabrieli (1557–1612) wrote music for several choirs (*canzoni*, sonatas) which provided a basis for the development of independent orchestral and chamber music.

A group of poets (among them O. Rinuccini, 1562–1621), musicians (E. di Cavalieri, 1550–1662, Jacopo Peri, 1561–1633, and others) and humanist scholars who met in the houses of counts Bardi and Corsi in Florence (the "Camerata fiorentina") were concerned to renew ancient tragedy with their music and to achieve a harmonious relationship between words and music. This gave rise in the 16th century to solo singing with a basso continuo accompaniment.

The first operas were now composed by Jacopo Peri ("Dafne", 1594) and Giulio Caccini ("Euridice", 1600).

Baroque

With the Baroque began a period which was of the greatest importance for the development of music throughout Europe right down to the 20th century. In the work of Claudio Monteverdi (1567–1643) the opera had its first flowering ("Orfeo", "L'Incoronazione di Poppea"). He made opera available to a wider public, a change reflected in the opening of Italy's first opera-house in Venice in 1637. Among Venetian operatic composers were Francesco Vacalli (1602–76) and Marc' Antonio Cesti (1623–69). Opera-houses were now also opened in Rome and Naples. Recitative and the *da capo* aria now evolved. The work of the leading representatives of *opera seria*, including Alessandro Scarlatti (1660–1725), Leonardo Vinci (1690–1730) and Leonardo Leo (1694–1744), influenced foreign operatic composers like Handel, Gluck and Mozart. *Opera seria*, however, soon degenerated into sterility, since it increasingly developed into virtuoso concert opera, in which the voices of the castrati and the ingenious stage machinery were more important than the content and the musical and dramatic expression.

From Naples and Rome *opera buffa* set out on its victorious progress through Europe. The works of Giovanni Pergolesi (1710–36; "La Serva Padrona"), Giovanni Paisiello (1740–1816; "The Barber of Seville") and Domenico Cimarosa (1749–1801; "The Secret Marriage") are still performed today.

Along with opera the oratorio and the cantata also developed (G. Carissimi, 1605–74; A. Stradella, 1641–82).

The instrumental music of the 17th century also evolved an expressive virtuoso style and a variety of new forms (sonata, concerto grosso, overture, suite, concerto with soloist). For long the keyboard instruments (organ, harpsichord) took pride of place, and Girolamo Frescobaldi (1583–1643) wrote numerous compositions for these instruments (*canzoni*, partitas, toccatas, etc.). From about 1650, however, the Italian tradition of violin-playing was established, beginning with Arcangelo Corelli (1653–1713) and fostered by the violin-making skill of the Amati, Stradivari and Guarneri families. The works of Antonio Vivaldi (*c.* 1678–1741), Domenico Scarlatti (1685–1757), Giuseppe Tartini (1692–1770), Luigi Boccherini (1743–1805) and Muzio Clementi (1752–1843), which gave a prominent place to stringed instruments, promoted the development of instrumental music as an independent form. Niccoló Paganini (1782–1840) carried virtuoso violin-playing to a peak of perfection.

In 19th century Italian music opera played a central part. The best known operatic composers in the first half of the century were Caetano Donizetti (1797–1848; "L'Elisir d'amore", "Lucia di Lammermoor", "Don Pasquale"), Vincenzo Bellini (1801–35; "Norma", "La Sonnambula") and Gioacchino Rossini (1792–1868; "The Barber of Seville", "William Tell", "The Thieving Magpie"). — 19th century

Giuseppe Verdi (1813–1901), whose early works (particularly "Nabucco") were very much in tune with the aspirations of the Risorgimento, was the outstanding Italian musical personality in the second half of the 19th century. The operas he composed between 1851 and 1853 ("Rigoletto", "Il Trovatore" and "La Traviata") made him famous in Italy, but it was only with his late works ("Don Carlos", 1867; "Aida", 1871; "Otello", 1887; "Falstaff", 1893) that he achieved international recognition and became accepted as one of the world's great operatic composers. — Giuseppe Verdi

Other composers who worked in Verdi's shadow were Arrigo Boito (1842–1918; "Mefistofele"), Umberto Giordano (1867–1948; "Andrea Chénier") and Amilcare Ponchielli (1834–1896; "La Gioconda").

The opera "Cavalleria Rusticana" by Pietro Mascagni (1863–1945) was seen as the first work in the style known as Verismo (musical naturalism), another representative of which was Ruggiero Leoncavallo (1858–1919; "Pagliacci"). — Verismo

The works of Giacomo Puccini (1858–1924; "La Bohème", "Tosca", "Madame Butterfly", "Gianni Schicchi", "Turandot") formed the last great high point of Italian opera. — Giacomo Puccini

Ermanno Wolf-Ferrari (1876–1948; "I Quattro Rusteghi") returned to the tradition of *opera buffa*.

In the 20th century instrumental music once again came into its own. The compositions of Ottorino Respighi (1879–1936) are notable for their rich musical colour. Ildebrando Pizzetti (1880–1968), Gian Francesco Malipiero (1882–1973) and Alfredo Casella (1883–1947) sought to achieve a synthesis between traditional and modern music. — 20th century

Goffredo Petrassi (b. 1904), Luigi Dallapiccola (1904–75), Mario Peragallo (b. 1910), Bruno Maderna (1921–73), who was the first composer to combine tape-recorded and instrumental music, and Luigi Nono (1924–90) largely follow the compositional principles of the modern Western European school (dodecaphony, serialism, punctualism).

The problem of Italy's Fascist past is reflected in the opera "La Speranza" (1970) by Franco Mannino (b. 1924).

Folk Traditions

Folk Traditions

Popular festivals

Although Italy has assimilated much of American and Northern
European culture, old traditions have been preserved in many parts of
the country, folk music and traditional costumes are still cherished,
and in spite of all external influences the old popular festivals have for
the most part retained their original character. A distinction must be
made between secular festivals (often of pagan origin) and religious
festivals. Some traditional festivals commemorating events in the
history of a town which had fallen into oblivion have been revived in
recent years, no doubt with the tourist trade in mind; but the local
people have shown themselves very ready to return to their ancient
traditions and enjoy the festivals for their own sake. In addition to well
known events like the Palio in Siena and the Giostra del Saracino in
Arezzo there are numerous local festivals all over Italy – village festivals, fishermen's festivals, vintage and harvest festivals – which give
visitors an interesting opportunity of observing the customs and way
of life of ordinary people.

Church festivals

An important part is played in Italian life by the various church festivals, which are usually celebrated with much more spontaneity than
in northern Europe and often take on the character of folk celebrations.
Particularly notable are the numerous processions on the occasion of
Corpus Christi, the Assumption and Holy Week. On Good Friday the
richly decked Santo Sepolcro (Holy Sepulchre) which is displayed in
all churches attracts large numbers of worshippers. In northern Italy
the Christmas tree is increasingly becoming a regular feature of the
Christmas celebrations, but in the south the *presepio* ("crib", Nativity
group) retains its almost exclusive role as the symbol of Christmas.
Children usually receive their presents at Epiphany (Epifania, January
6th). The Carnival is now celebrated only in a few places (e.g. at
Viareggio and San Remo); but some traditional features still survive
from earlier times, like the *mamutones* (fools, jesters) in Sardinia,
witches in Alto Adige and the "burning of Winter" in northern Italy.

Costumes

The old traditional costumes are still often worn at the various festivals celebrated throughout the year, particularly in country areas. At
any time of year, therefore, it is possible to see people wearing the old
traditional dress in the Abruzzi, Sardinia and many parts of Calabria
and Piedmont. The local costumes of Italy show remarkable variety. In
the Valle d'Aosta the peasants wear dark-coloured and rather severe
costumes reminiscent of French models, while in the Alto Adige with
its German-speaking population the traditional dress shows Austrian
and Bavarian features, including leather trousers and the typical
Tirolean hat. In central and southern Italy the variety and vivid colours
of the costumes are often almost overwhelming, and a diversity of
influences – Yugoslav, Greek and even Oriental – can be detected. The
women's costumes on Sardinia frequently include a veil.

Music in
everyday life

On festive occasions visitors may have an opportunity of hearing some
of the old traditional tunes which in everyday life now tend to be
crowded out by the hit tunes of the day. Music is an essential element in
Italian life, and this is particularly true of singing. A passer-by will
frequently hear the voice of some amateur singer from the courtyard of
a house, through an open window, or on a canal in Venice; and the cliché
of the baker singing as he makes his pizzas has some foundation in
reality. It is no accident that Italy is known as the land of *bel canto* and
the home of opera. Although the famous Neapolitan *canzoni* ("O sole
mio", "Torna a Surriento", "Tu ca' nun chiange", "Na sera e maggio",
etc.) can hardly be called folk songs in the proper sense of the term, they
do represent a curious and typically Italian combination of folk music,

50

pop song and musical composition. Genuine Neapolitan folk music is performed to high standards of musicianship by such groups as the Nuova Compagnia di Canto Popolare; and a great body of Italian folk music has been collected and recorded by the Ricordi firm of music publishers in Milan, the Italian Radio Corporation (RAI) and the Accademia di Santa Cecilia (the National Academy of Music) in Rome.

Italian folk music uses a number of characteristic instruments, often centuries old. Among wind instruments, in addition to the reed pipe and the fife (*piffero*), there are the triple-piped *launedda* and various kinds of Pan pipes. Different types of bagpipes, like the *zampogna*, are played by shepherds in the Abruzzi and Sardinia. Guitars and mandolines are also popular, as is the concertina, particularly in the country, where it often accompanies the *ballo liscio*.

Folk music

In earlier times dancing, often of ritual or religious significance, played an important part in Italian life. Although many of the old dances have not survived the centuries, a few, like the *ballo tondo* – a round dance, popular particularly in Sardinia, with some similarity to the Catalan *sardana* – have been preserved. The martial danze delle spade (sword dances) have also survived, and are danced with particular verve and vigour by the *spadonari* of Venaltio (May 17th), Giaglione (April 5th) and San Giorgio Canavese. The most popular Italian folk dances, however, are undoubtedly the Neapolitan *tarantella* and the *saltarello*, which both have love as their theme and are usually danced to a lively rhythm.

Dances

Suggested Routes

1. Through upper and central Italy to Rome (1800 km (1120 mi.))

From Domodossola, Lugano or Chiavenna travel first along ★★**Lake Maggiore**, Lake Lugano or ★**Lake Como**, then through the Po plain to ★★**Milan**. Continue along the motorway through the south of the Po plain to Binasco, then on the state road, passing close to the famous Certosa di Pavia and the old Lombard capital of **Pavia** and back on to the motorway. This leads across the **Apennines** and through a tunnel under the Giovi Pass to ★**Genoa**, the capital of Liguria, looking out from its magnificent position over the Mediterranean.

Continue by way of the Riviera di Levante along the Ligurian coast with its lush Mediterranean flora and through a number of resorts rich in tradition, such as Nervi and **Rapallo** and the foothills of ★**Portofino**, with their fine views. Beyond the resort of Sestri Levante the road turns inland to the port of **La Spezia**, Italy's largest naval base.

Soon after that the route leads along the edge of the Apuanian Alps, known for their marble quarries, to the large seaside resort of **Viareggio** and then on through the plains of Tuscany to ★★**Pisa** with its interesting buildings. From here follow the southern edge of the Apennines and visit the old Tuscany towns of ★**Lucca**, ★**Pistola** and **Prato** and the major spa resort of ★**Montecatini Terme**.

The route then continues on to ★★**Florence**, the old capital of Tuscany, beautifully situated in a wide valley basin and harbouring many rich art treasures, and thence through the charming Tuscany highlands to Poggibonsi and via the little town of ★★**San Gimignano** with its many towers to the equally interesting medieval town of ★**Volterra**, from where the road passes through Colle Val d'Elsa and the little walled mountain town of Monteriggioni to ★★**Siena**, famous for its art treasures.

Continuing through the highlands of southern ★**Tuscany**, where – just off the road – the monastery of Monte Oliveto Maggiore is worth a visit, the route leads on to San Quirico and thence to a road with panoramic views which winds through the little mountain towns of Pienza and **Montepulciano** to Chiusi. Now via the magnificent cathedral town of ★★**Orvieto**, built on a tufa crag, to Lake Bolsena lying in a former volcanic region and on to the town of **Viterbo** with its many fountains; then along the upper shore of the little Lago di Vico and around the almost circular Lago di Bracciano. Finally passing through the gently undulating Roman Campagna the route reaches the Italian capital ★★**Rome**, to visit which, even restricting oneself to the most important places of interest, at least three days should be allowed (to include an excursion via Ostia to Lido di ★**Ostia** in the Alban Mountains and via ★★**Tivoli** to **Subiaco** and back by way of Palestrina six days are needed).

On the way back from Rome to Upper Italy the road passes through the picturesquely situated little mountain towns of Civita Castellana and Nami, then via the busy industrial town of Terni, into the varied scenery of the Umbrian highlands, where away from the road the old towns of **Spoleto**, Trevi and Spello lie in charming situations on the slopes. A highlight of the trip is a visit to ★★**Assisi**, the town made famous by St Francis, and to ★**Perugia**, superbly situated high up on a hill.

The route continues to the medieval town of **Gubbio** and then later through the wild Furlo Gorge to ★**Urbino**, the interesting birthplace of the great Renaissance painter Raphael. Soon after that, north of

Routes in Italy

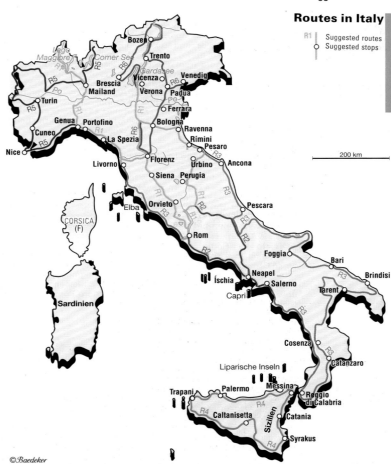

200 km

©Baedeker

Pesaro, the sandy and flat coast of the Adriatic is reached with the resorts of Cattolica and Riccione. From ★**Rimini**, well worth a visit to see its Roman buildings, the opportunity should be taken to make a detour to the little republic of ★**San Marino**.

There are now two equally charming alternative routes: the first includes a drive along the northern edge of the Apennines, thereby seeing the interesting buildings of the rich towns of **Forlì**, ★**Faenza**, ★★**Bologna** and ★**Modena**; then continue across the Po plain to the famous old town of ★★**Verona**, along the eastern – or better still the western – shore of ★★**Lake Garda**, with ford-like scenery in its northern part, to Riva and **Trient**, and thence through the Adige valley to ★**Bolzano**, the beautiful capital of South Tirol, and finally through the Isarco valley to the Brenner Pass, the Austro–Italian border since 1919.

53

Alternatively, from Rimini continue via the resorts of Cesenatico and Cervia, then through the Po plain, which is particularly wide here, to the town of ★★**Ravenna**, famous for the magnificent mosaics in its early Christian churches, and to the old Este residence of ★**Ferrara**. Soon on the far side of the Po ★★**Padua**, St Anthony's town is reached, and thence to Marghera, from where a dam leads to the unique lagoon city of ★★**Venice**. Beyond **Treviso** lies the edge of the Alps and on the far side of Vittorio Veneto the route takes us mainly through the broad Piave valley and across the Venetian Alps. Before the traditional winter sports resort of ★**Cortina d'Ampezzo** the magnificent ★★**Dolomites** come into view and can be seen all the way to Toblach. The route then passes through the town of Innichen near the border and returns in the direction of Lienz (Glocknerstrasse).

2. To central and lower Italy and Naples (2500 km (1550 mi.))

From Domodossola the route initially follows that described in Route 1 above as far as ★★**Milan**. Those who are not yet familiar with the ★**Riviera** should continue along this stretch; otherwise choose the del Sole autostrada through the interesting old towns of **Piacenza**, ★**Parma** and ★**Modena** to ★★**Bologna**, the chief town of the province of Emilia with a number of towers. From here a superb road leads across the **Apennines** to ★★**Florence**. Then continue via ★★**Siena** and ★★**Orvieto** to ★★**Rome**.

Continuing in a southerly direction, the route leads through the Roman Campagna into the once-volcanic Alban Mountains with their beautiful lakes and on to **Frascati**, known for its magnificent parks, and thence to Castelgandolfo, the Pope's summer residence. The Via Appia then crosses the flat, formerly marshy, Agro Pontino. Passing

Evening in the Tuscan countryside

Monte Circeo and close to the coast of the Tyrrhenian Sea it continues to Terracina on the border between Central and Lower Italy, then via Sperlonga to the port of Gaeta; from here the route passes Formia and the archaeological site of Minturnae and on to the antique ruins of Cumae. Continue along the Lago di Fusaro to Cape Miseno, with its fine views; from here via Bacoli and Baia with its ancient thermal baths to Pozzuoli, where the amphitheatre and nearby Solfatara are worth a visit. Soon the port of ★★**Naples**, situated in a magnificent gulf is reached, from where an excursion to the islands of ★★**Capri** and ★**Ischia** is recommended.

On the return journey from Naples visit the ruined town of ★★**Herculaneum** near the sea. Pass ★★**Vesuvius** and follow the road to ★★**Pompeii**. A magnificent coast road then leads round the Sorrento peninsula, from where excursions to ★**Sorrento** and, from the little town of ★**Amalfi** magnificently situated on the Gulf of Sorrento, to Ravello are recommended. Beyond **Salerno** and by way of Battipaglia the route continues to the splendid Temple of ★★**Paestum**, the southernmost point of this route.

From Paestum return to Salerno and then follow the direct state road or the motorway via Nocera to ★★**Naples**. Continue through the Volturno plain to ★**Caserta** with its palace, then via Santa Maria Capua Vetere to Capua and San Cataldo, the setting-out point for excursions to the famous Benedictine monastery of ★★**Montecassino**. The main stretch leads beyond San Cataldo via Venafro to Isernia and then on to Castel di Sangro. From here drive through the Abruzzo National Park by way of Opi to Celano, then on to ★**L'Aquila** (a worthwhile detour is to the Gran Sasso d'Italia). Continue by way of Rieti, the mountain lake of Piediluco and the Terni waterfalls to the provincial capital of Terni; then via ★**Rimini** to Brenner or to Innichen (cf. Route 1).

3. Around the Italian peninsula (4100 km (2550 mi.))

The initial details of the journey are as in Route 1, from the western Upper Italian lakes via ★★**Milan** and ★**Genoa** to ★★**Pisa**. From there drive to the large port of Livorno and along the mainly flat coast of the Tyrrhenian Sea, which – as far as Civitavecchia – was once the fever-infected land of the Marems. Next comes the little town of Follonica, then the provincial capital of Grosseto. Continue to Orbetello, with worthwhile detours to the foothills of Monte Argentario and to the ruins of the old Etruscan town of Cosa; then on to the port of Civitavecchia, from where ships leave for ★**Sardinia**. Continue along the coast, with detours to the Etruscan necropolis of Cerveteri, and later through the Roman Campagna to ★★**Rome**.

Then (as per Route 2) from Rome via ★★**Naples** and **Salerno** to ★★**Paestum**; through the mountainous countryside of the southern **Campania** to Sapri, which can also be approached from Paestum along a magnificent coastal road via Agropoli and Palinuro, and then on along a fine stretch of the west Calabrian coast, the southern part of which in particular is very charming. From Villa San Giovanni it is possible to make a detour via the Straits of ★**Messina** and then on to the spa town of ★★**Taormina**, high above the sea with a view of ★★**Etna**.

Back to Villa San Giovanni and to **Reggio di Calabria**, from where there is a worthwhile detour to be made to the wooded Aspromonte Mountains; then around the southern tip of **Calabria** and along the Ionian Sea as far as Catanzara Lido. Turn inland to Catanzaro and through the wooded Sila Mountains; near Cosenza the route joins the main road again. From here drive through the Crati valley and near Spezzano Albanese to the coast road along the Ionian Sea. Now continue along by the sea to Scanzano, then inland to Miglionico. Continue

Suggested Routes

to the very picturesque provincial capital of Matera and to Altamura, then via the little town of Alberobello, famous for its "trulli", to the port of **Taranto**. Then on to ★**Lecca**, known for its Baroque buildings, and via Maglie to Cape Santa Maria di Leuca, the southernmost cape in ★**Apulia**. Continue by way of Santa Cesarea Terme to Otranto and then again via Maglie back to Lecce and on to the important port of **Brindisi**.

From Brindisi the route runs close to the Adriatic and on to Monopoli, then inland to the magnificent Castellana caves and via Conversano back to the coast at Polignano a Mare. Continue along the Adriatic by way of ★**Bari**, the capital of Apulia, and **Trani** to ★**Barletta**, then inland via Andria to the massive Hohenstaufen palace of Caste del Monte. The route then goes via Minervino to **Foggia**, from where a tour around the foothills of Monte Gargano is recommended.

Beyond San Severo this part of the route nears the Adriatic coast once again, and this is followed as far as Marino di San Vito. Then through ★**Abruzzi** and via Scanno to **Sulmona**; along the western foot of the Maiella chain and – if possible, after making a detour to Chieti – to Pescara. Now either take the faster road along the coast or the more varied one through the interior via Ascoli Piceni and Macerata and the little pilgrimage town of ★**Loreto** to the harbour town of **Ancona**. Continue along the coast by way of Pesaro to ★**Rimini**; from there, as in Route 1, drive either to Brenner or to Innichen.

4. Grand journey through Italy and Sicily (5000 km (3100 mi.))

Initially, follow Route 1 from Domodossola, Lugano or Chiavenna via ★**Genoa** and ★★**Florence** to ★★**Rome**, and then continue as in Route 2 via ★★**Naples** to ★★**Paestum**, then as in Route 3 to Villa San Giovanni and take the ferry over the Strait of Messina (Stretto di Messina) to ★★**Sicily**. From the large port of ★**Messina** proceed either via the Colle San Rizzo or, preferably, around the Punta del Faro to the varied north coast of Sicily and follow the coast road. Detours are recommended to Milazzo (boats go to the ★**Lipari Islands**), to the pilgrimage church of the Madonna del Tindaro and the remains of the ancient town of Tyndaris, and also via Termini Imerese to the ruins of Soluntum. Then comes the magnificently situated Sicilian capital of ★★**Palermo**, which can also be reached direct from Naples by boat (and car ferry), but this means missing the coastal road scenery between Messina and Palermo.

Beyond Palermo follow the road running west, the next town being Monreale with its fine cathedral. Continue via Alcamo to the impressive temple of Segesta and then on to **Trapani**, from where a detour to Erice should not be missed. Then proceed to the port of **Marsala** at the western tip of the island, famous for its wine, and via Castelvetrano to the extensive ruins of ★**Selinunte**. Continue near to the south coast as far as ★**Agrigento** with its impressive temple ruins. From here either turn inland via Caltanissetta to Enna, then by way of Piazza Armerina with its interesting Roman villa, or from Agrigento hug the south coast via Gela and Ragusa to ★★**Syracuse** with the extensive remains of the ancient city. Follow the coast to ★**Catania**, Sicily's second largest city, where the road to Mount ★★**Etna**, with its splendid views, begins. From Etna return to Catania and then either direct via Acireale or around Etna to ★★**Taormina**, Sicily's largest health resort. Then follow the coast back to ★**Messina**.

From Messina return by ferry to Villa San Giovanni or to **Reggio di Calabria**, then as in Route 3 to Catanzaro and through the Sila Mountains to Cosenza. Continue through the interior of **Calabria**, the **Basilicata** region and southern **Campania** to Battipaglia, thus again reaching the stretch described in Route 2. On this, proceed via ★★**Naples** to ★★**Rome**, then via ★**Bologna** or ★★**Venice** to the Brenner or to Innichen (see Route 1); if time is short take the motorway from Battipaglia to Naples, beyond which the beautifully routed del Sole autostrada can be taken to Bologna.

5. Through western upper Italy (1700 km (1050 mi.))

This suggested itinerary (between 7 and 9 days if no long stays) takes in that part of Italy lying between the western Alps and the Ligurian Sea. From Chiavenna drive along the eastern shores of ★**Lake Como** and via Lecco to **Como**; from here take either the state road or the motorway to ★★**Milan**. Continue on the motorway to Chivasso, then by the Dora Baltea to Ivrea and up the ★**Aosta Valley** to Châtillon (detour to Breuil). From Châtillon proceed to **Aosta** with a detour to the Great St Bernard (road tunnel). Then by way of Pré-St-Didier to Courmayeur and Entrèves at the foot of Mont Blanc, through which there is also a tunnel. Return to Pré-St-Didier and via the Little St Bernard to Séez, then up the Isère valley and via the Col de l'Iseran to Lanslebourg. Then drive via Mont Cenis to Susa and by the Dora Riparia on to Ulzio (detour to Bardonecchia). From Ulzio via Cesana to Claviere and to Mont Genèvre; then back to Cesana and via Sestriere into the Chisone valley and down the valley to Pinerolo. From here pass Stupinigi Palace and on to ★**Turin**; then via Savigliano to Cuneo and by way of the Col di Tenda (tunnel) to Nice. From there continue along the ★**Riviera** (Riviera di Ponente) to ★**Genoa** and, as described in Route 1 but in the reverse direction, to ★★**Milan**, from where the return to Chiavenna is via Como.

6. Through eastern upper Italy (1500 km (930 mi.))

On this itinerary (6–7 days with no long stays) the visitor will get to know those parts of Upper Italy lying between Brenner, Lake Garda and Venice. From Brenner, as described in Route 1 but in the reverse direction, travel down the Isarco valley, then at Sterzing (Vipiteno) turn south-west over the Jaufenpass (Passo di Monte Giovo) to the famous old spa town of ★**Merano**. Continue via the Gampon ridge to Fondo and along Lake Molveno to the Ponte delle Arche. Drive on through the narrow pass known as the Gola de la Scaletta to Tione, then through the south of Judicaria, along Lake Idro to **Brescia** and via Salò and along the west bank of ★★**Lake Garda** to Riva. Now follow the road along the east bank of Lake Garda to Peschiera and on to ★★**Verona**. Continue through the Po plain, via **Mantua** and Carpi to ★**Modena**; from there cross the Apennines by way of the Abetone pass to ★**Pistola** and via **Prato** to ★★**Florence**. From here turn north again and proceed via ★★**Bologna** and ★**Ferrara** to ★★**Padua** and on to ★★**Venice**. Return to Padua and drive via Bassano (detour to Monte Grappa) and Levico to **Trento**. Then through the Adige valley to ★**Bolzano** and through the Sam valley by way of Penser Joch to Sterzing; from here the state road leads to Brenner (cf. Route 1).

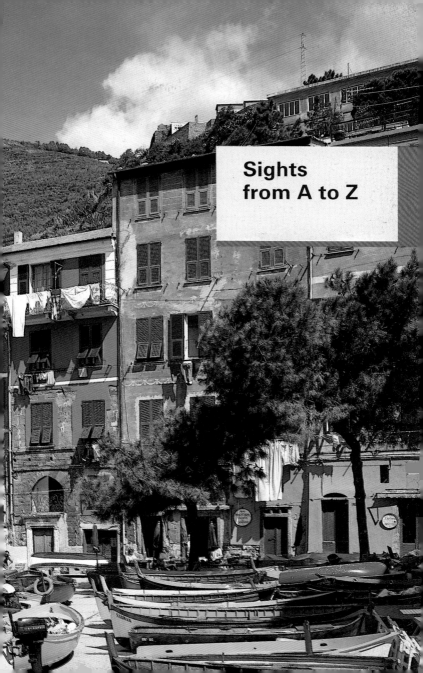

**Sights
from A to Z**

Tip   Some of the important museums in the larger towns and cities are open
                       only in the morning, (weekdays 9am–2pm, Sun. 9am–1pm); most are
                       closed Mon. Please note that the opening times can change at short
                       notice.

Advice   Visitors who have only one day to spend in a town or city are advised to
                       check in advance the days and times on which the museum they wish to
                       visit is open.

Abruzzi   J12

                       Region: Abruzzi/Abruzzo
                       Province: L'Aquila (AQ), Chieti (CH), Pescara (PE) and Teramo (TE)
                       Area: 10,794 sq. km (4152 sq. mi.). Population: 1,200,000

Location   The Abruzzi, the wildest and highest part of the Apennines in the east of
                       Central Italy extend from the watershed of the Central Apennines to the
                       Adriatic and take in the four provinces of L'Aquila, Pescara, Chieti and
                       Teramo. On the north they are bounded by the Marche, on the west by
                       Latium and on the south-east by Molise, with which they have been
                       combined since 1963 to form the administrative unit of Abruzzi e Molise.

Population   The is concentrated in the towns of the region – L'Aquila, Chieti, Lanciano,
                       Vasto, Teramo, Pescara, Sulmona and Avezzano. The rest is only thinly
                       populated.

Agriculture   With the exception of few areas, especially in the south and in the lower
                       regions, the largest part of the Abruzzi is sparsely wooded, has partly
                       karstic areas, a harsh climate, an abundance of snow and an infertile soil.
                       Arable farming is possible only in the valleys and depressions, particular-
                       ly in the Fucino basin; the mountain regions are good only for grazing
                       land.

Winter sports   In addition to agriculture the development of tourism is of great import-
                       ance particularly in the Gran Sasso for winter sports (cableway to Campo
                       Imperatore 2130 m (7029 ft)).

★Gran Sasso   The heart of the Abruzzi is formed by three mighty mountain chains, the
d'Italia   most easterly and highest of which contains the highest peaks in the
                       peninsula, in the Gran Sasso d'Italia group; Corno Grande 2912 m (9610 ft).
                       Between these mountain chains lie the central uplands of the Abruzzi, in
                       which the longitudinal valley of the Aterno, the high valleys of L'Aquila
                       and Sulmona and the wide and fertile Fucino basin form substantial inden-
                       tations. The north-eastern part, beyond the Gran Sasso massif, which is
                       occupied by an upland region traversed by numerous rivers, slopes down
                       gradually towards the Adriatic. Along the coast are many fine seaside
                       resorts.

★Abruzzi National Park

                       The southernmost part of the Abruzzi is occupied by the Abruzzi National
                       Park (Parco Nazionale d'Abruzzo) with its beautiful beech forests. It covers
                       an area of some 400 sq. km (154 sq. mi.) in the valley of the upper Sangro
                       and its numerous side valleys. With its network of footpaths and its moun-

                       ◀ *A picturesque fishing village in the Cinqueterre near La Spezia*

Houses huddled together in Abruzzi villages

tain huts it is ideally suited for tourists; another 200 sq. km (77 sq. mi.) belong to the nature reserve. The park was established in 1921 as a nature reserve to protect the landscape, flora and fauna of the Abruzzi; among the mountain animals which can still be seen here are the Abruzzi brown bear *(Ursus arctos marsicanus)*, the Abruzzi chamois *(Rupicapra rupicapra ornata)*, the Apennine wolf *(Canis lupus italicus)* and the golden eagle.

The central point of the park is the village of Pescasseroli; 1167 m, (3851 ft) in the Sangro valley – visited both by tourists who enjoy a summer vacation and winter sports enthusiasts – with its enclosures in which animals can live in natural surroundings; botanic garden and museum on the natural history of the park. The philosopher Benedetto Croce (1866–1955) was born here. **Pescasseroli**

About 5 km (3 mi.) south-east is the village of Opi, starting point for the rewarding climb of Monte Marsicano 2242 m (7398 ft).

In the northern Abruzzi lies Teramo (265 m (875 ft); population 51,500), the capital of the province of the same name (a road tunnel runs from Teramo to L'Aquila). In the centre of the town is the Piazza Orsini with the Town Hall, the Bishop's Palace and the cathedral (12th c.), which was restored in 1932. The cathedral has a Gothic doorway of 1332. Its interior is furnished in both Roman and Gothic style; worth seeing are a silver altar frontal by Nicola da Guardiagrele (1433–48) and a great polyptychon (1450) by Jacobello del Fiori. South-east of the cathedral are the remains of a Roman amphitheatre. **Teramo**

The west front of the cathedral faces on to the Piazza dei Martiri della Libertà, from which the Corso San Giorgio, the town's main street, runs to the municipal park.

Above the Pescara valley, in a situation affording extensive views, is Chieti 330 m (1089 ft); population 55,000, capital of the province of the same name and the see of an archbishop. In Piazza Vittorio Emanuele are the **Chieti**

Town Hall (collection of pictures) and the Gothic cathedral of San Giustino, with a Baroque interior. From the rear of the Town Hall the town's principal street, Corso Marrucino, runs south-west, passing near a group of three temples (to the right, 1st c.), to the municipal park and the Villa Comunale (views!). In the Villa Comunale is the National Museum of Antiquities (Museo Nazionale di Antichità), containing a remarkable collection of prehistoric and Roman material.

Just below Strada Marrucina, which flanks the east side of the town hill, is a large rock-cut Roman cistern, with the remains of the baths which it supplied.

Pescara

On the Adriatic coast, astride the River Pescara which reaches the sea here, is the provincial capital of Pescara (6 m (20 ft); population 132,000). The town was badly damaged during the Second World War but has been rebuilt on an impressive scale. In Piazza Italia, on the left bank of the river, is the imposing Palazzo del Governo. On the other side of the river, stands the Tempio della Conciliazione, built 1935–38 to commemorate the Lateran treaties. On the Corso Manthonè is the house where the poet Gabriele D'Annunzio (1863–1938) was born; inside (open to visitors) there are many relics. In the Museo Ittico (Via Paolucci), close to the Porto Canale, can be seen the skeleton of a sperm whale.

Adriatic coast

Along the Adriatic coast is a whole series of resorts, some of them with beautiful beaches. From north to south: Martinsicuro, Alba Adriatica, Tortoreto Lido (5 km (3 mi.) west, the medieval town of Tortoreto Alto), Giulianova, Roseto degli Abruzzi (formerly Rosburgo), Pineto (11 km (7 mi.)) west, the little town of Atri, with a Romanesque-Gothic cathedral dating from the end of the 13th c., contains fine frescoes), Silvi Marina, Montesilvano Marina, Francavilla al Mare, Ortona (ruins of a castle, fine views), San Vito Chietino (12 km (7¹/₂ mi.)) south-west, the walled town of

The Abruzzi National Park

Lanciano with the Gothic church of S. Maria Maggiori which was rebuilt in the 18th c., with a campanile dating from the 12th c.), Fossacesia Marina (near which is the Romanesque basilica of San Giovanni in Venere, 8th–13th c.) and Vasto, with several interesting churches and, in the cathedral square, the Palazzo d'Avalos (18th c.).

Agrigento   H21

Region: Sicily/Sicilia. Province: Agrigento (AG)
Altitude: 230 m (759 ft). Population: 52,000

Agrigento, capital of the province of the same name, lies half way along the south coast of Sicily – some 100 km (62 mi.) south-east of Marsala.
   With its magnificent ruined temples it is one of the most beautifully situated towns in Sicily. However, the skyline of the town itself has been drastically changed by the blocks of new housing developments, particularly on the south side of the old town.

Location

Agrigento was founded in 581 BC, under the name of Akragas by settlers from the Greek colony of Gela (80 km (50 mi.) south-east). Magnificently situated on a ridge between the rivers Akragas (San Biagio) and Hypsas (Santa Anna), it was celebrated by Pindar as "the most beautiful city of mortal men". On the north side of the hill, now occupied by the modern town, was the acropolis; to the south, on the land, sloping gradually towards the sea, lay the ancient city with extensive remains of its walls and temples. The town was mostly ruled by tyrants, one of whom, Phalaris (c. 549 BC), was notorious for his cruelty: he is said to have crucified his enemies to Zeus Atabyrios (the Moloch of Mount Tabor) by roasting them in a brazen bull. The town rose to wealth and power by trade with Carthage, and some of its citizens lived in princely state. Akragas reached its peak of prosperity as a free state under the leadership of Empedocles (who died c. 424 BC), but soon afterwards (406 BC) succumbed to the Carthaginians. The town was plundered and the temples were set on fire. Akragas had a new peak under the leadership of Timoleone, who defeated the Carthaginians in 340 BC. The Roman Agrigentum (from 210 BC) was a place of no importance. In AD 827 it was taken by the Saracens and grew to rival Palermo. In 1086 the Norman ruler Roger I established a bishopric here which developed during the Middle Ages into the richest in Sicily. Until 1927 the town was known by its Saracenic name of Girgenti.
   Agrigento was the birthplace of the writer Luigi Pirandello (1867–1936).

History

Old town

At the north-west corner of the old town, a huddle of narrow winding streets, stands the cathedral, built on the foundation of a temple of Jupiter of the 6th c. BC. It was begun in the 11th c., enlarged in the 13th–14th c. and largely remodelled in the 16th–17th c. A landslip in 1966 caused considerable damage but now it is mostly restored. At the end of the north aisle is the chapel of De Marinis, with the tomb of Gaspare de Marinis (1493). To the right of the choir is a fine silver reliquary (1639) with the remains of San Gerlando, first bishop of Agrigento.

Cathedral

By the steps – west of the cathedral – is the Museo Diocesano.

Museo Diocesano

To the south of the old town, in Piazza Pirandello, is the Museo Civico, containing medieval and modern art as well as paintings by Sicilian artists.

Museo Civico

The principal street of the town is the busy Via Atenea. It runs east to the Piazzale Aldo Moro, east of the old town. 1.5 km (1 mi.) farther east in a

Rupe Atenea

Agrigento

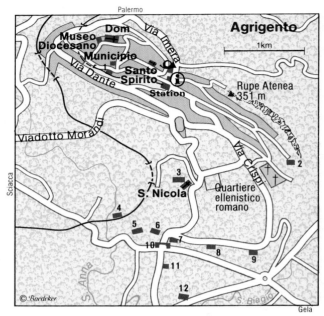

1 Museo Civico
2 Tempio di Demetra (San Biagio)
3 Museo Archeologico
4 Tempio di Vulcano
5 Tempio di Castore e Polluce
6 Tempio di Giove Olimpico
7 Tempio di Ercole
8 Tempio di Concordia
9 Tempio di Giunone
10 Porta Aurea
11 Tomba di Terone
12 Tempio di Esculapio

private garden is the Rock of Atenea (Rupe Atenea; 351 m (1158 ft)), from which there are extensive views.

Santo Spirito

North of the Via Atenea the church of Santo Spirito (13th c.) is worth visiting. It is decorated with fine stucco by Giacomo Serpotta.

Passeggiata Archeologica (Archaeological Tour)

The temple area is reached via the Piazzale Aldo Moro, immediately south of the Piazza Marconi with its railway station. The tour is signposted "Passeggiata Archeologica" and runs south-east along Via Crispi.

Cemetery

In 1 km (3/4 mi.) a road goes off on the left to the cemetery. At its south-east corner are remains of the Greek town walls.

Tempio di Demetra

From here it is only 500 m east on the stony ancient road to the Temple of Demeter (Tempio di Demetra) which stands on high ground. Originally built c. 470 BC, it was converted by the Normans into the little church of San Biagio. To the east below the terrace is a cave sanctuary of Demeter (c. 650 BC).

Greco-Roman city

Soon afterwards another road on the right branches off the Via Crispi. After 500 m a recently excavated section of the Greco-Roman city (4th c. BC to 5th c. AD) is reached; with fine wall paintings and mosaic pavements.

Close to the site is the Museo Archeologico Regionale with prehistoric finds, ancient sarcophagi, vases, coins and architectural fragments; particularly precious is a marble statue of an ephebe (c. 490 BC).

★Museo Archeologico Regionale

Immediately south of the museum is the little Gothic church of San Nicola (13th c.) with a fine doorway. Inside is a marble sarcophagus carved with scenes from the story of Phaedra and Hippolytus (2nd–3rd c. AD). Close to the church, to the west, is the so-called Oratory of Phalaris and a theatre built on a comitium (meeting-place).

San Nicola

Temple Area

1 km (½ mi.) beyond San Nicola the road reaches the entrance to the enclosed Temple Area (open at all times). To the right is the Temple of Zeus; immediately to the left of the road, near the south wall of the ancient city, the so-called Temple of Hercules (Tempio di Ercole; 6th c. BC), with eight columns – out of the original 38 – which were re-erected on the south side in 1923.

Tempio di Ercole

From the Temple of Hercules a new road runs east past the Villa Aurea (offices of the Temple Area administration; temporary exhibitions) to the Doric Temple of Concord (Tempio di Concordia) which was built in the 5th c. BC and converted into a church in the Middle Ages. With all its 34 columns still standing, it ranks with the Theseion in Athens as the best preserved ancient temple.

★★Tempio di Concordia

About 700 m farther east, magnificently situated above a steep escarpment at the south-east corner of the ancient city, near the road from Agrigento to Gela, is the so-called Temple of Iuno Lacinia (Tempio di Giunone; 5th c. BC), a classic example of the Doric style. The temple, actually dedicated to Hera, has 25 complete columns standing and nine others partly re-erected. 15 m east is the sacrificial altar.

★★Tempio di Giunone

Between the temples of Hercules and Zeus is the harbour gate, the so-called Porta Aurea, through which passes the road to Porto Empedocle (10 km (6 mi.) south-west) and the ancient port, which lies due south at the mouth of the Fiume San Biagio.

Porta Aurea

Outside the Porta Aurea is the so-called Tomb of Theron (Tomba di Terone), the remains of a tower-like Roman mausoleum (1st c. BC).

Tomba di Terone

Further to the south is the small Temple of Aesculapius (Tempio de Esculapio; 5th c. BC), from which there are extensive views.

Tempio di Esculapio

North-west of the Porta Aurea are the ruins of the unfinished Temple of Zeus (Tempio di Giove Olimpico; 5th c. BC). With its length of 113 m (371ft) it is the largest temple of Greek antiquity (Temple G at Selinunt 111 m (364 ft); Artemision at Ephesus 109 m (358 ft); Parthenon at Athens 70 m (230 ft)). The entablature was probably supported by the huge male and female Telamones or Atlas figures; one of them was restored ("il Gigante", 7.75 m (25½ft), lying on the ground). One of the Telamones can be seen in the Archaeological Museum.

Tempio di Giove Olimpico

West of the Temple of Zeus is the so-called Temple of Castor and Pollux (Tempio di Castor e Polluce) or Temple of the Dioscuri, of which four columns have been re-erected. A little way north is the Sanctuary of the Chthonic Divinities (Santuario delle Divinità Ctonie; 6th c. BC) a unique cult place dedicated to the divinities of the underworld, probably Demeter and Persephone. The remains of twelve altars and eight small temples in the form of treasuries have been excavated.

Tempio di Castor e Polluce

Farther to the north-west, beyond the railway, are the remains of the so-called Temple of Vulcan (Tempio di Vulcano, built c. 470 BC). From here there is a view of the range of temples.

Tempio di Vulcano

Surroundings

East of Agrigento, on a hill, lies the picturesque little town of Naro with fine remains of medieval buildings, among which are parts of the town walls and the Castello dei Chiaramonte.

Naro
35 km (22 mi.) E

★★Alto Adige (South Tirol)   E–H1–3

Region: Trentino-Alto Adige. Province: Bolzano (BZ)
Area: 7400 sq. km (2857 sq. mi.). Population: 422,000

The Alto Adige (Upper Adige) lies in the extreme north of Italy on the southern fringe of the Alps. The area extends north-south from the Brenner to the Saluner Klause, on the west it is bounded by the Resia (Rentschen) pass and the Stilfser Joch, and on the east by the Pusteria valley (Pustertal) and the Kreuzbergpass. The situation of the Alto Adige gives it a varied range of topography from the eternal snow of the great glaciated peaks of the Central Alps and the Ortles group (3902 m (12,877 ft)) to the Mediterranean climate and the vineyards of the Bolzano (265 m (875 ft)) and Merano area.

Location

The geological structure is determined by the girdle of ancient Alpine rocks (gneisses, granites, schists and quartz phyllites) in the north and west, the considerable area of dolomitic limestone crags in the east and the great spread of porphyries around Bolzano in the south, extending far into the neighbouring Trentino.

Geology

Scenery

Extending south from the Réesia (Reschen) pass is the upper Adige (Etsch) valley, which from here to Merano is known as the Val Venosta (Vintschgau), with the most massive peaks (about 3000 m (10,000 ft)) of the Eastern Alps, from which the Val Passiria (Passeiertal) branches off and runs north to the Passo di Monte Giovo (Jaufenpass, 2094 m (6910 ft)). Beyond this is Vipiteno (Sterzing) in the Isarco (Eisack) valley, which farther south is joined by the Pusteria (Puster) valley.

Between the Valtellina, the Val Venosta and the upper Noce valley (Val di Sole and Val di Non) extends the Ortles (Ortler) group, a range of mainly crystalline rocks but with its highest peaks, Ortles (Ortler, 3902 m (12,877 ft)) and the majestic Gran Zebrù (Königsspitze, 3859 m (12.735 ft)), built up from Triassic limestones. On the north side of the range are the Solda (Sulden), Martello (Martell) and Ultimo (Ulten) valleys, on the west the Valfurva and on the south the Péio and Rabbi valleys, all much glaciated in the upper reaches.

Ortles group

To the south of the Passo Di Tonale (1893 m (6214 ft)), bounded on the west by the Oglio valley (Val Camónica) and on the east by the Sarco valley, is the Adamello-Presanella group (Cima Presanella, 3556 m (11,735 ft)); Monte Adamello, 3554 m (11,728 ft), consisting mainly of tornalites, through which runs the wild Val de Génova with its waterfalls.

Adamello-
Presanella group

Along the east side of the Ortles and Adamella-Presanella groups runs the Valli Giudicarie (the middle valley of the Sarca and upper valley of the Chiesa or Chiem), one of the most striking fault lines in the Alps. To the

Brenta group

◀ *The Temple of Concord near Agrigento*

east of this line the land has sunk 2000 m (6660 ft) in places, so that here, in contrast to the crystalline Central Alps, the substance of the Etschbucht-gebirge which belongs to the Southern Alps and owes its name to its geological situation rather than to its geographical setting, is made up of Triassic and Jurassic dolomites and limestones. The best-known range is the dolomitic Brenta group (Cima Tosa, 3173 m (10,471ft)), which in spite of its geographical separation from the main Dolomites east of the Adige ranks equal with them in the magnificence of its mountain scenery.

The parallel chain to the east, the Etschgebirge, the northern part of which is called Nonsberger Alps, with the Monte Roén (Mendelgebirge, 2116 m (6983 ft)) being part of this, falls down in sheer limestone walls to the morainic uplands on the upper Adige in the north and the wide Adige valley, covered with later fluvial deposits.

Adige valley

South of the Pusteria valley and to a lesser extent in the north-eastern Sarentine Alps (Sarntaler Alpen) is a zone of quartz phyllites, mainly dark coloured. In Rasciesa (Raschötz, 2283 m (7534 ft)) and the southern Sarentine Alps this is overlaid by the Bolzano porphyries, hard reddish volcanic rocks of the Permian period.

Sarentine Alps

This porphyry zone, extending south as far as the Trento region and reach-ing its highest point in the Lagorai chain (Cima de Cece, 2772 m (9148 ft)) near Predazzo, is cut by deep valleys, notably the Val d'Ega (Eggental) at Bolzano and the Tires valley (Tierser Tal). The infertile porphyry has been covered, particularly on the Renón (Ritten) by old moraines, which have been eroded by heavy rain, leaving the famous "earth pillars" capped by their protective boulders.

Lagorai chain
Renón

The porphyries combine with melaphyres and sandstones of the late Permian, soft schists, clays and variegated marls of the Lower Triassic and intrusions of dark-coloured lavas and volcanic tuffs to form the undulat-ing basement formation, covered with beautiful Alpine meadows and coniferous forests, of the Dolomites.

Dolomites

The climate of the region reflects its geographical diversity, ranging from the Alpine conditions of the mountain valleys with their abundance of snow through the normal European climate of the intermediate areas to the Mediterranean type, with mild winters and sometimes very hot summers, of the wide valleys of the Adige and the Isarco with their south-ern exposure and their sheltered situation, protected from the north winds by the mountains. The Val Venosta in the west of the region has the repu-tation of being the driest valley in the Eastern Alps; in the north it has an Alpine climate, but in the southern part it approximates to the climatic pattern of Merano.

Climate

The population of the Alto Adige is mixed, consisting of Germans, Italians, and Ladins, the descendants of the original Rhaeto-Romanic inhabitants; and, lying as it does on one of the great European transit routes from north to south, it has suffered many vicissitudes in the course of its history, from the time of the Great Migrations to the present day.

Population

   The German-speaking population of 280,000 have German schools; they can develop their cultural life freely, and their language has equal status with that of the 124,000 Italians who live chiefly in the towns. The culture and language of the Ladins, some 18,000 in number, are also protected. Nearly the entire population (98 per cent) is Roman Catholic, no matter which ethnic group they belong to. Each linguistic group is entitled to a proportionate share of posts in the government service.

This begins with the finds of neolithic material in the south of the region and Bronze Age material in the Alpine territory. The indigenous population,

History

◀ *Springtime in the Alps*

known to the Romans as Rhaetians but subject also to Celto-Illyrian, Ligurian and Etruscan influences, were incorporated in the Roman Empire by Augustus in 15 BC and over the course of half a millennium were Romanised, at least in language. During the period of the Great Migrations this relatively thinly settled region, occupied by peoples who were now known as Raeto-Romanic, saw the passage of the invading Gothics and Lombards, but the first invaders to settle here were the Bajuwari, who had occupied the whole of the region by the end of the 6th c., making it a purely German-speaking area, along the fringes of which (the Dolomite valleys, the Val Venosta) the Rhaeto-Romanic population have contrived to survive down to modern times, perserving at least in part their language and their way of life as in the Val Gádera (Gadertal and Val Gardena (Gröden)).

The Alto Adige then became a part of the Frankish kingdom, and at the beginning of the 11th c. passed into the hands of the prince-bishops of Trento and Bressanone, whose lay governors, principally the Counts of Tirol, sought to unite their territories. These territories, lying on both sides of the Brenner, fell into the hands of the Habsburgs in 1363 and remained Austrian until 1918, with a short interruption during the Napoleonic period (Andreas Hofer's successful rising and subsequent defeat). Thereafter South Tirol became Italian against its will and was subjected to a process of denationalisation under Fascist rule. After the Second World War, under the Treaty of Paris, the region was granted a substantial measure of self-government.

Art

The vicissitudes of the region's history are reflected in its art and architecture, with examples of Romanesque (Val Venosta, San Cándido Cathedral), a rich range of Gothic (frescoes, altars with side panels), and major works of Renaissance and Baroque architecture. The Alto Adige is also notable for its numerous fortified castles.

Romanesque

A short survey of art and architecture can properly begin in the Val Venosta, which has mainly work in Romanesque style but also monuments dating back to the early days of Christianity, such as the crypt of Monte Maria (Marienberg) abbey, the Carolingian church of San Benedetto in Malles (Mals), numerous other churches in the valley which now stand empty, and above all San Prócolo at Naturno (Naturns), with the oldest surviving wall paintings in German-speaking territory. Other fine examples of Romanesque architecture which must be seen are the doorways in Castel Tirolo (Schloss Tirol) with their carved bestiary and the completely preserved cathedral at San Cándido (Innichen) in the Val Pusteria.

Gothic

Bolzano (Bozen) offers fine examples of Gothic, in particular its late Gothic cathedral and the altar by Michael Pacher (Coronation of the Virgin) in the old parish church of Gries. There are some fine exhibits to be seen in Bolzano Museum and the Diocesan Museum in Bressanone (Brixen). Both of these museums also contain Baroque pictures, while some of the finest painting to be found in the Alpine countries can be seen in the famous cloisters of the Franciscan and Dominican monasteries in Bolzano and in those of Novacella (Neustift) and above all Bressanone.

Baroque

The Alto Adige is poor in major buildings of the Baroque period, apart from the beautiful church at Dobbiaco (Toblach) in the Val Pusteria. The finest Baroque palace in the region, Castello Mareta (Wolfsthurn), lies in the Val Ridanna, a remote side valley near Vipiteno.

Folk art and traditions

Folk art and traditions have always been important to the inhabitants of the Alto Adige. In Teodone (Dietenheim), near Brunico (Bruneck), the regional folk museum has an interesting collection and an open air department. Fine examples of the craftmanship of the Alto Adige can also be seen in the Folk Museum in Innsbruck (Austria). Old traditions are well maintained by the many local bands with their smart costumes. The beautiful old peasant costumes are still worn in the Val Sarentina, during the ordinary working week and not merely on special occasions. The pre-Christmas period is celebrated here with an old tradition, the so-called "Klöckeln", an ancient fertility cult combined with later Christian elements. The Corpus Christi procession of Castelrotto (Kastelruth) is famous, and many towns and villages, particularly in the mountain valleys, still have impressive processions which show a characteristic combination of genuine piety with attachment to traditional practices.

Economy

The road and rail route over the Brenner and through the Isarco and Adige valleys is the most important north-south link in the Eastern Alps. The wide stretch of the Adige valley between Merano and the Salorno defile is also of great economic importance as the main area of production of the region's high-quality fruit (particularly apples and pears) and its renowned wines.

The wine-producing region extends from the Isarco valley in the north to the Salorno defile in the southern Adige valley, taking in part of the Val Venosta to the west and part of the Rienza valley to the east. It is divided into six main areas – the Isarco valley, the Val Venosta, the area round Merano, the Bolzano basin, the Upper Adige and the Adige valley. The total area under vines is over 6000 ha, which produce some 70 million litres of wine annually (85 per cent red, 15 per cent white). About four-fifths of the output is exported, mainly to Switzerland, Germany and Austria.

Wines

  Well known quality wines are Santa Maddalena (ruby-red, full-bodied, velvety), grown on the hillsides of the Bolzano basin; Merano (ruby-red, strong, well-rounded); and Lago di Caldaro (light red to ruby-red, light, harmonious).

A characteristic feature of vine-growing in the Alto Adige is the use of "pergolas" – wooden frames on which the vines grow, enabling large quantities of grapes to be produced in a relatively small area.

"Pergolas"

The wine is pressed with an ancient type of wine-press known as the "torkel". At the time of the vintage (September–October) the local people like to visit the wine-cellars and wine-shops to taste the new wine, accompanying it with walnuts, roast chestnuts and home-made bread.

"Torkel"

The "Alto Adige wine route" (Südtiroler Weinstrasse), 30 km (19 mi.) long, runs down the west side of the Adige valley from Castle Firmiano (Sigmundskron), west of Bolzano, to Frangarto, Cornaiano (Girlan), Appiano (Eppan: with San Michele/St Michael, San Paolo/St Pauls and Missiano/Missian), Caldaro (Kaltern), San Giuseppe (St Josef), Termeno (Tramin), Cortaccia (Kurtatsch), Magré (Margreid), Cortina all'Adige (Kurtinig: possible continuation via Rovere della Luna to Mezzocorona) and Salorno (Salurn).

Alto Adige wine route

The Bolzano area has the greatest concentration of commerce and industry (Bolzano Trade Fair; metal-working, particularly iron, aluminium and magnesium; engineering, vehicle manufacture; chemicals; textiles, leather goods, woodworking, canning). Merano has chemical plants (artificial fertilisers, etc.). There are numerous smaller industrial and craft establishments in the Isarco valley (Bressanone), Val Pusteria (Brunico) and the Val Venosta.

Industry

The economy of the region still depends mainly on the vigour and energy of its farming population. Corn-growing is steadily declining in favour of fodder crops (maize) and seed potatoes. In this region forestry is an important activity, while the extensive Alpine meadows provide pasture for

Agriculture

Amalfi

cattle (particularly dairy cows); Haflinger horses are prized both as working and as riding animals.

Tourism
One of the main pillars of the economy is now tourism, promoted by the incomparable beauty of the scenery, the excellent snow conditions in the high valleys in winter and the favourable climate. The region is well equipped for the tourist trade, with numerous funiculars, ski-lifts and other recreational facilities, a dense system of way-marked footpaths and routes for climbers, as well as ample accommodation for visitors, ranging from modestly priced rooms in private houses to first-class hotels offering every amenity.

Bolzano
See entry

Bressanone
See entry

Dolomites
See entry

Merano
See entry

Amalfi   J14

Region: Campania. Province: Salerno (SA)
Altitude: 0–11 m (0–36 ft). Population: 6000

Location
The seaside resort of Amalfi lies on the south coast of the Sorrento peninsula at the northern edge of the Gulf of Salerno – at the mouth of a deep gorge. Amalfi is one of the most popular holiday resorts in Italy, particularly favoured by the people of Naples.

History
According to legend Amalfi was founded by Constantine the Great. During the Middle Ages it was an independent state with a population of some 50,000, ruled by self-appointed dukes who later became hereditary. In 1077 the town was incorporated by Robert Guiscard in the Norman kingdom; through its active trade with the Orient it rose to influence and wealth. As a sea power Amalfi came into conflict with Pisa and Genoa. Amalfi's code of maritime law (Tabulae Amalfitanae) prevailed throughout the whole of the Italian Mediterranean from the 13th to the 16th c.

Sights

★Marina Grande
Along the coast runs a promenade and a beach. From the harbour, the Marina Grande, there are boat services to Naples, Capri and Salerno in the summer.

Town Hall
The houses cling to the bay. From the harbour it is a short distance by way of Piazza Flavio Gioia to the Town Hall; the façade is decorated with modern mosaic. The municipal museum (Museo Civico) is housed in the Town Hall; its major attraction is the so-called "Tavole amalfitane", a medieval document with the maritime law of ancient times. To the north lies the little Piazza del Duomo, from which a flight of 62 steps leads up to the cathedral.

Cathedral
The Cathedral of Sant'Andrea, originally built in the 9th c., was remodelled in Sicilian Lombard-Normanesque style in 1203; the campanile dates from 1180 to 1276. The magnificent portico, with pointed arches, was completely rebuilt in 1865. The front which was restored in 1890 is decorated with modern mosaic; the fine bronze door was cast in Constantinople in 1066. Inside there are ancient columns of Paestum, supporting the choir. The crypt contains the remains of the Apostle St Andrew, brought here in the 13th c.

Amalfi, on the beautiful Sorrento peninsula

To the left, in the portico, is the entrance to the cloister (Chiostro del Paradiso, 1266–68), which contains ancient sarcophagi, marble and mosaics.

About 500 m west of the cathedral, high above Amalfi (also reached by lift from the coast road), is the former Capuchin monastery (now a hotel) with a beautiful cloister and affording fine views.

Capuchin monastery

There is an attractive trip by motorboat (15 minutes) to a stalactitic cave, the Grotta di Amalfi, also known as the Grotta dello Smeraldo or Grotta Verde, west of the Capo Conca (fee).

★Grotta di Amalfi 1 km (¹/₂ mi.) W

Surroundings

On the coast road, beyond the Capo di Amalfi, at the mouth of a gorge of the Dragone, is the little town of Atrani (12 m (40 ft)). In the Piazza is the church of San Salvatore de' Bireto (10th c.), the church where the doges of Amalfi were crowned. Its Byzantine bronze doors were cast in Constantinople in 1087.

Atrani 1 km (¹/₂ mi.) E

From the east side of Atrani a winding road with two sharp bends ascends through orange-groves to Ravello (350 m (1155 ft)), an old town in a superb situation above the Amalfi coast. The town founded during the Norman period, had its heyday under the Anjou dynasty in the 13th c. when it had a population of 36,000; it possessed many churches, monastic houses and palaces.
    In the centre of the town is the Romanesque cathedral of San Pantaleone (begun in 1086, remodelled in Baroque style) with fine bronze doors (covered externally with wooden doors) by Barisanus of Trani (1179).

Ravello 6 km (4 mi.) N

The little town of Atrani lies on the coast road south of Amalfi

Inside there is a marble pulpit with a mosaic ground by Niccolo di Bartolomeo (1272). In the choir stands the bishop's throne, to the left the Capella di San Pantaleone in which some of the saint's blood is preserved.

South-east of the cathedral is the Villa Rufolo, in Saracenic style (11th c.), with a little pillared courtyard in the centre. The garden with its lookout terrace provided Wagner with the model for Klingsor's enchanted garden.

A walk (about eight minutes) from the cathedral, first south through an arcade, then up through the portico of the church of San Francesco (cloister in Romanesque style) and past the church of Santa Chiara leads to the Villa Cimbrone. An avenue runs through the beautiful park to the Belvedere Cimbrone, from which there are incomparable views of the Amalfi coast.

About 200 m north-east of the cathedral is the church of San Giovanni del Toro (12th c.; remodelled in Baroque style and modernised). Inside there is a mosaic pulpit adorned with Persian majolica (c. 1175); on the pulpit steps and in the crypt are frescoes of scenes from the life of Christ.

Ancona   H8

Region: Marche. Province: Ancona (AN)
Altitude: 16 m (53 ft). Population: 101,000

Location

Ancona, capital of the Marche region and the province of the same name, is picturesquely situated between foothills and the bay on the Italian Adriatic coast.

Importance

At present Ancona is an important traffic junction (railway; airport 13 km (8 mi.) west at Falconara) and a developing port: ferry services to Yugoslavia and Greece and the growing fishing industry mean a considerable economic upswing in recent years. The making of musical instruments contributes to this.

Ancona was founded by refugees from Syracuse about 390 BC under the name of Dorica Ancon (from the Greek *ankón*, bend or curve, after the promontory on which the town was built). In the 3rd c. BC it became a Roman colony, and in the reigns of Caesar and Trajan it was fortified and developed into a naval base. Although the town was presented to the Pope by Charlemagne in 774, and at the end of the 16th c. was incorporated in the Papal States, in practice it maintained its independence throughout the Middle Ages. Ancona has been the seat of a bishop since 462.

History

Harbour

The hub of the town's traffic is the Piazza della Repubblica. On its west side is the harbour, an oval basin the northern part of which is of Roman origin.

Piazza della Repubblica

At the north end of the breakwater is the Roman Arco di Traiano with an inscription recording that it was erected in AD 115 in honour of the Emperor Trajan and his wife and sister; to the west is the Arco Clementino (18th c.).

Arco di Traiano

At the south end of the harbour stands the former hospital, built on a pentagonal bastion; adjoining is the Porta Pia (1789). The modern port installations are situated to the north-west.

Porta Pia

Town centre

From the Piazza della Repubblica a street on the right leads past the theatre (1826) into the elongated Piazza del Plebiscito. In this square stands the Palazzo de Governo (15th c.) with the prefecture in and, approached by a flight of steps, is the Baroque church of Santa Domenico (18th c.); inside can be seen a painting of the crucifixion of Christ by Titian (1558).

Palazzo de Governo

To the west is the Loggia dei Mercanti (exchange), a late Gothic building with a façade by Giorgio Orsini (1451–59). Adjoining stands the beautiful Palazzo Benincasa (15th c.).

Loggia dei Mercanti

From the exchange a street on the right leads to the church of Santa Maria della Piazza (10th c.) which was erected in the 13th c. on foundations of two 5th/6th c. churches. It has an over-decorated façade (1210). Inside, the remains of the 6th c. floor have been let into the wall.

Santa Maria della Piazza

Farther north, in the Piazza San Francesco, is the church of San Francesco alle Scale with a Gothic doorway by Giorgio Orsini (1454). Note the "Assunta" by Lorenzo Lotto.

San Francesco alle Scale

From the Piazza San Francesco the Via Pizzecolli runs north to the church of del Gesù (18th c.) and the Palazzo Bosdari (1550), which houses the Pinacoteca Comunale (municipal picture collection). It contains work by Titian, Lotto, Crivelli and other masterpieces. In the modern art section are works by present-day Italian painters.

Pinacoteca Comunale

A little way north stands the Palazzo Ferretti (16th c.), which houses the Museo Nazionale delle Marche (state-run museum of the Marche region) with prehistoric and Roman material of the Marche region, particularly finds of tombs, such as vases, etc.

Museo Nazionale delle Marche

✶✶Ancona Cathedral

From the museum a walk up a flight of steps or a drive up a winding panoramic road, built after the destruction of the harbour district, leads to the top of Monte Guasco, on which stands the cathedral, built on the site

Ancona: the Romanesque porch and dome of the cathedral

of a temple of Venus. The domed cruciform church in Byzantine-Romanesque style (12th c.) is dedicated to San Ciriaco. The façade has a Gothic doorway, which is decorated with reliefs. In the crypt are the remains of an early Christian church (6th c.) and a temple (3rd c. BC).

Museo Diocesano

The diocesan museum is housed in a building to the left of the cathedral. Notable is the early Christian sarcophagus with carved decoration belonging to Flavius Gorgonius, a praetorian prefect (4th c.).

Surroundings

Numana
15 km (9¹/₂ mi.) S

A drive southwards on the coast road leads to the church of Santa Maria di Portonovo (11th c.) and to Monte Conero (572 m (1888 ft)) from which there are extensive views. From there the road continues to the picturesque village of Sirolo and the little seaside resort of Numana.

Aosta   B4

Region: Autonomous region of Valle d'Aosta (AO). Province: Aosta (AO)
Altitude: 583 m (1924 ft). Population: 37,500

Location

Aosta (French Aoste), capital of the autonomous region of Valle d'Aosta, lies some 100 km (62 mi.) east of Turin, in a fertile valley at the confluence of the Buthier and the Dora Baltea, ringed by an imposing circle of mountains, with Grand Combin to the north rising to 4314 m (14,153 ft).

The town, which has been a place of importance from time immemorial as the gateway to the Great and Little St Bernard passes, was originally built as the Roman fort of Augusta Praetoria Salassorum soon after 25 BC, and its plan still reflects the regular layout of the Roman station. It preserves numerous monuments dating from the Roman and medieval periods. It is still an important traffic junction at the meeting of the access roads to the Mont Blanc tunnel and the Great St Bernard pass.

Town

Sights

The old town is still surrounded by well-preserved Roman town walls, forming a rectangle 724 by 572 m (2375 by 1877 ft), with twenty towers. The east gate or Porta Praetoria, originally triple-arched, lies some 2.5 m (8¼ ft) below the present street level, with a spacious courtyard at the rear. Close by is the square tower of a medieval castle which belonged to the lords of Quart.

Porta Praetoria

From here it is only a few yards north-west to the stage wall, 22 m (73 ft) high, of the Roman theatre, actually four storeys high. In the neighbouring garden of a monastery there are some arches of the amphitheatre.

Teatro Romano

About 400 m east of the Porta Praetoria stands the Arch of Augustus (Arco di Augusto) with ten Corinthian pilasters.

Arco di Augusto

A little way north-west is the former collegiate church of Saint Ours (Collegiata di S Orso), originally built in the 10th c., remodelled in Late Gothic style at the end of the 15th c. with fine 11th c. frescoes and beautifully

Saint Ours

Aosta: Roman theatre (Teatro Romano)

carved choir stalls (16th c.). In front of the church is a fine campanile, partly built of Roman hewn stones (c. 1150); on the south side is a Romanesque cloister (1133) with fine carved capitals.

Museo
Archeologico
Regionale

Near the church – in Via S. Orso – can be found the Archaeological Museum (Museo Archeologico Regionale) containing Roman finds and objects.

Cathedral

In the centre of the town, at the point where the main roads of the Roman fort crossed, is the Piazza Chanoux with the Town Hall. A little way north-west stands the cathedral, erected in the 11th–12th c.; the present church originates from the 15th–16th c. It has a Renaissance façade (c. 1526) with a classical porch, added in 1837. The treasury (admission fee) houses the ivory diptych of the Emperor Honorius (406).

On the west side of the cathedral are remains of the Roman forum.

Surroundings

Lac de Chamolé
11 km (7 mi.) S

South of Aosta is Les Fleurs (1360 m (4488 ft)), which can be reached by cableway or by road (11 km (7 mi.)). From here there is a cabin cableway to the Conca di Pila (1800 m (5940 ft)), then a chair-lift to the Lac du Chamolé (2312 m (7630 ft)).

Great St Bernard

Location
34 km (21 mi.) NW

There is a very fine excursion north-west from Aosta on the SS27, with sharp turns and hairpin bends to the Vallée du Grand-St-Bernard up the Great St Bernard pass (2649 m (8148 ft)). There is also a road tunnel 5.8 km (3½ mi.) long, between St-Rhémy and Bourg-St-Bernard on the Swiss side. The pass, which lies between the Mont Blanc massif and the Valais Alps (small lake), marks the Italian–Swiss frontier. In Swiss territory is the hospice (dog breeding), founded by St Bernard (d. 1086).

Aosta Valley   A–B4

Region: Valle d'Aosta/Val d'Aosta.
Area: 3262 sq. km (1259 sq. mi.). Population: 113,600

Location

The autonomous region of the Aosta valley (Valle d'Aosta, Val d'Aosta) lies in the north-west of Italy – in the deeply eroded valley of the Dora Baltea and its beautiful side valleys. Set amid magnificent mountain scenery at the foot of the Mont Blanc massif and surrounded by the highest summits of the Alps, the Aosta valley ranks high among the regions of Italy for scenic beauty and grandeur.

Importance

The valley, important since ancient times as the access route to the principal Alpine passes, the Little and Great St Bernard, was guarded throughout its entire length by numerous castles and other fortified buildings, often very picturesquely situated.

History

The Aosta valley, strongly fortified by the Romans, became in 1191 part of Savoy, and together they passed temporarily to France in the early 19th c. and later to Piedmont. When it was incorporated in Italy in 1861, the French-speaking population resisted the threat of Italianisation in language and culture. The growth of separatist feeling finally led in 1948 to the recognition of the special status of the Aosta valley as an autonomous region.

The inhabitants of the Aosta valley speak a Franco-Provençal dialect; the use of pure French is declining. However, French has equal status with Italian as an official language and also in the cultural field. — Language

The beautiful scenery and the excellent snow to be found at the higher altitudes even in summer have promoted the development of a flourishing tourist trade. Other important sources of revenue are vine-growing at the lower levels, pasturing and some industry. — Economy

Pont-Saint-Martin to Entrèves (94 km (58 mi.)

The road from Turin, SS26 (also the A5 motorway), enters the autonomous region of the Aosta valley at Pont-Saint-Martin (345 m (1139 ft); Roman bridge from the 1st c. BC), where the River Lys, coming from the north, flows into the Dora Baltea. — **Pont-Saint-Martin**

From Pont-Saint-Martin an attractive detour (34 km (21 mi.)) can be made up the Valle di Gressoney, following the deeply indented and regularly dammed course of the Lys, via the village of Issime (14 km (9 mi.); 960 m (3168 ft)), which was founded by German-speaking settlers from the Valais in the 13th c., and the little holiday resort of Gressoney St-Jean (14 km (9 mi.); 1385 m (4571 ft)) to Gressoney-La-Trinité (1635 m (5396 ft)); from which a chair-lift leads to Punta Jolanda (2333 m (7699 ft); upper station 2247 m (7415 ft)) and also a cabin cableway to Lago Gabiet (2367 m (7811 ft); upper station 2342 m (7729 ft)). — **Gressoney-La-Trinité**

Gressoney-La-Trinité is known as a base for many interesting climbing excursions in the Monte Rosa range, particularly for the ascent (6–7 hours, guide required) of the Pointe Dufour (4634 m (15,292 ft)), the highest peak — **★Monte Rosa**

Mountain scenery near Gressoney-La-Trinité

in the Monte Rosa group. A chair-lift goes from Staval up to the Colle Bettaforca.

The Aosta valley road continues from Pont-Saint-Martin up the valley, which becomes steadily narrower. Beyond Donnaz (322 m (1063 ft)) the massive Fort Bard (391 m (1290 ft); 11th c.) stands on a hill on the right.

★Issogne Castle

10 km (6 mi.): Arnad (412 m (1360 ft)) with a ruined castle high above it (634 m (2092 ft)); beyond this, on the right bank of the Dora, is the castle of Issogne, built in 1480.

Verrès

4 km (2¹/₂ mi.): Verrès (391 m (1290 ft)) with an old castle, the Rocca (1390), picturesquely situated on a rocky hill.

Champoluc

From Verrès there is a rewarding excursion (27 km (17 mi.) north) up the valley of the River Evançon, the Valle di Challand. The route goes via the summer holiday resort of Brusson (16 km (10 mi.); 1338 m (4415 ft)) in the lower part of the valley to Champoluc (11 km (7 mi.); 1570 m (5181 ft)), the principal place in the upper part of the valley, known as the Val d'Ayas. This is also a popular summer and winter holiday resort with views of the twin mountains Castor (4230 m (13,950 ft)) and Pollux (4094 m (13,510 ft)) and the Breithorn (4171 m (13,764 ft), all of them south of the Matterhorn. A cabin cableway leads up to the Crest (1974 m (6514 ft)), then a chair-lift continues to 2500 m (8250 ft).

Beyond Verrès the Aosta valley road passes the castle of Montjovet, then runs through the picturesque Montjovet defile, beyond which there is a first glimpse of Mont Blanc.

Saint-Vincent

12 km (7¹/₂ mi.): Saint-Vincent (575 m (1898 ft)), is a popular summer holiday resort with a casino and mineral springs (recommended for liver and stomach disorders). Beyond this, perched on the left, is the castle of Ussel (c. 1350).

Châtillon

3 km (2 mi.): Châtillon (549 m (1812 ft); population 4700), is a charming village with a fine castle.

Valtournenche

From Châtillon there is a rewarding drive (27 km (17 mi.) north) up the Valtournenche, through which the River Matmoire (in Italian Marmore) flows down from the Matterhorn. The road runs through Antey St André (7 km (4 mi.); 1074 m (3544 ft)), beyond which the Matterhorn comes into sight, and Buisson (4 km (2¹/₂ mi.); 1128 m (3722 ft); cableway east to the Chamois, 1815 m (5997 ft): from there a chair-lift to Lago di Lod; 2015 m (6650 ft)) and comes to Valtournenche (7 km (4 mi.); 1528 m (5042 ft)), which is popular both with summer visitors and winter sports enthusiasts (chair-lift east to the Alpe Chanlève; 1850 m (6105 ft); cableway to Monte Molar, 2484 m (8197 ft).

Breuil (Cervinia)

The road continues through a gorge, just before which a footpath (10-minute walk) goes off to the Gouffre des Busserailles (waterfall; admission fee), 104 m (341 ft) long and 35 m (16ft) deep, and reaches Breuil or Cervinia (2006 m (6620 ft)), a winter sports resort which is also popular in summer (bobsleigh run 1540 m (5082 ft) to the Lac Bleu) with fantastic scenery.

★★Matterhorn

To the north is the mighty peak of the Matterhorn (Monte Cervino; 4478 m (14,777 ft); the climb with guide takes 12 hours), to the west the rock wall of the Grandes Murailles (3872 m (12,778 ft)). From Breuil there is a cableway east to the Plan Maison (2557 m (8438 ft)) and from there north-east to the Furggen ridge (3488 m (11,510 ft)) or alternatively east, either directly or via Cime Bianche (2823 m (9316 ft)), to the Plateau Rosà (3480 m (11,484 ft)). 1 km (¹/₂ mi.) north of the Plateau Rosà is the Theodul pass (3322 m (10,963 ft)), from which there are fine views, extending also into the Zermatt valley.

Castle of Fénis in the Aosta Valley

Beyond Châtillon the Aosta valley road affords open views of the fertile valley and the mountains around Aosta, with the three-peaked Rutor in the background. Farther on, above the mouth of the Val de Clavalité or Val de Fénis, in which the snowy peak of the Tersiva can be seen, stands the mighty castle of Fénis on the left (1330, with later additions) with a beautiful courtyard (15th c.) and wall paintings; inside there are 15th c. frescoes.

★Fénis Castle

12 km (7¹/₂ mi.): Nus (529 m (1746 ft)), a village at the mouth of the Vallée de St Barthélemy, with a ruined castle. On the slope above, to the left, the village of St Marcel (631 m (2082 ft)), at the mouth of the valley of the same name, comes into sight.

Nus

12 km (7¹/₂ mi.): see entry

Beyond Aosta the road to the Mont Blanc Tunnel leads further up into the valley of the Dora Baltea.

Aosta

6 km (4 mi.): Sarre (631 m (2082 ft)), is a village with a castle of 1710. This is a good base for a pleasant detour (28 km (17 mi.) south), up the Val de Cogne, past the castle of Aymavilles with its four towers (16th–17th c.; restored) and up the monotonous valley high above the ravine of the roaring Grand'Eyvie. Far below can be seen the Pont d'El, with a Roman aqueduct of the Augustan period, 120 m (396 ft) above the stream. The road then continues to Cogne (1534 m (5062 ft)), the chief town in the valley which is popular both as a summer and a winter holiday resort (iron mine; tunnel 6 km (3¹/₂ mi.) long on a mine railway to Aosta). From here there is a beautiful view to the south of Gran Paradiso (4061 m (13,401 ft); the climb by way of Valsavarenche takes 17 hours with guide) and to the north-west of Mont Blanc. Lift to Mont Cuc (2075 m (6848 ft)).

Sarre

Cogne is a good base for climbing expeditions, particularly in the fascinating Gran Paradiso National Park (Parco Nazionale de Gran Paradiso; 600 sq. km (231 sq. mi.); many ibexes and other animals), which occupies the northern part of the Graian Alps.

★Gran Paradiso National Park

81

Saint-Pierre Castle houses a regional museum

Saint-Pierre	Beyond Sarre the road continues past the castles of Saint-Pierre (17th c.; inside is the Scientific Museum with records of animals and plants, found in the Aosta valley), Sarriod de La Tour (14th c.) and the Tour Colin (13th c.). It then passes the junctions of the Val de Rhêmes and the Val Grisanche which run south to the French frontier, and enters the wild defile of Pierre Taillée (waterfalls); beyond this, on the hillside to the right, is the village of La Salle (1001 m (3303 ft)), with the castle of Châtelard (1171 m (3864 ft); 13th c.); ahead the towering mass of Mont Blanc can be seen. 22 km (13 mi.): Morgex (920 m (3036 ft)).
Pré-Saint-Didier	4 km (2½ mi.): Pré-Saint-Didier (1004 m (3313 ft)), a picturesquely situated village, has an arsenical chalybeate spring (36 °C (97°F)) at the point where the Thuile forces its way through precipitous cliffs into the Dora valley.
La Thuile	At Pré-Saint-Didier SS26 leaves the Aosta valley and runs south-west to La Thuile (1441 m (4755 ft)), the starting point for climbing the glaciated Rutor (3486 m (11,504 ft); 7–8 hours, with guide), passing the Rutor Falls (1934 m (6382 ft)). From Gollette (1496 m (4937 ft)) there is a cableway south-west to Les Suches (2180 m (7194 ft); mountain hut) and then a chair-lift to Mont Chaz Dura (2581 m (8517 ft)).
Little St Bernard Pass	The road then continues for another 13 km (8 mi.), with many bends and magnificent retrospective views to reach the Italian–French frontier at the little Lac Verney and the Little St Bernard Pass (2188 m (7220 ft)). Until 1947 the frontier was 2 km (1 mi.) farther south. Beyond Pré-Saint-Didier the Aosta valley road passes below the village of Verrand (1263 m (4168 ft)), with fine panoramic views.
Courmayeur	5 km (3 mi.): Courmayeur (1224 m (4039 ft)), a major tourist centre (particularly for winter sports enthusiasts), with mineral springs (chalybeate; spa establishments) lies at the foot of the Mont Blanc massif (Alpine Museum).

A chain of cableways leads from here first up to the Plan Chécrouit (1704 m (5623 ft)), from there to the Lago Chécrouit (2256 m (7445 ft)), then to the Cresta de Youla (2624 m (8659 ft)) and finally to the Cresta d'Arp (2755 m (9092 ft)); there is also a cableway to the Pré de Pascal (1912 m (6310 ft)) and a cabin cableway to the Val Vény.

Entrèves

4 km (2¹/₂ mi.) beyond Courmayeur is Entrèves (1306 m (4310 ft)), a magnificently situated village with open views of Mont Blanc to the north-west and the Dent du Géant (4014 m (13,246 ft)) and the Grandes Jorasses (4206 m (13,880ft) to the north-east; there is an even finer prospect 2 km (1 mi.) west from the pilgrimage church of Notre-Dame de la Guérison (1486 m (4901 ft); striking close view of the Brenva glacier). From La Palud (1 km (¹/₂ mi.) north-east) there is a very attractive drive (15 km (9 mi.)) with three cableways (1¹/₂ hours) by way of the Pavillon du Mont Fréty (2130 m (7029 ft)) and the Rifugio Torino (3322 m (10,963 ft)), below the Col du Géant (3354 m (11,068 ft)), then by the Punta Helbronner (3462 m (11,425 ft); passport control) to the Gros Rognon (3448 m (11,378 ft)) and to the Aiguille du Midi (3842 m (12,679 ft)) and so on to Chamonix.

★★Mont Blanc

Mont Blanc (in Italian: Monte Bianco, 4810 m (15,873 ft)), the highest peak in the Alps, over which the Italian–French frontier runs was first climbed in 1786 by Jacques Balmat of Chamonix and the village doctor, Michel Paccard; then in 1787 again by the Geneva scientist Horace-Bénédict de Saussure, accompanied by Balmat and 16 porters. The best starting point for the climb (10–12 hours, with guide) is Les Houches, a village 10 km (6 mi.) south-west of Chamonix.

★Mont Blanc Tunnel

The construction of the Mont Blanc Tunnel (Galleria del Monte Bianco; opened to traffic July 16th 1965) is very important, particularly for tourist traffic. The tunnel begins at Entrèves (altitude 1381 m (4557 ft)) above sea-level, and ends 11.6 km (7¹/₄ mi.) farther on at an altitude of 1274 m (4204 ft) above the hamlet of Les Pèlerins, a suburb of Chamonix. The tunnel (toll), which is open throughout the year, shortens the journey from Italy to western Switzerland and central and northern France by several hundred kilometres during the period from October to June when the high Alpine passes are closed.

Apennines   E7–L16

Location

The Apennines (Appennino, from the Celtic word *pen*, mountain) are the mountain range 1400 km (868 mi.) long and 30–150 km (19–93 mi.) wide, which extends in a long arc down the whole length of the Italian peninsula from the Alps at the Ligurian Gulf to the south-west tip of Calabria and continues into Sicily.

Geography

As a result of late folding during the early Tertiary period the outer side of the range facing the Po plain and the Adriatic has a more gradual slope, composed of sedimentary rocks, while the inner side, in consequence of later collapses, slopes down in a steeper scarp to the sea and the basins of Tuscany, Umbria and eastern Latinum. The northern Apennines, reaching their highest point in Monte Cimone (2163 m (7138 ft)), and the Central Apennines have more regular slopes and continuous summit ridges, which are crossed by several traffic routes at heights of between 650 and 1300 m (2145 and 4290 ft). The rocks are mainly of Cretaceous and Tertiary date. There are large expanses of sandstones and schists, clays and marls, with rounded summits and gentle slopes with only little variation, though when soaked with rain they are very vulnerable to landslides ("frane"). Sharper contours are produced by the dolomites and limestones, which have developed into rugged and contorted karstic land-forms, particularly in the Monti Sibillini (2478 m (8177 ft)) and the wild Abruzzi, which reach their

highest point in the Gran Sasso d'Italia (2914 m (9616 ft)). The lower Neapolitan Apennines, abutting at its southern end of the Abruzzi and the
Lucanian Apennines run slowly into the Calabrian Apennines, in which the
landscape pattern from the Crati valley onwards is formed by ancient rocks
such as granites, gneisses and micaceous schists; the Sila range (1929 m
(6366 ft)) and the Aspromonte (1956 m (6455 ft)) with their beautiful forests
of deciduous and coniferous trees are reminiscent of the upland regions of
central Europe.

Climate

The climate of the Apennines is relatively harsh at higher altitudes. Rain-fall
in the northern Apennines is very high, while in the lower areas the aridity
of the Mediterranean climate predominates. At the foot of the hills there are
numerous mineral springs. The water-level of the rivers is irregular.

Flora and fauna

At the foot of the Apennines the flora is of Mediterranean type, with
edible chestnuts and fruit-trees. Above this is a zone of open forests, with
beeches predominantly at the lower levels and conifers higher up. Long
human occupation, however, has destroyed many of the original forests,
which have been replaced over large areas by an evergreen macchia. In
consequence there is an almost total absence of the larger fauna; the wolf
is a protected species here. At heights above 1800 m (5940 ft) the slopes
are covered with carpets of stones.

Economy

Within the mountainous area settlement is confined to the basins and
valleys. The principal occupations are stock-farming (goats and sheep),
some modest arable farming and forestry.

Traffic

The numerous passes are very important as far as traffic is concerned.
Motorways cross them at heights of between 500 and 1000 m (1650 and
3300 ft) or pass through tunnels. Part of the Autostrada del Sole runs over
the Futa pass (903 m (964 ft)).

Apulia   K12–N16

Region: Puglia
Provinces: Bari (BA), Brindisi (BR), Foggia (FG), Lecce (LE) and Taranto (TA)
Area: 19,347 sq. km (7468 sq. mi.). Population: 4,000,000

Location

The region of Apulia (in Italian Puglia or Puglie) consists of the provinces
of Bari, Brindisi, Foggia, Lecce and Taranto; it lies east of the Apennines,
in the south-east of Italy, and extends as far as the spur (the Gargano hills)
and the heel of the Italian boot, the Salentine peninsula.

Landscape

The northern part of the region is occupied by the plain round Foggia,
the Tavoliere di Puglia, at the east end of which are the limestone hills
of the Gargano promontory (Monte Calvo; 1055 m (3482 ft)). In the centre
is the karstic limestone plateau, with numerous caves and swallow-holes,
of the Murge (altitude up to 680 m (2244 ft)), which merges in the south
into the varied terrain, partly flat and partly hilly, of the Salentine peninsula (up to 200 m (660 ft)).

Economy

Apulia is a purely agricultural region, its main crops being wheat on the
Tavoliere, tobacco around Lecce, vegetables on the coast; other important
agricultural products are grapes (wine and eating), almonds, figs and
olives. The itinerant grazing economy which once played an important
part is now confined to a few karstic hill regions. Large-scale water supply
schemes (the 3600 km (2232 mi.) long "Aquedotto Pugliese" through the
Apennines, partly in a tunnel) have promoted considerable development
of agriculture in this very dry but fertile region. There is fishing on the
coast (around Bari); in recent years modest industries, particularly petro-
chemicals, have been established here.

In ancient times the name of Apulia was confined to the Gargano hills. The
region was conquered by the Romans in 272 BC and together with Calabria
became Regio II, which played an important part in Roman trade with the
East. After the fall of the Roman Empire Apulia passed into the hands of
the Ostrogoths and later the Byzantines, and in 568 part of it was occupied
by the Lombards. Robert Guiscard conquered it for the Normans from
1141 onwards and was granted it as a fief by Pope Nicholas II. Under Roger
II it was united with the kingdom of Naples and Sicily and enjoyed a period of high prosperity under the Staufen dynasty. Foggia was a favourite
residence of Frederick II, also known as "Child of Pulli", who left behind
him fine buildings and objets d'art, foremost among them the Castel del
Monte. Apulia was united with Italy in the 19th c.

History

★★Zona dei Trulli

Every tourist should visit the Trulli country (Zona dei Trulli), an area of
some 1000 sq. km (386 sq. mi.) in the Murge region dominated by thousands of the curious dwellings called *trulli*, which are small round stone
built houses, often linked together in groups, with conical roofs of overlapping courses of stone (cf. the *nuraghi* of Sardinia).

The area takes in several towns: Alberobello (428 m (1412 ft); population
10,000), a picturesque little town with more than 1000 trulli in the Zona
Monumentale, including the church of Sant'Antonio, a modern building
built in trullo style, and the two-storey Trullo Sovrano in the north of the
town, the largest in Alberobello.

Alberobello

The little town of Locorotondo (410 m (1353 ft); population 13,000) is circular in plan.

Locorotondo

Between Locorotondo and Martina Franca is the Valle d'Itria, also with
numerous trulli.

★Valle d'Itria

The Lucanian Apennines

Under the pointed stone caps

Apulia is perhaps known mainly for an archaic form of architecture that is not found anywhere else in Italy. These are the *trulli*, small round stone-built houses, mostly of one storey, with conical roofs of overlapping courses of stone tiles which become smaller as they near the peak of the artificial dome. This simple geometric principle permits a variety of possible combinations – for example, some form farmhouses, their roofs surmounted with skittle-shaped mouldings; a line of several similar buildings form stables; even churches follow this same architectural pattern. While most of the trulli walls are of white limestone, the roofs with their stone pommels are in natural stone, often covered with mysterious signs and symbols. Whether these are magic charms of pagan origin, religious symbols or simply forms of decoration is hard to say. A settlement of trulli dwellings is certainly a mysterious and unusual sight.

The Zona dei Trulli is an area covering about 1000 sq. km (386 sq. mi.) on the carstic limestone plateau of the Murge and is home to more than a thousand of these curious buildings. The locality most favoured by visitors is Alberobello, named after a large oak forest that once stood here.

Martina Franca (431 m (1422 ft); population 44,000) is a town with charm- **Martina Franca**
ing Baroque buildings, for example the Palazzo Ducale (1669) and the
collegiate church of San Martino (18th c.).

Two other towns in the Zona dei Trulli are Cisternino (394 m (1302 ft); pop- **Fasano**
ulation 12,000) and Fasano (118 m (389 ft); population 37,000). Also worth
visiting is the park outside Fasano (1 km (³/₄ mi.)) which occupies an area
of 8 ha (20 acres). More than 600 animals (including lions) can be seen here.
Close to Egnazia, 9 km (5 mi.) north of Fasano, is one of the most important
Apulian sites.

At the southern end of the Zona dei Trulli close to the sea is Ostuni (218 m **Ostuni**
(719 ft); population 32,000), a picturesque little town with white, rustic
houses; on a hill stands the late Gothic cathedral (15th c.).

To the north of the Zona dei Trulli, 15 km (9 mi.) south-west of the port of **★★Grotte di**
Monopoli (9m/30ft; population 45,000), which has an 18th c. cathedral, are **Castellana**
the caves of Castellana (tours); they rank with the Postojna caves in Yugo- **Monopoli**
slavia as the finest stalactitic caves in Europe. The caves have a total length
of approximately 1.2 km (³/₄ mi.) – much more if the various ramifications
are included (two lifts). The finest cave is the Grotta Bianca (special
conducted tours), unsurpassed in Europe for its perfect condition and its
profusion of stalagmites and stalactites. Above the cave is a lookout tower
(28 m (92 ft) high, 170 steps); nearby a cave museum.

See Barletta   Castel del Monte

See entry   Lecce

L'Aquila   H11

Region: Abruzzi. Province: L'Aquila (AQ)
Altitude: 615–721 m (2093–2379 ft). Population: 69,000

L'Aquila, capital of the Central Italian region of the Abruzzi and of the   Location
province of l'Aquila, lies beyond the Aterno valley, surrounded by the
mighty limestone heights of the Abruzzi. It is the see of an archbishop.

L'Aquila was founded about 1240 by the Hohenstaufen emperor Frederick   History
II as a protection against the rebellious tribes of the Abruzzi. Charles I of
Anjou surrounded the town with walls which are partly preserved.

Sights

In the centre of the town is the spacious Piazza del Duomo, on the west   Cathedral
side of which is the cathedral of San Massimo (originally built in the 13th
c.; several times destroyed by earthquakes and rebuilt). It contains (to the
right of the entrance) a monumental effigy of Cardinal Agnifili (1480).

To the north is the little church of San Giuseppe, with the tomb of the   San Giuseppe
Camponeschi family (1432) by Gualterius di Alemania (Walter of
Germany).

Also north of the cathedral, in Piazza del Palazzo, is the former Palace of   Palace of Margaret
Margaret of Parma (1573; campanile), now occupied by the Court of   of Parma
Appeal.

South-east of Piazza del Palazzo is the porticoed street intersection known   ★San Bernardino
as the Quattro Cantoni, in the Corso Vittorio Emanuele II, the town's principal street. From here Via San Bernardino leads to the church of San

L'Aquila

Façade of the Church of San Bernardino

Bernardino (originally 1454), with a fine façade of 1527. It contains the tomb of Bernardino di Siena who died in l'Aquila in 1440.

★Santa Maria di Collemaggio

From San Bernardino we descend to the piazza, follow Via Fortebraccio straight ahead and continue through the Porta Bazzano to the magnificent church, formerly belonging to the Celestine order, of Santa Maria di Collemaggio, founded about 1280 by Pietro da Morrone, who was crowned here as Pope Celestine V in 1294. The church has a Baroque interior, with the Pope's Renaissance tomb (1517) and wall paintings by Ruter, a pupil of Rubens, depicting his life and deeds.

Parco del Castello

In the north-east of the town is the Parco del Castello with the beautiful Fontana Monumentale. From here there are far-ranging views of the Aterno valley and the Gran Sasso and Maiella range.

★Museum Nazionale d'Abruzzo

On the east side of the park is the Castello, built by the Spaniards in 1534, which now houses the Museo Nazionale d'Abruzzo (National Museum of the Abruzzi; entrance on the east side), with medieval and modern art as well as arts and crafts and paintings and sculpture from churches in the Abruzzi region. Particularly notable is its collection of Abruzzi majolica (17th–18th c.) from Castelli.

At the foot of the hill on the west side of the town, near the station and the Porta Rivera, is the Fontana delle 99 Cannelle (Fountain of the 99 Pipes; 1272), with sides of red and white marble, from which the water spouts through 99 different masks (male and female heads).

★Fontana delle 99 Cannelle

Surroundings

North of L'Aquila are the remains of the ancient city of Amiternum, which was first occupied by the Sabines and later by the Romans, with remains of a theatre, an amphitheatre and baths.

Amiternum
10 km (6 mi.) N

The route to the Gran Sasso d'Italia first passes the cemetery, with the convent church of Santa Maria del Soccorso, and then continues via the village of Assergi (church of Santa Maria Assunta, with a fine Gothic rose window), on the south-west slopes of the Gran Sasso group, to Fonte Cerreto (1105 m (3547 ft)), starting point of the cableway to the Gran Sasso d'Italia (3.2 km (2 mi.) long; 16 minutes). A panoramic road (27 km (17 mi.)) leads to the upper station of the cableway (2130 m (7029 ft)), on the western edge of the Campo Imperatore (1600–2200 m (5280–7260 ft); Albergo Campo Imperatore), a high valley 20 km (12 mi.) long and up to 5 km (3 mi.) wide which is an excellent walking and climbing centre and a popular winter sports area. Near the cableway station are the modern chapel of the Madonna della Neve and an observatory. Above the hotel (45-minute climb), on the Portelle ridge, is the Rifugio Duca degli Abruzzi (2301 m (7587 ft); views) from which it is another 4-hour climb to the Corno Grande or Monte Corno (2912 m (9610 ft)), the highest peak in the Gran Sasso d'Italia, the most elevated mountain range in the Italian peninsula, with sheer rock walls like those of the Calcareous Alps (road tunnel). From the summit there are views extending over the whole of Central Italy to the Adriatic in the east and over the Sabine hills, and on clear days as far as the Tyrrhenian Sea in the west.

★Gran Sasso d'Italia
48 km (30 mi.) NE

Another worthwhile trip is from L'Aquila to Avezzano. The road winds up the north-east slopes of Monte d'Orce (2206 m (7280 ft)), with many bends and fine retrospective views, and continues through the wide high valley between Monte Velino on the right and Monte Sirente on the left, with a number of villages which are popular summer and winter resorts. It then winds its way downhill, with attractive views of the little town of Celano (800 m (2640 ft)), with the ruins of an old church and a castle (Castello Piccolomini), and the wide Fucino basin. In the western part of the Fucino basin, formerly a lake which was drained in 1875, lies Avezzano (698 m (2291 ft); population 35,000). The town was almost completely destroyed by an earthquake in 1915 which claimed 30,000 lives. After being rebuilt it was again damaged in the Second World War. Worth a visit are the local museum and the museum of rural culture. Note also the gateway to Orsini castle, built in 1490 by Virgilio Orsini and restored after the earthquake.

Avezzano
62 km (38 mi.) S

An interesting excursion can be made to Albe (7 km (4 mi.) north), with the remains of the strongly fortified town of Alba Fucens (massive walls, baths, an amphitheatre and a basilica) and an 11th c. Romanesque church built into a temple of Apollo.

Albe

From Celano an excursion can be made to a wild gorge, the Gole di Celano by taking the Sulmona road south for 1.5 km (1 mi.) or to the Abruzzi National Park (see Abruzzi), then by a footpath on the left (15 minutes).

Gole di Celano

Aquileia   H4

Region: Friuli-Venezia Giulia. Province: Udine (UD)
Altitude: 5 m (17ft). Population: 3400

Aquileia

Location   Aquileia lies in central Italy – west of the place where the River Isonzo,
            flowing down from the Alps, flows into the Adriatic.

History   Founded by the Romans in 181 BC as a defensive post against the Celts,
            Aquileia became one of the great cities of ancient Italy, a major trading
            centre in the Gulf of Trieste and from the 6th c. the seat of a Patriarch. Later
            it lost its importance.

Sights

★★Cathedral   The most important monument of this great past is the cathedral, built at
               the beginning of the 11th c. on the site of an earlier church and remodelled
               in Gothic style at the end of the 14th c. It has a fine interior with a mosaic
               pavement (depicting humans, animals and plants) from the original
               church (4th c.). There are also a fine Renaissance pulpit and remains of
               11th c. frescoes in the apse. At the main entrance is an Easter Sepulchre
               (11th c.) and close by the entrance to the Cripta degli Scavi can be seen
               3rd c. mosaics.
               From the 73 m (241 ft) bell tower (11th and 14th c.) there are panoramic
               views.

Museo   From the military cemetery behind the chancel of the cathedral the Via
Paleocristiano Sacra, lined by cypresses, runs 700 m north to the site of the Roman river
               harbour. A little way north-east is the Museo Paleocristiano (with funeral
               urns); to the west the forum (partly reconstructed).

Amphitheatre   To the west of the cathedral are the remains of an amphitheatre, the
               Roman street of tombs, a Roman mausoleum (reconstructed) and a num-
               ber of partly excavated oratories with well-preserved mosaic pavements.

★Museo   South-west of the cathedral is the Museo Archeologico, containing
Archeologico   Roman material recovered by excavations, among which are precious
               stones, amber and glass (in the courtyard are many pyramidal urns).

Aquileia, Roman remains

Surroundings

South of Aquileia, on the spit of land south of the lagoon, the popular sea-side resort of Grado (2 m (7 ft); population 9650) can be found. Half way along the spit of land is the little fishing port, to the north lies the harbour canal, to the east, along the beautiful sandy beach (3 km (2 mi.) long; hot sand baths), is the hotel and villa quarter. Grado came into being as the re-sort of Roman Aquileia when the Patriarch fled here in 568 to escape the Lom-bards. The cathedral of Sant'Eufemia was built during this period with a mosaic pavement, a Romanesque pulpit and a silver frontal (Venetian; 1372). To the left of the cathedral stands the Baptistery (5th c.), and beyond this the church of Santa Maria delle Grazie, with a mosaic pavement.

Grado
11 km (6³/₄ mi.) S

The little town of Palmanova (26 m (86 ft); population 5600) is interesting because of its urban development. In 1593 it was built as a fort to a star-shaped nine-sided plan. The town can only be entered through one of the three gates. The Venetians built Palmanova as a bastion to protect them from the Habsburgs and the Turks. However, it was impossible to per-suade more than 2000 people to live in this artificial creation. An informa-tive exhibition of the town's history can be seen in the Museo Civico Storico (Borgo Udine 4c).

Palmanova
15 km (9 mi.) N

Arezzo   F9

Region: Toscana. Province: Arezzo (AR)
Altitude: 296 m (977 ft). Population: 92,000

Arezzo, capital of the province of the same name, lies in north-eastern Tuscany some 80 km (50 mi.) south-east of Florence and near the left bank of the Arno.

Location

Umbrians and the Etruscans settled on the hill which rises above the sur-rounding fertile countryside. The Roman military post was founded here by Gaius Maecenas (c. 70–8 BC); he was a friend of Augustus and used his influence to promote the poets who came to visit the Emperor's palace.
   Arezzo was the birthplace of Guido Monaco (Guido of Arezzo, c. 990–1050), who invented our system of musical notation, Francesco Petrarca (1304–74), the great poet and father of humanism and the satirical poet Pietro Aretino (1492–1556).

History

Sights

In the centre of the town is the Gothic church of San Francesco (13th–14th c.), dedicated to St Francis. The main feature of the church is the choir chapel with frescoes by Piero della Frances, painted during the period 1453–64, which depict scenes from the legend of the Cross.

★San Francesco

From San Francesco we go south-east along Via Cavour and then turn left up the Corso Italia to reach the Romanesque church of Santa Maria della Pieve (12th–14th c.) with a late Romanesque façade and a tower (59 m (165 ft)) completed in 1332. The principal feature is the polyptychon "Madonna and Saint", a masterpiece by P. Lorenzetti (1320).

★Santa Maria
della Pieve

Behind the church is the picturesque Piazza Grande, scene of the Giastro del Saracino, the medieval joust performed on the first Sunday in September. At the west side of the square stands the beautiful Palazzo del-la Faternità dei Laici (1375–1460), on the north side the Palazzo delle Logge, built in 1573 and named after the loggias which face the piazza.

★Piazza Grande

Opposite the west end of the Palazzo delle Logge, in the Corso Italia stands the Palazzo Pretorio (1322); it is decorated with the coats of arms of the former "podestá" (mayors).

Palazzo Pretorio

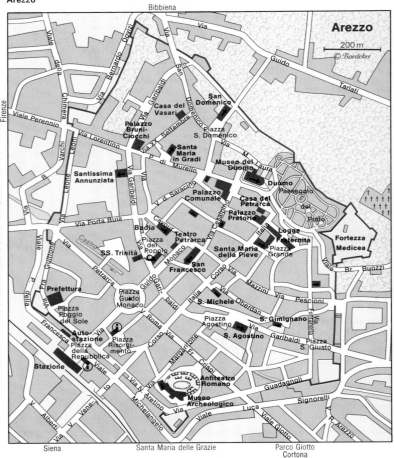

Casa del Petrarca	From the Palazzo Pretorio it is only a short way, skirting a beautiful park, the Passeggio del Prato, to the Via dell' Orto, with Petrarch's birthplace (Casa del Petrarca), on the left.
Palazzo del Comune	From the Casa del Petrarca it is only a few steps to the Palazzo del Comune (Town Hall, 1333, decorated with coats of arms) and from there to the cathedral.
★Cathedral	The cathedral, a Gothic building begun in 1277, has a modern façade. Inside, behind the high altar, can be seen the Arca di San Donato, a marble tomb of St Donatus, the martyr bishop of Arezzo. The tomb of Guido Tarlati, a warlike bishop of Arezzo (d. 1327), at the east end of the north aisle, is decorated with 16 bas-reliefs. Close to the tomb is a fine fresco by Piero della Francesco, dedicated to St Magdalene.

On the Piazza Grande stand the church of Santa Maria delle Pieve and the Palazzo delle Logge

North of the cathedral stands the Gothic church of San Domenico (13th-14th c.) with a fine campanile; on the high altar is a painted crucifix by Cimabue (1250–65).

San Domenico

Some 500 m north-west of the cathedral, in the Via Garibaldi, is the Palazzo Bruni-Ciocchi, containing the collections of the Galleria e Museo Medioevale e Moderno (Gallery and Museum of Medieval and Modern Art) with ceramics, majolicas and paintings (altarpiece by Luca Signorelli, 1520).

Museum of Art

In the south of the town near the remains of the Roman amphitheatre is the Archaeological Museum; it contains a collection of the famous "vasi aretini" (fragments of red clay urns with fine reliefs) and Etruscan reliefs on terracotta, urns, sarcophagi, amphoras and Roman mosaics.

★Archaeological Museum

Some 500 m south of the museum, stands the church of Santa Maria delle Grazie (15th c.), dedicated to the Madonna; the colonnaded portico is an Early Renaissance masterpiece.

Santa Maria delle Grazie

Ascoli Piceno   H10

Region: Marche. Province: Ascoli Piceno (AP)
Altitude: 154 m (508 ft). Population: 54,000

Ascoli Piceno, capital of the province of the same name, lies in the southern part of the coastal region of the Marches, in Central Italy, at the confluence of the rivers Castellano and Tronto. The town is some 30 km (19 mi.) from the Adriatic.

Location

Sights

Piazza del Popolo	The centre of the town is the picturesque Piazza del Popolo, in which the "Torneo cavalleresco della Quintana", a medieval joust preceded by a parade with musical accompaniment, is held on the first Sunday in August. In the Piazza is the Palazzo dei Capitani del Popolo (13th c., remodelled in 16th c.).
★San Francesco	On the north side of the Piazza del Popolo, here traversed by the Corso Mazzini, the long principal street of the town, stands the Gothic hall-church of San Francesco (1258–1371) with a doorway in Venetian Gothic style, and linked to it the crenellated Loggia dei Mercanti (covered market; 1513). On the north side are two beautiful cloisters.
Santi Vincenzo e Anastasio	Some 300 m north-west of the Piazza del Popolo are the Roma-nesque church of Santi Vincenzo e Anastasio (11th c.) with a façade of 64 square compartments, and the church of San Pietro Martire.
Ponte Romano Augustea	Farther north-west Via di Solestà leads to the Ponte Romano Augustea, a Roman bridge over the Tronto. A little way south-west stands the Palazzetto Longobardo (10th c.?) and adjoining it the Torre Ercolani, a tower 40 m (132 ft) high.
Porta Gémina	At the west end of the Corso Mazzini, in the Piazza di Cecco, is the Porta Gémina (1st c. BC), a double gate through which in Roman times the Via Salaria entered the town; near by are the remains of a Roman amphi-theatre.
Palazzo Comunale (Museum)	A little way south-east of the Piazza del Popolo is the Piazza dell'Arringo with the massive Palazzo Comunale (Town Hall; 1683–1745), which hous-es a Museum of Art containing paintings by Cola dell'Amatrice, Crivelli and Titian, etc. and a very valuable cope (worn by Catholic priests during the ritual duties) which was presented to the cathedral of Ascoli Piceno by Pope Nicholas IV in 1288.
★Cathedral	On the east side of the square is the Cathedral of Sant'Emidio, originally an early Romanesque building, which has been altered several times. The façade is attributed to Cola dell'Amatrice. In the large chapel in the south aisle is an altarpiece by Crivelli (1473). Note: impressive paintings of the Madonna and various apostles and saints are also to be seen. About 1470 the Venetian artist Crivelli settled in Ascoli Piceno and his work had a marked effect on the artistic development of the region. To the left, adjoining the cathedral, is the early Romanesque baptistery, an octagonal building.
Bridges	From the Piazza dell'Arringo the Corso Vittorio Emanuele runs east past the municipal park to the medieval bridge over the Castellano, the Ponte Maggiore. From here there is a fine view to the left of the Monte dell'Ascen-sione (1103 m (3640 ft)) and to the right of the Ponte di Cecco, a two-arched Roman bridge (restored after destruction in the Second World War).
Forte Malatesta	Close by the Ponte di Cecco is the old Forte Malatesta (1348).
Santissima Annunziata	Above the town to the south-west rises the monastic church of the Santissima Annunziata (views). There are even more extensive views from the castle "Fortezza Pia" (16th c.), farther to the west.

Surroundings

Monte Piselli 20 km (12 mi.) S	A road runs south from Ascoli Piceno and winds its way up to the Colle San Marco (694 m (2290 ft)). 5 km (3 mi.) farther south, beyond the Rigugio Paci (905 m (2987 ft)) is the starting point of the cableway up the Monte Piselli (1676 m (5531 ft)). From the summit there are magnificent views, on a clear day as far as the Dalmatian coast of Yugoslavia.

Assisi G9

Region: Umbria. Province: Perugia (PG)
Altitude: 403–500 m (1330–1815 ft). Population: 25,000

Assisi lies some 14 km (9 mi.) south-east of Perugia in the medieval region of Umbria. The town, the historic Roman city of Asisium, occupied artificial terraces on a westerly outlier of the Monte Subasio. — Location

The town, one of the most important places of pilgrimage in Italy, owes its fame to St Francis, born here in 1182, the son of a wealthy merchant. After spending his early years in a life of dissipation he devoted himself to abstinence, the service of the poor and the sick, and founded the Franciscan order; he died in 1226 in poverty. His life has since inspired works by famous artists (including Giotto). A free community since the 11th c., Assisi – like many Umbrian towns – fell under papal rule in the 14th c. With its well-preserved medieval streets and art treasures Assisi is one of Italy's great tourist sights. In September 1997 Umbria was shaken by a heavy earthquake which also caused damage in the town. — History

Sights

North-west of the town on the edge of the hill rises the Franciscan friary begun soon after the saint's death. The two-storey cloister was built by Pope Sixtus IV (1471–84) and is open to visitors, as is the treasury.

Part of the building is the impressive two-storeyed church, the Basilica di San Francesco, built over St Francis's tomb. The lower church is entered through a Renaissance portico and a Gothic door; it has a nave with side chapels, and the Romanesque vaulting gives it a crypt-like appearance. The walls are decorated with tempera frescos of *c.* 1260 that are among the finest examples of works by the early Italian school. On the south are scenes from Christ's Passion, beginning with the preparations for His Crucifixion, while on the north are episodes from the life of St Francis. — ★★Basilica di San Francesco

Worst affected by the earthquake of 1997 was the upper church, where two sections of the vaulted roof collapsed. The frescos by Cimabue, including a portrait of St Francis, were lost; also damaged but restorable are those by Giotto and Cavallini. Until the upper church is reopened only the lower church and crypt with the saint's tomb are open to visitors. An exhibition at the entrance to the friary gives an idea of what the upper church looked like before the earthquake.

South of the friary, beyond the Porta San Francesco, stands the church of San Pietro, with a fine doorway. — San Pietro

Leaving the lower church we go uphill to the left into the Via San Francesco and its continuation which lead to the Piazza del Comune, the town's main square, built on the site of the Roman forum. Under the Piazza del Comune, accessible via the Museo Civico (entrance on Via Portica) lies the interesting Roman site known as the Foro Romano. — ★Piazza del Comune

On the left is the portico of the Temple of Minerva, perhaps dating from the Augustan period, later converted into the church of Santa Maria della Minerva. — ★Temple of Minerva

Near the temple stands the Palazzo del Capitano del Popolo (13th c.).

At the end of the square, on the right, is the Palazzo Comunale or Palazzo dei Priori (Town Hall; 14th c.), which houses the municipal picture gallery (Pinacoteca). — Palazzo Comunale (Pinacoteca)

Assisi • San Francesco

10 m

© Baedeker

Chiesa Nuovo

A little way south, on a lower level, is the Chiesa Nuova (1615), a small church on a centralised plan, erected, it is said, on the site of St Francis's birthplace.

★San Rufino

From the Piazza del Comune the Via di San Rufino leads east to the cathedral of San Rufino (12th–13th c.), with a beautiful façade.

★Santa Chiara

South of the cathedral, in the Piazza Santa Chiara, stands the Gothic church of Santa Chiara (1265). Under the high altar is the open tomb of St Clare (d. 1253), the enthusiastic disciple of St Francis who founded the order of Clarissines or Poor Clares. In the Capella del Crocefisso on the left side of the nave hangs the "Speaking Cross" from the convent of San Damiano (see below), in front of which St Francis is said to have received the message from God to "go forth and rebuild my house".

Assisi, the birthplace of St Francis

Cathedral of San Rufino and church of Santa Chiara

From the Piazza di San Rufino the old Via Santa Maria delle Rose ascends to the Rocca Maggiore, a castle high above the town (re-built by Cardinal Albornoz in 1365), in which the Emperor Frederick II sometimes stayed during his youth. From here there are panoramic views.

Rocca Maggiore

South-east of the town centre is the little convent of San Damiano (305 m (1007 ft)), founded by St Francis, of which St Clare was the first abbess. On the small terrace, gay with flowers, in front of the convent, St Francis is said to have composed his famous "Canticle of the Sun". In addition to the church, the cloister with frescoes by Eusebio di San Giorgio (1507), the convent and the convent gardens are open to visitors.

Convento di San Damiano
2 km (1½ mi.) SE

Surroundings

South of Assisi on the SS75, is the small village of Santa Maria degli Angeli (218 m (719 ft)). The church of the same name, a massive domed structure in Renaissance style, built between 1569–1630 over St Francis' oratory (Porziúncola) and the cell in which he died: The nave and choir were re-erected after the earthquake in 1832 and the church was provided with a new façade in 1925–28.

★★Santa Maria degli Angeli
6 km (4 mi.) S

To the east of the sacristy is a small garden, in which it is said the roses have been thornless since an act of penance by the saint. Adjacent is the Cappella delle Rose with fine frescoes by Tiberio d'Assisi (1518), depicting scenes from the saint's life.

East of Assisi, charmingly situated in a small wood of holm-oaks above a ravine between the bare rock faces of Monte Subasio, is the hermitage of Le Carceri (791 m (2610 ft)), to which St Francis retired for his devotional exercises. The monastery dates from the 14th c.; visitors are also shown the saint's rock-bed.

★Le Carceri
4 km (2½ mi.) E

Il Poverello

Giovanni Battista, better known as Francis, was born in the winter of 1181/82, the son of Pietro di Bernardone, a wealthy merchant. His young years spent in the town of Assisi were overshadowed by the constant wars between the Emperor and the Pope. As a young man he set off to join a military expedition and to serve in the army of Gualtieri III. In Spoleto, the first stage of his long journey, he fell ill and, shaking with fever, heard the voice of the Lord calling him to return to Assisi. From then

Fresco of St Francis by Cimabue

onwards he devoted himself to the care of the poor and lepers and himself began to beg. When praying one day in the little half-decayed church of San Damiano he heard the voice of God ordering him to "go and rebuild my house". At first Francis took the words literallly and set to work to improve the little church – with the help of money from his father. This led to a disagreement with the latter, following which Francis publicly renounced his parents and his friends; he took off his clothes and threw them at his father's feet, saying that in future he would know only one father – his Father in Heaven.

As an outward sign of his declaration of poverty and abstinence, the former nobleman now went about barefoot and in a simple brown coat tied around the waist. Soon his "little army" of followers (il poverello) had won a number of adherents, most of them, like himself, members of the urban upper class. For them – said to have been twelve in number, like Jesus' disciples – he drew up a rule in a wretched little hut at Rivotorto near Assisi; in 1223 the Pope approved this rule. As the first monastic order in the Western world the Franciscans devoted themselves to preaching and serving their fellow men, especially the poor and the sick. After working as a missionary in the south of France and a long stay in the Holy Land, Francis returned home in 1220. In answer to the question which tormented him of whether he was following the right path, God gave him a sign in 1224; on Mount La Verna Christ appeared to him and gave him the marks (*stigmata*) of His wounds. Two years later Francis fell sick and, on October 3rd 1226 he died in the Porziuncola oratory in Santa Maria degli Angeli near Assisi. His death-bed was the bare floor.

The charisma of this man, who was said to have been able to talk to animals as well as to humans, is still felt today, perhaps because St Francis, he was canonised in 1228, lived the way many merely preach – loving his neighbour and in a spirit of true compassion and brotherhood.

From the monastery it is an hour and a half's climb to the broad ridge of Monte Subasio (1290 m (4257 ft); panoramic views). The drive over Monte Subasio to Spoleto (see entry) is also a fine experience.

Asti   C6

Region: Piemonte. Province: Asti (AT)
Altitude: 123 m (404 ft). Population: 74,000

Asti, the Roman Asta, lies in the valley of the Tarano, some 55 km (34 mi.) from Turin.
    The town, seat of a bishop and one of the most powerful city-republics of northern Italy in the Middle Ages, lies in the very fertile wine-producing area of the Montferrato, which is particularly known for its sparkling wine, Asti Spumante.

Location

Sights

At the east end of the Corso Vittorio Alfieri, the principal street of the town, are the Romanesque baptistery of San Pietro (12th c.) and the former church of San Pietro in Consavia (1467), decorated with beautiful terracotta. The cloister and other parts of the church house the Archaeological and Paleontological Museum.
    Near the Town Hall stands the Romanesque-Gothic church of Chiesa de San Secondo (13th–15th c.) with a notable crypt (7th c.).

★ Baptistery of San Pietro

In the western part of the main street can be found the Palazzo Alfieri (museum); inside is the room in which the dramatist Vittorio Alfieri (1749–1803) was born.

Palazzo Alfieri

Near the Palazzo Alfieri is the Romanesque-Gothic cathedral, built 1309–48 on the site of an earlier church. It has a brick façade, and the south doorway is decorated with statues. The spacious interior contains Baroque paintings. The Romanesque campanile originates from 1266. On the north side of the cathedral is the Baroque church of San Giovanni with a 9th c. crypt.

Cathedral

In Asti there are a number of tower houses belonging to noble families, among them the Torre Troiana and the Torre dei Comentini, both in the west of the town.

Tower houses

The Palazzo Mazzetti on Corso Vittorio Alfieri houses the municipal picture gallery displaying works by contemporary artists. This building also houses the "Museo del Risorgimento".

Museums

Bari   L13

Region: Puglia. Province: Bari (BA)
Altitude: 4 m (13ft). Population: 343,000

Bari, capital of the region of Apulia and the province of the same name, lies in southern Italy – on the Adriatic coast. It is the largest city in Apulia and the second largest in southern Italy after Naples.
    The port of Bari, a leading commercial and industrial centre (petrochemicals and shipbuilding), is particularly important by virtue of its trade with the eastern Mediterranean. It is also the see of an archbishop and possesses a university and a naval college.

Location

The picturesque old town, with its narrow winding streets, frequently spanned by arches, lies to the north, on a promontory between the old and

Tower

Bari

The old harbour of Bari adds to the atmosphere of this Adriatic town

new harbours. To the south is the spacious and regularly planned new town, which has developed considerably since 1930, when the Levant Fair was first held here.

History

The ancient Barium was a place of little importance. Until it was captured by Robert Guiscard in 1071 it was used by the Byzantines as their main base in southern Italy. From 1324 it was an almost independent fief which finally passed to the kingdom of Naples in 1558.

New town

Museo Archeologico Nazionale

The centre of the new town is the palm-shaded Piazza Umberto I. On its west side is the imposing building of the university, with a well-stocked library (160,000 volumes), and the interesting Museo Archeologico Nazionale.

Piazza Garibaldi

From the north side of the square the new town's principal traffic artery, Via Sparano, coming from the station, runs north past the modern church of San Ferdinando into the busy Corso Vittorio Emanuele II, which separates the new town from the old. 100 m along the Corso Vittorio Emanuele II to the left is the Piazza Garibaldi, the traffic centre of the town. On the right is the prefecture, on the left the Town Hall, which also houses the Teatro Piccinni.

From the east end of the Corso Vittorio Emanuele II the Corso Cavour, lined with fine buildings, leads towards the station.

★Lungomare Nazario Sauro

The east end of the Corso Vittorio Emanuele II is also the starting point of the Lungomare Nazario Sauro, a magnificent seafront promenade which runs along the old harbour.

Pinacoteca Provinciale

1 km (1/2 mi.) southwards along the Lungomare Nazario Sauro is the palace of the provincial administration in which is the picture gallery

100

(Pinacoteca Provinciale). Most of the pictures are older scenes of Bari and the surrounding area, together with works by Moretto da Brescia, A. Vaccaro, C. Maratta, Giovanni Bellini ("Martyrdom of St Peter"), Vivarini, Paolo Veronese, Tintoretto, and others.

Old town

In the centre of the old town rises the cathedral of San Sabino (originally 1170–78), with important remains of Norman ornaments. In the crypt is an elaborately adorned painting of the Madonna; the archives include two parts of a large exsultet roll (the Catholic Easter liturgy; 11th c.). ★San Sabino

A little way north of the cathedral is the church of San Nicola, a large pilgrimage church begun in 1087 but not completed until 1197, which is one of the finest achievements of Romanesque architecture in Apulia. ★★San Nicola

Inside, above the high altar, is a tabernacle (12th c.) and to the right of the altar is a "Madonna with Saints" by Vivarini (1476). In the apse is the tomb (1593) of Bona Sforza, wife of King Sigismund II of Poland and last duchess of Bari (d. 1558) and a marble bishop's throne. The crypt with 26 different columns contains a silver altar (1684) underneath which is a vault containing the remains of the popular Saint Nicholas of Bari (c. 350), patron of seamen, prisoners, pupils and children (principal feast May 8th).

To the west of the old town is the Castello, originally a Byzantine-Romanesque building, reconstructed by Frederick II in 1233. Bona Sforza converted it into a palace in the 16th c.; later it was used as a prison and signal station. The building now houses an interesting museum with copies of Apulo-Norman sculptures (plus temporary art exhibitions). Castello (Museum)

From the Castello the wide Corso Vittorio Veneto runs west past the Great Harbour (Gran Porto or New Harbour) to the grounds of the Levant Fair (Fiera de Levante), 2.5 km (1½ mi.) away on the seafront. Great Harbour

The Castello, Bari

Bari to Gravina di Puglia (55 km (34 mi.))

Bitetto

About 15 km (9 mi.) south-west of Bari is the little town of Bitetto (139 m (459 ft); population 9000) with the cathedral of San Michele (14th c), a building in late Apulo Romanesque style.

Altamura

From here it is another 29 km (18 mi.) south-west over the Murge plateau to Altamura (478 m (1577 ft); population 53,000), a town still partly surrounded by its old walls. There is an imposing cathedral, built by Frederick II in 1231 and renewed in the 14th and 16th c. It has a richly decorated doorway (1312) on the main façade. Inside are a pulpit, a bishop's throne (16th c.) and beautifully carved choir-stalls (1543).

Gravina di Puglia

About 11 km (7 mi.) west of Altamura is Gravina di Puglia (338 m (1115 ft); population 37,000), picturesquely situated above a deep gorge (gravina) with an interesting cathedral (15th c. choir-stalls), the church of Santa Sofia (tomb of a duchess of Gravina; 1518) and a municipal museum. Outside the town, in a gorge, is the rock-hewn church of San Michele with remains of Byzantine paintings; another rock-hewn church is beyond the viaduct. On a hill north of the town are the ruins of a Hohenstaufen castle, which was built by Frederick II in 1231.

Bitonto

Location
17 km (10½ mi.) W

West of Bari lies Bitonto (118 m (389 ft); population 51,000), with well-preserved town walls. In the centre of the old town is the cathedral (c. 1200), perhaps the finest example of Apulian Romanesque architecture. Particularly beautiful are the richly decorated main doorway and the delicately pillared gallery on the south side. Inside there are two fine pulpits. Beneath the church is a crypt supported by 24 columns. East of the cathedral stands the Palazzo Vulpano Sylos (Renaissance courtyard; 1500).

Barletta   L13

Region: Puglia. Province: Bari (BA)
Altitude: 15 m (50 ft). Population: 90,000

Location

The busy port of Barletta, one of the principal towns of Apulia, lies on the Adriatic coast between Foggia and Bari.

Sights

San Sepolcro

At the junction of Corso Vittorio Emanuele and Corso Garibaldi, Barletta's busiest traffic intersection, stands the church of San Sepolcro (end 13th c.), an early Gothic building on the Burgundian model with a rich treasury.

★Barletta statue

In front of the church is a bronze statue, over 5 m (16 ft) high, of a Byzantine emperor (perhaps Valentinian I; d. 375), the finest piece of colossal sculpture in bronze from ancient times. The Venetians brought it back from Constantinople to Italy in the 13th c. and left it after a shipwreck on the beach of Barletta.

Museo Civico

North-east of the church is the Municipal Museum (Museo Civico) with a picture gallery.

Bronze statue of Emperor Valentinian I (?)

★Santa Maria Maggiore

A little way to the north-east, at the end of the narrow Via del Duorno, the continuation of the Corso Garibaldi, is the cathedral of Santa Maria Maggiore. The façade and campanile (13th c.) are built in Romanesque style, while the other parts of the building, including the choir, were added in the 14th–15th c. The church contains a tomb of the count of Barby and Mühlingen (d. 1566), with an inscription in German and a fine pulpit and tabernacle (both 13th c.).

Castello

Beyond the cathedral is the massive Castello, originally built by the Hohenstaufens in the 13th c., with four bastions added in 1537.

Sant'Andrea

North-west of the cathedral stands the church of Sant'Andrea with a Romanesque doorway (13th c.).

Porta Marina

On the promontory north of the town is the Porta Marina (1751); to the east of this is the harbour and to the west the bathing beach.

Excursion from Barletta via Castel del Monte (90 km (56 mi.))

Andria

There is an attractive drive south to Castel del Monte. The road comes first in 12 km (7 mi.), to Andria, once the favourite residence of the Emperor Frederick II; the crypt of the cathedral contains the tombs of Iolante of Jerusalem (d. 1228) and Isabella of England (d. 1241 at Foggia), the second and third wives of the emperor. The church of Sant'Agostino has a richly decorated doorway (14th c.).

★★Castel del Monte

From Andria it is another 18 km (11 mi.) to the Castel del Monte or Casteldelmonte (540 m (1782 ft)), the most imposing Hohenstaufen castle in Italy, built about 1240 as a hunting lodge for Frederick II, probably to his own design. The massive limestone structure, in early Gothic style, is an exact octagon, with a beautiful courtyard and eight towers; on each floor there are eight rooms of the same size, which originally had rich marble decoration. The rooms on the upper floor, with particularly fine windows, are believed to have been the emperor's apartments. Later the castle served as the prison of his grandsons, the sons of Manfred. From the roof there are panoramic views extending as far as Monte Gargano.

Minervino Murge

There is another attractive drive west of Castel del Monte (21 km (13 mi.)) to Minervino Murge (429 m (1416 ft); population 14,000), splendidly situated on the highest part of the Murge. Because of the extensive views from

Castel del Monte, Frederick II's hunting lodge

here it is also called "Balcony of Apulia". The town has a castle and a small cathedral. In a park outside the town is a large war memorial, the Faro votivo ai Caduti. From the north side of the park there are fine views of the town and surroundings.

Canosa di Puglia   16 km (10 mi.) north of Minervino Murge is Canosa di Puglia (105 m (347 ft); population 31,000), built on the site of the important Roman town of Canusium. There are remains of Roman walls, a town gate (to the west, outside the modern town) and the ruins of an amphitheatre of some size (near the station). The principal church, San Sabino, contains eighteen ancient columns; in the choir is a marble bishop's throne supported by elephants (1078–89, by Romualdus) and in the nave a marble pulpit (*c.* 1120). In the court to the south (entered from the south aisle) is the chapel, with a massive bronze door by Rogerius of Melfi, where Prince Boemond of Taranto (d. 1111), ruler of the Latin principality of Antioch is buried.

Cannae   From Canosa di Puglia it is 22 km (14 mi.) north-east back to Barletta. About half-way, off the road to the left, is the cemetery of the ancient town of Cannae, the place where Hannibal defeated the Romans in 216 BC (museum; medieval cemetery of the 9th–11th c.).

Basilicata   K–L14

Region: Basilicata. Province: Potenza (PZ) and Matera (MT)
Area: 9992 sq. km (3858 sq. mi.). Population: 611,000

Location   The region of Basilicata or Lucania, consisting of the provinces of Potenza and Matera, lies in southern Italy. Most of it is occupied by the southern

Neapolitan Apennines, with many rivers, mountain chains and tableland. The region is bounded in the north by Apulia, in the south by Calabria and in the west by Campania; it is open to the Tyrrhenian Sea in the Gulf of Policastro and to the Ionian Sea in the Gulf of Taranto.

In spite of the relatively fertile soil, which yields wheat, maize, vines, olives and edible chestnuts, many of the inhabitants of the region still live in poverty.

Despite the establishment of Greek colonies and Hellenistic settlements   History
on the coast of the Ionian Sea in the 8th–7th c. BC and the fact that the area was later Romanised, becoming Regio III of the Roman Empire, Basilicata remained throughout its history an area of only little consequence.

The region suffered severe damage in an earthquake in November 1980.

Sights

Potenza (819 m (2703 ft)), capital of the more westerly province and of the   **Potenza**
region of Basilicata, lies above the River Basento on a ridge between two valleys. It was severely damaged in an earthquake in 1857 and again during the Second World War, but has since largely been rebuilt. In the centre of the old town (1980 further earthquake damage), on the main street, Via Pretoria, is the Piazza Matteotti; a little way to the north-east stands the 18th c. cathedral. Just off the west end of the Via Pretoria rises the Romanesque church of San Michele (11th c.). To the north of the town the Museo Archeologico Provinciale, with finds from tombs, architectural fragments from the temple of Apollo Lyceus at Metaponto, is worth visiting.

There is a rewarding trip along the road which runs north via Castel Lagope-   **Castel Lagopesole**
sole (756 m (2495 ft)) with a well-preserved castle in Gothic style, built by Frederick II about 1242 on an eminence (829 m (2736 ft)) west of the former Lake Lagopesole to Rionero in Vulture (656 m (2165 ft); population 12,500).

From here it is 6 km (4 mi.) north-west to Monte Vulture (1330 m (4389 ft)),   **★Monte Vulture**
an extinct volcano visible from all over Apulia.

10 km (6 mi.) west of Rionero are the two small lakes of Monticchio (in the   **Monticchio**
double crater of an extinct volcano; 650 m (2145 ft); 38 m (125 ft) deep); on the smaller lake are the former Capuchin monastery of San Michele and a hydro-electric station. Between the two lakes are the ruins of the abbey of San Ippolito (12th c.). 7 km (4½ mi.) away, on the western slopes of the Monte Valtura, is the little spa of Monticchio Bagni (540 m (1782 ft)).

From Rionero the road continues north 9 km (5½ mi.) to Rapolla (438 m   **Rapolla**
(1445 ft)), a spa (recommended for rheumatism) with a beautiful Gothic cathedral.

From Rapolla a detour (20 km (12 mi.) east) can be made to Venosa (415 m   **★Venosa**
(1370 ft); population 12,000), an ancient Samnite town, from 291 BC the Roman colony of Venusia and the birthplace of the poet Horace.

Excavations have brought to light considerable remains of the town dating from the Roman Imperial period. Square stone blocks from the amphitheatre were used in the 12th c. in the construction of the convent of the Santissima Trinità, founded in 1046, which is situated to the north-east of the town. The original church was intended by the Norman duke Robert Guiscard (d. 1085) as a family burial place but remained unfinished. It contains 11th c. frescoes, the tomb of Robert Guiscard's wife, Roman inscriptions and fragments of sculpture.

To the north, on the road to the station, are Jewish catacombs (4th–5th c.) with inscriptions in Hebrew, Latin and Greek. In the centre of the town stands a 15th c. castle.

About 6 km (4 mi.) north-west of Rapolla, on a much-eroded lateral crater of   **Melfi**
Monte Vulture, is the little town of Melfi (531 m (1752 ft); population 16,000),

the market town of an extensive wine-producing and olive-growing area. It has a fine 12th c. cathedral, modernised in 1851; adjoining it is the former Archbishop's Palace. The Norman castle above the town houses the Museo Nazionale Archeologica, which contains a magnificent Roman sarcophagus from Rapolla, made in Asia Minor of a Roman lady (AD 165–170).

Matera

Matera, the chief town of the more easterly province of Basilicata (399 m (1317 ft); population 55,000), is picturesquely situated above a rocky gorge. The town is on the site of a prehistoric settlement, remains of which can be seen in the National Museum. The lower old town is made up of the two quarters of Sasso Barisano and Sasso Caveoso. Most of the houses here, known as *sassi*, are hewn from the rock and built in tiers on the hillside. They are a confusion of small walls, steps, gables and chimneys. In 1960 most of the occupiers were re-housed, and today the sassi are occupied largely by squatters. However, it is intended to restore them and use them for a variety of events. The sassi di Matera are on the UNESCO list of protected buildings.

On the highest point of the old town stands the 13th c. cathedral. Its façade is decorated with a rosette in stone symbolising the Wheel of Life. Inside can be seen a fragment of a fresco of the Madonna della Bruna, the patron saint of Matera. Other old churches nearby include those of San Giovanni Battista (13th c.), dedicated to John the Baptist, and San Francesco d'Assisi (stucco, paintings, etc.). In the monastery complex adjoining the church of Santa Chiara is the Museo Nazionale (rich finds from various eras).

In the region around Matera there are a number of small churches hewn out of the rock, suggesting that at one time monks, sheep-rearing communities, etc. lived here.

The Strada Panoramica runs along the top of the gorge past the church of San Pietro Caveoso to the church of Santa Maria de Idris (Byzantine frescoes), on the rocky hill of Montorrone.

Matera: sassi, *charming houses built into the rock*

Tavole Palatine, remains of a Doric temple near Metaponto

Metaponto

Near the north-west coast of the Gulf of Taranto is Metaponto, with the remains of the famous Greek city of Metapontion, the Roman Metapontum. The town, probably founded by Archaean settlers at the beginning of the 7th c. BC, became in the 6th c. a centre of Pythagorean teaching, the home of the great mathematician and philosopher Pythagoras, who is said to have died here in 497 BC at the age of 90. To the north of the town are the Tavole Palatine, the remains of a Doric temple, with fifteen of the original 36 columns still standing. The Antiquarium can display at any one time only a selection of the rich store of finds recovered in the excavations of recent years. Most of the material comes from the sacred precinct containing the remains of four large temples, which probably collapsed when they were undermined by rising ground-water in the 3rd c. BC.

A remarkable feature of the area is the carefully planned layout of the fertile plain, with regular field boundaries, roads and water channels and more than 300 Greek farmsteads, eleven of which have been excavated. The theatre (3rd c. BC), the walls of which were pulled down and the stones removed at an early period, had a semicircular cavea and Doric columns, anticipating some of the main features of the Roman theatre.

Benevento   J13

Region: Campania. Province: Benevento (BN)
Altitude: 135 m (446 ft). Population: 62,000

Benevento, chief town of its province, lies in Campania, some 50 km (31 mi.) north-east of Naples. The town, beautifully situated on a flat-topped hill between the rivers Savato and Calore, is the economic and communications centre of the fertile Benevento basin.

Location

The town was originally called Maleventum, but after the "Pyrrhic victory" of King Pyrrhus of Epirus over the Romans in 275 BC and the establishment

History

of a Roman military colony in 268 BC it was given the more auspicious name of Beneventum. Situated at the junction of the Via Appia with four other Roman roads, it developed into one of the most important towns in southern Italy, and from the 6th to the 11th c. it was the seat of powerful Lombard dukes. Thereafter the town belonged to the Papal State (with a short interruption under Napoleon) until it became part of Italy in 1860.

It has been the see of an archbishop since 969.

Sights

Cathedral	The town's principal street, running from north-west to south-east, is the Corso Garibaldi, in which stands the cathedral (founded *c.* 1200), which was completely destroyed in 1943 apart from the façade and the campanile but has since been rebuilt.
Teatro Romano	South-west of the cathedral are the remains of a Roman theatre (2nd c. AD); operatic performances now take place here.
Ponte Leproso	Another 500 m south-west is the Ponte Leproso, still incorporating part of the Roman bridge which carried the Via Appia over the Sabato.
★★Arco di Traiano	East of the cathedral along Corso Garibaldi is the Town Hall, beyond which (to the left, along Via dell'Arco di Traiano) rises the Arch of Trajan (Arco di Traiano), the so-called Porta Aurea, dedicated by the senate and people of Beneventum to the "best of princes" in AD 114 in anticipation of his return from the Parthian wars. The arch, built of Greek marble, stands 15.5 m (51 ft) high and is excellently preserved. One of the finest of its kind, it is decorated with reliefs glorifying the emperor.
Santa Sofia	Farther east along Corso Garibaldi is the Piazza Santa Sofia (officially Piazza Matteotti), where stands the church of Santa Sofia, a circular structure of the Lombard period (*c.* 760; 12th c. doorway).
★Museo del Sannio	Adjoining the church is the beautiful cloister of a former convent of Benedictine nuns, now housing the interesting Museo de Sannio, which contains a very fine prehistoric and early historical department, including Samnitic and Greco-Roman finds and Egyptian sculpture, as well as a rich coin collection and medieval and modern pictures.
Rocca dei Rettori	Still farther east, in Piazza IV Novembre, is a 14th c. castle, the Rocca dei Rettori, which contains the historical section of the museum. There are fine views from the municipal park.

Bergamo   D4

Region: Lombardia. Province: Bergamo (BG)
Altitude: 249–365 m (822–1205 ft). Population: 115,000

Location	The provincial capital of Bergamo lies north-east of Milan at the foot of the Bergamo Alps. It consists of an old town of narrow winding streets on a hill, defended by bastions erected in the 16th c., and a lower town extending out on to the Po plain with modern buildings and busy industries (textiles, cement, printing).
History	Originally a Gallic settlement and recorded in 200 BC as the Roman Municipium Bergomum, the town achieved no great importance until the Lombard period. In 1167 it became a member of the Lombard league of towns; then in 1264 it passed under the control of Milan and from 1427 it belonged to Venice. From 1814 Bergamo was controlled by Austria until

it was liberated by Garibaldi in 1859. In the 16th c. the theatre form known as the "commedia dell'arte" came to the fore in Bergamo.

Lower Town

The centre of the Lower Town (Città Bassa; 249 m (822 ft)) is the Piazza Matteotti, with beautiful gardens, parks and monuments, adjoining which on the north-west is the imposing Piazza Vittoria Veneto, with the Torre dei Caduti, a war memorial.

Piazza Matteotti

On the south-east side of Piazza Matteotti are the twin Neo-Classical gate-houses of the Porta Nuova (view of the upper town), from which the wide Viale Papa Giovanni XXIII runs south to the station. This street and the Viale Vittoria Emanuele II, which leads from the Piazza Vittorio Veneto to the upper town, form Bergamo's principal traffic artery.

Porta Nuova

East of Piazza Matteotti, in the busy avenue called the Sentierone, stands the Teatro Donizetti and in the east side of the Piazza Cavour is a monument to the Bergamo-born composer Gaetano Donizetti (1797–1848).

Teatro Donizetti

At the north-east end of the Sentierone is the church of San Bartolomeo (17th c.; façade 1901). Inside there are fine choir-stalls and behind the high altar Lorenzo Lotto's "Madonna with Child and Saints", one of his chief works.

San Bartolomeo

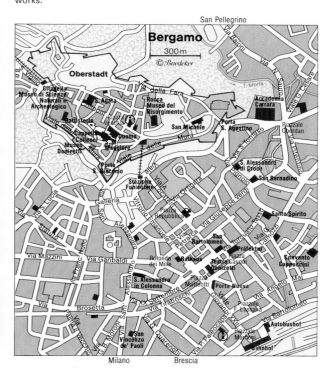

The commedia dell'arte

Can there be anyone who has not seen a harlequin, the jester dressed in a striped costume? Picasso painted pictures portraying the theme of the *commedia dell'arte* in a new way, sometimes melancholy, including such paintings as "Two Harlequins" and "Pierrot with Mask". Other figures from the commedia dell'arte appear in etchings by the Spaniard Jacques Callot (the "Balli di Sfessania" cycle); they are based on sketches which Callot made in Florence. Some genre scenes by Antoine Watteau reflect the influence of the the Italian commedia dell'arte, including his picture showing the figure of "Gilles", which can be seen in the Louvre in Paris.

The harlequin, or *arlecchino* in Italian, is one of the best known figures from the commedia dell'arte, a special form of impromptu comedy performed by wandering troupes in Upper Italy between 1550 and 1750. The plot and sequence of scenes were clearly laid down, but improvisation provided scope for deviation. The individual scenes were linked together by *lazzi*, pranks, tomfoolery and jokes. The fact that the actors represent stock "types" and dress accordingly is a salient feature.

The name of "Harlequin", the cunning servant, is thought to come from the description of the Devil as "Hellequin" the bump on Harlequin's head is supposed to be the remains of his shrunken horns. In addition there are Brighella, the sly farmer born in Bergamo, and the chamber-maid Colombina, the female equivalent of Arlecchino and Brighella, together with the show-off Pulcinella, a stupid and lazy fellow easily recognised by his protruding hooked nose, and the villain Mezzettino who plays the guitar. One should also not forget Zanni, who portrays either a sly schemer or a fool. The beginning and end of all dramatic plots involve the lovers (*amorosi*), with the audience playing an active part in their fortunes. Often the servant is also involved in the intrigues.

Some of the players in the commedia dell'arte wore masks. The question is often asked as to whether the commedia dell'arte designed its own masks or whether they can be traced back to those worn in carnivals. Probably both are true. One well-known thespian says of the masks "The mask brings us to the very threshold of the mystery of theatre ... The mask is a ritual".

Action was the keyword in commedia dell'arte. In no way was it a "learned" form of theatre, aimed at conveying values or a form of instruction. Therefore it is not surprising that the comedy was wide in scope. The absurd and comical figures on which tricks are played include the two old men, Pantalone and Dottore. Pantalone is often the caricature of a Venetian merchant whose costume – red trousers and cloak – he wears. He also has a long nose and a pointed beard. Dottore, who could be a jurist from Bologna or a doctor, personifies an academic rather than the ordinary man in the street. Capitano also adds to the interest; he purports to be a bragging officer famous for his heroic deeds and his bravery, while in fact he is just a loud-mouth whose amorous adventures are doomed to failure.

Baedeker Special

Some features of the commedia dell'arte found their way into the theatre of other European countries, especially in France. The influence came from Italian actors who, as early as the 16th century, toured in France and often performed before kings and the nobility. For quite a time the "theâtre italien" existed side by side with the "theâtre français" in Paris until 1697. The French comedy-writer Molière (1622–73), who managed his own theatrical group, introduced an element of farce into his plays, especially early on in his career; one only has to think of such readily remembered figures as Harpagnon in "L'Avare" (The Miser), or the main character in "Le Malade Imaginaire".

Traces of commedia dell'arte could also be found in Austrian literature, such as the character of Hanswurst in Stranitsky's work of the same name. From Hanswurst evolved the comical figure seen in the Viennese popular theatre. With the introduction of singing roles such farcical characters appeared in the form of *opera buffa*.

In the 18th century the routine followed by the commedia dell'arte became more clearly established. As popular tastes had changed there were clamours for reform. Critics of improvisation included Carlo Goldoni who reproached the commedia dell'arte on the grounds that its plays were offensive, silly and irrational. His aim was to introduce character comedy.

Even though commedia dell' arte in the narrow sense of the term no longer exists, it still plays an important role in the life of the Italians in particular and in contemporary life in general, as its characters still provide material for the satirist. For example, an unsuccessful politician may be compared with Fritellino, the master of the empty purse and the eternal loser. The British "Punch" is derived from Pulcinella, and "Bajazzo" from Pagliaccio. On the other hand, a highly-regarded troupe known as the "Bread and Puppet Theatre", which lays much emphasis on improvisation and gestures, has come to the fore in the United States.

◀ *Pulcinella*

Bergamo

Santo Spirito	From San Bartolomeo Via Torquato Tasso runs to the church of the Santo Spirito, which has another "Madonna" by Lotto (1521) and a painting by Previtali which depicts John the Baptist and other saints.
San Bernardino in Pignolo	A short distance north, in the steep Via Pignolo, is the little church of San Bernardino in Pignolo, with a "Madonna Enthroned" by Lotto (1521) in the choir. Higher up are a number of palaces with beautiful Early Renaissance courtyards.
★Accademia Carrara	In Via San Tommaso, which goes off Via Pignolo on the right, is a palace housing the Accademia Carrara, with a picture gallery with fine works by Lorenzo Lotto, Palma il Vecchio, Giovanni Battista Moroni, Vittore Carpaccio, Jacopo and Giovanni Bellini, Andrea Mantegna, Girolamo Romani Romanino, Giovanni Battista Tiepolo, Titian, Paolo Veronese, Raffael Santi, Sandro Botticelli, Luca Signorelli and Carlo Crivelli as well as works by Albrecht Dürer and Anton van Dyck. From here a stepped lane leads up to the Porta Sant'Agostino.

Upper Town

Porta Sant'Agostino	From Piazza Vittorio Veneto the Viale Vittorio Emanuele II runs past the lower station of the funicular and through the Porta Sant'Agostino into the Upper Town (Città Alta, 325–365 m (1073–1205 ft)).
Piazza Mercato delle Scarpe	From the gate we keep straight ahead, past the church of Sant'Agostino on the right, and then bear left and continue steeply uphill on the Via di Porta Dipinta, past the beautiful churches of San Michele al Pozzo Bianco and Sant'Andrea (inside the latter is a "Madonna Enthroned with Saints" by Moretto), to the Piazza Mercato delle Scarpe, with the upper station of the funicular on the left.
Rocca Museum	From here Via alla Rocca, to the right, ascends to the Rocca (14th c.), an old bastion, with the Museo del Risorgimento e della Resistenza (documents of Italy's recent history). From the castle keep and the adjoining Parco della Rimembranza there are very fine views.
★Piazza Vecchia	From the Piazza Mercato delle Scarpe the narrow Via Gombito, in which is a patrician tower-house, the Torre di Gombito (c. 1100), leads to the Piazza Vecchia, which together with the neighbouring Piazza del Duomo (cathedral square) forms the architecturally impressive centre of the Upper Town.
Palazzo della Ragione	Between the two squares is the Palazzo della Ragione (late 12th c.; largely rebuilt 1538–54), with an open colonnade. Adjoining is the Torre del Comune (lift). On the north side of the Piazza Vecchia is the Palazzo Nuovo (Municipal Library), a late Renaissance building.
★Santa Maria Maggiore	In the Piazza del Duomo the church of Santa Maria Maggiore, begun in 1137 as a Romanesque basilica, has a stepped-back tower over the crossing and a picturesque choir. On the south and north sides are doorways guarded by lions, with beautiful Gothic canopies (1353 and 1360). Inside there are fine choir-stalls in Renaissance style, Baroque stucco-work and tapestries on the walls of the side-aisles and choir. The church also contains the tomb of the composer Donizetti.
★Capella Colleoni	Adjoining the church is the Capella Colleoni in early Lombard Renaissance style, with a lavishly decorated marble façade, built 1470–76 to house the tomb of the condottiere Bartolomeo Colleoni. Inside are the tombs of Colleoni and his daughter Medea (d. 1470), both by Amadeo; ceiling paintings by Tiepolo (1732) and fine choir-stalls.
Baptistery	To the right of the Capella Colleoni is the Baptistery (1340), an octagonal building, originally in Santa Maria Maggiore, re-erected here in 1898.

View of Bergamo

Opposite is the cathedral of Sant'Alessandro (1459; choir 1560; dome and façade modern), with fine pictures by Tiepolo, Previtali and Moroni and beautiful Baroque choir-stalls.

Cathedral

From the Piazza Vecchia the narrow Via Colleoni runs north-west to the Citadel, which houses a museum of natural science and archaeology (Museo di Scienze Naturali e Museo Archeologico).

Archaeological Museum

Beyond it is the Porta Sant'Alessandro, from which Viale delle Mura (near-by, on the left, is the Donizetti Museum) leads round the wa ls (fine views) to the Porta San Giacomo, the most handsome of the town gates, and so back to the Porta Sant'Agostino, the starting point for the walk through the upper town.

Viale delle Mura

San Pellegrino Terme

In the Bergamo Alps is the spa of San Pellegrino Terme (358 m (1181 ft)), which also attracts visitors because of its beautiful situation in the wooded Brembo valley and its equable climate. Its widely renowned alkaline mineral water (recommended for gout and stomach, liver and urinary disorders) comes from three springs (26°C (79°F)) on the right bank of the Brembo (pump room, Kursaal, casino, theatre). From the Kursaal a funicular runs up in 10 minutes to San Pellegrino Vetta (653 m (2155 ft); restaurant).

Location
24 km (15 mi.) N

Bologna   F6–7

Region: Emilia-Romagna. Province: Bologna (BO)
Altitude: 55 m (165 ft). Population: 401,000

Bologna

Location

Bologna, capital of the region Emilia-Romagna and the province Bologna, lies in the fertile Upper Italian plain under the northern end of the Apennines.

The town is the see of an archbishop and has a famous university. It has a character all its own, with its long arcaded streets, its brick-built palaces, its numerous old churches, its curious leaning towers and the remains of its 8 km (5 mi.) circuit of 13th and 14th c. walls.

History

The town, known to the Etruscans as Felsina, became a Roman colony in 189 BC; the city centre still shows the regular layout of a Roman camp. It was declared a free city by the Emperor Henry V in 1116, and thereafter became a member of the Lombard League and took an active part in the struggle against the Hohenstaufens. The Imperial School of Bologna, which is said to have been in existence as early as the 5th c., became a university in the 13th c. – the oldest in Europe – and attracted students from many lands; in the 14th c. it pioneered the teaching of human anatomy.

The noble families of the town, who were in constant conflict with the Papacy, managed to assert their authority in the 14th c., but in 1506 Pope Julius II was able to incorporate the town in the Papal State. In 1530 Charles V was crowned Emperor here – the last imperial coronation on Italian soil. In 1796 the town was incorporated in Napoleon's Cisalpine Republic. In 1816 it reverted to Papal rule, and in 1860 finally became part of a united Italy. During the last war there was heavy fighting near Bologna.

Economy

Bologna's principal industries are the manufacture of pasta and sausages (particularly mortadella), shoe manufacture, chemicals, engineering and precision instruments. The world's largest fair of children's and young people's books is held here annually.

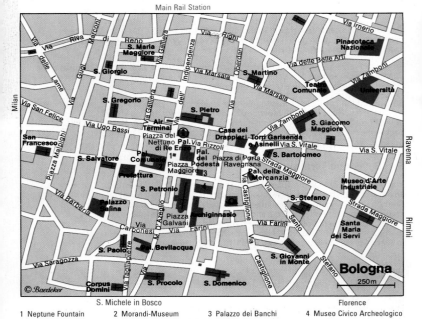

1 Neptune Fountain   2 Morandi-Museum   3 Palazzo dei Banchi   4 Museo Civico Archeologico

114

The town is also famous for its culinary specialities, chief among them is the meat sauce *à la bolognese*.

The characteristic feature of the architecture of Bologna is the use of brick. The first buildings of any consequence date from the Gothic period (church of San Petronio). The Renaissance and Baroque are abundantly represented, outstanding among local architects being Fioravante Fioravantini (d. after 1430) and his son Rodolfo, known as Aristotele (d. 1486), Pellegrino Tibaldi (d. 1597) and Sebastiano Serlio (1475–1522), one of the great architectural theorists of the late Renaissance. Serlio's school of theatre architects and painters achieved an international reputation in the 17th and 18th c. through the work of the Bibiena family of Tuscany, laying the foundations of modern stagecraft.

Architecture

Sculpture was practised mainly by artists from other parts of Italy. Michelangelo worked in San Domenico in 1494.
In painting, the first artist to attain more than local fame was Francesco Francia (1450–1517). Later the academy founded by Lodovico Carracci (1555–1619) and carried on by Annibale and Agostino Carracci fostered the school known as Eclecticism, whose leading representatives were Guido Reni (1575–1642), Domenichino (1581–1668) and Guercino (1581–1666).

Art

Town centre

The life of the town centres around two adjoining squares (both pedestrian precincts), the Piazza Maggiore and the Piazza del Nettuno. In the Piazza del Nettuno is the Neptune Fountain by Giambologna (1563–67), one of the finest fountains of the 16th c.

★Piazza Maggiore and Piazza del Nettuno

From the Piazza del Nettuno the busy shopping street Via dell'Indipendenza leads to the station. In this street, on the right, is the cathedral of San Pietro (the Metropolitana), founded in 910, with a choir by Pellegrino Tibaldi (1575) and a nave, remodelled in Baroque style (17th c.). It contains some fine treasures, including two marble lions from the Romanesque doorway, a "Mourning of Christ" and an "Annunciation of Our Lady" by I. Carraci. Beyond the choir is the Archbishop's Palace.
Parallel to the Via dell'Indipendenza to the west is Via Galleria, with many old aristocratic mansions.

San Pietro

The west side of the Piazza del Nettuno and Piazza Maggiore is occupied by the Palazzo Comunale (Town Hall), an extensive Gothic building begun in 1290 and largely rebuilt in 1425–30. Above the main entrance (1555) is a bronze statue (1580) of Pope Gregory XIII, a native of Bologna. On the second floor is the Municipal Art Gallery (Collezione Comunale d'Arte).

Palazzo Comunale Art Gallery

In 1993 the Morandi Museum was opened on the upper floor of the Palazzo d'Accursio. On display are over 200 paintings, water-colours, drawings and etchings by the Bolognese painter G. Morandi (1890–1964), mainly donated by his family. His studio has also been reconstructed here together with his extensive library.

★★Morandi Museum

Nearby the Town Hall is the Gothic Palazzo di Re Enzo (restored in 1905), in which Enzo, the poet son of Frederick II, was kept prisoner from 1249 to 1272.

Palazzo di Re Enzo

On the north side of the Piazza Maggiore is the former Palazzo del Podestà (1201; rebuilt from 1484 onwards in Early Renaissance style), with a tower, Torre dell'Arengo dating from 1212.

Palazzo del Podestà

The south side of the Piazza Maggiore is dominated by San Petronio, the largest church in Bologna, which is dedicated to the town's patron saint.

★San Petronio

Palazzo Comunale (now an art gallery), on the Piazza Maggiore

Begun in 1390 it was not completed according to the original plan, work being suspended about 1650 after the construction of the nave. The sculpture on the main doorway of the unfinished façade is by Jacopo della Quercia (1425–38). The interior ranks as the supreme achievement of Gothic architecture in Italy. Note the pieta by Amico Aspertini (1519) and the various wall-paintings.

★Museo Civico Archeologico

To the south of San Petronio, in Via dell'Archiginnasio (No. 2), is the Archaeological Museum (Museo Civico Archeologico), with a collection of prehistoric and Etruscan material from the surrounding area, and other antiquities; the museum has the finest Egyptian department after those of Turin and Venice (Rooms III–V). The Greek department (Room VI) contains a head of Athena Lemnia (copy of a work by Phidias, 5th c. BC).

Palazzo Galvani

From the museum the Via dell'Archiginnasio, with the Portico del Pavaglione and its numerous shops, runs south to the Piazza Galvani, where stands a marble statue of the Bologna-born physiologist Luigi Galvani (1737–98), discoverer of the "Galvanic discharges" (though he himself interpreted them wrongly). On the left is the Archiginnasio (1562–63), until 1803 occupied by the university (with the old anatomy lecture-room, the Teatro Anatomico) and now housing the Municipal Library (600,000 volumes).

★Palazzo Bevilacqua

To the south-west, in Via d'Azeglio, is the Palazzo Bevilacqua, built in 1474–82 in the Early Renaissance style of the Florentine palaces, with a fine courtyard and a beautiful façade.

Piazza San Domenico

Via d'Azeglio runs by way of Via Marsili to the Piazza San Domenico, in which are two columns bearing statues of Saint Dominic and the Virgin, and the Gothic tombs of two learned lawyers Rolandino de' Passeggeri (d. 1300) and Egidio Foscherari.

On the south side of the square is the church of San Domenico (begun *c.* 1221; façade unfinished), with an interior remodelled in Baroque style, containing the tomb of St Dominic (d. in Bologna 1221), a marble sarcophagus with carving by Nicola Pisano, Arnolfo di Cambio and Fra Guglielmo (1267); cover by Niccolò dall'Arca (d. 1494); the angel on the right, the figure of St Petronius on the cover and the youthful St Proculus (to rear) are early works by Michelangelo (1494). Fine intarsia (mosaic woodwork) choir-stalls (1541–51).

★San Domenico

To the left of the choir, between the first and second chapels is a wall monument to King Enzo ("Hencius Rex", d. 1272; restored 1731).

In the sacristy is the Museo San Domenico.

Museo San Domenico

From the Piazza del Nettuno Via Rizzoli runs east to the Piazza di Porta Ravegnana, on the south side of which is the beautiful Gothic Palazzo della Mercanzia (1384), home of the Chamber of Commerce.

Palazzo della Mercanzia

In the middle of the square are the Leaning Towers, two plain brick towers (Torre degli Asinelli and Torre Garisenda) originally built for defensive purposes, which have become a landmark and an emblem of the city. The Torre degli Asinelli (1119; 498 steps), 97.6 m (322 ft) high, leans 1.23 m (4 ft) from the vertical; the Torre Garisenda (begun end of 11th c.), 48 m (158 ft) high, is 3.22 m ($10^3/_4$ ft) aslant.

★Leaning Towers

From the Piazza di Porta Ravegnana five streets radiate to the gates on the east side of the town – Via Castiglione, Via Santo Stefano, Strada Maggiore, Via San Vitale and Via Zamboni.

Piazza di Porta Ravegnana

In Via Santo Stefano is the basilica of Santo Stefano, a complex of eight buildings of which three have frontages on the street – the Chiesa del

Via Santo Stefano Santo Stefano

The Gothic Palazzo di Re Enzo, near the town hall

117

Bologna

Crocifisso, now the principal church, originally Romanesque but rebuilt in 1637, with an external pulpit (12th c.) and a crypt (1019); the church of Santo Sepolcro, an octagonal building on a centralised plan containing the tomb of St Petronius, bishop of Bologna in the 5th c.; and the Romanesque church of Santi Vitale e Agricola (founded 5th c.; present building 1019; façade 1885), with the 13th c. Chiesa della Trinità. Behind San Sepolcro is the Cortile di Pilato, a pillared courtyard of 1142 (marble basin, 741), adjoining which is a two-storey cloister.

Strada Maggiore
Casa Isolani

In Strada Maggiore, immediately left, is the church of San Bartolomeo (1530; interior 17th c.). Farther along, on the right (No. 19), is Casa Isolani, a 13th c. aristocrat's mansion with a projecting upper storey supported on oak beams. Opposite (No. 24) is the Palazzo Sampieri, with admirable frescoes from the story of Hercules by Carracci and Guercino. Next door (No. 26) is the house of the composer Gioacchino Rossini, who lived mostly in Bologna between 1825 and 1848 (commemorative tablet).

Palazzo Davia-Bergellini

In Strada Maggiore (No. 44) is the Palazzo Davia-Bargellini (1638–1658), with a Picture Gallery and Museum of Industrial Art.

Santa Maria dei Servi

Almost opposite is the church of Santa Maria dei Servi (begun 1346), with a beautiful portico; inside is a "Madonna Enthroned" by Cimabue.

Piazza Carducci

Some 500 m south-east of the church, in Piazza Carducci, is the house which belonged to Giosuè Carducci (1835–1907), the most popular Italian poet of the 19th c.; to the right, on the town walls, is a monument to the poet (1928).

Via Zamboni
San Giacomo Maggiore

In the Via Zamboni (No. 13) is the Palazzo Malvezzi-De' Medici (1560), now the headquarters of the provincial administration. Farther along, on the right, is the church of San Giacomo Maggiore (originally 1267; rebuilt c. 1500), which contains the tomb of the jurist Antonio Bentivoglia (d. 1435), by Jacopo della Quercia. To the left of this, is the Capella del Bentivoglia, containing a "Virgin Enthroned" by Francesco Francia. The Oratory of Santa Cecilia behind the apse of the church, has beautiful frescoes by Lorenzo Costa, Francesco Francia and their pupils (1504–06). Farther along Via Zamboni, on the left, stands the Teatro Comunale (1756–63), an opera-house.

University

Opposite the Teatro Comunale is the former Palazzo Poggi, with a façade and ceiling paintings by Pellegrino Tibaldi (1569), which has been occupied since 1803 by the University (with some 40,000 students). Farther north-east is the finely planned "University City".

★Pinacoteca Nazionale

To the north of the university, in Via delle Belle Arti (No. 56), is a former Jesuit college which now houses the National Picture Gallery (Pinacoteca Nazionale), with some of the best works of Bolognese painters of the 14th–18th c., the 17th c. being particularly well represented. Outstanding among other works are a "Madonna with Saints" by the Ferrarese artist Francesco del Cossa, one of his finest works, and a masterpiece by Raphael, "St Cecilia"; there are also works by Guido Reni, Guercino, Perugino, Vasari and Carracci, as well as pictures by Venetian masters, including Tintoretto, Palma il Giovane, Cima da Congliano and Vivarini.

San Martino

At the west end of the Via delle Belle Arti stands the Carmelite church of San Martino (Gothic, 13th–16th c.); in the first chapel on the left can be seen a "Madonna with Saints" by Francesco Francia.

★San Francesco

In Piazza Malpighi, to the west of the town centre, is the Gothic church of San Francesco, built 1236–63 on the model of French churches, with a tower erected 1397–1402. It contains a large Gothic marble altar (1388).

Basilica Madonna di San Luca near Bologna ▶

Bolzano

Textile Museum	500 m south-east, in the Palazzo Salina (Via Barberia 13), there is a Textile Museum.

Suburbs

Museum of Modern Art	Outside the town to the north lie the exhibition grounds with the Museum of Modern Art.
San Michele in Bosco 1 km (¾ mi.) S	From the south town gate Porta San Mamolo a road leads to Via Cadivilla, at the end of which stands the former monastery of San Michele in Bosco (124 m (409 ft)). Note the organ of 1524 and the frescoes in the sacristy. From the monastery there are fine views.
Basilica Madonna di San Luca 4 km (2½ mi.) SW	500 m west of the Porta Saragozza, the south-west town gate, begins a colonnade (built 1674–1739) of 666 arches, 3.5 km (2 mi.) long, which extends by way of Meloncello (where a branch goes off to the Certosa) to the Monte della Guardia (reached also by a motor road), with the pilgrim-age church of Madonna di San Luca. From here there are beautiful views as far as the Adriatic Sea and the Apennines, and in clear weather the Alps.

Bolzano   F2–3

Region: Trentino-Alto Adige. Province: Bolzano (BZ)
Altitude: 165 m (545 ft). Population: 98,000

Location	Bolzano (in German Bozen), capital of the autonomous province of the same name, lies in a fertile basin at the junction of the River Isarco (Eisack), coming from the Brenner, with the Talvera (Talfer), coming from Val Sarentina. The Isarco, thus reinforced, flows into the Adige (Etsch) to the south of the town. To the east is the magnificent Catinaccio group, with the Torri del Vaiolet, typical Dolomite peaks.
	Situated at the intersection of through routes and popular mountain roads, Bolzano's convenient location makes it an excellent base from which to explore the region.
	Bolzano is the chief commercial, industrial and tourist centre of the mainly German-speaking region of Alto Adige (South Tirol).
	The old town, lying within the confluence of the Talvera and the Isarco, is with its handsome Renaissance and Baroque buildings, its picturesque oriel windows, inner courts and staircases, a typical Germanic town. To the west of the Talvera, nearby Gries and Quirain, are typical Italian residential districts. South of the Isarco is Bolzano's industrial zone.
History	Bolzano was the Roman Bauzanum. In 680 it was taken by the Lombards and in 740 by the Franks, and later became the seat of Bavarian Lords of the Marches. For a time it belonged to the bishopric of Trient, which was compelled to cede it to the count of Tirol in the 13th c. It came under Habsburg rule in 1363, and thereafter shared the destinies of Tirol until 1919, when it passed to Italy. In 1948 the provinces of Bolzano and Trento were formed into the autonomous region of Trentino-Alto Adige, and German was granted the status of a second offical language in the province of Bolzano. Since 1964 Bolzano has been the seat of the bishopric of Bolzano and Bressanone.

Old town

Piazza Walther	The central feature of the town is the Piazza Walther (Waltherplatz), named after the German minnesinger Walther von der Vogelweide (c. 1170–1230), with a monument to the poet (1889; Heinrich Natter). At the south-west corner of the square is the Gothic parish church (14th–15th c.), which, like its counterpart in Bressanone, has the status of a cathedral. It has an ele-gant tower 65 m (215 ft) high (1504–19) and a Lombard doorway; fine
Parish church	

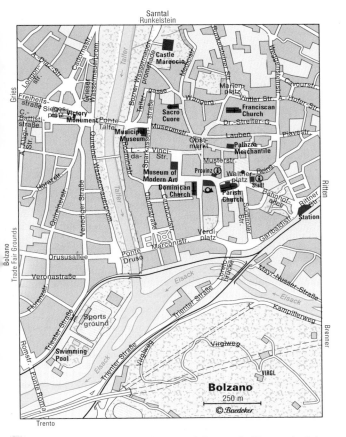

Sarntal
Runkelstein

Castle
Mareccio

Maria
platz

Franciscan
Church

Sacro
Cuore

Victory
Monument

Ponte
Talfe.

Municipal
Museum

Palazzo
Merchantile

Obst
markt

Lauben

Museum of
Modern Art

Provinz

Walther
platz

Dominican
Church

Parish
Church

Station

Verdi
platz

Ponte
Druso

Drususallee

Veronastraße

Sports
ground

Swimming
Pool

Virglweg

VIRGL

Bolzano

250 m

© *Baedeker*

Trento

Gries

Bolzano
Trade Fair Grounds

Ritten

Bremer

interior with a Late Gothic pulpit (1513–14) decorated with carved reliefs
and frescoes of the 14th–15th c.

To the west of the Piazza Walther is the Gothic Dominican church (13th c.;   Dominican church
remodelled in 1498 as a hall-church with three naves), with fine late 14th c.
frecoes.

In the adjoining St John's Chapel are frescoes of the school of Giotto   ★St John's Chapel
(1330–50), including a fine "Triumph of Death".
   The cloister of the former Dominican monastery (now the Conservatoire)
has frescoes by Michael Pacher and other artists.

To the north of Piazza Walther is the arcaded Via dei Portici (Laubengasse)   Via dei Portici
the town's principal shopping and commercial street (pedestrian precinct
with textile shops, perfumeries and boutiques), with fine 17th c. town
houses. The fine Palazzo Mercantile (1708–27; now the Chamber of
Commerce) on the south side of the street, is the only example of an Italian
palazzo in Bolzano.

121

Bolzano

The central feature of Bolzano: Piazza Walther with the parish church

Town Hall

At the east end of Via dei Portici in a small square stands the Town Hall, a building in Baroque style erected in 1907; at the west end of the street is the fruit market, with a Neptune Fountain (1777).

Franciscan monastery

A little way north of the fruit market stands the Franciscan monastery. Its church (originally 13th–15th c.), has 20th c. stained-glass windows; concerts are held in the adjoining late Romanesque cloisters (14th c.). In the Lady Chapel is a fine Late Gothic altar of carved wood by Hans Klocker (c. 1500).

Farther east stands the Late Gothic church of the Teutonic Order (Deutschhauskirche).

Museum of Modern Art

The west end of the pedestrian precinct leads into the Via Sernesi; here can be found the Museum of Modern Art, with contemporary sculptures in the courtyard (temporary exhibitions).

Municipal Museum

From the fruit market the Via del Museo runs west to the Municipal Museum, with archaeological material, peasant house interiors, traditional costumes, folk art and works by local artists.

Alto Adige (South Tirol) Archaeological Museum

From the Municipal Musuem it is not far to the Alto Adige Archaelogical Musuem, where the ancient and early history of the area is documented. The centrepiece of the exhibition is the famous glacier mummy known as "Otzi"; its age is estimated at 5300 years.

Castel Mareccio Castel Sant'Antonio

From the Lungotalvera Bolzano, which begins at the Municipal Museum and follows the east bank of the Talvera for 1.3 km (³/₄ mi.), there are fine views of Monte Sciliar and the Catinaccio group. A little way along this promenade, on the right, is Castel Mareccio (Schloss Maretsch, 13th–16th c.), with five towers, now a Congress Centre. At the north end of the promenade is the 17th c. Castel Sant'Antonio (Schloss Klebenstein).

North-east above Castel Sant'Antonio on a precipitous porphyry crag stands the 13th c. Castel Roncolo (361 m (1191 ft)), with frescoes of the 14th–15th c. Since 1893 the castle has belonged to the community of Bolzano.

Castel Roncolo

New town

To the west of the Talvera extends the predominantly Italian new town. Just west of the Talvera Bridge is a large triumphal arch, the Victory Monument (Monumento della Vittoria, 1928).

Monumento della Vittoria

To the left is the Viale Venezia, which runs south to the Lido (open-air and indoor swimming pools and other sports facilities),1 km ($\frac{1}{2}$ mi.) away. A little way west of this are the grounds of the Bolzano Trade Fair, with the Palazzo della Fiera (at present an ice-rink).

Bolzano Trade Fair

From here the Corso Italia runs north past the massive Law Courts to the Piazza Mazzini, where it meets the Corso Libertà, a street which runs west, lined by tall arches, from the Victory Monument and continues to the main square of Gries.

Gries

The suburban district of Gries (273 m (901 ft)), lies at the foot of the hill of Guncinà (Guntschna-Berg) and was formerly a popular winter resort noted for its mild climate. The old central area is surrounded by numerous villas set in trim gardens.

On the east side of the main square of Gries is a Benedictine monastery, originally built as a castle, with a beautiful church in late Rococo style (1769–78; ceiling paintings and altarpiece by Martin Knoller). Not far to the north-west stands the old Parish Church of Gries (15th–16th c.). The chief feature of the interior and at the same time one of the most important Gothic works of art in the Alto Adige is the beautifully carved altarpiece by Michael Pacher with a representation of the Coronation of the Virgin, now to be seen in the Erasmus Chapel. Also of interest is a 12th c. Romanesque-Byzantine crucifix.

Benedictine monastery
Old Parish Church

★★Pacher Altar

To the north of the Old Parish Church in Gries is the beginning of the Passeggiata del Guncinà, an attractive path which winds its way up the hill and ends at the Reichrieglerhof hotel (45 minutes). The hotel can also be reached by road (3.5 km (2 mi.)) from the Victory Monument by way of Via Cadorna and Via Miramonti.

★Passeggiata del Guncinà

Beyond the St Anton Bridge are Castel Sant'Antonio and the beginning of the Passeggiata Sant'Osvaldo, which climbs through the vineyards, affording fine views, to a height of 400 m (1320 ft) and then runs down past the picturesque wine village of Santa Maddalena to the suburban district of Rencio (Rentsch) on the road to the Brenner (1$\frac{1}{4}$ hours).

★Passeggiata Sant'Osvaldo

A little way north of the St Anton Bridge over the Talvera a cableway and a well engineered panoramic road lead up to San Genesio Atesino (Jenesien; 1087 m (3587 ft); also reached on a narrow road), a village which is a popular health resort with magnificent views of the Schlern and the Dolomites.

San Genesio Atesino

Bolzano to Collalbo (17 km (11 mi.))

North-east of Bolzano is the Renón (Ritten), an extensive porphyry plateau lying between the Talvera and the Isarco, reached by an excellent road (17 km (11 mi.)) from Bolzano.

★Renón

Bolzano

Auna di Sotto   12 km (7 mi.): Auna di Sotto (Unterinn, 908 m (2996 ft)), where a narrow road (5 km (3 mi.)) branches off, past the little Lago di Castro, to Soprabolzano (Oberbozen, 1220 m (4026 ft)), which can also be reached by cableway from Bolzano.

Collalbo   5 km (3 mi.): Collalbo (Klobenstein, 1190 m (3927 ft)), which, like Soprabolzano, is a popular summer resort, with superb views of the Dolomites. To the north, in the Fosco gorge beyond Longomoso (Lengmoos), are interesting earth pyramids which are reached in 30 minutes.

Bolzano to Sterzing over the Passo di Pennes (67 km (42 mi.))

A beautiful run on an excellent engineered road. Leave Bolzano by way of Via Castel Roncolo and Via Beato Arrigo (on left; then past Castel Sant'Antonio (on left: road to San Genesio cableway), and below Castel Roncolo (on right) over the Talvera to join the road which comes in from Gries on the left.

Continue north on this road, passing on the right a covered wooden bridge carrying an old road over the river, and beyond this, in the valley, the old moated Castel Novale (Schloss Ried); then up the Val Sarantina (Sarntal), which narrows in places into a gorge between sheer walls of porphyry, with 24 tunnels. The road passes the extensive ruins of Castel Sarentino (Schloss Rafenstein; 16th c.; 692 m (2284 ft)) on the left and Castel Vanga (Schloss Wangen) on the right. Soon afterwards Monte San Giovanni, a massive porphyry crag 230 m (759 ft) high, with the old church of San Giovanni, can be seen ahead.

10 km (6 mi.): Locanda alla Posta (Gasthaus zur Post Halbweg). The road continues up the valley, which here widens out.

5 km (3 mi.): Ponticino (Bundschen-Dick; 923 m (3046 ft)) with houses built for workers in the hydro-electric power station.

1 km (¹/₂ mi.) farther on, on the right, is the Pino inn (Gasthaus Fichte), and soon afterwards lower down on the left the little spa of Bagni di Serga (Bad Schörgau: chalybeate water).

Sarantino   4 km (2¹/₂ mi.): Sarantino (Sarnthein; 981 m (3237 ft)), the chief place in the valley, a beautifully situated little town which is a favourite summer holiday resort. Two castles stand here: Regino (Reineck, 13th c.) and Kränzelstein. The little church of San Cipriano contains over-painted 16th c. frescoes. Picturesque local costumes are worn on Sundays.

The road continues from Sarantino up the Val Sarantina to the Passo di Pennes.

Campolasta   3 km (2 mi.): Campolasta (Astfeld; 1023 m (3376 ft)), a pretty village at the junction of two valleys – to the right the Valdurna (Durnholzer Tal), with the village of the same name, situated on the beautiful Lago di Valdurna (Durnholzer See; 12 km (7 mi.); 1568 m (5174 ft)); to the left the pretty Val di Pennes (Penser Tal). Going up the Val di Pennes, the road climbs gradually, coming in 9 km (6 mi.) to the Alpenrose inn (on left). It then continues past a reservoir and the modest Edelweiss inn, running along the slope of the hillside.

Pennes   18 km (11 mi.): Pennes (Pens; 1459 m (4815 ft)), a straggling village, which is the chief settlement of the valley.

The road then climbs more steeply up the bare hillside, with three sharp bends: to the left is the Corno Bianco (Weisshorn; 2705 m (8927 ft)).

★Passo di Pennes   10 km (6 mi.): Passo di Pennes (Penser Joch; 2211 m (7296 ft)), with magnificent views, particularly of the peaks in the Ötz and Stubai valleys (Zuckerhütl; 3507 m (11,573 ft)).

Dosso   Beyond the pass the road descends (gradient of 10 per cent), at first high up on the bare slopes above the Val di Dosso (Eggertal). In 8 km (5 mi.), below the Schönblick inn, it comes to the hamlet of Dosso (Egg), with a chapel. It then runs down through forest country, with picturesque glimpses of the Isarco valley (Sterzing, Burg Sprechenstein).

Then a steep descent (13 per cent) into the Isarco valley, joining the road from the Passo di Monte Giovo shortly before reaching the parish church of Sterzing.

17 km (11 mi.): Sterzing (Vipiteno; 948 m (3128 ft)), an old village popular as a summer and winter sports resort. In the Multscher Museum there are painted panels and carvings by the Master of Ulm.

Sterzing

★Bordighera   B8

Region: Liguria. Province: Imperia (IM)
Altitude: 5 m (17ft). Population: 12,000

The little town of Bordighera lies on the Riviera di Ponente near the French frontier, some 30 km (19 mi.) east of Nice and 10 km (6 mi.) west of San Remo.

Location

The town has long been a popular health resort and has become equally popular as a seaside resort.

Bordighera is famed for the date-palms *(Phoenix dactylifera)* that grow here because of the mild climate, though the dates seldom ripen sufficiently to be edible. Large quantities of branches are supplied to Roman Catholic churches in spring for Palm Sunday. The Vatican is also supplied with palm leaves from here.

Flora

Flower-growing is also an important local industry.

This part of the Riviera is also called "Riviera dei Fiori" (the Riviera of Flowers).

Sights

Bordighera consists of the picturesque old town (Città Vecchia), high above Capo Sant'Ampelia, and the newer districts west of the cape.

The main traffic artery of Bordighera is Via Vittorio Emanuele, in which are the theatre and the Chiesa di Terrasanta. From this street various side streets climb up to the Via Romana. In one of these side streets, in Via Regina Margherita, is the Museo Bicknell, which houses Liguria's archaeological collections (over 50,000 books, a large photographic archive, collection of rubbings of rock-drawings from Monte Bego, and complete reconstruction of a 2nd c. Roman tomb). To the right of the entrance is a memorial tablet to Charles Bicknell. From the Via Romana there are charming views of beautiful palm-gardens. It ends in the west at the Rio Borghetto, in the east at the Spianata del Capo, on top of the promontory, from which there are magnificent views: of the Ospedaletti bay to the north-east and Ventimiglia, the Côte d'Azur and the peaks of the Maritime Alps, usually snow-capped, to the west. At the foot of the cliff-fringed promontory is a seafront promenade, the Lungomare Argentina.

Museo Bicknell

Just north of the Spianata del Capo is the old town, a huddle of narrow winding streets, still with the old town gates. (Note the parish church of S. Maria Maddalena on the Piazza del Popolo.) From here the Via dei Colli runs west above the little town, affording superb views.

Old town

Surroundings

In the outlying district of Arziglia, to the east, near the mouth of the Sasso valley and the Kursaal, are the Vallone Gardens (private property), laid out

Arziglia

Bormio

Bicknell Museum: rubbings of rock drawings from Monte Bego

by a German gardener named Ludwig Winter (d. 1912), where palms are cultivated for their leaves.

About 1.5 km (1 mi.) east, on the road to Ospedaletti, is the Madonna Garden, also laid out by Winter (and also private property, but open to visitors all the year round).

Sasso

From the Via dei Colli a road runs north above the Sasso valley to the fortress-like village of Sasso, situated on the summit of a hill.

Seborga

Some 8 km (5 mi.) farther on is the little village of Seborga, once a fortified mountain village owned by the Courts of Ventimiglia, it was later taken over by Benedictine monks who founded a mint here. The village commands extensive views.

Bormio   E3

Region: Lombardia. Province: Sondrio (SO)
Altitude: 1225 m (4430 ft). Population: 4000

Location

Bormio (formerly Worms) lies in the Veltlin (Italian Veltellina) at the north-west foot of the Ortles group and at the western end of the pass across the Stilfser Joch, close to the Italian–Swiss frontier.

Town

The little town popular as a health resort, tourist centre and winter sports resort, has a fine old centre. In its surroundings are several mineral springs which can be used for therapeutic purposes.

Sights

In the Piazza Cavour, east of the centre of the village, is the Baroque parish church, the Chiesa Collegiata SS. Gervasio e Protasio; (17th c.); to the left stands the loggia of the Kuèerc, the former court of justice, behind which is the Torre Civica (town tower).

Parish church

North-west of the parish church, in Via Buon Consiglio, is the Palazzo De Simoni, which houses the municipal museum, the Museo Civico, with a historic collection.

Museo Civico

At the extreme northern end of Bormio, in Via Monte Ortigara, is a mineralogical museum (Museo Mineralogico Naturalistico Valli di Bormio).
    Near the museum, in Via Sertorelli, can be found the Botanical Garden.

Museo Mineralogico

A short way to the south of the river is Combo with the Santuario del Crocifisso (or Sant'Antonio Abbate; 14th c.); the interior is decorated with 15th and 16th c. frescoes.

Santuario del Crocifisso

Outside the village, to the west, are the sports stadium and ice rink, built to a pentagonal plan.

Sports stadium

Bagni di Bormio

Bagni di Bormio (1318 m (4349 ft)), the popular spa district of Bormio, consists of the Bagni Vecchi (old baths) and the Bagni Nuovi (new baths).

Location
3 km (2 mi.) N

The seven springs of the Bagni Vecchi, mentioned by Pliny, in the Dolomites beyond the deep gorge of the Adda. Interesting are the so-called "piscine", bathing basins, rock-hewn by the Romans.

Bagni Vecchi

The Bagni Nuovi are situated on a mountain terrace. Their radioactive water, containing traces of gypsium, issues at temperatures between 38 and 41°C (94 and 99°F) and is recommended for rheumatism, asthma and arteriosclerosis.

Bagni Nuovi

Bormio 2000

At the south edge of Bormio is the lower station of the cableway which goes up to Bormio 2000 near the tree line. The second section leads to Bormio 3000, immediately at the foot of the Cima Bianca (3012 m (9940 ft)). The surrounding area offers superb winter sports facilities, including an artificial snow-making installation.

From Bormio 3000 a 45-minute climb can be made up to the Vallecetta.

Bormio 3000

Also in this area is a cableway to the Ciuk (1620 m (5346 ft)), from where a chairlift continues to La Rocca (2126 m (7016 ft)).

La Rocca

Brescia   E4

Region: Lombardia. Province: Brescia (BS)
Altitude: 149 m (492 ft). Population: 194,000

Brescia, capital of the province of the same name, second in importance only to Milan among the towns of Lombardy, lies below two foothills of the Brescian Alps, some 25 km (15 mi.) west of Lake Garda.
    The picturesque old town, surrounded by gardens, has Roman remains dating from the early Empire and fine Renaissance buildings. Following

Location

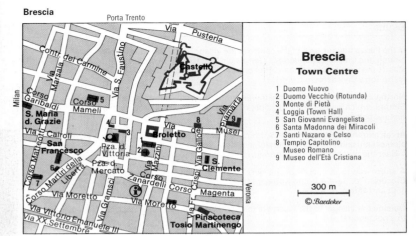

Brescia

Porta Trento

Brescia
Town Centre

1 Duomo Nuovo
2 Duomo Vecchio (Rotunda)
3 Monte di Pietà
4 Loggia (Town Hall)
5 San Giovanni Evangelista
6 Santa Madonna dei Miracoli
7 Santi Nazaro e Celso
8 Tempio Capitolino
  Museo Romano
9 Museo dell'Età Cristiana

300 m

© Baedeker

Station

heavy damage during the Second World War some parts of the town have been rebuilt with wider streets and larger squares.

History

The ancient Brixia became a Roman colony in the time of Augustus under the name of Colonia Augusta Civica and rose to prosperity as a result of its situation on the road which ran from Bologna through the Alps by way of the Splügen pass. During the Middle Ages it was an active member of the Lombard league of towns. From 1428 to 1797 it belonged to Venice.

Brescia produced two notable painters – Alessandro Bonvicino, known as Il Moretto (1498–1554), whose colouring vies with that one of the Venetians, and Girolama da Romano, known as Il Romanino (c. 1485–after 1562). Their works are well represented in the town's churches and in the Pinacoteca.

Economy

The town's industries include textiles and hardware, and it is also an important market centre for the agricultural products of the fertile surrounding area.

Piazza del Duomo

Duomo Nuovo

In the Piazza del Duomo is the 17th c. cathedral, the Duomo Nuovo, with a central dome of 1825.

★Rotonda

On its south side is the Rotonda or Duomo Vecchio, a massive circular structure crowned by a dome (11th–12th c.) containing works by Moretto and Romanino. Beneath the transept lies the Cripta di San Filastrio; the columns have capitals of the former Basilica di S Maria Maggiore (6th and 9th c.).

Broletto

To the north of the Duomo Nuovo is the Broletto (1187–1230), the old Town Hall, now housing the prefecture, with the Torre del Popolo.

★Loggia

To the west of the Piazza del Duomo is the Piazza della Vittoria, the town's central square (rebuilt c. 1930). Behind the Post Office lies the Piazza della Loggia, one of the most picturesque squares in northern Italy. On its west side is the superb Loggia (Town Hall), begun in Early Renaissance style

The Duomo Nuovo and Duomo Vecchio (Rotonda)

(1492–1508) and completed between 1526 and 1674 (windows by Palladio). Opposite on the east side can be seen a façade with a 16th c. clock-tower.

On the south side is the Monte di Pietà (pawnshop), with a beautiful Early Renaissance loggia (15th c.).

The life of the town centres on the Corso Zanardelli, on the south side of the Piazza del Duomo. On its north side, behind some houses, is the Teatro Grande (18th c.), with a handsome auditorium and foyer.

Teatro Grande

From the Broletto steps lead up to the Castello, an old stronghold of the Visconti family, surrounded by a park (zoo, observatory); the Castello houses the Risorgimento Museum. A tunnel, the Galleria Tito Speri, under the castle hill leads to the developing district of Borgo Trento.

Castello

Via dei Musei

From the Broletto the Via dei Musei, once the Via Aemilia, the main street of the Roman town, runs east to the Tempio Capitolino, a Corinthian temple built in AD 73, in the reign of Vespasian, and dedicated to Jupiter, Juno and Minerva, with a pronaos of eight columns and three cellas. The three cellas contain a collection of Roman inscriptions.

★Tempio Capitolino

Behind it is the Museo Romano, with Roman material from Brescia and the surrounding area, including a bronze statue, almost 2 m (7 ft) high, of a winged Victory, dating from the period of construction of the temple, and six Roman bronze busts (2nd–3rd c.).

Museo Romano

Farther east, in Via Piamarta, is the Museo dell'Età Cristiana (Museum of Christian Antiquities), in the former church of Santa Giulia, with religious

Museo dell'Età Cristiana

129

art, including carved ivories of the 3rd–5th c. and a gold cross which belonged to the Lombard king Desiderius (8th c.).

Immediately east of this is the 9th c. church of San Salvatore, which has a beautiful crypt (42 columns).

Galleria d'Arte
Moderna
In the western cloister of the former convent of Santa Giulia is the Galleria d'Arte Moderna, with works of the 19th c. Adjoining stands the remarkable Romanesque church of S Maria in Solario (12th c.).

Sights in the west of Brescia

Santa Maria dei
Miracoli
In the Corso Martiri della Libertà, to the south-west of the town, is the little church of Santa Maria dei Miracoli (restored), with an elegant Early Renaissance vestibule (1487–1508) and an impressive interior.

Santi Nazaro e
Celso
A little way south-west stands the church of Santi Nazaro e Celso (1780), with altarpieces by Moretto and a "Resurrection" by Titian behind the high altar.

San Francesco
To the north is the Gothic church of San Francesco (1254–65) with fine pictures by Romanino and a beautiful Gothic cloister (1393).

San Giovanni
Evangelista
North-west of the Piazza della Vittoria is the church of San Giovanni Evangelista, with paintings by Moretto and Romanino.

Madonna delle
Grazie
Farther west stands the former convent church of Santa Maria delle Grazie, with a sumptuous interior and a beautiful cloister.

★Pinacoteca Tosio
Martinengo
About 500 m south-east of the Teatro Grande, in Piazza Moretto, is the Pinacoteca Tosio Matinengo, with masterpieces by Brescian artists, including pictures by Moretto and Romanino and paintings by Lotto, Foppa and Raffael.

Surroundings

Monte Maddalena
13 km (8 mi.) E
From Brescia a road with many bends leads to Monte Maddalena (875 m (2888 ft)), from which there is a panoramic prospect extending as far as Monte Rosa.

★**Lake Iseo**
The Lago d'Iseo (Lake Iseao; alt. 185 m (611 ft); area 62 sq. km (24 sq. mi.); 251 m (824 ft) deep), is an attractive lake rich in fish, and known to the Romans as Lacus Sebinus. It is one of the most beautiful Alpine lakes, dominated on the east by Monte Gugliemo (1949 m (6432 ft); climbed from Marone in 4¹/₂ hours). The largest river flowing into the lake is the Oglio, which leaves it again at Sarnico.

In the middle of the lake lies the steep sided Monte Isola (559 m (1845 ft), an island 3 km (2 mi.) long, covered with dense chestnut forests. On the highest point stands the pilgrimage church of the Madonna della Ceriola (views). At the south-east extremity of the island lies the fishing village of Peschiera Maraglio, at its north-western end the village of Siviano, at its south-western tip Sensole.

On the south side of the lake the little port of Iseo (198 m (653 ft)) has an interesting parish church and an old Scaliger castle. At the northern end of the lake the small town of Lovere (208 m (686 ft); population 7000) boasts the fine Renaissance church of Santa Maria in Valvendra (15th c.; Baroque interior) and the Accademia Tadini, a picture gallery. From the lakeside promenade there are beautiful views.

**Darfo Boario
Terme**
13 km (8 mi.) north-east of Lovere, in the Val Carmonica, lies the spa of Darfo Boario Terme with chalybeate springs. From here there is an attrac-

In Lake Iseo lies Monte Isola, covered in dense chestnut forests

Rock drawings near Capo di Ponte in the Val Comonica

tive excursion to the north-west, through the 10 km (6 mi.) long Dezzo gorge, known as the "Via Mala Lombarda", to Dezzo.

Breno

Breno (343 m (1132 ft); population 6000) is situated 13 km (8 mi.) north-east of Darfo Boario Terme. It is the chief town of the Val Camonica, with a ruined castle and the two churches of San Salvatore and Sant' Antonio. To the north rises a fine dolomitic peak, the Corna di Concarena (2549 m (8412 ft)), to the north-east the Pizzo Badile (2435 m (8036 ft)), the "Matterhorn of the Val Camonica".

★Parco Nazionale della Incisioni Rupestri

At Capo di Ponte, in the Val Camonica, lies the Parco Nazionale della Incisioni Rupestri (National Park of the Rock Paintings); in this area can be seen numerous rock paintings made by the former inhabitants, the Camuni (a total of 876 scenes from the late Bronze and Iron ages). These rock paintings are included in the UNESCO list of protected items.

Lago d'Idro

From Breno a beautiful road, narrow and sometimes steep, leads south-east (49 km (30 mi.)) via Campolaro to the Passo di Croce Domini (1895 m (6254 ft)), and then through the Valle Sanguinara and the Valle Caffaro to the mountain village of Bagolino (778 m (2567 ft)) and beyond this to the church of Sant'Antonio on the charming Lago d'Idro (10 km (6 mi.)) long, 122 m (400 ft) deep), known to the Romans as Lacus Eridius.

Lake Garda

See entry

Bressanone

F2

Region: Trentino – Alto Adige. Province: Bolzano (BZ)
Altitude: 562 m (1855 ft). Population: 16,000

Location

Bressanone (German Brixen), the third largest town of the Alto Adige, lies in a broad part of the Isarco valley on the Brenner motorway. It is here that the River Rienza, coming from the Pusteria valley, flows into the Isarco.

History

Bressanone was founded in 901 on the remains of an old settlement. In 970 Bishop Albuin transferred the seat of the bishopric to Bressanone; the first Ottonian cathedral was built c. 990. In 1091 the town became the centre of the Bressanone diocese; the town wall was erected in the 12th c. and farther north the Neustift convent was founded. In 1179 Frederick I granted the Bishop the right to mint coins, to conduct markets and to levy taxes, as well as full legal jurisdiction. In 1348 the town was afflicted by the plague; in 1444 many buildings were destroyed in a fire. The famous humanist and theologist Cusanus (Nikolaus van Kues) was from 1450 to 1451 bishop of Bressanone.

Building of the Baroque cathedral was begun in 1745, but is was not consecrated until 1758. From 1797 onwards during the Napoleonic Wars the town was occupied by the French; however, after the defeat of the French army in the battle of Spinges the occupying forces withdrew.

The German deputation order of 1803 put an end to ecclesiastical sovereignty in Bressanone; from 1806 to 1814 the town was under Bavarian rule and then it became part of Tyrol.

Sights

★★Cathedral

The eastern edge of the Old Town is dominated by the Baroque Cathedral of the Assumption. Its plain, flat façade reveals a Lombard influence; the Neo-Classical portico supported on pillars and columns was not added until 1785. The lower sections of the two west towers are relics of its Romanesque predecessor.

Interior

The interior with its vaulted roof is flanked on each side by chapels separated by marble-clad columns. The ceiling of the nave has a giant fresco by Paul Troger (1750); he was also responsible for the painted ceiling in the choir.

From the right of the portico a corridor leads to the cloisters, which were originally built in the Romanesque period (around 1200). Special mention should be made of the magnificent and partly restored frescoes on the vaulted ceiling, dating from the Gothic period (1390–1510) and portraying scenes from the Old and New Testaments.

Cloisters

On the southern edge of the cathedral and cloister complex stands the church of St John, a Romanesque building from the period after 1200, with a Gothic vaulted ceiling and 13th–15th c. frescoes.

Church of St John

To the north of the cathedral on its left will be found the original Parish Church of St Michael dating from *c.* 1500. In 1757–58 the interior was renovated in the Baroque style and the ceilings painted by Josef Hauzinger. In the churchyard, in a niche in the outside wall of the cathedral, is a figure in memory of the poet Oswald von Wolkenstein (1377–1445).

Parish church

South-west of the cathedral stands the former royal episcopal palace (Hofburg), now restored. There was a castle here from 1260, which gave place in 1595 to a new Renaissance palace, which was not finally completed until 1710; the latter stages of construction show Baroque influence.

★★ Court Palace

In the typical inner courtyard with its three-storeyed loggias stand terra-cotta figures (1600) by the master sculptor from Schongau, Hans Reichle.

The collection in the Bressanone Museum in the palace includes the cathedral treasury, medieval and modern works of art, paintings and porcelain, and a world-famous collection of cribs.

Diocesan Museum

The Court Palace in Bressanone houses a fine museum

Brindisi

Seminary — South-east of the cathedral precincts stands the block of buildings housing the seminary. It was founded in 1607 and the buildings are Baroque. In 1764 the church of the Crucifixion was built on to the existing main façade. The interior contains frescoes by Franz Anton Zeiller.

Cusanus Academy — Adjoining the priests' seminary are the buildings of the Cusanus Academy which was officially opened in 1962.

★★Novacella

3 km (2 mi.) N — The Augustinian New Cathedral Chapter (Novacella) was founded in 1124 and completely renewed only fifty years later. There are several blocks of buildings enclosing two courtyards. At the entrance to the monastic precinct stands the Romanesque Chapel of St Michael ("Engelsburg" or Castle of the Angels), a unique Romanesque round building with battlements. There is space to park in the courtyard at the back. An arched gateway leads into the monastery courtyard proper where stands a pretty octagonal Renaissance fountain with its canopy decorated with frescoes. Guided tours Easter–Nov. Mon.–Sat.; Dec.–Mar. Mon.–Fri.

Monastic church — The triple-naved Basilica to Our Lady dates from the time when the monastery was first built in the late 12th c.; it underwent considerable changes during the Baroque period, however, especially between 1734–37. The ceiling frescoes are by Matthias Günther.

The monastery's late Baroque library with its multicoloured parquet floor, rocaille ornamentation and delicate gallery deserves special attention; the Gothic cloisters with their frescoes and the panelled pinacoteca are also worth seeing.

Brindisi   M14

Region: Puglia. Province: Brindisi (BR)
Altitude: 15 m (50 ft). Population: 95,000

Location — The port of Brindisi, the Roman Brundisium, lies at the head of a wide inlet on the east coast of Apulia near the Adriatic – some 55 km (34 mi.) north-east of Taranto or 100 km (62 mi.) south-east of Bari. The town, capital of the province of the same name and see of an archbishop, has been since ancient times an important centre of trade with the Eastern Mediterranean.

The poet Virgil died here in 19 BC on his way back from Greece.

Harbour — The sheltered Inner Harbour consists of two arms – to the west the Seno di Ponente, 600 m (198 ft) long, with extensive quays and a bathing beach, and to the east the Seno di Levante, 450 m (1485 ft) long, in which very large vessels can berth. A channel 525 m (1733 ft) long connects both arms with the Outer Harbour, the entrance to which is divided into two by the islet of Sant'Andrea, with a 15th c. fort.

Sights

Piazza del Popolo — The life of the town centres on the Piazza del Popolo. A little way south stands the church of Santa Lucia, with a Byzantine crypt (frescoes) and catacombs.

Marine Station — From the Piazza del Popolo the Via Garibaldi runs north-east to the Piazza Vittorio Emanuele, which overlooks the Seno di Levante. On the right is the Marine Station (Stazione Marittima; ferry services to Greece).

Colonna Romana — The Viale Regina Margherita, to the left, leads to a marble column, 19 m (63 ft) high, marking the end of the Via Appia (constructed from 312 BC onwards), the "Queen of Roads", which ran from Rome via Taranto to

Brindisi. Only the lower half of a second column, partly destroyed in 1528, is left.

A little way south-west of the column is the cathedral, with a 12th c. mosaic pavement which was remodelled in Baroque style.

Cathedral

Adjoining the cathedral is the Archaeological Museum (Museo Archeologico Provinciale), with medieval sculpture, Roman portrait statues, etc. Also near the cathedral are the 14th c. Palazetto Balsamo, with a richly decorated balcony and the former baptistery of San Giovanni al Sepolcro (11th c.).

Archaeological Museum

Farther south-west is the Norman church of San Benedetto (c. 1100), with a Romanesque side doorway and a cloister (fine relief carving).

San Benedetto

About 500 m west of the cathedral, above the western harbour gate, is the Castello Svevo (not open to the public), built by Frederick II in 1227, with massive round towers (15th c.).

Castello

Surroundings

There is a boat trip from Viale Regina Margherita across the Seno di Ponente to the Monumento al Marinaio d'Italia, a naval war memorial (brick tower; 1933), in the form of a ship's rudder, 53 m (175 ft) high (lift; fine views from the top).

Monumento al Marinaio d'Italia

North-west of Brindisi (3 km (2 mi.)) is the former convent church of Santa Maria del Casale (late 13th c./early 14th c.), with a beautiful doorway and geometric patterns in multi-coloured stone on the façade; inside there are some fine Byzantine frescoes.

★ Santa Maria del Casale

Cagliari   D17

Region: Sardegna. Province: Cagliari (CA)
Altitude: 10 m (33 ft). Population: 225,000

Cagliari (in Sardinian Casteddu), capital of the autonomous region of Sardinia and the province of Cagliari, lies on the south coast of the island on the wide Gulf of Cagliari.

Location

The oldest part of the town, which was founded by the Phoenicians and became the Roman "Carales", is known as the Castello (Sardinian Casteddʼe susu). It clings picturesquely to the slopes of a precipitous hill, around the foot of which are the newer districts and suburbs of the town. To west and east are two large lagoons, the Stagno di Santa Gilla and the Stagno di Molentargius (salt-pans).

Town

Town centre

The tree-shaded Via Roma runs along the busy harbour quay, with the railway station and the modern Town Hall (two towers; in the interior murals by F. Filgari) at its north-west end. From the Town Hall the wide Largo Carlo Felice goes north-east, gently uphill, to Piazza Yenne, from which the busy Corso Vittorio Emanuele runs north-west. In Via Tigello, a side street off the Corso Vittorio Emanuele, are the remains of three Roman houses.

Town Hall

Via G. Manno, a shopping and commercial street popularly known as the Costa, descends south-east from Piazza Yenne to the Piazza della Costituzione. A little way off the Via Garibaldi, which begins here, is the church of San Domenico, with a beautiful cloister.

Piazza della Costituzione

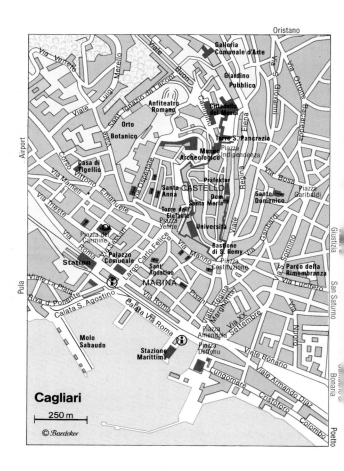

Cagliari

250 m

© Baedeker

★Viale Regina Elena

From the Piazza della Costituzione, the beautiful Viale Regina Elena, affording fine views, runs north below the sheer east side of the old bastion to the Giardino Pubblico.

★Bastione San Remy

A flight of marble steps, the Passeggiata Coperta, climbs to the Bastione San Remy, a magnificent terrace (fine views), laid out on the medieval bastions, which are preserved in part. Higher up, to the north, is the Bastione Santa Caterina, which also commands extensive views.

Torre dell'Elefante

From the Bastione Santa Caterina Via dell'Università leads north-west to the university (founded 1956; fine library) and the massive Torre dell'Elefante (1307), a fine building in medieval Sardinian style.

Cathedral

From the Bastione San Remy we pass through the gate of the old Torre dell'Aquila into the narrow Via Lamarmora, the main street of the old town, which runs north along the steep hillside, linked with parallel streets to

Cagliari, overshadowed by the medieval town

right and left by steep lanes or dark archways and flights of steps. Half-way along is the terraced Piazza del Palazzo, above the east side of which is the cathedral of Santa Cecilia, built by the Pisans in 1312, with beautiful old doorways in the transepts. Inside, on either side of the entrance, are the two halves of a pulpit from Pisa Cathedral, a masterpiece of 12th c. Pisan sculpture by Guillelmus, which was presented to Cagliari in 1312.

At the north end of Via Lamarmora is the Piazza dell'Indipendenza, in which are the Torre San Pancrazio (erected in 1305 to defend the old bastion; view) and the Museo Archeologico Nazionale, with Punic, Greek and Roman material as well as the largest collection of Sardinian antiquities. Of particular interest in Room I are the bronze statues found in the nuraghi (dolmens). On the upper floor are pictures of the 14th to 18th centuries.

★Museo Archeologico Nazionale

Adjoining the museum is the 16th c. Chiesa della Purissima, built in Gothic-Aragonian style.

Chiesa della Purissima

From the museum, Viale Buon Cammino runs north through the outer courtyard of the Citadel and along the ridge of the hill. In 500 m a road leads down on the left to the Roman amphitheatre arena (50 by 34 m (165 by 112 ft)), constructed in a natural depression in the rock, which is now used as an open-air theatre. To the south-west lies the Botanic Garden.

★Amphitheatre

North-west of the Piazza dell'Indipendenza is the new Cittadella dei Musei (Museum), built on the remains of older buildings, with a fine collection of Eastern Art.

Cittadella dei Musei

Nearby the museum is the Municipal Art Gallery, which contains modern masterpieces of the most important Sardinian artists. Adjoining is a Sardinian ethnographical museum.

Municipal Art Gallery

Cagliari

San Saturno   East of the centre, in Piazza San Cosimo, is the church of San Saturno, also called Santi Cosma e Damiano. The church (founded in the 6th c.; enlarged in the 11th–12th c.), is dedicated to St Saturnus.

Santuario di Bonario   Farther south stands the Santuario di Bonario, where the famous painting "Madonna di Bonario" can be seen; adjoining the sacristy is a small museum (votive pictures).

Surroundings

Dolianova

20 km (12 mi.) NE   At Dolianova (212 m (700 ft)) stands the Romanesque–Gothic Basilica S Pantaleone (12th–13th c.), with a notable façade; some of the decoration has Arabic features.

Uta

22.5 km (14 mi.) W   The village of Uta, situated on the road to Iglesias, is worth visiting for its Romanesque church of Santa Maria (12th c.), the finest country church in Sardinia.

Capo Carbonara

50 km (31 mi.) SE   There is an attractive trip (7 km (4½ mi.) south-east), passing close to Monte San Elia (139 m (459 ft)) and the extensive Molentargius salt-pans to the Spiaggia di Poetto, Cagliari's popular bathing beach, which extends for 10 km (6 mi.) along the Golfo di Quartu.

     From here the road traverses an extensive agricultural development area, then beyond the hamlet of Flumini a beautiful stretch of road keeps close to the indented coast, passing many old watch-towers and *nuraghi* (dolmens), to Capo Carbonara, the extreme south-easterly point of Sardinia (views), with the Torre Santa Caterina (115 m (378 ft)). Nearby is the Fortezza Vecchia (17th c.).

Tour of the Iglesiente (*c.* 200 km (124 mi.))

Sante Gilla   Another rewarding excursion is a tour of the Iglesiente, the hilly region in the south-west of the island. Leave Cagliari on SS195, which runs south-west along the spit of land between the Stagno di Santa Gilla and the sea and past the large Santa Gilla salt-pans.

★Nora   At the village of Sarroch (20 km (12½ mi.)) is a very characteristic nuraghi. 7 km (4½ mi.) farther on is Pula, from which a road leads south (4 km (2½ mi.)) to the remains of the Phoenician and later Roman town of Nora, on a narrow peninsula (forum, amphitheatre, baths, temples, foundations of villas, well-preserved mosaic pavements).

Teulada   After some time the road leaves the coast. 38 km (23 mi.) from Pula it crosses a pass (301 m (993 ft)), with the Nurag de Mesu, and comes in another 14 km (9 mi.) to the attractively situated little town of Teulada, chief place of the southern part of the Iglesiente, known as Sulcis. About 36 km (22 mi.) from Teulada SS195 joins SS126 at San Giovanni Suergiu.

Sant'Antioco   From San Giovanni Suergiu there is an interesting excursion (11 km (7 mi.) south-west) to the volcanic island of Sant'Antioco (109 sq. km (42 sq. mi.)) with the popular little seaside resort of the same name (15 m (50 ft); population 13,000). On either side of the castle is a well-preserved Phoenician

Remains of the Phoenician-Punic fort on Monte Sirai

cemetery (5th–3rd c. BC; museum). North-west of Sant'Antioco is Calasetta (29 m (96 ft)), a little place of rather Oriental appearance, the inhabitants of which managed, like those from Carloforte on the neighbouring island of San Pietro, to preserve the language and costumes of Genoa.

Beyond San Giovanni Suergiu the tour of the Iglesiente continues north on SS126, which comes in 6 km (4 mi.) to Carbonia (population 33,000), a new town founded in 1938 in the middle of the Sardinian coalfield. 4 km (2½ mi.) north-west of Carbonia, on Monte Sirai, the remains of a Phoenician-Punic fort have been uncovered. In another 11 km (7 mi.) a road branches off on the left to the little ports of Portoscuso (tuna fishing) and Portovesme, from which there are boats to Carloforte (10 m (33 ft)); population 6000).

Carbonia

13 km (8 mi.) beyond the turning for Portoscuso and Portovesme is Iglesias (176 m (581 ft); population 30,000), an old episcopal town in the centre of the Iglesiente which still preserves remains of its medieval walls and has a Mining Academy (museum). In the Piazza del Municipio stands the cathedral built by the Pisans in 1288, and to the south of the square is the medieval church of San Francesco. Above the town to the east rises the Castello Salvaterra (14th c.).
From Iglesias it is 56 km (35 mi.) east on SS130 to Cagliari.

Iglesias

Calabria

Region: Calabria
Provinces: Catanzaro (CZ), Cosenza (CS) and Reggio di Calabria (RC)
Area: 15,080 sq. km (5281 sq. mi.). Population: 2,000,000

The region of Calabria occupies the south-west of the peninsula, the toe of the Italian boot, between the Ionian and Tyrrhenian seas.

Location

Calabria

Landscape

The region is traversed by the Calabrian Apennines – three massive ranges of granite and gneiss belonging to an ancient mountain rump. In the north is the Sila (Botte Donato, 1930 m (6369 ft)) and in the south the Aspromonte range (Montalto, 1956 m (6455 ft)), separated by an expanse of low-lying land, once marshy and malaria-ridden, which is caught between the Golfo di Squillace and the Golfo di Santa Eufemia. Along the west coast of northern Calabria, separated from the Sila by the fertile Crati valley, extends the Calabrian Coastal Chain (Catena Costiera), falling down to the sea in precipitous cliffs.

The lower uplands are covered with dense mixed forests of beeches and pines (representing about 40 per cent of the total area of Calabria), which give the landscape an almost Central European character. There are few beaches along the coasts, which are much indented by bays and coves. The region has been frequently devastated by violent earthquakes, particularly along the Strait of Messina.

Economy

Economically Calabria is one of the most under-developed parts of Italy. The overwhelming majority of the population live by agriculture. In the fertile low-lying land a mixed agriculture of Mediterranean type predominates, producing wheat, olives, citrus fruit, wine and figs; at the higher levels only pasturing is possible. The only minerals of any consequence are rock salt (at Lungro) and sulphur (at Strongoli). A number of dams in the Sila range supply electric power for the industrial area around Crotone.

History

In ancient times the name of Calabria was given to the Salentine peninsula, the "heel" of Italy between the Gulf of Taranto and the Adriatic, which was occupied by the Iapyges and conquered by Rome in 272 BC. Present-day Calabria was then the land of the bruttii, and formed part of magna graecia from the 8th c. BC until occupied by Rome during the second Punic War. After the fall of the Ostrogothic kingdom it passed to Byzantium and was given the name of Calabria after the loss of the Salentine peninsula. In the 9th and 10th c. Calabria suffered repeated Saracen raids. It was conquered by the Normans in 1060, and later became part of the kingdom of Naples until its union with Italy in 1860.

Sights

Sila range

A very rewarding trip can be made into the Sila range. La Sila consists of three parts – the main range, Sila Grande, the Sila Piccola to the south, and along the northern edge of the range the Sila Greca, named after the Albanians of the Greek Orthodox faith who have been settled here since the 15th c. The Sila is a plateau-like massif of ancient rocks with a total area of 3300 sq. km (1274 sq. mi.) and an average height of 1300–1400 m (3900–4620 ft), rising to 1930 m (6370 ft) in Botte Donato, which presents a precipitous face to the Crati valley, but falls away gradually towards the Gulf of Taranto. Its extensive forests of chestnuts, beeches, oaks, black spruces and pines are still inhabited by wolves as well as by numerous black squirrels. Since 1927 the rivers have been harnessed to provide electricity by the construction of dams which form large artificial lakes; the most attractive of these are Lago Arvo (1280 m (4224 ft)) and Lago Ampollino.

On the high plateaux, with their extensive areas of grazing, the trim houses of the new settlers who have been established here under the government's land reform form a striking contrast to the wretched cottages of the past.

Rossano

In the north of the Sila Greca, picturesquely situated on a hillside a few kilometres from the sea, is Rossano (275 m (908 ft); population 33,000), once capital of Calabria and still the see of an archbishop. On a crag to the south-east of the town is the church of San Marco, a church of Byzantine type on a centralised plan, with five domes, dating from the Norman period. The Museo Diocesano contains a valuable 6th c. Gospel manu-

The Calabrian landscape

script. From the terrace half-way along Via Garibaldi there is a very fine view of Monte Pollino and the Apulian plain.

About 32 km (20 mi.) north-west of Rossano, in the lower course of the Crati, not far from the sea, are the remains of the ancient city of Sybaris, founded in 709 BC by Achaeans, which became proverbial for its luxury but was destroyed in 510 BC by the people of Croton. Systematic excavations have been carried out here since 1960 by Milan Technical College and Pennsylvania University.

Sybaris

To the south of the Sila range, near Lago Ampollino, lies San Giovanni in Fiore (1049 m (3462 ft); population 20,000), the centre of the Sila region and a summer resort, renowned for its beautiful costumes and craft work.

San Giovanni in Fiore

In the Sila range three regions are under protection orders and together form the Parco Nazionale della Calabria. They are the regions around the town of Fossiata and Monte Gariglione and a part of the Aspromonte. The commonest tree found in the forests is the pina iaricio, which gives the landscape a northern appearance. The fauna is worthy of note: in addition to the Apennine wolf, the Bonetti eagle and the rare black woodpecker may be seen. There are good roads within the national park.

★Parco Nazionale della Calabria

Catanzaro

The capital of the region is Catanzaro (320 m (1056 ft); population 100,000), well-known as industrial centre and the see of an archbishop, beautifully situated on a plateau which falls away to the south, east and west. In the centre of the town are the cathedral and the church of San Domenico or Chiesa del Rosario, (richly decorated with good pictures and sculpture). There are very fine views from Via Bellavista, on the south side of the town, and the municipal gardens to the east.

Calabria

Catanzaro Marina

13 km (8 mi.) south of Catanzaro, on the coast of the Ionian Sea between the mouths of the rivers Corace and Fiumarella, is the port and seaside resort of Catanzaro Marina (5 m (17 ft)).

On the Gulf of Squillace is the Robinson Club Calabria.

Tiriolo

About 17 km (11 mi.) west of Catanzaro, in a delightful setting, is the little town of Tiriolo (690 m (2277 ft); population 5000), renowned for the beautiful costumes of its women and for its embroidery and lace. Above the town to the north-east (30-minute climb) is Monte di Tiriolo (838 m (2765 ft)), with a ruined castle. From here there are fine views.

Paola

34 km (21 mi.) north-west of Catanzaro, in a gorge near the coast and on the hillside above, is the little town of Paola (94 m (310 ft); population 17,000).

1.5 km (1 mi.) north-west of Paola is the convent of San Francesco di Paola (1416–1507, founder of the mendicant order of the Minims), built in the 15th c. across a gorge and enlarged in the 17th c.

There is also an attractive drive from Paola (17 km (11 mi.)) to the Passo Crocetta (979 m (3231 ft); view).

Tropea

About 70 km (43 mi.) south-west of Catanzaro is the little town of Tropea (61 m (201 ft); population 7000), an elegant seaside resort on the Tyrrhenian Coast, with a fine cathedral.

Cosenza

In the fertile Crati valley in north-west Calabria lies Cosenza (240 m (792 ft); population 107,000), once capital of the Bruttii (Cosentia), now a provincial capital and the see of an archbishop. The Visigothic leader Alaric died in Cosentia in AD 410 and was buried with his treasure in the bed of the River Busento. To the north-west – on the slopes of the castle hill – lies the handsome new town; the old town with its narrow winding streets is built on the tongue of land within the confluence of the Crati and the Busento. In the winding main street, Corso Telesio, is the early Gothic cathedral (consecrated 1222), in which the unhappy Hohenstaufen king Henry VII was buried in 1242; in the north transept is the tomb of Isabella, wife of Philip III of France, who died in Cosenza in 1271.

From the municipal gardens on the south side of the old town the road climbs north-west to the Castello (385 m (1271 ft); view), with walls 3 m (10 ft) thick which nevertheless were not strong enough to withstand the frequent earthquakes (particularly severe in 1783 and 1905).

Crotone

On the east coast of northern Calabria is the port and industrial town of Crotone (43 m (142 ft); population 60,000), in antiquity the famous Achaean colony of Croton, founded in the 8th c. BC, which was ruled in the 6th c. BC by Pythagoras and his disciples. Noteworthy is the cathedral with a Byzantine Madonna and treasury. Near the Castello is the Museo Archeologico Statale (Via Risorgimento), with prehistoric and classical material.

Capo Colonna

From Crotone an interesting excursion can be made (11 km (7 mi.)) to Capo Colonna which has the remains of a temple of Hera Lacinia. The rounding of this cape by the Romans in 282 BC led to the outbreak of the Pyrrhic War. In 203 BC Hannibal sailed from here, leaving a record of his deeds in the temple.

Reggio di Calabria

See entry

Locri

On the east coast of southern Calabria, 3 km (2 mi.) south of the resort of Locri (5 m (17 ft); population 13,000), are the remains of the ancient Greek city of Lokroi Epizephyrioi (signposted "Scavi di Locri"), famous for the code of laws compiled by Zaleucus (c. 650 BC). Near the coast road are the foundations of a temple rebuilt in Ionic style in the 5th c. BC, and on the hill of Mannella, to the north of the excavation site, are remains of the town walls. There are also a notable theatre, a Doric temple and a pre-Greek and Greek cemetery.

Campania   H–K13–15

Region: Campania
Provinces: Avellino (AV), Benevento (BN), Caserta (CE), Napoli (NA) and
    Salerno (SA)
Area: 13,595 sq. km (5249 sq mi.). Population: 5,608,000

The region of Campania covers an area, extending from the Neapolitan   Location
Apennines (Monte Cervati, 1898 m (6263 ft)) to the coast of the Tyrrhenian
Sea, here much indented (gulfs of Gaeta, Naples, Salerno and Policastro).
It is a fertile low-lying region, well watered by the rivers Garigliano,
Volturno and Sele.
    Violent volcanic activity (Vesuvius) has left its marks on the area.

The extraordinary fertility of the soil, the mild climate and the availability   Landscape
of water earned the region the name of "Campania Felix" in ancient times.
It has long been one of the most densely populated parts of Italy and is intensively cultivated (wheat, fruit, vines, vegetables, tobacco).

The original inhabitants were an Italic people, the Osci. In the 8th c. the   History
Greek colonies of Kyme, Dikaiarchia and Neapolis (Magna Graecia) were
established on the coast. At the end of the 6th c. Campania was occupied
by the Etruscans; in 430 BC it was captured by the Samnites, and in 338 BC
by the Romans. Under the Empire it was much favoured by noble Romans
as a place of residence, and the wealth and ostentation of this period has
been preserved in the ruins of Herculaneum and Pompeii. In the early
medieval period Campania was divided into Lombard and Byzantine
spheres of influence, but was reunited by the Normans in the 12th c. and
thereafter passed to the kingdom of Sicily and the kingdom of Naples.

The most important towns in Campania are Naples and Salerno (see   Towns
entries).

★★Capri, Island of   J14

Region: Campania. Province: Napoli (NA)
Area: 10.5 sq. km (4 sq. mi.). Population: 13,000

Regular service several times daily from Naples (taking car not worth   Ferries
while; use prohibited in summer); also hydrofoil service. Also services
from Sorrento, Positano, Amalfi and Ischia.

The Island of Capri, one of the most beautiful and most visited of the   Location
islands in the Tyrrhenian Sea, is in fact an extension of the peninsula of
Sorrento, and lies at the southern end of the Gulf of Naples.

In Roman times, when it was known as Caprae, it was a favourite resort of   Roman holiday
the emperors Augustus and Tiberius.

The island, about 6 km (4 mi.) long and between 1 and 2.5 km (1/2 and   Island
1 1/2 mi.) wide, has rugged limestone crags rising to a height of 589 m
(1944 ft) above the sea. The only places of any size are the picturesque
little towns of Capri and Anacapri.

The island has rich flora, including the acanthus, whose leaves form the   Flora
characteristic ornament of Corinthian capitals.

Capri

The regular boats land their passengers in the picturesque port of Marina   Marina Grande
Grande, on the north coast of the island. From here a funicular (5 minutes),

a stepped footpath (30 minutes) and a road (3 km (2 mi.)) leads up to the town on Capri (124 m (409 ft); population 8000), the island's capital, situated on a saddle between the hills of Il Capo to the east, Monte Solaro to the west, San Michele to the north-east and Castiglione to the south-west.

Certosa di San Giacomo

The central feature of the town is the little Piazza Umberto I ("the Piazza" for short), at the top of the funicular from Marina Grande. From here it is a short walk past the steps leading up to the church of Santo Stefano (1683) and along the main shopping street to the Certosa di San Giacomo (founded 1371, restored 1933), a former Carthusian house, which houses the Museo Diefenbach, with late Romanesque pictures by Diefenbach (1851–1915). The adjoining church of San Giacomo has a Gothic doorway, 17th c. frescoes and two cloisters (access to the Belvedere).

★Punta Tragara

From the Hotel Quisisana it is a 15 minutes' walk to the terrace on Punta Tragara, the south-east promontory of the island, which commands a picturesque view of the south coast and the three stacks known as the Faraglioni.

Salto di Tiberio

From Capri a very attractive footpath, the Via Tiberio (45 minutes), runs north-east to the promontory of Il Capo. Immediately beyond a gateway is the rock known as the Salto di Tiberio (297 m (980 ft)) from which legend has it that the tyrannical Emperor Tiberius had his victims thrown into the sea (view). To the right are the substructures of an ancient lighthouse.

★Villa di Tiberio

In the extreme north-east of the island are the remains of the Villa de Tiberio or Villa Iovis, rising in terraces to the top of the hill, in which Tiberius is said to have lived from AD 27 until his death in 37.

Santa Maria del Soccorso

On the adjoining promontory is the chapel of Santa Maria del Soccorso, with a conspicuous figure of the Virgin; magnificent views from the top.

★Arco Naturale

From the Villa di Tiberio a footpath to the right leads in 15 minutes to the Arco Naturale, a natural archway in the rock (view), from which steps run down to the Grotta di Matromania, perhaps a sanctuary of the nymphs. From the cave a foothpath (45 minutes) runs along above the sea, with views of the Monacone, a rocky islet, and the Faraglioni, and so back to Punta Tragara.

Steep cliffs and an azure sea – a scene that charmed the Roman Emperor Tiberius

South-west of Capri is the little harbour of Marina Piccola, reached by a wide footpath, the Via Krupp. The path begins west of the Certosa and runs below the beautiful Parco Augusto (terrace with fine views) and round the steep-sided Castiglione to join (15 minutes) the road from Capri, on which it is a 10-minute walk to the harbour of Marina Piccola on the south coast of the island.

Marina Piccola

Excursion to Anacapri

Anacapri, in the west of the island, is reached either by a beautiful road (3.5 km (2 mi.); bus service) which winds its way up the rocky slope from the town of Capri or from Marina Grande on an ancient flight of over 500 steps, the so-called Scala Fenicia (not all usable) to the viewpoint of Capodimonte, 10-minute walk east of the town. Above the viewpoint is the Castello di Barbarossa, the ruins of a castle destroyed by the pirate Khaireddin Barbarossa in 1535.

★Capodimonte

On the slopes of Capodimonte is the conspicuous Villa San Michele, home of the Swedish doctor and author Axel Munthe (1857–1949).

Villa San Michele

Anacapri (275 m (908 ft)), a little town of almost Oriental aspect, straggles over the plateau, surrounded by vineyards. The church of San Michele has a fine majolica pavement (1751). In the Piazza is the town's principal church, Santa Sofia.

★★Anacapri

Half an hour's walk south-west of the town is the viewpoint of Belvedere di Migliara, about 300 m (990 ft) above the sea.

Belvedere di Migliara

From Anacapri a chair-lift (12 minutes) and a footpath (1 hour) lead up to the top of Monte Solaro (598 m (1973 ft); restaurant), to the south-east, the

Monte Solara

highest point on the island, from which on clear days there are magnificent views extending as far as the Abruzzi.

★★Blue Grotto

About 3 km (2 mi.) north-west of Anacapri is one of Capri's great tourist attractions, the Blue Grotto (Grotta Azzurra), which can be reached either by boat from Marina Grande or by the Via Pagliaro (3 km (2 mi.)) from Anacapri. This, the most famous of Capri's caves, was carved out of the rock in prehistoric times by the constant battering of the sea, and as a result of the sinking of the land is now half-filled with water. The entrance, only about 1 m (39 in.) high, can be negotiated only by small boats when the sea is calm. The cave is 54 m (178 ft) long, 30 m (99 ft) wide and 15 m (50 ft) high, with 14 to 22 m (46 to 66 ft) depth of water. When the sun is shining it is filled with an extraordinary blue light (at its best from 11am to 1pm).

Excursion round the island

Another very attractive excursion is a boat trip round the island (1½–2 hours by motorboat, 3–4 hours by rowing boat), which allows visitors to see the other caves around the coasts of Capri. The finest are the Grotta Bianca and the Grotta Meravigliosa above it (on the east coast near the Arco Naturale), the Grotta Verde at the foot of Monte Solara and the Grotta Rossa. A boat trip to the Faraglioni is also worthwhile.

★Carrara   E7

Region: Toscana. Province: Massa-Carrara (MS)
Altitude: 100 m (330 ft). Population: 67,000

The town of Carrara lies in a valley in the Apuan Alps only a few kilometres from the Ligurian Sea.

Location

Carrara is famous for the 400 marble quarries around the town which provide employment for most of its population. The stonemasons' workshops are of great interest.

Marble quarries

Sights

In the north of the town is the Cathedral of Sant'Andrea (11th–14th c.), with a fine Romanesque and Gothic façade, the lower part of which consists of half-columns and pointed arches; the centre part of the doorway is richly decorated. Inside note the multi-coloured marble pulpit, the 14th c. "Annunciation of Our Lady" and other marble sculptures. There are fine views from the bell-tower.

Cathedral

To the south, in Via Roma, the town's principal street, is the Accademia di Belle Arti, with pictures and marble sculptures. 500 m west of the cathedral is the Church of the Madonna delle Grazie, with sumptuous marble decoration.

Academy of Fine Art

South-west of the town's centre is the Museo Civico del Marmo (Municipal Marble Museum) with six departments, demonstrating the history of marble, from antiquity to its present-day artistic and technical uses.

Museo Civico del Marmo

◀ The Blue Grotto – a must for any visitor to Capri

Carrara

Marble quarry near Carrara

★Carrara marble quarries

Every tourist should visit the marble quarries in the three valleys which meet at Carrara, the Colonnata, Fantiscritti and Ravaccione valleys. They can be reached on reasonably good roads. The quarries were already being worked in Roman times, but achieved their widest fame through Michelangelo, who greatly prized the marble of Carrara. Particularly impressive are the quarries at Piastre (4 km (2½ mi.) east), which yield the fine marmo statuario.

The marble is shipped from the nearby Mediterranean ports (Marina di Carrara) to places all over the world.

Surroundings

Massa
7 km (4½ mi.) SE

South-east of Carrara is Massa (65 m (215 ft); population 66,000), chief town of the province of Massa-Carrara, which also has large marble quarries. Notable are the former Palazzo Ducale (now a prefecture), a fine Baroque build-ing of 1701, the cathedral and, north-east of the town (15 minutes), the massive 15th–16th c. castle, from which there are fine views. 5 km (3 mi.) south-west is the seaside resort of Marina di Massa, with a long beach.

Pietrasanta
18 km (11 mi.) SE

Farther south-east of Carrara is the town of Pietrasanta (14 m (46 ft); population 26,000), beautifully situated among hills.

It is the principal resort of the Versilia region, the district between Massa and Viareggio. The campani¹e of the 13th–14th c. cathedral of San Martino is unfinished. Adjoining the cathedral is the baptistery with a fine font (1509). In the cathedral square is the Archaeological Museum (Museo Archeologico Versiliese).

There are numerous good hotels at Marina Pietrasanta (4 km (2½ mi.) south-west).

Sarzana

See La Spezia, Surroundings

Caserta   J13

Region: Campania. Province: Caserta (CE)
Altitude: 68 m (224 ft). Population: 69,000

The provincial capital of Caserta, the "Versailles" of the Bourbon rulers of   Location
Naples, lies at the foot of the Monti Tifatini in the northern part of the
Campanian plain – some 30 km (19 mi.) north of Naples.

Sights

Opposite the station is the former Royal Palace (247 m (925 ft) long, 41 m   ★Palazzo Reale
(135 ft) wide; 1200 rooms and 1790 windows), a magnificent residence in
the manner of Versailles built by Luigi Vanvitelli for King Charles III of
Naples and Sicily from 1752 onwards. The interior, with its well-preserved
decoration and furnishings, forms a museum of the Bourbon dynasty
which ruled the kingdom of the Two Sicilies (1734–1860). Particularly fine
are the Grand Staircase (116 steps), the Cappella Reale, the Royal
Apartments and the Theatre. In the Second World War the Palace served
as the headquarters of the Allied Middle East Command; on April 29th
1945 the German armies in Italy signed the surrender document here.

Behind the palace is the park, with magnificent fountains adorned with   Park
statues, and the magnificent "Grand Cascade". From the terrace beyond
the beautiful English Garden (45 minutes' walk north of the palace) there
are very fine views.

Surroundings

The interior of the Palazzo Reale in Caserta is modelled on that of the Palace of Versailles

Catania

Caserta Vecchia

About 10 km (6 mi.) north-east of Caserta is the dilapidated village of Caserta Vecchia (401 m (1323 ft)), originally founded by the Lombards, which has retained its medieval character. It boasts a castle of the counts of Caserta and a cathedral (12th–13th c.), built in Normano-Sicilian style, with a fine campanile (1234).

Santa Maria di Capua Vetere
7 km (4 mi.) W

From Caserta there is an interesting trip (7 km (4 mi.) west) to the developing town of Santa Maria di Capua Vetere (36 m (119 ft); population 32,000), on the site of the ancient capital of Campania, Capua, which was originally founded by the Etruscans. As the centre of this fertile region Capua became a wealthy and powerful city renowned for its luxury, but after its destruction by the Saracens in the 9th c. the town was moved to its present-day site. In the north-west of the town is the amphitheatre, built in the reign of Augustus (1st c. AD) and restored by Hadrian, which was the largest in Italy until the building of the Colosseum in Rome. Under the arena (76 m (251 ft) long, 46 m (152 ft) across) are well-preserved substructures (passages, cages for wild beasts). Near the amphitheatre are the remains of a fine triumphal arch (three arches), dedicated to the Emperor Hadrian (2nd c. AD).

★Mitraeum

About 500 m south, in an underground passage, is a mithraeum (2nd c. AD), a shrine of the Persian god of light, Mithras, richly decorated with paintings.

Cathedral

About 500 m south-east is the cathedral of Santa Maria Maggiore, with columns from the amphitheatre.

Capua

5 km (3 mi.) north-west of the ancient city of Capua Vetere, in a bend of the River Volturno, is the modern town of Capua (25 m (83 ft); population 19,000), the see of an archbishop, built on the site of the ancient Capua after its destruction in the 9th c. and held for many years by Norman rulers. In the centre of the town, near the Volturno, is the cathedral, rebuilt after its destruction during the Second World War, the only parts which survived unscathed being the campanile and the 11th c. forecourt, with its ancient columns (3rd c.). Nearby is the Campanian Provincial Museum, the most important archaeological museum in Campania after the National Museum in Naples.

Sant'Angelo in Formis

5 km (3 mi.) east, on the western slopes of Monte Tifata (604 m (1993 ft)), lies the village of Sant'Angelo in Formis, with a Romanesque basilica built in 1058 on the site of a temple of Diana Tifatina. The beautiful portico has Oriental pointed arches. The church contains ancient marble columns and fine frescoes of the school of Montecassino (11th c.).

Catania

Region: Sicilia. Province: Catania (CT)
Altitude: 10 m (33 ft). Population: 378,000

Location

Catania, capital of the province of the same name, lies half-way along the flat eastern coast of Sicily to the south-east of Mount Etna. It is Sicily's second largest town after Palermo and one of the most important ports in Italy, shipping the produce of the wide and fertile Piana di Catania, the principal grain-growing region in Sicily.

Catania possesses a university and is the see of an archbishop.

Catania is a town of imposing modern aspect, having been almost completely rebuilt, with long straight streets, after a devastating earthquake in 1693. The wealth of the city is demonstrated by its fine Baroque churches and large aristocratic mansions, frequently rebuilt after earthquake damage.

History

Katana was founded about 729 BC by Greek settlers from Naxos, and was one of the first places on the island to be taken by the Romans (263 BC). Under Roman rule it grew into one of the largest towns on Sicily, but during

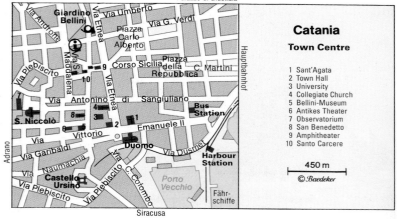

Palazzo di Giustizia

Catania

Town Centre

1 Sant'Agata
2 Town Hall
3 University
4 Collegiate Church
5 Bellini-Museum
6 Antikes Theater
7 Observatorium
8 San Benedetto
9 Amphitheater
10 Santo Carcere

450 m

© Baedeker

Siracusa

the early medieval period it declined into insignificance, recovering its prosperity only in the 14th c. under Aragonese rule. The 1693 earthquake, which affected the whole of Sicily, was particularly destructive in Catania.

Sights

The central feature of the town is the beautiful Piazza de Duomo, in the centre of which is a fountain with an ancient elephant, carved from lava, and bearing a granite Egyptian obelisk. On the east side of the square rises the 18th c. cathedral (choir apses and east wall of transept 13th c.). In the interior (by the second pillar on the right) lies the tomb of the composer Vincenzo Bellini (1801–35), a native of Catania. To the right, in front of the choir (beautiful choir-stalls), is the chapel of St Agatha, with the tomb of the Spanish viceroy Acuña (d. 1494).

Cathedral

Across the street from the cathedral, to the north, stands the abbey of Sant'Agata with a Baroque church.

Sant'Agata

About 500 m south-west of the Piazza del Duomo, in Piazza Federico di Svevia, is the Castello Ursino, lying close to the sea, which was built for Frederick II about 1240 and later, in the 14th c., became the residence of the kings of Aragon. Thereafter it served as a prison and as barracks, and since 1934 has housed the Museo Civico, with a fine collection including Greek sculptures of the 5th–4th c. BC

Castello Ursino

Museo Civico

From the south-west corner of the Piazza del Duomo the busy Via Garibaldi runs past the Piazza Mazzini, to the Porta Garibaldi (1768).

Via Garibaldi

To the north, in Via Vittorio Emanuele, a wide street 3 km (2 mi.) long, is the Piazza San Francesco, with the Bellini Museum, the house in which the composer was born.

Piazza San Francesco

Immediately to the west (entrance from the Via Teatro Greco) stands the Ancient Theatre (Teatro Romano), on Greek foundations, most of it now underground. On its west side is the Odeon, a small and well-preserved Roman theatre for rehearsals and musical competitions.

Teatro Romano

151

Catania

Piazza del Duomo

★San Nicola

In Via Crociferi, which runs north from the Piazza San Francesco, are two churches with Baroque façades, San Benedetto and Chiesa dei Gesuiti (both on the left). On the right stands the church of San Guiliano.

About 500 m west, in Piazza Dante, is the former Benedictine monastery of San Nicola (founded 1518, rebuilt 1735), used from 1866 as a barracks and a school.

The monastery church, with an unfinished façade, is a massive Baroque structure. From the lantern of the dome (internal height 62 m (205 ft)) there are extensive views. There are also fine views from the observatory which adjoins the church on the north-west.

Via Etnea

From the Piazza del Duomo Via Etnea, the town's wide principal street, runs north for 3 km (2 mi.), interrupted by a series of spacious squares, with a prospect of Etna in the background. Immediately on the left stands the Town Hall.

University

Nearby the Piazza dell'Universitá on the left, is the University, founded in 1444, in a fine building erected in 1818. Farther on is the Collegiate Church, with a fine Baroque façade (1768). The next square is the palm-shaded Piazza Stesicoro, with a monument to Bellini.

Anfiteatro

On the left side of the square are the remains of a Roman amphitheatre (perhaps 2nd c. AD), partly demolished during the reign of Theodoric in order to provide material for building the town walls; only the north end is visible. The amphitheatre, with its unusually large arena (70 × 50 m (231 × 165 ft)) was second only to the Colosseum in Rome.

San Carcere

A little way to the west is the church of San Carcere (13th c. doorway).

Giardino Bellini

Farther along Via Etnea, on the left, a few steps beyond Piazza Stericoro, is the main entrance to the Giardino Bellini, an attractive public garden (pleasant views from the terrace).

Along the north side of the Villa Bellini runs the tree-lined Viale Regina Margherita, which with its eastward continuation the Viale XX Settembre and the wide Corso Italia, beginning at the beautiful Piazza Verga (with the modern Law Courts), forms the main traffic artery, 6 km (4 mi.) long, of the northern part of the city.

At its eastern end is the Piazza Europa, which looks down on to the sea and from which a magnificent coast road (lookout terraces) leads north to the suburban district of Ognina, with the little Porto d'Ulisse in a sheltered bay.

★Porto d'Ulisse

★★Etna

The most rewarding excursion from Catania is the ascent of Etna or the subsidiary craters of Monti Rossi, or alternatively the trip round the volcano (see entry).

Cefalù   J19

Region: Sicilia. Province: Palermo (PA)
Altitude: 16 m (33 ft). Population: 13,000

The little port of Cefalù, picturesquely situated under a bare limestone crag which falls sheer down to the sea, lies on the northern coast of Sicily, some 50 km (30 mi.) from Palermo (west) and 100 km (62 mi.) from Messina (east). It has preserved much of its character and charm. Cefalù is the seat of a bishop.

Location

The Romanesque cathedral of Cefalù

Cefalù

Sights

★★Cathedral
On the east side of the town's principal street, the Corso Ruggero, which runs north towards the sea, is the spacious Piazza del Duomo, with the Town Hall and the cathedral, one of the finest buildings of the Norman Period, which was begun by King Roger in 1131–32.

The interior (74 m (244 ft) long), has fifteen granite columns plus one of cipollino, all with beautiful capitals. The apse contains magnificent mosaics, including one of the Saviour (1148), as well as the "Virgin with Four Archangels", and the "Twelve Apostles". In the south aisle is a fine 12th c. font. The cloister (beautiful capitals) is entered from the north aisle.

Museo Mandralisca
A short way west of the Piazza del Duomo is the little Museo Mandralisca, with antiquities from the Lipari Islands and fine pictures, including the "Picture of an Unknown Person" by Antonello da Messina (1470).

La Rocca
At the north end of the Corso Ruggero is the starting point of the climb (1 hour) of the crag known as the Rocca (269 m (888 ft)), which is composed almost entirely of fossils; remains of a medieval castle and of an ancient polygonal structure known as the Tempio di Diana (9th c. BC). From the highest point, on which are remains of a Norman castle, there are magnificent views.

Santuario di Gibilmanna

15 km (9 mi.) S
South of Cefalù is the Santuario di Gibilmanna (17th–18th c.), a place of pilgrimage (Museum of Franciscan art and culture).

Cerveteri   G11

Region: Lazio. Province: Roma (ROMA)
Altitude: 81 m (267 ft). Population: 21,000

Location
The little country town of Cerveteri, now a place of no particular importance, occupies the site of the ancient Caere, once one of the leading Etruscan cities, on a tufa ridge 45 km (28 mi.) north-west of Rome. The empire of the Etruscans, who were artists and skilled artisans, reached its peak in the 6th c.

Sights

Little remains of the original city. In the Piazza Santa Maria is the medieval Rocca, a castle which is partly built on Etruscan walls of the 4th c. BC

Museo Nazionale Cerite
Opposite stands the 16th c. Palazzo Ruspoli, which houses the Museo Nazionale Cerite, containing material from the Etruscan cemeteries round the town; the most important items, however, are in Rome (Etruscan Museum in the Vatican, Villa Giulia Museum).

★Banditaccia Cemetery

To the north of the town, extending along the edge of the tufa hill known as the Banditaccia, is a large Etruscan cemetery (7th–1st c. BC); a city of the dead which bears impressive witness, in the scale of the necropolis and the richness of the buried goods, to the importance attached by the Etruscans to the cult of the dead. On either side of a "main street" some 2 km (1½ mi.) long, with a number of side streets, lie hundreds of tombs, including huge tumuli up to 30 m (99 ft) in diameter and many tomb chambers hewn from the rock in the form of dwelling-houses, often with several rooms. Many tombs have holes showing the point of entry of early tomb-robbers (a torch should be taken).

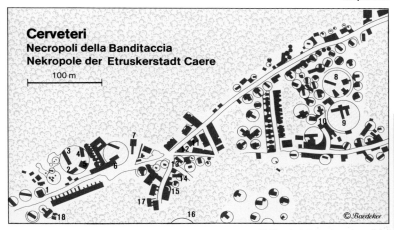

Cerveteri
Necropoli della Banditaccia
Nekropole der Etruskerstadt Caere

100 m

8
9
10
7
3 4
2
5 1
6
2
1
13
12
14
15
17
16
18

© Baedeker

1 Tomba dei Capitelli	7 Tomba dei Rilievi	13 Tumulo della Quercia
2 Tumulo dei Letti e Sarcofagi	8 Tumulo del Colonello	14 Tumulo dei 2 Ingressi
3 Tomba della Capanna	9 Tumulo Mengarelli	15 Tumulo della Cornice
4 Tomba dei Dolii	10 Tumulo Maroi	16 Grande Tumulo della Tegola Dipinta
5 Tomba dei Vasi Greci	11 Tomba di Marce Ursus	17 Tomba dei 6 Loculi
6 Tomba dei 13 Cadaveri	12 Tomba della Casetta	18 Tombe della Spianata

The most impressive gravestones include those of the Tomba dei Capitelli, Tomba dei Dolii, Tomba dei Vasi Greci, Tomba dei 13 Cadaveri, Tomba dei Rilievi, Tomba della Casetta, Tomba dei Letti e Sarcofagi, as well as the Tumulo della Cornice and the Tumulo Ophelia Maroi.

Of the underground tombs, particular mention should be made of the Tomba dei Rilievi, with painted bas-relief representations of everyday objects.

★Cinqueterre   D7

Region: Liguria. Province: La Spezia (SP)
Population: 7000

The very picturesque coastal region known as the Cinqueterre, fringed by tall and precipitous cliffs, lies between La Spezia and Levanto on the Gulf of Genoa, the so-called Riviera di Levante, with the five villages ("cinque terre") of Monterosso al Mare, Vernazza, Corniglia, Manarola and Riomaggiore, of which Monterosso al Mare, a medieval fishing village, is the largest.

Location

These picturesque villages, linked with one another only by a narrow winding country road but accessible individually by road, railway or boat, have in consequence of their remoteness preserved their old-world aspect. With their beautiful setting and their pleasant climate they have a charm and a character all their own.

The inhabitants live by agriculture (vines, olives) and fishing.

★Landscape

This charming coastal stretch, with its steeply sloping vineyards, should be explored on foot. Numerous footpaths link Monterosso al Mare with the other villages of the Cinqueterre. The walk *par excellence* is the Sentiero Azzurro from Monterossa to Riomaggiore (Blue Walk; 12 km (7½ mi.)), a stretch that is well sign-posted.

Walks

The Cinqueterre, a picturesque section of the coast between La Spezia and Levanto

The Five Villages

Monterosso al Mare

The main features of the pretty chief village situated behind the railway line are the Loggia del Podestà (14th c.) and the tower of the parish church of San Giovanni Battista, built as a Genoese watch-tower.

High above Monterosso, on the road to Vernazza, lies the pilgrimage church of the Madonna di Soviore which is worth a visit (magnificent view).

Vernazza

Vernazza, undoubtedly the prettiest of the villages, snuggles behind a rocky cliff in a cleft in the valley. A piazza with colourful houses opens onto the small harbour. In 1182 Vernazza fought on the Genoese side against Pisa. A few sections of the old Genoese fortifications, walls and a round tower have been preserved.

Corniglia

Corniglia, the only one of the Cinqueterre lying above sea-level (193 m (633 ft)), is laid out similarly to the villages in the Ligurian hinterland.

The little road from Vernazza to Corniglia crosses a narrow mountain ridge on which is perched the hamlet of San Bernardino. San Bernardino, with the pilgrimage church of the same name (good view of the whole region), can be reached from Corniglia in an hour.

Manarola

On the upper edge of Manarola, which since 1806 has formed part of Riomaggiore, stands the Gothic church of the Natività di Maria Vergine, the front of which boasts a magnificent rose of Carrara marble. Opposite the church are the free-standing bell-tower and a 16th c. watch-tower

Riomaggiore

Riomaggiore, the easternmost place in La Spezia and the easiest to reach, has expanded considerably as the result of tourism. It became known largely because of the painter Telemaco Signorini who often stayed here from 1860 onwards and painted the village several times. Inside the parish church of San Giovanni (14th c.) are a pulpit with marble reliefs and a wooden crucifix; above the Renaissance doorway can be seen a 15th c.

triptych. On a hill in the north-west of the village are remains of the 15th/16th c. castle.

Città di Castello   G9

Region: Umbria. Province: Perugia (PG)
Altitude: 288 m (950 ft). Population: 38,000

Città di Castello lies on the Tiber in northern Umbria – some 50 km (30 mi.)   Location
north of Perugia. It is a busy commercial centre (tobacco growing, printing
industry) and has some important art collections.

Sights

The central feature of the town, which is still partly surrounded by its old
walls, is the Piazza Matteotti, enclosed by fine old palaces, among which
the Palazzo Vitelli (16th c.). Close to the Palazzo Vitelli stands the Palazzo
Albizzini (15th c.), in which are displayed the works of the Italian "arte
povera" artist Alberto Burri (d. 1995).

To the west of the Piazza Matteotti is the Piazza Gabriotti, in which stands   Cathedral
the fine rusticated Palazzo Comunale (Town Hall). Beyond this, on the
west, is the Cathedral of Santi Florido e Amanzio, originally 11th c. but
remodelled in Renaissance style in the 15th and 16th c. The treasury contains an embossed silver antepedium with designs in silver-gilt (c. 1150).
   On the west side of the square is the little Giardino Pubblico.

South-east of the cathedral is the Gothic church of San Domenico (1424),   San Domenico
with old frescoes and a pretty monastic courtyard.

View over Città di Castello

Cividale dei Friuli

★Pinacoteca Comunale

Near the church by the town wall stands the fine Palazzo Vitelli della Cannoniera, which contains the municipal picture collection, with numerous altarpieces (13th–15th c.), a maestà by the master of Cittá di Castello (13th c.), early work by Raffael and the "Martyrdom of St Sebastian" by Luca Signorelli.

San Francesco

North of Piazza Matteotti stands the church of San Francesco (1273; interior refurbished in the Baroque style in 1707), with a Vitelli Chapel built by Vasari.

Cividale del Friuli   H3

Region: Friuli-Venezia Giulia. Province: Udine (UD)
Altitude: 138 m (455 ft). Population: 11,000

Location

Cividale del Friuli, formerly capital of Friuli, lies a little way east of Udine, on the River Natisone below the Julian Alps, which have belonged to Yugoslavia since 1947.

With its early medieval buildings, it has much of interest to offer the visitor. The town suffered some damage in an earthquake in May 1976.

History

Cividale, the Roman Forum Iulii – which gave its name to the region of Friuli – was from 569 to 774 the seat of Lombard dukes, and from 730 the residence of the Patriarch of Aquileia. After his conquest of the Lombard kingdom in 774 Charlemagne made it the seat, under the name of Civitas Austriae, of a line of Frankish margraves, the most important of whom, Berengarius I, ruled Italy as king from 888 to 924, with Cividale as his capital.

Even after the seat of the Patriarchate was transferred to Udine in 1238 Cividale remained for centuries the most important place in Friuli by virtue of its command of major Alpine passes. In 1419 the town was occupied by the Venetians, who in 1439 compelled the Patriarch to renounce his secular authority. Thereafter the town fell into a steady decline. In 1752 the Patriarchate was replaced by the archbishopric of Gorizia and Udine.

Sights

Cathedral

In the Piazza del Duomo, in the centre of the town, stands the cathedral (originally 8th c.; remodelled in Early Renaissance style by Pietro and Tullio Lombardi from 1502 onwards). It contains the remains of an octagonal baptistery (8th c.), the altar of Duke Ratchis (8th c.), a Romanesque silver-gilt antependium (c. 1200) and a large crucifix.

Notable are the crypt and the Museo Cristiano.

Town Hall

Also in the Piazza del Duomo are the Palazzo del Comune (Town Hall) and the Palazzo Pretorio (formerly Palazzo del Provveditore), built by Palladio.

★Museo Archeologico Nazionale

Opposite the cathedral is the Museo Archeologico Nazionale, with valuable Lombard antiquities (fine gold ornaments) and prehistoric, Roman and medieval material (including two psalters which belonged to St Elizabeth of Thuringia, d. 1231).

★Tempietto

At Porta Brossana is the former Benedictine convent of Santa Maria in Valle, picturesquely situated on the banks of the Natisone, with the Tempietto, the front part of a Lombard church destroyed by a spate of the river (stucco reliefs of the 8th–9th c.; frescoes of the 14th/15th c.; 14th c. choir-stalls).

Lower down, on the river bank, is the church of Santi Pietro e Biagio, with the remains of ancient frescoes.

Surroundings

There is a rewarding excursion through steep and narrow roads to the Santuario di Castelmonte (618 m (2039 ft)), the most famous pilgrimage centre in Friuli.

Santiuario di Castelmonte
10 km (6 mi.) E

Como   D4

Region: Lombardia. Province: Como (CO)
Altitude: 202 m (667 ft). Population: 95,000

Como, capital of the province of the same name, some 50 km (31 mi.) north of Milan, lies at the southern end of Lake Como, surrounded by rocky hills, which are partly forest-covered. The town is an important centre of the silk industry.

Location

Como was founded by the Romans in 195 BC, on the site of an earlier settlement, as the frontier fortress of Comum, directed against the Rhaetians. During the Middle Ages the town – which in 1058 had the status of an episcopal see independent of Milan – was the key to Lombardy and an important base of the German emperors. In 1451 it passed to the control of Milan.

History

Sights

The town's life centres on the Piazza Cavour, by the harbour, from which the short Via Plinio runs south-east to the Piazza del Duomo. On the east side of this square is the Broletto (1215), formerly a lawcourt, now a banqueting hall.

The interior of Como cathedral

Lake Como

★Cathedral

Adjoining it to the south-east is the cathedral, built entirely of marble (originally erected 1396, remodelled in Renaissance style 1426–1596; dome over crossing 1730–70). On either side of the principal doorway, which has fine sculptured decorations, are statues (1498) of Pliny the Elder and Younger, natives of Como. South-east of the cathedral in Via Vittorio Emanuele II, Como's principal street, is the Romanesque church of San Fedele (12th c.). Opposite it is the Town Hall.

Museum

Farther south, in the Palazzo Giovio, is the Musei Civici, with archaeological finds and documents on local history. Via Vittorio Emanuele II runs south to end at the town walls; on the south-east side of the old town are three well-preserved 12th c. towers.

Sant'Abbondio

About 500 m from the south-west corner of the town walls is the twin-towered church of Sant'Abbondio, a basilica in Lombard Romanesque style (11th c.; modernised in 1587). The choir contains 14th c. frescoes.

Volta memorial

A little way south-west of Piazza Cavour is Piazza Volta, with a statue of the physicist Alessandro Volta (1745–1827), a native of Como who was born in No. 50 Via Volta.

Tempio Voltiano (Museum)

At the north-east corner of the Giardino Pubblico, on the shores of the lake, stands the Neo-Classical Tempio Voltiano, with the Volta Museum, the exhibits in which include the first voltaic pile.

Surroundings

Brunate

From the Piazza Vittoria it is 5 km (3 mi.) by road (also funicular) to the villa suburb of Brunate (716 m (2363 ft)), on a terrace on the hillside, with beautiful views of Como, the plain extending as far as Milan, the Pre-Alps and the mountains from Monte Rosa to Monviso.

San Maurizio

There are even more extensive views from San Maurizio (871 m (2874 ft)), 2.5 km (2 mi.) above Brunate.

Monte Boletto

From Brunate there is a footpath (2 hours) to the top of Monte Boletto (1234 m (472 ft); views).

★Lake Como   D3–4

Region: Lombardia
Province: Como (CO). Altitude: 198 m (653 ft)

Location

Lake Como (Lago di Como or Lario), the Roman Lacus Larius, lies 50 km (31 mi.) north of Milan between the Lugano and the Bergamo Alps. Narrow and fjord-like, the lake fills the glaciated valley of the Adda, which flows through it from end to end. From its northern end to its southern tip at Como the lake is 50 km (31 mi.) long; at its half-way point, between Menaggio and Varenna, it is 4 km (2¹/₂ mi.) wide; it has an area of 146 sq. km (56 sq. mi.); and its greatest depth is 410 m (1353 ft), making it the deepest lake of northern Italy.

Landscape

On the south-west arm, the Lago di Como, are numerous villas surrounded by beautiful gardens and vineyards. The rather more austere south-east arm, the Lago di Lecco, with the outflow of the Adda, is less crowded with visitors. On the steep hillsides bordering the lake, rising to 2610 m (8613 ft) in Monte Legnone, are plantations of chestnuts and walnuts, the green of their foliage contrasting strongly with the greyish tints of the olives. The inhabitants live by fishing, the production of wine and oil, and by industry (ironworking, marble-quarrying, textiles).

Lake Como, one of the most scenic places in Upper Italy

Boat services (from Bellano throughout the year): Between Colico and Como, with varying ports of call on both sides of the lake; between Bellano and Como; between Varenna and Lecco. In summer there are also hydrofoil services.

Boat services

Tour of the lake (250 km (155 mi.))

Leave Como on the Lugano road, going north-west and in 2 km (1¼ mi.) turn into SS340, which runs up the west side of the lake. On the right of the road is the Neo-Classical Villa Olmo (1782–97; damaged by fire 1983); now used for exhibitions, concerts and congresses; fine views from the park.

★ Villa Olmo

3 km (2 mi.): Cernobbio (201 m (663 ft); population 7500), with many villas set in beautiful gardens and the palatial Villa d'Este (1568; now a hotel). From here a narrow road winds its way up (16 km (10 mi.)) to Monte Bisbino (1325 m (4373 ft); views), on which there is a pilgrimage church.

Cernobbio

22 km (14 mi.): Lenno, the most southerly place in the district of Tremezzina, over which towers Monte Crocione (1641 m (5415 ft)). From here an attractive visit can be made to the Punta di Balbianello or Punta d'Avedo, a long promontory projecting into the lake, with the Villa Arconati (late 16th c.; access only by boat), from the terrace of which there are beautiful views.

Lenno

3 km (2 mi.): Tremezzo, a popular resort in a warm and sheltered situation on the lake, surrounded by beautiful gardens.

Tremezzo

500 m: Villa Carlotta (formerly Sommariva, named after Charlotte, Duchess of Meiningen, mother of an earlier owner; now the property of the State). The palace built in 1747 contains Thorwaldsen's famous marble frieze of

★ Villa Carlotta

161

A magnificent villa near Tremezzo on Lake Como

The Villa d'Este reflects past splendour

Alexander the Great's triumphal entry into Babylon, and sculptures by Canova. The gardens are a riot of southern vegetation (azaleas in bloom in May).

550 m: Cadenabbia (201 m (663 ft)), with a Romanesque church, many villas and a beautiful lakeside promenade.   **Cadenabbia**

4 km (2½ mi.): Menaggio (203 m (670 ft); population 3000), one of the most popular resorts on Lake Como. The road then passes the rocky walls of the Sasso Rancio.   **Menaggio**

12 km (7 mi.): Dongo (208 m (686 ft)), outside which Mussolini and his mistress Clara Petacci were caught by partisans in 1945 while fleeing to Switzerland. They were shot on the following day at Mezzagra, near Lenno.   **Dongo**

4 km (2½ mi.): Gravedona (201 m (663 ft)) with the Romanesque-Lombard church of Santa Maria del Tiglio (12th c.).   **Gravedona**

10 km (6 mi.): Gera Lario (208 m (686 ft)), the most northerly place on Lake Como.
   4 km (2½ mi.) beyond Gera Lario the road joins SS36. coming from Chiavenna, which runs down the east side of the lake to Milan.   **Gera Lario**

8 km (5 mi.): Colico (209 m (690 ft)), dominated by the mighty Monte Legnone.   **Colico**

7 km (4½ mi.): The abbey of Piona, an old Cluniac monastery, with a fine 11th c. church (restored), contains Byzantine frescoes and an interesting Romanesque-Gothic cloister (1257).   **Piona Abbey**

4 km (2½ mi.): Dervio (202 m (667 ft)), from which a detour can be made to Monte Legnone (2610 m (8613 ft): 18 km (11 mi.) by road, then a 4-hour climb).   **Dervio**

8 km (5 miles: Varenna (220 m (726 ft)), situated on an promontory at the mouth of the Valle d'Esino, with beautiful gardens and quarries of black marble; magnificent views of Bellagio on a promontory and of the three arms of the lake. The Villa Monastero (park) is occupied by the Italian Institute of Hydrobiology.   **Varenna**

11 km (7 mi.): Mandello del Lario (214 m (706 ft)), on a delta running far out into the lake at the foot of the jagged Grigna Meridionale, with one of the largest motorcycle factories in Italy (Moto Guzzi).   **Mandello del Lario**

10 km (6 mi.): Lecco (214 m (706 ft)), an industrial town magnificently situated at the south-east tip of Lake Como, at the outflow of the River Adda. In the Largo Manzoni is a monument to the novelist Alessandro Manzoni (1785–1873), author of "I Promessi Sposi", the scene of which is partly set in Lecco.   **Lecco**
   East of Lecco are the Piani d'Erna (1329 m (4386 ft)), reached by cableway or by road. To the north is the Piano dei Resinelli (1272 m (4198 ft)), from which the Grigna Meridionale (2184 m (7207 ft)) can be climbed (2½ hours).
   At the south-west end of Lecco we leave SS36 and turn right into a road which runs below the precipitous slopes of Monte Moregallo (1276 m (4211 ft)), passing through a number of tunnels.

16 km (10 mi.): Bellagio (229 m (756 ft)), a very popular spa on the west side of the Punta di Bellagio, one of the great beauty spots of the north Italian lakes. On the promontory is the Villa Serbelloni, with a park (conducted tour) from which there are views of the three arms of Lake Como. Farther along the road are the park of the Villa Melzi and the gardens of the Villa Trotti.   **Bellagio**

Nesso 14 km (9 mi.): Nesso (275 m (908 ft)), a picturesque village at the mouth of the Val di Nesso, with a waterfall 20 m (66 ft) high.

Villa Pliniana 8 km (5 mi.): Below the road on the right, in Molina bay, is the Villa Pliniana (1570), named after a spring mentioned by Pliny the Younger that daily changes its level.

Torno 4 km (2½ mi.): Torno (225 m (743 ft)), a finely situated village on a rocky promontory, surrounded by villas. Near the picturesque harbour is the church of Santa Tecla, with 15th c. frescoes.

7 km (4½ mi.): Como.

Cortina d'Ampezzo G2

Region: Veneto. Province: Belluno (BL)
Altitude: 1224 m (4039 ft). Population: 8000

Location The internationally renowned tourist centre of Cortina d'Ampezzo, Italy's most popular winter sports resort, lies at the eastern end of the Strada delle Dolomiti in a wide valley enclosed by the high peaks of the Dolomites.

The Winter Olympics 1956 took place in Cortina d'Ampezzo.

Sights

★Parish church In the Corso Italia, the lively main street of Cortina (pedestrian precinct), is the fine parish church (18th c.), with ceiling paintings and wall paintings in the choir by Franz Anton Zeiller (1774) and an altar dedicated to the Virgin by Andrea Brustolon (1724).

Cortina d'Ampezzo lies at the eastern end of the Strada delle Dolomiti

A short distance south-east, in the Casa de Ra Regoles, are the Mario Rimoldi Collection (contemporary art) and the Museum (fossils; material of folk interest), with works by De Chirico, De Pisis, Guttuso, Morandi.

| Casa de Ra Regoles

Farther south-east, by the cemetery, is the beautiful Baroque church of the Madonna della Difesa.

To the north of Cortina is the Olympic Ice Stadium (Stadio Olimpico del Ghiaccio) with a memorial to the French geologist Dieudonné Dolomieu (1750–1801), after whom the Dolomites are named.

| Olympic Ice Stadium

To the south of the town, on the road to Pieve di Cadore, a little way off, to the right, is the Olympic Ski Jump (Trampolino Olimpico di Salto "Italia").

| Olympic Ski Jump

Cableways west of the valley

A cableway (Freccia del Cielo) runs from the Ice Stadium to the Col Druscié (1770 m (5841 ft)) and Ra Valles (2470 m (8151 ft)); from here there is a double chair-lift to Bus Tofana 2823 m (9316 ft)) with a connection to the Tofana di Mezzo (3244 m (10,705 ft); upper station 15 minutes below the peak).

| ★★Tofana

There is a chair-lift from Campo Corono (1220 m (4026 ft)) via Colfiere (1462 m (4825 ft)) to the Col Druscié; two parallel lifts from Rumerlo (1678 m (5537 ft)) via the Rifugio Duca d'Aosta (2098 m (6923 ft)) to the Forcella Pomedes (2282 m (7531 ft); mountain hut).

| Forcella Pomedes

From the Piazza Roma (near the parish church), a cableway leads to Pocol-Belvedere (Belvedere on the Crepa; 1539 m (5079 ft)); the hotel complex of Pocol rises above the valley of Cortina d'Ampezzo.

| Pocol-Belvedere

Cableways east of the valley

A chair-lift from Guargnè (1304 m (4303 ft)) goes via the Col Tondo (1437 m (4742 ft)) to the Rifugio Mietres (1710 m (5643 ft)).

| Rifugio Mietres

From the bus station a cableway leads via Mandres (1480 m (4884 ft)) to the Rifugio Faloria (2123 m (7006 ft)) and from there to the Capanna Tondi di Faloria (2327 m (7679 ft)).

| Capanna Tondi di Faloria

See Dolomites

| Strada delle Dolomiti

Cortona   F–G9

Region: Toscana. Province: Arezzo (AR)
Altitude: 500–650 m (1650–2145 ft). Population: 23,000

The town of Cortona lies close to the eastern border of Tuscany, north of the Lake Trasimene in Umbria, and 30 km (19 mi.) south of Arezzo.

| Location

Cortona is one of the oldest towns in Italy. It was one of the twelve cities of the Etruscan League, and later became a Roman colony. During the Middle Ages it passed through various vicissitudes before coming under the control of Florence in 1411. The painter Luca Signorelli (d. 1523) was born in Cortono in 1441 or 1450.

| History

Old town

The central feature of the walled old town is the Piazza della Repubblica, on the west side of which stands the Palazzo Comunale (Town Hall; 13th c., with later rebuilding), with a broad flight of steps.

| Palazzo Comunale

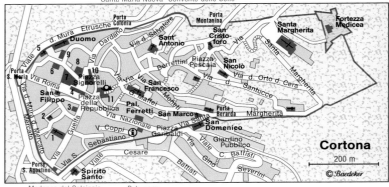

Arezzo
Santa Maria Nuova Convento delle Celle

Cortona

200 m

© Baedeker

Madonna del Calcinaio   Palazzone
Lago Trasimeno

1 Sant' Agostino
2 San Benedetto
3 Palazzo Mancini-
   Sernini

4 Palazzo Comunale
5 Chiesa
   del Gesù
   (Museo Diocesano)

6 Palazzo Tommasi
7 Palazzo Casali
   (Museo dell' Acca-
   demia Etrusca)

8 Teatro Signorelli
9 Palazzo Vescovile
10 Palazzo Fierli
11 Palazzo del Popolo

Palazzo Pretorio	To the north-west of the Town Hall is the Piazza Signorelli, with the Palazzo Pretorio, the façade of which bears the coats of arms of former podestàs; it now houses the Accademia Etrusca (founded 1726) and the Museum of Etruscan Antiquities (Etruscan bronze candelabrum; 5th c. BC).
Cathedral	North-west of the Piazza Signorelli, in the Piazza del Duomo (extensive views), stands the cathedral (originally Romanesque, remodelled in Renaissance style by Giuliano da Sangallo, 1456–1502).
★Museo Diocesano	Opposite the cathedral, in the former Baptistery (or Chiesa del Gesù), is the Museo Diocesano, which contains some fine pictures, including works by Fra Angelico, Luca Signorelli, Pietro Lorenzetti and other artists, and a Roman sarcophagus of the 2nd c. AD.
Town walls	To the east of the cathedral, from the Porta Colonia, there is an impressive view of the town walls (2.6 km (1½ mi.) long; lower parts Etruscan).
Santa Maria Nuova	1 km (½ mi.) north-east, below the Porta Colonia, is the church of Santa Maria Nuova (16th c.), a Renaissance building with a quadrangular plan (high dome).
San Francesco	The church of San Francesco is to the east of the town (begun in 1245 in Gothic style and remodelled in the 17th c.) has a remarkable reliquary of the Holy Cross on the high altar and a Byzantine ivory picture of the 10th c.
★San Domenico	From the Piazza della Repubblica the Via Nazionale runs south-east to the Piazza Garibaldi, outside the town walls. To the east of this square, on the north side of the Giardino Pubblico (public park), stands the 15th c. church of San Domenico, originally part of a Dominican convent, with pictures by Signorelli and a winged altar by Lorenzo Ghiberti (14th–15th c.).
★Madonna del Calcinaio	From the Piazza Garibaldi a twisting road with four sharp bends descends for 3 km (2 mi.) to the southern slope of the town hill, on which stands the church of Santa Maria del Calcinaio, a beautiful domed building on a

cruciform plan by Francesco di Giorgio of Siena. The church was dedicated to a miraculous Madonna (originally on the wall of a *calcinaio*, limepit).

High above the town rises the Fortezza Medicea (fortress of the Medici family), the north-eastern corner pillar of the town wall. From here there are magnificent views.

Fortezza Medicea

A little way below the fortress, clinging to the hill, are the buildings of the Santuario di Santa Margherita (pilgrimage church), with the tomb of St Margaret of Cortona (dates from 1362; her silver reliquary is on the high altar).

Santuario di Santa Margherita

Surroundings

The village of Castiglion Fiorentino (12 km (7½ mi.) north-west) is picturesquely situated on a hill, surrounded by medieval town walls (14th and 15th c. towers).

Castiglion Fiorentino

Cremona   E5

Region: Lombardia. Province: Cremona (CR)
Altitude: 45 m (148 ft). Population: 74,000

The provincial capital of Cremona lies in the fertile North Italian plain just north of the Po, near the mouth of the River Adda, some 70 km (43 mi.) south-east of Milan, the capital of Lombardy.

Location

The town is famous for the violin makers who worked here, particularly in the 16th–18th c. The violins made by Niccolò Amati, Antonio Stradivari, Guarneri de Gesù and other violin-makers are famous for their sound.
   Today efforts are made to perpetuate this musical tradition by means of concerts, etc. In Cremona there is an Institute of Professional Violin Makers, and in the cultural centre exhibitions on the same theme are held.
   Cremona was also the birthplace of the composer Claudio Monteverdi (1567–1643). There is a musical college named after him.

Violin makers

The Gallic settlement on this site became a Roman colony in 218 BC, and in later centuries suffered destruction on many occasions – by Vespasian's army (in AD 70), by the Goths and the Lombards, and during the struggle between Guelfs and Ghibelines. The town was an important base of the emperor Frederick II. In 1334 it passed to Milan.

History

Piazza del Comune

In the Piazza del Comune, in the centre of the picturesque old town, stands the town's principal landmark, the imposing Torrazzo (1267), an octagonal tower 111 m (366 ft) high, from which there are extensive views. There is a fascinating violin workshop, the "Bottega della Torre", on the first floor.

★Torrazzo

East of the Torrazzo, linked with it by a Renaissance loggia (begun 1497, completed in the 18th c.), is the cathedral, in Lombard Gothic style (1107–90), which has a richly sculptured façade embellished with columns. It contains frescoes (1506–73) by Pordenone, Boccaccino and others and many Biblical scenes. Note the beautiful relief decoration on the two pulpits (19th c.).

★Cathedral

Adjoining the cathedral are the octagonal Baptistery (1167), with a font by L. Trotti (16th c.) and the subterranean Campo Santo.

Baptistery

Cremona cathedral, built in Lombard Gothic style

★Palazzo Comunale

On the west side of the square is the Gothic Palazzo Comunale (Town Hall, 1206–45), which contains four violins by the famous Cremonese violin-makers. To the left of the Town Hall is the Gothic Loggia dei Militi (1292).

San Pietro al Po

About 250 m west stands the church of San Pietro al Po (1563–68), the interior of which contains rich stucco ornament and ceiling paintings by Antonio Campi (d. 1591). In the neighbouring convent is a representation of the "Miracle of the Loaves and Fishes" (*c.* 1550).

Piazza Roma

Palazzo Fodri

North of the cathedral is the Piazza Roma, laid out with gardens, on which the life of the town is centred (memorial stone to Stradivarius). From here the Corso Mazzini leads to the Palazzo Fodri (15th–16th c.; formerly a pawnshop), a fine Renaissance mansion with a notable loggia.

Museo Civico

North-west of the Piazza Roma, in Via Ugolani Dati, we find the imposing Palazzo Affaitati (1561), a massive Late Renaissance building with a Baroque courtyard and staircase, which now houses the Museo Civico, with numerous works by the Cremona school of painters (15th–18th c.) founded by Boccaccio Boccaccino (*c.* 1467–1525), as well as archaeological finds, ceramics, and Cremona terracotta work. The old town has fine churches and palaces, many of them with terracotta decoration.

Stradivarius Museum

The Palazzo Affaitati (corner Via Ugolani Dati/Via Palestro) houses the Stradivarius Museum, with more than 700 examples by the famous violin maker of Cremona. Antonio Stradivarius, called Stradivari (1644–1737), was a pupil of Niccolò Amati, and had the ability to appreciate the acoustic quality of various types of wood. Stradivarius acquired great wealth, and the Italians still use the expression "as rich as Stradivari".

Surroundings

East of Cremona is the church of San Sigismondo, a superb Early Renaissance building by Bartolomeo Gadia (1463), with frescoes and pictures by Camillo Boccaccio, the younger Campi and others.

San Sigismondo
2 km (1¼ mi.) E

★★Dolomites

F3–G2

Regions: Trentino-Alto Adige and Veneto
Provinces: Bolzano (BZ), Trento (TN) and Belluno (BL)

The Dolomites are a range of mountains in the eastern part of the Alps, situated in northern Italy, actually in the Alto Adige – east of Bolzano and Trento.

Location

The magnificent range of mountains called the Dolomites after the French geologist Dieudonné (or Déodat) Dolomieu (1750–1801) is one of the most beautiful and most visited parts of the Alps. Taken in its widest sense, the range is bounded by the rivers Isarco, Adige, Brenta, Piave and Rienza. Scattered among the mountains are beautiful little lakes, including the Lago di Braies, Lago di Carezza, Lago di Misurina, Lago di Landria and Lago d'Alleghe.

The famous Alpine glow, bathing the Alps in the flaming red of the setting sun, is particularly beautiful in the Dolomites. The real Alpine glow, when the rock faces and snowfields are clad in brilliant hues of yellow, purple and red, occurs only very rarely, and then only for five to ten minutes after sunset, when there is a light haze in the west and dusk has already fallen in the valleys.

Alpine glow

Dolomite peaks

Dolomites

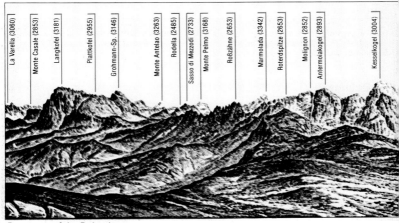

La Varella (3060) | Monte Casale (2853) | Langkofel (3181) | Plattkofel (2955) | Grohmann-Sp. (3146) | Monte Antelao (3263) | Rodella (2485) | Sasso di Mezzodi (2733) | Monte Pelmo (3168) | Roßzähne (2653) | Marmolada (3342) | Roterdspitze (2653) | Molignon (2852) | Antermoiakogel (2893) | Kesselkogel (3004)

Panorama of the Dolomites

Flora	The natural flora of the Dolomites is of Alpine character. The valley floors and gentler slopes are mostly covered with arable land and pasture, while the steeper slopes, up to 2200 m (7260 ft), are wooded – mostly with conifers but in the southern Dolomites also deciduous trees. Above the tree level are great expanses of upland meadows spangled with Alpine flowers.
Population	The Isarco valley and its side valleys and the Val Pusteria were settled from the 6th c. onwards by German-speaking Bajuwari (Bavarians), while at the same time Italians advanced into the region from the south. The Rhaetians, speaking a Romance language and now known as Ladins, withdrew into the inner valleys of the Dolomites, and are now mainly found in the Val Gardena and Val Gadera. There are newspapers and magazines in the Ladin language which is derived from Latin. The Ladins are noted for their fine wood-carving, particularly in the Val Gardena.
Legends	Legends of giants and dwarfs, witches and ghosts, princes and heroes have grown up in the Dolomite area, most of them originating from the the Ladin region.
Tourism	The main source of income of the population, apart from stock-farming and forestry, is alpine tourism, particularly winter sports.
	The Dolomites are remarkably easy of access, thanks to the valleys which cut deeply into the mountains and to an excellent network of roads (for example the Strada delle Dolomiti). In addition to large and widely famed winter sports and health resorts, such as Cortina d'Ampezzo, Corvara and San Martino di Castrozza, there are numerous small and middle-sized resorts and a host of remote mountain hotels and inns.
	The military roads of the First World War, many of them still in good condition, make it possible even for non-climbers to reach the heights and enjoy the extensive views they offer. The summits are being brought within easier reach by the steadily increasing numbers of cableways and lifts of various kinds.
★★Dolomiti Superski	The area between the Isarco valley, the Val Pustera and the Val di Fiemme forms the greatest skiing area in the Alps, the so-called "Dolomiti Superski", a Mecca for skiers. Some 500 lifts give access to 1000 km (620 mi.) of pistes, descents through deep snow and cross-country skiing, and all can

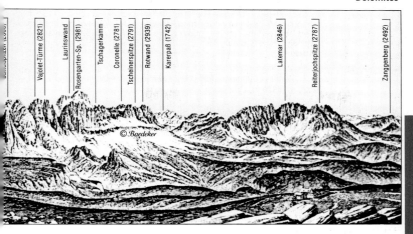

Vajolet-Türme (2821) · Laurinswand · Rosengarten-Sp. (2981) · Tschagerkamm · Coronelle (2781) · Tscheinerspitze (2791) · Rotwand (2939) · Karerpaß (1742) · Laternar (2846) · Reiterjochspitze (2787) · Zanggenberg (2492)

© Baedeker

be used with a single ski pass. The cableways extend for some 100 km
(62 mi.).

★★Dolomite Road

The 110 km (68 mi.) Dolomite Road runs from Bolzano to Cortina d'Ampezzo
(see entries).

Not far from Bolzano (see entry) we cross the Brenner motorway and climb   **Karneld**
the gorge in the Eggen valley through which flows the Karneld stream. On
a steep rocky height on the left stands Karneld Castle (13th c., restored
about 1880; chapel and frescoes) above the village of the same name. In
Kardaun is the Eisack power station, beyond which a road bridge crosses
the Eggen valley waterfall. Then the valley broadens out; near Birchabruck
(Ponte Nova; 877 m (2728 ft)) there is a fine view of the Laternar (on the
right) and the Rosengarten (on the left). Beyond Birchabruck the Dolomite
Road leaves the Eggen valley and ascends the Welschofen valley.

The village of Welschofen, picturesquely situated on the hillside, is popular   **Welschofen**
both as a summer and as a winter sports resort. From the Hainzer sawmill
a chair-lift goes up to the Frommer Alm (1730 m (5678 ft)) and continues to
the Kölner Hütte, (2337 m (7679 ft)). From the Cologne Path (Kölner Weg) it
is about 1¼ hours to the Paolina Hut (2127 m (6981 ft)) above the Karer Pass
(see below).

After almost 6 km (4 mi.) we reach the little hotel settlement of Karersee   **★Carezza Lake**
(Carezza al Lago; 1609 m (5281 ft)) not far above the Carezza Lake (Lago di
Carezza; 1530 m (5121 ft); nature reserve), in which are reflected the rough
rocky walls of the Laternar (2794 m (8611 ft)) which rises in the south. In
the north-east towers the Rotwand (2806 m (9209 ft)).

The Dolomite Road now continues downhill above meadows to the Passo   **Passo di**
di Costalunga (1753 m (5753 ft)) on the German/Ladin language frontier   **Costalunga**
between the Laternar and the Rotwand.
   High above the top of the pass stands a monument to the Dolomite
pioneer Theodor Cristomanos.

Dolomites

Vigo di Fassa

On the far side of the summit of the pass is Vigo di Fassa (1382 m (4536 ft)), a popular holiday and winter sports resort on the slopes above the Fassa valley. In the 15th c. parish church in the community of San Giovanni can be seen frescoes dating from the 16th c. Above the village is a military cemetery.

Pozza di Fassa

Further up the Fassa valley in which flows the River Avisio lies the resort of Pozza di Fassa (1290 m (4234 ft)), with a chair-lift to the Buffaure slope (2020 m (6629 ft); ski-lifts).

★Campitello di Fassa

Campitello di Fassa, dominated by the jagged peaks of the Langkofel, is much visited both in summer and in winter. A chair-lift goes up to the Col Rodella (2387 m (7834 ft)); it takes about 15 minutes to climb to the Rodella (2485 m (8156 ft); refuge hut).

Canazei

At the end of the Val Lastie lies Canazei a very popular touring base and winter sports resort of the upper Fassa Valley.

Pecol

A cableway leads to Pecol on the road over the Pordoi ridge where there is an extensive skiing area. A chair-lift ascends to the Belvedere (2389 m (7841 ft); refuge hut). From the Pordoi ridge the Viel dal Pan track leads in 2^1/2 hours via the Viel dal Pan Refugio (2346 m (7746 ft); refuge hut) to the Refugio Marmolada/Castiglioni on the artificially dammed Fadaia Lake (2046 m (6715 ft)).

Fadaia Pass

On the road leading south from Canazei to the Fadaia Pass is the village of Alba (cableway to Ciampac, 2136 m (7010 ft); skiing area). The road to the pass reaches the picturesque mountain village of Penia (1556 m (5107 ft)) and, above Pian Trevisam (1717 m (5635 ft); Refugio Villetta Maria), continues to the Fedaia Lake (see above).

Malga Ciapela

On a two-hour mountain tour over the Baita Robinson (1828 m (5999 ft)) we reach the Refugio Contrin (2016 m (6617 ft)). The path continues in 4^1/2 hours above the Ombretta Pass, (2704 m (8875 ft)) then below the mighty south wall of the Marmolada along to the Refugio O. Falier (2080 m (6827 ft)) and on to the hotel settlement of Malga Ciapela (1446 m (4746 ft)) on the east side of the Marmolada.

★Sasso Pordoi

This stretch via Pecol (see above) continues uphill with numerous bends to the Pordoi Col (2239 m (7348 ft)), the highest point on the Dolomite Road. It offers a magnificent view; in the east are the Ampezzo Dolomites with Tofana. From the Pordoi Col there is a cableway to the Sasso Pordoi (2950 m (9682 ft)). From here it is another 1^1/2 hours via the Refugio Forcella Pordoi (2850 m (9354 ft)) to Piz Boè (3151 m (10,342 ft)), the highest peak of the Sella group.

Arabba

The Dolomite Road winds its way down from the Pordoi ridge and in 10 km (6 mi.) reaches Arabba (1602 m (5258 ft)), primarily a winter sports resort at the foot of the Sella group.

Porta Vescovo

A cableway (with a chair-lift in winter running parallel to it) leads to Porta Vescovo (2510 m (8238 ft); mountain hut), a depression between the Belvedere (2650 m (8697 ft)) and the Mesola (2739 m (8989 ft)), from which there is an impressive view over the Fedaia Lake (see above) on the north flank of the Marmolada.

Livinallongo Valley

The Dolomite Road now follows the Livinallongo Valley watered by the Cordevole river, first along the floor of the valley and later high on the northern slope and over a gorge. Then we reach Pieve di Livinallongo, the administrative centre of the extensive district of Livinallongo del Col di Lana. South-east below Pieve is the Sacrario di Pian di Salesi, an Italian military cemetery. The road to it continues south to Caprile and Alleghe on the lake of the same name.

To the north above Pieve di Livinallongo towers the Col di Lana (2462 m (8080 ft)) which can be reached on foot in three hours via the Refugio Gaetani (1835 m (6022 ft)). The summit was the scene of intense fighting in 1915 to 1918; Italian alpine troops drove a tunnel under the positions of the Austrian Imperial infantry on the summit and on April 17th/18th 1916 blew it up. Near the summit stands a memorial chapel and remains of the military positions; from the top there is an exceptional panorama.

★Col di Lana

Beyond Pieve di Livinallongo the Dolomite Road turns north and climbs the Passo di Falzarego (Falzarego Pass (2177 m (7145 ft)), which is overlooked on the west by the Sasso di Stria ("witches' rock"; 2477 m (8130 ft)), on the east by the curiously named Cinque Torri ("five towers"; 2362 m (7752 ft)) and on the south by Nuvolauo (2575 m (8451 ft)). North of the pass a cableway goes up to the Piccolo Lagazuoi (2728 m (8953 ft)).

Falzarego Pass

From the Falzarego Pass a road leads north-west along the beautiful Lago di Valparola to the Valparola ridge (2192 m (7194 ft)), overlooked on the north-east by the Lagazuoi (2803 m (9199 ft)), then winds downhill to Armentarola (1640 m (5382 ft)); from here we continue through the charmingly situated village of San Cassiano (1537 m (5044 ft)) to the village of La Villa (Stern; 1483 m (4867 ft)), high in the valley of the Gader.
    The Dolomite Road continues in curves and S-bends steadily downhill; on the left is the mighty rock wall of Tofana (see Cortina d'Ampezzo, mountain railways).

Lago di Valparola

5 km (3 mi.) beyond the summit of the pass a road branches off to the Refugio Cinque Torri (2131 m (6994 ft)); from here there are climbs on the rocks of the Cinque Torri ("five towers"; main summit 2362 m (7752 ft)). About 15 minutes west of the hut is the Refugio Scoiattoli (2230 m (7319 ft); ski-lift), from where a chair-lift descends to the Refugio Bai de Dones (1900 m (6236 ft)) on the Dolomite Road.

Cinque Torri

About 7 km (4½ mi.) beyond the summit of the Falzarego Pass a 6 km (4 mi.) long military road branches off to the Refugio Cantore (2545 m (8353 ft)), the starting point for climbing the Tofana (see Cortina d' Ampezzo, cableways).
    Via Pocol, it is then 9 km (5½ mi.) to the winter sports resort of Cortina d'Ampezzo (see entry).

★★Tofana

★Elba, Island of   E10

Region: Toscana. Province: Livorno (LI)
Area: 223 sq. km (86 sq. mi.). Population: 30,000

Regular services (including car ferries) run several times daily from Piombino to Portoferraio and between Livorno and Portoferraio. In summer there are also hydrofoil services from Piombino and Livorno to Portoferraio.

Ferries

The Island of Elba (Isola d'Elba), the largest of the islands off Tuscany, lies in the Ligurian Sea 10 km (6 mi.) south of the mainland port of Piombino.
    Elba, 27 km (17 mi.) long, up to 18.5 km (11 mi.) wide, consists mainly of granite and porphyry, and has considerable deposits of high-quality iron ore, particularly in the eastern part of the island, with a metal content of 40–80 per cent.

Location

The possession of the iron-mines of Elba enabled the Etruscans to assert their dominance in Italy, and the mines were later worked by the Romans. Together with the tuna and anchovy fisheries and agriculture (fruit, vines) the working of iron was one of the island's main sources of income until 1982 when it finally came to a halt, most of the sites being exhausted.

Economy

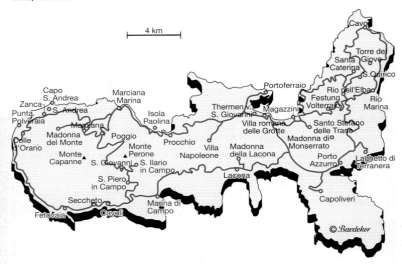

© Baedeker

Resort	Elba's mild and equable climate, its great scenic beauty and the excellent conditions for scuba diving off its cliff-fringed coast have drawn increasing numbers of visitors to the island in recent years.
History	Elba belonged to Pisa from the 11th c. onwards; then in 1284 it passed to Genoa, later to Lucca and in 1736 to Spain. After Napoleon's defeat in 1814 he was granted full sovereign rights over the island, and lived there from May 3rd 1814 to February 26th 1815. Elba was returned to the Grand Duchy of Tuscany by the Congress of Vienna.

Portoferraio

The chief place of the island, Portoferraio (10 m (33 ft); population 11,500), lies on a promontory on the west side of the entrance to a wide bay on the north coast. In the main street, Via Garibaldi, stands the Town Hall and a little way north-east, in Via Napoleone, the Misericordia church, in which a mass is said for Napoleon's soul on May 5th every year; it contains a reproduction of his coffin and a bronze cast of his death-mask. On the highest point in the town is the Piazza Napoleone, from which there are fine views. To the west rises Forte Falcone (79 m (261 ft)), to the east, above the lighthouse, Forte Stella (48 m (158 ft)), both originally built in 1548 and later completed by Napoleon. On the seaward side of the square is the simple Villa dei Molini, Napoleon's official residence, which contains his library.

Villa Napoleone	About 6 km (4 mi.) south-west of Portoferraio, set amid luxuriant vegetation on the slopes of the wooded Monte San Martino (370 m (1221 ft)), is situated the Villa Napoleone, the emperor's summer residence (fine views from terrace).
Pinacoteca Foresiana	Near the summer residence is a building which houses the Pinacoteca Foresiana, with works by Antonio Canova ("Galatea"), Guido Reni and Salvatore Rosa.

The island is dominated by the ruins of Volterraio castle

Drive through Elba

A road runs west from Portoferraio to the seaside resort of Procchio, in the bay of the same name, and the village of Marciana Marina (18 km (11 mi.)), another popular resort.

Procchio
Marciana Marina

About 4 km (2½ mi.) inland is the fort of Poggio (359 m (1185 ft)), and 4 km (2½ mi.) west of this the village of Marciana (375 m (1238 ft); ruined castle), a summer resort surrounded by centuries-old chestnut trees.

Poggio
Marciana

From here there is a cableway up Monte Capanne (1019 m (3363 ft)), the island's highest peak (views).

Monte Capanne

From Poggio there is an attractive walk up Monte Perone (630 m (2079 ft)), to the south-east (1 hour).

Monte Perone

On the east coast is Rio Marina (population 2500) with large open-cast iron workings.

Rio Marina

Picturesquely situated in a long inlet lies the little fishing port of Porto Azzurro (population 3000), which was fortified by the Spaniards in the 17th c.

Porto Azzurro

Worth visiting is the charming mining and wine producing village of Capoliveri, situated on a promontory in the south-east of the island.

Capoliveri

On the lonely south coast is the popular seaside resort of Marina di Campo, finely situated in the Golfo di Campo.

Marina di Campo

Region: Emilia-Romagna
Provinces: Bologna (BO), Ferrara (FE), Forli (FO), Modena (MO), Parma
(PR), Piacenza (PC), Ravenna (RA) and Reggio nell'Emilia (RE)
Area: 22,124 sq. km (8542 sq. mi.). Population: 3,947,000

Location

Emilia-Romagna, the south-eastern part of the north Italian plain occupies
the area extending from the River Po to the Apennines and then eastward
to the Adriatic coast.
It comprises the provinces of Bologna, Ferrara, Forli, Modena, Parma,
Piacenza, Ravenna and Reggio nell'Emilia.

Economy

The high fertility of the soil and the advantages of its situation in an area of
passage traversed by ancient traffic and trade routes between the Adriatic,
northern Italy and the Gulf of Genoa enabled this region, and particularly
the larger towns, to attain considerable prosperity from an early period.
Emilia-Romagna is still one of Italy's most highly developed regions. The
main elements in its agriculture are meat and dairy farming, tomatoes and
fruit, wine, sugar-beet, maize and rice. Its industries have an international
reputation – petro-chemicals, based on the recently developed resources
of oil and natural gas in the Po plain, engineering, car manufacture,
textiles, boots and shoes. On the Adriatic coast fisheries and the tourist
trade also make important contributions to the economy of the region.

History

Emilia, the western part of the region, derives its name from the Roman Via
Aemilia (now Via Emilia), a military road running from Rimini along the
south edge of the north Italian plain via Bologna, Parma and Piacenza to
Tortona which was built by the consul Marcus Aemilius Lepidus in 187 BC
to protect the Roman provinces north of the Apennines. After the Lombard
conquest of northern Italy the south-east part of the region, including Forli
and Ravenna, remained in Byzantine hands under the name of Romagna.

Touring

The modern Via Emilia is an attractive route, passing through a series of
important towns with much of interest to offer, such as Piacenza – Parma
– Reggio nell'Emilia – Modena – Bologna – and Forli (see entries).

Sights

★ Fidenza

Between Piacenza and Parma is Fidenza (72 m (236 ft); population 25,000),
the ancient Fidentia Iulia, which was known between 387 and 1927 as
Borgo San Donnino.

Cathedral

The fine cathedral is in Lombard Romanesque style (12th c.), with lion
doorways and statues of prophets on the unfinished façade. Inside, to
right of the entrance, there is a Romanesque holy-water stoup.

Salsomaggiore
Terme

About 10 km (6 mi.) south-west of Fidenza is Salsomaggiore Terme (165 m
541 ft); population 18,000), a spa attracting many visitors between March
and November, with springs (high iodine, bromine and salt content) which
are effective in the treatment of disorders of the joints, muscles, heart and
nerves.

Tabiano Bagni

5 km (3 mi.) east of Salsomaggiore Terme, it is a sulphur spa.

Cesena

See Forli, Surroundings

Enna   J20

Region: Sicilia. Province: Catania (CT)
Altitude: 931 m (3072 ft). Population: 30,000

The town of Enna, previously known as Castrogiovanni, reverted to its classical name in 1926. It is picturesquely situated on a horseshoe-shaped plateau in the Monti Erei, in the centre of Sicily, and has been aptly called the "belvedere" or the "navel" of the island.

Location

Sights

The main square, the Piazza Vittorio Emanuele, lies on the north side of the town, with the church and convent of San Francesco (15th c. campanile) and a terrace commanding fine views. From the smaller Piazza Crispi, to the west, there is a superb view of the little town of Calascibetta, 3 km (2 mi.) north-west. From the Piazza Vittorio Emanuele the south-east section of the town's main shopping street, Via Roma, passes the Theatre and the Town Hall and reaches the Piazza Mazzini.

Piazza Vittorio Emanuele

On the north side of the Piazza Mazzini stands the cathedral or Chiesa Madre (begun in 1307) which has a picturesque interior (14th c.), with four half-columns and eight full columns on bizarrely carved bases. Beyond the cathedral is the Museo Alessi, which houses the cathedral treasury containing Greco-Roman material and medieval paintings.

Cathedral

The Via Roma ends at the Castello di Lombardia, a huge pile, with three courtyards, which still preserves six of its original twenty towers. From the platform of the Torre Pisana there are magnificent views, particularly at sunset: to the east the towering mass of Etna, to the north the Monti Nebrodi and the Madonie range, to the south the Lago di Pergusa and, on clear days, the distant Mediterranean.

Castello di Lombardia

The south-east section of the Via Roma runs from the Piazza Vittorio Emanuele past the churches of San Cataldo and San Tommaso to the Giardino Pubblico, in the centre of which, on a hill, is the octagonal tower of a castle built by Frederick II of Aragon (c. 1300; fine views).

Enna to Caltagirone via Piazza Armerina (c. 70 km (43 mi.))

A fascinating excursion from Enna is via the Lago di Pergusa to Piazza Armerina (35 km (22 mi.); population 25,000), a town also known as Chiazza to the Sicilians, with a handsome cathedral and the Norman church of Sant'Andrea (1096; fine 12th–15th c. frescoes), 1 km (1/2 mi.) north.

Piazza Armerina

6 km (4 mi.) south of the Piazza Armerina is the site of the Villa Romana del Casale, a magnificent example of a Roman country house of the late Empire (3rd–4th c. AD; occupied until about 1200), with baths, a peristyle and a basilica. The villa is notable for its splendid series of mosaics, particularly in the Triclinium (dining room), that are among the largest and best of their kind.

★★**Villa Romana del Casale**

In the vicinity of the Piazza Armerina are other excavations of the ancient city of Morgantina, with a Greek theatre, extensive Agora and remains of a shrine, plus the town walls, 10 km (6 mi.) long.

★**Morgantina**

From Piazza Armerina it is well worth continuing south-west (32 km (20 mi.)) to visit Caltagirone (568 m (1874 ft); population 62,000), which is famous for its majolica and terracotta work. It has an interesting Museum of Ceramics.

Caltagirone

Caltanisetta

South-west of Enna is Caltanisetta (588 m (1940 ft); population 65,000), a provincial capital and the most important town in the interior of Sicily (sulphur mines). The main square of the town is the Piazza Garibaldi, in which are the cathedral (consecrated 1622; frescoes by Borremans, 1720;

Location
34 km (21 mi.) SW

splendid Maundy Thursday procession) and the Town Hall (Museo Civico). Beyond the Town Hall are the Law Courts, in Baroque style. From the Piazza Garibaldi the Corso Umberto I runs south into the Viale Regina Margherita, in which are the Palazzo del Governo and the Villa Amadeo gardens. In the east of the town are the disused church of Santa Maria degli Angeli (13th–14th c.) and the ruins of the Aragonese castle of Pietrarossa. On Monte San Giuliano (727 m (2399 ft); view), to the north of the town, stands a statue of Christ 18 m (59 ft) high.

★★Etna   J20

Region: Sicilia. Province: Catania (CT)

Location

Etna (3343 m (11,032 ft)), also called "Mongibello" (from the Italian *monte* and the Arabic *giaba,* mountain) lies in the east of the island of Sicily – close to the coast and north-west of Catania. It is Europe's largest active volcano and after the Alpine peaks the highest mountain in Italy. The area has been designated as a National Park.

Etna is one of the youngest geological features in Sicily and rises in the form of a truncated cone probably where an arm of the sea existed in Tertiary times. The almost circular base is 40 km (25 mi.) in diameter and 165 km (102 mi.) in circumference.

Flora

The upper slopes have only a meagre cover of vegetation; the porous rock allows water to sink down rapidly to lower levels, where it meets an impervious bed of rocks and emerges in many places as springs. Oranges and lemons are grown up to about 500 m (1650 ft), olives and vines to 1300 m (4290 ft). Above this are forest trees and macchia up to 2100 m (6930 ft), sometimes with recent lava flows cutting through them. The summit region up to the snow line is a dull black wasteland glistening in the sun.

Etna, Europe's largest volcano

View of the crater

There are more than one hundred known eruptions of Etna. The volcanic vents, more than 260 in number, are mostly on the flanks of the mountain. Major activity occurs at intervals of four to twelve years (the most recent eruption was in 1992).

Eruptions

On the south slope of Etna stands the solar power station "Eurhelios" (surface 6000 sq. m (64,586 sq. ft).

Eurhelios

Ascent of Etna

The little town of Nicolosi (698 m (2303 ft); population 3850) on the south side of Etna, is the starting point for the ascent to the subsidiary craters of the Monti Rossi (948 m (3128 ft); the climb takes 45 minutes to 1 hour; view). The walls of the crater show clear volcanic stratification; to the north-west, at the foot of the Monti Rossi, is the Grotta delle Palombe (lava cave).

Nicolosi

From Nicolosi the road runs first north-west and then north between lava flows and comes in 17 km (11 mi.) to the turning (1 km (¹/₂ mi.), left) to the Grande Albergo Etna and in another 1 km (¹/₂ mi.) to the Casa Cantoniera (roadman's house) which now houses the vulcanological and meteorological station of Catania University; nearby is the restaurant and Rifugio-Albergo G. Sapienza. Opposite the rifugio is the lower station of a cableway which is once again threatened by outbreaks of lava, and which only goes up to a little over 2600 m (8580 ft) (at present not in operation; ascent by cross-country vehicle). Observatory (2943 m (9712 ft)) destroyed in 1971.

Rifugio-Albergo G. Sapienza

The crater of Etna, which is filled with gases, is always changing its shape by eruptions. It is impossible to get very close to the crater. As Etna is never really inactive the area is declared dangerous to visitors; the climb leads through a rugged moonlike landscape.

Crater

Valle del Bove

South-east of the former observatory is the beginning of the Valle del Bove (Valley of the Ox), a black and desolate chasm (5 km (3 mi.) wide) surrounded on three sides by rock walls up to 1200 m (3960 ft) high.

Experienced climbers can go down (with guide) through the Valle del Bove to Zafferanda Etnea (600 m (1980 ft)).

Drive round Etna (c. 144 km (89 mi.)

A drive round Etna, starting from Catania also possible by rail), is very rewarding. The road runs via Misterbianco (213 m (703 ft); population 15,000), Paternò (225 m (743 ft); population 46,500) with a castle built by Roger I in 1073 (renovated 14th c.; well-preserved interior), towering above the town, to Adrano (588 m (1940 ft); population 34,000), beautifully situated on a lava plateau, with a Norman castle containing an Archaeological Museum and the convent of Santa Lucia, 15th–17th c.

About 9 km (5½ mi) south-west of Adrano, picturesquely situated on a steep hill above the Simeto valley, with a magnificent view of Etna, is the little town of Centuripe (730 m (2409 ft); population 6750), formerly Centorbi, with the so-called Castello di Corradino (1st c. BC). The Archaeological Museum contains finds from the ancient Siculan town of Centuripae which rose to importance in the late Hellenistic-Roman period and was destroyed by Frederick II in 1233 (interesting is the Hellenistic-Roman house "Contrada panneria", with paintings of the 2nd–1st c. BC).

From Adrano the road continues via Bronte (760 m (2508 ft); population 20,000), Maletto (960 m (3168 ft); old castle), Randazzo and Linguaglossa (600 m (1980 ft); population 4500) to Fiumefreddo (62 m (205 ft)). Then back to Catania on the motorway A18 or SS114.

Faenza   F7

Region: Emilia-Romagna. Province: Ravenna (RA)
Altitude: 35 m (116 ft). Population: 54,000

Location

Faenza lies in the Po plain between Bologna and Rimini – about 45 km (28 mi.) north-west of Bologna and 55 km (34 mi.) south-east of Rimini.

Economy

Faenza is famous for the faience (majolica) which is named after the town. The great age of this ware was in the 15th and 16th c., and it is only in recent years that the craft has again been practised and deliberately promoted. There are now at least 60 ceramic workshops in the town.

Sights

The town, still surrounded by its old town walls, suffered severe war damage, but this has been almost completely made good. The main street is the Corso Giuseppe Mazzini, at the east end of which are two elongated squares joining one another at right angles – the Piazza della Libertà to the north and the Piazza del Popolo to the south. In the Piazza della Libertà are the Torre dell'Orologio (Clock-Tower) and a beautiful fountain of 1621.

Cathedral

Notable is the cathedral (1474–1513) in Early Renaissance style, with the tomb of St Savinus (by Benedetto da Maiano; 1476) to the left of the high altar.

Town Hall

In the Piazza del Popolo are the Town Hall (left) and the Palazzo del Podestà (right; 1256), both with high arcades.

Pinacoteca
Museo Civico

In a palace in Via Santa Maria dell'Angelo are the Pinacoteca, with paintings by old masters of Emilia and Romagna (wooden statue of St Hiero-

Faenza is famous for its painted majolica (faience)

nymus by Donatello and his pupils) and the Museo Civico. A building in Corso Matteotti (No. 2) houses the modern department of the Museo Civico (Fattori, Signorini, Rodin, De Pisis, Morandi and others).

In Viale Baccarini we find the richly stocked Ceramic Museum (Museo delle Ceramiche), with majolica of the area and ceramics from all over the world.

★Museo delle Ceramiche

Fano   G–H8

Region: Marche. Province: Pesaro e Urbino (PS)
Altitude: 14 m (46 ft). Population: 53,000

Fano, the ancient Fanum Fortunae, built on the site of a temple of Fortuna, and now a popular seaside resort, lies on the Adriatic, south-east of Pesaro.

Location

Sights

Fano is still surrounded by its medieval walls and a deep moat. The central feature of the town is the Piazza XX Settembre, in which are the Palazzo della Ragione (built in 1299 and used since 1862 as a theatre) and the Torre Civica. On the south side of the square is the beautiful Fontana della Fortuna (1593).

★Palazzo della Ragione

181

The Palazzo Malatesta, at the north end of the square, is the municipal museum, and also contains a lapidarium, a coin collection and a small collection of pictures.

Cathedral

North-west of the Piazza XX Settembre is the Piazza Mercato, from which Via dell'Arco d'Augusto leads to the Romanesque cathedral of San Fortunato; inside are 16 frescoes by Domenicchino (1623).

★Arco di Augusto

Near the cathedral the triumphal triple Arch of Augustus (Arco di Augusto; 1st c.; still well-preserved) spans the street. The original form of the arch can be seen on the façade of the adjoining church of San Michele (Renaissance doorway).

Santa Maria Nuova

To the south of the Piazza XX Settembre stands the church of Santa Maria Nuova, which contains two pictures by Perugino, a "Sacra Conversazione" (3rd altar right: 1497) and an "Annunciation" (2nd altar left).

Ferrara   F6

Region: Emilia-Romagna. Province: Ferrara (FE)
Altitude: 9 m (30 ft). Population: 138,000

Location

Ferrara, capital of the province of the same name, lies 5 km (3 mi.) south of the River Po in the fertile north Italian plain. The distance from Ferrara to the Adriatic coast is about 50 km (31 mi.). There are good roads linking Ferrara to Bologna, Ravenna, Padua and Venice.

Ferrara, see of an archbishop, and with a small university, was once the splendid capital of the dukes of Este and an important trading centre. Its wide streets, forbidding castle and sumptuous Renaissance palaces still bear witness to the great days of its past. The Old Town of Ferrara was recently included in the UNESCO List of World Cultural Heritage Sites.

History

The town first appears in the records at the time of the Great Migration. In 1332 it fell into the hands of the Este family, one of the oldest noble houses in Italy (961–1598), which reached its period of greatest splendour in the 16th c. Ariosto (1474–1533), the greatest Italian poet of the day, and the poet Torquato Tasso (1544–95) lived at the brilliant Renaissance court. Girolamo Savonarola was born in Ferrara in 1452. In 1598 the town was incorporated in the Papal State and in 1860 it was united with the Kingdom of Italy.

Town centre

★Castello Estense

In the centre of the town is the picturesque Castello Estense, the four-towered moated castle of the Este family, begun in 1385 and partly rebuilt after 1554. The castle contains frescoes by pupils of Dosso Dossi (1489/90–1542). The roof gardens are also open to visitors.

Piazza Savonarola

South of the Castello is the Piazza Savonarola, with a monument to Savonarola, the great preacher and reformer. Here, too, we find the Palazzo Comunale, once the palace of the dukes of Este (originally built in 1243, rebuilt in the 14/15th c.), with a façade of 1924.

★Cathedral

A little way south-east of the Castello rises the cathedral, with a magnificent façade in Lombard Romanesque style (12th–14th c.); it contains pictures by artists of the Ferrara school; near the altar are two 15th c. bronze statues (St Maurelius and St Georg); in the transept are busts of the apostles, and a very fine painting of "Mary with the Saints". Over the narthex is the Cathedral Museum, with pictures and sculptures, including the "Madonna del Melograno" by Jacopo della Quercia, as well as a Dutch tapestry by J. Karcher, based on drawings by G. Filippi and Garafola.

The Castello Estense in the centre of Ferrara

About 500 m south-east of the cathedral stands the church of San Francesco, a brick-built Early Renaissance building (15th c.) roofed with a series of domes. Immediately east is the University (founded 1391).

San Francesco

Sights in the south

Farther south-east, in Via Scandiana, is the Palazzo Schifanoia (late 14th c.; remodelled in 1466–93), an Este summer residence, now incorporating the Municipal Museum (Museo Civico), with miniatures, medals and fine frescoes by Francesco del Cossa and his pupils (c. 1470).

Municipal Museum

About 500 m south of the Palazzo Schifanoia is the Palazzo di Ludovico il Moro (16th c.; unfinished), with a beautiful courtyard and fine frescoes, early examples of trompe-l'oeil painting (c. 1500). It now houses the Archaeological Museum (Museo Civico d'Arte Antica), which has a splendid collection of vases and other finds from the Greek-Etruscan necropolis of Spina, near Comacchio (see Surroundings).

Archaeological Museum

South-west of San Francesco, in Via delle Scienze (No. 17), is the Palazzo del Paradiso, occupied from 1586 to 1962 by the university and now by the Biblioteca Comunale Ariostea, with Ariosto's tomb and some of his manuscripts.

Biblioteca Comunale Ariostea

Sights in the north

In the north of the town, at the intersection of Corso Ercole I d'Este with Corso Rosetti/Corso di Porta Mare, are two fine palaces. On the north-west corner is the Palazzo Sacrati or Prosperi (c. 1500), with a fine doorway.

Palaces

Opposite, to the south, is the Palazzo dei Diamanti, a superb example of Early Renaissance architecture (1492–1567) which takes its name from the

National Gallery

The impressive Romanesque cathedral in Ferrara

Idyllic lagoons in the Valli di Comacchio

faceted stones of its façade. It now contains the National Gallery, with works by 15th–16th c. painters of the Ferrara school.

About 500 m north-west, at Via Ariosto 65, is the house in which Ariosto lived; on the first floor is the room where the poet died.

Ariosto's house

Farther north-east is the Certosa, a former Carthusian house founded in 1452 and dissolved in 1796, now a cemetery; here also is a fine 15th–16th c. church.

Certosa

From the Certosa it is only a few steps to the building complex of the Palazzo Massari-Palazzina Cavalieri di Malta, which houses the Boldini Museum (Museo Boldini e dell'Ottocento Ferrarese) and works by other painters of Ferrara. Boldini (1842–1931) painted portraits and scenes of the Parisian street-life.

Boldini Museum

The Palazzo Massari contains the Municipal Collection of Contemporary Art (Civica Galleria d'Arte Moderna).

Art Collection

Surroundings

Comacchio (population 21,500), a picturesquely situated town, is the centre of the Valli di Comacchio, which consists of thirteen islands connected by canals. Near Comacchio is the site of two cemeteries of the Greek-Roman port of Spina (4th–3rd c. BC).

Comacchio
57 km (35 mi.) SE

North of Comacchio lies the Benedictine abbey of Santa Maria di Pomposa (founded in the 7th c.), of importance during the Middle Ages but abandoned in the 17th c. because of the prevalent malaria. The church, built in the 8th–9th c. and enlarged in the 10th–11th c., has an impressive atrium and a 48 m (158 ft) campanile; inside are a mosaic floor and 14th c. frescoes. Near the church are the chapter-house with well-preserved frescoes, the refectory (c. 1420) and the Palazzo della Ragione (now a college of agriculture).

★Abbazia Santa Maria di Pomposa

★★Florence

F8

Region: Toscana. Province: Firenze (FI)
Altitude: 50 m (165 ft). Population: 436,000

Much of the centre of Florence is barred to cars. Visitors are permitted to drive to their hotel and unload their luggage, but must then remove their vehicle from the prohibited zone.

Advice

Florence (in Italian Firenze), the old capital of Tuscany, called "la Bella", and now a provincial capital, a university town and the see of an archbishop, is picturesquely situated on both sides of the River Arno, surrounded by foothills of the Apennines.

Location

While in ancient times the life of Italy was centred on Rome, from the Middle Ages to our own day Florence has been its intellectual centre. Here the Italian language and Italian literature were created, and here Italian art attained its finest form. With its astonishing abundance of art treasures, its historical associations and its beautiful surroundings, Florence is one of the world's greatest tourist centres.

Art treasures

The Etruscan and Roman town of Florentina played no great part in history. At the beginning of the 13th c. the fortunes of war and the industry of its people (wool, silk) made it the leading town in Central Italy, but the ruling noble families were weakened by continual internecine strife between

History

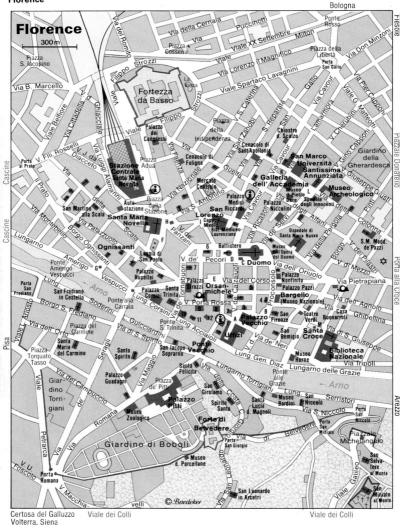

Florence

300 m

A Piazza della Signoria
B Piazza San Firenze
C Piazza del Duomo
D Piazza San Giovanni
E Piazza della Repubblica·
F Piazza Santa Maria Novella
G Piazza Ognissanti

H Piazza dell' Unità Italiana
I Piazza Madonna degli
  Aldobrandini
K Piazza San Marco
L Piazza della Santissima
  Annunziata
M Piazza Santa Croce

1 Loggia dei Lanzi
2 Palazzo Fenzi
3 Palazzo Uguccione
4 Badia Fiorentina
5 Casa di Dante
6 Santa Maria
  Maggiore

7 San Gaetano
8 Mercato Nuovo
9 Palazzo Davanzati
10 Palazzo Spini-Ferroni
11 Santi Apostoli
12 Palazzo di Parte
   Guelfa

Guelfs (followers of the Pope) and Ghibelines (followers of the Hohenstaufens). The town's craft guilds grew steadily in strength and in 1282 their
leaders, the priori (convenors) gained control of the city's government.

In 1434 power fell into the hands of the wealthy merchant family of the
Medici, whose leading members Cosimo (1434–64), the "father of his
country" (pater patriae), and Lorenzo the Magnificent (1469–92), brought
the republic to its greatest prosperity and made it a brilliant centre of art
and learning. In 1494 the Medici were driven out, and four years later, in
1498, the great preacher and reformer Girolamo Savonarola was burned
at the stake in the Piazza della Signoria. In 1512 the Medici returned
to Florence under the protection of Spanish troops, but in 1527 they
were again expelled. Only three years later, however, after the capture of
the town by Charles V (1530), Alessandro de'Medici was installed as
hereditary duke. After his murder in 1537 he was succeeded by Cosimo I,
who became Grand Duke of Tuscany in 1569.

After the house of Medici became extinct in 1737 the Grand Duchy
passed to the house of Lorraine, which held it, with an interruption during
the Napoleonic period (1810–14), until 1860. Tuscany then became part of
the kingdom of Italy, and Florence enjoyed a fresh period of prosperity as
temporary capital of the new kingdom (1865–70).

The city did not suffer much during the Second World War, except for
the destruction of the bridges across the River Arno, which were blown up
by the Germans, but the most beautiful one, the Ponte Vecchio, was not
damaged and the other bridges have been rebuilt in their original style. In
November 1966 flooding of the River Arno caused severe damage to
many historic buildings and the flood cost many lives.

In literature Florence is associated with Dante Alighieri (1266–1321), author   Literature
of the "Divine Comedy" and creator of the Italian literary language;
Giovanni Boccaccio (1313–75), whose "Decameron" provided the model
for Italian prose; and Francesco Petrarca (Petrarch), who played a major
part in preparing the way for humanism.

From the end of the 13th c. Florence played a leading part in the develop-   Art
ment of art. Arnolfo di Cambio (d. 1302), the great forerunner of the
architects of the Renaissance, worked on Santa Croce and the cathedral,
and Giotto (1266–1337), father of modern painting, began his career here.
Among his principal pupils were Taddeo Gaddi (d. 1366) and Orcagna
(d. 1368), also noted as a sculptor.

The year 1402 can be regarded as marking the beginning of the
Renaissance (competition for the north door of the Baptistery), although
in architecture the new spirit did not find full expression until 20 years
later. Filippo Brunelleschi (1377–1446) applied his knowledge of ancient
architecture to meet new requirements, and was followed by Leon Battista
Albert (1404–72).

The sculptors of the Florentine Renaissance included Lorenzo Ghiberti
(1378–1455), Luca della Robbia (1400–82), noted for his glazed terracotta
reliefs, and above all Donatello (1386–1466), the greatest master of the
century. After Donatello's death the leading sculptor was Andrea
Verrocchio (1436–88), also noted as a painter.

The pioneers of Renaissance painting were Masaccio (1401–28), Andrea
del Castagno (1423–65) and Paolo Uccello (1397–1475). Outstanding in
fervour of religious feeling was Fra Angelico da Fiesole (1387–1455), who
influenced Fra Filippo Lippi (1406–69) and Benozzo Gozzoli (1420–97). The
zenith of the Florentine Early Renaissance was reached in the work of
Andrea Verrocchio, the brothers Antonio and Piero del Pollaiuolo (1429–98,
1443–c. 1495), Sandro Botticelli (1444–1510), Fra Filippo's son Filippino
Lippi (c. 1459–1504) and Domenico Ghirlandaio (1449–94). Of the three
great masters of Italian art the Tuscans Leonardo da Vinci and Michelangelo received their training in Florence, and here too Raphael shook off
the trammels of his earlier years; from 1506 all three were working in
Florence. About the same time Lorenzo di Credi (1459–1537), Piero di

View of Florence with the cathedral and the Palazzo Vecchio

Cosimo (1462–1521), Fra Bartolomeo (1472–1517) and the talented colourist Andrea del Sarto (1486–1531) were also working in Florence, as were Franciabigio and Pontormo. Among painters of a slightly later period were Agnolo Bronzino (1503–72), Alessandro Allori (1535–1607) and Giorgio Vasari (1511–74), noted for his "Lives of the Artists". Leading sculptors of this period were Benvenuto Cellini (1500–71), also famous as a goldsmith, and Giovanni Bologne (c. 1524–1608; actually Jean Boulogne Duai).

★★Piazza della Signoria

The old centre of Florentine life is the Piazza della Signoria, the former forum of the Republic which has had its present form since 1386. The Palazzo Vecchio and the Loggia dei Lanzi are the dominating buildings on the south side of the square.

The Palazzo Vecchio (old palace), the Town Hall, a castle-like building with a 94 m (310 ft) tower, was built for the Signoria between 1298 and 1314 as Palazzo dei Priori – probably in accordance with a plan by Arnolfo di Cambio – and extended to the rear in the 16th c.

★★Palazzo Vecchio

To the left of the entrance can be seen a modern copy of Michelangelo's "David" (original in Galleria dell'Accademia); in the outer courtyard (remodelled 1454) is a copy (original on second floor) of the "Boy with a Fish" by Andrea del Verocchio.

On the first floor the Salone dei Cinquecento (1495) houses Michelangelo's marble group "Triumph of Virtue over Vice" (c. 1520). The state apartments (Quartieri Monumentali) are on the first and second floors.

◀ *Florence: the impressive Cathedral*

Magnificent pillars in the inner courtyard of the Palazzo Vecchio

The Neptune Fountain in the Piazza della Signoria

At the north-west corner of the palazzo in front of the Neptune Fountain (Fontana del Nettuno; 1563–75) is a stone slab marking the spot where Savonarola was burned at the stake.

Fontana del Nettuno

Adjoining the Palazzo Vecchio is the Loggia dei Lanzi (originally Loggia dei Signori; 1376–82), an open hall designed for addressing the people, named after Cosimo I's German pikemen. In the loggia are a number of sculptures, including Giovanni da Bologna's marble group "Rape of the Sabine Women" (1583) and Benvenuto Cellini's bronze "Perseus with the Medusa's Head" (1553).

★Loggia dei Lanzi

On the east side of Piazza della Signoria is the former chamber of commerce (Mercanzia; 1359); to the north the 16th c. Palazzo Uguccioni; at the west side of the square the Palazzo Fenzi (1871), an imitation of the early Florentine palaces.

Palazzi

From the Piazza della Signoria the busy Via del Calzaiuoli ("Street of the Hosiers") runs north to the Piazza del Duomo.

Via del Calzaiuoli

At the junction of the Via de'Lamberti, on the left, stands the mighty three-storeyed church of Orsanmichele (Or San Michele), built in 1284–91 as a corn exchange, and rebuilt 1337–1404. The exterior is decorated with important pictures by Verrocchio, Ghiberti, Donatello and others.

★Orsanmichele

A little way north-east of the Piazza della Signoria, in Piazza San Firenze, stands the fortress-like Palazzo del Podestà commonly known as the Bargello, which was the headquarters of the chief of police (bargello) and a prison. Since 1865 the building has housed the Museo Nazionale del Bargello, devoted to the history of Italian culture and modern times, with an excellent collection of Florentine Renaissance sculpture. The courtyard with its pillared hall, a fine flight of steps and walls decorated with coats of arms, is a fine example of a medieval castle courtyard.

★★Museo Nazionale del Bargello

Opposite the Bargello, to the west, is the Badia Florentina, an old Benedictine abbey, founded in 978, with a delicate pointed campanile.

Badia Florentina

At the south-east side of the Piazza Firenze stands the Baroque building complex of San Firenze; the church was rebuilt in 1633–48.

San Firenze

Via Dante Alighieri, to the north of the Bargello, leads to the so-called houses of Alighieri (Case degli Alighieri); it is assumed that Dante was born in one of them. The house No. 4 is called Casa di Dante and contains a Dante Museum.

Casa di Dante (Dante Museum)

★★Uffizi

South of the Palazzo Vecchio and the Loggia dei Lanzi, extending towards the Arno, stands the Palazzo degli Uffizi, built in 1560–74 by Vasari. Today it houses the Galleria degli Uffizi (Uffizi for short), the world-famed art collection, founded by the Medici, the former rulers of Florence and the Grand Dukes of Tuscany. Gradually it became the most important art collection in Italy and one of the greatest in the world, with some 4000 pictures. They provide an almost complete survey of Florentine painting and also include major works by north Italian, particularly Venetian, painters, as well as outstanding pictures by Dutch and old German masters including ancient paintings. There are also valuable sculptures, as well as tapestries, drawings, jewellery, weapons, scientific instruments and archaeological finds.

Palazzo degli Uffizi

From the Uffizi the Vasari corridor (Corridoio del Vasari or Vasariano), with an interesting gallery of self-portraits, leads across the Ponte Vecchio to the Palazzo Pitti (see page 198).

Corridoio del Vasari

Florence/Firenze

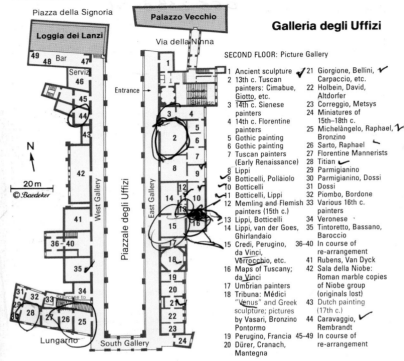

Piazza della Signoria

Palazzo Vecchio

Loggia dei Lanzi

Via della Ninna

Galleria degli Uffizi

SECOND FLOOR: Picture Gallery

1 Ancient sculpture
2 13th c. Tuscan painters: Cimabue, Giotto, etc.
3 14th c. Sienese painters
4 14th c. Florentine painters
5 Gothic painting
6 Gothic painting
7 Tuscan painters (Early Renaissance)
8 Lippi
9 Botticelli, Pollàiolo
10 Botticelli
11 Botticelli, Lippi
12 Memling and Flemish painters (15th c.)
13 Lippi, Botticelli
14 Lippi, van der Goes, Ghirlandaio
15 Credi, Perugino, da Vinci, Verrocchio, etc.
16 Maps of Tuscany; da Vinci
17 Umbrian painters
18 Tribuna: Médici "Venus" and Greek sculpture; pictures by Vasari, Bronzino Pontormo
19 Perugino, Francia
20 Dürer, Cranach, Mantegna
21 Giorgione, Bellini, Carpaccio, etc.
22 Holbein, David, Altdorfer
23 Correggio, Metsys
24 Miniatures of 15th–18th c.
25 Michelàngelo, Raphael, Bronzino
26 Sarto, Raphael
27 Florentine Mannerists
28 Titian
29 Parmigianino
30 Parmigianino, Dossi
31 Dossi
32 Piombo, Bordone
33 Various 16th c. painters
34 Veronese
35 Tintoretto, Bassano, Baroccio
36–40 In course of re-arrangement
41 Rubens, Van Dyck
42 Sala della Niobe: Roman marble copies of Niobe group (originals lost)
43 Dutch painting (17th c.)
44 Caravaggio, Rembrandt
45–49 In course of re-arrangement

FIRST FLOOR: Copper engravings

★★Piazza del Duomo

Squares — The Via de' Calzaiuoli runs from the north end of the Piazza della Signoria to the Piazza del Duomo (on the right) with the cathedral and the campanile; to the left is the Piazza San Giovanni with the Baptistery.

Misericordia — Immediately on the right, at the corner of the cathedral square, is the Oratory of the Misericordia, a charitable fraternity which succoured the poor and the sick and buried the dead.

Loggia del Bigallo — To the left, at the corner of Piazza di San Giovanni, we find the Gothic Loggia del Bigallo, which was built in 1352–58.

★★Baptistery — In the centre of the Piazza San Giovanni is the Baptistery (Battisterio San Giovanni), an octagonal structure which was probably founded on the remains of a Roman building and was rebuilt in the 11th–13th c., when it was clad externally and internally with variegated marble.

★★Bronze doors — It is famous for the three gilded bronze doors with relief decoration (the original gilding was uncovered in 1948): the south door by Andrea Pisano (1330–36), the north door (1403–24) and the principal door facing the cathedral (1425–52), the Porta del Paradiso ("Gate of Paradise") by Lorenzo Ghiberti.

In the interior are superb mosaics by several Florentine artists of the 13th c.

Piazza del Duomo

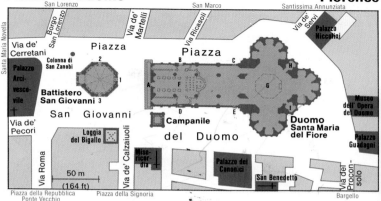

BAPTISTERY
1 East Doorway
(Porta del Paradiso)
2 North Doorway
3 South Doorway (entrance)

CATHEDRAL
A Portale Maggiore
B Porta dei Cornacchini
C Porta della Mandorla
D Porta del Campanile

E Porta dei Canónici
F Santa Reparata (Crypt)
G Dome
H Old Sacristy
I New Sacristy

The Florentine Cathedral (Cattedrale di Santa Maria del Fiore, so called after the lily which is the emblem of Florence), a mighty Gothic building, was begun by Arnolfo di Cambio in 1296, continued by Francesco Talenti from 1357 onwards and consecrated in 1436. The octagonal dome (1420–34) is Filippo Brunelleschi's master-work. The building, clad externally with variegated marble, is 169 m (554 ft) long, the width of the crossed wings is 104 m (341 ft), the height of the dome is 91 m (300 ft); to the top of the lantern (finished 1461) it is 107 m (353 ft). The façade dates only from 1875 to 1887.

★★Florentine Cathedral

The spacious interior is dominated by the strict Gothic forms and impresses with its bareness.

Steps lead down to the old cathedral of Santa Reparata (4th–5th c.), which has been excavated since 1965.

Santa Reparata

It is well worth the trouble of climbing up to the dome as the view is even more magnificent than from the campanile.

Dome

The quadrangular campanile (82 m (271 ft)) high; begun in 1334 by Giotto and finished in 1387), faced with coloured marble, is one of the finest in Italy. There is sculpture by Donatello and his assistant Rosso (1420) and by Andrea Pisano and Luca della Robbia (1437).

Campanile

The entrance to the Cathedral Museum (Museo dell'Opera del Duomo) is opposite the choir of the cathedral, in the courtyard of the house No. 9 (on the right). It contains art from the cathedral and the baptistery, among which the choir gallery with the famous relief of children by Lucca del Robbia and Donatello.

★Cathedral Museum

A little way south-east of the cathedral square, in Via del Proconsolo are two fine palaces, No. 2 the imposing Palazzo Nonfinito ("unfinished palace"; 1592) which since 1869 has housed the Museum of Ethnology

Museum of Ethnology

Florence

Detail from the bronze doors of the Baptistery

(Museo Nazionale di Antropologia ed Etnologia), and No. 10 the Palazzo dei Pazzi dating from 1470, a building with interesting architectural detail.

Town centre

Centro	The area south-west of the cathedral, the so-called Centro (centre) was modernised at the end of the 19th c.
Piazza della Repubblica	The town's traffic centre, the scene of lively activity, particularly in the evening, is the Piazza della Repubblica.
Mercanto Nuovo	From the south-east corner of the square Via Calimara runs south to the Mercanto Nuovo (new market), a loggia-like building dating from 1547–51, at present a craft market (hand embroidery, etc.).
Museo della Casa Fiorentina Antica	In the Piazza Davanzati stands the mighty 14th c. Palazzo Davanzati with the Museo della Casa Florentina Antica (Museum of the Florentine House), which provides a good impression of Florentine everyday life in the Middle Ages.
Via de' Tornabuoni	At the west side of the Centro is the busy Via de' Tornabuoni with its fine palaces and elegant shops.
★Palazzo Strozzi	Particularly interesting is the Palazzo Strozzi, a magnificent example of Florentine palace architecture, built in 1489–1536, with an interesting courtyard by Cronaca. On the façade there are fine wrought-iron lanterns, torch holders and rings. In the palace temporary art exhibitions are held.
Santa Trinità	In Via de' Tornabuoni to the south stands the church of Santa Trinità, originally one of the oldest Gothic churches in Italy, rebuilt in the 13th–15th c. with a façade of 1593.

Opposite the church to the south-west, on the banks of the River Arno, stands the Palazzo Spini-Ferroni, built in 1289 and restored in 1874, the largest medieval palace in Florence.

Palazzo Spini-Ferroni

North-west behind the church of Santa Trinità, between Via del Parioni and the River Arno (Lungarno Corsini), stands the 17th c. Palazzo Corsini, with a privately owned art collection.

Palazzo Corsini

From Palazzo Strozzi Via della Vigna Nuova runs west to the Palazzo Rucellai (erected in 1446–51), one of the finest Florentine Renaissance palaces.

Palazzo Rucellai

Near the Palazzo Rucellai is the old church of San Pancrazio which houses a museum, with work of the painter and sculptor Marino Marini (1901–80; 176 pictures, sculptures and other work). Marini's fame is based on his horse and rider compositions.

Marini Museum

*Piazza di Santa Maria Novella

To the north-west of the town centre is the spacious Piazza di Santa Maria Novella with the Loggia Di San Paolo (1489–96) and two obelisks, which served in the past as the finishing-post in chariot races.

On the north side of the square stands the Dominican church of Santa Maria Novella, a Gothic building (1278–1350) with an inlaid marble façade and a Renaissance doorway. In the choir are frescoes which rank as Domenico Ghirlandaio's finest work.

*Santa Maria Novella

To the left of the church is the entrance to the cloisters (Chiostri monumentali di Santa Maria Novella); on the north side of the "Green Cloister" we find the former chapter-house, known as the Cappellone degli Spagnoli (Spanish chapel; c. 1355).

Cloisters

North-west of Santa Maria Novella is the Piazza della Stazione (station square) with the Stazione Centrale di Santa Maria Novella (1935), Florence's central station.

Stazione Centrale

South-west of Santa Maria Novella in Piazza Ognissanti which leads to the Arno, stands the church of Ognissanti, one of the first Baroque churches in the town (originally 13th c.; rebuilt in the 16th and 17th c.); inside there are fine frescoes by Botticelli (St Augustinus) and Ghirlandaio (St Hieronymus).

Ognissanti

From the Piazza dell'Unità Italiana, on the east side of Santa Maria Novella, the short Via del Melarancio leads east to the church of San Lorenzo, originally consecrated by St Ambrose in 393 as Florence's first cathedral (rebuilt in Romanesque style in the 11th c.). The present building, in the form of an early Christian basilica with columns, was re-erected in 1421 by Brunelleschi and his successors. The inside wall of the façade is by Michelangelo. In the north transept is the Old Sacristy (by Brunelleschi, 1421–28), an early work of Renaissance architecture, with sculpture by Donatello. Adjoining the church to the left is an idyllic cloister with a double-columned hall.

*San Lorenzo

North-west from the cloister a staircase leads up to the Biblioteca Mediceo Laurenziana (in a 16th c. building), which was founded in 1444 by Cosimo the Elder, with several thousand manuscripts of Greek and Latin classical authors collected by the Medici.

Biblioteca Mediceo Laurenziana

Behind the church of San Lorenzo, in the Piazza Madonna degli Aldobrandini, is the entrance to the Medici Chapels (Capelle Medicee). From the

*Medici Chapels

crypt a staircase leads up to the Chapel of the Princes (Capella dei Principi), decorated with fine stone mosaics, which was built in 1604–10 to house the sarcophagi of the Grand Dukes of Tuscany.

★New Sacristy

On the left a passage leads to the New Sacristy (Sagrestia Nuova), a square, domed edifice, built by Michelangelo (1520–24) as the mausoleum of the Medici family. It contains the tombs of a son and grandson of Lorenzo the Magnificent.

★Palazzo Medici-Riccardi

At the north-east corner of the Piazza San Lorenzo rises the massive Palazzo Medici-Riccardi, which was built for Cosimo the Elder in 1444–52 and extended in the 17th and 18th c.

Medici Museum

In the courtyard is the entrance to the chapel, with fine frescos by Benozzo Gozzoli (c. 1460), and to the Medici Museum (Museo Medicco) with relics of the Medici family who occupied the palace until 1537.

★Museo di San Marco

From the east side of the Medici Palace Via Cavour runs north-east to the Piazza San Marco, in which are the church of San Marco and the monastery of San Marco, now the Museo di San Marco, rebuilt in the 15th c. for the Dominicans, with notable frescos by Fra Angelico da Fiesole.

★Galleria dell'Accademia

South of San Marco, at Via Ricasoli 52, is the Accademia di Belle Arti (Art Academy), with the Galleria dell'Accademia, a study collection which supplements the Uffizi and the Galleria Pitti (13th–16th c. Tuscan painting). Its most notable feature is the famous David ("il Gigante"), carved from a single block of stone by the youthful Michelangelo (1501–03; copies in the Piazza della Signoria and the Piazzale Michelangelo).

★Santissima Annunziata

From the Piazza San Marco the Via Cesare Battisti runs past the former university to the magnificent church of the Santissima Annunziata (originally 1250, remodelled 1444–60; entrance replaced 1601). The forecourt contains frescos by Andrea de Sarto (1505–14) which rank among the finest achievement of the Florentine High Renaissance.

The interior of the church is partly Baroque. Beyond the door, leading from the north transept into the cloister (Chiostro dei Morti) is a fresco by Andrea del Sarto ("Madonna del Sacco", 1525), one of his late masterpieces.

Spedale degli Innocenti

To the east, opposite the church, is the foundling hospital of Spedale degli Innocenti, an early example of Renaissance architecture, begun in 1419 by Brunelleschi. Between the arches are coloured medallions with infants in swaddling clothes by Andrea della Robbia (c. 1463).

Archaeological Museum

South-east of the Santissima Annunziata stands the Palazzo della Crocetta (1620) which houses the Museo Archeologico Centrale dell'Etruria (entrance Via della Colonna No. 38), the Archaeological Museum founded in 1870, with a fine collection of Etruscan and Greco-Roman material and a notable Egyptian collection.

★Santa Croce

On the south-east side of the old town, near the Arno, we find the church of Santa Croce, a Franciscan church begun in 1295 but not completed until 1442, with a façade of 1857–63. The spacious interior contains the tombs of many famous Italians, including Michelangelo, Alfieri, Macchiavelli, Rossini, Cherubini and Galileo. Notable are the remains of the frescos in the choir chapels by Giotto and his pupils and the magnificent marble pulpit by Benedetto da Maiano (1472–76).

★Pazzi Chapel Cloisters

On the far side of the first cloister is the Pazzi Chapel (Cappella de' Pazzi; by Brunelleschi, 1430), an early work of the Renaissance; to the left on the façade are Arno high-water level marks (November 4th 1966: 4.9 m (16 ft). The second cloister (Secondo Chiostro) is one of the finest examples of the Early Renaissance.

Adjoining the first cloister, to the south, is the former refectory, which houses the rich Church Museum (Museo dell' Opera di Santa Croce).

Adjoining the church of Santa Croce to the south, is the building complex of the National Library (Biblioteca Nazionale Centrale, 1911–35). It is one of the largest and most important libraries in Italy, with more than four million volumes, among which are precious manuscripts, incunabula, musical compositions, atlases and geographical maps.

A little way north of Santa Croce, in Via Ghibellina 70, is the Casa Buonarotti which Michelangelo bought for his nephew Leonardo di Buonarotti, whose son furnished it and turned it into a memorial to Michelangelo in 1620. The museum contains early work by the master as well as copies of his work, also drawings, manuscripts, pictures and other relics.

About 200 m west of the Central Library, at the end of Corso de' Tintori (Via de Benci 6), is the Museo della Fondazione Horne. This museum is based on the gift of the British art critic Herbert Percy Horne (1864–1916) and contains a valuable collection of pictures, drawings, sculpture and furniture, as well as ornaments and utensils of the 14th–16h centuries.

Only a few steps south of the Museo Horne the Ponte alle Grazie (fine views) leads to the northern bank of the Arno.

Some 200 m south-west of the Piazza della Signoria the narrowest part of the Arno is spanned by the Ponte Vecchio (old bridge), the oldest of the bridges, leading to the southern bank. The bridge was so wide that arcades were built on both sides; soon apartments and shops appeared (butchers were able to throw their waste into the river). By the end of the 16th c. Grand Duke Ferdinand I decreed that only goldsmiths' shops were to be allowed on the bridge, a regulation which is still in force today.

Ponte Vecchio, the "Old Bridge" across the Arno, famous for its goldsmiths' workshops

Florence

★★Palazzo Pitti

South-west of the Ponte Vecchio, at the foot of the Boboli hill, stands the imposing square building of the Palazzo Pitti, begun by Luca Pitti c. 1458 and extended in the 16th–18th c.

★★Galleria Palatina

In the left-hand half of the first floor the famous Pitti Gallery (Galleria Palatina), founded by the Medici in the 16th and 17th c., now contains hundreds of pictures, including masterpieces by Raphael, Fra Bartolommeo, Andrea del Sarto and Titian. Adjoining the gallery are ten of the former Royal Apartments (Appartamenti Reali; 18th–19th c.).

Carriage Museum

On the ground floor is the Silver Chamber, with silver and gold work as well as other precious objects which belonged to the Medici. There is also a Carriage Museum (Museo delle Carrozza), with carriages of the Duca di Modena, Francescos II and King Ferdinand of Naples.

Gallery of Modern Art

On the second floor the Gallery of Modern Art (Galleria d'Arte Moderna) contains 19th and 20th c. works, mostly by Tuscan artists, and also present-day sculpture.

Costume Gallery

The Palazzina della Meridiana contains an interesting costume gallery.

★Boboli Gardens

To the south of the Palazzo Pitti extend the Boboli Gardens (Giardino di Boboli; 4.5 ha (11 acres). The beautiful park, decorated with fountains and

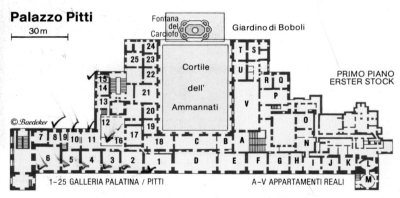

Palazzo Pitti

30 m

© Baedeker

Fontana del Carciofo

Giardino di Boboli

Cortile dell' Ammannati

PRIMO PIANO
ERSTER STOCK

1–25 GALLERIA PALATINA / PITTI   A–V APPARTAMENTI REALI

1 Sala di Venere
  Tizian, Tintoretto
2 Sala di Apollo
  Van Dyck, Rubens,
  Reni, del Sarto,
  Tizian, Tintoretto
3 Sala di Marte
  Tintoretto, Reni,
  Tizian, Rubens,
  Murillo, Veronese
4 Sala di Giove
  Raffael, Bordone,
  Rubens, del Sarto,
  Perugino, Guercino
5 Sala di Saturno
  Raffael, Perugino,
  Ghirlandaio
6 Sala dell'Iliade
  Velázquez, Raffael

7 Sala della Stufa
  Fresken von
  Rosselli, Cortona
8 Sala dell'Educa-
  zione di Giove
  Caravaggio, Allori
9 Bagno di Napoleone
10 Sala di Ulisse
  Raffael, Reni, Lippi
11 Sala di Prometeo
  Signorelli, Lippi,
  Botticelli, Reni
12 Corridoio d. Colonne
13 Sala della Giustizia
  Veronese, Tizian
14 Sala di Flora
  Canova, Bronzino
15 Sala dei Putti
  Jordaens, Rubens

16 Galleria Poccetti
  Pontormo, Rubens,
  Ribera, Dughet
17 Sala della Musica
18 Sala Castagnoli
19 Sala delle Allegorie
20 Sala delle Belle Arti
21 Salone d'Ercole
22 Sala dell'Aurora
23 Sala di Berenice
24 Sala di Psiche
25 Sala della Fama

A Vestibolo
B Sala degli Staffieri
C Galleria delle Statue
D Sala delle Nicchie
E Sala verde
F Sala del trono

G Sala celeste
H Cappella
I Sala dei pappagalli
J Sala gialla
K Camera da letto
L Gabinetto da
  toletta
M Sala da musica
  e da lavoro
N Camera da letto
O Salotto di
  ricevimento
P Sala di Bona
Q Sala della Temperanza
R Sala della Prudenza
S Sala della Giustizia
T Sala della Carità
U Sala della Speranza
V Sala da ballo

The Sala dell'Iliade in the Palazzo Pitti

statues extends up a slope and from the terraces there are attractive views of Florence.

The Casino del Cavaliere houses a fine Porcelain Museum.

Porcelain Museum

Above the gardens to the south-east rises the Forte del Belvedere (Forte di San Giorgio), which was built by Bernardo Buontalenti in 1590–95.

Forte del Belvedere

North-east of the Palazzo Pitti stands the church of the Santo Spirito (begun in 1436 to a plan by Brunelleschi and completed in 1487), with a campanile of 1543. Notable features are the sacristy (1489–92), numerous altarpieces and two 16th c. cloisters.

Santo Spirito

Farther west is the former Carmelite monastic church of Santa Maria del Carmine, almost completely rebuilt in 1782 after a fire. The Brancacci Chapel contains famous frescos on the lives of the Apostles (by Masolino and Masaccio 1424–27) which marked the beginning of Renaissance painting.

Santa Maria del Carmine

★Viale dei Colli

The Viale dei Colli, laid out from 1868 onwards, which runs along the south side of the town from the Porta Romana to the Piazza Francesco Ferrucci, with a total length of almost 6 km (3¾ mi.), is one of Italy's finest promenades.

The road winds its way up through magnificent scenery to the Piazzale Michelangelo, with a spacious terrace from which there is a famous view of the town and the Arno valley.

★★Piazzale Michelangelo

Above the square to the south is the monastic church of San Miniato al Monte, conspicuous from afar with its inlaid marble façade, one of the

San Miniato al Monte

Roman theatre in Fiesole

finest examples of Tuscan Romanesque architecture of the 11th–12th c. In the apse is a fine mosaic (1297); the crypt contains frescos by Taddeo Gaddi.

To the right of the church rises a fortress built by Michelangelo in 1529 (now an Olivetan monastery), the walls of which surround a cemetery.

From the terrace there are fine views.

Le Cascine

Almost 2 km (1¼ mi.) west of the Ponte Vecchio, at the Piazza Vittorio Veneto, is the beginning of the municipal park called le Cascine (originally the estates of the Medici and the Lorena), which extends along the northern bank of the Arno (swimming pool, cycle circuit and horse race course).

★Fiesole

8 km (5 mi.) NE

The little town of Fiesole which was originally an Etruscan town and later the Roman Faesulae, still preserves parts of its massive walls. In the centre of the town is the cathedral (11th and 13th c.), in Tuscan Romanesque style, and behind it are the remains of a Roman theatre and an Etrusco-Roman temple (museum of antiquities). From the terrace of the church of Sant'Alessandro, a little way west of the cathedral in the municipal park, there is a very fine view of the low-lying country around Florence.

Foggia   K13

Region: Puglia. Province: Foggia (FG)
Altitude: 74 m (244 ft). Population: 158,000

Foggia, chief town of the province of the same name, which was also   Location
known as "Capitanata", is situated in the northern part of the Adriatic
coastal region of Apulia, south of the Monte Gargano promontory. Once
a favourite residence of the Emperor Frederick II, it is both the geographical and the economic centre of the extensive Apulian plains, the Tavoliere
di Puglia.

Almost all the town's medieval buildings were destroyed in an earthquake in 1731. With its wide tree-lined streets and its many new buildings,
including those erected after the Second World War to make good the
severe destruction which the town had suffered, Foggia is now a town of
very modern appearance.

Sights

The hub of the town's traffic is the Piazza Cavour, to the east of the centre.
Adjoining the east side of the square, beyond a colonnade, is the municipal
park, extending eastwards. From the Piazza Cavour Viale XXIV Maggio,
lined by fine buildings, runs north-east to the station.

To the west of the Piazza Cavour is the Piazza Umberto Giordano, from
the far end of which the busy Corso Vittorio Emanuele, Foggia's principal
street, leads into the old town centre. 300 m (990 ft) west it is crossed by
another busy street, the Corso Garibaldi, along which, to the south-west,
are the Prefecture and the Town Hall.

A little way north of the Prefecture is the cathedral, built about 1172 in   Cathedral
Romanesque style but rebuilt in Baroque style after the 1731 earthquake.

Farther north, in Piazza Nigri, is the Municipal Museum (Musei Civici)
which contains archaeological and folklore material as well as a collection
of modern pictures.

★Round the Monte Gargano promontory (c. 230 km (143 mi.))

There is a very attractive trip around the Monte Gargano promontory
(1056 m (3485 ft)), the "spur" of the Italian boot, a hilly tongue of land
which extends 65 km (40 mi.) into the Adriatic and, geologically, already
belongs to the Dalmatian limestone formations.

Leave Foggia on SS89 (the "Gargánica"), which runs north-east through   **Lido di Siponto**
the extensive and well-cultivated Apulian plain. In 27 km (17 mi.), on the
right, is San Leonardo, formerly a lodge of the Teutonic Order but now a
farmhouse (Masseria), with a square Romanesque church (richly sculptured 12th c. doorway). Soon afterwards the road reaches the coast at Lido
di Siponto (5 m (17ft)), the Roman Sipontum, which was abandoned in the
13th c. Among the remains is the cathedral of Santa Maria Maggiore
(consecrated 1117), on a square ground plan, with an interesting crypt.

43 km (27 mi.) from Foggia the road comes to Manfredonia (5 m (17 ft);   **Manfredonia**
population 54,000), a port founded in the 13th c. by King Manfred, son of
Frederick II, in place of the abandoned town of Sipontum, and now the see
of an archbishop. After its destruction by the Turks in 1620 it was rebuilt
on a regular plan with streets intersecting at right angles. Interesting
features are the cathedral, the 13th c. church of San Domenico, a 13th c.
castle and the Museo Archeologico Nazionale del Gargano. There are boat
services several times weekly to the Tremiti Islands (4–5 hours).

About 7 km (4¹/₂ mi.) beyond Manfredonia the road forks: to the left is the   Detour
shorter road through the hills, to the right the longer but scenically more
attractive coast road.

9 km (5¹/₂ mi.) from the fork the hill road reaches Monte Sant'Angelo (796 m   **Monte
(2627 ft); population 17,000), the centre of the Gargano area. This little town   Sant'Angelo**

Foggia

is charmingly situated with a fine ruined castle (1494) and the pilgrimage church of San Michele Arcangelo which is visited by something like a million pilgrims every year. The church occupies a cave in the centre of the town which according to legend was chosen as a shrine by the Archangel Michael himself when he appeared to St Lawrence, archbishop of Sipontum, in 493. From the vestibule beside the campanile (1273) 86 steps lead down to the church, which has Biblical scenes on bronze doors and an inscription recording that they were cast in Constantinople. The church contains a fine 12th c. bishop's throne. Near the church is the so-called "tomb of Rothari" (a Lombard king), a curious domed building (c. 1200) which was probably a baptistery. Nearby is the church of Santa Maria Maggiore (begun 1170), with a beautiful doorway (1198).

San Giovanni Rotondo

About 5 km (3 mi.) beyond Monte Sant'Angelo a road goes off on the left to San Giovanni Rotondo (566 m (1868 ft); population 23,000), situated below Monte Calvo (1056 m (3485 ft)), the highest summit in the range. On the west side of the town is the modern church of Santa Maria delle Grazie, to the left of which is a Capuchin monastery famous as the home of Padre Pio da Pietrelcina (d. 1968), who bore the stigmata from 1918 until his death. The monastery is visted by large numbers of pilgrims seeking a cure for their ailments, and there is a modern hospital adjoining.

★ Foresta Umbra

Beyond the turning for San Giovanni Rotondo the main road winds its way uphill and then crosses the karstic plateau of Monte Gargano and down through the magnificent beech forest of Foresta Umbra to the coast, joining the coastal road from Manfredonia 43 km (27 mi.) beyond San Giovanni.

Vieste

The more attractive coast road (19 km (12 mi.) longer), running partly inland and partly above the coast, through magnificent scenery, comes in 49 km (30 mi.) to the picturesque little port of Vieste (43 m (142 ft); population 13,000). The castle, built by Frederick II, has a fine view of the coast.

Peschici

5 km (3 mi.) farther on is the picturesque little town of Peschici situated on a crag rising sheer from the sea. The road then continues, with many bends, to Bellariva, where it is joined by the road from Monte Sant'Angelo.

San Menaio

18 km (11 mi.) beyond Bellariva is San Menaio (10 m (33 ft)), a seaside resort, with villas set amid pine-woods.

Rodi Garganico

About 7 km (4¹/₂ mi.) farther on is the port of Rodi Garganico (42 m (139 ft); population 4000). From here there are boat services (approximately 1¹/₂ hours) to the beautiful Tremiti Islands, 22 nautical miles north-west.

Lago di Varano

Soon afterwards the road skirts a coastal lagoon, the Lago di Varano (12 km (7¹/₂ mil.) long, 8 km (5 mi.) across), which is separated from the sea by a long spit of sand – dunes known as the "Isola", and passes either to the south or to the north along the dunes. It then continues through barren hill country to join the motorway to Foggia either at Poggio Imperiale (45 km (28 mi.)), at the west end of the Lago di Lesina, or at San Severo (65 km (40 mi.)).

Lucera

18 km (11 mi.) W

West of Foggia, on a plateau above the wide Apulian plain, is Lucera (219 m (723 ft); population 34,000), the ancient Luceria. The town was developed into an important stronghold, the key to Apulia, by the Emperor Frederick II, and populated by 20,000 Saracens brought in from Sicily between 1233 and 1245. Most of the population was killed by Charles II of Anjou around 1300.

Notable are the Gothic cathedral, built by Charles II of Anjou after 1300 on the site of the old Saracen mosque (inside a wooden 14th c. crucifix) and the Museo Civico Giuseppe Fiorelli, with coins, inscriptions, numerous terracottas, a beautiful statue of Venus of the 1st c. AD and other treasures.

About 1 km (¹/₂ mi.) west of the town, beyond the beautiful Giardino Pubblico, is a castle (251 m (828 ft)) built by Frederick II in 1233 and rebuilt by Charles I of Anjou, a well-preserved example of medieval military architecture, from the top of which there are far-ranging views.

East of Lucera, at the foot of a hill, is a Roman amphitheatre.

17 km (11 mi.) south of Lucera is the little town of Troia (439 m (1449 ft); population 8000), with an interesting cathedral (begun 1092) showing Toscanian Pisan influence. The two bronze doors are by Oderisius of Benevento, 1119 and 1127. Also in Troia can be seen the remains of the old town walls.

Troia

Foligno   G10

Region: Umbria. Province: Perugia (PG)
Altitude: 234 m (772 ft). Population: 53,000

The industrial town of Foligno lies on the left bank of the River Topino, in the fertile Umbrian plain – some 35 km (22 mi.) south-east of Perugia and 25 km (16 mi.) north of Spoleto.

Location

The earliest printed book in Italy was published here (in Italian) in 1472 – the first edition of Dante's "Divine Comedy".

The Old Town suffered serious damage as a result of the 1997 earthquake in Umbria.

Sights

In the centre of the town is the spacious Piazza della Repubblica, on the east side of which is the cathedral of San Feliciano (1133; closed at present), with a beautiful façade and a Neo-Classical interior (1770). The altar canopy is a copy of the bronze baldachin designed by Bernini for St Peter's in Rome.

Cathedral

Facing the cathedral, to the south-west, stands the 17th c. Town Hall.

On the north side of the square is the Palazzo Trinci (14th–15th c.), in which are the Archaeological Museum, a library and an interesting collection of pictures (closed at present).

Palazzo Trinci (museums)

On the south side of the Piazza della Repubblica stands the Palazzo Comunale, built in the 13th c.; note the Neo-Classical façade. It is believed that Italy's first printing press was housed in the elegant Palazzo Orfini (1515; fine Renaissance doorway), on the right of the Palazzo Comunale.

Palazzo Comunale

Palazzo Orfini

From the Palazzo Trinci Via A. Gramsci runs past the fine Palazzo Deli (1510; on the right) to the former 13th c. church of San Domenico and the old church of Santa Maria Infraportas; inside three representations of the crucifixion.

Other sights

A little way north is the Scuola d'Arti e Mestieri (School of Arts and Crafts), in the courtyard of which are casts of monuments of Umbrian art. Adjoining the school the church of San Niccolò houses some fine paintings.

In a narrow lane to the south-east of the cathedral is the former Oratorio della Nunziatella (15th c.), with a fine fresco of the Baptism of Christ by Perugino.

Surroundings

The abbey of Sassovivo (Abbazia di Sassovivo), standing in splendid isolation, was founded by Benedictine monks in the 11th c. Particularly remarkable is the Romanesque cloister with 128 filigree spiral columns.

★Abbazia
Sassovivo
6 km (3³/₄ mi.) E

Bevagna
10 km (6 mi.) SW

South-west of Foligno, in the valley of the Clitunno, lies the little town of Bevagna (210 m (693 ft); population 4500). In the picturesque main square are the churches of San Silvestro and San Michele, with early medieval façades.

★Montefalco

From Bevagna it is 7 km (4¹/₂ mi.) up a winding road, with sharp bends, to the little walled hill-town of Montefalco (473 m (1561 ft); population 5500), with churches which contain fine examples of Umbrian painting: outside the town gate the monastic church of Santa Chiara, inside the gate the church of Sant'Agostino and in the town the former church of San Francesco (now a museum), with frescos by Benozzo Gozzoli (1452).

There are also frescos by Gozzoli in the church of San Fortunato, 1.5 km (1 mi.) south of the town.

★Spello
5 km (3 mi.) NW

North-west of Foligno, picturesquely situated on the lower slopes of Monte Subasio, is Spello (280 m (924 ft); population 7800), the ancient Hispellum, which still preserves part of its walls and gates, among which the Porta Venere of the Augustan period. From the Porta Consolare, with three portrait-statues, a street leads up to the church of Santa Maria Maggiore (1285), with a number of notable works of art – in the Cappella Baglioni frescoes by Pinturicchio (1501), as well as majolica flooring from Deruta (1566); on the high altar a magnificent marble tabernacle by Rocco da Vicenza (1515); in the sacristy and presbytery are frescoes by Pinturicchio. Above Santa Maria rises the church of Sant'Andrea (13th c.), which has further frescos by Pinturicchio.

Trevi
11 km (7 mi.) S

South of Foligno, off SS3 to the east, is Trevi (412 m (1360 ft); population 7300), the Roman Trebiae, magnificently situated on the slopes of a steep hill. In the central Piazza Mazzini stands the Palazzo Comunale (14th/15th/16th c.) with an open arcaded hall on the ground floor. The Via San Francesco leads to the Franciscan church of San Francesco (1288), which houses the municipal picture collection and documents the town's history. Contemporary Italian works of art can be seen in the Trevi Flash Art Musuem in the Palazzo Lucarini (opened in 1993).

Outside the town stands the church of San Martino, with fine frescoes by Lo Spagna and Pier Antonio Mazzastris and a beautiful view of Trevi. Below the old town, on the link road to the state road no. 3, stands the Renaissance church of the Madonna della Lacrime, famous for its "Adoration of the Three Kings" by Perugino.

Forlì   G7

Region Emilia-Romagna. Province: Forlì (FO)
Altitude: 34 m (112 ft). Population: 110,000

Location

Forlì, capital of the upper Italian province of the same name, lies on the Via Emilia between Bologna and Rimini – some 55 km (34 mi.) south-east of Bologna and 45 km (28 mi.) from Rimini.

The town, the Roman city of Forum Livii and in the late medieval period an independent republic.

Sights

In the centre of the town the large Piazza Saffi is surrounded by fine palaces. On the west side of the square stands the Town Hall, beside it is the Gothic Palazzo del Podestà (1460).

San Mercuriale

At the east corner of the square stands the Romanesque church of San Mercuriale (12th–13th c.), with a fine campanile. Inside are paintings and other works of art. To the right of the church is the cloister of the old Benedictine abbey (16th c.).

From Piazza Saffi the Corso Garibaldi runs north-west to the cathedral of Santa Croce (rebuilt 1841).

From Piazza Saffi the Corso della Repubblica leads south-west to the municipal Pinacoteca and the museums, in a palace dating from 1172. In the Pinacoteca works by Guercino (c. 1590 to 1666), Melozzo da Forlì (1438 to 1494) and Beato Angelico can be seen. The Museo Archeologico contains prehistoric, Etruscan and Greek finds. There is also a display of faience and a history section.

Museums

At the end of the Corso della Repubblica is the spacious Piazzale della Vittoria, with a war memorial (1932) in the form of a tall marble column.

Piazzale della Vittoria

In the south-west of the town is the citadel, the Rocca di Ravaldino (1361).

Citadel

Surroundings

On Via Emilia, in the area between Revenna, Forli and Rimini, lies the walled town of Cesena (40m/131ft; population 90,000). Note the famous Biblioteca Malatestiana (1452), the Gothic cathedral (15th c.) and, built on a hill, the Rocca Malatestiana, a largely rebuilt 14th/15th c. fortification.

Cesena

Frascati   G12

Region: Latium/Lazio. Province: Roma (ROMA)
Altitude: 322 m (1063 ft). Population: 20,000

The little town of Frascati lies some 20 km (12 mi.) south-east of Rome on the north-west slopes of the Alban Hills. Frascati, the most important of the so-called "Castelli Romani", is a town famous for its healthy climate, which makes it a favourite summer resort with the people of Rome.

Location

It is notable also for the many fine villas, belonging to old noble families, mostly dating from the 16th and 17th c., set in magnificent parks and gardens.

Architecture

Sights

The focal point of the town is the Piazza Roma, with the adjoining Piazza Marconi. To the south is the beautiful park of the Villa Torlonia (destroyed in the Second World War).

Villa Torlonia

Above the south-east side of the Piazza Marconi stands the Villa Aldobrandini or Belvedere (1598–1604), in a magnificent park (terrace with extensive views; grottoes, fountains, cascade).

★Villa Aldobrandini

A little way north of the Piazza Roma is the Piazza San Pietro, the main square of the old town, with a beautiful fountain and the cathedral of San Pietro (16th–17th c.). Inside, note the Madonna, Baroque altar and tomb of Charles Edward Stuart (1788) near the main door.

Piazza San Pietro

Outside the town, to the south-east, is the splendid Villa Rufinella or Tuscolana, built by cardinal Rufini in accordance with a plan by Luigi Vanvitelli. The villa and park are not open to the public.

Villa Rufinella

Surroundings

About 1 km (¹/₂ mi.) east of Frascati we find the entrance to the picturesque park of the Villa Falconieri, built by Borromini in 1545–48 (frescos).

Villa Falconieri

2 km (1¹/₄ mi.) east of Frascati stands the Villa Mondragone (1573–75), since 1865 a Jesuit seminary, with magnificent cypresses. It was here that, in 1852, Pope Gregory III approved the Gregorian calendar named after him.

Villa Mondragone

Friuli

Tusculum
5 km (3 mi.) SE

From Frascati a recently constructed panoramic road winds its way uphill through beautiful scenery and areas of forest to the remains of ancient Tusculum, 5 km (3 mi.) south-east. This was the birthplace of Cato the Elder and a favourite resort of Cicero. Held during the early Middle Ages by warlike counts, it was destroyed by Rome in 1191. There are remains, much overgrown, of an amphitheatre, a theatre, the forum, a well-house and a stretch of the old town walls.

It is a 15-minute walk up the hill above the site to a ruined castle (670 m (2211 ft)), which commands extensive views.

Rocca di Papa
8 km (5 mi.) S

There is a very attractive trip from Frascati to the little town of Rocca di Papa, with numerous summer residences (620–720 m (2046–2376 ft); population 9000), picturesquely perched on a rock on the outer margin of a large extinct crater known as the Campo di Annibale, and surrounded by beautiful woods.

Monte Cavo

From Campo di Annibale it is possible either to walk (45 minutes) or drive (6.5 km (4 mi.)) to the summit of Monte Cavo (949 m (3132 ft); television transmitter), the second highest of the Alban Hills, from which there are far-reaching views (particularly clear after rain) of most of Latium. Here there stood in antiquity a temple of Jupiter, the shrine of the Latin League.

Friuli

G–H3–4

Regions: Friuli-Venezia Giulia
Provinces: Pordenone (PN) and Udine (UD)

Location

The north Italian region of Friuli, in the basins of the Tagliamento and the lower Isonzo, extends from the Carnic and Julian Alps to the Adriatic.

Together with the eastern part of the old province of Veneto (provinces of Trieste en Gorizia) it now forms the region of Friuli-Venezia Giulia, which occupies 7846 sq. km (3029 sq. mi.) (population 1,200,000).

History

The region, originally occupied by an Illyrian tribe, the Carni, was conquered by Rome around 150 BC. Its name comes from the Roman town of Forum Iulii (Cividale del Friuli). Later a Lombard duchy, in the time of Charlemagne it was held by a Frankish margrave, in 952 it passed to Bavaria, in 976 to Carinthia, and in 1077 was a gift to the Patriarchate of Aquileia. In the 15th c. the western (and larger) part was conquered by Venice, while the smaller eastern part was granted to the counts of Gorizia as a fief and in 1500 passed to Austria, which in 1797 also acquired the territory held by Venice. Italy secured the Venetian territory in 1866 and the county of Gorizia in 1918, but in 1947 was compelled to cede the eastern part, predominantly inhabited by Slovenes, to the former Yugoslavia.

Much of the region was ravaged by a series of earthquakes in 1976 in which more than 1000 people lost their lives, and many valuable works of art and architecture as well as complete villages were destroyed. In many places many houses, streets, castles and palaces have since been rebuilt or restored.

Population

Of the 1.2 million inhabitants of the region of Friuli-Venezia Giulia some 520,000 are Friulians (in Italian "Friulani", in Friulian "Furlani"), the descendants of Rhaetians who were Romanised at an early date. They speak Friulian, a Rhaeto-Romanic dialect.

Economy

The economy is traditionally based on agriculture (including viticulture), but many Friulians now find employment in other parts of Italy in building or other trades.

Tourism

In the mountains the opening up of new skiing areas has made tourism an increasingly important element in the economy of the region. The favourite winter sports resorts are Piancavallo, Forni di Sopra, Ravascletto, Sella Nevea and the area around Tarvisio. In Sella Nevea there is a summer ski-school.

On the Adriatic coast there are a great number of popular seaside resorts, including Grado, nearby which bird's nesting areas (lagoon) and small fishing islands (see Aquileia) can be found, and Lignano Sabbiardoro, with a wide beach.

Interesting to visit are the towns of Aquileia, Cividale del Friuli and Udine (see entries).

Towns

★★Lake Garda

E4–5

Regions: Lombardia, Veneto and Trentino-Alto Adige
Provinces: Brescia (BS), Verona (VR) and Trento (TN). Altitude: 65 m (215 ft)

With an expanse of 370 sq. km (143 sq. mi.) of deep blue water, Lake Garda (Lago di Garda), the Roman Lacus Benacus, is the largest of the north Italian lakes (52 km (32 mi.) long, 5–16.5 km (3–10 mi.) wide, up to 346 m (1142 ft) deep), lying in a deeply eroded valley between Venetia and Lombardy. Its main feeder in the north is the River Sarca, and its outlet at the south end is the Mincio, which flows into the Po.

Location

The northern part of the lake is narrow and fjord-like; towards the south end the shores slope down gradually to the extensive morainic cirque left by the old Garda glacier. The east side of the lake is separated from the Adige valley by the 80 km (50 mi.) long limestone ridge of Monte Baldo (2200 m (7260 ft)). The west side, hemmed in towards its northern end by sheer rock faces, opens out between Gargnano and Salò to form the beautiful and fertile coastal strip known as the Riviera Bresciana.

Until 1918 the northern tip of Lake Garda, with Riva and Torbole, belonged to Austria.

Landscape

The climate in the area of Lake Garda is extraordinarily mild, and snow is rare. The lake is seldom entirely calm, and in a storm coming from the north can be rough. In fine weather a very cold wind known as the ora blows around midday in winter and spring.

Sailing and surfing is popular on the lake.

Climate

The vegetation is luxuriant on the more sheltered stretches of the lakeside, in places almost Mediterranean. Olives grow up to 300 m (1000 ft), and palms, cedars, magnolias and agaves flourish in the gardens.

The lake fish are excellent.

Flora and fauna

Round Lake Garda (c. 135 km (84 miles))

The lake is surrounded by fine modern roads. Along the west side runs the famous "Gardesana Occidentale", a masterpiece of modern road engineering, with numerous galleries and tunnels hewn from rock, and also a route of great scenic beauty, while on the east side there is the "Gardesana Orientale".

Gardesana Occidentale

Gardesana Orientale

The tour of the lake begins at the little town of Riva del Garda (70 m (231 ft); population 13,000), a summer and winter resort and congress centre at the north-west tip of the lake. To the west of the town is the precipitous Rocchetta (1527 m (5039 ft)), with a Venetian watch-tower.

Riva del Garda

The town's busiest traffic intersection is the square by the harbour, with arcades and a massive old clock-tower. To the east, by the lakeside, is the little Piazza Carducci. Nearby stands the old moated castle of the Scaliger

Lake Garda

Riva, the embarkation point for boat trips around the lake

family, the Rocca (12th–15th c.). On the road to Arco is the church of the Inviolata, with a Baroque interior (1603).

On the south side of the town is the Ponale hydro-electric power station (88,000 kW), fed by water brought from the Lago di Ledro, 585 m (1930 ft) above Riva, in a pipeline 6 km (3³/4 mi.) long.

Riviera Bresciana — 29 km (18 mi.) from Riva on the road which follows the west side of Lake Garda, on the lower slopes of a precipitous hill, is the attractive village of Gargnano (98 m (323 ft)), where the Riviera Bresciana begins. The Villa Feltrinelli, a little way north of the lakeside promenade, was occupied by Mussolini from September 1943 to April 1945 (it is now a department of the university of Milan).

Bogliaco — 2 km (1¹/4 mi.): Bogliaco, with the large country house of Count Bettoni (park).

Toscolano-Maderno — 6 km (3³/4 mi.): Toscolano-Maderno (70 m (231 ft)). In Maderno are the Romanesque church of Sant'Andrea (12th c.) and the Palazzo Gonzaga (17th c.). Beautiful views from the lakeside promenade.

Gardone Riviera — 4 km (2¹/2 mi.): Gardone Riviera (70 m (231 ft)), which attracts many visitors with its mild climate and luxuriant southern vegetation; magnificent Hruska Botanic Garden; bar serving whisky specialities.

About 1 km (³/4 mi.) north surrounded by beautiful gardens is Gardone di Sopra (130 m (429 ft)). Near the church (view from the terrace) is the Villa Vittoriale degli Italiani, the last home of Gabriele d'Annunzio (1863–1938), with mementoes of the poet.

Salò — 3 km (2 mi.): Salò (75 m (248 ft); population 10,000), charmingly situated in a long narrow bay under Monte San Bartolomeo (568 m (1874 ft)). This was the birthplace of Gasparo da Salò (1542–1609), inventor of the violin, and from September 8th 1943 the seat of the Fascist government of Italy

("Republic of Salò"). The Gothic parish church of Santa Maria Annunziata (1453) is worth seeing.

21 km (13 mi.): Desenzano del Garda (67 m (221 ft); population 20,000) at the south-west tip of Lake Garda, has an old castle and remains of a Roman villa of the 4th c. AD (mosaics).
    From Desenzano SS11 runs along the south end of the lake.

Desenzano del Garda

In 4.5 km 3 mi.) a road on the right leads to the village of San Martino della Battaglia (110 m (363 ft)), 5 km (3 mi.) south-east, where a Piedmontese army, allied with the French, defeated the Austrians or June 24th 1859 (commemorative tower, war museum).

San Martino della Battaglia

About 11 km (7 mi.) south is the village of Solferino (132 m (436 ft)); here a French army led by Napoleon III defeated the Austrians on the same day (museum, ossuary). From the Rocca, above the village, there are extensive views. The sufferings of the wounded in the battle of Solferino gave Henri Dunant the idea of founding the Red Cross.

Solferino

2.5 km (1½ mi.) beyond Desenzano on SS11 a road goes off on the left (3.5 km (2 mi.)) to the picturesque little town of Sirmione, on a long promontory reaching out into the lake. The Roman poet Catullus (84–54 BC) had a villa here. The town which is also visited for its sulphur springs has a large and picturesque castle of the Scaligers (13th c. restored); fine view from the tower.

★Sirmione

About 1 km (½ mi.) north is the Punta di Sirmione, with a terrace from which there are fine views, built on late Roman substructures ("Grotte di Catullo").

Punta di Sirmione

7 km (4½ mi.): Peschiera del Garda (68 m (224 ft); population 9000), is a strongly fortified little town at the south-east corner of Lake Garda, at the outflow of the River Mincio.

Peschiera del Garda

Sirmione has a stately castle dating from the time of the Scaligers

Lake Garda

From Peschiera the road continues up the east side of the lake.
In 9 km (5$\frac{1}{2}$ mi.) it reaches Lazise (76 m (251 ft)); population 5000), with medieval town walls and a Scaliger castle (14th c.).

Bardolino

5 km (3 mi.): Bardolino (68 m (224 ft)), famous for its wine. To the left of the road is the little Romanesque church of San Severo (8th and 12th c.), with frescoes (12th and 13th c.).

Garda

4 km (2$\frac{1}{2}$ mi.): Garda (69 m (228 ft); population 3500), a small old town. A footpath leads up in 45 minutes to the Rocca (294 m (970 ft)), on the site of an earlier castle which gave its name to the lake.

★San Vigilio

About 3 km (2 mi.) beyond Garda is the promontory of San Vigilio (fine views), set amid cypresses (1540; no admission).

Torri del Benaco

5 km (3 mi.): Torri del Benaco (68 m (224 ft)), with the medieval Castello Scaligero (1383).

San Zeno di Montagna

From Torri del Benaco an attractive excursion can be made to the summer holiday resort of San Zeno di Montagna, 9km/5$\frac{1}{2}$ miles north-east (583 m (1924 ft)), situated high above the lake (views) on the south-west slopes of the Monte Baldo range.

Malcesine

11 km (7 mi.): Malcesine (90 m (297 ft)), in a fine situation below the rugged cliffs of Monte Baldo (2200 m (7260 ft)). At the north end of the town, almost sheer above the lake, is a Scaliger castle (13th–14th c.). A cableway leads to the Bocca Tratto Spin (1720 m (5676 ft)).

Torbole

14 km (8$\frac{1}{2}$ mi.): Torbole (85 m (281 ft)), a picturesque little fishing village lying under bare crags at the north-east corner of Lake Garda.
4 km (2$\frac{1}{2}$ mi.): Riva

Boat trip

A trip on Lake Garda is an attractive way of seeing both sides of the lake. There are boats from Riva to Desenzano which call at various places on the east and west sides of the lake, and also from Toscolono-Maderno via Garda to Peschiera del Garda or Desenzano. Hydrofoils operate from Riva to Desenzano.

Lago di Ledro

From Riva there is a very rewarding trip up the Ponale Road to the Lago di Ledro, 10 km (6 mi.) west. The road winds its way up above the west side of Lake Garda, with several sharp bends and magnificent views, skirts the cliffs of the Rocchetta and passes through a number of tunnels. At Pieve di Ledro (660 m (2178 ft)), at the west end of the lake, are the remains of a Bronze Age settlement.

★Lago di Molveno

46 km (29 mi.) N

A road runs north from Riva through magnificent scenery fo the hamlet of Foci del Varone, near which is the Cascata del Varone, a waterfall in a gloomy gorge, and Ponte delle Arche (26 km (16 mi.); alt. 401 m (1323 ft)), an old road intersection where SS237 runs east through the magnificent Sarca gorge to Trento and west through the wild Gola della Scaletta to Tione. 20 km (12 mi.) farther north from Ponte delle Arche is the beautiful blue Lago di Molveno (alt. 821 m (2709 ft); 4 km (2$\frac{1}{2}$ mi.) long, up to 119 m (393 ft) deep), below Monte Gazza (1990 m (6567 ft)) to the east and the precipitous crags of the Brenta group to the west. At the north end of the lake is Molveno, a summer holiday resort, with a chair-lift to Pradel (1342 m (4429 ft)) and the Palòn di Torre (1530 m (5049 ft)), to the north.

About 4 km (2½ mi.) north of Molveno is the holiday and winter sports **Andalo**
resort of Andalo (1042 m (3439 ft)), with views of the Brenta group. From
here there is a cableway to Malga Terlago (1772 m (5848 ft)) and Pian del
Dosson, and from there a chair-lift to the Paganella (2126 m (7016 ft)).

Arco

North-east of Riva, on the right bank of the Sarca, is the old town of Arco, 6 km (3¾ mi.) NE
a resort set in luxuriant southern vegetation, which attracts many visitors of Riva del Garda
in winter as well as summer by reason of its mild climate. In the Kurpark,
south of the church, is a bronze monument to the painter Giovanni
Segantini (1858–99), who was born in Arco. To the west are two beautiful
promenades, one planted with magnolias and the other with palms; the
Kurcasino is between the two promenades. On a cypress-clad rock (284 m
(937 ft)) are the ruins of a castle (view).

★Genoa   C7

Region: Liguria. Province: Genova (GE)
Altitude: 25 m (83 ft). Population: 676,000

Genoa (in Italian Genóva), capital of the region of Liguria, lies in the Gulf of   Location
Genoa (Golfo di Genova), the northern bay of the Ligurian Sea. Genoa is a
conurbation (Greater Genoa) extending from Nervi to Voltri for a distance
of 35 km (22 mi.) along the coast. It is Italy's leading port and centre of
maritime trade, ranking with Marseilles as one of the two principal Mediterranean ports. It is also a university town and the see of an archbishop.
  Genoa, known as "la Superba" on account of its splendid marble palaces, has a magnificent situation, particularly when seen from the sea,
rising in a wide arc on the lower slopes of the Ligurian Apennines. The various parts of the town are linked by five road tunnels and high bridges, and
two huge tower blocks form striking landmarks in the town centre.
  The old town is a maze of narrow streets, many of them steep, which are
filled with the colourful and noisy activity of a Mediterranean town. The
new parts of the town with their tall modern buildings, gardens and villas
lie in the plain at the mouth of the River Bisagno and on the higher ground
to the north and west. The tall lighthouse on the west side is the emblem
of the town.

Genoa's economy revolves mainly around the port, which was extended   Economy
in the mid-1950s to supply the industrial regions of Milan and Turin.
Container trans-shipment has also increased. Besides being the exit point
for oil pipelines to Switzerland and Germany, the nearby districts of
Sampierdarena, Cornigliano and Multedo are the main centres of heavy
industry, together with Cristoforo Colombo airport built over the sea.
Other major industries include papermaking, textiles and transport.

Genoa first appears in history in 218 BC as capital of the Ligurians. In the   History
10th c. AD it was an independent republic, which in 1284, after almost 200
years of war, finally defeated its most dangerous competitor, Pisa, in the
naval battle of Meloria. In the 14th c. the Genoese fought with Venice for
control of the trade with the East, but were decisively defeated at Chioggia
in 1381. During this period the town was torn by internal disputes and fell
into the hands of foreign masters. The independence of the republic was
restored by Admiral Andrea Doria (1466–1560) in 1528, but Genoa's power was now in decline. In 1684 the town was bombarded by a French fleet,
and in 1746 it was occupied for some months by Austrian troops. In 1805
the "Ligurian Republic" was incorporated in the Napoleonic Empire, and
ten years later (1815) became part of the Kingdom of Sardinia and
Piedmont. In 1860 Genoa finally became a part of Italy. In the Second
World War it was a centre of the resistance movement.

Genoa

Famous natives of Genoa include the Italian freedom fighter and revolutionary Giuseppe Mazzini (1805–72), the national hero Giuseppe Garibaldi (1807–82), son of a Genoese from Nice, Christopher Columbus (Christoforo Colombo, 1451–1506), discoverer of America, and the great virtuoso of the violin Niccolò Paganini (1782–1840).

Art

The old palaces of the nobility, more numerous and more splendid in Genoa than in any other Italian town, give some impression of the magnificent life-style of the 16th and 17th c. The pattern of the Genoese palace, with its grandiose distribution of architectural masses and its skilful use of rising ground, was set by the Perugian architect Galeazzo Alessi (1512–72) and his successors.

The churches of Genoa, many of them of very ancient origin, were mostly rebuilt during the Gothic period and adorned with Pisan and Lombard sculpture.

Outstanding Genoese painters were Luca Cambiaso (1527–85) and Bernardo Strozzi, called "Il Prete Genovese" (1581–1644).

Inner city

Piazza De Ferrari

The hub of the city is the Piazza De Ferrari, surrounded by public buildings, banks and the offices of the big shipping lines, and with the busiest streets in Genoa radiating from it in all directions.

Opera

On the north-east side of the square is the Neo-Classical Teatro Carlo Felice (1828), one of the largest opera-houses in Italy (burned down during the Second World War and re-opened in 1991; guided tours). In front of the opera-house stands an equestrian statue of Garibaldi (1893).

★ Picture Gallery

To the right of the theatre stands the Accademia Lingustica di Belle Arti (picture gallery), with a museum, containing works of art, particularly sculptures from Genoa and Liguria.

Exchange

On the east side of the Piazza De Ferrari is the Exchange (Borsa), an imposing Neo-Baroque building (19th c.). From here the city's principal street, Via XX Settembre, runs south-east, lined by fine modern buildings and arcades containing numerous shops.

Piazza Dante

From the right-hand side of the Exchange a short street, Via Dante, leads south to Piazza Dante, with two modern tower blocks.

Porta Soprana

On the west side of Piazza Dante is the Gothic Porta Soprana or Porta di Sant'Andrea, the south-east town gate (1155). The little house in front of it to the right is known as the Casa di Colombo (Columbus's House), in which Columbus spent his childhood.

Piazza Matteotti

A short distance south-west of the Piazza De Ferrari is Piazza Matteotti, in which stands the fine Jesuit church of Santi Ambrogio e Andrea (1588–1637) which contains pictures by Rubens and Reni.

★ Doge's Palace

On the north side of the square is the former Doge's Palace (Palacio Ducale), a group of buildings dating from the 13th c. It has been converted into an exhibition and function centre and opened in 1992. The frescos by Carlone and Tiepolo have been restored.

San Matteo

From here Via Tommaso Reggio (left of the palace) and the Salita all'Arcivescovado lead to the little Gothic church of San Matteo (1278), with many relics of the noble Doria family (on the façade inscriptions in their honour, in the crypt the tomb of Andrea Doria). To the left of the church is a beautiful early Gothic cloister (1308–10).

Genoa: the cathedral of San Lorenzo ▶

Genoa

Palaces

In the square in front of the church are several palaces of the Doria family, some of them faced with black and yellow marble; and in the narrow surrounding streets, once the most aristocratic part of the town, are numerous other noble mansions.

★★San Lorenzo

From Piazza Matteotti the busy Via San Lorenzo runs north-west to the harbour. Immediately on the right is the Cathedral of San Lorenzo, originally a Romanesque pillared basilica (1100–1160), remodelled in Gothic style in 1307–12 and crowned with a Renaissance dome by Galeazzo Alessi in 1557. It contains fine pictures and sculpture. In the north aisle is the large Cappella San Giovanni Battista (1450–65), the earliest example of Renaissance architecture in Genoa.

Under the cathedral lies the Treasury.

★Santa Maria di Castello

Between the 12th and 16th c. a complex of churches and convents was built on Castello Hill. The centre is the Romanesque church of Santa Maria (12th c.), with a Roman frieze in the main doorway. From the sacristy a three-storey cloister is open to the public; note the Loggia dell'Annunziazione on the first floor, with the fresco "The Annunciation of Our Lady", and the ceiling paintings. Museum of religious art.

★San Agostino

Note the church of San Agostino, badly damaged in the Second World War and rebuilt. To the right of the church are two cloisters with the Museo di Scultura e Architettura di S. Agostino (Genoese sculpture from the Middle Ages to the 18th c.).

★Museo Chiossone

From the Opera-House the busy Via Roma, in which are various entrances to the Galleria Mazzini, a shopping arcade, runs east to the Piazza Corvetto. From here the Via XXV Aprile runs north to the Piazza Fontane Marose. On higher ground to the north-west of this square is the Villetta di Negro park (view), with the Museo Edoardo Chissone which contains a collection of Oriental art (3rd c. BC to 19th c.).

Garibaldi–Via Cairoli–Via Balbi to Piazza Acquaverde

From the west side of Piazza Fontane Marose a major traffic artery formed by Via Garibaldi, Via Cairoli and Via Balbi runs north-west to Piazza Acquaverde and the station. Laid out in the 16th and 17th c., this area contains a number of churches and Genoa's finest palaces, approached by magnificent flights of steps which are one of the particular sights of Genoa.

★Via Garibaldi Palaces

In the narrow Via Garibaldi, designed by Galeazzo Alessi, are a succession of palaces, with fine collections of pictures. On the right (No. 9) is the former Palazzo Doria Tursi, now the Palazzo Municipale (Town Hall), begun in 1564. It contains Niccolò Paganini's violin and manuscripts by Christopher Columbus. On the left (No. 18) is the Palazzo Rosso, a splendid 17th c. mansion which belonged to the Brignole-Sale family (17th c.), containing a picture gallery on the first and second floors; notable particularly for its fine family portraits (works by Van Dyck, Paris Bordone, Bernardo Strozzi, Veronese, Moretto, Titian, Tintoretto, Caravaggio, etc.). Almost opposite (No. 11) is the Palazzo Bianco, a Brignole palace (originally 1548, altered after 1712), which also houses a notable picture gallery, with works by Italian, Dutch and Flemish masters.

Via Cairoli

Crossing the Piazza della Meridiana, we enter the wide Via Cairoli with its many antique and bookshops, etc.

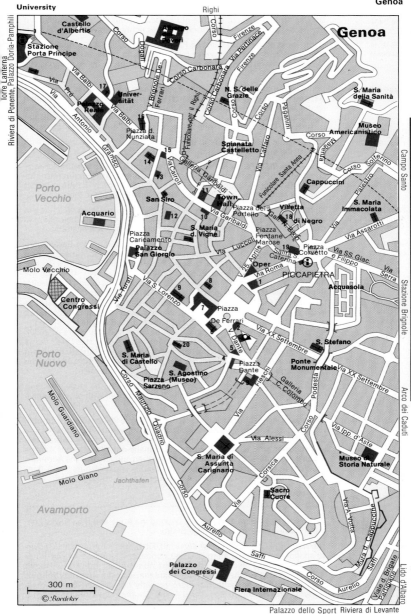

Genoa

San Siero
Off this street, to the left, is the old cathedral (San Siero: remodelled in Baroque style 1586), the interior of which is richly decorated with frescos.

★ Galleria Nazionale
South-west of the church, in the Palazzo Spinola, is the National Gallery (Galleria Nazionale), with works by Antonello da Messina, Anthonis van Dyck, etc. as well as valuable sculpture and a triptych by Joos van Cleve (1485).

Largo della Zecca
Via Cairoli meets the Largo della Zecca, from which a road tunnel, the Galleria Giuseppe Garibaldi, runs to the Piazza Corvetto; the same tunnel continues on the other side of Piazza Portello as Galleria Nino Bixio. On the right-hand side of the Largo della Zecca is the lower station of the funicular to the Righi (302 m (997 ft)), one of Genoa's most beautiful viewing points.

Palazzo Balbi
On the south side of the Largo della Zecca stands the Palazzo Balbi, with an unusual and distinctive staircase (1750).

Casa di Mazzini
Beyond the Balbi Palace is Via Lomellini, which runs south past the Baroque church of San Filippo Neri (completed 1712) to the Casa di Mazzini, the birthplace of Giuseppe Mazzini, the founder of "Young Italy", with the Museo del Risorgimento containing relics of the freedom fighter of the Risorgimento.

Santissima Annunziata
The Largo della Zecca joins the Piazza della Annunziata, in which is the magnificent church of the Santissima Annunziata, originally belonging to the Capuchins (built 1522–1620; Neo-Classical colonnade of 1843).

★ Via Balbi Palaces
West of the church is the beginning of Via Balbi, laid out by Bartolomeo Bianco in the early 17th c. and lined with splendid palaces. Immediately on the right (No. 1) is the Palazzo Durazzo-Pallavicini (c. 1620), with a Rococo entrance hall and a fine staircase of 1780. On the left (No. 4) stands the Palazzo Balbi-Senarega (1620 onwards) with a fine courtyard, from which there is a view of the orangery. No. 5 (on right) is the Palazzo dell'Università, begun in 1634–50 as a Jesuit college, with the finest courtyard and gardens in Genoa. In the atrium are six bronze figures (The Virtues) and six bronze reliefs (The Sufferings of Our Lord) by Giovanni da Bologna (1579). To the left of the university stands the church of San Carlo (sculpture of 1650). Opposite is the Palazzo Reale (begun 1650), with fine staircases, large balconies and a richly decorated interior (pictures, tapestries). From 1822–24 it was the residence of the House of Savoy-Piedmont. View of the harbour and Piazza Statuto from the beautiful garden terrace.

Main Station
Via Balbi leads north-west to the Piazza Acquaverde, the large square in front of the main station, the Stazione Porta Principe, with an impressive monument to Columbus (1846–62).

★ Palazzo Doria-Pamphili
To the west is the Piazza del Principe, in which is the Palazzo Doria-Pamphili or Palazzo del Principe, built in 1522–29 as a country house for Doge Andrea Doria. The façade facing on to the street, has a large doorway with a Latin inscription in praise of Andrea Doria. Originally only the lakeside garden with the Neptune and Triton fountains was open, but recently the Admiral's Apartments have also been opened to the public (guided tours Sat. 3–6pm and Sun. 10am–1pm, but subject to change at short notice).

Harbour area

Marine Station
To the south of Piazza del Principe, beyond Via Adua and the railway line, is the Stazione Marittima (Marine Station).

Harbour
The Harbour (27 km (17 mi.) wharves, 40,000 employees, annual turnover 40 million tonnes including 300,000 containers) consists of the inner harbour or Porto Vecchio, constructed about 1250, the Porto Nuovo (1877 onwards), the naval harbour (Darsena) and the outer harbour, or Avamporto, together with the more recently constructed Bacino della Lanterna and Bacino di San Pier d'Arena. On the edge of Porto Vecchio rises the tower "Lanterna" (1543; 76 m (251 ft)), the symbol of the city.

The eastern part of the harbour, along Corso Maurizio Quadrio, is occupied by the Porticciolo Duca degli Abruzzi, used by yachts and sailing boats. The whole harbour is enclosed by breakwaters, the Diga Foranea dell'Aeroporto, the Diga di Cornigliano, the Diga Foranea and the Molo Duca di Galliera. There are very attractive boat trips around the harbour (about two hours).

Porticciolo Duca degli Abruzzi

The eastern part of the old harbour was converted into a leisure, exhibition and congress centre for the Columbus celebrations in 1992. The buildings include the "Grande Bigo", a 60 m (200 ft) construction, and the Aquarium (Acquario di Genova), with marine animals of all kinds in a largely natural environment.

Aquarium

At the west end of the harbour is the international Cristoforo Colombo Airport, built on an artificially-laid peninsula.

Airport

From Piazza del Principe Via A. Gramsci runs alongside the high-level motorway which skirts the inner harbour to Piazza Caricamento, in which is the Gothic Palazzo di San Giorgio (c. 1260), occupied from 1408 to 1797 by the Banca di San Giorgio, an influential bank which financed the Genoese republic (beautiful courtyard).

Palazzo San Giorgio

Panoramic roads

From the former bank Via F. Turati runs south past the warehouses of the free port to the Piazza Cavour, the starting point of the Circonvallazione a Mare, a seafront highway (now flanked by the high-level motorway) laid out in 1893–95 in the place of the outer walls. Under the names of Corso Maurizio Quadrio and Corso Aurelio Saffi the highway passes the grounds

★Circonvallazione a Mare

Genoa: cruise ships in the old harbour

of the International Trade Fair, on land recently reclaimed from the sea, to the Piazza della Vittoria.

Churches

A little way south-east of Piazza Cavour is the Romanesque church of Santa Maria di Castello. In the adjoining Dominican monastery is the small Museo di Santa Maria di Castello (good pictures). Farther east are the Romanesque church of San Donato and the early Gothic church of Sant'Agostino, both with fine campaniles. From here Via Eugenio Ravasco and a viaduct 30 m (99 ft) high lead south to the conspicuous domed church of Santa Maria Assunta di Carignano, begun in 1552 to the design of Galeazzo Alessi and completed about 1600, a smaller edition of the plan adopted by Bramante and Michelangelo for St Peter's in Rome. Under the dome are four large Baroque statues. From the dome there are magnificent views of the city and the harbour.

★Passeggiata a Mare

From Piazza della Vittoria the Viale delle Brigate Partigiane, built over the bed of the Bisagno and lined by tall modern blocks, leads south to join the Passeggiata a Mare, a fine promenade which runs along the seafront under the names of Corso G. Marconi and Corso Italia. 2 km (1¼ mi.) along this road, near its east end, is the Lido d'Albaro, a beautifully situated recreation park.

Circonvallazione a Monte

From the Piazza Corvetto the Via Assarotti runs east up to Piazza Manin, the starting point of the beautiful Circonvallazione a Monte.

Museum of America

In the Corso Solferino is the Museum of America (Museo Americanistico), with a fine collection of pre-Columbian art.

Castello d'Albertis

The road runs west along the slopes of the hill to the Spianata del Castelletto (79 m (261 ft); two lifts down to the town), from which there are fine views, and then above the imposing buildings of the 17th c. Albergo dei Poveri (poorhouse) to the Corso Ugo Bassi, near which stands the fortress-like Villa Castello d'Albertis (Museum of Archaeology and Ethnology).

Surroundings

Cimitero di Staglieno
3 km (2 mi.) N

North of the Piazza della Vittoria, up the Bisagno valley, is the beautifully situated Campo Santo or Cimitero di Staglieno, one of the most famous cemeteries in Italy. In the lower arcades are numerous monuments, richly decorated and often overloaded with ornament. Steps lead to the upper arcades, the central feature of which is a domed rotunda. Above this, in the Boschetto dei Mille, is the tomb of Giuseppe Mazzini.

★Madonna della Guardia
10 km (6 mi.) N

North of Genoa, on a prominent conical hill, stands the 19th c. pilgrimage church of the Madonna della Guardia (804 m (653 ft)). The main celebration is held on August 29th, the day (in 1940) when the Virgin Mary appeared to a farmer in the village of Livellato.

Gorizia   H4

Region: Friuli-Venezia Giulia. Province: Gorizia (GO)
Altitude: 86 m (284 ft). Population: 38,000

Location

The provincial capital of Gorizia lies just on the Slovenian frontier at the west end of the karstic limestone country, where the fertile valley of the Isonzo emerges into the plain of Friuli.
 Gorizia is the see of an archbishop.
 The old town lies around the castle on its hill (148 m (488 ft)); the newer districts adjoin the station.

Economy

The fruit and wine trade, as well as some industry (cotton, silk, paper, furniture) and tourism are important features of the economy.

From 1500 until 1918 the country of Gorizia belonged to Austria. During the First World War, lying as it did on the important road to Austria, it was almost continuously in the front line and was largely destroyed. In 1947 the eastern suburbs of the town, with the Montesanto station, were transferred to what was then Yugoslavia. On the other side of the frontier the town is known as "Nova Gorica". History

Sights

At the foot of the north-west side of the castle hill is the triangular Piazza della Vittoria, in which are the Prefecture and the Jesuit church of Sant' Ignazio (17th c.). From here Via Rastello runs south to the cathedral (originally 14th c.; completely rebuilt 1927), with a treasury containing gold and silver objects of the 12th–14th c. Cathedral

From the Piazza del Duomo a road climbs east to the Castello, once the seat of the counts of Gorizia. Nearby is the Museo di Storia e Arte, which houses exhibits of local history, archaeology and applied art. In the Borgio Castello is the Museo della Grande Guerra, (patriotic relics of the First World War). Castello

Isonzo battlefields

From Gorizia the battlefields of the Isonzo, where twelve battles were fought in 1915–17, can be visited (though some of the battle area now lies within the former Yugoslavia).

3.5 km (2¹/₄ mi.) north, on a hill (175 m (578 ft)) beyond the Isonzo, is the military cemetery of Oslavia, laid out in 1938, with an ossuary containing the remains of 60,000 Italians who fell in the First World War. **Oslavia Military Cemetery**

11 km (7 mi.) from Gorizia on the Trieste road a minor road branches off to San Martino del Carso (163 m (538 ft)) and Monte San Michele (277 m (914 ft)); far-ranging views), with old military positions and a small war museum. **Monte San Michele**

★★Gubbio G9

Region: Umbria. Province: Perugia (PG)
Altitude: 478–529 m (1577–1746 ft). Population: 32,000

The Umbrian town of Gubbio, the Roman Iguvium, lies some 40 km (25 mi.) north of Perugia, at the mouth of a gorge on the north-east edge of a fertile basin, under Monte Calvo (983 m (3244 ft)) and Monte Ingino (906 m (2990 ft)). Location
 The old surrounding wall is intact. Gubbio is known for its numerous pottery studios and its spectacular festival held on May 15th, including a race in which three heavy wooden candles are pulled through the streets (corsa dei ceri).

Sights

The medieval Old Town boasts some mansions, narrow lanes (such as Via Galeotti), steep flights of steps and many beautiful stone houses. A number of these old houses have "doors of the dead", a second small door near the main door, said to have been used for the removal of the dead. Townscape

The tour of the town begins at the large mendicant church on the Piazza Quaranta Martiri (mainly 13th c.). The campanile is 15th c.; inside the church is a fresco cycle by O. Nelli (c. 1410). San Francesco

Gubbio: ruins of the Palazzo dei Consoli

★ Piazza della Signora

The central feature of the town is the Piazza della Signora, laid out on the slope of the hill on massive supporting pillars. It is dominated by the Palazzo dei Consoli (1332–37), one of the most beautiful Gothic palaces in Umbria; it was built by Gattapone of Gubbio, as was the Palazzo Pretorio opposite (commenced in 1349, but never completed). The Palazzo dei Consoli houses the Municipal Picture Gallery and also the Archaeological Museum. The latter contains the "Iguvine Tablets" – seven out of an original nine bronze tablets (2nd c. BC) with inscriptions partly in Umbrian, Etruscan and Latin, providing information on the political, social and religious life in Umbria.

Palazzo Ducale Cathedral

To the north, above the Piazza della Signoria, can be seen the Gothic Palazzo Ducale, built 1471–74 on the model of the Ducal Palace in Urbino. Note the grand courtyard. From the small gardens there is a magnificent view over the Old Town. Opposite, partly built into the hillside, stands the 13th c. cathedral, with older sculptures on the façade. Inside are 16th c. altarpieces. There is a small museum in the former canon's house.

★ Via dei Consoli

Largo Bargello

From the Piazza della Signoria the busy Via dei Consoli, with its many beautiful old houses and numerous small pottery studios and souvenir shops, leads to the north-western Old Town with its narrow lanes. On Largo Bargello, with its Iguvine fountain, the Fontana dei Matti, stands the Gothic Palazzo del Bargello (early 14th c.). At the end of the street is the church of San Domenico (consecrated 1278; 15th c. frescoes).

Santa Maria Nuova

The pretty Via XX Settembre leads to the south-east of the town, where the church of Santa Maria Nuova (14th c.) boasts a major fresco, the "Madonna del Belvedere", by Ottaviano Nelli (1403). Other frescos by Nelli can be seen in the church of Sant'Agostino, to the south-east outside the Porta Romana town gate.

Roman theatre, mausoleum

The Roman theatre, which seated about 600 spectators, and the mausoleum lie outside the medieval centre.

From the cathedral a steep street leads up to the monastery of Sant'Ubaldo (820 m (2690 ft)), on the slopes of Monte Ingino (alt. 906 m (2973 ft); cable railway). From the monastery the mountain peak can be climbed in 20 minutes (fine view).

Sant'Ubaldo

Surroundings

Monte Cucco, east of Gubbio (approach by main roads 298 and 3), is 1566m/5140ft high, making it the highest peak in the Umbrian Apennines and a favourite beauty spot. On its eastern slope, at an altitude of 1390m/4562ft, lies the Grotta del Monte Cucco, one of Italy's largest karst caves with some magnificent dripstone formations.

Monte Cucco

★★Herculaneum

J14

Region: Campania. Province: Napoli (NA)
Altitude: 44 m (145 ft). Population: 61,000

The remains of Roman Herculaneum lie within the area of modern Ercolano (until 1969 known as Resina), 8 km (5 mi.) south-east of Naples, near the Gulf of Naples in a bay of the Tyrrhenian Sea.
    Although much of Herculaneum is still buried under the modern town, it offers a vivid impression of the aspect of an ancient city. comparable with the remains of Pompeii and Ostia.

Location

Probably founded by Greek settlers under the name of Herakleion and later occupied by Oscans, Etruscans and Samnites, Herculaneum fell into Roman hands in 89 BC. In AD 63 it suffered severe damage in an earthquake, and in AD 79 it was buried under ashes and pumice during an eruption of Vesuvius. At that time the town, a favourite summer resort of the Romans, had a population of perhaps 6000. Subsequent eruptions increased the depth of ashes and lava to between 12 and 30 m (40 and 100 ft). The hardness of this covering, in contrast to the situation at Pompeii, hindered the activity of plunderers in antiquity.

History

From 1719 onwards shafts were sunk into the site at random, yielding some splendid finds which now rank among the principal treasures of the National Museum in Naples, including papyrus rolls and bronze statues. Systematic excavations carried on since 1927 have brought to light the sumptuous villas of wealthy merchants, the furnishings of which have so far as possible been left in situ.
    In contrast to the mostly single-storeyed buildings of Pompeii, the houses of Herculaneum are mostly of two or three storeys, with much use of wood in half-timbered construction, doors and staircases. Extensive excavations are still in progress.
    Severe damage took place during an earthquake in November 1980.

Excavations

Scavi d'Ercolano

From the main entrance (general view) at the north-east corner of the excavation site, the Scavi d'Ercolano, a road 400 m long leads to the south end of Cardo III, which runs through an area excavated in the 19th c. On the left is the House of Aristides, a sumptuous country villa, and beyond it the House of Argus, with wall paintings and a pillared garden.

Opposite, on the right-hand side of Cardo III, the Large Inn, a patrician house converted into an inn, has a terrace overlooking the sea. Farther along, on the right, is the House of the Skeleton (wall paintings, mosaics),

Large Inn

Herculaneum

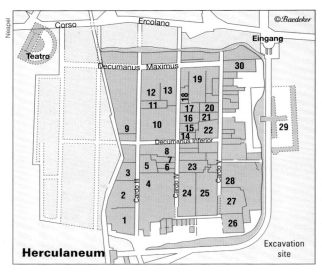

1 House of Aristides
2 House of Argus
3 House of the Genius
4 Large Inn
5 House of the Skeleton
6 House of the Bronze Herm
7 House of Wickerwork
8 House of the Wooden Partition
9 House of Galba
10 Baths
11 House of the Two Atria
12 Sacello degli Augustali
13 Salon of Nero
14 Samnite House
15 Cloth-Merchant's Shop

16 House of the Charred Furniture
17 House of the Mosaic of Neptune and Amphitrite
18 House of the Fine Courtyard
19 House of the Bicentary
20 House of the Corinthian Atrium
21 House of the Wooden Shrine
22 House with the Large Doorway
23 House of Alcoves
24 House of the Mosaic Atrium
25 House of the Deer
26 Suburban Baths
27 House of the Gem
28 House of the Relief of Telephus
29 Palaestra
30 Aula Superiore

and on the left the House of the Genius, a fine patrician mansion with a garden enclosed by colonnades.

Recent excavations

Half-way along its length Cardo III is crossed by the Decumanus Inferior, along which are the recent excavations. Beyond the crossing, on the left of Cardo III, is the House of Galba, another fine patrician mansion, with a cruciform water-basin.

Sacello degli Augustali

At the north end of Cardo III, on right, the Sacello degli Augustali, a square shrine lit by an opening in the roof, was originally dedicated to Hercules, patron of Herculaneum, but later consecrated to the Imperial cult (fine frescos).

Baths

Along the Decumanus Inferior to the right is the Cloth-Merchant's Shop, with a wooden hand-press (restored). To the left are the Baths, much of the structure well preserved, with separate sections for men and women.

Overall view of the Herculaneum archaeological site

At the corner of the Decumanus Inferior and Cardo IV is the Samnite House, one of the oldest patrician mansions in the town, with regular paving and rich stucco and fresco decoration.
    Adjoining is the House with the Large Doorway.

Samnite House

On Cardo IV, immediately on the right, is the House of the Wooden Partition, a patrician house of Samnite type (without a peristyle or colonnaded court). The bedrooms still contain bedsteads and a wooden chest. The adjoining Casa a Graticcio, was a more modest house with interior walls of wattle. Immediately to the south is the House of the Bronze Herm, named after a bronze herm (head of Hermes) which is probably a portrait of the owner of the house.

House of the Wooden Partition

In the southern section of the street, on left, is the House of the Mosaic Atrium, a spacious and sumptuously furnished mansion.

House of the Mosaic Atrium

Adjoining it on the east is the House of the Deer.
    In the northern part of the street, on the right, is the House of the Charred Furniture, and beyond it the House of the Mosaic of Neptune and Amphitrite. Nearby are the House with the Fine Courtyard, and opposite a building called the Salon of Nero.

House of the Deer

To the south-east, on the far side of Cardo V, the House of the Gem is beautifully painted in reddish-brown tones, and adjoining it on the south-east are the Suburban Baths (Terme Suburbane).

Suburban Baths

To the north-east of the House of the Gem, towards the sea, is the House of the Relief of Telephus, one of the most elegant mansions in the town, with a spacious colonnaded atrium containing a marble basin and a colonnade leading into the park.

House of the Relief of Telephus

On the east side of the town is the extensive complex of the Palaestra.

Palaestra

Mosaic in Herculaneum

★House of the Bicentenary

On the Decumanus Maximus (only partly excavated), parallel to the Decumanus Inferior on the north, the House of the Bicentenary contains on the first floor the oldest known Christian cross. It derives its name from the fact that it was uncovered in 1938 some 200 years after excavations were started.

★★Ischia, Island of   H14

Region: Campania. Province: Napoli (NA)
Area: 46 sq. km (18 sq. mi.). Population: 45,000

Ferries

Several times daily (including car ferries) to and from Naples, Capri, Procida and Pozzuoli. Hydrofoil services.

Location

The volcanic island of Ischia, lying at the entrance to the Bay of Naples, is the largest island in the vicinity of Naples. It was known to the Greeks as Pithekousa, to the Romans as Aenaria and from the 9th c. as Iscla.

Scenery

An island of luxuriant vegetation (vineyards, fruit orchards, pinewoods), Ischia is of great scenic beauty, particularly on the north side. Its strongly radioactive hot springs attract many visitors seeking a cure for gout or rheumatism.

Tour of the island

★Ischia

Ischia (population 17,000), the chief place on the island, is picturesquely situated on the north-east coast; it consists of the two districts of Ischia Ponte and Ischia Porto. In Ischia Ponte a mighty Castello stands on a 91 m (300 ft)-high rocky crag accessible by a stone causeway.

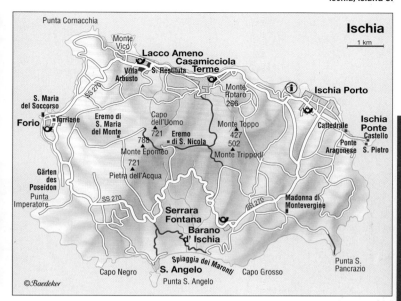

Ischia

1 km

About 2 km (1¼ mi.) west is the busier spa and seaside resort of Ischia Porto with the island's oldest harbour, a former crater lake.

Ischia Porto

4 km (2½ mi.) west of Ischia Porto, half-way along the north coast of the island, Casamicciola Terme (3 m (10 ft); population 6500, surrounded by gardens and vineyards, is situated on the lower slopes of Monte Epomeo, with hot springs (65°C (149°F)) and a good bathing beach. A walk along Via Borbonica (fine views) or an excursion to Monte Rotaro are well worthwhile.

Casamicciola Terme

In the north-west of the island lies the resort of Lacco Ameno (population 4000). The town's emblem is the mushroom-shaped rock ("Il Fungo") which rises out of the sea near the harbour. A small museum provides information on the old Greek colony excavated near Lacco Ameno. The best-known hot mineral springs are those of Santa Restituta and Regina Isabella.

Lacco Ameno

On a flat spur of land on the west coast of Ischia lies the little old town of Forio (population 20,000). It has a pretty whitewashed seafarers' church of the Madonna del Soccorso and a crenellated defensive tower, "Il Torrione", built in 1480 as a protection against pirates.

Forio

From Forio a beautiful road (20 km (12 mi.)) leads through the southern part of the island. It passes above the Gardens of Poseidon (magnificent bathing facilities, with thermal springs) and continues via Panza (155 m (512 ft)).

★Gardens of Poseidon

At Panza a road goes off to the village of Sant'Angelo (hot springs), picturesquely situated on the slopes of a promontory.

★Sant'Angelo

The road continues to Serrara (366 m (1208 ft)), Fontana (452 m (1492 ft)) and Barano d'Ischia (212 m (700 ft); large beach with hot springs), past a 16th c. aqueduct and so back to Ischia Ponte.

Barano d'Ischia

225

Panoramic view of Ischia Porto

From Fontana there is a rewarding climb (1 hour) up Monte Epomeo (789 m (2604 ft), a massive volcano (extinct since 1302), with an almost vertical north face, in the centre of the island (panoramic views).

★**Monte Epomeo**

Prócida, Island of

With an area of 3.75 sq. km (1¼ sq. mi.), Prócida is the third and smallest island in the Bay of Naples, after Ischia and Capri (see entry). It lies north-east of Ischia, between the latter and Capo Miseno, and is also of volcanic origin. It is formed of two adjoining craters, the southern rims of which have been invaded and eroded by the sea, leaving two bays on the south-east coast. The Bay of Chiaiolella to the south-west may have been formed by another smaller crater, while a fourth gave rise to the neighbouring islet of Vivara.

Location

On the north-east side of the island lies the little town of Prócida, with a modern harbour (Sancio Cattolico) and the old fishing harbour of Corri-cella, a charming district of pastel-washed houses with domes, terraces and the characteristic external staircases.

Prócida

On a precipitous crag above Corricella lies the medieval fortified upper town known as Terra Murat. From here and from the Punta dei Monaci there are extensive views of the island.

★Corricella

From the town a narrow road 3 km (2 mi.) in length leads to Chiaiolella Bay, with a sheltered harbour and a fine beach.

Chiaiolella

Offshore to the west lies the little islet of Vivara (109 m (360 ft)), which is connected to Prócida by a bridge. Olive trees grow well here and there are wild rabbits. A nature park is being laid out.

Vivara

◄ *Castell Aagonese towers above the houses of Ischia Ponte*

Region: Latium/Lazio
Provinces: Roma (ROMA), Frosinone (FR), Latina (LT), Rieti (R) and
Viterbo (VB)
Area: 17,203 sq. km (6640 sq. mi.). Population: 5,156,100

Location

The historic area and the present-day region of Latium occupies the west side of the Central Apennines, extending south-west from the Monti Sabini to the coast of the Tyrrhenian Sea between the mouths of the River Chiarone in the north and the Garigliano in the south. The centre of Latium is the densely populated city of Rome.

Mountains and lakes

Most of the region is occupied by four volcanic massifs of the Quaternary era, in the craters of which four large lakes and a number of smaller ones have been formed. To the north-west are the Monte Volsini (639 m (2109 ft)), with the Lago di Bolsena; farther south-east the Monti Cimini (1053 m (3475 ft)), with the Lago di Vico, and the Monti Sabatini (612 m (2020 ft)), with the Lago di Bracciano; and south-east of Rome the Monti Albani or Alban Hills (948 m (3128 ft)), with the Lago Albano.

Tiber Maremma

Through the fertile volcanic soil of the region the Tiber has carved out its wide bed. Along the coast extends the Maremma, a broad strip of alluvial soil, once marshy and malaria-ridden, which has been drained and brought under intensive cultivation. This varied geological and geographical pattern has made Latium a region of great scenic diversity.

Agriculture and fishing

The main elements in the economy are still arable and sheep-farming. The lower-lying areas produce corn, vegetables and sugar-beet, while the volcanic soils of the uplands yield citrus fruits, olives and good quality grapes.
   Along the coast (e.g. at Civitavecchia) fishing is of some economic importance.

Industry

In recent years there has been a rapid development of modern industry, particularly around Rome, in the Sacco and Liri valleys and in the catchment area of the Autostrada del Sole – chemicals and pharmaceuticals, metal-working, textiles, building materials, etc. There are thermo-electric power stations at Civitavecchia and Borgo Sabatino. A considerable contribution is also made to the economy by tourism, particularly in and around Rome.

History

Present-day Latium was occupied in early antiquity by Etruscans and, around the mouth of the Tiber, by the Latin peoples, who formed a league of 30 republics under the leadership of the city of Alba Longa. During the 6th and 5th c. BC the rising city of Rome became a member of the Latin League and steadily increased in influence until, after the transfer of the federal sanctuary to the Temple of Diana on the Aventine, it became de facto the leading city of the League. The Latin towns sought to counter the predominance of Rome by force of arms (Latin War, 340–338 BC, but were defeated. Thereupon the League was dissolved and the various towns became subject to Rome, on varying terms, and thereafter shared the destinies of Rome.

Rome

The main centre of attraction in Latium is Rome (see entry).

Segni

On the road from Rome to Frosinone and on to Naples there are numerous places of interest. 19 km (12 mi.) south-east of Rome on SS6 (the Via Casilina), which runs parallel to the motorway, a minor road leads south via Collefero (225 m (743 ft); population 18,000), with a castle on a hill, to the little town of Segni (668 m (1841 ft); population 8000), situated on an outlier of the Monti Lepini, with extensive views. This was the very ancient city of Signia, and preserves most of its 2 km (1¹/₄ mi.) circuit of town walls dating from the 6th c. BC, with the remarkable Porta Saracinesca to the north-west. On the acropolis stands the 13th c. church of San Pietro, built on the central cella of an ancient temple.

11 km (7 mi.) farther along SS6 a road goes off to Anagni (424 m(1399 ft); **Anagni** population 18,000), on a hill 6 km (3³/₄ mi.) north-east, still surrounded by Roman walls. This was the ancient Anagnia, capital of the Hernici, and in the Middle Ages was frequently the residence of the Pope. The cathedral of Santa Maria (11th c., rebuilt in the 13th c.) contains a mosaic pavement by Magister Cosmas (1226), an Easter candlestick and a bishop's throne by Vassalletto (1263); in the crypt are old frescoes and an altar by Cosmas and his sons; to the right of the choir is the Diocesan Museum. Also of interest is the 13th c. Town Hall.

Farther along the main road is the old town of Ferentino (393 m (1297 ft; **Ferentino** population 18,000), with almost completely preserved town walls (5th–2nd c. BC); on the south side the Porta Sanguinaria and on the east side the Porta Maggiore or Porta di Casamira. On the highest point in the town, the old acropolis, are the Bishop's Palace and the cathedral, which has a mosaic pavement by Magister Paulus (c. 1116). To the north-east, near the Porta Sanguinaria, stands the church of Santa Maria Maggiore (12th–13th c.; fine doorway).

12 km (7¹/₂ mi.) beyond Ferentino we reach the provincial capital, Frosinone **Frosinone** (291 m (960 ft); population 46,000), picturesquely situated on a hillside above the Cosa valley, with remains of ancient buildings.

16 km (10 mi.) east is the Cistercian abbey of Santi Giovanni e Paolo di **★Santi Giovanni e** Casamari (1203–17), which ranks with Fossanova as one of the finest **Paolo di Casamari** achievements of early Burgundian Gothic in Italy.

42 km (26 mi.) beyond Frosinone on SS6 a side road branches off to **Aquino** the village of Aquino (106 m (350 ft), the ancient Aquinum, home of the satirist Juvenal (c. AD 60–140) and of the scholastic philosopher Thomas Aquinas (1226–74), known as the "Doctor Angelicus" or "Doctor Ecclesiae", who was born in the castle of Roccasecca (10 km (6 mi.) north) and trained in Montecassino abbey. On the Via Latina, which passed here, are remains of the Roman city. Near the river is the 12th c. church of Santa Maria della Libera, a Lombard foundation built on the ruins of a temple of Hercules, with a fine doorway (friezes, mosaics, frescoes).
   12 km (7¹/₂ mi.) farther along is the little town of Cassino (see Montecassino).

On SS155 (Via Prenistina), which also leads from Rome to Frosinone **Palestrina** north of SS6, we reach in 40 km (25 mi.) Palestrina (450 m (485 ft); population 14,000), the ancient Praeneste and one of the oldest towns in Italy, birthplace of the greatest Italian composer of church music, Giovanni Pierluigi da Palestrina (1525–94; tomb in St Peter's, Rome). In 1630 the town fell into the hands of the noble Barberini family. Almost the whole area of the present-day town was occupied by the massive temple of Fortuna Primigenia, the seat of a frequently consulted oracle, which was built on four terraces on the slope on the hill, and of which there are considerable remains. On the second terrace, by the cathedral, are the well-preserved remains of the Antro delle Sorti ("Cave of Destiny") and the Aula dell'Ora-colo, home of the oracle. On the fourth terrace, above the massive arches of the third, stands the Palazzo Barberini (15th and 17th c.; Archaeological Museum), on the site of the shrine of Fortuna, with magnificent views extending as far as Rome.

From here a road (3 km (2 mi.) winds its way up to the village of Castel San **Castel San Pietro** Pietro Romano (752 m (2482 ft)), linked with Palestrina by ancient walls, **Romano** with the massive ramparts of its acropolis and a ruined 15th c. castle. From the Spianata delle Torricelle there are panoramic views.

Latium

Fiuggi

39 km (24 mi.) from Palestrina on SS115, situated among beautiful forests of chestnut trees, is Fiuggi (621–747 m (2049–2465 ft)); population 8000), the most popular spa in southern Italy, with radioactive thermal springs (120°C (248°F)). 3.5 km (2 mi.) north is the medieval part of the town, Fiuggi Città (747 m (2465 ft)).

Alatri

7 km (4½ mi.) beyond Fuggi on the main road is Alatri (502 m (1657 ft); population 23,000), the ancient Aletrium, which has the finest surviving circuit of ancient walls. Especially well preserved are the walls (4th c. BC) of the acropolis, built of huge polygonal blocks: note in particular the south-west gate, the Porta dell'Areopago, with a lintel slab 5 m (16½ ft) long and 1.60 m (5¼ ft) thick. On the castle hill are the cathedral and the church of Santa Maria Maggiore.

12 km (7½ mi.) beyond Alatri is Frosinone.

Cisterna di Latina

In the southern part of Latium is the little town of Cisterna di Latina (81 m (267 ft); population 17,000).

Cori

From here, 10 km (6 mi.) north-east, on an outlier of the Monti Lepini, is the little town of Cori (384 m (1267 ft); population 10,000), the ancient Cora. The town, which claims to have been founded by the Trojan Dardanus, preserves considerable remains of its ancient polygonal walls (5th c. BC). In the upper town stands the church of Sant'Oliva, built on ancient foundations, with a two-storey cloister, ancient columns and unusual ceiling paintings (16th c.). Higher up, by the church of San Pietro, is the antechamber of the so-called Temple of Hercules (1st c. BC), probably in fact dedicated to the three Capitoline deities, Jupiter, Juno and Minerva. From here there are beautiful views over the town to the sea, the plain and Monte Circeo. Below the temple (30-minute walk) are the remains of another temple dedicated to Castor and Pollux.

★Ninfa

12 km (7½ mi.) east of Cisterna di Latina is Ninfa, a ruined town still partly surrounded by its walls. The town, mostly dating from the 12th and 13th c. (castle of the Caetani family with an imposing tower, monastery, two small churches) was abandoned in the 17th c. on account of malaria. The enclosed area, with a garden of botanic interest, is open only from April to October on the first Saturday in the month; it is private property.

★Norba

8 km (5 mi.) north of Ninfa, at Norba (417 m (1376 ft); population 4000), are the remains (15 minutes' walk on a hill track) of the old Volscian city of Norba, which became a Latin colony in 492 BC and was destroyed by supporters of Sulla during the Roman civil wars. The site, surrounded by a polygonal wall 2.5 km (1½ mi.) long (4th c. BC), contains the remains of four temples (museum).

Sermoneta

8 km (5 mil.) north-east of Ninfa is the little medieval town of Sermoneta (257 m (848 ft); population 6500), dominated by a castle which belonged to the Caetani family from 1297 onwards, but which was taken over by Pope Alexander VI (Borgia) in 1500–03 for his daughter Lucrezia and was fortified by Cesare Borgia (14th–15th c. frescoes). The cathedral contains a Madonna ascribed to Benozzo Gozzoli.

★Gaeta

In the extreme south of Latium, charmingly situated on a rocky promontory in the gulf of the same name, the port of Gaeta (10 m (33 ft); population 25,000), was until 1861 the principal strong point of the kingdom of Naples and Sicily. The cathedral of Sant'Erasmo has a campanile in Sicilian Romanesque style (1279). Inside, behind the high altar, is a banner presented by Pope Pius V to Don John of Austria, the victor of Lepanto and opposite the principal doorway an Easter candlestick with Late Romanesque reliefs (c. 1200), is borne on four lions. A short distance west of the Piazza stands the large church of San Francesco. The church of the Santissima Annunziata

Gaeta Cathedral

to the north was originally built in 1320 (Baroque façade); to the south is the Citadel, with the Angevine Tower.

On the highest point of the promontory (171 m (564 ft)) rises the Mausoleo di Lucio Munazio Planco, the imposing tomb of Lucius Munatius Plancus (d. after 22 BC), who worked successively for Caesar, Antony and Augustus. At the south-west tip of the promontory (2 km (1¼ mi.); extensive views) is the Montagna Spaccata, with a cleft in the rock which according to tradition was caused by the earthquake at the death of Christ. From the new pilgrimage church steps lead down to the beautiful Grotta del Turco (admission fee), on the sea.

On the west side of the promontory is an excellent bathing beach, the Spiaggia di Serapo.

In the surroundings of Gaeta are many places with remains of Roman Villas.

About 20 km (12 mi.) south of Gaeta is the resort of Baia Domizia.

About 6 km (3¾ mi.) north of Gaeta, the pretty little town of Formia is charmingly situated on the Golfo di Gaeta; it is a resort much frequented by Italians in summer. At the west end of the town, near the sea, is the Villa Rubino or Villa di Cicerone, which once belonged to the kings of Naples.

Formia

On a promontory 15 km (9 mi.) west of Gaeta lies the picturesque fishing village of Sperlonga, still partly surrounded by walls, with a good bathing beach.

★**Sperlonga**

Outside the town, in an olive-grove, the very interesting Museo Archeologico Nazionale di Sperlonga houses an excellent collection of original Greek sculpture in marble. Most of the items, found in the Grotta di Tiberio, are now reduced to the condition of huge torsos. The finest piece is the "Ship of

★Museo Archeologico Nazionale

Odysseus", by the sculptor responsible for the famous Laocoön group now in Rome, which depicts Odysseus and his companions struggling with the marine monster Scylla. Between the museum and the sea are remains of the Emperor Tiberius's villa and of ancient basins hewn from the rock, which were used for the rearing of fish (aquationes). Close by is the entrance to the Grotta di Tiberio, in which the Emperor Tiberius is supposed to have caroused with his friends. Since 1957 some 7000 fragments of Greek statues have been discovered here.

Itri

15 km (9 mi.) north of Gaeta is the little town of Itri (170 m (561 ft); population 8000), formerly notorious as a centre of brigandage and birthplace of the bandit Fra Diavolo, the hero of Auber's opera. Some of the houses in the town are built into the substructures of the Via Appia; above it towers a massive ruined castle.

Tomb of Cicero

In the vineyards between Itri and Formia is a round tower known as the Tomb of Cicero, who was murdered at the age of 64 in this area, near his country estate at Formia, in the year 43 BC.

Fondi

14 km (9 mi.) north-west of Itri is Fondi (8 m (26 ft); population 20,000), still partly surrounded by ancient walls. In the Corso Appio Claudio, the main street which runs through the whole length of the town on the line of the old Via Appia, are the church of Santa Maria Assunta, with an early Renaissance doorway, and the Gothic church of San Pietro, with a pulpit and bishop's throne of the 13th c. On the south-east side of the town is the Palazzo del Principe (15th c.), with the crenellated 13th c. Castello opposite.

Rieti

80 km (50 mi.) north-east of Rome is the provincial capital of Rieti (402 m (1327 ft); population 44,000), situated on a fertile plateau, fringed by hills, on the right bank of the River Velino. Along the north side of the town stretch defensive walls and towers. In the central Piazza Vittorio Emanuele is the Palazzo Comunale with the Museo Civico. To the south-west stands the cathedral (completed 1458, almost completely altered in the 17th c.), with a 13th c. campanile. Inside, in the fourth chapel on the north side, is a statue of St Barbara by Bernini. From the Piazza del Duomo there are fine views. Behind the cathedral lies the Bishop's Palace, with the beautiful Loggia Papale (13th c.).

Terminillo

From Rieti attractive trips can be made into the Monti Reatine, particularly to Terminillo (21 km (13 mi.) north-east: cableway, chair-lift, ski-lifts), a popular summer resort and winter sports centre, much favoured by the people of Rome (the "montagna di Roma"). From Monte Terminillo (2216 m (7313 ft)), the highest peak in the Monti Reatini, there are panoramic views extending to the Gran Sasso and Maiella, and on clear days as far as the Adriatic and the Tyrrhenian Sea.

Civita Castellana

In northern Latium, situated at the west end of a tufa plateau surrounded by deep gorges, is the ancient town of Civita Castellana (145 m (479 ft); population 15,000), capital of the Faliscan territory lying between Etruria and Latium. In 241 BC the Faliscan town, known to the Romans as Falerii Veteres, was destroyed by Roman forces and the inhabitants transferred to a new settlement at Falerii Novi, from which they later returned. The noteworthy 12th c. cathedral of Santa Maria has a beautiful porch of 1210 and some ancient columns in the crypt. In a commanding situation to the west of the town stands the Citadel, built by Pope Alexander VI in 1494–1500 to the design of Antonio da Sangallo the Elder; in the large arcaded courtyard are decorative paintings by the Zuccaro brothers (16th c.). The Citadel houses the Archaeological Museum of the Faliscan Territory.

Falerii Novi

6 km (3³/₄ mi.) west are the remains of Falerii Novi, founded in 240 BC to rehouse the inhabitants of the older town of Falerii Veteres, which has preserved its complete circuit of walls (2.1 km (1¹/₄ mi.) long, with nine gates

and 50 towers). Within the walls, near the Porta di Giove on the west side, the ruined abbey of Santa Maria di Falleri has ancient columns in the nave. Near the Porta del Bove, to the south-east are the remains of a theatre, the forum and a swimming pool.

Another attractive place in northern Latium is the Lago di Bolsena (alt. 305 m (1007 ft); area 114 sq. km (44 sq. mi.); up to 151 m (496 ft) deep), known to the Romans as Lacus Vulsiniensis. The lake occupies the crater of a collapsed Tertiary volcano. In the southern half of the lake are two little rocky islets, Bisentina (361 m (1191 ft)) and Martana (377 m (1244ft)). On the island of Martana the Gothic queen Amalasuntha, only daughter of Theodoric the Great, was strangled in her bath in the year 535 on the orders of her co-Regent Theodahad.

★Lago di Bolsena

At the north-east corner of the lake the picturesquely situated little town of Bolsena (348 m (1148 ft); population 4000) lies below the site of Etruscan Volsinium, political centre of the league of twelve Etruscan cities (remains of a wall of dressed stone), and the Roman Volsinium Novum, built in 263 BC. An ancient road paved with basalt blocks leads up (30 minutes) to the scanty remains. Features of interest in Bolsena itself are the 13th c. Castello and the church of Santa Cristina (13th c.) to the south of the town. The church has a fine Renaissance façade (c. 1500) with two terracotta reliefs by Andrea della Robbia above the doors. In the interior is the Grotta di Santa Cristiana, with the saint's tomb, and, under the high altar, the stone with which she was drowned in the year 278. The altar is known as the Altare del Miracolo, following the "miracle of Bolsena" in 1263, when a Bohemian priest who had doubted the doctrine of transubstantiation (i.e. the transformation of bread and wine into the body and blood of Christ in the mass) was convinced of his error by the appearance of drops of blood on the consecrated Host. To commemorate the event Pope Urban IV made the feast of Corpus Christi (which had recently been initiated in Belgium) a universal festival of the Church (1264) and caused the splendid cathedral of Orvieto to be built.

Bolsena

South-east of Bolsena, on a subsidiary crater just inland from the lake, is Montefiascone (590 m (1947 ft); population 12,000), noted for the famous sweet white wine "Est Est Est". The cathedral of Santa Margherita (by Sanmicheli, 1519) has an octagonal dome. From the gardens around the castle above the town there are extensive views. To the north-east, below the town on the Orvieto road, is the double church of San Flaviano (12th c.), with 14th c. frescoes.

Montefiascone

Also in northern Latium is the beautiful Lago di Bracciano (alt. 279 m (921 ft); area 57.5 sq. km (22 sq. mi.); up to 165 m (541 ft) deep, the ancient Lacus Sabatinus, which, like Lake Bolsena, was created by the explosion and subsequent collapse of a volcanic cone.

Lago di Bracciano

Above the lake to the south-west is the little town of Bracciano (279 m (921 ft); population 11,000), with the massive five-towered Castello Orsini Odescalchi (built 1470, in the possession of the princely Odescalchi family since 1696), a fine example of a fortified medieval castle. Notable interior and pillared courtyard; from the wall-walk there are magnificent views of the lake.

Bracciano

See entry.

Cerveteri

★Lecce

N15

Region: Puglia. Province: Lecce (LE)
Altitude: 49 m (162 ft). Population: 94,000

Lecce

Location

The provincial capital of Lecce lies mid-way along the Salentine peninsula, the heel of the Italian boot, in the southern most part of Italy – some 30 km (19 mi.) south-east of Brindisi.

Lecce is one of the most interesting towns in southern Italy, notable for its magnificent Baroque buildings erected by local architects using the beautiful and easily worked yellow limestone of the area.

Sights

Piazza Sant'Oronzo

In the centre of the town is the Piazza Sant'Oronzo, with an ancient column bearing a statue of the saint, and marking the end of the Via Appia. To the west of the column is the Palazzo del Sedile, a loggia built in 1592, and adjoining it the doorway of the little church of San Marco (founded 1543). On the south side of the square are the excavated remains of a Roman amphitheatre (2nd c. AD).

Castello

South-east of the Piazza Sant'Oronzo is the Castello, built by Charles V in 1539–48, on a trapezoid ground-plan.

South of the town centre in the Piazza Vittorio Emanuele stands the 18th c. church of Santa Chiara and farther south the church of San Matteo (built *c.* 1700), with a bizarrely curved façade.

★Piazza del Duomo

From the Piazza Sant'Oronzo the Corso Vittorio Emanuele II runs west, past the Theatine church of Sant'Irene (1639), into the Piazza del Duomo, with the cathedral of Sant'Oronzo (1658–70; tower 70 m (231 ft) high), the Bishop's Palace and the Seminary, which has a richly decorated façade and a courtyard containing a fountain.

Santa Maria del Rosario

500 m south of the Piazza del Duomo is the large Dominican church of Santa Maria del Rosario (1691–1728).

A magnificent palazzo in Lecce

To the south of the town, in Piazza Argento, is the Palazzo Argento, which houses the Provincial Museum (ancient vases, terracottas, statues and pictures).

Museo Provinciale

North of Piazza Sant'Oronzo in the Piazza della Prefettura the magnificent Baroque church of Santa Croce has an elaborately decorated façade (begun 1548, completed 1697 onwards) and a fine interior. Adjoining it on the north is the extensive and richly ornamented façade of the Celestine convent (13th c.) which belonged to the church; now Palazzo del Governo.

★Santa Croce

From the Palazzo del Governo we go north along Via Umberto I and in 100 m turn left into Via Principe di Savoia to reach the Porta di Napoli, on the west end of the old town, a triumphal arch erected in 1548, and a memorial to Charles V. North-west of this is the Campo Santo, with the church of Santi Nicolò e Cataldo, founded by the Norman Count Tancred in 1180, with a superb Romanesque doorway in the centre of the Baroque façade of 1716 showing Arabian influence. The harmonious interior, with strong influence of French Gothic, has beautiful capitals.

★★Santi Nicolò e Cataldo

Gallipoli

There is an attractive drive over the Apulian plain, passing through the little country town of Galatone (59 m (195 ft); population 14,000), with a cathedral and the Baroque church of the Crocifisso, to Gallipoli (14 m (46 ft); population 22,000), a little port beautifully situated on a rocky island in the Golfo di Taranto and linked by a bridge with its modern suburb on the mainland. At the east end of the bridge is a fountain of 1560, with ancient reliefs. Beyond the bridge, to the left, is the Castello (16th c.), from which the main street, Via Antonietta de Pace, runs across the town. In this street, on the left, stands the cathedral (1629–96), with fine choir-stalls, and, on the right, the Municipal Museum.

38 km (24 mi.) SW

A pleasant trip from Gallipoli is on a road, partly hewn from the rock, along the "Riviera Neretina" to the little resort of Santa Maria al Bagno, which lies 12 km (7½ mi.) north. In another 2 km (1¼ mi.) the road comes to the hamlet of Santa Caterina Riviera.

Santa Maria al Bagno

Lecce to Capo Santa Maria di Leuca
(c. 65 or 100 km (40 or 62 mi.))

Another attractive trip is from Lecce to Capo Santa Maria di Leuca, either on the direct road (65 km (40 mi.)) via Maglie (81 m (267 ft)) or on the longer but scenically superior coast road (about 100 km (62 mi.)).

The coast road traverses the seaside resort of San Cataldo which has a good beach and a lighthouse, and comes to Otranto (15 km (9 mi.); population 5000), a little fishing town beautifully situated in a bay. Under the name of Hydrus or Hydruntum, often referred to in the ancient sources as a port of embarkation for Apollonia in Epirus, Otranto was destroyed by the Turks in 1480. From the Castello, built in 1495–98, there is a view across the Straits of Otranto (75 km (47 mi.) wide) to the mountains of Albania. The cathedral of the Santissima Annunziata (begun 1080) contains ancient columns with 12th c. capitals, a unique mosaic pavement, completely preserved, with representations of the months and of heroic subjects (1163–66) and a five-aisled crypt. In a side street in the upper part of the town is the little church of San Pietro (10th–11th c.), with a Byzantine dome and frescos, depicting the saints and scenes of the life of Christ.

Otranto

From Otranto the road continues, running inland for part of the way and then winding its way along the coast, to Santa Cesarea Terme (56 m

Santa Cesarea Terme

Leghorn

(185 ft)), a popular resort, charmingly situated above the sea. It has four springs of sulphureous water (36°C (97°F)) in large caves in the cliffs.

Stalactitic caves

From here there is an interesting boat trip (4–5 km (2¹/₂–3 mi.) south), along the rocky coast with its numerous coves to two stalactitic caves which were inhabited in prehistoric times, the Grotta Romanelli and the Grotta Zinzulusa.

Capo Santa Maria di Leuca

Beyond Santa Cesarea Terme the road continues along the rocky coast to the little fishing port of Castro Marino, below the fortified village of Castro, and Capo Santa Maria di Leuca (59 m (195 ft)), the south-eastern tip of Italy, named after its white limestone cliffs (Greek ákra leuká). On the cape is the church of Santa Maria de Finibus Terrae ("St Mary of the Ends of the Earth"), with an altar constructed of stone from the temple of Minerva which stood here, and an image of the Virgin which is revered as miraculous. From the lighthouse there are magnificent views, extending in clear weather as far as Albania.

West of the cape is the little seaside resort of Leuca and to the south-west Punta Ristole.

There are attractive boat trips along the magnificent rocky coast with its numerous caves.

Leghorn   E8

Region: Toscana. Province: Livorno (LI)
Altitude: 3 m (10 ft). Population: 176,000

Location

Leghorn (in Italian Livorno), capital of its province and the most important harbour in Tuscany, is situated on the low-lying coast of the Tyrrhenian Sea, some 20 km (12 mi.) south of Pisa.

History

Leghorn owed its rise to the Medici, who during the 16th and 17th c. offered asylum to refugees from many lands.

The city is of modern aspect, and the heavy destruction of the Second World War has left it with no great monuments of the past. Leghorn was the birthplace of the painter Amedeo Modigliani (1884–1920).

Sights

Piazza Grande

The central feature of the old town is the long Piazza Grande, now surrounded by modern buildings. At its southern end stands the cathedral, rebuilt in accordance with the original plan; in the centre of the square is the Palazzo Grande (1951) and at the north-east corner the Town Hall. From here Via Cairoli runs south to the Piazza Cavour, the new centre of the city's traffic, which is partly laid out over a canal, the Fosso Reale.

Via Grande

Leghorn's main street, the Via Grande, cuts across the Piazza Grande; at its east end is the Piazza della Repubblica, with statues of Ferdinand III (d. 1824) and Leopold II (d. 1870), the last Grand Dukes of Tuscany. Immedi-ately north of the square is the Fortezza Nuova (bastion; 1590), surrounded by canals.

Harbour

The harbour, at the west end of the old town, is one of the most important ports of the Mediterranean. The old part of the harbour is called Porto Mediceo in honour of its founders. On the north side of the Piazza Michele, flanking the docks, stands a statue of Grand Duke Ferdinand I (1587–1609) by Giovanni Bandini, which, because of the bronze figures on the plinth (by Pietro Tacca, 1624), is also called "Monumento dei Quattro Mori" (monument of the four moors).

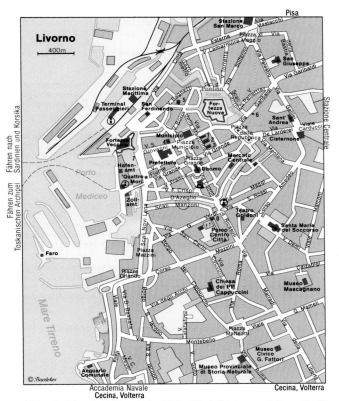

Livorno
400m

Pisa

Fähren nach
Sardinien und Korsika

Fähren zum
Toskanischen Archipel

1 Chiesa degli Armeni   3 Chiesa dei Greci Uniti   5 Santa Caterina   7 Darsena Vecchia
2 Chiesa della Madonna   4 Chiesa di San Giovanni   6 Garibaldi-Monument   8 Chiesa Valdese

At the northern end of the harbour and its docks is the Fortezza Vecchia (old bastion; 1534), with a massive tower.

Fortezza Vecchia

The southern boundary of the docks is the starting point of the beautiful Viale Italia which runs south, along the coast, past parks and beaches. In the Terrazza Mascagni is the Aquarium (Aquarino Comunale); adjoining it is a marine research institute.

Viale Italia

South-east of the old town, set amid a park, is the Museo d'Arte Contemporanea (Museum of Contemporary Art), with works by mainly Italian artists (temporary exhibitions).

Museo d'Arte Contemporanea

The Museo Civico, in the park of the Villa Fabbricotti to the south of the new town, contains works by the Macchiaioli, a group of painters formed in the mid-19th c., whose principal aim was to overcome academic restrictions. Modern art is also on display including paintings by Modigliani.

Museo Civico

Liguria   B–D6–8

Region: Liguria
Provinces: Genova (GE), Imperia (IM), La Spezia (SP) and Savona (SV)
Area: 5416 sq. km (2090 sq. mi.). Population: 1,700,000

Location
The region of Liguria, with Genoa as capital, lies on the southern slopes of the arc of mountains which extends around the Gulf of Genoa (Ligurian Sea) from the Ligurian Alps in the west to the Ligurian Apennines in the east.

History
The region, originally occupied by Ligurians, was Romanised in the 2nd c. BC. Fragmented during the early medieval period into numerous Lombard and Frankish principalities, it fell from the 12th c. onwards under the control of Genoa, then growing in strength as a sea power. In 1805 Liguria was annexed by Napoleon, and in 1814 it was assigned by the Congress of Vienna to Piedmont, becoming part of the new united Italy.

Scenery
The mountains which here fall steeply down to the sea provide almost complete protection against unfavourable weather from the north, and the region's southern exposure gives it a mild and sunny climate, particularly along the coastal strip known as the Riviera, with its palm-trees and magnolias, which has long been a favourite winter resort.

Population
The population of the region is mainly concentrated in the industrial areas around the ports of Genoa, La Spezia (see entry) and Savona. In the country regions, with only moderately productive soil, vegetables and fruit are grown, as well as the flowers (also used in the manufacture of perfume) for which the region is renowned.

Tourism
Tourism is of great economic importance along the whole of the Riviera (see entry).

★Lipari Islands   J–K18–19

Region: Sicilia. Province: Messina (ME)
Area: 117 sq. km (45 sq. mi.). Population: 13,000

Ferries
Regular services from Milazzo and Messina as well as from Palermo and Naples to Lipari, Vulcano, Salina and Panarea, with connections several times weekly to Filicudi and Alicudi. Car ferries from Milazzo, Messina and Naples.

Location
The Lipari Islands (Isole Lipari), also known as the Aeolian Islands (Isole Eólie) after the Greek wind god Aeolus, lie between 30 and 80 km (19 and 50 mi.) off the north coast of Sicily in the Tyrrhenian Sea.
    They form an archipelago of seven larger islands and ten uninhabited islets, the tips of mountains of volcanic origin rising from the sea-bed far below.

Holiday resort
The islands were long used as penal colonies and places of banishment. In more recent times their mild climate and unusual scenery have attracted increasing numbers of visitors. They offer excellent scuba diving.

Lipari

The largest and most fertile of the islands is Lipari (area 38 sq.km/ 14 sq.miles, population 11,000). In the more southerly bay on the east coast lies the little town of Lipari (5 m (17ft); population 4500), the chief place of the island. To the south of the harbour, on a rocky promontory, is the Castello, within which are the cathedral (1654) and three other churches. Adjoining the cathedral, in the former Bishop's Palace, is the Museo Eoliano containing rich finds of the prehistoric period and historical times from recent excavations on the island (painted Greek vases, a statuette of Isis, tombs, etc.). To the west of the cathedral, on an excavation site in front of the Immacolata Church, can be seen a series of building levels ranging in date from the Early Bronze Age (17th c. BC) through the Iron Age (11th–9th c. BC) and the Hellenistic period to Roman times (2nd c. AD). North of the Castello is the fishermen's quarter; to the south the warehouses in which the island's exports, including pumice-stone, currants, Malvasia wine, capers and figs, are stored to await shipment.

3 km (2 mi.) north of Lipari, beyond Monte Rosa (239 m (789 ft)), the village of Canneto (10 m (33 ft)) is the centre for the extraction, processing and export of pumice-stone. The pumice quarries in the valley of the Fossa Bianca, north-west of the village (45 minutes) are an interesting sight.

Canneto

West of Canneto (1½ hours), beyond the massive lava flows at Forgia Vecchia, rises Monte Sant'Angelo (594 m (1960 ft)). From its summit, roughly in the centre of the archipelago, there is the best panoramic view of the Lipari Islands.

Monte Sant'Angelo

At Piano Conte, in a valley near the west coast, are the hot springs of San Calogero (62°C (144°F); steam baths).

From Lipari there is an attractive walk (1½ hours) to San Salvatore (3 km (2 mi.)), on the southern tip of the island, and from there back to Lipari along the west side of Monte Guardia (369 m (1218 ft)).

Vulcano

To the south of the island of Lipari, separated from it by the Bocche, a strait 1 km (½ mile wide, on the west side of which is the basalt cliff of Pietralunga (60 m (198 ft)), the island of Vulcano (area 21 sq. km (8 sq. mi.); population 400) offers excellent opportunities for studying volcanic phenomena. On the north side of the island is Vulcanello (123 m (406 ft)), with three craters, which rose out of the sea in 183 BC. In the depression south of the hill are the harbours of Porto di Ponente (to the west) and Porto di Levante (to the east). On the shore beside Porto di Levante is a curiously shaped rock, the remnant of an old volcano, riddled with caves for the extraction of alum. The sea-water, here strongly radioactive, is warm and sometimes boiling as a result of under-water emissions of steam.

From the Gran Cratere (391 m (1290 ft); climbed from Porto di Levante in 1 hour) to the south of the depression, there are magnificent views; half-way up are numerous fumeroles. The crater, which since the eruptions of 1880–90 has the characteristics of a solfatara, measures 200 by 140 m (656 by 505 ft) and is 80 m (262 ft) deep.

Farther south is the cone of Monte Aria (499 m (1647 ft)), the island's highest peak.

Salina

4 km (2½ mi.) north-west of Lipari lies the island of Salina (area 27 sq. km (10½ sq. mi.); population 2000), with two extinct volcanoes, Monte de Porri (860m/2838ft) to the north-west and Monte Fossa delle Felci (962m/3175ft) to the south-east.

Islands of Filicudi and Alicudi

Filicudi   20 km (12 mi.) of Salina is the island of Filicudi (775 m (2558 ft); area 9 sq. km (3½ sq. mi.); population 150). On its west coast a fine cave (Grotta del Bue Marino) with basalt pillars can be visited.

Alicudi   13 km (8 mi.) farther west is the island of Alicudi (663m/2188ft; area 5 sq. km (2 sq. mi.)), with a population of some 130 shepherds and fishermen.

Panarea

The small group of islands between 14 and 21 km (9 and 13 mi.) north-east of the island of Lipari may have been a single island before the volcanic eruptions of 126 BC. The largest of the group, Panarea (421 m (1389 ft); area 3.5 sq. km (1¼ sq. mi.); population 250) has hot springs. At Punta Milazzese, the southernmost tip of the island, are the foundations (excavated 1948) of 23 huts belonging to a Bronze Age village (14th–13th c. BC), the best preserved in Italy.

4 km (2½ mi.) north-east of Panarea is a small uninhabited rocky island, Basiluzzo (cultivation of capers).

Stromboli

14 km (9 mi.) north-east of Basiluzzo is the island of Stromboli (area 12.5 sq. km (5 sq. mi.) population about 350), reputed in ancient times to be the home of the wind-god Aeolus. On the north-east coast the chief place of the island, Stromboli (20 m (66 ft)), comprises the districts of Piscità, San Vincenzo and Ficogrande.

Glowing lava spouting from the Stromboli crater

Like the crater on Vulcano, Stromboli (926 m (3056 ft)), is one of the few   ★Volcano of
European volcanoes that are still active; its red glow can be seen from a   Stromboli
long way off. The ascent (3 hours), recommended to be undertaken from
the north side, is a fascinating experience. The crater, to the north of the
highest peak, emits at frequent intervals huge bubbles of lava which ex-
plode with a thunderous noise, throwing up showers of stones which fall
back into the crater or roll harmlessly down the Sciara de Fuoco, a slope
descending on the north-west side at an angle of 35° to the sea and continuing for some distance below the surface. Only every few years are
there more violent eruptions which cause damage to the cultivated parts
of the island. When the vapour is not too thick it is possible to go down to
the brink of the crater and look in.

1.5 km (1 mi.) north-east of the village of Stromboli is the basalt cliff of   Strombolicchio
Strombolicchio, rising 56 m (185 ft) sheer from the sea (steps cut in rock).

Livigno   E2

Region: Lombardia. Province: Sondrio (SO)
Political status: duty free zone
Altitude: 1800–2250 m (5940–7385 ft). Population: 4700

The valley of Livigno is situated in the northernmost part of Lombardy;   Location
through it flows the River Spöl, which in Swiss territory to the north joins
the River Inn (Rhaeto-Romanic "En"). This once remote area has developed into a very popular holiday region, particularly for winter sports.
Another attraction to visitors is its duty free status.

The high valley is accessible all year through the Munt-La-Schera Tunnel   Access
(closed at night; toll), the starting point of which is in the Münstertal in
Switzerland (access from Vinschgau via Glurns and Taufers). During the
summer access is also possible by way of the Stilfser Joch and/or from
Tirano, through the Swiss Val Poschiavo and over the Forcola di Livigno
(2330 m (7647 ft)).

Scenery

Livigno has a number of fine old wooden houses. In the north of the area
is the Lago del Gallo (Lago di Livigno; 1806 m (5960 ft)), an artificial lake
which provides electricity for Switzerland. The tunnel to the Punt La
Drossa ends at the Ponte del Gallo (Rhaeto-Romanic "Punt dal Gal"); in
the fine Swiss National Park. The River Adda connects two other lakes,
outside the customs-free zone, the Lago di San Giacomo (1946 m (6422 ft))
and the Lago di Cancano (1900 m (6270 ft)), with Lago di Gallo.

Cableways

Chair-lift from Ponte di Bondio (1822 m (6013 ft) to the Alpe Eira (Motto-   East side of the
lino; 2400 m (7920 ft), then chair-lift to Monte della Neve (2785 m (9191 ft);   valley
upper station 100 m (330 ft) below the summit); chair-lift from Rin del Ciuk
(2112 m (6970 ft)) to Monte Sponda (2521 m (8319 ft)); chair-lift from
Trepalle to the Alpe Eira, etc.

Cableway from San Rocco (1875 m (6188 ft) to the Balta Pel (2200 m (7260 ft));   West side of the
from here to the Lac Salin (2761 m (9111 ft)); chair-lift from Tagliede (1972 m   valley
(6508 ft) to Costaccia (2355 m (7772 ft).

241

Lodi   D5

Region: Lombardia. Province: Milano (MI)
Altitude: 88 m (289 ft). Population: 42,000

Location
The town of Lodi, situated on the right bank of the Adda in the fertile Po plain, is some 20 km (12 mi.) south-east of Milan.

History
Lodi was founded by Frederick Barbarossa in 1158 after the destruction of Lodi Vecchio. Throughout the Middle Ages it was one of Milan's bitterest opponents. In 1311 it came under the sway of the Visconti family (see Milan, History).

Sights

★Cathedral
In the Piazza della Vittoria, in the centre of the town, rises the Romanesque cathedral (12th c.); it has a beautiful pillared doorway with figures of Adam and Eve and Romanesque reliefs in the crypt, together with the tomb of St Bassianus.

★Church of the Incoronata
A little way north-west of the Piazza della Vittoria stands the church of the Incoronata, a fine building (1488–94) on a centralised plan, with four panels by Bergognone ("The Childhood of Christ") on the second side altar to the right, an organ gallery of 1507 and richly carved choir-stalls (c. 1700).

Museo Civico
North of the Piazza della Vittoria the Museo Civico houses a rich collection (archaeology, pottery and pictures).

★San Francesco
To the north-east of the cathedral, in Piazza Ospedale, we find the beautiful church of San Francesco, in Lombard Gothic style (13th c.), with frescoes

Lodi cathedral: the Crypt

Santa Maria della Croce, near Crema

on the pillars in the interior. To the right of the church the Ospedale Maggiore has an Early Renaissance fine pillared courtyard.

Surroundings

West of Lodi is Lodi Vecchio (82 m (271 ft); population 5000), the Roman Laus Pompeia, destroyed by the Milanese in 1111 and 1158, after which it declined into an unimportant little country town. There are two interesting churches – San Bassiano (11th c.), restored in Gothic style in 1322, with 15th c. frescoes, and the Badia di San Pietro.

Lodi Vecchio
7 km (4½ mi.) W

North-east of Lodi is situated the busy little town of Crema (79 m (261 ft); population 35,000), with a Romanesque cathedral (13th c.), a 16th c. Town Hall, the Palazzo Vescovile (paintings) and the Augustinian monastery of S Agostino with the Museo Civico and the Palazzo Terni de Gregory.

1 km (½ mi.) north of the town on the Bergamo road is the church of Santa Maria della Croce, built 1490 onwards under the influence of Bramante. Inside, note the ceiling frescoes and figures of saints.

Crema
16 km (10 mi.) NE

Lombardy

C–E3–5

Region: Lombardia
Provinces: Bergamo (BG), Brescia (BS), Como (CO), Cremona (CR), Milano (MI), Mantova (MN), Pavia (PV), Sondrio (SO) and Varese (VA)
Area: 23,859 sq. km (9200 sq. mi.). Population: 8,900,000

The historic territory and modern region of Lombardy extends from the High Alps (Bernina massif, Ortles, Adamello group) in the north by way of

Location

243

the Bergamo and Brescia Alps to the Po plain, and includes the central part of that plain between the rivers Sesia and Mincio, bounded on the south by the Apennines.

The province's capital is Milan.

Economy

Southern Lombardy, in the plain of the Po and the flat pre-Alpine uplands, is one of Italy's most highly developed industrial regions (chemicals and pharmaceuticals, metal-working, car manufacture, engineering and light engineering, textiles, leather goods) as well as one of its most productive agricultural regions (corn, rice, maize, market gardening, fodder crops). The hill regions are mostly devoted to dairy and pastoral farming, while the Valtinella is noted for its wine. Tourism makes a major contribution to the economy in the area around the beautiful Alpine lakes (lakes Maggiore, Como and Garda) and in the mountains (winter sports, climbing). The population is mainly concentrated in the densely settled conurbations centred on Milan, Brescia, Pavia and Varese.

History

After the fall of the Western Roman Empire Lombardy (Langobardia) became in the 7th c. the heartland of the Langobards or Lombards and in 951 a kingdom, with its capital at Pavia. The conflict between the Lombard League and the Hohenstaufen rulers of Germany in the 12th and 13th c. led to the division of the Lombard towns between the Guelfs and Ghibellines, with a consequent internal decline and a splitting up from the kingdom. From the 14th c. Milan established its dominance in western Lombardy, while Venice gained control of the eastern part of the territory. In 1535 Milan passed to the Spanish Habsburgs and in 1797, as the Cisalpine Republic, to France. The Congress of Vienna assigned Lombardy and Venetia to Austria as a Lombard-Venetian kingdom. Finally in 1859 Austria was compelled to cede Lombardy, and after 1866 Venetia as well, to the kingdom of Italy.

Sights

The tourist attractions of northern Italy include not only towns such as Milan, Pavia, Bergamo, Brescia, Cremona and Mantova (see entries) but also the Alpine lakes – lakes Como, Garda and Maggiore (see entries) – with their beautiful scenery and favoured climate.

★Lake Lugano

In addition there is also Lake Lugano (Lago di Lugano or Lago Ceresio; alt. 274 m (904 ft); area 50 sq. km (19 sq. mi.); greatest depth 288 m (748 ft)), most of which is in Switzerland.

Porlezza

On the north-east arm of Lake Lugano is the village of Porlezza (271 m (894 ft)), from which an attractive road runs along the south side of the lake, via the little village of Osteno, to Lanzo d'Intelvi (907 m (2993 ft)), a summer resort in the upper reaches of the Valle d'Intelvi. A short distance north-east is Belvedere di Lanzo (887 m (2927 ft)), from which a funicular runs down to Santa Margherita on the lake.

Campione d'Italia

On the east side of Lake Lugano, within Swiss territory, is the Italian enclave of Campione d'Italia , with a popular casino and the church of the Madonna dei Ghirli (14th c.; fine frescoes).

Lakes

The town centres in Lombardy, which boast a large number of historical places of interest are worth visiting. The large lakes in north Italy are also attractive: Bergamo, Brescia, Lake Como, Cremona, Lake Garda, Lake Maggiore, Lodi, Mantua, Milan, Pavia, Varese. See entries.

★Loreto   H9

Region: Marche. Province: Ancona (AN)
Altitude: 127 m (419 ft). Population: 11,000

The little town of Loreto lies on a hill near the Adriatic Sea, some 20 km (13 mi.) south of Ancona.

Location

Since the 14th c. it has been Italy's second most important place of pilgrimage after Rome.

According to legend the Virgin's house in Nazareth, the Santa Casa, was transported by angels to Trsat near Rijeka (Fiume) in the former Yugoslavia in 1291, then in 1294 to a "laurel wood" (lauretium) at Recanati and in 1295 to its present site in Loreto.

History

In 1586 Pope Sixtus V gave the town a municipal charter and the right to build walls. Since 1920 the Madonna of Loreto has been the patroness of airmen.

★Santuario della Santa Casa

In the Piazza della Madonna, with a beautiful 17th c. fountain, stands the Santuario della Santa Casa, a Gothic hall-church with a fortress-like exterior begun in 1468 under Pope Paul II and continued in 1479–86 by the Florentine Giuliano da Maiano; the dome dates from 1500. The handsome façade, showing influence of Late Renaissance, was added in 1583–87. The three bronze doors are decorated with figures and bas reliefs. A bronze statue of Pope Sixtus V stands on the left in front of the façade.

The interior of the church was altered from 1526 onwards. To the left of the entrance is a beautiful font (1607). Adjoining the south transept are the two sacristies, with celebrated wall paintings: on the right frescos by Melozzo da Forli (1438–94), on the left much restored frescos by Luca Signorelli and an assistant together with a marble fountain by Maiano. In the choir apse ("Capella dei Tedeschi") are paintings by Ludwig Seitz (1893–1908).

Interior

In the centre of the church, under the dome, is the Santa Casa, a simple brick building (4.2m (13¾ ft) high, 8.8 m (28¾ ft) long, 3.9 m (12¾ ft) wide)

Santa Casa

Piazza della Madonna in Loreto

surrounded by a high marble screen designed by Bramante (16th c.). On the walls are scenes of the life of the Madonna and of the transportation of the Santa Casa to Loreto.

Museum

Opposite the Santuario, in Piazza della Madonna is the Palazzo Apostolico, with a picture collection, tapestries (from designs by Raphael) and majolica from Urbino.

★Lucca   E8

Region: Toscana. Province: Lucca (LU)
Altitude: 17 m (56 ft). Population: 90,000

Location

The provincial capital of Lucca, the see of an archbishop, lies in the north-west of Tuscany, on the left bank of the River Sergio, almost 25 km (16 mi.) inland from Viareggio. The Alpi Apuane are to the north of the town, the Monti Pisani to the south.
   Lucca was the home of the sculptor Matteo Civitali (1436–1501) and the composer Giacomo Puccini (1858–1924), whose birthplace is now a museum and open to the public.

History

The ancient Lucca, which became a Roman colony in 177 BC, belonged after the fall of the Roman Empire to the Ostrogoths, the Lombards and the Franks in turn. It later became capital of the marquisate of Tuscia, and subsequently fell into the hands of the Scaligers and Florence. In 1369 the town purchased its freedom from Charles IV for 100,000 gold florins, and thereafter it remained independent until the French invasion in 1799. In 1805 Napoleon gave Lucca together with Massa-Carrara as a principality to his sister Elisa Bacciocchi. In 1817 it passed to the house of Bourbon-Parma as a duchy, and in 1847 was ceded to Tuscany.
   Lucca played a prominent part in the history of architecture from the Lombard period onwards; but its early medieval churches, partly built with ancient material, were altered and restored in the 12th c.

Sights

Piazza Napoleone

The central feature of the town is the Piazza Napoleone, the largest square in Lucca, laid out under Elisa Bacciocchi. On the west side of the Piazza Napoleone stands the Palazzo della Provincia, the old ducal palace (begun in 1578, continued in 1728), the courtyard of which is unfinished.

★ Cathedral

From Piazza Napoleone Via Duomo runs south-east to the Piazza San Martino, in which stands the cathedral of San Martino, founded in the 6th c. and mainly dating in its present form from the 12th c. (nave remodelled in Gothic style in 14th c.). On the richly decorated Romanesque façade (1204), to the right of the principal arch, is St Martin with the beggar (copy; the original is inside the church). In the vestibule are reliefs, probably early works by Nicola Pisano. The cathedral has pictures and fine sculpture, including work by Jacopo della Quercia and Matteo Civitali. The Tempietto, a small octagonal chapel (by Civitali, 1482–84) in the north aisle contains an ancient crucifix (11th–12th c.) from the Holy Land known as the Volto Santo, displayed only on certain feast days in May and September.
   Beyond the cathedral is the Archbishop's Palace, rebuilt in the 18th c., with a fine library. Behind it is the graceful Gothic chapel of Santa Maria della Rosa (1309).

San Giovanni

A little way west of the cathedral is the 12th c. church of San Giovanni with a fine relief of the Madonna (1187) above the doorway. The interior is divided by rows of columns into three naves; notable is the old baptistery at the end of the north transept.

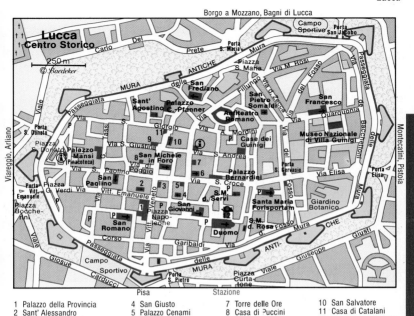

Borgo a Mozzano, Bagni di Lucca

1 Palazzo della Provincia	4 San Giusto	7 Torre delle Ore	10 San Salvatore
2 Sant' Alessandro	5 Palazzo Cenami	8 Casa di Puccini	11 Casa di Catalani
3 Palazzo Pretorio	6 San Cristoforo	9 Palazzo Orsetti	12 Museo d. Cattedrale

From the Piazza Napoleone the busy Via Vittorio runs north to the Piazza San Michele, on the site of the ancient forum. On the right-hand side of this street is the Palazzo Pretorio (begun 1492), in Early Renaissance style. On the north side of the square the church of San Michele (12th c.) has a high Pisan-style façade; on top of the ground floor, separated by arches with half-columns, are four arcaded galleries. The gable is crowned with a statue of the Archangel Gabriel, flanked by two angels.

★San Michele in Foro

Opposite San Michele in Via di Poggio is the birthplace of Giacomo Puccini (Casa Natale di Giacomo Puccini).

House of Puccini

A short distance west of the House of Puccini stands the 17th c. Palazzo Mansi which houses the notable Pinacoteca Nazionale (National Picture Gallery), with pictures by Veronese, Tintoretto, Bergognone, G. Reni and other painters of the school of Tuscany.

Pinacoteca Nazionale

East of Piazza San Michele in Via Fillungo stands the Romanesque church of San Cristoforo (11th–12th c.). To the north is the Chiesa San Salvatore or Chiesa della Misericordia, also 11th–12th c.

Churches

Via Fillungo leads north past a number of old towers, belonging to noble families, to the Piazza San Frediano, on the west side of which is the church of San Frediano, said to have been founded in the 6th c. by an Irish saint, Frigidianus. It was rebuilt in Romanesque style from 1112 onwards. On the façade is a 12th c. mosaic of Christ enthroned with Apostles. The church contains a 12th c. font with fine reliefs by Robertus and a marble altar by Jacopo della Quercia (1422); adjoining the church is an impressive campanile with open arcades.

★San Frediano

Lucca

San Michele in Foro

The mosaic façade of San Frediano

The "Anfiteatro Romano" in Lucca

A short distance south-east of Piazza San Frediano is the Piazza del Mercato, originally the arena (80 × 53.5 m (262³/₄ × 175¹/₂ ft) of the Roman amphi– theatre, on the foundations of which the houses around the square have been built. Two series of 54 arches can still be seen on the north-east side. | Anfiteatro Romano

To the east of the amphitheatre stands the church of San Pietro Somaldi, a pillared basilica of the late 12th c. (façade 13th c.). Farther east is the church of San Francesco (1228). | Churches

South of the amphitheatre in Via Guinigi is a mighty tower, the top of which is overgrown. It is part of the building complex called the Case del Guinigi, which comprised town houses of the noble families who ruled Lucca in the beginning of the 15th c., a period of peace and prosperity. | Case dei Guinigi

A little way south-east of the building complex is the 13th c. church of Santa Maria Forisportam. The church owes its name to the fact that it was built outside the port ("forisportam"). Inside there is an Early Christian sarcophagus, now used as a font. | Santa Maria Forisportam

To the east of the church, at the end of Via Santa Croce, is the old Porta San Gervasio, a remnant of the town's second circuit of walls (13th c.), with two massive round towers. | Porta San Gervasio

To the east of the town in Via della Quarquonia is the 15th c. villa built for Paola Guinigi which now houses the Museo Nazionale (National Museum), with a large art collection. Of interest are the Etruscan and Roman sculptures, sculptures from the medieval churches of Lucca and paintings by several Italian masters. | ★Museo Nazionale di Villa Guinigi

The present ramparts (4.2 km (2¹/₂ mi.) long), now shaded by fine old trees, were built between 1504 and 1645. There is an attractive walk around the | ★Ramparts whole circuit ("Passeggio delle Mura Urbane"), affording charming views of the town with its numerous towers and of the beautiful surrounding hills.

San Guiliano Terme

13 km (8 mi.) SW   South-west, prettily situated under the west side of the Monti Pisani, is the spa of San Guiliano Terme (10 m (33 ft); population 27,000), with radioactive sulphur springs.

Bagni di Lucca

25 km (16 mi.) N   North of Lucca, Bagni di Lucca (150 m (495 ft); population 9000), comprises a number of separate villages, known as early as the 10th c. as the "Baths of Corsena", with springs containing salt and sulphur (37–54°C (99–129°F): season May–September). The principal village is Villa, once a residence of the dukes of Lucca, with its own thermal spring. The village of Bagni Caldi is the most important spa, with a warm spring, the "Doccione" (54°C (129°F)), in a cave.

★★Lake Maggiore   C3–4

Regions: Lombardia and Piedmonte
Provinces: Varese (VA) and Novara (NO).
Altitude: 194 m (640 ft)

Location   Lake Maggiore (Lago Maggiore), known to the Romans as Lacus Verbanus, lies in north Italy; the northern part of the lake, with the town of Locarno, is in Switzerland. The distance between the southern tip of the lake and the town of Novara is about 30 km (19 mi.).

Scenery   Lake Maggiore, with an area of 212 sq. km (82 sq. mi.) (length 65 km (40 mi.), breadth 3–5 km (2–3 mi.), greatest depth 372 m (1228 ft)), is the second largest of the north Italian lakes. Less intricately patterned than Lake Como and without the sheer rock faces of the northern part of Lake Garda, it nevertheless offers scenery of southern splendour which may lack the grandeur of the other lakes but is perhaps even more appealing. The east side belongs to Lombardy and the west side to Piedmont. The lake's principal tributaries are the Ticino and the Maggia to the north and the Toce on the west side. The river which flows out of the southern end is the Ticino. The northern part of the lake is enclosed by mountains, for the most part wooded, while towards the south the shores slope down to the plain of Lombardy. In clear weather the water in the northern part of the lake is green, in the southern part deep blue.

Climate   The climate is mild. From midnight until morning the tramontana blows, usually coming from the north; from midday until evening the inverna blows from the south.

Flora   The trees of Lake Maggiore, like that of lakes Garda and Como, include numerous subtropical species: figs, olives and pomegranates flourish in the mild climate, and in August the myrtle blooms. On the Borromean Islands lemons, oranges, cork-oaks, sago-palms and carob-trees grow.

Tourism   The most popular tourist areas are around Locarno and on the western arm of the lake between Pallanza and Stresa, where the magnificent Borromean Islands with their subtropical parks are the main attraction. There is an attractive drive around the lake on an excellent road.

Ispra   Near the east side of the lake, at Ispra, is the first Italian atomic research centre, now a Euratom research centre, with an atomic reactor (1959) and a tower 120 m (396 ft) high belonging to a meteorological station.

Another very worth-while excursion is a boat trip on the lake (services throughout the year). The boats ply between Locarno and Arona (also hydrofoil services), calling alternately at places on the west and east sides; between Cannobio and Stresa, and between Verbania and Stresa. There are also car ferry services.

Boat services

Sights

On the west side of Lake Maggiore, beautifully situated near the Borromean Islands, lies Verbania (205 m (677 ft); population 32,000), a town formed by the amalgamation of Pallanza and Intra together with other adjoining villages. It attracts large numbers of visitors with its mild climate and beautiful scenery.

Verbania

The district of Pallanza lies on both sides of the Punta della Castagnola (magnificent view from the park of the former Eden Palace Hotel).

Just offshore, to the west, is the little island of San Giovanni.

On the lakeside road is the Kursaal with its park (fine views). Beyond this, by the lake, is the mausoleum of General Cadorna (1850–1928), commander-in-chief of the Italian army during the First World War. To the north stands the parish church of San Leonardo (16th c. restored). Farther west are the Palazzo di Città (Town Hall) and the landing-stage, from which there are good views of the Borromean Islands (with Isola Madre in the foreground) and Monte Mottarone.

Pallanza

About 1.5 km (1 mi.) north, at the foot of Monte Rosso (693 m (2287 ft)), the domed church of the Madonna di Campagna, contains frescoes by Lanino and the Procaccini.

Madonna di Campagna

On a hill 1 km (1/2 mi.) north of the Punta della Castagnola is the park of the Villa San Remigio (no admission) and nearby is the little Romanesque church of San Remigio (11th c.). Immediately north is the magnificent park of the Villa Taranto, laid out after the Second World War (open: April–October, good guide book, with plan; boat landing-stage), with botanical research laboratories and numerous rare and exotic plants.

★★ Villa Taranto

North-east of Pallanza, between the Torrente San Bernardino and the Torrente San Giovanni, is the industrial district of Intra, with the fine church of San Vittore. From here there is a car ferry across the lake to Laveno.

Intra

North of Intra rises Monte Zeda (2157 m (7118 ft); extensive views), which can be climbed in seven hours.

★ Monte Zeda

From Intra a panoramic road runs 13 km (8 mi.) north to the village of Premeno (840 m (2772 ft)), a summer holiday resort.

Premeno

About 13 km (8 mi.) north-east of Intra Cannero Riviera (226 m (746 ft)) is beautifully situated on the shores of the lake amid vineyards, orchards and olive-groves. The climate here is the mildest on the lake, and lemon and orange trees can survive the winter in the open. There is also a beautiful beach.

Cannero Riviera

Farther north, on rocky islets in the lake, are the ruins of the two Castelli di Cannero, built by Lodovico Borromeo in 1519 in place of earlier castles which had been held by brigands.

★ Castelli di Cannero

7 km (4 1/2 mi.) north of Cannero – also on the west bank of Lake Maggiore – on a plateau at the mouth of the wide, cool Valle Cannobina, the old town of Cannobio (214 m (706 ft)) has picturesque narrow streets. Notable are the Palazzo della Ragione (1291) and near the landing-stage the Santuario della Pietà, a Renaissance church in the manner of Bramante (on the high altar "Christ bearing the Cross" by Gaudenzio Ferrari, c. 1525).

Cannobio

Also on the west side of Lake Maggiore, south of its western arm, the little town of Stresa (210 m (693 ft); population 5000) looks on to the Borromean Islands. Stresa is the largest resort on Lake Maggiore after Locarno. Cooler and windier than other places on the lake, it is busiest during the warmer part of the year. The long lakeside road affords beautiful views of the lake and the Borromean Islands.

Stresa

The life of Stresa centres on its lakeside promenade (fine views), on which are the parish church and most of the large hotels.

About 1 km ($^1/_2$ mi.) south, above the landing-place, is the Collegio Rosmini (267 m (881 ft)), an educational institution run by the Rosminians; in the church is the tomb of the priest and philosopher A. Rosmini (1797–1855). 500 m farther on is the beautiful park of the Villa Pallavicino (closed in winter), with luxuriant vegetation and an interesting menagerie.

★Park of the Villa Pallavicino

From Stresa a toll road, the Borromea (about 30 km (19 mi.); also a cableway), runs up via Gignese (707 m (2333 ft)), with an unusual Umbrella Museum, to the summit of Monte Mottarone (1491 m (4920 ft)), from which the view embraces the chain of the Alps from Monte Viso to Ortles, with Monte Rosa to the west (particularly fine in the morning).

★Monte Mottarone

Half-way up, at the hamlet of Alpino (768 m (2534 ft)), a road branches off to the Giardino Alpinia (807 m (2663 ft)), 500 m north, with some 2000 species of plants (magnificent views).

Giardino Alpinia

From Stresa there is a very attractive boat trip to the Borromean Islands.

★★Borromean Islands
★Isola Bella

The boat calls first at Isola Bella which owes its present appearance to Count Vitaliano Borromeo, who between 1650 and 1671 transformed what had been a barren rock, with a parish church and a few houses, by building up terraces of fertile soil and creating a splendid summer residence. The palace, left unfinished, contains magnificent state apartments, numerous pictures (including some good Lombard works of the 16th and 17th c.) and a gallery of 17th c. Flemish tapestries. The Italian-style garden (beautiful views), rises in ten terraces to a height of 32 m (106 ft) and is covered with luxuriant southern vegetation – lemon and orange trees, cherry-laurels, cedars, magnolias, cork-oaks, sago-palms, carob-trees, camellias, oleanders, etc.

About 500 m north-west of Isola Bella is the Isola dei Pescatori or Isola Superiore, with a picturesque fishing village.

Isola dei Pescatori

Between the Isola dei Pescatori and Pallanza lies Isola Madre, which, like Isola Bella, belongs to the Borromeo family. It has beautiful English-style grounds surpassing even Isola Bella in the variety and luxuriance of their vegetation. On the highest point is an uninhabited palace (view).

★Isola Madre

About 4 km (2$^1/_2$ mi.) north-west of Stresa is Baveno (205 m (677 ft)), a popular resort, with a fine parish church. From the lakeside promenade there is a picturesque view of the lake with the Borromean Islands. At the southern end of the town stands the large Villa Branca, which belongs to the manufacturer of the well-known vermouth Fernet Branca, with a beautiful park (no admission).

Baveno

About 13 km (8 mi.) south of Stresa is Meina (214 m (706 ft)), with the splendid Villa Farragiana (museum). An eminence south of the village – between Meina and Arona – is crowned by the "San Carlone", a 23 m (76 ft) high statue of St Charles Borromeo (1538–84), Cardinal-Archbishop of Milan, who played an important part in the moral revival of Catholicism.

Meina

On the east side of the lake, opposite the statue, is Angera, with an old Visconti castle (view).

Angera

◄ The Borromean Islands, picturesquely situated in Lake Maggiore

Domodossada

From Stresa or Verbania there is an attractive drive (42 or 45 km (26 or 28 mi.)) first along the Lago di Mergozzo, a former arm of Lake Maggiore which was cut off by soil deposited by the River Toce, then continuing up the valley of the Toce to Domodossola (272 m (898 ft); population 20,000), a little hill town, with a pretty market-place and a notable collegiate church with three naves portal with 15th c. frescoes.

Macugnaga

Half-way to Domodossola a road goes off, passes through Piedimulera and continues up the Anzasca valley (gold-mines), the upper part of which has been occupied since the 13th c. by German-speaking settlers from the Valais, to Macugnaga (1327 m (4379 ft)), a holiday resort in a magnificent situation below the east face of Monte Rosa.

Mantua   E5

Region: Lombardia. Province: Mantova (MN)
Altitude: 19 m (63 ft). Population: 53,000

Location

The provincial capital Mantua, former residence of the Gonzaga family, lies south of Lake Garda in the Po plain on the lower course of the Mincino, which here forms a marshy lake divided into three parts: Lago Superiore, Lago di Mezzo and Lago Inferiore.

The town is still surrounded by a ring of walls and bastions. Today it is a relatively prosperous industrial town, especially in the sphere of plastics.

History and art

Originally founded by the Etruscans, the town was noted in antiquity only as the home of the poet Virgil (70–19 BC). It rose to some importance in the 12th and 13th c. under the Hohenstaufen Emperors.

From 1328 the town was ruled by the Guelf house of Gonzaga, who acquired the title of marquis in 1433 and of duke in 1530 and made Mantua one of the most refined and cultivated of princely capitals, a great centre of art and learning. Marquis Lodovico (1444–78) summoned the Florentine architect Leon Battista Alberti to Mantua, and in 1463 enrolled Andrea Mantegna, leader of the Padua school of painters, in his service; the beautiful and accomplished Isabella d'Este (1490–1539), wife of Giovanni Francesco II, carried on a lively correspondence with the great men of the day; and Raphael's outstanding pupil, Giulio Romano (1492–1546), came to Mantua in 1524 and was active as an architect and painter.

After the Gonzaga line died out (1707) the town passed to Austria, as one corner of the defensive "quadrilateral" of Peschiera–Verona–Legnago–Mantua and held it until 1866 (except for a brief interlude during the Napoleonic period). The Austrian patriot Andreas Hofer was shot in Mantua in 1810 on Napoleon's orders (memorial tablet, outside the town, to the north).

Sights

★★Sant'Andrea

In Piazza Mantegna, in the centre of the town, stands the church of Sant'Andrea, a masterpiece of Early Renaissance architecture built by Leon Battista Alberti in 1472–94, with a transept and choir of 1600, and a dome of 1782. The white marble façade, in the style of a classical temple, has beside it the earlier Gothic tower of red brick (1413). The interior, with its massive barrel vault, is of imposing effect. In the first chapel on the left is the tomb of Mantegna, with a bronze bust; in the last chapel on the right are frescoes by Giulio Romano.

From Piazza Mantegna the arcaded Corso Umberto I, the town's principal shopping and business street, leads west to Piazza Cavallotti, from which the Corso della Libertà, a wide street built over an old canal, runs to Piazza Martiri di Belfiori.

Adjoining Piazza Mantegna on the east in the Piazza delle Erbe, are the Torre dell'Orologio (clock-tower), the Palazzo della Ragione (13th c., with much later alteration) and the little Romanesque church of San Lorenzo (11th c.) on a circular plan.

Palazzo della Ragione

To the north, in the medieval Piazza Sordello (at one time the political and artistic centre of the town), are two crenellated Gothic palaces, the Palazzo Guervieri (12th–13th c.), with the 55 m (182 ft) high Torre della Gabbia, and the 13th c. Palazzo Bonacolsi or Palazzo Castiglioni. Adjoining is the Baroque Bishop's Palace (18th c.).

Palaces

On the north-east side of Piazza Sordello stands the cathedral of San Pietro, originally built in Romanesque style as the burial church of the marquises of Canossa and the Gonzaga family, remodelled in Gothic style between 1393 and 1401 and reconstructed internally to the design of Giulio Romano after a fire in 1545; it has fine Baroque façade (1756). Behind the church stands a Romanesque campanile.

Cathedral

Opposite the cathedral the massive Palazzo Ducale, the sumptuous residence of the Gonzagas and one of the most splendid palaces in Italy, now houses a number of important museums and collections – the Municipal Collection of Antiquities (Greek and Roman sculpture); the Museo Medievale e Moderno (mainly medieval and Renaissance sculpture); and the Galleria, a valuable collection of pictures displayed in a series of rooms richly decorated with frescos and ceiling paintings. Outstanding among these rooms are the Appartamento degli Arazzi, with nine tapestries made in Brussels about 1528 (scenes from the life of SS Peter and Paul) after cartoons by Raphael; the Gallery of Mirrors; the Appartamento del Paradiso, from which there are beautiful views of the lakes. On the ground floor are the rooms occupied by Isabella d'Este, the Gabinetti Isabelliani, with richly sculptured ceilings.

★★Palazzo Ducale

Rich paintings line the walls of the Palazzo Ducale

Magnificent frescoes by Mantegna in the Castello San Giorgio

Castello San Giorgio	At the north-east corner of the Palazzo Ducale stands the palace church, Santa Barbara, in High Renaissance style (1565) and the older castle, the massive Castello San Giorgio (1395–1406). On the first floor the Camera degli Sposi contains magnificent frescos by Mantegna (1474), depicting the brilliant life of the court of Lodovico and his wife Barbara of Hohenzollern. On the ceiling are fine trompe-l'oeil paintings.
Monument to Virgil	North-west of Piazza Sordello is the Piazza Virgiliana, with a monument (1927) to the poet Virgil, who was born near Mantua, in Andes (now Pietole).
Palazzo di Giustizia	In the south of the town, at Via Carlo Poma 11, is the Palazzo di Giustizia (16th c.), with colossal hermae (heads of the god Hermes) on the façade.
San Sebastiano	South of the Palazzo di Giustizia the church of San Sebastiano was the first Renaissance church built on a Greek cross plan (1460–1529) as a votive church for Ludovic II.
★Palazzo del Te	Farther south still is the single-storey Palazzo del Te, built 1525–35 by Giulio Romano as a country house for the Gonzagas and decorated with frescoes and stucco work under his direction. The interior rooms are worthy of note: they include the Sala dei Cavalli, the walls of which are decorated with paintings of royal horses, the Sala di Psiche with representations of Amor and Psyche, and the Sala di Giganti.

Surroundings

Santa Maria degli Angeli	On the Cremona road (3 km (2 mi.) west), lying off the road on the right, on the Lago Superiore, the church of Santa Maria degli Angeli (1429) is in Lombard Gothic style, with a beautiful altarpiece by Mantegna.

A short distance farther on, near the west end of the Lago Superiore, stands the Gothic pilgrimage church of Santa Maria delle Grazie (1399). The over-furnished interior contains 44 figures in wood and wax of notable visitors to the shrine (including Charles V) and a fine altarpiece ("St Sebastian") by F. Bonsignori.

Santa Maria delle Grazie
7 km (4½ mi.) W

There is a rewarding trip to the little town of San Benedetto Po (18 m (59 ft)); population 8000), with a former Benedictine monastery (Abbazia di Polirone) founded in 1007 by Marquis Tedaldo of Canossa and dissolved in 1789. The church, originally built in Gothic style was remodelled by Giulio Romano as a splendid Renaissance building with an octagonal dome over the crossing and a fine portico; in front of the presbytery are floor mosaics (12th c.). The internal furnishings are mainly 16th c. Note the terracotta figures by Antonio Begarelli in the nave and choir. In the monastery buildings grouped around the cloisters are remains of some Renaissance frescos. Some rooms of the monastery house the Museo della Cultura Popolare Padana, with 10,000 items on display documenting the life and work of the people of Mantua and the neighbouring provinces of Modena and Reggio nell'Emilia. The exhibits include puppet theatres, evidence of the spiritual and religious life, as well as objects portraying the everyday lives of the farmers and craftsmen.

San Benedetto Po
20 km SE

Marche   G–H8–10

Region: Marche
Provinces: Ancona (AN), Ascoli Piceno (AP), Macerata (MC), Pesaro e Urbino (PS)
Area: 9693 sq. km (3741 sq. mi.). Population: 1,424,000

The region of Marche (the Marches) in Central Italy covers mountainous country, consisting partly of inhospitable terrain (Monte Vettore, 2476 m (8171 ft)) but mostly of very fertile uplands, which extends between the rivers Foglia and Tronto down the eastern slopes of the Appennino Umbro-Marchigiano to the Adriatic coast. The capital of the region is Ancona, at one time one of Italy's most influential towns.

Location

The people earn their living from agriculture and horticulture (wheat, barley, maize, fruit, vegetables, vine) and from stock raising (cattle and pigs). Along the coast fishing and shipbuilding are of some importance.
    The production of majolica is a traditional industry, particularly at Pesara and Urbino and new industries are being developed including both light and heavy engineering.
    Tourism makes a major contribution to the economy in the seaside resorts along the Adriatic coast.
    While in the past a small number of towns in the region, particularly Urbino and Ancona, gained prosperity and influence, the entire region of the Marches which already first in the records in the 10th c., was without any notable importance.

Economy

Sights

Apart from the towns along the Adriatic coast and Ascoli Piceno it is well worth visiting the provincial capital of Macerata (314 m (1036 ft); population 44,000), which occupies a commanding situation cn high ground between the rivers Chienti and Potenza. The central feature of the town is the Piazza della Libertà, in which are the Palazzo Comunale (statues of toga-clad figures and inscriptions from Helvia Ricina in courtyard), the Prefecture (in a 16th c. Gonzaga palace), the beautiful Loggia dei Mercanti

Macerata

Beautiful landscape of the Marche

(16th c.) and the Theatre. From the Piazza della Libertà the Corso della Repubblica leads to the Piazza Vittorio Veneto, with the Biblioteca Comunale, which contains the municipal collection of pictures (including works by the local painter Paganini, Carlo Crivelli, Allegretto Nuzi da Fabriano and Lanfranco). Also of interest are the cathedral and the Sferisterio Festival Theatre (theatrical and operatic productions). There is also a small university.

Fermo

South of Macerata is the town of Fermo (319 m (1053 ft); population 35,000), the see of an archbishop, with churches containing a number of fine pictures. At Porta San Francesco are remains of the town's ancient cyclopean walls. In the Piazza del Popolo, reached by steep lanes running up from the Porta San Francesco, are the Town Hall and the Palazzo degli Studi (library, museum, picture gallery). On the commanding Rocca is the 13th c. cathedral, in the porch of which is the Gothic tomb of Giovanni Visconti (d. 1366) by Bonaventura da Imola. Nearby are remains of the ancient theatre. Under the church of San Domenico, below the Piazza del Popolo, is an ancient cistern (1st c. AD). Also worth a visit are the churches of San Agostino (13th c.) and San Francesco (13th–15th c.).

Iesi

In the north of the region, 30 km (9 mi.) south-west of Ancona, is Iesi (96 m (317 ft); population 42,000), birthplace of the German Emperor Frederick II of Hohenstaufen (1194–1250) and Giovanni Battista Pergolesi (1710–36), composer of the "Stabat Mater". The main features in the town, which is still surrounded by medieval walls, are the fine Palazzo della Signoria, in Early Renaissance style (1487–98; fine pillared courtyard), a Roman and medieval museum and the Pinacoteca, which contains pictures by Lorenzo Lotto.

Ancona, Ascoli Pisceno, Fano, Loreto, Pesaro, Urbino; see entries.

Marsala G20

Region: Sicilia. Province: Trapani (TP)
Altitude: 12 m (40 ft). Population: 80,000

The port and commercial town of Marsala, situated at the western tip of   Location
Sicily, is best known for its rich golden-yellow dessert wine.
  The principal wine-making establishments (stabilimenti or bagli: visitors
admitted) lie along the shore to the south of the town. The Woodhouse
establishment near the station was named after its English founder, who
introduced wine-making to Marsala about 1773. 500 m farther south is
Florio, the town's most famous wine-making establishment, and another
500 m beyond this Ingham-Whitaker. Other leading firms are Rallo and
Pellegrino.

Sights

The hub of the town's traffic is the Piazza della Repubblica, with the beau-   Cathedral
ti-ful 18th c. Old Town Hall, built in the form of a loggia, and the cathedral
of San Tomaso, dedicated to St Thomas of Canterbury, which contains fine
sculpture by Antonello Gagini and eight magnificent 16th c. Flemish tapestries, displayed only on certain feast days.
  From the Piazza della Repubblica the town's main street, Via XI Maggio,
runs north-west past the monastery and church of San Pietro (16th c.) to
the Porta Nuova. On a house on the left is a plaque commemorating the
second visit in 1862 by Garibaldi, whose victorious campaign against the
Bourbons had begun two years earlier, on May 11th 1860, with his landing in Marsala harbour. Beyond the Porta Nuova, to the right, are the Villa
Cavallotti gardens, at the north end of which is a belvedere affording wide
views.

Below the belvedere and along the Viale Vittorio Veneto, which continues   Insula Romana
the line of Via XI Maggio, are remains of the ancient Lilybaeum, including
fragments of the town walls. Off the road to the right are the ruins of the
Insula Romana, living quarters of the 3rd c. AD, with a fine animal mosaic
in the associated baths. From the end of the avenue there is a beautiful
view of the sea and the coast; and from Capo Boeo or Capo Lilibeo, a little way south-west, there are more extensive views north-east over the old
harbour to Monte Erice and north-west of the Isole Égadi.

A museum in Capo Lilibeo contains the remains of a Punic ship which was   Museum
found in 1969 near the island of Langa dello Stagnone.

Half-way between the cape and the Porta Nuova, off the road to the right,   Grotta della Sibilla
is the church of San Giovanni Battista, from which steps lead down to the
"Grotta della Sibilla" (Roman mosaic).

San Pantaleo

On the island of San Pantaleo are the remains of the Punic city of Mozia,   **Mozia**
founded in the 8th c. BC and destroyed in 397 BC. Preserved are the crenel-   about 10 km
lated town walls and towers, a shrine with an altar and a cemetery.   (6 mi.) N

★Merano F2

Region: Trentino-Alto Adige. Province: Bolzano (BZ)
Altitude: 324 m (1069 ft). Population: 35,000

Merano

Location	Merano is situated at the outflow of the River Passirio into the broad valley of the Adige which emerges from the Val Venosta.
Economy	Merano in the Alto Adige is the largest health resort on the south side of the Eastern Alps, with its main season in spring and autumn for the grape cure and with radioactive thermal springs.
History	Merano came into the hands of the counts of Tirol in 1233, and in 1310, together with the Passirio and Ultimo valleys, was formed into a separate burgraviate. From 1317 to 1420 it was capital of Tirol.

Sights

Piazza del Teatro	At the south-west corner of the old town, near the right bank of the Passirio, is the Piazza del Teatro, Merano's busiest square, with the Municipal Theatre (by Martin Dülfer, 1899–1900). From here the Corso della Libertà runs west to the station and east, past the Kursaal, to the Piazza della Rena. The busy Via delle Corso, which bounds the old town on the west, runs north from the Piazza del Teatro to the Piazza del Grano and beyond this to the Porto Venosta.
Via dei Portici	From the Piazza del Grano the old-world Via dei Portici (Laubengasse), a busy shopping street, runs east through the old town, lined with arcades (the Portici di sinistra or Berglauben to the left and the Portici di destra or Wasserlauben to the right). Half-way along the Portici di sinistra is the Town Hall (1928–32).
Castello Principesco	Behind the Town Hall stands the Castello Principesco (1480), still with its original furnishings and a collection of musical instruments.
Municipal Museum	A little way north-west of the castle, at Via Galilei 5, is the rich Municipal Museum, with prehistoric material, local history, medieval sculpture and modern pictures.

The Salvar Baths in Merano

At the east end of the Via dei Portici is the Piazza del Duomo, with the Gothic parish church of San Nicolò (14th–15th c.), whose characteristic campanile dominates the town. From here the old Porta Bolzano leads into the Piazza della Rena.

San Nicolò

On the left bank of the Passirio the district of Maia Bassa (Untermais) is reached from the Piazza della Rena by way of the Ponte Nazionale. Immediately beyond the bridge is the Late Gothic church of the Santo Spirito (15th c.).

Maia Bassa

A little way west are the Salvar Baths (1971), with an indoor bath (radio-active water, 30–35°C (86–91°F), an outdoor pool, sauna facilities, a treatment centre, a restaurant and a Congress Centre.

Salvar Baths

From the Santo Spirito church Via Cavour climbs east to the select villa suburb of Maia Alta (Obermais), in which are many old aristocratic residences such as Castello di Nova (Trautmannsdorf), Castello Rametz (vine-growing estate), Castello Labers (hotel), Castello Rundegg (hotel), Castello Planta (pension) and Castello Gaiano (Schloss Goyen).

Maia Alta

Promenades

Along the broad embankment on the right bank of the Passirio runs the Passeggiata Lungo Passirio, in the centre of which is the Kursaal (1907). Farther west is the Protestant Church of Christ (1885). The Passeggiata Lungo Passirio is continued eastward by the sheltered Passeggiata d'Inverno.

Passeggiata Lungo Passirio

From the Ponte Nazionale the Passeggiata d'Estate follows the left bank of the Passirio and is linked by a bridge with the Passeggiata d'Inverno on the right bank. The two promenades run upstream to the Ponte Romano (1616), from which the Passeggiata Gilf continues along the right bank to the gorge under Castello San Zeno.

Passeggiata d'Estate

From the Ponte Romano and the Passeggiata Gilf we can continue on the Passeggiata Tappeiner, a beautiful high-level promenade which begins at the medieval Torre della Polvere and runs for 4 km (2½ mi.) at a height of some 150 m (495 ft) above Merano (magnificent views, particularly from the Torre della Polvere) along the slopes of Monte Benedetto (Küchelberg, 531 m (1752 ft)). There is a chair-lift up the hill from near the Castello Principesco, and it makes an attractive trip to take the lift up and walk down. From Monte Benedetto there is a footpath (30 minutes) to the village of Tirolo.

★Passeggiata Tappeiner

Surroundings

From the Porta Passiria a good road (4 km (2½ mi.)) runs north-east along-side the Passeggiata Gilf and past Castello San Zeno (12th and 13th c.), and then turns north-west up the slopes of Monte Benedetto to the village of Tirolo (1596 m (5267 ft); cableway up La Mutta, 1350 m (4455 ft)).
   From here it is a 25 minutes' walk, passing above Castel Fontana and through a narrow gorge 52 m (172 ft) long, to the 12th c. Castel Tirolo (Schloss Tirol, 647 m (2135 ft)), the residence in the 12th and 13th c. of the counts of Tirol (who died out in 1253), which has given its name to the whole region of Tirol. The castle now houses the Regional Museum with an archaeological department.

★Castel Tirolo

West of Castel Tirolo (30 minutes) is Castello Torre (Schloss Thurnstein (551 m (1818 ft); with a beautiful view). Lower down is Castello Fontana (Brunnenburg; restored in 1904).

Castello Torre

Scena

3.5 km (2 mi.) north of Maia Alta, above the village of Scena, at the mouth of the Passirio valley, the Castello di Scena (Schloss Schenna, 14th–16th c.;

★Castello di Scena

View of Merano and Monte Benedetto

596 m (1967 ft)) commands magnificent views. The castle (admission charge) contains a collection of arms and armour, Renaissance furniture, portraits of members of princely families and Andreas Hofer's cradle.

Churches

At the village of Scena (587 m (1937 ft)) are the castle-like parish church (1914–31; adjoining it the old Gothic church) and next to it the small Neo-Gothic parish church of St John (1869), with the tomb of Archduke John of Austria (1782–1859) and his wife Anna. The building is known as one of the best examples of Neo-Gothic architecture in Alto Adige.

Monte Scena

2 km (1¼ mi.) north-east of Scena is a cableway up Monte Scena (Taser; 1460 m (7082 ft)).

Avelengo

From Maia Alta a road runs south-east to the village of Avelengo (Hafling; 1298 m (4283 ft)), famous for the horses which are bred here.

★Merano 2000

North-east of Avelengo, now easily accessible by various cableways and lifts, is the extensive skiing area of Merano 2000. From the outlying district of Falzeben (1610 m (5313 ft)), to the north-east, reached by a road (6 km (3¾ mi.)) from Avelengo or the upper station of the cableway, a chair-lift (lower station at Rosa Alpina inn) runs up to the Malga Pivigna (Pifinger Köpfl, 1905 m (6287 ft)), which can also be reached by a cableway from the Val di Nova (Naiftal: lower station 4 km (2½ mi.) east of Merano). From here there is a cableway to Sant'Osvaldo (Kirchsteiger Alm, 1938 m (6395 ft)), from which there are chair-lifts north-east to the Kesselwand-Joch (2265 m (7475 ft): ski-lift in winter) and south-east to Monte Catino (Mittager, 2234 m (7372 ft)).

Merano to the Giogo di San Vigilio

The road runs west from Maia Bassa past the sports ground, crosses the Adige and continues south along the west side of the broad Adige valley. On the hillside to the right is the prettily situated village of Marlengo (Marling, 370 m (221 ft)), from which a footpath, the "Waalweg", following the line of an irrigation canal half-way up the slope, runs north to Tel (Töll) or south below Castello Monteleone (open: Sat.–Thurs.) to Lana di Sopra. | **Marlengo**

In another 8 km (5 mi.) the road reaches Lana di Sopra (Oberlana), the most northerly part of the large village of Lana (population 7000), at the mouth of the Val d'Último (Ultental), which attracts visitors who want a quiet holiday either in summer or in winter (reservoirs). | **Lana**

From Lana di Sopra a cableway runs up in 7 minutes to the Hotel Monte San Vigilio (Vigiljoch, 1486 m (4904 ft)), from where there are magnificent views of the Adige valley and the Dolomites.

From the upper station of the cableway there are two possibilities – either by chair-lift (15 minutes) to the Dosso dei Lárici (Larchbühel, 1824 m (6019 ft)) or on an easy winding footpath to the Albergo al Giogo. From here it is only a few minutes' climb to the old chapel of San Vigilio on the Giogo di San Vigilio (Vigiljoch, 1795 m (5924 ft)), from where there are fine views of the Val Venosta, the Ötztal and the Texel group.

2 km (1¼ mi.) south of Lana di Sopra by way of Lana di Mezzo (Mitterlana) is Lana di Sotto (Niederlana), the parish church of which has a richly gilded Gothic altar of carved wood, the largest in Tirol, by the Merano sculptor Hans Schnatterpeck (1503–11; conducted visits from 10am onwards). The Romanesque church of Santa Margherita is also of interest. | **Lana di Sotto**

★Messina
K19

Region: Sicilia. Province: Messina (ME)
Altitude: 5 m (17 ft). Population: 266,000

The port of Messina, capital of the province of the same name and the see of an archbishop, lies near the north-east tip of Sicily on the busy Strait of Messina, with its western districts extending along the foothills of the Monti Peloritani. | Location

After the great earthquake in 1908 which killed some 60,000 people and destroyed 91% of its houses Messina was rebuilt with wide streets.

Messina was founded by Greek settlers about 730 BC on the site of an earlier Siculan settlement and named Zankle ("sickle") after the shape of the harbour. | History

It was renamed Messana about 493 BC, when is was occupied by Greek refugees.

It was destroyed by the Carthaginians in 396 BC and subsequently rebuilt, and became a Roman town in 264 BC. It was captured by the Saracens in AD 843 and by the Normans in 1061. Under the Normans the town enjoyed a long period of prosperity, which continued into the 17th c. under Spanish rule.

Thereafter Messina suffered a rapid decline, due partly to internal conflicts but mainly to the town's bitter rivalry with Palermo, the process being hastened by a plague in 1740 and severe earthquakes, particularly in 1783. Its subsequent recovery was promoted by its favourable situation on one of the most important traffic routes in the Mediterranean.

Sights

From the Marine Station on the south side of the harbour it is a short distance west to the north end of the town's main street, Viale San Martino, | Viale San Martino

Messina

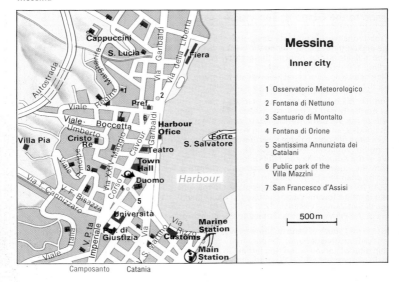

Messina

Inner city

1 Osservatorio Meteorologico

2 Fontana di Nettuno

3 Santuario di Montalto

4 Fontana di Orione

5 Santissima Annunziata dei Catalani

6 Public park of the Villa Mazzini

7 San Francesco d'Assisi

500 m

Camposanto   Catania

which cuts through the southern part of the city. In 400 m it crosses the tree-shaded Piazza Cairoli, Messina's busiest traffic intersection, and in another 1.5 km (1 mil.) it joins the spacious Piazza Dante.

Camposanto

On the west side of the square is the Camposanto (or Cimitero), one of Italy's most beautiful cemeteries. On top of the hill is an Ionic colonnade, the Pantheon of the town's leading citizens, from which there are fine views of the city and the strait.

Cathedral

From Piazza Cairoli the broad Corso Garibaldi runs north. 1.5 km (1 mi.) along this street Via I Settembre leads left into the large Piazza del Duomo, the centre of the old town, with the richly decorated Orion Fountain (1547–51) by Giovanni Angelo Montorsoli, a pupil of Michelangelo. On the east side of the square, dominating the town, is the cathedral, originally built by Roger II in the 12th c., destroyed in 1908 and rebuilt in its original form in 1919–29, incorporating architectural fragments from the ruins, and again rebuilt after being damaged by fire in 1943. The interior is 93 m (306 ft) long. In the apse is a beautiful mosaic, a reproduction of the 13th c. original which was destroyed in 1943. Adjoining the church rises the 60m (198 ft) high campanile (1933), on the main front of which is an elaborate astronomical clock, with numerous moving figures. The lion, above, roars at noon; the cock, below, crows. The clock was the work of the Strasbourg clock-maker Ungerer.

Santissima Annunziata dei Catalani

A short distance south-east of the cathedral, in Corso Garibaldi, a beautiful Norman church, the Santissima Annunziata dei Catalani (12th c.) is to be found. Beside the church is a bronze statue of Don John of Austria, son of the Emperor Charles V and hero of the battle of Lepanto (1571), under whose leadership the Spaniards and Venetians defeated the Turks.

Piazza Antonello

North-west of the cathedral is the circular Piazza Antonello, with the Palazzo Municipale, the Town Hall and the Head Post Office.

Villa Mazzini

From Piazza Antonello Corso Cavour runs north, passing the Teatro Vittorio Emanuele, to the Villa Mazzini public gardens (with an aquarium), on the

View across the Strait of Messina

Santissima dei Catalani; The Apse

north side of which stands the Palazzo del Governo (prefecture). West of the gardens is the church of San Francesco d'Assisi (1254; rebuilt).

★Museo Regionale

From the north-east corner of the gardens the Viale della Libertà runs north past the buildings of the Fiera di Messina (fair) and along the seafront to the Museo Regionale, which contains material salvaged from the Municipal Museum after the 1908 earthquake, together with sculpture and pictures from the hundred or so churches which were also devastated at the same time. Particularly notable items in room IV are a "triptych of St Gregory" by Antonello da Messina (1479; badly damaged in 1908), the central panel of which depicts a Madonna enthroned, and two sculptures by G. Montorsoli, depicting Neptune, and Scylla, the sea monster which is said to have devoured shipwrecked sailors.

Circonvallazione a monte

There is a pleasant drive around Messina on the Circonvallazione a monte, which, under various names, describes a circuit above the west side of the town, passing the Santuario di Montalto, a pilgrimage centre, and the modern church of Cristo Re.

Torre di Faro

15 km (9 mi.) NE

There is also a very attractive trip (15 km (9 mi.)) along the coast road, which runs north-east, between villas and gardens, passes two salt-water lagoons, the Pantani, also known as the Laghi de Ganzirri, and comes to the village of Torre di Faro, on the Punta del Faro, Sicily's north-eastern tip, with fine views from the lighthouse.

Tour

From Torre di Faro the coast road continues around the most northerly cape in Sicily; then the return to Messina is over the Colle San Rizzo (465 m (1535 ft)).

★★Milan   D4–5

Region: Lombardia. Province: Milano (MI)
Altitude: 122 m (403 ft). Population: 1,400,000

Location

Milan (Milano), capital of Lombardy and Italy's second largest city, lies in the north-west of the Po plain at the junction of several important traffic routes from the Alps.

Economy

Milan is Italy's principal industrial centre, its most important railway junction and its leading banking and commercial city. It was one of the largest silk markets in Europe and also a State and a Catholic university; it is the see of an archbishop.
    The main industries are textiles, the manufacture of cars, machinery and rolling-stock, chemicals (the Montecatini group) and papermaking.

City

Milan is a city of predominantly modern aspect. Even the old town centre around the Piazza del Duomo, though it still has many narrow old streets, is traversed by wide arteries radiating in all directions. Between the old town and the outer ring of bastioni, on the line of the Spanish ramparts built in 1549, is a zone of more modern streets, and farther out are the city's steadily expanding suburbs including "Milano 2" and "Milano 3". Since the Second World War large modern buildings, including tower blocks, have been erected in every part of the city.

History

Milan, founded by Celts about 400 BC, was conquered by Rome in 222 BC and thereafter, as Mediolanum, became the second most important town in northern Italy (after Verona). Later it became one of the capitals of the Lombard and Frankish kingdoms. As capital of the Lombard League it led the opposition to the Hohenstaufens. In consequence it was destroyed by

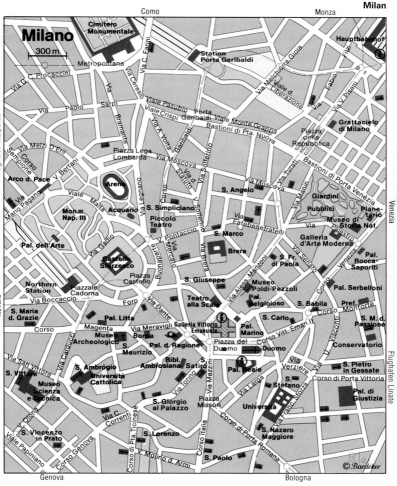

Como   Monza

Frederick Barbarossa in 1162, but was rebuilt five years later. Internal feuds between the nobility and the people led to the dominance of the Visconti family, who won control of much of northern Italy; and in 1395 Gian Galeazzo (d. 1402) gained the ducal title. In 1450 the Viccntis were succeeded by the dynasty founded by the mercenary leader Francesco Sforza, but the Sforza line died out in 1535, and the duchy then passed to Spain under Charles V. In 1714, after the War of the Spanish Succession, it was assigned to Austria, which apart from an interlude of French occupation in Napoleonic times (1796–1814) held on to it until 1859, in spite of repeated popular risings. In 1919 Mussolini founded the Fascist party in Milan; and in April 1945 the body of the fallen dictator was put on show in Piazzale Loreto. In the 1990s Milan has several times been the scene of outrages. In July 1993 an explosive device was detonated in the city, costing several lives and leading to demonstrations and strong protests throughout the country. The mayor of Milan said the "political Mafia" was responsible. In 1994 the "czar of the media", Silvo Berlusconi, entered politics and made his voice heard.

Art

Remains of early Christian architecture have been preserved in one or two churches, notably San Lorenzo and Sant'Ambrogio. 13th c. buildings are to be found mainly in the Piazza dei Mercanti. The Gothic period is represented almost exclusively by the cathedral.

Around 1450 the Florentines Filarete and Michelozzo brought the Tuscan Early Renaissance to Milan (Ospedale Maggiore). The heyday of Milanese art began with the coming of Bramante and Leonardo da Vinci, who produced his major works here between 1485 and 1500; and these two masters influenced the work of subsequent generations of painters, including Andrea Solario, Bramantino, Luini, Sodoma and Gaudenzio Ferrari. The present aspect of central Milan is due to the architects of the Late Renaissance and Baroque periods, particularly Galeazzo Alessi and Pellegrino Tibaldi, the Neo-Classical architect Giuseppe Piermarini and two practitioners of the Empire style, Luigi Canonica and Luigi Cagnola. A competent Neo-Classical painter was Andrea Appiani.

Piazza del Duomo

The life of Milan centres on the Piazza del Duomo, flanked on the north and south sides by palatial buildings, designed by Mengoni and erected from 1876 onwards. Near the west end is an equestrian statue of Victor Emanuel II (1896). Under the square are the foundations of the Basilica di Santa Tecla (4th–5th and 7th c.; "winter church") and the 4th c. baptistery (Battisterio di San Giovanni alle Fonti), which were discovered during the construction of the Metropolitana (access from the cathedral).

Adjoining the Piazza del Duomo to the north-west is the Piazza dei Mercanti, beyond which is the Piazza Cordusio. From the cathedral to the Piazza Cordusio extends an underground passage, with numerous shops.

★Galleria Vittorio
Emanuele II

On the north side of the Piazza del Duomo, giving access to the Piazza della Scala, is the Galleria Vittorio Emanuele II, designed by Giuseppe Mengoni and built in 1865–77. It was then the largest shopping arcade in Europe (195 m (645 ft) long, dome 48 m (158 ft) high; restored in 1988–89). It is known to the inhabitants of Milan as "il salotto" (the salon).

★★Cathedral

The cathedral of Santa Maria Nascente, a cruciform basilica faced with white marble, is one of the world's largest and most magnificent churches. With a length of 157 m (516 ft) and a façade 61.5 m (201 ft) wide, it covers an area of 11,700 sq. m (125,937 sq. ft) and can accommodate a congregation of 40,000.

The dome rises to 68 m (224 ft), and its total height including the statue of the Virgin known as the "Madonnina" is 108.5 m (358 ft). The roof is adorned with 135 pinnacles, the exterior with 2245 marble statues. Building, in Gothic style, began in 1386 but made slow progress (dome completed c. 1500, spire 1765–69, façade under Napoleon 1805–13). The imposing bronze doors are modern: the one to the left dates from 1840 and the large central door from 1908; the reliefs on two other doors were carried out between 1948–51, and the last one in 1965.

Galleria Vittorio Emanuele II ▶

The Gothic cathedral, the symbol of Milan

The rather dark interior, in striking contrast to the brilliant and richly patterned exterior, nevertheless makes a powerful impression with its 52 gigantic pillars. The stained-glass windows in the nave (mostly 15th–16th c.) are the largest in the world; the eight windows in the dome date from 1968. 15th c. stained glass windows can be seen in the south aisle.

In the north transept is a fine seven-branched bronze candelabrum by Nicholas of Verdun (c. 1200), and on the east wall of the south transept is a statue, by Marco Agrate (1562), of St Bartholomew, flayed. Note also the wall-tomb of Gian Giacomo Medici (d. 1555).

In the octagonal Borromeo chapel leading off the crypt is the Scurolo di San Carlo with the reliquary of San Carlo Borromeo, richly adorned with gold and jewels.

Treasury

In the south sacristy is the valuable treasury, with gold and silver work (4th–17th c.).

View

A walk on the roof of the cathedral is an impressive experience, offering magnificent views, which extend on clear days to the mountains flanking the west side of the Po plain. (Access outside the cathedral, on the west side of the north transept: 158 steps, or lifts on east side of transept; then 73 steps to the platform of the dome.)

Palazzo Reale

Museo del Duomo

On the south side of the cathedral is the Palazzo Reale, the former Royal Palace, built in 1788 on the site of an earlier palace which had belonged to the Visconti and Sforza families. On the ground floor is the Museo del Duomo (Cathedral Museum).

Museo d'Arte Contemporanea

The rooms on the second floor house the Civico Museo d'Arte Contemporanea, the City's Art Museum, with works by modern Italian painters.

To the rear of the palace stands the old palace church, San Gottardo in Corte (c. 1330), with a fine tower (campanile). To the east the Archbishop's Palace (remodelled by Pellegrino Tibaldi, 1570 onwards) has a fine colonnaded courtyard.

Adjoining the Palazzo Reale on the west is the Palazzo del Turismo, to the south of which is the Piazza Diaz, surrounded by modern buildings, including a 16-storey office block.

Palazzo del
Turismo

South-east of Piazza Diaz, in an area rebuilt since the Second World War (with the Torre Velasca, a 99 m (27 ft) high office block erected in 1958), is the old Ospedale Maggiore, a brick building 285 m (936 ft) long, the town's first hospital, begun in 1456 by Antonio Filarete and continued from 1465 onwards in Gothic and Renaissance style. It now houses the Rector's Office and two faculties of the State university.

★Ospedale
Maggiore

500 m east of the Ospedale Maggiore, between the broad Corso di Porta Vittoria and Via San Barnaba, rises the massive Palazzo di Giustizia (Law Courts), completed in 1940.

Palazzo di
Giustizia
(Law Courts)

★Piazza della Scala

In Piazza della Scala is a monument to Leonardo da Vinci (1872). On the north-west side of the square stands the Teatro alla Scala (1775–78), one of the largest and most important opera-houses in the world. To the left of the main building is the Museo Teatrale, with material on the history of the theatre; it incorporates a Verdi Museum with numerous mementoes of the composer (d. in Milan 1901).

Teatro alla Scala

On the south-east side of the square, opposite the Scala, the Palazzo Marino (by Galeazzo Alessi, 1558–60) is now the headquarters of the municipal administration.

Palazzo Marino

Behind the Palazzo Marino, in Piazza San Fedele, stands the fine Jesuit church of San Fedele, begun by Pellegrini in 1569 under San Carlo Borromeo.

San Fedele

Beyond San Fedele, in the beautiful Piazza Belgioioso, is the fine Palazzo Belgioioso, built by Piermarini in 1781.

Palazzo Belgioioso

At the corner of Via Morone (No. 1) is Manzoni's House, with the room in which the novelist Alessandro Manzoni (1785–1873) worked and in which he died.

Manzoni's House

Almost opposite (Via Manzoni 12), in an elegant old patrician house, the Museo Poldi-Pezzoli contains pictures by Botticelli, Mantegna, Piero della Francesca, Guardi and other artists; there are also Flemish and Persian carpets, tapestries, jewellery, silver, bronzes and weapons.

★Museo Poldi
Pezzoli

Corso Vittorio Emanuele to Corso Venezia

From Piazza Belgioioso the Corso Matteotti, with fine modern buildings, runs east to the Piazza San Babila, which has been considerably enlarged since the Second World War, with large modern blocks and the little Romanesque church of San Babila. From the south-west corner of the square the Corso Vittorio Emanuele (pedestrian precinct), lined with elegant shops, leads towards the cathedral.

Piazza San Babila

Immediately on the right-hand side of the Corso is the church of San Carlo al Corso, a circular building modelled on the Pantheon (by Carlo Amati, 1836–47).

San Carlo al Corso

Milan

From Piazza San Babila the line of Corso Vittorio Emanuele is continued north-east by the broad Corso Venezia.

Palaces

On the right-hand side, at the corner of Via San Damiano, are the Palazzo Serbelloni (1793) and the Palazzo Rocca-Saporiti (1812), both in Neo-Classical style.

Museo Civico di
Storia Naturale

Almost opposite the Palazzo Rocca-Saporiti is the Museo Civico di Storia Naturale (Museum of Natural History), notable in particular for its large collection of birds (25,000 specimens). Behind the museum extend the Giardini Pubblici, with an interesting planetarium.

Porta Venezia

The Corso Venezia joins the Piazzale Oberdan, in which are two little gatehouses of the Porta Venezia. From here the busy Corso Buenos Aires continues the line of Corso Venezia north-east to the circular Piazzale Loreto.

Central Station to the Piazza Cavour

Central Station

1 km (1/2 mi.) north-west, at the end of the broad Via Andrea Doria, is the Central Station, an imposing building richly clad in marble (by Ulisse Stacchini, started in 1912), and one of the largest stations in Europe.

Museo delle Cere

In the station is the Museo delle Cere (Wax Museum), with wax figures of famous Italian and foreign personalities.

Pirelli Building

Facing the station, to the south-west, is the 32-storey Pirelli Building (1955–59), 127 m (419 ft) high (conducted tours).

Piazza della
Repubblica

From the station Via Pisani runs south-west to the spacious Piazza della Repubblica, laid out from 1931 onwards on the site of the old railway station and now surrounded by huge modern buildings, including the 31-storey "Grattacielo di Milano", 114 m (376 ft) high, built in 1955.

Porta Garibaldi
Station

From the north-west corner of the square the wide Viale della Liberazione leads to the Porta Garibaldi Station, 1 km (1/2 mi.) away, which relieves pressure on the Central Station.

Giardini Pubblici

From the Piazza della Repubblica the Via Turati runs south to the Piazza Cavour, a busy traffic intersection at the south-west corner of the beautiful Giardini Pubblici, the Municipal Gardens laid out in 1783–86. On the south-east side of Piazza Cavour are three tower blocks, including the 22-storey Centro Svizzero (completed 1952).

Galleria d'Arte
Moderna

A little way east of the Piazza Cavour, to the west of the Natural History Museum, stands the Neo-Classical Villa Comunale (or Villa Reale; 1790), which houses the Galleria d'Arte Moderna, a museum of modern art (19th and 20th c. painting including works by Carrà, De Chirico, Modigliani, Morandi, etc.). In a separate hall is the Museum Marino Marini (paintings and sculpture). From Piazza Cavour the Via Alessandro Manzoni runs south to the Piazza della Scala.

Palazzo di Brera

Accademia di
Belle Arti

West of Piazza Cavour and north-west of Piazza della Scala, in Via Brera, is the Renaissance Palazzo di Brera (1651–1773), originally a Jesuit college, which has been occupied since 1776 by the Accademia di Belle Arti. In the courtyard can be seen a monument to Napoleon I by Canova (1809).

The palace contains a library (800,000 volumes) founded in 1770 and an observatory.

On the first floor is the Pinacoteca di Brera, one of Italy's finest picture galleries, which contains among many other exhibits futuristic paintings of the 20th c. The picture collection was founded as a didactic collection of the Art Academy and its principal exhibits were formed by pictures from churches and acquisition from Rome. Only some of the rooms of the Pinacoteca are open to the public. ★★**Pinacoteca di Brera**

The chief strength of the Pinacoteca di Brera lies in the works by the north Italian masters. Notable among 15th c. pictures are works by Mantegna ("Madonna in a Ring of Angels' Heads" and "Lamentation"). The Venetian masters are represented by Carlo Crivelli (including "Enthroned Madonna della Candeletta"), Gentile ("Preaching of St Mark in Alexandria"), Giovanni Bellini ("Lamentation" and two Madonnas) and Cima da Conegliano.

Pictures from later periods include works by Paolo Veronese, Titian ("Count Antonio Porcia" and "St Jerome") and Tintoretto ("Finding of St Mark's Body" and "Descent from the Cross", and portraits by Lorenzo Lotto and Giovanni Battista Moroni.

The Lombard masters, disciples of Leonardo da Vinci, are well represented, with works by Bramantino, Sodoma, De Predis, Boltraffio and Andrea Solario.

Artists of the Ferrarese school include Ercole de' Roberti ("Madonna with Saints") and Dosso Dossi.

Coreggio of Parma is represented by a "Nativity" and an "Adoration of the Kings".

There is an excellent representation of the Umbrian school, including works by Gentile da Fabriano ("Coronation of the Virgin with Saints"), Piero della Francesca ("Madonna with Saints and Duke Federico da Montefeltro") and Bramante (eight frescoes "Christ of the Column").

The most famous picture in the gallery is Raphael's "Marriage of the Virgin" ("Lo Sposalizio"), the finest work of his first period.

There are also important works by 17th and 18th c. artists.

Outstanding among foreign masters are Rembrandt (portraits of women, including "The Artist's Sister"), Van Dyck ("Princess Amalie of Solms"), Rubens ("Last Supper") and El Greco ("St Francis").

Piazza dei Mercanti

From the Piazza della Scala the Via Santa Margherita runs south-west into the Piazza dei Mercanti, centre of the old town of Milan. In the centre of the square is the single-storey Palazzo della Ragione (1228–33), originally a law court, with an equestrian statue of the builder on the south side. The Palazzo dei Giureconsulti (1564), on the north side of the square, has a clock-tower dating from 1272. On the south side is the Gothic Loggia degli Osii (1316), a marble-fronted building from which judgements and proclamations were issued in the Middle Ages. Palazzo della Ragione

Piazza Cordusio

North-west of the Piazza Mercanti the oval Piazza Cordusio is the meeting-place of important streets. To the south-east the Via Orefici, lined with shops, leads to the Piazza del Duomo; to the west the Via Meravigli goes past the Exchange to the church of Santa Maria delle Grazie; to the north-west the Via Dante leads to the Castello and from here an underground shopping arcade extends to the Piazza del Duomo.

South of Piazza Cordusio is the Palazzo dell'Ambrosiana (1603–09), with a famous library (700,000 printed volumes, 35,000 manuscripts, 2000 incunabula) and an important picture gallery founded in 1618 by Cardinal-Archbishop Federico Borromeo (works by Leonardo da Vinci, including "Portrait of a Musician", and by Botticelli, Raphael, Titian, "Adoration of the Magi", Tiepolo and Caravaggio). Palazzo dell'Ambrosiana

Milan

San Satiro

South-east of the Palazzo dell'Ambrosiana is the little church of San Satiro (by Bramante; 1478 onwards), with an older campanile and a modern façade. The interior has a choir seen in perspective. The baptistery in the south aisle is a gem of Lombard Early Renaissance architecture by Bramante (1480–88). At the end of the north transept is the curious little domed Capella della Pietà (9th c.), decorated with terracotta ornaments and figures.

Largo Cairoli

The Largo Cairoli at the north-western end of Via Dante is crossed by the broad Foro Buonaparte, which has a bronze equestrian statue of Garibaldi. From there the short Via Beltrami continues into the beautiful Piazza Castello.

★Castello Sforzesco

Musei del Castello Sforzesco

The Castello Sforzesco, held successively by the Viscontis and the Sforzas, was built in 1368, demolished by the people of Milan in 1447 and rebuilt from 1450 onwards. The Torre de Filarete, on the nearside (70 m (231 ft) high), is a reproduction (1905) of the original gate-tower. The Castello houses the Musei del Castello Sforzesco, with a collection of sculpture which consists mainly of medieval and modern works together with some Early Christian material and graves. Its greatest treasure is the "Pietà Rondanini", Michelangelo's last masterpiece, brought here in 1953 from the Palazzo Rondanini in Rome. Other important items are the unfinished tomb of Gaston de Foix of Bambaia and the large tomb, with an eques–trian statue, of Bernabò Visconti (d. 1385) by Bonino da Campione. There is also a collection of decorative art, as well as pictures by old masters (including Bellini, Correggio, Mantegna, Bergognone, Foppa, Lotto, Tintoretto and Antonello da Messina), prehistoric and Egyptian antiqui-ties, a collection on musical history and an armoury.

Park

Between the two rear courtyards of the Castello is a passage leading to the park, laid out in 1893–97, once the pleasure garden of the dukes of Milan and later a military training ground. In the north-east of the park is the Arena, an amphitheatre constructed in 1807 for sporting and other events. To the south-east is an interesting Aquarium.

★Santa Maria delle Grazie

South-west of the Castello, past the Northern Station and along Via Boccaccio and Via Caradosso, can be found the church of Santa Maria delle Grazie, in the Corso Magenta. This is a brick-built Gothic structure (begun about 1465), with a choir and a massive six-sided dome in the finest Early Renaissance style designed by Bramante (1492 onwards). During the repair of war damage in the dome old sgraffito paintings were brought to light. At the end of the north aisle is the Baroque chapel of the Madonna delle Grazie, with an altarpiece of the Madonna.

★★"Last Supper" by Leonardo da Vinci

In the refectory of the former Dominican monastery is Leonardo da Vinci's "Last Supper" (the Cenacolo Vinciano), his most famous work, painted on the wall in tempera between 1495 and 1497: a dramatic presentation of the scene which was quite novel and marked an important new stage in the development of art. The painting is much damaged from the flaking off of the paint and during the last decades has been restored several times, a process which will probably never be fully completed.

San Vittore al Corpo

To the south of Santa Maria delle Grazie, in Via San Vittore, stands the beautiful church of San Vittore al Corpo, an early Christian foundation,

The Castello Sforzesco now houses a number of museums ▶

"The Last Supper" by Leonardo da Vinci

which was remodelled by Galeazzo Alessi in Late Renaissance style (1530 onwards), with a sumptuous Baroque interior.

★★Museo Nazionale della Scienza e della Tecnica

Adjoining it on the east is the Leonardo da Vinci National Museum of Science and Technology, housed in a former Olivetan monastery. The museum, opened in 1953, illustrates the history of science and technology down to modern times. Of particular interest are the Leonardo da Vinci Gallery; the department of physics, with apparatus used by Galileo, Newton and Volta and the departments of optics, acoustics, telegraphy, transport, shipping, railways, flying, metallurgy, motor vehicles, clocks and watches, and timber. There is also a library and reading room (film presentations).

★★Sant'Ambrogio

The church of Sant'Ambrogio east of the National Museum was founded in 386 by St Ambrose. The present church is a masterpiece of Romanesque architecture (12th c.; choir 9th c.). Notable features of the interior are the pulpit, restored about 1200, with late Romanesque carving, and the casing (paliotto) of the high altar, a masterpiece of Carolingian art (made in 835 at either Milan or Rheims).

Museum

On the north-west side of the church are the Museo di Sant'Ambrogio and a monumental war memorial (1930).

University

The Catholic University of the Sacred Heart (del Sacro Cuore), adjoining the church on the south-east, was founded in 1921 and has two cloisters by Bramante.

Museo Archeologico

In the former monastery, the Monastero Maggiore, is the Milan Archaeological Museum, with Greek, Etruscan and Roman finds. Note the Buddha statue and the Roman sculptures on the ground floor, including one of Maximilian (3rd c.), a bronze head and a female statue with folded drapes.

Sights

South-east of Sant'Ambrogio, in the Corso di Porta Ticines, San Lorenzo, a fine building on a centralised plan, dates from the Early Christian period; it has a Renaissance dome (1574) and the chapel of St Aquilinus (4th c. mosaics). In front of the church a portico of sixteen Corinthian columns, the largest surviving monument of Roman Mediolanum, has been re-erected.

San Lorenzo
Maggiore

500 m farther south the church of Sant'Eustorgio, a Romanesque basilica (12th–13th c.) has a fine campanile (1297–1309) and a façade which was added in 1863. Beyond the choir is the Cappella Portinari (by Michelozzo, 1462–68), the earliest example of Renaissance architecture, with frescoes by Vincenzo Foppa. In the chapel is the marble tomb (1339) of St Peter Martyr, a Dominican monk murdered in 1250.

★ Sant'Eustorgio

A toy museum (Museo del Giocattolo e del Bambino) was opened in 1989 at Via Ripa Ticinese (No. 27). On display are some 200 games and toys dating from 1700 to 1950.

Toy Museum

Just north of the church of San Lorenzo the Corso di Porta Ticinese runs into the Piazza Carrobbio. In Via Torino, which runs north-east from this square to the Piazzo del Duomo, stands the church of San Giorgio al Palazzo, with paintings by Bernardino Luini.

San Giorgio al
Palazzo

In north-western Milan, at the Porta Volta, lies the Cimitero Monumentale (opened 1866), Italy's most splendid cemetery, with numerous highly elaborate marble tombs.

★ Cimitero
Monumentale

Surroundings

South-east of Milan is Chiaravalle Milanese, noted for its Cistercian abbey church, a fine brick edifice with a tall tower; it was founded by St Bernard of Clairvaux in 1135 and remodelled between 1170 and 1221 and has magnificent Baroque choir-stalls of 1640, an elegant little cloister and a cemetery.

**Chiaravalle
Milanese**
7 km (4½ mi.) SE

South-east of Milan, in the commune of San Donato Milanese, is Metanopoli (188 m (620 ft)), also called "Capital of Methane" or "Oil City", a satellite town which has grown up since 1940 with the headquarters or branch establishments of the leading Italian oil companies, such as ENI (Ente Nazionale Idrocarburi), SNAM (Società Nazionale Metanodotti), AGIP (Azienda Generale Italiana Petroli, with departments of mining and atomic research) and ANIC (Azienda Nazionale Idrocarburi).

Metanopoli
8 km (5 mi.) SE

North-east of Milan, on the River Lambro, is the industrial town of Monza (162 m (535 ft); population 124,000), which together with Pavia was the place of coronation of the Lombard kings from the 11th c. In the Piazza Roma stands the old Town Hall ("Arengario") of 1293, and close by the cathedral, founded in 590 and rebuilt in the 13th and 14th c. in Lombard Gothic style, with a beautiful façade and a harmonious interior. In the Cappella di Teodolinda are frescos and the famous "Iron Crown", said to be the royal crown of the Lombards, with which the German emperors were crowned as kings of Italy. Under the little cloister on the left side of the cathedral the Museo Serpero contains the rich Cathedral Treasury.

Monza
15 km (9 mi.) NE

To the north of Monza stands the Villa Reale, built 1777–80 in Classical style by G. Piermarini (formerly a royal castle; small picture gallery). Nearby is the main entrance to the Parco Reale, through which flows the River Lambro. In the extensive park are the Mirabello racecourse and the well-known motor-racing circuit, as well as golf-courses and polo pitches.

Villa Reale

Lake Maggiore, Varese, Lake Como, Como; see entries.

Modena   E6

Region: Emilia-Romagna. Province: Modena (MO)
Altitude: 34 m (112 ft). Population: 178,000

Location

The provincial capital of Modena, lies between the rivers Secchia and Panaro near the southern edge of the north Italian plain on the Via Emilia. It is an important commercial and industrial centre and has a university.

Town centre

The town centre has wide arcaded streets and large squares, and the old fortifications have given place to beautiful avenues and gardens.

History

Originally a Celtic settlement of the Boii, the town, lying astride the ancient Via Aemilia, became a Roman colony in 183 BC under the name of Mutina. In 1288 it came into the hands of the house of Este, who acquired the ducal title in 1452 and remained rulers of Modena until 1796.

The motor-car manufacturer Enzo Ferrari was born in Modena in 1898.

Sights

★ Cathedral

The main traffic artery of the town is the Via Emilia, on the line of the old Roman road. Just off the south side of this street, in the central Piazza Grande, stands the imposing Cathedral, a basilica begun in 1099 in Romanesque style, consecrated in 1184 and completed in the 13th c., with beautiful sculpture on the exterior walls and in the interior. On the side facing the Corso Duomo can be seen a magnificent rose window (13th c.), marble lions supporting the porticus, and four reliefs at the side of the main door and above the side doors. They number among the earliest Romanesque sculptures in Italy and represent phases in the history of mankind. The interior is notable for some good pictures and for sculptures of the Passion (13th c.) on the choir screen and the pulpit. In the crypt, its roof supported by 30 slender columns, is a realistic group representing the "Adoration of the Infant Christ" by Guido Mazzoni (after 1480).

★ Torre
Ghirlandina

On the north side of the cathedral, in the Piazza del Torre, rises the 88 m (290 ft) high Torre Ghirlandina (slightly off the perpendicular), one of the finest campaniles in northern Italy and a distinctive city landmark.

Museo Lapidario
del Duomo

Also on the north side of the cathedral stands the Museo Lapidario del Duomo, which has Romanesque metopes from the cathedral roof.

San Giovanni
Battista

North-west of the cathedral, along Via Emilia, is the Piazza Matteotti, a large square on the west side of which, at the corner of Via Emilia, stands the church of San Giovanni Battista, a plain domed building (1730) containing, to the left of the high altar, a beautifully painted terracotta of the "Lamentation" by Mazzoni (1477–80).

Sant'Agostino

A little farther along Via Emilia is the Baroque church of Sant'Agostino. To the right of the entrance is a "Lamentation", an early work by Antonio Begarelli, the major Renaissance sculptor in the Emilia region.

Palazzo dei Musei

The Palazzo dei Musei, farther west along Via Emilia, houses the municipal collections.

In the courtyard is the Museo Lapidario with Roman finds including sarcophagi.

On the ground floor the Museo Civico del Risorgimento contains mementoes of the fight for freedom in the 19th c.

On the first floor can be found the Biblioteca Estense, with more than 380,000 volumes, 1640 incunabula and a valuable collection of manuscripts. Particularly notable is a 15th c. Bible which belonged to Borso d'Este, with more than a thousand pages illustrated by French artists, and the "Sphaera", a masterpiece of Lombardian miniature painting.

★Biblioteca Estense

The second floor contains several collections: the Museo Civico (archaeology and ethnology), the Museo Estense, with medallions, terracotta sculpture, statuettes, porcelain, musical instruments, etc. and the Galleria Estense.

The Este Picture Gallery is famous for its large collection of early Emilian and Tuscan art, including 15th c. pictures of the Po as well as Modena art of the 15th c., with works by Correggio, Dosso Dossi, Titian, Tintoretto, Guercino, Veronese, Velázques, Giovanni di Paolo, Bassano, Domenichino, Strozzi, Rosa, Guardi and other artists.

★Este Picture Gallery

Other terracottas by Begarelli can be seen in the church of San Francesco, near the south-west corner of the old town, and in the church of San Pietro (1476), in the south-east of the old town.

Northern part of the old town

In the north of the old town in Piazza Roma, about 500 m north-east of the cathedral, rises the massive Palazzo Ducale, begun in 1634 in accordance with a plan by Bartolomeo Avanzini, an excellent example of secular architecture of the 17th c. The balustrade is decorated with numerous figures, depicting the virtues and figures of mythology; the doorway is flanked by massive figures of Hercule and Aemilius Lepidus. The Palazzo Ducale is now a military academy and is not open to the public.

Palazzo Ducale

North-east of the Palazzo are the palace gardens, today a public park (Giardini Pubblici), with a botanic garden. Notable is a 17th c. villa, built to a plan by the famous architect Gaspare Vigarini for the dukes of Este. The villa, a long building, the central part of which is crowned by an octagonal domed tower has been used for exhibitions for many years.

Giardini Pubblici

Surroundings

North of Modena is the interesting town of Carpi (28 m (92 ft); population 60,000). In the centre of the town is the large Piazza dei Martiri, in which stand the New Cathedral (begun 1514; façade 1667), the Loggia, the 15th c. Colonnades (52 arches) and the old Castello (now partly occupied by a museum) of the Pio family, who ruled here from 1327 to 1525; in the second courtyard is a memorial to the victims of the Second World War. Behind the Castello is the Old Cathedral, founded in 751, La Sagra (Romanesque interior, with a 12th c. pulpit), adjoining which is a campanile of 1221.

Carpi
18 km (11 mi.)

At Nonantola (24 m (79ft); population 11,000) stands the well-known Abbazia di Nonantola, founded in the 8th c. and dedicated to St Silvester. It was destroyed several times by fire and rebuilt, the latest building in Romanesque style dating from the 12th c. The abbey was restored in the 20th c., in particular the crypt, the vault of which is supported by 64 small columns decorated with capitals. The south aisle of the abbey church is decorated with 15th c. wall paintings by a master of Modena. The church treasury includes manuscripts with miniatures and gold work. Notable is the relief on the doorway with scenes from the Gospels and episodes from the history of the abbey.

★**Abbazia di Nonantola**
10 km (6 mi.) NE

Molise J–K12–13

Region: Molise
Provinces: Campobasso (CB) and Isernia (IS)
Area: 4438 sq. km (1713 sq. mi.). Population: 333,000

Location
The region of Molise, one of the poorest and remotest in Italy, lies in the Neapolitan Apennines (Appennino Napolitano) in eastern Central Italy.

Bounded on the north by the region of Abruzzi, with which it is linked by historical and cultural tradition and with which it was combined until 1963 to form the region of Abruzzi e Molise, Molise extends from the karstic hills of the Monti del Matese (Monte Miletto, 2050 m (6765 ft)) in the south-west to the edge of the wide Apulian plain in the east and the Adriatic to the north-east. The inhabitants gain a modest subsistence from arable and pastoral farming.

Sights

Campobasso
The principal town in the region is Campobasso (701 m (2313 ft); population 50,000), capital of the province of the same name and the see of an archbishop. Above the town are the ruins of the Castello di Montforte (16th c.; view). Also of interest is the Romanesque church of San Bartolomeo. The Museo Provinciale Sannitico recently opened in the Palazzo Mazzarotta.

Sepino
South of Campobasso, near the border with Apulia, is the village of Sepino (698 m (2303 ft)).

Saepinum
About 3 km (2 mi.) north of Sepino are the remains of the old Roman town of Saepinum. Excavations have brought to light a theatre, a basilica, the forum, the baths and the town walls with four towers.

Isernia
The capital of Molise's other province is Isernia (423 m (1396 ft); population 21,000), also the see of a bishop.

Excavations
Near the town are the excavated remains (uncovered in 1979) of a Palaeolithic settlement over a million years old. The site is open to visitors; fossils, tools and geological specimens are on display in the Museo Nazionale della Pentria.

Abbazia di San Vincenzo
About 20 km (13 mi.) north-west of Isernia in the Volturno valley are the ruins of the Abbazia di San Vincenzo, founded about 700 and destroyed by the Saracens in 880. The crypt, with fine frescoes (9th c.), has been preserved.

Pietrabbondante
30 km (19 mi.) north-east of Isernia, at Pietrabbondante, are the excavated remains of a Samnite town (theatre, temple, etc.).

★Montecassino H12

Region: Latium/Lazio. Province: Frosinone (FR)
Altitude: 519m/1703ft. Population: 20,000

Cassino
The town of Cassino lies between Rome (110 km (68 mi.) north-west) and Naples (about 80 km (50 mi.) south-east), in southern Latium.

The town is noted chiefly for the great abbey of Montecassino which towers above it on a hill. During the Second World War there was bitter fighting around Cassino, and the town was completely destroyed and rebuilt on a new site slightly farther south.

Abbey of Montecassino

The road to the abbey of Montecassino (9 km (5¹/₂ mi.)) winds steeply up the hill in hairpin bends from the west side of the town. Just outside the town, on the left of the road, are the remains of the Roman Casinum, including the massive ruins of an amphitheatre, a mausoleum and a theatre. At the next bend, on the right, are the ruins of the Rocca Ianula (193 m (637 ft)), built 949–86.

Just before the monastery, on the right, is a road leading to the Polish military cemetery, with over 1000 graves. Beyond this are pre-Roman polygonal walls (4th–3rd c. BC).

On the summit of the hill (519 m (1713 ft)) is the abbey of Montecassino, founded by St Benedict in 529, and acknowledged as the cradle of the Benedictine order, which became a great centre of learning and art.

During the Second World War the hill of Montecassino was a cornerstone of the German defensive line from October 1943 to May 1944, and on February 15th 1944 the abbey was almost completely destroyed by an Allied air attack, although the Germans had declared that it was clear of troops. The abbey has since been rebuilt in its original form, the only surviving features of the old buildings being the crypt, with paintings from the school of Beuron (1898–1913), and the tombs of St Benedict and his twin sister St Scholastica (both c. 480–543). The contents of the valuable library (80,000 volumes), the abbey's archives and many pictures were removed to safety in the Vatican during the fighting.

Since 1980 there has been a museum adjoining the monastery, displaying Roman and Etruscan finds, medieval manuscripts, drawings and engravings with views of the monastery as well as paintings and statues from various epochs.

Monastery museum

Above the abbey is Monte Calvario (593 m (1557 ft)), crowned by a Polish war memorial, from which there are magnificent views.

Monte Calvario

The famous Benedictine Monastery of Montecassino

★Montecatini Terme   E8

Region: Toscana. Province: Pistola (PT)
Altitude: 27 m (89 ft). Population: 22,000

Location

The famous spa of Montecatini Terme lies in the north-west of Tuscany, some 30 km (19 mi.) east of Lucca, in the fertile but in summer very hot Nievole valley (Val die Nievole).

Montecatini Terme is Italy's leading spa, attracting large numbers of visitors, mainly Italians, throughout the whole year (high season July–August). The baths and mineral springs (temperature 19–25°C (66–77°F); water containing sulphur and sodium carbonate) have been used for treatment since the 14th c.

Sights

Piazza del Popolo

The central feature of the town is the Piazza del Popolo with the Neo-Classical church of Santa Maria Assunta; a little way north-west is the Kursaal.

Spa area

The wide Viale Verdi runs north-east from the Piazza del Popolo to the spa centre. At the edge of the large spa park are several thermal baths – to the left the Stabilimento Excelsior, built in 1915 and enlarged in 1968, the Terme Leopoldine (1775; rebuilt 1927) and the Stabilimento Tamerici; at the end of the street is the Stabilimento Tettucio (1927), a large building with fine colonnades. In Viale A. Diaz, opposite the Stabilimento Regina, is the Accademia d'Arte, with a small museum.

North-west of the Stabilimento Tettucio are the smaller houses, the Torrettas and the Rinfresco. At the north-east corner of the spa park is the lower station of the cableway up to Montecatini Alto (see below).

The spa area of Montecatini Terme

About 260m/285yd above the thermal bath, on the top of a h ll, is the old- **Montecatini Alto**
world village of Montecatini Val di Nievole (usually called Montecatini 5 km (3 mi.) NE
Alto). It can be reached either by funicular from Montecatini Terme or by
road.

On the access road from the thermal bath is the entrance to the Grotta Grotta Maona
Maona, a dripstone cave discovered in the 19th c.

Only ruins remain of the Castello Montecatini Alto. Castello

★Parco di Pinocchio

North-west of Montecatini Terme, near the village of Collod , is the Parco 14 km (9 mi.) NW
di Pinocchio. Between a fairytale park and playgrounds can be found a
monument to Pinocchio. The adventures of the famous character, created
by the Florence-born writer Carlo Collodi (originally Carlo Lorenzini) who
grew up in Collodi, are known all over the world.

Monte Gargano

See Foggia.

Montepulciano   F9

Region: Toscana. Province: Siena (SI)
Altitude: 605 m (1997 ft). Population: 14,000

The little town of Montepulciano lies on a hill in eastern Tuscany, about Location
70 km (43 mi.) south-east of Siena and 20 km (12 mi.) west of Lake Trasimene
(Lago Trasimeno) in the region of Umbria.
  Montepulciano is one of the most attractive little towns in Central Italy,
with its walls and its beautiful Gothic and Renaissance buildings.

Sights

The life of the town centres on the Piazza Grande, on the south side of Cathedral
which is the cathedral, begun in 1570 by Bartolomeo Ammannati and
completed by Ippolito Scalza, with the exception of the façade, in 1630.
Inside to the left of the main doorway, is a recumbent figure of Bartolomeo
Aragazzi (the secretary of Pope Martin V; 15th c.) from the magnificent
tomb by Michelozzo di Bartolomeo (1427–36) which was taken down,
parts of it being dispersed about the cathedral and some parts being lost.
Behind the main altar is a fine triptych by Taddeo di Bartolo ("Assumption
of the Virgin Mary"; 1401).

To the right of the cathedral stands the Palazzo Comunale (Town Hall; Palazzo Comunale
14th c.), a massive building, with fine views from the tower.

To the left of the cathedral is the Palazzo Contucci, begun in 1519 by Palaces
Antonio da Sangallo the Elder and completed by Peruzzi. Inside can be
seen fine frescoes by Andrea Pozzo (1642–1709).
  Opposite the cathedral is the Palazzo Tarugi, the town's finest Renaissance palace, and to the left of it a fountain of 1520.

North of the Piazza Grande, in Via Ricci (on right), is the Palazzo Neri-Orselli Museo Civico
(14th c.), with the Museo Civico (municipal museum), with fine medieval

Montepulciano
Old Town

1 Sant' Agnese
2 San Bernardo
3 Palazzo Avignonesi
4 Palazzo Bucelli
5 Santa Luccia
6 Palazzo Cervini
7 San Francesco
8 Palazzo Ricci
9 Palazzo Neri Orselli
  (Museo Civico)
10 Palazzo del
   Capitano del Popolo
11 Palazzo Tarugi
12 Palazzo Comunale
13 Palazzo Contucci
14 Teatro Policiano
15 Casa del Poliziano
16 Chiesa Il Gesù
17 Santa Maria dei Servi

200 m

© *Baedeker*

and Renaissance pictures, also some terracotta work by Andrea della Robbia.

Via di Voltaia	To the east of Piazza Grande Via dell'Opio with its northward continuation, Via di Voltaia, forms the main street of the town which is lined with fine palaces and churches.
Palazzo Cervini	At the north end of Via di Voltaia, on the right, is the Palazzo Cervini, by Antonio da Sangallo the Elder. The palace was commissioned by Cardinal Marcello Cervini, later Pope Marcellus II, but remained uncompleted.
Sant'Agostino	The church of Sant'Agostino is reached by way of Via di Gracciano, north of the Palazzo Cervini. It has a Renaissance façade by Michelozzo di Bartolomeo and inside there are a notable wooden crucifix (15th c.) and a number of pictures, particularly of the 16th–17th c.
★San Biagio	The church of San Biagio, about 2 km (1¼ mi.) south-west of the town, at the end of a long avenue lined with cypresses, is a centralised structure which was built in 1518–45 by Antonio da Sangallo the Elder, but it still shows the influence of Bramante. The church is built of gold-coloured travertine, and is considered one of the finest buildings of the Renaissance.

Pienza

14 km (9 mi.) W	West of Montepulciano is Pienza, named after Pope Pius II (b. here in 1405), who adorned the town with splendid buildings, mainly designed by Bernardo Rossellino, the leading Florentine architect of the day.

San Biagio, near Montepulciano

Piazza Pio II, surrounded by 15th c. buildings, offers a harmonious picture of Early Renaissance architecture. On the south side of the square is the cathedral, which contains a number of fine pictures, including works by the Sienese painter Matteo di Giovanni and by Lorenzo Vecchietta, and beautiful Gothic choir-stalls. In the crypt is a font by Rossellino. The Bishop's Palace to the right, adjoins the Cathedral Museum (with a cope which once belonged to Pius II). Opposite the cathedral, to the north, are the Palazzo Comunale (Town Hall) and the Palazzo Ammannati. To the left of the cathedral is the Palazzo Piccolomini, (display-rooms, library, coin collection) from the roof-garden of which there are magnificent views.

★Piazza Pio II

Chiusi

South-east of Montepulciano, above the Chiana valley, lies the little walled town of Chiusi, the former Chamars or Clevsin, one of the twelve towns of the Etruscan League and a bitter opponent of Rome about 500 BC. During the Middle Ages the population was devastated by malaria.

23 km (14 mi.) SE

In the Piazza del Duomo is the Museo Etrusco, with a rich collection of material from the Etruscan tombs of the area, including funeral urns, bronze and clay masks and pitchers.

★Museo Nazionale Etrusco

The cathedral (6th c., rebuilt in the 12th c.), opposite the museum, is built almost entirely with stone from Roman buildings (18 antique columns). A walk round the town affords attractive views.

Cathedral

Scattered around the outskirts of the town are about 400 notable Etruscan tombs. Some of them are accessible to the public; information from the Etruscan National Museum.

★Etruscan tombs

~~.u uella~~ Scimmia	On the road to the Lago di Chiusi can be found the early 5th c. BC. Tomba della Scimmia (called "Tomb of the Ape" after a detail of the wall paintings which depicts scenes of funeral ceremonies).

Region: Campania. Province: Nápoli (NA)
Altitude: 10 m (33 ft). Population: 1,207,000

Location	The south Italian port town of Naples (Nápoli), principal town of the region of Campania and of the province of Nápoli, lies on the north side of the Bay of Naples, on the Tyrrhenian Sea, extending along the lower slopes of attractive hills.
Architecture	The old town with its narrow streets and stepped lanes and its tall balconied houses is fringed on the west and north by extensive villa suburbs and on the east by an industrial zone. In recent years much of the city has been redeveloped with new buildings and realigned streets, particularly in the area around the harbour, the Rione Santa Lucia.

Naples possesses many historical monuments going back almost 3000 years, particularly the treasures, to be seen in the National Museum, garnered from the cities engulfed by Vesuvius; the port of Naples is of major importance for southern Italy.

In November 1980 there was severe damage from earthquakes. |
| History | Naples was originally a Greek foundation. As early as the 8th c. BC the site was occupied by the Rhodian settlement of Parthenope, near which settlers from Kyme (Latin Cumae), itself a colony established by Ionians from Euboea, founded the "old town", Palaiopolis, in the 7th c. In the 5th c. the "new town", Neapolis, was founded, mainly by incomers from Chalcis on Euboea. In 326 BC the three settlements became allies of Rome and were amalgamated. Although favoured by Rome for its faithfulness to the alliance, Neapolis preserved its independence and its distinctive Greek characteristics until late in the Imperial period. The town became a favourite residence of the Roman magnates, and Virgil composed some of his finest poetry here.

During the period of the Great Migration, in 543, the town fell into the hands of the Goths, but returned to Byzantine rule in 553 and thereafter succeeded in asserting its independence until conquered by the Normans in 1139 and incorporated by Roger II in his kingdom of Sicily. Roger's grandson Frederick II of Hohenstaufen founded the university in 1224. In the reign of Charles of Anjou (1266–85) Naples became capital of the kingdom. In 1442 Alfonso I of Aragon reunited the kingdoms of Sicily and Naples. From 1503 to 1707 Naples was the residence of Spanish viceroys. Following the War of the Spanish Succession the territory passed in 1713 to the Habsburgs, and after the War of the Austrian Succession (1734) to the Bourbons, with whom it remained until its incorporation in the new united Italy in 1860. |

Old town

Teatro San Carlo	The city's busiest traffic intersection is the Piazza Trieste e Trento, on the east side of which stands the Teatro San Carlo (1737), one of the largest theatres in Europe (2900 seats). Immediately north is the Galleria Umberto, a shopping arcade built in 1887–90.
San Francesco di Paola	Adjoining the Piazza Trieste e Trento on the south is the large Piazza del Plesbiscito, occupied on the west side by the church of San Francesco di Paola (1817–46), an imitation of the Pantheon in Rome.
Palazzo Reale	Along the east side of the Piazza del Plesbiscito is the Palazzo Reale, the former Royal Palace, begun in 1600 by Dominico Fontana and restored in

Capua
Galleria Nazionale

Benevento
Aeroporto

Naples

Albergo
dei Poveri

S. Maria
d. Angeli

Orto
Botanico

Staz.

Piazza
L. Poderico

S. Maria
della Sanità

Via S. Antonio Abate

S. Maria
d. Fede

S. Maria
dei Miracoli

Foria

S. Giovanni a
Carbonara

Via S. Giovanni a Carbonara

Pretura

Bus Station

S. Francesco

Porta Capuana

Museo
Nazionale

Cavour

S. Maria
d. Grazie

Duomo

Castel
Capuano

Central Station

Piazza
G. Garibaldi

Accademia
Belle Arti

Via Pisanelli

Via Tribunali

Via Duomo

Porta
Nolana

Convitto
Naz.

Cappella
Pontano

Tribunali

San Pietro
Martire

Station
S.F.S.M.

Piazza
Dante

S. Domenico
Magg.

Archivio
di Stato

Santa Croce

Gesù
Nuovo

S. Chiara

Gesù
Vecchio

Piazza
Nicola Amore

Piazza del
Mercato

S. Maria
del Carmine

Spirito
Santo

Pal.
Gravina

Università

Marina

Via Marinella

Staz.
Cumana

Pal.
Penna

Borsa

Nuova

Port Office

Via A. Diaz

Incoronata

Town Hall

Bacino del Piliero

Molo del Carmine

Molo Cesario Console

Galleria
Umberto

Castel
Nuovo

Marine Station

Molo Martello

Prefettura

Palazzo
Reale

Piazza del
Plebiscito

Giardini
Pubblici

Molo Angioino

Avamporto Amm. Caracciolo

San Francesco
di Paola

N

300 m

Fontana dell'
Immacolatella

Molo San Vincenzo

Castel
dell' Ovo

Via Partenope

Pompei

Ercolano

1 Teatro San Carlo
2 La Pietà del Turchini
3 Sant' Anna dei Lombardi
4 Donna Regina
5 San Paolo Maggiore
6 Santissimi Severino e Sossio
7 Palazzo Filomirino
8 Galleria Principe di Napoli
9 Palazzo della Provincia
10 Santa Maria la Nova

11 Conservatorium
12 San Pietro a Maiella
13 San Giorgio Maggiore
14 Sant' Agostino della Zecca
15 San Pietro Martire
16 Palazzo Merigliano
17 San Lorenzo Maggiore
18 Girolomini
19 SS. Annunziata
20 San Pietro ad Aram

© Baedeker

Metropolitana

Galleria Umberto, a shoppers' paradise

1837–41. On the façade (169 m (555 ft)) are eight marble statues of the various kings who ruled Naples. The palace contains a grand staircase of white marble (1651), a theatre, seventeen richly appointed state apartments and the valuable Biblioteca Nazionale (1,500,000 volumes, 12,000 manuscripts, 5000 incunabula).

★Castel Nuovo   Behind the palace to the north-east, on the south side of the Piazza del Municipio, is the five-towered Castel Nuovo, also known as the Maschio Angioino, once the residence of kings and viceroys of Naples. Originally built by Charles I of Anjou in 1279–82, it was enlarged by Alfonso I of Aragon and has recently been restored. The entrance is formed by a splendid Early Renaissance triumphal arch, with rich sculptured decoration, erected between 1453 and 1467 in honour of the entry of Alfonso I of Aragon. In the courtyard is the Gothic church of Santa Barbara (or Cappella Palatina), and to the left of this the large Baron's Hall.

Town Hall   In the centre of the Piazza del Municipio, which is laid out in gardens, stands an equestrian statue of Victor Emmanuel II (1897). On the west side of the square is the fine Town Hall (1819–25), originally built to house government departments.

San Giacomo degli Spagnoli   Adjoining the Town Hall the church of San Giacomo degli Spagnoli (1540) has behind the high altar, the sumptuous tomb of Viceroy Don Pedro de Toledo, founder of the church.

Harbour

To the east of the palace and the Castel Nuovo extends the Harbour, divided into separate docks and basins by a series of piers and breakwaters, which is always a bustle of activity. Extending east from the Piazza del Municipio

Castel Nuovo, once a royal residence

is the Molo Angioino, on which is the Marine Station. To the west of this is the Eliporto (Heliport), from which there are regular helicopter services to Capri, Ischia, Capodichino Airport (7 km (4¹/₂ mi.) north), etc. Farther south, from the quay on the Calata di Beverello, boats sail to Ponza, Capri and Ischia.

Santa Lucia

To the west of the Piazza del Plesbiscito, on the slopes of Pizzofalcone and extending down to the sea, lies the district of Santa Lucia. South of the wide Via Santa Lucia this is an area of modern streets laid out on a regular plan, but to the north of that street it is a picturesque huddle of narrow stepped lanes in which the traditional Neapolitan way of life can be observed at any time of the day but particularly in the evening.

From the south-east corner of the Piazza del Plesbiscito a succession of streets runs round the east and south sides of the Santa Lucia district – first Via Cesario Console, which passes the Giardini Pubblici; then Via Nazario Sauro and Via Partenope, in which there are several large luxury hotels; and finally, beyond the Piazza della Vittoria, Via Caracciolo, which affords magnificent views of the Bay of Naples.

From Via Partenope a causeway and a bridge lead to a little rocky islet on which stands the Castel dell'Ovo, begun in the 12th c., completed by Frederick II and rebuilt in the 17th c. On the causeway is the Porto di Santa Lucia.

Castel dell'Ovo

★Villa Comunale

Between Via Caracciolo and the fine Riviera di Chiaia to the north extends the Villa Comunale, a park laid out in 1780, almost 1.5 km (1 mi.) long, which

Aquarium

Santa Lucia and Castel dell'Ovo

is the city's most popular promenade. Half-way along we find the Zoological Station, an important biological research institution founded by a German scientist, Anton Dorn, in 1870. In the central block is an Aquarium with 31 tanks which give an excellent survey of the fauna of the Bay of Naples.

Villa Pignatelli

North-west of the Aquarium, in a park just north of the Riviera di Chiaia, is the Villa Pignatelli, once the residence of Prince Diego Aragona Pignatelli Cortes, with a richly appointed interior in the styles of the 18th and 19th centuries (open to visitors; a fine collection of furniture and chinoiserie).

Via Toledo

From the Piazza Trieste e Trento the Via Toledo, named after Don Pedro de Toledo who built it, the city's principal traffic artery and a scene of constant bustle and activity, runs north for a distance of 2 km (1¼ mi.), rising gently uphill. It is crossed by numerous streets and lanes, many of those on the left being stepped lanes climbing up to the Corso Vittorio Emanuele (4 km (2½ mi.) long: beautiful views) and to the Castel Sant'Elmo. The streets on the right, descending to the harbour, are the centre of the city's business and commercial life. At the end of Via Roma, the continuation of Via Toledo, is the spacious Piazza Dante.

Via Medina to Piazza Gesù Nuovo

Via Medina

From the Piazza del Municipio the Via Medina runs past the 14th c. church of the Incoronata. Near the end of Via Medina, on the left, is the 32-storey Grattacielo della Cattolica (1958), and a little way farther north the Piazza Matteotti, with the Post and Telegraph Office (by Vaccaro, 1936), one of the finest achievements of modern Italian architecture. In a little square just east of this building stands the church of Santa Maria la Nova (16th c.; beautiful interior), with two Renaissance cloisters of the monastery to which it belonged.

The line of Via Medina is continued north-west by Via Monteoliveto. At the end of this street is the fine Palazzo Gravina (1513–49), which houses the Academy of Architecture. The street runs into the Piazza Monteoliveto, with the church of Monteoliveto or Sant'Anna dei Lombardi, begun in 1411 and later continued in Early Renaissance style; it contains eight good terracottas (15th–16th c.) and beautiful 16th c. choir-stalls.

Via Monteoliveto

From the Piazza Monteoliveto the Calata Trinità Maggiore leads to the Piazza Gesù Nuovo, with a gilded statue of the Virgin (1748). On the north side of the square is the Jesuit church of Gesù Nuovo (1584), and to the south-east the church of Santa Chiara (founded 1310), which contains the tomb (1343–45) of Robert the Wise (1309–43) and other fine Gothic tombs belonging to members of the house of Anjou. The Nuns' Choir, behind the high altar, was used by the Poor Clares until 1925. In the adjoining Franciscan monastery is a beautiful cloister (Chiostro delle Clarisse) decorated with Capodimonte majolica.

Gesù Nuovo

Piazza San Domenico Maggiore

To the east of the Gesù Nuovo, in Piazza San Domenico Maggiore, is the church of San Domenico Maggiore (c. 1300), which in spite of later alteration is still one of the most interesting churches in Naples, with much Early Renaissance work. In the Cappellone Crocifisso are a 13th c. "crucification" and a 15th c. "Burial of Christ". The sacristy contains 45 sarcophagi belonging to members of the house of Anjou.

San Domenico Maggiore

The Capella Sansevero (museum), a little way east, was built in 1590 as the burial chapel of the Sangro family and elaborately embellished in Baroque style in the 18th c.; it contains some fine sculpture, including a "Christ in a winding-sheet" by Sammartino (1753).

★Capella Sansevero

From Piazza San Domenico Maggiore the Via San Biagio dei Librai runs east: 300m/330yd along this street, on the left, is Via San Gregorio Armeno, in which stands the little church of San Gregorio Armeno (1580), one of the richest Baroque churches in Naples, with a cloister.

San Gregorio Armeno

Via Biagio continues north-east and leads into Via del Duomo. Along this street to the right is the Palazzo Cuomo, a fine Early Renaissance building (1464–90) which now houses the Museo Filangieri, with arms, majolica, porcelain, enamel-work and pictures. On the opposite side of the street, a little farther north-east, is the church of San Giorgio Maggiore, founded in the 5th c. and rebuilt in the 17th c.

Palazzo Cuomo Museum

Between the Piazza Bellini and the cathedral, the Via dei Tribunali, which runs north parallel to Via San Biagio, becomes the "Decumano Maggiore" (the Decumanus Maximus was the main east-west arterial road from the Roman camp) and forms the first section of the planned Museo Aperto (open-air museum).

Decumano Maggiore

★Cathedral

400 m north, on the right-hand side of Via del Duomo, stands the cathedral, dedicated to St Januarius (San Gennaro), patron saint of Naples. Originally built between 1294 and 1323 in French Gothic style, it was considerably restored and altered after an earthquake in 1456. In the centre of the front,

The cloister of Santa Chiara, with its majolica decoration

which dates from 1877 to 1905, is an older doorway (1407). In the south aisle is the sumptuously appointed chapel of St Januarius (1608–37), on the principal altar of which is a silver bust containing the skull of St Januarius, bishop of Beneventum, who was martyred in 305, in the time of Diocletian. In the tabernacle are two vessels containing the saint's blood, which is believed to have the power of liquefaction. The liquefaction, which, according to the legend, occurred for the first time when the saint's remains were transferred to Naples in the time of Constantine is said to take place twice a year on several successive days celebrated as special festivals (particularly on the first Saturday in May in the church of Santa Chiara and on September 19th in the cathedral). The saint's tomb can be seen in the richly decorated Confessio (1497–1506) under the high altar.

Archbishop's Palace

To the left of the cathedral stands the Archbishop's Palace, and to the north of this, in Largo Donnaregina, is the Baroque church of Santa Maria Donnaregina (1649; no admission). Adjoining this church on the north is the older Gothic church of the same name (entrance at Vico Donnaregina 25), restored 1928–34, with the tomb of Queen Mary of Hungary (d. 1323) and fine frescoes by Giotto's contemporary Pietro Cavallini and his school (c. 1308) in the elevated nuns' choir.

Girolamini, San Paolo Maggiore

West of the cathedral, in Via dei Tribunale, are two fine Baroque churches – the church of the Girolamini (Hieronymites) or of San Filippo Neri (1592–1619), with a collection of pictures, and San Paolo Maggiore (1590–1603), built on the ruins of a temple of the early Empire (remains on the façade).

San Lorenzo Maggiore

To the south of San Paolo Maggiore, in Via San Gregorio Armeno, is the restored Gothic church of San Lorenzo Maggiore (1266–1324), with the fine tomb of Caterina d'Austria (d. 1323), and other tombs and frescoes. The adjoining Franciscan monastery, in which Petrarch stayed in 1345, has a notable cloister and a chapter-house decorated with frescos.

The Castel Capuano, usually known as the Vicaria, at the east end of Via dei Tribunali was a Hohenstaufen and later an Angevin stronghold which has been occupied since 1540 by law courts.

Opposite the north-east corner of the Castello is the domed church of Santa Caterina a Formiello (1519–93) and farther east the Porta Capuana, a beautiful Renaissance gateway (1485; further work 1535).

500 m north-west of the Castel Capuano, in Strada Carbonara, the former church of San Giovanni a Carbonara (begun 1343, enlarged in the 15th c., recently restored) contains the Gothic tomb of King Ladislaus (d. 1414).

South-east of Naples

A short distance south-east of the Porta Capuana in the spacious Piazza Garibaldi is the Central Station, built in 1960–64 some 250 m east of the old station.

From here the Corso Garibaldi runs south to Piazza G. Pepe, to the right of which stands the church of Santa Maria del Carmine, containing the tomb of Conradin of Hohenstaufen, Frederick II's grandson, who was beheaded at the age of sixteen. Above the tomb is a statue of Conradin from a design by Thorwaldsen (1847).

North-west of Santa Maria del Carmine, in the Piazza del Mercato, is the church of Santa Croce al Mercato, on the spot on which Conradin was executed on October 29th 1268 on the orders of Charles I of Anjou. Inside the church, to the left of the entrance, a commemorative porphyry column can be seen.

From Piazza Garibaldi the broad Corso Umberto I runs south-west to the University, with its massive main building (1908) facing the street and behind it the former Jesuit college (1605) which was the only university building from 1777 to 1908. To the east is the church of Santi Severino e Sossio (1494; rebuilt 1731 onwards).

Corso Umberto I runs into the Piazza Giovanni Bovio, with the new Exchange and an old Fountain of Neptune.

★★Museo Archeologico Nazionale

From Piazza Dante the Via Enrico Pessina, the continuation of Via Roma, leads to the Museo Archeologico Nazionale (National Museum), with one of the world's finest collections of antiquities. The building, originally erected in 1585 as a barracks and from 1616 the home of the university, was converted in 1790 to house the royal collections. It contains the art treasures of the kings of Naples, the Farnese collections from Rome and Parma, the collections from the palaces of Portici and Capodimonte and material from Pompeii, Herculaneum and Cumae.

The ground floor is devoted mainly to the collection of sculpture in marble. Items of particular importance are the figures of Harmodius and Aristogeiton, a marble copy of a bronze group by Critius and Nesiotes (477 BC) which stood in the Agora in Athens; the so-called Hera Farnese, the head of a statue of Artemis in the earlier severe style; Orpheus and Eurydice with Hermes, a copy of a famous relief from the time of Phidias; and Pallas Athene, a copy of an original from the time of Phidias.
   In the Galleria del Toro Farnese are the Farnese Hercules, a colossal statue 3.17 m (3½ ft) high (after a 4th c. original) found in the Baths of Cara-

calla in Rome, and the Farnese Bull, the largest marble group which has come down to us from antiquity, a copy of a Rhodian work by Apollonius and Tauriscus (3rd–2nd c. BC).

Mosaics

On the mezzanine floor is the collection of ancient mosaics, mainly from Pompeii. Among the most notable items is the famous Alexander's Battle, a mosaic 6.20 m (20 ft) long (copied from an important painting of the 4th c. BC) which was found in Pompeii in 1831. It shows Alexander, with his horsemen, charging the Persian king Darius at the battle of Issus (333 BC) and transfixing a Persian general who has been thrown from his horse, while Darius in his chariot prepares for flight.

Bronze sculpture

On the first floor, in the central Salone dell'Atlante, is the Farnese Atlas. Here, too, is the collection of bronze sculpture, mostly from Herculaneum (recognisable by the dark patina) but also from Pompeii (with green oxidation). Particularly notable are "Apollo playing a lyre" (a 5th c. original from the Peloponnese, found in the Casa del Citarista in Pompeii), a "Dancing Faun" from the Casa del Fauno in Pompeii and the so-called "Narcissus", actually the youthful Dionysus, a masterpiece of the school of Praxiteles.

Wall paintings

Also on the first floor are the collection of ancient wall paintings, mainly from Herculaneum, Pompeii and Stabiae, and the small bronzes (household utensils, etc.), together with terracottas and a large model of Pompeii (1879) on the scale of 1:1100.

The famous collection of erotic art from Pompeii can be seen by appointment only for the purposes of study.

Corso Amedeo di Savoia

Santa Maria della Sanità

From the National Museum Via Santa Teresa degli Scalzi and the Corso Amedeo di Savoia run north, slightly uphill, to the park of Capodimonte, 2 km (1¼ mi.) away. In 750 m it comes to the Ponte della Senità, a viaduct (lift) which carries the road over the low-lying Sanità district. Below, to the right, is the large domed church of Santa Maria della Sanità (1602–13), with the Catacombs of San Gaudioso (5th c.).

★Catacombs of San Gennaro

The Corso Amedeo di Savoia ends at a roundabout, the Tondo di Capodimonte, on the west side of which is the entrance to the 2nd c. Catacombs of San Gennaro. Like the Roman catacombs, these consist of a maze of passages and tomb chambers, but are more ambitious architecturally and have finer paintings than their Roman counterparts. The church of San Gennaro extra Moenia dates from the 5th c. (restored).

Madre del Buon Consiglio

From the Tondo di Capodimonte the Via Capodimonte, to the left, leads in 200 m to the imposing pilgrimage church (on the left) of the Madre del Buon Consiglio (1920–60).

★Capodimonte Park

Palazzo Reale Museo di Capodimonte

Beyond this the road curves up to the Porta Grande, the main entrance to the magnificent Capodimonte Park. In the park is the Palazzo Reale di Capodimonte (1738–1838), commanding fine views. With over a hundred rooms, the palace houses the Capodimonte Museum (Galleria dell'Ottocento), with 19th c. pictures, arms and armour, porcelain, furniture, ivories and bronzes.

★★Galleria Nazionale

Also in the palace is the National Gallery (Galleria Nazionale), one of the finest collections in Italy, with more than 500 pictures, including works by Titian (portraits of members of ruling families from the Farnese collection), Mantegna, Caravaggio, El Greco, Bellini and Neapolitan artists of the 17th and 18th c.

Vomero

To the west of the old town, on a plateau above the Corso Vittorio Emanuele, the district of Vomero, built from 1885 onwards, can be reached by a number of streets and three funiculars. In the southern part of this district is the Villa Floridiana public park, with the Museo Nazionale della Ceramica Duca di Martina, which contains enamels, ivories, pottery and porcelain from many different countries.

Villa Floridiana Museum

On the eastern edge of the Vomero plateau rises the Castel Sant'Elmo (224 m (739 ft)), built in 1329 and extended in the 16th c., with massive walls and underground passages hewn from the rock; it is now used for exhibitions and general events.

Castel Sant'Elmo

To the east of the castle is the former Carthusian monastery of San Martino (1325; rebuilt in the 17th c.), with the Museo Nazionale di San Martino. Notable features are the church, richly decorated with marble and pictures of the 17th and 18th c., the sacristy, the treasury, the Chiostro dei Procuratori and the main cloisters, with 60 columns of white marble. The museum contains porcelain, cribs, including the Presepe di Cuciniello, a state coach of Charles III's reign (18th c.) and relics of the history of Naples and southern Italy in the 18th and 19th c.
   From the room known as the Belvedere there are superb views of Naples, its bay and Vesuvius extending to the Apennines.

*Carthusian monastery Museum

*Camaldoli

The best view of Naples and its beautiful surroundings is to be had from the Camaldulensian monastery of Camaldoli, north-west of the city on the highest point in the Phlegraean Fields (458 m (1511 ft)). The monastery was founded in 1585. The prospect from the terrace on a clear day is one of the finest in Italy.

11 km (7 mi.) NW

The same view can be enjoyed from the Belvedere della Pagliarella, 500 m south, reached in 15 minutes by a footpath through the scrub.

Belvedere della Pagliarella

*Posillipo

South-west of Naples is Posillipo, a ridge of hills 6 km (4 mi.) long, covered with villas and gardens, between the Bay of Naples and the Bay of Pozzuoli, with magnificent views. The name comes from a villa called Pausilypon ("Sans-Souci") which belonged to the notorious epicure Vedius Pollio and later to Augustus.

12 km (7 mi.) SW

From Via Caracciolo, which ends in Mergellina, the Via di Posillipo runs south-west above the sea. Climbing slightly, it comes in 4 km (2½ mi.), after passing the end of Via Boccaccio, to the Parco della Rimembranze (153 m (835 ft)), lying at the south-west end of the ridge almost vertically above the sea and the rocky volcanic island of Nisida. From the road encircling the park there are beautiful views.

Parco della Rimembranze

Via Boccaccio runs uphill into Via Manzoni, from which Via Petrarca continues gently downhill, affording extensive views, to Via Orazio. On the upper part of this road to the left is the pilgrimage church of Sant'Antonio, from which there is a famous view of Naples. Beyond this the road de-scends to the suburb of Mergellina, with a picturesque harbour, Porto Sannazzaro (hydrofoil services to Capri and Ischia). A little way north, at the exits of two tunnels through the hill of Posillipo, are the Piazza Sannazzaro and the Piazza di Piedigrotta, where stands the church of Santa Maria di Piedigrotta (13th c.), with a Renaissance cloister (famous traditional fiesta

Mergellina

from September 5th–13th: principal celebrations on September 7th). To the west of the church, immediately beyond the railway underpass, is the entrance (on the left) to the Parco Virgiliano, in which are the tomb of the poet Giacomo Leopardi (1798–1837) and a Roman structure (actually the columbarium of an unknown family) known as the Tomb of Virgil (70–19 BC), who had a villa on Posillipo and desired to be buried there.

Fuorigrotta

From the entrance to the park the Galleria delle Quattro Giornate leads west to the suburb of Fuorigrotta, with huge blocks of apartments, a stadium (1959) seating 100,000 spectators, the new buildings of the Technical University (1965) and the Mostra d'Oltremare complex, a large exhibition centre, with two theatres, a swimming pool, an illuminated fountain, a zoo and a large amusement park, Edenlandia.

Pozzuoli

27 km (17 mi.) W

West of Naples, over the Posillipo, is Pozzuoli (28 m (92 ft); population 71,000), a port situated on the slopes of a tufa ridge projecting into the sea, on the edge of the area of volcanic hills known as the Phlegraean Fields. Founded in the 6th c. BC by Greeks from Samos, it passed in the hands of the Romans in 318 BC and as Puteoli developed into the principal Italian port for trade with Egypt and the East. In the old town, which is situated on a peninsula, is the cathedral of San Procolo (destroyed by fire in 1964; not open to the public), which was built on the site of a temple of the 3rd–2nd c. BC and has ancient columns. It contains the tomb of the composer Pergolesi (1710–36).

★Serapeum

500 m north, on the sea, is the so-called Serapeum, an ancient market (macellum), which preserves some columns of its colonnade. South-west of the Serapeum are baths. In the harbour to the north-west remains of a

Solfatara, a semi-extinct volcano

temple with 14 columns and a sculptor's workshop were discovered on the sea-bed. Above the old town, on the left of the road to Naples, is the Roman Amphitheatre (149 m (492 ft) long, 116 m (381 ft) across; seating for 40,000). Particularly impressive are the underground passages which housed the machinery and the wild beasts' dens.

1.5 km (1 mi.) east, near the road from Naples, is the entrance to the Solfatara, a semi-extinct volcano (only recorded eruption 1198). This is a circular area enclosed by tufa hills, with numerous fissures which emit steam and sulphurous gases. The ground sounds hollow. The temperature of the largest fumarole is 162°C (324°F), of the smaller ones around 100°C (212°F). The volume of vapour is considerably increased if a piece of burning paper or a torch is held at the mouth of one of the vents.

Solfatara

6 km (4 mi.) west of Pozzuoli is Baia (population 6000), prettily situated on the west side of the Bay of Pozzuoli. As Baiae this was the most fashionable watering-place of Imperial Rome, and impressive palaces dating from this period have been excavated. At the near end of the town, amid vineyards to the right of the road, is the so-called Temple of Mercury, a large circular building with a vaulted roof open in the centre, adjoining which are the Baths of Mercury. Farther on, to the right, are the Baths of Sosandra, with the semicircular Theatre of the Nymphs and a statue of Sosandra. Immediately west are the Baths of Venus, opposite the so-called Temple of Venus.

Baia

2 km (1¼ mi.) south-east of Baia along the west side of the Bay of Pozzuoli (on the left the 16th c. Castello di Baia) we come to Bacoli (population 25,000). On a tongue of land 500 m east is a two-storey Roman structure known as the Cento Camerelle, the upper storey of which was a cistern.

Bacoli

500 m south of Bacoli, above the Mare Morte, is the Piscina Mirabilis, an excellently preserved Roman reservoir 70 m (231 ft) long by 25.5 m (84 ft) wide, with a vaulted roof borne on 48 massive pillars.

★Piscina Mirabilis

From the nearby village of Miseno it is a half hour's climb to the top of Monte Miseno (167 m (551 ft)), a curiously shaped crater rising out of the sea, described by Virgil as the tomb of Aeneas's trumpeter Misenus, from which there is one of the finest views of the Bay of Naples and Gaeta.

Miseno

There are also very fine views from Capo Miseno (79 m (261 ft)), half an hour south. Near here was Lucullus's villa, in which the Emperor Tiberius died.

Capo Miseno

★Cumae

The remains of Cumae (Italian Cuma, Greek Kyme), the oldest Greek settlement in Italy, founded in the 9th or 8th c. BC and destroyed by the Saracens

Location
35 km (22 mi.) W

in the 9th c. AD. The site has been excavated since 1926. Beyond a short tunnel, to the right, is the so-called Roman Crypt, a tunnel of Augustan date, 180 m (591 ft) long, which runs under the acropolis to the sea. Opposite this, to the left, is the entrance of the Cave of the Sibyl (Antro della Sibilla), described by Virgil (Aeneid VI, 43 ff.) as having a hundred entrances and a hundred issues, "from which resound as many voices, the oracles of the prophetess". This is a passage hewn from the rock, 131 m (439 ft) long, 2.5 m (2³/₄ ft) wide and 5 m (17 ft) high, with numerous side passages opening on to the sea which provide light and air. At the far end is the actual cave of the oracle, a square chamber with three vaulted recesses. From the Cave of the Sibyl a ramp leads up to the acropolis. The road leads past a lookout terrace to the remains of the Temple of Apollo and beyond this, on the summit of the hill, the ruins of a Temple of Jupiter which was used as a church in early Christian times. From the top of the hill there are magnificent views of the sea, extending as far as Gaeta and the Isole Ponziane, and of the Phlegraean Fields to the east.

On the south side of the excavated area is the Amphitheatre (129 m (423 ft) long, 104 m (342 ft) across, 21 rows of seats).

To the south-east is the Lago del Fusaro, linked with the sea by two canals, a shallow lake (8 m (26ft) deep) which is used for oyster-culture.

★★Naples to Amalfi and Salerno (c. 97 km (60 mi.))

One excursion which no visitor to Naples should miss is the beautiful drive on SS18 to Amalfi and Salerno (the motorway is shorter but less attractive).

Portici

10 km (6 mi.) east of Naples is Portici (26 m) 86 ft); population 83,000), with a former royal palace which now houses the Faculty of Agriculture of Naples University.

Herculaneum

1 km (¹/₂ mi.): main entrance to the excavations of Herculaneum (see entry).

Torre del Greco

3 km (2 mi.): Torre del Greco (51 m (168 ft); population 105,000), which has in the course of its history been repeatedly covered with lava or destroyed by earthquakes.

Torre Annunziata

8 km (5 mi.): Torre Annunziata (14 m (46 ft); population 60,000), with a villa painted in Pompeian style, a relic of the Roman town of Oplontis. This is the starting point for the ascent to Vesuvius.

Castellammare di Stabia

9 km (5¹/₂ mi.): Castellammare di Stabia (5 m (17 ft); population 73,000), a port built at the foot and on the lower slopes of an outlier of Monte Sant'Angelo, occupying the site of the Roman Stabiae, which was destroyed together with Pompeii in AD 79 (recent excavations; museum). The town is a favourite resort of the Neapolitans on account of its mineral springs, impregnated with sulphur and carbonic acid gas. In the Piazza del Municipio is the 16th c. cathedral. In the south-west of the town are the harbour, with a long breakwater, and the spa establishments, with a ruined castle (13th c.) on the hill above. In the Scanzano district, above the cathedral to the east, are the new Baths.

Monte Faito

Above Castellammare to the south-east (30 minutes) is the beautiful park of the Villa Quisisana ("Here you recover your health"); the house is at the south-east end of the park. From here there is an attractive drive (12 km (7 mi.); also cableway) up Monte Faito (1131 m (3732 ft); view), to the south.

Beyond Castellammare the Amalfi road runs close to the coast again, affording magnificent views of the Bay of Naples, Vesuvius and the steep rock coast of the Sorrento peninsula.

Meta

15 km (9 mi.): Meta (111 m (366 ft); population 7000). The road then goes over a pass (310 m (1023 ft)) in the Monti Lattari to reach the south side of the

Positano, which developed from an artists' colony

Sorrento peninsula, looking on to the Bay of Salerno. The following stretch of road as far as Salerno, blasted out of the rocky coast high above the sea, is one of the most beautiful roads in the world, its charm enhanced by the many little towns and villages in a rather Oriental style of architecture which cling to the precipitous slopes. Out to sea, as the road reaches the coast, can be seen the little "Isles of the Sirens", usually known as Li Galli.

13 km (8 mi.): Positano (30 m (99 ft); population 3000), a very picturesque little town extending up the steep rocky slopes above the sea, with square flat-roofed houses reminiscent of the Saracen period. From here the road continues along the wild and rugged coast, passing several old watch-towers on the coast below. **Positano**

15 km (9 mi.): Amalfi (see entry). **Amalfi**

Beyond Amalfi the road skirts the Capo d'Amalfi and along a stretch which is almost entirely blasted out of the cliffs or carried over gorges on viaducts, affording splendid views. **Capo d'Amalfi**

4 km (2¹/₂ mi.): Minori, once the arsenal of Amalfi has a Roman villa (1st c. AD) with well-preserved wall paintings. **Minori**

1 km (³/₄ mi.): Maiori (15 m (50 ft); population 6000), a popular resort at the mouth of the Tramonti valley. On the coast near the town are a sulphur spring and a number of stalactitic caves, including the Grotta Pandona, which resembles the Blue Grotto on Capri. **Maiori**

10 km (6 mi.): Cetara (15 m (50 ft), a fishing village picturesquely situated in a deep ravine which was the first settlement established by the Saracens. **Cetara**

8 km (5 mi.): Salerno (see entry). Salerno

Naples to Nola and Montevergine (55 km (34 mi.))

Nola

There is also a very attractive trip (28 km (17 mi.) east) from Naples to Nola (34 m (112 ft); population 32,000), where St Paulinus (354–431), a native of Bordeaux and an accomplished poet, is said to have invented the church-bell (hence the Italian word for a bell, campana, Nola being in Campania); his feast, the Festa dei Gigli ("Feast of Lilies"), is celebrated with great pomp on the last Sunday in June. In the Piazza del Duomo is a bronze statue of Augustus, who died here in AD 14. The cathedral, built over the remains of an ancient temple and rebuilt in 1870 after a fire, has a fine crypt. In the Piazza Giordano Bruno is a monument to the philosopher Giordano Bruno, born in Nola in 1548, who was burned at the stake in 1600 in Rome as a heretic.

Montevergine

20 km (12 mi.) east of Nola on the road to Avellino is a side road leading north (5 km (3 mi.)) to the pilgrimage centre of Montevergine (1270 m (4191 ft); cableway from Mercogliano). In the church of the monastery founded by St William of Vercelli in 1119 on the ruins of a Temple of Cybele are a number of fine tombs and, in the south aisle, a chapel with a figure of the Virgin venerated as miraculous; the head of the figure is Byzantine. Pilgrimages take place at Easter and on September 7th–8th.

It is a 45 minutes' climb from the monastery to the top of Montevergine (1493 m (4927 ft)), crowned by a large cross, from which there are magnificent views of the Bay of Naples and Salerno and the mountains of the interior.

Novara   C5

Region: Piemonte. Province: Novara (NO)
Altitude: 159 m (525 ft). Population: 101,000

Location

The provincial capital of Novara lies in the Piedmontese plain between the rivers Sesia (to the west) and Ticino (to the east). The distance between Novara and the more easterly situated city of Milan is some 40 km (25 mi.).

Novara is an industrial town with a varied range of industry and a large map-making institute (De Agostini).

Sights

Cathedral

The town is surrounded by a ring of attractive boulevards on the line of the old fortifications. In the centre of the town, in the arcaded Via Fratelli Rosselli, stands the cathedral, built between 1865 and 1869 in place of an earlier church. The relief on the main altar is by Thorwaldsen.

It has an attractive cloister, entered from the south aisle. There is an important museum, the Museo Lapidario and to the west of the cathedral, opposite the imposing entrance court is a 5th c. baptistery, with 10th c. frescoes.

Broletto

North of the cathedral, reached by way of the beautiful courtyard of the Broletto (Municipal Museum and Art Gallery), is the Corso Italia, one of the town's two main traffic arteries (the other being the Corso Cavour).

San Gaudenzio

A little way north of the Broletto, at the end of Via Gaudenzio Ferrari, the church of San Gaudenzio (by Pellegrino Tibaldi, 1577) has a prominent dome (1875–78). Inside are some fine frescos, a wooden crucifix by Gaudenzio Ferrari and a painting of St Gaudenzio by Pelagio Palagi (c. 1830). Note also the silver sarcophagus of St Gaudenzio, patron saint of Novara.

Piazza Martiri della Libertà

West of the cathedral is the large Piazza Martiri della Libertà, with the Teatro Coccia and the Palazzo del Mercato (1840). On the south side is the rebuilt Castello Sforzesco, once the residence of the ruling Milanese princes.

Surroundings

There is a very attractive drive (north-west) up the Sesia valley to Varallo
Sesia (450 m (1485 ft); population 8000), charmingly situated in the Pre-Alps
at the mouth of the narrow valley of the Mastallone, the birthplace of the
painter Gaudenzio Ferrari (c. 1480–1546). The collegiate church of San
Gaudenzio is picturesquely situated on a crag and another fine church,
the church of Santa Maria delle Grazie, has frescos by Gaudenzio Ferrari
(1507–13).

Varallo Sesia
56 km (35 mi.) NW

At Santa Maria begins the ascent, with Stations of the Cross, to the Sacro
Monte (608 m (2006 ft)). On the summit of the hill are 44 chapels with
painted terracotta groups and frescos depicting scenes from the scriptural
story; in the 38th chapel is a Crucifixion by Gaudenzio Ferrari.

★Sacro Monte

36 km (22 mi.) beyond Varallo, beautifully situated at the head of the Sesia
valley, is Alagna Valsesia, from which a cableway (20 minutes) runs up via
Zaroltu (1825 m (6023 ft)) and the Bocchetta delle Pisse (2406 m (7940 ft))
to the Punta Indren (3260 m (10,758 ft)), a southern outlier of Monte Rosa.

Alagna Valsesia

North of Novara is Lake Orta, the Roman Lacus Cucius (area 18 sq. km
(6¼ sq. mi.), greatest depth 143 m (472 ft)), the southern end of which is
particularly beautiful.

Lake Orta
45 km (28 mi.) N

In a picturesque setting at the foot of the Monte d'Orta or Sacro Monte di
San Francesco (401 m (1323 ft); 20 pilgrimage chapels; view of Monte Rosa)
is the little town of Orta San Giulio (293 m (967 ft); population 1000). In the
main square is the Town Hall (1592); from the west end of the square there
is a beautiful view of the Isola San Giulio, with a church traditionally said to
have been founded by St Julius in 390 (rebuilt in the 11th and 12th c.). There
is a pleasant drive up Monte Mottarone (1491 m (4920 ft)), from which there
are panoramic views.

Orta San Giulio

Isola San Guilo in Lake Orta

Orvieto

<table>
<tr><td>Vercelli
23 km (14 mi.) S</td><td>South of Novara is the old town of Vercelli (131 m (432 ft); population 53,000), the Roman Vercellae; it is the see of an archbishop, the centre of the largest rice-growing area in Europe and has many fine old churches. In the north of the town, near the station, stands the cathedral, remodelled in Baroque style, with the exception of the tower, from the 16th c. onwards; the cathedral library contains valuable manuscripts. A short distance south-west is the imposing four-towered church of Sant'Andrea (1219–24), one of Italy's first buildings in Gothic style. The adjoining Cistercian abbey has a beautiful cloister. In the southern part of the town is the Dominican church of San Cristoforo, with frescoes by Gaudenzio Ferrari. The Museo Borgogna has fine work of Renaissance painters from Vercelli and its surrounding, as well as pictures by other Italian painters.

South of Vercelli, on the road to Casale, were the Campi Raudii, where the Roman consul Marius defeated the Cimbri in 101 BC.</td></tr>
</table>

Novara to Vigevano (55 km (34 mi.))

<table>
<tr><td>Magenta</td><td>31 km (19 mi.) east of Novara is Magenta (138 m (455 ft); population 24,000), scene of the famous battle on June 4th 1859 in which the French and Piedmontese defeated the Austrians, who thereupon withdrew from Lombardy (church of San Martino, built in 1903 to commemorate the victory; charnel-house).</td></tr>
<tr><td>Abbiategrasso</td><td>9 km (5½ mi.) south of Magenta in Abbiategrasso (120 m (396 ft); population 27,000) stands the fine parish church of San Maria Nuova (façade by Bramante, 1497).</td></tr>
<tr><td>Vigevano</td><td>12 km 7 mi.) south-west of Abbiategrasso is Vigevano (116 m (383 ft); population 66,000). In the Piazza Ducale, the central square designed by Bramante, are arcades which still preserve remains of their Early Renaissance decoration. Other features of interest are the 16th c. cathedral, the Visconti castle, rebuilt by Bramante and da Vinci in 1491–94, and the Church of San Pietro Martire with a fine campanile.</td></tr>
</table>

★★Orvieto   G10

<table>
<tr><td></td><td>Region: Umbria. Province: Terni (TR)
Altitude: 325 m (1073 ft). Population: 22,000</td></tr>
<tr><td>Location</td><td>The Umbrian town of Orvieto lies some 100 km (60 mi.) north of Rome. The town was built on a tufa crag which rears up out of the Paglia valley. The white wine of Orvieto is renowned.</td></tr>
<tr><td>History</td><td>Founded by the Etruscans, the town was known in late antiquity as Urbibentum or Urbs Vetus, and later became a stronghold of the Guelf party, where the Popes frequently sought refuge.</td></tr>
</table>

Sights

<table>
<tr><td>★★Cathedral</td><td>The cathedral (begun before 1285), in the south-east of the town, in the Piazza del Duomo, one of the most splendid examples of Italian Gothic architecture, was built in alternating courses of black basalt and greyish-yellow limestone and decorated by the finest artists of the day. It was founded in 1290 in honour of the "miracle of Bolsena" and consecrated in 1309. The façade, begun in 1310 but not completed until the 16th c., is decorated with scenes from the Old and New Testaments by Sienese artists (14th c.) and mosaics of overwhelming richness (originally 14th c., mostly restored in the 19th c.) including the "Coronation of the Virgin" on the tympanum. The intricately carved modern bronze doors are by Emilio Greco (1969).</td></tr>
</table>

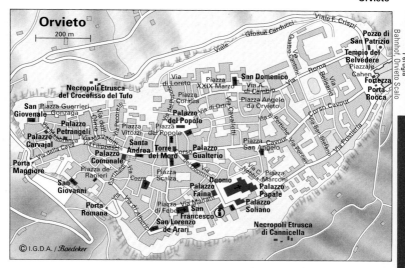

In the richly decorated interior is the Cappella Nuova or Cappella della Madonna di San Brizio, with frescoes (in particular, the "Last Judgment"), begun by Fra Angelico da Fiesole in 1447 but mainly painted by Luca Signorelli from 1499 onwards, which are among the supreme achievements of 15th c. painting.

Cappella Nuova

Behind the altar of the Cappella del Corporale is a reliquary (1338) containing the bloodstained chalice-cloth of the "miracle of Bolsena", which is displayed only on Easter Day and Corpus Christi.

Reliquary

To the right of the cathedral is the Palazzo Soliano (1297–1301), which now houses the Museo Archeologico Nazionale with Etruscan finds from the Orvieto region displayed in five rooms. The Museo dell'Opera del Duomo containing pictures and sculpture, etc. from the cathedral is also worth seeing.

Palazzo Soliano

Facing the cathedral is the Palazzo Faina which houses the Municipal Museum, with a collection of Etruscan and Greek vases.

Palazzo Faina

From the cathedral the Via del Duomo runs north-west into the Corso Cavour, the main street of the town, which traverses it from east to west. At the junction of the two streets rises the Torre del Moro, a quadrangular tower over 40 m (132 ft) high. Opposite stands the Palazzo Gualterio with a highly-decorated Late Renaissance doorway (1550).

★Corso Cavour

A short distance north of the Torre del Moro is the Piazza del Capitano del Popolo (markets held on Thurs. and Sat.), with the 11th c. Palazzo del Popolo, built in volcanic tufa stone; in front of the crenellated façade is a flight of steps.

★Palazzo del Popolo

At the west end of Corso Cavour is the busy Piazza della Repubblica, with the church of Sant'Andrea (12-sided 11th c. tower) and the massive Palazzo Comunale (12th c.; façade rebuilt in 16th c.).

Palazzo Comunale

303

Orvieto: the beautiful marble façade of the Cathedral

★Western part of the old town

Narrow lanes and tufa stone houses make this part of the town very attractive. In Via della Cava (house No. 7) visitors can see underground rooms carved out of the rock. From Porta Maggiore, which is the oldest town gate and was also hewn from the rock, a walk can be taken along the former fortifications to the little church of San Giovanni (fine views).

★Pozzo di San Patrizio

At the east end of the town, to the north of the Fortezza (now public gardens), can be seen the Pozzo di San Patrizio (1527–37 by Sangallo the Elder), a well 61 m (201 ft) deep with two separate spiral staircases winding round the shaft, one for the descent and the other for the ascent of the donkeys which brought up water from the well.

Etruscan buildings and necropolis

Near the Pozzo di San Patrizio are the remains of the Tempio Etrusco.
Below the north side of the town, to the left of the road to the station, is an interesting Etruscan necropolis (Tombe Etrusche del Crocifisso del Tufo), with tombs mostly dating from the 5th and 6th c. BC.
Another Etruscan necropolis can be found to the south of the town (Tombe Etrusche di Cannicella).

★★Ostia
G12

Region: Lazio. Province: Roma (ROMA). Altitude: 3 m (10ft).

Ostia, the port of ancient Rome, now lying 5 km (3 mi.) inland from the Tyrrhenian Sea and close to Fiumicino Airport, is the largest excavation site in Italy after Pompeii.

Location

The excavated remains of Ostia give a vivid picture of life in the port which supplied Rome. Ancient Ostia was founded about the 4th c. BC in an area of salt-pans at the mouth (ostia) of the Tiber. From about 300 BC it was the principal Roman naval base, and under the Empire developed into a considerable town of 50,000 inhabitants and was Rome's largest suburb and commercial port, through which the city's supplies of corn were brought in.

History

After the fall of the Roman Empire Ostia fell a victim to decay and the ravages of malaria. The harbour silted up, and in 1558 the Tiber changed its course.

The present town of Ostia (population 5000) is dominated by a castle (1486), built to protect the harbour. An irregular triangle in plan, it has strong walls, bastions on the side facing the river and a massive keep in typical Italian Renaissance fortification style. The Renaissance church of Santa Aurea was built at the same time.

Ostia Antica

★Ostia Scavi

The excavated remains date mainly from the 2nd–4th c. AD, i.e. the period following the destruction of Pompeii. In contrast to Pompeii with its single-storey houses occupied by separate families Ostia's swarming population was housed in blocks of apartments (insulae) several storeys high, with numerous windows opening on to the street and on to the interior garden and often with loggias and balconies facing the street – typical examples of the architecture of Imperial Rome.

Excavation area

Just beyond the main entrance of the excavation area of Ostia Scavi (closed Mondays), along the ancient Via Ostiensis and in the parallel street to the south, the Via delle Tombe (even more impressive), are rows of tombs, both individual tombs, sometimes of considerable size, and columbaria with niches for large numbers of urns. The Via Ostiensis leads to the remains of the Porta Romana, the most important of the town's three gates.

Tombs

The Decumanus Maximus, the main street of ancient Ostia, more than 1 km (1/2 mi.) long starts here. Beyond the gate, on the left, is the Piazzale della Vittoria, named after the statue of Minerva Victoria (1st c. AD) which was found here; on the right can be seen the ruins of a corn store (horrea) dating from the 1st c. BC.

Decumanus Maximus

Further along, at the corner of Via dei Vigili (on right), are the Baths of Neptune, with heating arrangements at the north-east corner (good general view from a terrace on the first floor). At the end of Via dei Vigili, on the left, are the Watchmen's Barracks (2nd c. AD), with an imposing central courtyard.

Baths of Neptune

Continuing along the Decumanus past the Baths, we come to the Theatre, originally built in the time of Augustus and enlarged under Septimius Severus, with seating for 2700 spectators. From the highest tier of seating there is a good view of the excavations, particularly of the Piazzale delle Corporazioni immediately north of the theatre, with the columns of the Temple of Ceres. Along the east side of this square are the offices (scholae) of the various shipping corporations trading with overseas ports, mainly in Africa.

Theatre

To the west of the theatre is the House of Marcus Apuleius Marcellus (2nd–3rd c. AD), with a peristyle and atrium of Pompeian type. Adjoining it on the north is a shrine of Mithras.

Shrine of Mithras

Ostia

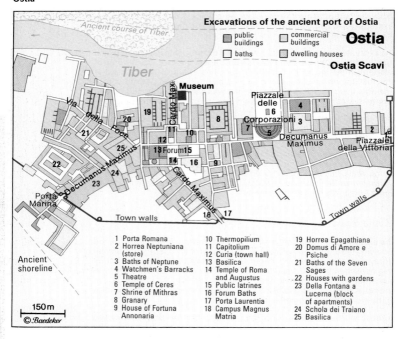

Excavations of the ancient port of Ostia

- public buildings
- commercial buildings
- baths
- dwelling houses

Ostia

Ostia Scavi

Ancient course of Tiber

Tiber

Museum

Piazzale delle Corporazioni

Decumanus Maximus

Piazzale della Vittoria

Via della Foce

Cardo Max.

Decumanus Maximus

Cardo Maximus

Forum

Porta Marina

Town walls

Town walls

Ancient shoreline

150 m

© Baedeker

1 Porta Romana	10 Thermopilium	19 Horrea Epagathiana
2 Horrea Neptuniana (store)	11 Capitolium	20 Domus di Amore e Psiche
3 Baths of Neptune	12 Curia (town hall)	21 Baths of the Seven Sages
4 Watchmen's Barracks	13 Basilica	22 Houses with gardens
5 Theatre	14 Temple of Roma and Augustus	23 Della Fontana a Lucerna (block of apartments)
6 Temple of Ceres	15 Public latrines	24 Schola dei Traiano
7 Shrine of Mithras	16 Forum Baths	25 Basilica
8 Granary	17 Porta Laurentia	
9 House of Fortuna Annonaria	18 Campus Magnus Matria	

Temples

Farther along the Decumanus, on the right, are four small temples built on an older substructure, with a large granary (Grandi Horrea) to the west. Beyond this, also on the right-hand side of the Decumanus, is a well-preserved Thermopolium, a bar with a stone counter containing basins for cooling the drinks and tiers of shelves for drinking vessels.

Capitolium

Beyond the Thermopolium, to the right, the imposing Capitolium (2nd c. AD) was the religious centre of the town. Standing on a high brick base, this was the only building of ancient Ostia which remained above ground throughout the Middle Ages.

Forum

To the south of the Capitolium is the Forum, in the centre of the town at the intersection of the Decumanus with the Cardo Maximus, the principal transverse street. On the south side of the Forum are the remains of the Temple of Roma and Augustus (1st c. AD), with a statue of the victorious Roma. To the west, beyond a basilica, is a rotunda (3rd c. AD) in the style of the Pantheon. South-east of the Forum are large 2nd c. Baths.

Horea Epagathiana

In a road running parallel to the Cardo Maximus, west of the forum, will be found the Horrea Epagathiana, impressive privately-owned warehouses with a handsome gateway and a two-storey arcaded courtyard.

Domus di Amore e Psiche

Opposite, in the Domus di Amore e Psiche, a typical dwelling with inner courtyard, is a well-preserved marble floor.

Baths of the Seven Sages

Nearby, in Via della Foce, lie the Baths of the Seven Sages, with a beautiful mosaic floor in the central domed room, portraying hunters and animals. Nearby are remains of the multi-storey House of the Charioteer.

The Roman theatre in Ostia

Returning to the Decumanus Maximus, on the right can be seen first the 4th c. Christian basilica, so far the only Christian church found in Ostia. Opposite lies the Schola di Traiano (2nd/3rd c.), the meeting place of shipowners and mariners and named after a statue of Trajan found there. Prior to its erection dwellings stood here; in the south-eastern corner there still stands a peristyle with a nymphaeum.

Basilica Schola di Traiano

On the same side of the Decumanus Maximus is the 108 m (354 ft) long block of apartments known as Della Fontana a Lucerna, with shops on the ground floor. Opposite lies a Garden Town. The mosaic floors and heated bathrooms suggest that these apartment blocks were built to a high standard. The Decumanus Maximus ends at the Porta Marina (car park).

Garden Town

When returning to the entrance to the excavation site it is worth making a detour to the south town gate, the Porta Laurentina. There, on the town wall, lies the traingular Campus Magnae Matris, with remains of the Temple of Kybele.

Campus Magnae Matris

Lido di Ostia

South-west of Ostia Antica, on the Tyrrhenian Sea, the seaside resort of Lido di Ostia has a beach 7 km (4 mi.) long.

4 km (2½ mi.) SW

From here a road runs south-east past the Parco di Castel Fusano to the resort of Lido di Castel Fusano, 4 km (2½ mi.) from Lido di Ostia, at the end of the expressway from Rome, the Via Cristoforo Colombo.

Lido di Castel Fusano

★Padua   F5

Region: Veneto. Province: Padova (PD)
Altitude: 12 m (40 ft). Population: 215,000

Padua

Location

The provincial capital of Padua (Padova) lies 30 km (19 mi.) west of Venice on the edge of the Euganean Hills.

Architecture

The older part of the town has a medieval aspect with its narrow arcaded streets, ancient bridges over the many arms of the River Bacchiglione and the Byzantine domes of its churches.

History and art

Under the early Empire the Roman Patavium was one of the wealthiest cities in Italy. It was destroyed by the Huns in 452, but thereafter enjoyed a further period of prosperity. In 1164 it became the first town in northern Italy to free itself from Hohenstaufen rule. During the subsequent conflicts it usually supported the Guelfs. In 1318 it passed into the hands of the house of Carrara, and in 1405 was annexed by Venice.

The Roman historian Livy lived in Padua and died there in AD 7. In the early 13th c. the eloquent preacher St Antony (b. in Lisbon 1195, d. 1231 at Arcella, 2.5 km (1½ mi.) north of Padua) lived and worked in Padua. The town's importance during the medieval period and at the Renaissance rested mainly on its university, founded in 1222 and extended by Frederick II in 1238, which became the first centre of humanism and also exerted a great attraction on artists.

During the 14th c. the finest works of art produced in Padua were by incomers like Giotto, Giovanni Pisano and Altichiero; and the great flower-

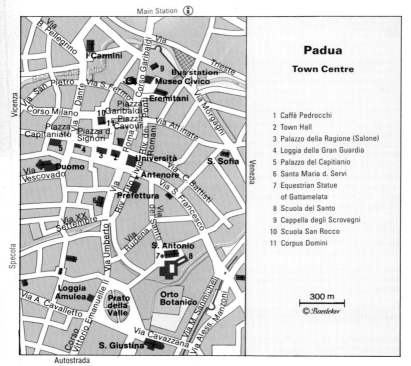

Padua

Town Centre

1 Caffè Pedrocchi
2 Town Hall
3 Palazzo della Ragione (Salone)
4 Loggia della Gran Guardia
5 Palazzo del Capitaniano
6 Santa Maria d. Servi
7 Equestrian Statue
  of Gattamelata
8 Scuola del Santo
9 Cappella degli Scrovegni
10 Scuola San Rocco
11 Corpus Domini

300 m

© Baedeker

ing of art in the 15th c. was due to Florentine artists, among them Donatello, Paolo Uccello and Andrea del Castagno, who influenced sculptors as well as the great painter Andrea Mantegna (1431–1506).

Sights

In the centre of the old town is the Piazza Cavour, from which the busy Via III Febbraio runs south. On the right is the Neo-Classical Caffè Pedrocchi (rebuilt after the Second World War), which when it was first opened in 1831 was the largest café in Europe. It played an important part in the history of the Risorgimento, and is still the resort of professors and students of the university.

Piazza Cavour

Beyond this, farther south, stands the Palazzo Municipale (Town Hall), with a façade of 1930 and an older building to the rear (16th c.).

Palazzo Municipale

Opposite the Town Hall, on the east side of Via III Febbraio, is the University, built in the 16th c. In the colonnaded courtyard (1552) and inside the building are numerous names and coats of arms of distinguished graduates. Beside the Great Hall are the chairs of Galileo and other famous professors, and the Anatomy Theatre (1594), the oldest of its kind.

University

From the university two streets run west, leading respectively to the Piazza delle Frutta and the Piazza delle Erbe. Between the two squares we find the Salone or Palazzo della Ragione, built 1218–19 as a law court, now an exhibition and conference hall (entrance from the Piazza delle Erbe, on the right). The huge hall, rebuilt in 1430, contains a large wooden horse (c. 1466), a copy of Gattamelata's horse in Donatello's famous statue, and astrological frescoes (15th c. restored) on the walls.

★Salone

Farther west is the Piazza dei Signori, in which can be seen the Loggia del Consigli or Loggia della Gran Guardia, an elegant Early Renaissance building with an open loggia below and a closed upper storey (1496–1523).

Piazza dei Signori Loggia del Consigli

On the west side of the square is the Palazzo del Capitanio, formerly the seat of the Venetian governor, with a fine clock-tower and remains of a Late Gothic loggia which belonged to the earlier Carrara palace.

Palazzo del Capitanio

To the west of the Piazza dei Signori stands the cathedral, a High Renaissance building (1552–77) with an unfinished façade. To the right of the cathedral the elegant brick-built Baptistery (13th c.) has interesting frescoes by Giusto de' Menabuoi (c. 1375).

Cathedral

South-west of the university, beyond the wide modern streets (Riviera Vittorio Tito and Riviera dei Ponti Romani) built over an arm of the Bacchiglione, is the Prefecture. In front of this is a medieval sarcophagus (1233), popularly called the Tomb of Antenor, the mythical founder of Padua. To the east is the Via del Santo, which runs south to the Piazza del Santo, with the church of Sant'Antonio (Basilica del Santo), known as "il Santo" for short, containing the Tomb of St Antony of Padua, a shrine visited by countless pilgrims. The massive structure (13th–14th c.), a pillared basilica which shows a fantastic mingling of Romanesque, Gothic and Byzantine features, is highly picturesque, with its two slender towers, the conical dome over the crossing and seven other round domes (heightened in 1424).

★★Church of Sant'Antonio

The interior contains interesting works of art. In the north aisle is the Cappella di Sant'Antonio (1500–46), with nine 16th c. high reliefs (scenes from the life of St Antony, by Jacopo Sansovino, Antonio and Tullio Lombardi and others); within the altar, hung with numerous ex-votos, are the saint's remains. The high altar, originally by Donatello (1443–50), was subsequently removed but restored in 1895 with the original sculpture

Interior

Villas in Veneto

The country houses and villas in the hilly countryside beyond Venice and along the Brenta canal, which connects it with Padua, are a most memorable and vivid link with the past. Nestling magically among vineyards and fruit groves at the foot of the Dolomites, their special charm comes from the subtle mixture of Roman and Renaissance features embodied in their architecture.

Even today, when Veneto has become one of Italy's most economically prosperous regions, the visitor can still sense the aristocratic composure and opulent contentment of days gone by, when the Venetian *doges* came here in summer to relax. They financed this luxury retreat from the income derived from a flourishing agricultural economy.

For many years now industrial firms have established themselves in the hinterland of Venice, Mestre and Marghera being prize examples of the ugliness associated with such developments. Between Treviso and Vicenza lies a profusion of new buildings, factories and petrol stations, while within the towns' precincts one can still find the remains of Roman castles. The old streets lined with plane trees casting a welcome shade are becoming fewer by the year. In the hills just a few miles away, however, garlands of grape-vines swing between mulberry trees and voluptuous sandstone goddesses recline enticingly in fertile gardens containing ponds and caves.

About 3000 Venetian villas still remain, some being used as museums. Many are privately owned and are open to visitors at week-ends, such as the Villa Barbaro in Maser, famous for its frescoes by Paolo Veronese and its beautiful stucco work by Alessandro Vittoria. This villa, intended as a residence for the Barbaro family, reflects the Palladian villa style – a portico with tall Ionic columns, flanked by domestic wings with a pillared hall. Many villas can only be admired from the outside, such as Palladio's "La Rotonda" with its four temple-like façades. Many have fallen into decay and some are now used as workshops.

Some villas have been converted to hotels or restaurants for the connoisseur. Here those prepared to pay the price for such luxury can savour something of the dolce vita enjoyed by the Renaissance patricians.

In these buildings Venetian history comes alive. In the years between 1389 and 1420 Venice succeeded in bringing a number of regions on the Italian mainland under its yoke, thus boosting the self-confidence of the Venetian people. For the first time in their history they had set foot on the mainland and so no longer had to face the hazards of transporting foodstuffs by sea. The great architects and artists of Venice were busy fitting out and furnishing the new villas and country houses. Andrea Palladio, the genial architect to whom Vicenza owes its fame, built for the Venetians villas reminiscent of the country's Roman past. They owe their restrained beauty to the building regulations laid down by the town council; "Villas yes, palaces no!"

The villas in which tourists can find accommodation form a pleasant base for excursions to Venice in the hot season. In the evenings, when a damp, hot haze lies over the lagoon, an airy villa in the countryside offers a welcome retreat. The price paid for a good villa hotel on the mainland is similar to that asked for a very average room in Venice itself.

The charges are very reasonable at Villa Revedin near Osoppo, which also boasts a good fish restaurant, Villa Ducale in Dolo on the Brenta canal, and Villa Michelangelo in Arcugnano near Vicenza. Luxurious and correspondingly expensive are Villa Cipriani in Asolo and "Da Alfredo al Toulà" in Ponzano Veneto near Treviso (restaurant). In Villa Giustinian, also known as "Roncade Castle", in Portobuffole near Treviso, visitors can chose between small, reasonably-priced rooms or luxury suites, while enjoying the pleasures of an elegant restaurant and wine-cellar. The villa is surrounded by a wall with battlements and towers, signs of its medieval origin.

The majority of the villas stand along the Brenta canal, the old link between Venice and Padua. Visitors can explore the charming surrounding countryside by car or excursion boat, the *burchiello*. Some 70 feudal country mansions are concentrated along a few miles of the canal bank. These include the villa known as "La Malcontenta", which Palladio built for the Poscari family between 1550 and 1560. According to legend, it was here in the 14th century that a noblewoman of the house of Poscari was banished into exile to atone for the dissolute life she had led. It was thus that the villa obtained its name of "La Malcontenta". Napoleon lived in the Villa Nazionale (Villa Pisani), and Hitler and Mussolini held their first meeting here.

The hilly countryside between Treviso and Vicenza conceals many villas which are well worth seeking out. Here, too, can be found some of the best wine in the region, including the sparkling *prosecco*.

In the hills high above Thiene lies Anrea Palladio's first villa, "Piovene Porto Godi", named after the founding family whose descendants still occupy it today. Plain and elegant in design, it lies in a magnificent 19th century garden and still provides an example of the greatest luxury any Venetian could desire – plenty of space.

Padua

(angel musicians, entombment and bronze figures by Donatello). On the left of the altar is a magnificent bronze candelabrum by Briosco (1507–15). Beyond the ambulatory in the Cappella del Tesoro or Cappella delle Reliquie (1690) are fine examples of goldsmith's work.

On the south side of the church are four beautiful cloisters (13th–16th c.), the first of which in particular contains many old gravestones.

Museo Antoniano

The Museo Antoniano houses the church's art collection.

★★Equestrian statue of Gattamelata

To the side of the church stands the equestrian statue of Gattamelata. Donatello, the talented sculptor of the Early Renaissance, who worked in Padua from 1441 to 1453, created the bronze statue between 1447 and 1453 in honour of Erasmo da Narni. The latter was commander-in-chief of the Venetian army (against Milan) and his diplomatic skill earned him the name of "Gattamelata" (spotted cat).

Scuola di Sant'Antonio

On the south side of the Piazza del Santo is the Scuola di Sant'Antonio, on the first floor of which are seventeen frescos (mostly repainted) depicting the saint's miracles. In the adjoining Oratorio San Giorgio are frescoes by Altichieri and Avanzi.

Botanic Garden

South of the Scuola di Sant'Antonio lies the Botanic Garden, one of the oldest in Europe.

Basilica di Santa Giustina

A short distance from the Botanic Garden in the centre of a spacious square, the Prato della Valle, is an oval planted with trees which contains 82 statues of distinguished citizens of Padua and students of the university. In the south-east corner stands the imposing church of Santa Giustina (1518–87), in High Renaissance style. Behind the high altar is a fine painting by Paolo Veronese ("Martyrdom of St Justina", c. 1575); there are fine carved stalls (c. 1560) in the choir.

Padua: Basilica of St Anthony's Cathedral

Just north of Piazza Cavour is the busy Piazza Garibaldi, from which Via Emanuele Filiberto, runs west to the Piazza dell'Insurrezione, now the city's busiest traffic intersection; this was laid out after the Second World War and is surrounded by tall modern buildings. To the south are the church of Santa Lucia and the Scuola di San Rocco (frescoes).

Piazza dell'Insurrezione

North-east of Piazza Garibaldi is the former Augustinian church of the Eremitani (13th c., restored after war damage), with remains of frescoes by Mantegna in the Cappella Ovetari.

Chiesa degli Eremitani

Immediately north of the church is the chapel of the Madonna dell' Arena, built in 1303–05 as the chapel of a palace which was demolished around 1820; the chapel is also known as the Cappella degli Scrovegni, and contains Giotto's splendid frescos (scenes from the life of the Virgin and the life of Christ; 1303–06), which are his earliest, largest and best preserved work. Particularly fine are the "Kiss of Judas" and the "Lamentation" in the third row, depicting the Passion with great dramatic force. On the altar is a "Madonna with Two Angels", a fine statue by Giovanni Pisano.

★Cappella degli Scrovegni

Between the two churches is the Museo Civico. The art gallery has painting by Giotto, Bellini, Titian, Veronese and Tintoretto as well as works by Flemish painters.

Museo Civico

Surroundings

A rewarding trip can be made south-west through the Euganean Hills (Colli Euganei), a volcanic range rising abruptly out of the plain and reaching a height of 603 m (1990 ft) in Monte Venta.
   There are numerous hot springs and a number of popular spas in the hills, among them the world-famous thermal resort of Albano Terme (14 m (46 ft); population 17,000), the Roman Aquae Patavinae or Fons Aponi, where hot radioactive springs (87°C (189°F)) deposit mud of volcanic origin, which, when pulverised and mixed into a paste with hot water, is known as "fango" and is used in the treatment of gout and rheumatism.

Albano Terme
10 km (6 mi.) SW

4 km (2¹/₂ mi.) west of Albano Terme is the Abbazia di Praglia (alt. 21 m (69 ft)), a Benedictine abbey founded in 1080 and restored in the 15th–16th c., with a Renaissance church.

★Abbazia di Praglia

Another popular spa with hot springs is Montegrotto Terme (10 m (33 ft)), where the remains of Roman baths and a theatre have been brought to light.

Montegrotto Terme
14 km (9 mi.) SW

6 km (4 mi.) farther south, on the A 13, is Battaglia Terme, another spa in the surroundings of Padua.

Battaglia Terme

South-west of Padua, under Monte Calaone (415 m (1370 ft)), is the little town of Este (15 m (50 ft); population 18,000), the Roman Ateste, which was held from c. 1050 to 1275 by the princely family of Este. The Museo Nazionale Ateastino, in the former Palazzo del Castello or Palazzo Mocenigo (16th c.), has rich prehistoric and Roman collections. Adjacent is the 14th c. Castello Carrarese, surrounded, particularly on the east side, by massive walls. Also of interest is the 18th c. Cathedral of Santa Tecla, which has a picture of the saint by Tiepolo in the choir; it shows St Tecla praying for the town to be saved from the plague (1630).

Este
30 km (19 mi.) SW

15 km (9 mi.) farther west is Montagnana (16 m (53 ft); population 10,000), with medieval town walls and 24 battlemented towers, best seen from the ring road which makes a circuit of the town. Outside the Porta Padova, on the east side of the town, is the Villa Pisani (by Palladio, 1560). In the town centre are the Gothic Romanesque cathedral (15th c.) and the Palazzo Pretorio (16th c.), now the Town Hall.

Montagnana

Paestum

Arquà Petrarca   About 8 km (5 mi.) north-east of Montagnana is the medieval village of Arquà Petrarca (80 m (264 ft)) where Francesco Petrarca (Petrarch) (1304–74) died. His tomb (1380) and the 14th c. house in which he lived are open to the public.

Padua to Venice (30 km (19 mi.))

Stra   There is a very attractive excursion from Padua along the canalised River Brenta (boat services in summer). The road first reaches Stra (8 m (26 ft)), a favourite resort of the Venetians in summer. At the far end of the village, in a park to the left of the road between the Brenta canal and its tributary the Veraro, stands the 18th c. Villa Pisani or Villa Nazionale. Composed of five wings grouped around two inner courtyards, there are over 100 rooms with beautiful Empire furniture, paintings, wall and ceiling paintings, with a splendid ballroom containing a large ceiling painting by Tiepolo (1762).

Mira   The road then continues east alongside the navigable Brenta canal (Naviglio di Brenta), past a series of country houses and villas surrounded by parks. Beyond Stra, at the straggling village of Mira (6 m (20 ft)), the road crosses a broad lateral canal, the Taglio Nuovissimo di Brenta, and in another 15 km (9 mi.) reaches the Piazzale Roma in Venice (see entry).

★★Paestum   K15

Region: Campania
Province: Salerno (SA). Altitude: 18 m (59 ft)

Location   The site of Paestum lies in southern Campania, in a plain nearby the Gulf of Salerno, a bay on the Tyrrhenian Sea.
    With its ruined temples and its cemeteries, this site possesses the finest remains of Greek architecture on the mainland of Italy.

History   Paestum was founded by Greeks from Sybaris under the name of Poseidonia about 600 BC. In the 4th c. BC it passed into the hands of the Lucanians, and in 273 BC became a Roman colony.
    In the time of Augustus it already had a bad name for the malaria-ridden marshland which surrounded it, and after the devastation of the region by the Saracens in the 9th c. its inhabitants abandoned the town, taking with them a relic of St Matthew which had according to tradition been preserved in Paestum since the 4th c., and founded a new settlement on the neighbouring hills at Capaccio, of which Paestum with its few modern houses is now a part.
    The deserted town was despoiled of its columns and sculpture by the Norman leader Robert Guiscard, and thereafter was forgotten until the 18th c., when there was a revival of interest in classical Greek art.

Sights

Town walls   The site of the ancient city is enclosed by a magnificent circuit of town walls 4.75 km (3 mi.) long, with four gates and a number of towers (a walk round the walls is recommended for the fine views of the site and the sea).

★★Museum   In the centre of the area, on the east side of the state road, is the Museum, with prehistoric material, painted pottery and fine metopes from the Temple of Hera on the Sele, north of Paestum, and the archaic Treasury, including Greek statues and pictures. Also to be seen are grave-paintings found in the nearby necropoli, as well as Greek statues and paintings.

314

Paestum: A Doric temple

Immediately south of the museum the state road cuts across the Amphi-   Amphitheatre
theatre of the Roman period, the rounded end of which can still be
distinguished. Some 300 m farther south, on the right, is the entrance to
the site, near the south side of the ancient city.

★★Site (Zona Archeologica)

Opposite the entrance is the magnificent Temple of Hera (misnamed   Temple of Hera
Temple of Neptune), a consummate example of the mature, strictly disciplined architecture of the 5th c. BC, reflecting the Greek ideal of harmony
and proportion. The stone is a porous limestone to which the passage of
time has given a beautiful yellow tone. At the east end of the temple the
tip of an earlier oval structure emerges from the ground. 10 m east are the
remains of the sacrificial altar associated with the temple.

To the south of the Temple of Hera can be seen the misnamed Basilica, the   Basilica
oldest temple on the site, dated by the marked swelling of the columns
and the form of the capitals to the second half of the 6th c. BC. As with the
Temple of Hera, there are remains of an earlier oval temple at the east end
and, 27 m farther east, a sacrificial altar 21 m (69 ft) wide.

Just beyond the west end of the basilica is a section of the ancient Via   Via Sacra
Sacra which ran across the city from north to south.

200 m north of the Temple of Hera is the Forum (150 m 495 ft long, 57 m   Forum
(189 ft) across), which was surrounded by a colonnade of late Doric
columns.
   North of the Forum are the massive substructures of the Tempio Italico
(273 BC), with one re-erected column.

Temple of Ceres	Still farther north the so-called Temple of Ceres has traces of stucco and painting on the gable, which shows Ionic influences.

★★Cemeteries

Tomb paintings	Outside the town walls three large cemeteries, with tomb paintings of the highest quality, have been discovered since 1968.

On the south side are tombs of the 5th c. BC, the heyday of Magna Graecia, with frescoes in the style of the classical vase-painters ("Tomb of the Diver").

To the north are 70 tombs dating from the 4th c. (the period of Lucanian predominance) painted in vivid colours, with scenes from everyday life which throw fresh light on the discovery of colour, of light and shade and of spatial representation in Western art.

On the west side a cemetery was found, covering an area of 2.5 ha (6 acres) with thousands of 3rd c. tombs painted in a style which demonstrates that even during the Roman period southern Italy still belonged to the Greek (Hellenistic) cultural sphere.

Altogether more than 500 tomb paintings have been discovered so far.

★★Palermo   H19

Region: Sicilia. Province: Palermo (PA)
Altitude: 19 m (63 ft). Population: 715,000

Location	Palermo, capital of the region of Sicilia and principal port of the island, lies in a bay on the north coast of Sicily. It is bounded on the south and west by the artificially irrigated plain known as the Conca d'Oro ("Golden Shell"), with a wide arc of imposing mountains forming the background.
Architecture	Although Palermo now has the aspect of an entirely modern city, it preserves a distinctive character, thanks to its Norman buildings with their rather Oriental style of architecture and the Baroque architecture it has inherited from the period of Spanish rule. The old town with its narrow and twisting side streets is still the scene of a vigorous popular life. Its numerous gardens and palm-shaded promenades give it a particular charm.
History	Palermo, founded by the Phoenicians and known to the Greeks as Panormos, became the principal Carthaginian base in Sicily until its capture by the Romans in 254 BC. In AD 553 the Byzantine general Belisarius recovered it from the Ostrogoths, and thereafter it remained in Byzantine hands until its capture by the Saracens in 830. The Saracens were followed in 1072 by the Normans, who were in turn succeeded in 1194 by the Hohenstaufens and in 1266 by the house of Anjou, whose brief period of rule was ended by the popular rising known as the Sicilian Vespers in 1282. Palermo then came under Aragonese and Spanish rule, passed to the Bourbons in the 18th c. and was finally liberated by Garibaldi on May 27th 1860. Palermo is the see of an archbishop and has a university.

Sights

★Quattro Canti	The busiest traffic intersection in the old town is the square, laid out in 1609, known as the Quattro Canti ("Four Corners") or Piazza Vigliena, at the crossing of the Via Vittorio Emanuele, which runs accross the city from north-east to south-west for a distance of 2 km (1¼ mi.), and the Via Maqueda, which runs from the station to the newer parts of the city, offering views of the long rows of uniform buildings, all set against a background of great scenic beauty. At the southern corner of the Quattro Canti is the church of San Giuseppe dei Teatine (1612–45), a massive

pillared basilica with a sumptuous Baroque interior. Adjoining it on the south is the University.

Beyond this to the south stands the imposing church of the Gesù (1564–1633), also in Baroque style.

Church of the Gesù

From the Quattro Canti Via Vittorio Emanuele runs south-west to the Piazza della Cattedrale. On the north-west side of this square, which is surrounded by a stone balustrade erected in 1761, with sixteen large statues of saints, stands the cathedral, originally Romanesque but frequently enlarged, with a beautiful south front (1300–59) and a dome finished in the 18th c.

★Cathedral

In the south aisle are six royal tombs – the majestic porphyry sarcophagi, surmounted by temple-like canopies, of the Emperor Frederick II (d. 1250: on the left), his father Henry VI (d. 1197: on the right), Roger II (d. 1154: behind, on the left), his daughter the Empress Constance (behind on the right), William, son of Frederick II of Aragon (in niche on the left) and

Royal tombs

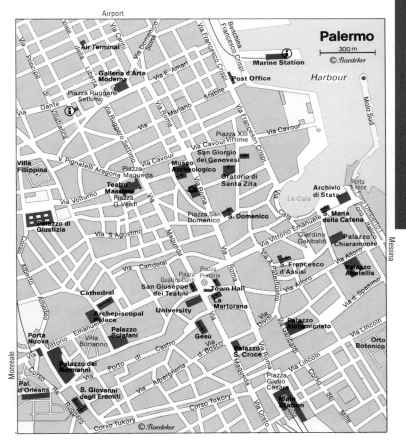

Constance of Aragon, wife of the Emperor Frederick II (by the wall, to the right). In the chapel to the right of the choir a silver sarcophagus contains the remains of St Rosalia, the city's patron saint. The sacristy, at the end of the south aisle, houses the rich Cathedral Treasury; the crypt is also of interest.

Diocesan Museum

Immediately south-west of the cathedral is the Archbishop's Palace (Palazzo Arcivescovile, 15th c.), with the Diocesan Museum (entrance in courtyard to the right).

Palazzo dei Normanni

On the opposite side of the Via Vittorio Emanuele is the Piazza della Vittoria, with the palm-shaded park of the Villa Bonanno (remains of Roman houses). The west side of the park is occupied by the Palazzo dei Normanni, the former royal palace, a fortress-like building originally dating from the Saracen period which was remodelled by the Norman kings. The last gateway on the left gives access to the palace courtyard (Renaissance arcades).

★★ Cappella Palatina

On the first floor is the famous Cappella Palatina (on the right), dedicated to St Peter, which was built by Roger II in 1132–40. This is surely the most beautiful palace chapel in the world with its splendid mosaic decoration and its mingling of Western and Oriental elements, including the ceiling painted in Oriental style. The glass mosaics on a gold ground which cover the walls depict scenes from the Old Testament, the life of Christ and the lives of the apostles Peter and Paul.

Near the chapel rises the Torre di Santa Ninfa, with a 15 m (50 ft) high room on the ground floor which was probably the strong-room of the Norman kings.

On the second floor is an observatory, from the roof of which there is a fine view of Palermo. There are also good views from the balconies of

Palermo Cathedral

318

various rooms in the palace (conducted tour). Particularly interesting is King Roger's room, with mosaics (*c.* 1170; hunting scenes).

Just beyond the Palazzo dei Normanni (on north) the Via Vittorio Emanuele is spanned by the Porta Nuova (1535), the upper storey of which (accessible from the palace) affords another magnificent view.   Porta Nuova

At the south-eastern corner of the Piazza della Vittoria is the Palazzo Sclafani (1330) and at the south-western corner a monument to Philip V (1856).   Palazzo Sclafani

Just south of the Palazzo dei Normanni is Palermo's most unusual ruined church, San Giovanni degli Eremiti (1132), a building of decidedly Oriental aspect with its five tall red domes. Adjoining the church are the remains of a small mosque. On its north side is a picturesque cloister, with tropical plants.   San Giovanni degli Eremiti

West of the church, in the Piazza dell'Indipendenza, the Villa d'Aumale or Villa d'Orléans, now the offices of the autonomous region of Sicily, has a beautiful park.   Villa d'Aumale

Piazza Pretoria

On the east side of San Giuseppe dei Teatini is the Piazza Pretoria, with a Florentine fountain (1555–75) in the centre. On the south side of the square stands the Palazzo del Municipio (Town Hall). At the east corner is the side entrance to the church of Santa Caterina (Baroque interior), with its main front on Piazza Bellini. In this square also, a flight of steps leads up to the little church of Santo Cataldo (1161), in Byzantine style, with a dome.   Palazzo del Municipio

On its east side is the fine church of La Martorana (1143), also known as Santa Maria dell'Ammiraglio after its founder Georgios Antiochenos, grand admiral of the Norman king Roger I, with excellent Byzantine   ★La Martorana

The beautiful cloister of San Giovanni degli Eremiti

Magnificent buildings in the Piazza Pretoria

mosaics and fine painting in the vaulting. The campanile is in the Arabic style.

Harbour district

Santa Maria della Catena

The eastern section of the Via Vittorio Emanuele cuts across the busy Via Roma (200 m east of the Quattro Canti), a modern street driven through the old town from north to south, and comes to the church of Santa Maria della Catena (*c.* 1500; beautiful portico), on the left. It then runs into the Piazza Santo Spirito, closed on the seaward side by the ruins of the Porta Felice.

Porta Felice

Piazza Marina

West of Santa Maria della Catena lies the picturesque boating harbour, La Cala, and to the south is the Piazza Marina, almost entirely occupied by the tropical Giardino Garibaldi. The Palazzo Chiaramonte, usually known as Lo Steri, on the east side of this square, was built between 1307 and 1380 and later became the residence of the viceroy.

★Galleria Regionale della Sicilia

To the south-east, in Via Alloro, is the Palazzo Abatellis (1495), with a crenellated tower and a Gothic doorway. The palace now houses the Galleria Regionale della Sicilia, which gives a comprehensive view of Sicilian painting from the Middle Ages to modern times. Particularly notable is a magnificent wall painting, the "Triumph of Death", by an unknown 15th c. master (in Room II).

★Foro Umberto I

Along the seafront to the east and south-east of the Porta Felice extends the Foro Umberto I, a broad boulevard which affords magnificent views of the Bay of Palermo and is a popular resort of the citizens on summer evenings. At the southern end of the Foro Umberto I is the beautiful Villa Giulia park, also known as La Flora (laid out in 1777). On the west side of this the Botanic

Garden has a magnificent variety of plants including date and coconut palms, banana trees and fine stands of bamboos and papyrus.

Piazza Giuseppe Verdi

From the Quattro Canti Via Maqueda runs north-west to the busy Piazza Giuseppe Verdi, lying between the old and the new town, with the Teatro Massimo (1875–97), one of the largest theatres in Italy (3200 seats).

★Teatro Massimo

From the Piazza Verdi Via Ruggero Settimo continues through the new town to Piazza Ruggero Settimo, with monuments to Sicilian patriots. On the north-east side of the square, in the Politeama Garibaldi, is the Galleria d'Arte Moderna E. Restivo, with works by Sicilian artists.

Galleria d'Arte Moderna E. Restivo

From the Teatro Massimo Via della Bara runs east to the Piazza dell'Olivella, in which are the Olivella church (1598) and the Archaeological Museum (Museo Archeologico Nazionale), one of Italy's finest museums, housed in a former monastery of the Compagnia di San Filippo Neri. In addition to prehistoric material and an Etruscan collection the museum contains many important classical antiquities, among them the famous metopes from Selinunte (c. 550–450 BC), 56 water-spouts in the form of lions' heads from Himera (5th c. BC) and fine Greek bronzes, including Heracles and the Cerynaean hind, a fountain group from Pompeii excavated in 1805, and a large ram from Syracuse.

★Museo Archeologico Nazionale

Piazza San Domenico

From the east side of the Archaeological Museum Via Roma runs south past the Head Post Office (on right) to the Piazza San Domenico, in which is a 30 m (99 ft) high marble column bearing a statue of the Virgin (1726). On the east side of the square stands the church of San Domenico (14th c., rebuilt 1636–40). It contains a number of good pictures and many monuments to prominent Sicilians. In the chapel to the right of the choir is a charming relief of the "Virgin with Angels" by Antonio Gagini. Adjoining the church is a picturesque cloister (14th and 16th c.).

San Domenico

Behind San Domenico, in Via Bambinai, the Oratorio della Compagnia del Rosario di San Domenico (entrance at No. 16, on the right), has stucco decoration by Giacomo Serpotta (1656–1732). On the high altar is the "Madonna del Rosario" (1624–25), by Van Dyck.

To the north of the Oratorio in the church of Santa Zita, founded in 1369, can be seen a triptych (cona; 1517) by Antonio Gagini. Immediately behind the church, in Via Valverde, is the Oratorio della Compagnia del Rosario di Santa Zita, with stucco-work by Serpotta.

Santa Zita

North-east of Santa Zita is the church of San Giorgio dei Genovesi (1591). From here Via Francesco Crispi runs north to the busy harbour.

San Giorgio dei Genovesi

Surroundings

1.5 km (1 mi.) west of the Porta Nuova, on the edge of the town, is the Convento dei Cappuccini (1621), with underground passages which contain mummies and skeletons of ecclesiastics or well-to-do citizens in the clothes they wore during life (and which are sometimes renewed by the descendants). No further burials of this kind have been permitted since 1881.

Convento dei Cappuccini

500 m north of the convent is a former Norman palace, the Palazzo della Zisa, a plain building based on Arab models, which was erected by William I and his son William II between 1154 and 1166. On the ground floor is a

Palazzo della Zisa

square garden room with a fountain decorated with Byzantine mosaics and high stalactitic vaulting.

Santa Maria di Gesù

4 km (2½ mi.) S — From the former Minorite house of Santa Maria di Gesù, on the lower slopes of Monte Grifone (832 m (2746 ft)) there is perhaps the finest view of Palermo and the Conca d'Oro, particularly in the morning light.

San Martino delle Scale

13 km (8 mi.) SW — South-west of Palermo is the former Benedictine monastery of San Martino delle Scale. The present buildings date from 1770–86; the church was erected in 1590.

Spianata della Sacra Grotta

13 km (8 mi.) N — There is a rewarding trip to the Spianata della Sacra Grotta, a cave converted into a church in 1625. According to the legend St Rosalia, daughter of Duke Sinibaldo and niece of King William II, withdrew to this remote hermitage, at the age of only fourteen.

★**Monte Pellegrino** — From here a steep path ascends south-east (30 minutes) to the summit of Monte Pellegrino (606 m (2000 ft); two television towers), from which there are panoramic views.
From the Spianata della Sacra Grotta a good road descends, with many bends and fine views, to Mondello (8 km (5 mi.); see below).

Tour round Monte Pellegrino (c. 30 km (19 mi.))

La Favorita — There is also a very attractive tour around Monte Pellegrino. The road runs north past the former royal country house of La Favorita (park, orangery), near which is the little Palazzina Cinese, with the interesting Museo Etnografico Siciliano Pitrè (folk traditions).

Mondello — From here the route continues along the foot of Monte Pellegrino on the southern slopes of Monte Gallo (527 m (1739 ft)), to Mondello, a seaside resort (good sandy beach) lying on the Bay of Mondello between Monte Gallo and Monte Pellegrino. From Mondello the return route runs along the coast, around the Punta di Priola, past the Cimitero Monumentale (or Cimitero dei Rotoli), Palermo's largest cemetery, and through the coastal suburbs of Arenella and Acquasanta to Palermo.

Piana degli Albanesi

24 km (15 mi.) S — Another excursion, through country of particular scenic beauty, is to Piana degli Albanesi, formerly called Piana dei Greci. The little town was founded by Albanian settlers in 1488, and the people still preserve their distinctive dialect and the Eastern rite of the Catholic Church. The town is the seat of a bishop whose diocese extends to all the Albanians in Italy. Picturesque Albanian costumes are worn on feast-days.

Ustica

67 km (42 mi.) N — There is an attractive trip by boat (several times weekly) or hydrofoil (several times daily) to the volcanic island of Ustica (area 9 sq. km (3½ sq. mi.); population 1200). The highest point on the island is the Punta

Maggiore (244 m (805 ft)), a remnant of the old crater rim. The island is attracting increasing numbers of visitors with its beautiful scenery.

On its eastern tip is the only settlement, Ustica (49 m (162 ft); hotels), with the harbour. To the south accessible only by boat, are a number of caves – the Grotta Azzurra, the particularly beautiful Grotta dell'Acqua and the Grotta Pastizza.

Monreale, Bagheria; see Sicily.

★Parma   E6

Region: Emilia-Romagna. Province: Parma (PR)
Altitude: 52 m (172 ft). Population: 170,000

Parma, the former capital of the duchy of Parma, now a provincial capital and seat of an university, lies at the foot of the Apennines in the North Italian plain on the banks of the River Parma, a tributary of the Po.

In spite of its long history, the town, situated on the old Roman main road, the Via Aemilia, is a city of modern aspect, with straight streets on a regular plan. In the town centre, on the right bank of the Torrente Parma, fine new squares have been laid out. On the other bank of the river lies the old town, Parma Vecchia, with the Palazzo Ducale and a park. The area is also known for its Parma ham and Parmesan cheese.

Location

Parma became a Roman colony in 183 BC. During the Middle Ages it became a place of some consequence through its woollen mills and its university. The town, always on the Guelf side, belonged to Milan from 1341 to 1512, when it was annexed to the States of the Church. In 1545 Pope Paul III granted the duchies of Parma and Piacenza to his natural son Pier Luigi Farnese. When the Farnese male line died out in 1731 the duchies passed to a collateral line of the Bourbons. They came under French rule in 1806, and in 1816 were granted to Napoleon's wife Marie Louise for life, reverting to the Bourbons on her death. After the expulsion of the Bourbons in 1860 the territory was incorporated in the new kingdom of Italy.

The painter Antonio Allegri, known as Correggio (1489–1534), the great master of chiaroscuro, lived and worked in Parma.

History

Sights

The central feature of the town is the Piazza Garibaldi in which stands the Palazzo del Governatore, with a façade dating from 1760 and an astronomical clock. Nearby is the Palazzo del Municipio (Town Hall; 1627–73).

Piazza Garibaldi

The university, south-west of the Piazza Garibaldi, has various natural history collections.

University

Opposite, to the south-east, is the Pinacoteca Stuard, the finest private collection in Parma, with works by Tiepolo, Canaletto and Tintoretto.

Pinacoteca Stuard

From Piazza Garibaldi the busy Strada Cavour runs north. On the right the short Strada al Duomo leads to the Piazza del Duomo. Immediately on the left of this square is the Bishop's Palace, on the right the Baptistery, a massive octagonal marble building begun in Romanesque style by Benedetto Antelami in 1196–1216 (the doorways, with reliefs of scriptural subjects, are his work) and completed in Gothic style in 1260; it contains 13th c. high reliefs and frescoes.

★Baptistery

On the east side of the square is the cathedral, a Romanesque pillared basilica dating from the 12th c., whose wide façade forms an impressive

★Cathedral

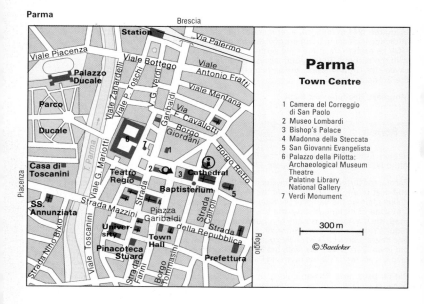

Parma

Brescia

Parma
Town Centre

1 Camera del Correggio
  di San Paolo
2 Museo Lombardi
3 Bishop's Palace
4 Madonna della Steccata
5 San Giovanni Evangelista
6 Palazzo della Pilotta:
  Archaeological Museum
  Theatre
  Palatine Library
  National Gallery
7 Verdi Monument

300 m

© Baedeker

Campanile	group with the adjoining campanile (63 m (208 ft) high) of 1284–94. In the dome is a huge fresco of the "Assumption of the Virgin" by Correggio (1526–30). In the south transept is a relief by Benedetto Antelami of the "Descent from the Cross" (1178), originally on a pulpit.
	In the crypt are some beautiful pillars and early Christian floor mosaics.
San Giovanni Evangelista	Behind the cathedral stands the convent church of San Giovanni Evangelista, a Renaissance building (1510) with a Baroque façade of 1607 and a slender tower of 1614. It contains fine frescoes by Correggio (in the dome; 1521–23) and his pupil Parmigianino.
	Beside the convent is the Storica Farmacia di San Giovanni Evangelista, an old chemist's shop, with a Renaissance interior and ceramic containers (16th–18th c.).
Palazzo della Pilotta	From the Piazza del Duomo the Strada al Duomo and Strada Pisacane lead west to the Piazzale Marconi, which was much enlarged after the Second World War. On the west side of this square is the Palazzo della Pilotta (Pilotta palace), a huge brick building begun in 1583 but left unfinished, which has a fine courtyard. It derives its name from the fact that a ball-game like the Basque game of "pelota" used to be played in the three inner courtyards.
★Museums	In the Palazzo are the Galleria Nazionale, the Museo Archeologico Nazionale and – in the Palazzo Farnese of the Pilotta palace – the Biblioteca Palatina, the Bodoni Museum (printing) and a Picture Gallery (Galleria Nazionale), with important works by Correggio ("Madonna del San Girolamo" and "Madonna della Scodella"), Parmigianino, Fra Angelico, Giulio Romano, Cima da Conegliano, Tiepolo, Canaletto, Carracci, El Greco including a drawing (study of a head) by Leonardo da Vinci.

Parma: the octagonal Baptistery ▶

Parma

Teatro Farnese	On the same floor is the Teatro Farnese, built entirely in wood by Aleotti, a pupil of Palladio, in 1618–28; it was then the largest theatre in the world (4500 seats).
Verdi memorial	In front of the Palazzo della Pilotta stands a memorial to the composer Giuseppe Verdi, who hailed from the town of Le Roncole in the province of Parma.
Museo Glauco Lombardi	On the east side of the Piazza della Pace is the Museo Glauco Lombardi, housed in the Palazzo di Riserva, which contains an art collection with works of the 18th–19th c.
Camera di San Paolo	A short distance east of the Piazzale Marconi, in a former Benedictine nunnery, is the Camera di San Paolo (St Paul's room), with well-preserved frescos by the young Correggio (1518–19: Diana; the Goddess of Love, with the famous "putti del Correggio").
Teatro Regio	South of the Piazzale Marconi, on the right-hand side of Strada Garibaldi, is the Teatro Regio (Royal Theatre; 1821–29), one of Italy's finest theatres.
Madonna della Steccata	Opposite the Teatro Regio is the fine domed church of the Madonna della Steccata (1521–39), modelled on St Peter's in Rome (Greek-cross plan). Inside there are fine frescos on the triumphal arch and on the dome.
Museo d'Arte Ciinese	In the south of the town, near the citadel, is the interesting Museo d'Arte Cinese (Chinese art), with a Museum of Ethnology.

Oltre Torrente

Santissima Annunziata	From Piazza Garibaldi Strada Mazzini runs west over the Ponte di Mezzo (fragments of the old Roman bridge, rebuilt, in underpass) spanning the River Parma into the Oltre Torrente district or Parma Vecchio, the oldest part of the town. At the near end of Strada Massimo d'Azeglio, on the left, is the church of the Santissima Annunziata, a Baroque building (1566) with an unusual ground-plan and a boldly designed dome (1626–32).
Santa Croce	At the end of the street, also on the left, the Romanesque church of Santa Croce contains good 17th c. frescos.
House of Toscanini	A short distance north of the church at Borgo Rodolfo Tanzi 13 is the birth-place of the conductor Arturo Toscanini (1867–1957).
Parco Ducale	Farther north, extending to the banks of the Parma, is the large Parco Ducale, in the north-east corner of which is the Palazzo Ducale (1564).

Surroundings

Torrechiara 18 km (11 mi.) S	There is a fine trip to the Apennine village of Torrechiara, which has a 15th c. castle magnificently situated above the valley of the Parma (Camera d'Oro, with beautiful painted wall tiles and frescos by Benedetto Bembo).
Brescello 20 km (12 mi.) NE	North-east of Parma, on the banks of the River Po, is Brescello, the town in which the stories of Don Camillo and Peppone (by Giovanni Guareschi, 1908–68; starring Fernandel and Gino Cervi) were filmed. In the main square is a statue of Hercules dating from the Renaissance period.
Sabbioneta 30 km (19 mi.) NE	North-east of Parma is the interesting little town of Sabbioneta (18 m (59 ft)), which Vespasiano Gonzaga (1531–91) made the very model of a small princely residence of the Renaissance period (fortifications, Palazzo Ducale, Palazzo del Giardino, Chiesa dell'Incoronata; theatre in which performances are given in summer).

Pavia   D5

Region: Lombardia. Province: Pavia (PV)
Altitude: 77 m (231 ft). Population: 77,000

The old Lombard town of Pavia, now a provincial capital, lies on the River   Location
Ticino near its junction with the Po, in the western part of the north Italian
plain. It is linked with Milan by a shipping canal, the Naviglio di Pavia.
    With its old brick buildings it has preserved much of its medieval aspect
and is notable particularly for its beautiful churches in Lombard Romanesque style. Of its once numerous towers, the fortified residences of
noble families, few now remain, but it still has remains of the ramparts and
bastions of the Spanish period.
    Pavia is the seat of a university.

Pavia, the Roman Ticinum, was a favourite residence of Theodoric the   History
Great, and after the fall of Ravenna became for a short time the Ostrogothic
capital. From 572 to 774 it was capital of the Lombard kingdom. From the
7th c. the town was known as Papia. During the Middle Ages many kings
of Italy were crowned in the church of San Michele, as were the emperors
Henry II and Frederick Barbarossa. The town remained for the most part
faithful to the emperor, until it was handed over to the Visconti family by
Charles IV in 1359. Francis I of France was defeated and taken prisoner at
Pavia in 1525. In the 18th c. the town was taken over by the Austrian
Habsburg line.

Sights

In the centre of the town, in the Strada Nuova, Pavia's main street, is the   University
university, founded in 1361 on the basis of an earlier law school established
in the 11th c. The present building was begun in the 14th–15th c. and
enlarged in the 18th c. In the five courtyards are monuments and memo-
rials to famous professors and students; in the second courtyard are a
statue of Volta (1878) and reliefs from the tombs of professors. The library,
founded about 1770, contains some 370,000 volumes. Beyond the first
courtyard there is a picturesque view of three old brick towers, formerly
belonging to noble families.

To the west of the university stands the huge church of Santa Maria del   Santa Maria del
Carmine, an early Gothic brick structure surrounded by chapels.   Carmine

A short distance north of the church, in Piazza Petrarca, stands the Palazzo   Palazzo Malaspina
Malaspina.

South-west of the university is the Piazza della Vittoria, in which is the   Broletto
12th c. Broletto, the old Town Hall.

Near the Broletto stands the cathedral, built on a central plan with an apse   Cathedral
and three aisles. It was begun in 1488 by Cristofora Rocchi with the
collaboration of Amadeo and Bramante in Early Renaissance style. Inside
note particularly the paintings: "Madonna with Rosary", a "Madonna with
Child" and Saint Anthony and John the Baptist. Also of interest is the
pulpit with reliefs of the life of Saint Siro. In the entrance is the "Adoration
of the Magi", by Daniele Crespi.

The 78 m (257 ft) high brick-built tower Torre Civica (11th c.), originally the   Torre Civica
clock-tower of an older church, collapsed on the morning of March 17th
1989 and buried four people.

Inner courtyard of Pavia University

San Teodoro

From the cathedral we go south along Via dei Liguri and then turn right into Via Pietro Maffi to reach the Romanesque church of San Teodoro (12th c.), which has frescoes including a view of Pavia (1522), immediately left, and a fine crypt (12th c.).

★ San Michele

550 m east of San Teodoro, on the far side of the Strada Nuova, is the old coronation church of San Michele (1155), in Lombard Romanesque style, with a beautiful façade (rich ornaments and figural reliefs in a series of bands, surmounted by a gabled gallery) and fine interior with a 10th c. silver crucifix and remains of a mosaic floor in the presbytery.

Ponte Coperto

At the south end of the Strada Nuova, on the banks of the Ticino, is the Piazzale Ponte Ticino, from which the Ponte Coperto (built 1354, restored after war damage) leads into the suburban district of Borgo Ticino.

★ Castello Visconteo

A short distance east, on the north-east side of the town stands the Castello Visconteo (1360–65), a square building with a spacious courtyard; it houses the Municipal Museum (archaeological finds, sculpture) and the Picture Gallery (Pinacoteca Malaspina) with some 500 paintings, including works by Bellini, Crivelli and Correggio.

★ San Petro in Ciel d'Oro

A short walk from the Castello is the old convent church of San Pietro in Ciel d'Oro (1132; restored 1875–99), in Lombard Romanesque style. In the choir is the splendid marble tomb (1362) of St Augustine (354–430).

★★ Certosa di Pavia

North of the town (10 km (6 mi.)), on the road to Milan, is the Certosa di Pavia, the most famous Carthusian house after the Grande Chartreuse near

Grenoble, founded by Gian Galeazzo Visconti in 1396, suppressed in 1784, but reoccupied between 1843 and 1881 and again since 1968. A tour of the monastery needs the permission of the Soprintendenza ai Monumenti di Milano. At the entrance is a good restaurant.

In the forecourt the old Pharmacy now produces a liqueur (tasting room). To the south is the Foresteria, built about 1625 to accommodate distinguished visitors (museum, with pictures, etc.). *Foresteria*

Building of the church, on the east side of the courtyard, was started in 1396 in Gothic style and continued by Guiniforte Solari (d. 1481) from 1453 onwards. The famous marble façade, a masterpiece of north Italian Early Renaissance architecture, was begun in 1491 to the design of Giovanni Antonio Amadeo (1447–1522) and carried on by Benedetto Briosco in 1500–07; the upper part, however, was left unfinished about 1550. The plinth is adorned with medallions of Roman emperors. Above the windows are niches with numerous statues. *Church*

The nave, flanked by aisles, is still entirely Gothic in character, but the transepts, choir and dome show Renaissance features. The altarpieces and decoration of the side chapels are mainly 17th c.; the splendid choir screen dates from around 1600. Outstanding among the many works of art in the church are the marble recumbent figures of Lodovico Sforza, il Moro (d. 1508) and his wife Beatrice d'Este (d. 1496) by Cristoforo Solari (in north transept); the richly decorated altar (1568) and stalls (1486–98) designed by Bergognone in the choir; a Renaissance fountain (1490) in the lavatorium; to the right of the choir the magnificent tomb of Gian Galeazzo Visconti (d. 1402), begun in 1494 by Gian Cristoforo Romano and Benedetto Briosco but not completed until 1562 (by Galeazzo Alessi and others). In the New Sacristy an "Assumption" by Andrea Solario, and in the Old Sacristy; an ivory polyptychon with scenes from the Old and New Testaments.

Certosa di Pavia, a famous Carthusian convent

Perugia

Cloisters

An elegant Early Renaissance doorway (1466) leads from the south aisle into the Front Cloister (Chiostro Piccolo), with marble colonnades and charming terracotta decoration (1462–72). From the west side there is a fine view of the nave and south transept of the church.

Around the Great Cloister, to the rear, are 24 small apartments for monks.

★Perugia   G9

Region: Umbria. Province: Perugia (PG)
Altitude: 493 m (1627 ft). Population: 150,000

Location

Perugia, capital of its province and of the region of Umbria, lies on a hill between the Trasimenian Sea and the Tiber valley.

The town is worth visiting not only for the beauty of its setting but also for its fine old buildings. It is the see of an archbishop and a university town, with a University for Foreigners.

History

The ancient Perusia, one of the twelve cities of the Etruscan federation, came under Roman rule in 310 BC, and in the middle of the 3rd c. AD was raised to the status of a military colony under the name of Augusta Perusia. Considerable sections of the Etruscan walls, which extended for 2.8 km (1¾ mi.) round the town, have been preserved. In 547 Perusia was captured by the Ostrogothic king Totila. In the 13th and 14th c. it was the most powerful city in Umbria. From 1534 until the unification of Italy in 1860 it belonged to the States of the Church.

Art

Perugia is renowned as the principal centre of the Umbrian school of painting, the leading members of which, Pietro Vannucci, called Perugino (1446–1523), and Bernardino Betti, called Pinturicchio (1455–1513), both worked here. The young Raphael worked in Perugino's studio until 1504.

Tip

The town centre is closed to cars.

Sights

★Piazza IV
Novembre

The main square of Perugia is the picturesque Piazza IV Novembre, in the centre of which is the Fontana Maggiore (1277–80), one of the most beautiful fountains of the period, with reliefs by Nicola and Giovanni Pisano. On the west side of the square is the Archbishop's Palace with the Museum of Natural History, and beyond it the vaulting of the so-called Maestà delle Volte, a relic of the Palazzo del Podestà which was burned down in 1534.

From the Piazza IV Novembre the medieval Via delle Volte runs to the Piazza Fortebraccio.

★San Lorenzo

On the north side of the Piazza IV Novembre stands the cathedral of San Lorenzo, a 15th c. Gothic hall-church, with an unfinished façade. On the steps leading up to the entrance, to the left, is a bronze statue of Pope Julius III (1555). Inside there are fine choir-stalls (1486–91) and a banner depicting a view of Perugia.

Museo Capitolare

The Museo Capitolare to the left of the cathedral houses sculpture, valuable missals and pictures, including a "Madonna Enthroned" by Signorelli (1995: closed until further notice).

San Severo

East of the cathedral the church of San Severo contains a fresco by Raphael (1505), the Trinity.

★Palazzo dei
Priori

On the south side of the cathedral is the Palazzo dei Priori, also known as the Palazzo Comunale (Town Hall), a massive building in Italian Gothic style (1293 and 1333), with its main front on the Corso Vannucci. On the side fac-

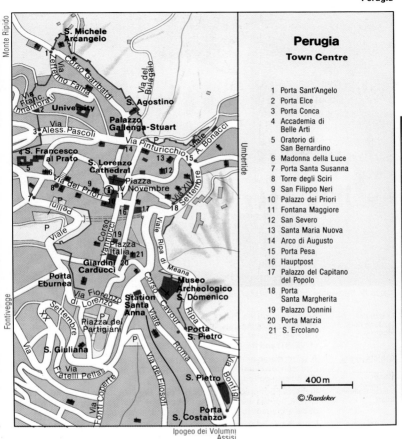

Perugia
Town Centre

1 Porta Sant'Angelo
2 Porta Elce
3 Porta Conca
4 Accademia di Belle Arti
5 Oratorio di San Bernardino
6 Madonna della Luce
7 Porta Santa Susanna
8 Torre degli Sciri
9 San Filippo Neri
10 Palazzo dei Priori
11 Fontana Maggiore
12 San Severo
13 Santa Maria Nuova
14 Arco di Augusto
15 Porta Pesa
16 Hauptpost
17 Palazzo del Capitano del Popolo
18 Porta Santa Margherita
19 Palazzo Donnini
20 Porta Marzia
21 S. Ercolano

400 m

© Baedeker

Ipogeo dei Volumni
Assisi

ing the Piazza IV Novembre are a griffin (the heraldic emblem of Perugia), a 14th c. bronze lion, and chains, all of which commemorate a victory over the Sienese in 1358. On the first floor of the palace, which is entered through the richly decorated main doorway in the Corso, is the splendid Sala dei Notari, on the second floor the Municipal Library (150,000 volumes), and on the third floor the Galleria Nazionale dell'Umbria with paintings by Perugino and Pinturicchio, Benedetto Bonfiglio (d. 1496), Bartolomeo Caporali (d. about 1509), and other artists, sculptures by di Cambio, di Duccio, etc., and a small majolica collection. The Sala del Collegio della Mercanzia is also worth a visit.

Only a few yards from the Palazzo dei Priori is the Collegio del Cambio, the old Exchange, the audience chamber of which is decorated with frescoes by Perugino.

Collegio del Cambio

Piazza IV Novembre with the Palazzo dei Priori and Fontana Maggiore

Palazzo del Capitano del Popolo	South-east of the Piazza IV Novembre is the Piazza Matteotti, built on massive substructures, some of which date from the Etruscan period. On the east side of the square are the Palazzo del Capitano del Popolo (1472–81) and the Old University (1453–83).
Arco d'Augusto	A short distance north of the cathedral the Arco d'Augusto, one of the Etruscan town gates, bears an inscription. "Augusta Perusia", dating from the Roman period.
Palazzo Gallenga Stuart	In Piazza Fortebraccio, outside the gate, the Palazzo Gallenga Stuart (18th c.) now houses the University for Foreigners (language courses and introductory courses to Italian history, art and literature).
Sant'Arcangelo	From Piazza Fortebraccio the Corso Garibaldi runs north-west, passing the church of Sant'Agostino, to the Porta Sant'Angelo. To the north of this gate is the church of Sant'Arcangelo, a round church (5th–6th c.) of great architectural interest, with sixteen ancient columns in the nave.
★Oratorio di San Bernardino	From the Corso Vannucci Via dei Priori, entered through an archway under the Palazzo Comunale, runs west past the medieval Torre degli Sciri and the little Renaissance church of the Madonna della Luce to the Piazza di San Francesco, in which, straight ahead, is the Oratorio di San Bernardino, with a magnificent façade of coloured marble and terracotta (by Agostino di Duccio, 1457–61).
Prefecture	Corso Vanucci, the town's main street, leads south from the Town Hall to the Piazza Italia, in which stands the Prefecture, built on the site of the Papal citadel, demolished in 1860. From the terrace on the south side there are magnificent views of the Umbrian plain, with Assisi, Spello, Foligno and Trevi, and of the Tiber valley.
Porta Marzia	From the Piazza Italia Via Marzia leads south-east past the substructures of the former citadel to the Porta Marzia, at the beginning of the lower town, a remnant of one of the Etruscan town gates.

The Arco di Augusto dates from Etruscan times

Here is the entrance to what is left of the old 16th c. fortress, the Rocca Paolina (escalator to the lower town). Beyond this in Viale dell'Indipendenza, is the little Gothic church of Sant'Ercolano (1297–1326).

Rocca Paolina

Continue along Corso Cavour to the church of San Domenico, a brick structure begun in 1305 and altered in 1621–34, with a huge Gothic window and the tomb of Pope Benedict XI (1304).

San Domenico

In the adjoining monastery is the Museo Archeologico Nazionale dell' Umbria, with Roman and Etruscan antiquities, including the Cippus Perusianus, one of the longest known Etruscan inscriptions.

Museo Archeologico Nazionale dell'Umbria

Corso Cavour ends at the finely decorated Porta San Pietro, the inner gate of which dates from the 14th c. and the outer gate from the 15th c.

Porta San Pietro

Outside the gate, in Borgo XX Giugno (on the left), we find the fine church of San Pietro, an early Christian structure rebuilt in the 12th c., containing eighteen ancient columns, beautiful choir-stalls (1535) and many pictures of the early Umbrian school and of the 17th c.

★San Pietro

To the south-west of the church, extending to the Porta San Constanzo, lies the Giardino del Frontone (views).

East of Perugia, 1 km (3/4 mi.) before Ponte San Giovanni (189 m (624 ft)), is a modern building which houses the entrance to the underground Tomb of the Volumnii (Ipogeo dei Volumni), one of the finest tombs in Etruria, dating from the 2nd c. BC. It imitates the plan of an ancient house, with nine chambers grouped round a central space, which contain urns with extraordinarily expressive carvings.

★Tomb of the Volumnii

Nearly 15 km (9¹/₂ mi.) south of Perugia, in the middle of a well-known wine-producing region lies the little town of Torgiano (219 m (720 ft); population

Torgiano
15 km (9¹/₂ mi.) S

4900). The local wine museum, established by the Lungaroti family in an old palazzo in the town centre, is of interest.

Deruta   On the E45, 20 km (12½ mi.) south of Perugia, the town of Deruta (218 m (717 ft); population 7600), epitomises ceramic manufacture in Umbria. Hand-made majolica objects, painted in traditional patterns, can be purchased in the many craft shops in the town centre. A few beautiful old examples are on display in the Museo delle Maioliche on the first floor of the Palazzo Communale. Of interest is the small church of the Madonna del Bagno, on the E45 2 km (1¼ mi.) south of Deruta (Casalina exit), which has more than 600 majolica votive plaques.

Pesaro   G8

Region: Marche. Province: Pesaro e Urbino (PS)
Altitude: 11 m (36 ft). Population: 91,000

Location   Pesaro, capital of the province of Pesaro e Urbino and a very popular sea-side resort, lies at the mouth of the River Foglia, on the north-west Adriatic coast between Rimini and Ancona.

History   In the 16th and 17th c. Pesaro was the residence of the Della Rovere family, dukes of Urbino, and a centre of art and literature, famous for its majolica factories. The composer Gioacchino Rossini (1792–1868) was born here.

Sights

Palazzo Ducale   The life of the town centres on the Piazza del Popolo, in which are the Town Hall and the Palazzo Ducale (begun about 1461 for the Sforzas, completed in the 16th c. for the Della Rovere). A little way south-east is the Santuario della Madonna delle Grazie, known as San Francesco, with a beautiful Gothic doorway. Farther along are the spacious Piazza Matteotti and the adjoining Giardino Cialdini, a public park, with a 15th c. fortress, the Rocca Constanza, now used as a prison. In Via Rossini, which runs from the Piazza del Popolo to the seafront, is Rossini's birthplace (Casa di Rossini, No. 34, on the right), containing a number of pictures and caricatures. From here it is only a short distance to the 13th c. cathedral.

Musei Civici   To the west of the cathedral, in the Palazzo Toschi-Mosca, are the Musei Civici, with a notable collection of pictures (works by Bellini, "Coronation of the Virgin", and Marco Zoppo) and an outstanding collection of majolica, the finest in Italy.

Surroundings

Villa Imperiale   6 km (4 mi.) north of Pesaro, on the road to Gabbice, lies the Villa Imperiale, an impressive Renaissance building (1486) surrounded by a park (guided tours only).

Gradara   Gradara, 15 km (9½ mi.) north-west of Pesaro, is a pretty little medieval town with a 13th c. castle. It is said to be the scene for Dante's tragedy of the lovers Francesca and Paolo.

★Piacenza   D5

Region: Emilia-Romagna. Province: Piacenza (PC)
Altitude: 61 m (201 ft). Population: 104,000

The provincial capital of Piacenza lies in the north Italian plain near the   Location
right bank of the Po, some 50 km (31 mi.) south-east of Milan.
   The town has a well-preserved circuit of mid-16th c. walls 6.5 km (4 mi.)
long.

Piacenza was founded by the Romans in 219 BC, under the name of Colonia   History
Placentia, to defend the Po crossing against the Gauls. During the Middle
Ages it was a member of the Lombard League, and thereafter belonged to
the Viscontis, the Sforzas and (from 1521) the States of the Church. From
1545 onwards the Farnese duchy of Piacenza together with the duchy of
Parma formed an independent principality, which was incorporated in the
Kingdom of Italy in 1859.

Sights

The life of Piacenza centres on the picturesque Piazza dei Cavalli, named   Piazza dei Cavalli
after the prancing Baroque equestrian statues of dukes Alessandro and
Ranuccio Farnese (1587–92, 1592–1622), by the Tuscan sculptor Francesco
Mocchi (1612–29).

On the south-west side of the square is the Palazzo del Comune, called "il   ★Palazzo del
Gotico" (Town Hall), built from 1280 onwards, the model for many other   Comune
Italian town halls. On the ground floor is an arcade with five pointed
arches; above this a large hall with round-arched windows richly decorated with terracotta; the attic is crowned with battlements.

Opposite stands the Neo-Classical Palazzo del Governatore (1781), now   Palazzo del
the chamber of trade.   Governatore
   On the south-east side of the square, set a little way back, is the large
brick Gothic church of San Francesco (1278).

From the Piazza dei Cavalli Via XX Settembre (closed to cars) leads south-   ★Cathedral
east to the cathedral, begun in 1122 in Lombard Romanesque style and
completed in the mid 13th c. under Gothic influence, with three beautiful
doorways. The bell-tower dates from 1333. The dome is decorated with
frescos (prophets and sibyls) by Guercino. The crypt has 108 columns. On
the left of the cathedral stands the Bishop's Palace.

A short way east of the cathedral is the church of San Savino (1107), with   San Savino
early ribbed vaulting and a Baroque façade (1721). The choir and crypt
have mosaic pavements (12th c.).

South-west of the Piazza del Duomo, at the end of Via Chiapponi, is the   Sant'Antonio
church of Sant'Antonio (11th–12th c., with much later alteration), the
former cathedral, with a large Gothic porch of 1350. Opposite is the Teatro   Teatro Verdi
Verdi (1803/04: Classical façade).

300 m farther south-west in Via S. Siro is the Galleria d'Arte Moderna Ricci   Galleria d'Arte
Oddi, a fine building (1931) with a collection of pictures by Italian masters   Moderna
of the 19th c.

From the Piazza dei Cavalli the busy Corso Cavour, Piacenza's main street,   Palazzo Farnese
runs north-east to the massive Palazzo Farnese, begun in 1558, continued
in 1564 by Vignola and finished in 1602. The restored building houses the
Municipal Museum (Museo Civico), with an archaeological section containing Etruscan bronzes, Roman and medieval sculpture, ceramics, glass
and much more besides.

To the north-west, near the northern edge of the town, is the church of San   San Sisto
Sisto (1499–1511), in Early Renaissance style, with a Baroque façade and a
fine Ionic colonnade. It was for this church that Raphael painted the "Sistine Madonna" (c. 1515), which was sold to Dresden in 1754 and replaced

by a copy (c. 1725). In the north transept is the tombstone (designed in 1593) of Margaret Duchess of Parma, wife of Ottavio Farnese.

Madonna di Campagna

Near the north-western edge of the town is the church of the Madonna di Campagna, an Early Renaissance church on a centralised plan (by Alessio Taramello, 1522–28) containing frescos by Pordenone (1528–31).

Surroundings

Collegio Alberoni
3 km (2 mi.) SE

South-east of Piacenza, on the road to Parma, the Collegio Alberoni has an interesting picture gallery, library (100,000 volumes) and observatory.

Bobbio

In the convent at Bobbio, 44 km (27 mi.) south-west of Piacenza, is the tomb of the Irish monk and missionary Columban, who died here in 615. The fine church treasure is housed in the neighbouring Museo di Colombano. The town also has sulphur and salt baths.

Castell'Arquato
25 km (16 mi.) SE

Castell'Arquato is a town with a number of medieval features. Particularly notable are the Palazzo Pretorio (1293), the collegiate church (12th c.; small museum in the cloister) and the remains of the castle.

Piedmont   A–C 4–7

Region: Piemonte
Provinces: Torino (TO), Alessandria (AL), Asti (AT), Cuneo (CU),
    Novara (NO) and Vercelli (VC)
Area: 25,399 sq. km (9804 sq. mi.). Population: 4,300,000

Location

Piedmont, in northern Italy, occupies the upper Po basin and the adjoining pre-Alpine moraine and hill region, bounded on the south, west and north by the mighty mountain arc of the Apennines and the Alps, which here reach their highest points in Mont Blanc, Monte Rosa, the Gran Paradiso and the Matterhorn.
    The region takes in six provinces with Turin as its capital.

Economy

The geographical diversity of the region is reflected in different economic patterns. The upland area round Turin, Ivrea and Biella, with good communications and adequate energy supplies (hydro-electric power from the mountains, natural gas in the Po plain, oil from Genoa), is one of the most progressive industrial areas in Italy. The main elements in a very varied range of industries are metal-working, the manufacture of machinery and cars, the textile industry which developed out of the famous silk-manufacturing industry of earlier days, leather goods and foodstuffs.
    Agriculture is still predominant on the fertile alluvial soil of the Po valley, where fruit-growing, arable farming (wheat, maize, rice, fodder crops) and cattle-rearing achieve high yields through the application of modern methods. Vine-growing is important, particularly in the Monferrato. White truffles – the finest and most expensive form of this delicacy – are found in the Alba area.
    In the hill regions tourism has developed rapidly in recent years, supplementing the traditional pastoral farming and the relatively unproductive mining (lead, zinc, copper, coal).

History

Originally occupied by a number of different peoples, Piedmont ("foot of the mountain") was Romanised in the time of Augustus. After the fall of the Roman Empire it was held successively by the Lombards (Langobardi) and the Franks. It was devastated by the Magyars in 899 (massacre of Vercelli) and later by the Saracens. Thereafter it split up into a patchwork of coun-

Vineyards in Piedmont

ties, duchies and marquisates, the most important of which in the 10th c. were Ivrea and Turin, joined by Saluzzo and Monferrato in the 12th c. In the 11th c. most of the present-day Piedmont passed to the house of Savoy (French Piémont) as a result of a dynastic marriage; and the territory became in the 13th c. the county, and in 1416 the duchy, of Piedmont. Thereafter it was disputed between the Habsburgs and France, owing its importance and the vicissitudes of its subsequent history largely to its control of the western Alpine passes (the Great and Little St Bernard). In 1720 Piedmont acquired Sardinia in exchange for Sicily, and as the kingdom of Sardinia played a leading part in the unification of Italy. In 1861 Victor Emmanuel II (1849–78), son of the last king of Sardinia, became king of Italy, with Turin, the old Piedmontese capital, as capital of the new kingdom until 1865.

Sights

The most attractive tourist areas in Piedmont are to be found in the mountains – the Graian, Cottian and Ligurian Alps – and around Lake Maggiore (see entry), all of them of great scenic beauty.

The principal towns of interest to visitors are Turin, Novara and Asti (see entries), but there are many others. In eastern Piedmont, between Vercelli and Alessandria, is the old town of Casale Monferrato (116 m (383 ft); population 41,000), from the 14th to the early 18th c. the residence of the marquises and later dukes of Monferrato. In the centre of the town is the imposing Town Hall (1778), and to the north of this the Romanesque cathedral of Sant'Evasio, with a beautiful porch (12th c.) and a number of fine works by Lombard sculptors in the interior, as well as a Romanesque silver-clad wooden crucifix, and Romanesque floor-mosaics in the perambulatory. Between the cathedral and the bridge over the Po stands the church of

Casale Monferrato

San Domenico, with remains of frescoes and paintings (including "The Battle of Lepanto", 1630, by Giovanni Crosio and a fine cloister. To the west, near the river, is the old Castello (15th–16th c.).

Cuneo

In southern Piedmont is another interesting town, Cuneo (535 m (1766 ft); population 56,000), beautifully situated on a wedge-shaped plateau above the junction of the rivers Gesso and Stura di Demonte. In the centre of the town is a large arcaded square, the Piazza D. Galimberti, lying on the town's main traffic artery, formed by Via Roma and Corso Nizza in the newer south-western part of the town. The cathedral, in Via Roma, has a Neo-Classical façade. Farther north, in Piazza Virginio, are the Loggia dei Mercanti (14th c., restored) and the former Franciscan church (now a warehouse), in Late Romanesque transitional style (1227) with a Gothic tower (1399) and a doorway of 1481. Nearby is the church of Santa Croce, on an elliptical ground-plan (1715). The Municipal Museum (Museo Civico) contains numerous prehistoric and Roman finds. From the promenades on the line of the old fortifications there are fine views of the Alps.

Mondovi

27 km (17 mi.) east of Cuneo is Mondovi (population 22,000), which had a university from 1560 to 1719. From the industrial lower town, Mondovi-Breo (395 m (1304 ft)), a road and a funicular lead to the upper town, Mondovi-Piazza (550 m (1815 ft)), with an 18th c. cathedral (sumptuous interior) and the fine Baroque church of the Gesù, also 18th c. From the Belvedere (571 m (1884 ft)), with a 14th c. Gothic tower, one can enjoy impressive Alpine views.

Santuario di Vicoforte

6 km (4 mi.) south-east of Mondovi is the Santuario di Vicoforte (512 m (1690 ft)), a magnificent pilgrimage church (1596–1733; façade and towers 19th c.). The central feature is All Saints Chapel; in the four side-chapels are the tombs of members of the House of Savoy.

Saluzzo

The old town of Saluzzo (342 m (1129 ft); population 17,000), 35 km (22 mi.) north of Cuneo, on an outlier of Monte Viso, was from the 12th to the 16th c. the chief place in the county of Saluzzo. In the lower town is the cathedral of San Chiaffredo (1491–1501), with a large crucifix (1500) in the choir. In the upper town (395 m (1304 ft)) are the Palazzo del Comune (1462); the Casa Cavassa, a Renaissance mansion which now houses the Municipal Museum, and the church of San Giovanni, in French Gothic style, containing many works of sculpture of the Lombard school and the tomb of Lodovico II (d. 1504). From the old Castello Via Griselda leads to the Belvedere, a terrace from which there are splendid views of the Alps.

Manta

4 km (2 1/2 mi.) south is the village of Manta (464 m (1531 ft)), with a castle containing fine 15th c. frescos.

Asti, Lake Maggiore, Novara, Turin. See entries.

★★ Pisa · E8

Region: Toscana. Province: Pisa (PI)
Altitude: 4 m (13 ft). Population: 103,000

Location

Pisa, capital of the province of the same name, and the see of an archbishop, lies in the northern part of the Tuscanian coast astride the Arno – 10 km (6 mi.) from the Tyrrhenian Sea, which has retreated as a result of the deposition of soil by the river.

History and art

Pisa, the Roman Pisae, originally an Etruscan trading station, became a Roman colony in 180 BC. From the 11th c. onwards it developed into one of the leading maritime and commercial powers in the Mediterranean, rivalling Genoa and Venice. It took the lead in the struggle against Islam,

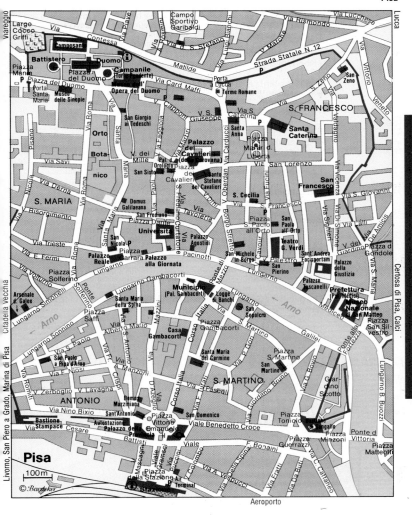

Pisa

100m

© Baedeker

defeating the Muslims in Sardinia, Sicily and Tunis and playing a prominent part in the Crusades. The town celebrated its victories by the erection of splendid buildings. The building of its cathedral in the 11th c. marked a new epoch in Tuscan art and architecture. Pisa also took a leading place in sculpture, with Nicola Pisano (c. 1220-after 1278), the great forerunner of the Renaissance; and Nicola's son Giovanni (1265–1314), his pupil Arnolfo di Cambio (d. about 1302) and Giovanni's pupil Andrea Pisano (1273–1348) formed links with the art of Florence.

The fall of the Hohenstaufens was a heavy blow for the town, which supported the Ghibelline cause. In the long-continued conflict with Genoa the Pisan fleet suffered a decisive defeat off the island of Meloria in 1284. Internal partisan struggles led to the occupation of the town by the Florentines in 1406; and Pisa finally lost its earlier importance at the end of the 17th c. when Livorno became the leading port in Tuscany.

Pisa is the birthplace of the brilliant mathematician and scientist Galileo Galilei (1564–1642).

Sights

★★Campo dei Miracoli

In the north-west of the town, enclosed on two sides by the old battlemented town walls, is the Piazza del Duomo or Campo dei Miracoli, with the cathedral, the Leaning Tower, the Baptistery and the Campo Santo – a harmoniously composed group of buildings of unrivalled beauty.

★Cathedral

The cathedral, a Romanesque basilica of white marble with transepts and an elliptical dome over the crossing, was built after a Pisan naval victory over the Saracens at Palermo (1064–1118) and restored in 1597–1604 after a fire. The most magnificent part is the façade (12th c.), the upper part of which has four pillared galleries. The bronze doors of the main entrance (usually closed) date from the end of the 16th c., the door of the south transept (Porta di San Ranieri), decorated with reliefs from scriptural history, from 1180.

Inside the cathedral there are ancient columns on both sides of the nave. The nave has a richly gilded Renaissance coffered ceiling.

★Pulpit

The pulpit (by Giovanni Pisano, 1302–11) is decorated with nine vigorous reliefs (New Testament scenes, Last Judgment).

Campo dei Miracoli   Pisa

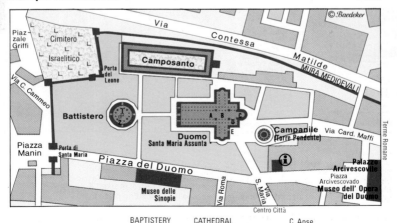

BAPTISTERY	CATHEDRAL	C Apse
1 Font	A Pulpit by G. Pisano	D Sagrestia dei Cappellani
2 Pulpit by	B Bronze lanterns	E Tomb of Emperor Henry VII
N. Pisano	by B. Lorenzi	F Porta di San Ranieri

Campanile, Cathedral and Baptistery

The beautiful bronze lamp (1587) is said to have given Galileo the idea of the pendulum as it swung to and fro.

In the south transept is the splendid Cappella di San Ranieri, with the sarcophagus of the town's patron. To the left is the tomb of the Emperor Henry VII, by Tino da Camaino (1315).

The choir contains fine Renaissance choir-stalls and pictures by Andrea del Sarto and Sodoma. In the apse are fine mosaics, one of which represents the "Head of John the Evangelist" by Cimabue (1302).

The Treasury is kept in the Sacristy (Sagrestia dei Cappellani).

At the west end of the cathedral is the almost entirely marble-clad Baptistery, a circular structure built between 1153 and 1278, originally Romanesque but with 14th c. Gothic additions. In the interior, under the conical dome, are a marble font by Guido Bigarelli and the famous pulpit by Nicola Pisano (1260).

★Baptistery

★★Leaning Tower

Near the east end of the cathedral stands the celebrated Leaning Tower (Torre Pendente), a campanile built between 1173 and 1350, with a series of several superimposed pillared galleries. The tower, which was built on alluvial land, leans to the south-east and is at present 5°30′ off the vertical; see Baedeker Special page 342. Galileo Galilei, who was born in Pisa, carried out experiments here relating to the law of free-fall. Since 1990 climbing the tower has been prohibited, and safety measures have been introduced, including the use of steel hawsers.

Along the north side of the Piazza del Duomo is the Campo Santo, the most famous cemetery of its kind, a colonnaded quadrangle (126 m (1414 ft)

★Campo Santo

Pisa's Leaning Tower

The first thing to mention about this extravagance is its date. According to the inscription a start was made on building the famous Leaning Tower of Pisa on August 9th 1174. However, at that time the town employed a rather unusual calendar – instead of January 1st the year began on Lady Day (March 25th) of the previous year. So it would be more correct to say that its construction really began in 1173.

The architect was aware that the ground of what was then a sea-port was badly waterlogged and therefore not very stable, and so he laid only flat foundations. However, when only the lower storeys had been built it was found that the vertical axis was already inclining towards the south-east, and attempts were made to correct this by building higher walls on one side. Consequently, as well as leaning the campanile became slightly curved. To counteract the asymmetric sinking of the foundations ballast was added to the other side (a stabilising measure still being considered today) and the builders then cautiously continued with the construction. It was a hundred and eighty years after the foundation stone had been laid that the belfry was finally added to the almost 55 m (180 ft) high tower.

Since then the degree of inclination has constantly increased – in the more recent past by about a millimetre each year, with the result that the tower is now a good four and a half metres (fifteen feet) out of true or, to put it another way, its axis deviates by at least five degrees from the vertical. Consequently there is a lot of speculation as to whether and when it will collapse. There are even said to be some crafty locals who try to sell an insurance policy to tourists who park their cars nearby to provide cover for possible damage to them if it does fall down!

The danger clearly does exist, and suggestions as to how the tower can now actually be stabilised or even straightened are legion. There is no lack of people with far-fetched ideas as well as highly-skilled specialist engineers who are applying their minds to the problem. For example, it has been suggested that the tower might lean on a supporting metal construction, be anchored by steel rods to secondary concrete foundations sunk some way away, or that the ground on which it stands should be drained so that it does not give so much. However, to date all attempts to stabilise it, including the injection of 90 tonnes of cement into the ground in 1934, have in fact had the opposite effect to that which was intended. In 1990 the tower was closed to visitors. It became clear that an end must be put to the slow tipping of the campanile. As a precaution, in the spring of 1992 18 steel ropes were wrapped around the tower in order to stabilise it provisionally. The special-ist German firm of Deutsche Montan-Technologie submitted plans to raise one side with the aid of computer-controlled hydraulic presses and to force concrete into the resultant wedge-shaped gap that will be formed. The foun-dations will remain sloping but the bell-tower will be pulled closer to the vertical. On the other hand, the engineer Fritz Leonhardt, who built the Stuttgart television tower, advises compressing the ground on the north side by means of a giant concrete slab with steel traction anchorages in order to straighten the building. But only to a certain degree, for a completely straight "Leaning Tower" in Pisa is inconceivable – it would be pure sacrilege.

long by 52 m (171 ft) across) in Tuscan Gothic style, built by Giovanni di Simone in 1278–83 and completed in 1463. Earth for the cemetery had been brought from Jerusalem in 1203.

The cemetery, in the form of a cloister, is surrounded by arcades and has tall round-arched windows filled with beautiful tracery overlooking the central courtyard. The world-famous frescos on the walls (notably by Benozzo Gozzoli) were mostly destroyed by melted lead from the roof during a fire caused by Allied bombing on July 27th 1944, but some have been restored and are displayed in the cloister and in two adjoining rooms. Some of the Etruscan, Roman and medieval sculpture disposed round the cloister is of high artistic value. The pavement is composed of gravestones. ★Frescos

On the south side of the Piazza del Duomo stands the Museo delle Sinopie, with sketches (sinopie) for the frescos of the Campo Santo. ★Museo delle Sinopie

East of the Piazza del Duomo is the Cathedral Museum (Museo dell'Opera del Duomo), with art of the buildings situated in the Piazza and the valuable treasury including embroideries, tombs, silver church objects, sculpture and pictures. ★Museo dell'Opera del Duomo

In the Piazza dei Cavalieri in the centre of the old town are the church of Santo Stefano dei Cavalieri (1565–96), the Palazzo dei Cavalieri and a marble statue of Grand Duke Cosimo I (1596). Piazza dei Cavalieri

North-east is the tree-shaded Piazza Martiri della Libertà, at the north-east corner of which stands the church of Santa Caterina (begun 1251), with a façade in Pisan Gothic style. Santa Caterina

A little way to the south-east the Gothic convent church of San Francesco (13th c.) has a fine campanile and 14th c. frescos. San Francesco

Along each bank of the Arno extends a busy riverside street (Lungarno), under various names. In the Lungarno Mediceo, on the right bank, stands the 13th c. Palazzo dei Medici, now the Prefecture. Lungarno Mediceo

Immediately east of this is the church of San Matteo, with the former Benedictine nunnery of San Matteo, now housing the Museo Nazionale. Its collection mainly contains Pisan sculpture and pictures of the Tuscan school of the 12th to 15th c. ★Museo Nazionale di San Matte

At the west end of the Lungarno Mediceo is the Piazza Garibaldi, from which runs the Borgo Stretto, a busy street flanked by arcades. At the near end of this street, on the right, stands the church of San Michele in Borgo, with a beautiful façade in Pisan Gothic style (14th c.). San Michele in Borgo

In Lungarno Pacinotti is the Gothic Palazzo Agostini (15th c.), built in brick. A short distance north-west is the university (1493), with an Early Renaissance courtyard. University

North-west of the university, on the south side of the Botanical Garden, is the Domus Galilaeana (house of Galileo), a memorial to the Pisa-born scientist and mathematician Galileo Galilei (library and study). Domus Galilaeana

Sights on the left bank of the Arno

On the left bank of the Arno, at the west end of the Lungarno Sonnino, is the church of San Paolo a Ripa d'Arno, a basilica built about 1200 with a very fine façade. San Paolo a Ripa d'Arno

500 m east stands the church of Santa Maria della Spina, in French Gothic style, built in 1230 and enlarged in 1323, an elegant little church with ★Santa Maria della Spina

Church of Santa Maria della Spina on the bank of the Arno

external sculpture by pupils of Giovanni Pisano. Inside there are statues by Tommaso Pisano. The church owes its name to the fact that the interior contains a thorn (spina) of Christ's crown of thorns which was brought by the Pisans from the Holy Land.

Still farther east, at the Ponte di Mezzo, are the Gothic Palazzo Gambacorti (now Town Hall) and the Logge di Banchi (1605).   Palazzo
                                                                           Gambacorti

A little way east of the Town Hall is the octagonal church of San Sepolcro (12th c.).

★San Piero a Grado

According to legend on his way to Rome the Apostle Peter landed at this   5 km (3 mi.) SW
place which was then situated on the coast. It is said that he is the founder
of the Ecclesia ad gradus (church on the steps).

The three-aisled basilica probably dating from the 11th c., was erected over the remains of a previous building, which were discovered during excavations. Inside there are 14th c. frescoes: the lower part has portraits of popes, the centre part scenes from the life of Petri and the upper part the "heavenly" Jerusalem.

★Certosa di Pisa

East of Pisa is the Certosa di Pisa, a Carthusian house founded in 1366 and   14 km (9 mi.) E
rebuilt in Baroque style in the 17th and 18th c. Interesting features are the
two cloisters (15th and 16th c.) and the pure Baroque style of the church.

◄ *The famous Leaning Tower of Pisa is to undergo repairs*

345

In the northern part of the complex a nature and local museum (Museo di Storia Naturale e del territorio dell'Università di Pisa) has been installed. Its collections cover zoology, anatomy, geology and palaentology.

Pistoia   E8

Region: Toscana. Province: Pistoia (P)
Altitude: 65 m (215 ft). Population: 92,000

Location

The provincial capital of Pistoia lies at the north-west end of Tuscany on the southern slopes of the Apennines, some 28 km (17 mi.) north-west of Florence.

History

Pistoia was the Roman Pistoria. During the Middle Ages it was the scene of bitter conflicts between Ghibellines and Guelfs, and in 1295 it came under Florentine rule – a subjection confirmed in 1530. The town's surviving medieval buildings demonstrate the vigorous spirit of enterprise of even the smaller Tuscan towns. In the older churches the influence of the Pisan style, widely diffused in the 12th c., is still predominant, but from the 14th c. the artists working here came almost exclusively from Florence.

Sights

★Cathedral

In the centre of the rectangular area occupied by the old town is the Piazza del Duomo, on the south side of which stands the cathedral of Santi Zeno e Jacopo, a 12th–13th c. Romanesque building. The campanile was originally a fortified tower (1200), to which three orders of columns, Pisan-style, were later added. In the porch, added in 1311, is a terracotta medallion of the Madonna with Angels by Andrea della Robbia (1505). Inside, to the left of the entrance, is the fine tomb of Cardinal Niccolò Forteguerri (d. 1473), designed by Andrea Verrocchio and in the Cappella del Sacramento, to the left of the choir, is a Madonna by Lorenzo di Credi (1485). To the right of the choir in the Cappella di San Iacopo can be seen a rich silver altar (13th-14th c., with over 600 small figures, depicting scenes from the Old and New Testaments.

Palazzo dei Vescovi

Adjoining the north aisle of the cathedral is the old Palazzo dei Vescovi (Bishop's Palace; 14th c.) which houses the Cathedral Chapter Museum (Museo Capitolare) containing pictures and goldsmiths' and silversmiths' work, as well as geological finds.

★Baptistery

The Gothic Baptistery (14th c.) opposite the cathedral has an external pulpit and a fine Early Renaissance wooden door.

Palazzo del Podestà

Adjoining the baptistery is the 14th c. Palazzo del Podestà or Palazzo Pretorio, with a picturesque arcaded courtyard; in the arcades and on the façade are the coats of arms of podestàs of the past, sent from Florence.

Palazzo del Comune Museo Civico

On the north side of the Piazza del Duomo stands the Gothic Palazzo del Comune (1294-1385), also with a beautiful courtyard. The Museo Civico on the top floor contains pictures, sculpture and material recovered by excavation.

Palazzo Respigliosi

Further east stands the Palazzo Respigliosi (16th c.), with the Museo Clemente Respigliosi (17th c. panel painting), and also the new Diocesan Museum (vestments, liturgical objects, paintings).

San Bartolomeo in Pantano

North-east of the Palazzo del Comune stands the 12th c. church of San Bartolomeo in Pantano, a pillared basilica in Tuscan Romanesque style, with a fine interior including a pulpit (1250) with eight reliefs from the life of Christ.

In the nearby Piazza dello Spedale, to the north-west of the town, is the Ospedale del Ceppo (13th or 14th c.). In the porch is a frieze of terracotta reliefs, coloured and glazed by Giovanni della Robbia and his pupils. (1514–25).

West of the hospital stands the church of Sant'Andrea, a 12th c. pillared basilica in Pisan style. The pulpit, one of Giovanni Pisano's principal works, is supported by seven porphyry columns (two of them standing on lions). The wooden crucifix is also by Giovanni Pisano.

★Sant'Andrea

A short distance west of Sant'Andrea, in the spacious Piazza San Francesco d'Assisi, the church of San Francesco, a Gothic convent church begun in 1294, has frescoes in the chapter-house modelled on Giotto's frescoes at Assisi (14th c.; restored in 1930). In the main choir chapel are 14th c. wall paintings, depicting scenes from the life of St Francis.

San Francesco

From San Francesco we go south on Via Bozzi and Via Curtatone e Montanara and then turn right along Via della Madonna to reach the church of the Madonna dell'Umiltà (1494–1522), with a beautiful porch and an octagonal dome added by Vasari in 1561 on the model of the dome of Florence Cathedral.

★Madonna dell'Umiltà

South of Pistoia

To the east of the Piazza Gavinana, the town's busiest traffic intersection, is the church of San Giovanni Fuorcivitas (1160–70), in Tuscan Romanesque style. It contains a pulpit (c. 1270) by Fra Guglielmo da Pisa and a terracotta group (the "Visitation") by Lucca della Robbia (c. 1445).

★San Giovanni Fuorcivitas

From the church Via Cavallotti leads south to the convent church of San Domenico (1380), with remains of 14th c. frescoes and fine monuments.
   Diagonally opposite stands the Chiesa del Tau, now the headquarters of the Marino Marini Foundation (pictures and sculptures).

San Domenico

A little way east, in the broad Corso Silvano Fedi, is the church of San Paolo (c. 1302), with a fine Pisan-style façade.

San Paolo

★★Pompeii   J14

Region: Campania. Province: Napoli (NA)
Altitude: 16 m (53 ft). Population: 23,000

The ruined city of Pompeii lies 20 km (12 mi.) south-east of Naples at the foot of Vesuvius, near the Gulf of Naples.
   It is the finest example of a Roman town and its way of life, presented to modern eyes by excavation. In 1997 it was included in the UNESCO list of World Cultural Heritage Sites.

Location

To the east of the ancient site is the newer settlement, known until 1929 as Valle di Pompei, with a conspicuous domed church, Santa Maria del Rosario, which is visited by countless pilgrims (particularly on May 8th and on the first Sunday in October).

Valle di Pompei

Pompeii, probably founded by the Oscans, an Italic people, became Roman after the Samnite wars (290 BC), and by the 1st c. AD was a prosperous provincial capital with a population estimated at 20,000. In AD 63 much of the town was destroyed by a severe earthquake, and rebuilding had not been completed when an eruption of Vesuvius in AD 79 covered the whole town, as well as Herculaneum and Stabiae, with a layer of ash and pumice-stone up to 7 m (23 ft) thick – though a proportion of the population were able to escape in time. The town was now abandoned, after some at least of the survivors had recovered objects of value from the loose covering of ash.

History

Pompeii

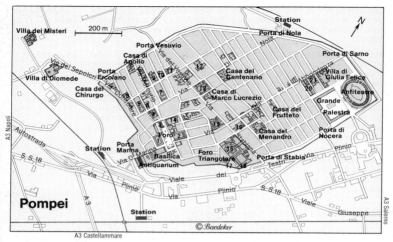

1 Temple of Apollo
2 Building of Eumachia
3 Temple of Jupiter
4 Forum Baths
5 House of Pansa
6 House of Tragic Poet

7 House of Faun
8 House of Sallust
9 House of Labyrinth
10 House of Vettii
11 House of Gilded Cupids
12 House of Silver Wedding

13 Central Baths
14 Macellum
15 Stabian Baths
16 Large Theatre
17 Doric Temple
18 Gladiators' Barracks

19 Casa del Citarista
20 House of Marcus Loreius Tiburtinus
21 House of Venus

Since the 18th c. something like three-fifths of the total area of the town (the walls of which had a perimeter of 3.1 km (2 mi.) have been recovered by large-scale excavation, carried out systematically from 1860 onwards. Although the buildings are in a ruinous state and it is only in the more recently excavated areas (since 1911) that the internal arrangements and domestic equipment have, as far as possible, been left as they were found. Visitors to Pompeii get a more immediate and more vivid impression of ancient life – in luxurious mansions and more modest houses, in the markets and the streets, in baths, theatres and temples – than on any other ancient site; and much of what they see will strike them as astonishingly modern.

In November 1980 a severe earthquake caused considerable damage.

Site

In modern times the site has been divided into several regions (I–IX) separated by the principal streets. The blocks (insulae) within the regions are, like them, numbered with Roman numerals (in the plan with Arabic numerals); individual houses have Arabic numerals.

The streets are paved with polygonal slabs of lava, with raised pavements on either side. At intersections and at other places along the streets are stepping-stones designed to help pedestrians to cross. Deep ruts in the paving bear witness to heavy traffic. At many street corners are fountains for public use. The inscriptions on the outside walls of houses, in the manner of modern posters, mostly relate to municipal elections.

Roman house

The Roman house was entered from the street by a narrow passage (fauces, ostium), often flanked by shops and workshops (tabernae), leading into a large court or atrium with a roof which sloped inwards. In the centre of the roof was a square opening (compluvium), below which, sunk into the ground, was a basin for catching rain-water (impluvium). On each side, and

Pompeii was a flourishing town until its destruction in 79 BC ▶

348

Pompeii AD 79

"Several days previously we had felt the earth move without attaching undue importance to it, because we who lived in Campania were used to this. However, that night the earth shook so violently that it seemed as if everything would collapse around us.

"My mother came running into my room, but I was already up and about to go and wake her in case she was still asleep. We went out into the courtyard which separated the house from the sea. . . . A friend of my uncle, who had just arrived from Spain, saw me and my mother sitting there and me reading. He reproached us for not showing any particular concern and me for lack of sense, but I still did not lift my eyes from my book. It had been daylight for over an hour, yet the light was still vague and seemed to be fading.

"Some of the houses round about had already collapsed and so, although we were in the open air, it seemed sensible to flee the town for fear of being crushed. The frightened populace ran after us; in their panic and fear each of them blindly followed the others rather than making his or her own decision as to where to go. . . .

"It also seemed to us as though the sea had swallowed itself and been pushed back by the earthquake. There was no doubt that the beach had widened, and numerous fish were stranded on dry land. On the opposite bank the hot whirlwind ripped the grey-black clouds into long fiery strips which looked like lightning but were even more magnificent. . . .

"It was not long before those same clouds sank down to earth and covered the sea. They encased Capri so that it could no longer be seen at all, and soon after that the foothills of Misenum were lost from view. My mother pressed close to me uttering words of comfort and begging to me to flee and save myself because I was still so young; she said she was an old woman and did not want to feel she was to blame for my death if I stayed. However, I replied that I only wanted to be saved if I was with her. I then took her hand and forced her to hurry. She followed me with difficulty and complained that she was slowing me down.

"It had already begun to rain ashes, although they were not yet thick. I looked around me and saw behind us a thick cloud of smoke which spread along the ground like a river and was almost on our heels. 'Let us go back', I said, 'until we can see again and not be crushed underfoot by the horde of people following us'. Scarcely had we done so than it became as night, not a moonless and cloudy night but the night as in a closed room without any light. You should have heard the women crying, the children whining and the men shouting! One would be trying to find his parents just by the sound of their voices, others seeking their children, one bemoaning his own fate, the other that of those near and dear to him. Others were fleeing for their lives. Many prayed to the gods, others swore there were no gods any more and that the end of the world was nigh. Liars who themselves believed the truth of what they were saying said they had come from Misenum which had been devoured by fire.

"Finally a half-light began to appear, but not the light of a dawning day, rather like the reflection of a nearby fire. But no fire came; instead it became dark once more and we were covered in a fresh cloud of ashes. Now and again we stood up and shook the ashes from us, otherwise we would have been crushed and suffocated by them. Terror and fear knew no end, as the ground continued to tremble. Many went mad and uttered prophesies of disaster while joking about their own misfortune and that of others."

For this graphic report on the facts of that day we must thank the Roman author Gaius Plinius Caecilius Secundus, who was about eighteen years of age when Vesuvius erupted. That which he described in his writings has been confirmed by archaeologists who since the 18th century have been engaged in uncovering the once flourishing towns of Pompeii and Herculaneum which became covered in a thick layer of solid ash. Dwelling houses have been unearthed, with their contents still just as they were when their occupants fled. The corpses of those killed left hollows in the ashes which archaeologists filled with plaster of Paris, thus preserving true likenesses of the victims of the volcano. Many still had their clothing preserved, and some were carrying valuables which they had grabbed as they fled. In their "History of Vesuvius", published in 1929, the vulcanologists I. Friedländer and G.B. Alfano came to the conclusion that, of the estimated population of Pompeii of 20,000, the majority were able to escape.

Vesuvius in the 18th century

View from the Tower of Mercury in Pompeii

sometimes in front, were bedrooms (cubiculae); on each side too were alae, open spaces originally designed for the statues of ancestors. The fourth side of the atrium was entirely occupied by a large open apartment, the tablinum. Beyond the front portion of the house, in which visitors were received, lay the private apartments used by the family; these were built round a garden-like courtyard, known as the peristylium from the columns which enclosed it. Beyond this there was sometimes a garden (viridarium). Opening off the peristylium were the triclinium (dining-room) and sitting-room (oecus). The position of the kitchen (culina) and cellars varied. Many houses also had an upper floor with balconies.

It is interesting to compare the Pompeian single-storey house occupied by one family with the blocks of apartments built round a large central court-yard which became general under the Empire and are found at Ostia but not at Pompeii.

Tour

Main entrance	The main entrance to the site (open daily) is near the Pompeii-Villa dei Misteri railway station. 300 m from the entrance is the Porta Marina, the ancient gate at the south-west corner of the town.
Antiquarium	Immediately beyond the gate, on the right, is the Antiquarium, containing excavated material from Pompeii dating from the pre-Samnite period to Roman times. Particularly impressive are the casts of human bodies and of a dog found buried under the ashes.
★Forum	Beyond the Antiquarium, also on the right, is the Basilica, used as a market and a law-court. To the left is the Temple of Apollo, surrounded by 48 Ionic columns. Beyond these two buildings is the Forum, the principal square of the Roman town, which was enclosed by colonnades. At the north end of

the forum is the Temple of Jupiter, on a base 3 m (10 ft) high. At the north-east corner is the Macellum, a hall for the sale of foodstuff. Down the east side are the Shrine of the Lares, the Temple of Vespasian (probably dedicated originally to Augustus) and the Building of Eumachia, probably a hall for the sale of wool. On the south side of the forum is the Curia, the meeting-place of the town council, flanked by three other rooms.

Beyond the forum the Via dell'Abbondanza, one of the principal streets of the ancient town, continues east, to the right of the Building of Eumachia, towards the new excavations. The second street on the right (Via dei Teatri) leads to the tree-shaded Triangular Forum, intended mainly for theatre-goers, which is entered through a fine arcade. On the south side of this little square are the remains of a Greek temple; facing this, to the east, are barracks for gladiators. | Triangular forum

Adjoining the northern half of the Triangular Forum, built into the sloping ground, is the Large Theatre (Teatro Grande), which could seat some 5000 spectators and is now used for "Son et lumière" shows in summer. From the top row there are fine views. | ★Large Theatre

Adjoining this the better preserved Little Theatre (Teatro Piccolo), the earliest example of a roofed Roman theatre (*c.* 75 BC); with seating for 1500, was used mainly for musical performances. | ★Little Theatre

On the east side of the Little Theatre is the Via Stabiana, which runs north-west. Immediately on the left is the little Tempio di Giove Meilichio. To the west of this, in the Via del Tempio d'Iside, the Temple of Isis has an in-scription scratched on its walls by the French novelist Stendhal (Henri Beyle) during a visit in 1817. | Temples

Beyond this, on the east side of the Via Stabiana, is the Casa del Citarista, one of the largest houses in Pompeii. Just beyond this the Via Stabiana joins the Via dell'Abbondanza.

100 m along the Via dell'Abbondanza to the right is the beginning of the New Excavations (Nuovi Scavi), in which wall paintings and furniture have been left in place and in many cases the upper storey with its balconies and loggias has been preserved by the insertion of girders. In this area there are many election "posters" and other casual inscriptions painted on the walls, with the help of which the former director of excava-tions, Della Corte, was able to compile a "directory" containing 550 names. This part of the town dates from Pompeii's final period and was mostly occupied by tradesmen. Among the establishments to be seen here are an ironmonger's shop; beyond this to the right a fuller's and dyer's workshop (Fullonica di Stefano), with two restored pressing machines; and beyond this, to the south, the House with the Cryptoporticus, with a magnificent painted frieze (in a passage leading to the cellar) depicting 20 episodes from the "Iliad" and other Homeric poems. | Nuovi Scavi

Still farther south is the large and well-preserved House of Menander which belonged to a wealthy merchant; it was named after a likeness of the Greek comic playwright Menander in a niche in the magnificent peristylium. Adjoining this is the charming little House of the Lovers. | ★House of Menander

Farther along the Via dell'Abbondanza, on the left, is the Thermopolium, a tavern fully equipped with drinking vessels, a kettle, a stove and a lamp, with the last customer's money still on the counter. Beyond this, on the left, is the interesting House of Trebius Valens, the front wall of which is covered with inscriptions; and beyond this again, on the right, is the rich House of Marcus Loreius Tiburtinus, with a restored double door and an interesting interior.

Farther east, to the south of the Via dell'Abbondanza, are the most recent excavations (1951–59). Of particular interest in this area are the House of | ★Painting of Venus

353

Pompeii

Venus (Casa della Venere), with a fine painting of Venus; the House of the Orchard (Casa del Frutteto); and the Villa di Giulia Felice.

Necropolis

Farther south, outside the Porta di Nocera, we come to a necropolis (cemetery), such as lay outside the walls of all ancient towns.

Palaestra

South of the House of Marcus Loreius Tiburtinus is the Palaestra, with colonnades round three sides (each 140 m (459 ft) long) and a swimming pool in the centre.

Amphitheatre

Immediately east of this is the massive Amphitheatre (136 m (446 ft) long, 104 m (341 ft) across, seating for 12,000 spectators), the oldest surviving Roman amphitheatre (80 BC).

★Stabian Baths

At the corner of the Via dell'Abbondanza and the Via Stabiana are the Stabian Baths (Terme Stabiana), the largest and best-preserved baths in Pompeii (entrance from Via dell'Abbondanza). The entrance leads into the colonnaded palaestra, with a swimming pool on the left; on the right are the male and female baths, separated by the stoves for heating the water. Each establishment has a circular cold bath (frigidarium), a changing room (apodyterium) with racks for clothing, a warm bath (tepidarium) and a hot (Turkish) bath (caldarium) heated by air-ducts in the floor and walls.

Houses

Immediately north of the baths is the House of Siricus (entrance from Vicolo del Lupanare); next door is a bakery. On the threshold is the inscription "Salve lucrum" ("Long live profit!"); fine paintings in the interior. Farther along the Via Stabiana, on the right, is the House of Marcus Lucretius, also with well-preserved paintings.

In another 100 m the Via Stabiana crosses the Via di Nola, one of the principal streets of the town, and 100 m farther on again comes to an intersection at which the Vicolo delle Nozze d'Argento (on the right) leads to the House of the Silver Wedding (fine atrium and peristylium) and the Vicolo di Mercurio (on the left) leads past the House of the Vettii to the House of Sallust.

House of the Gilded Cupids

Farther along the Via Stabiana, also called the Via del Vesuvio in its northern section, is the elegant House of the Gilded Cupids (Casa degli Amorini dorati), with a garden which still preserves its original marble decoration. The Via Stabiana ends at the Porta del Vesuvio; from the hill outside the gate there is a fine view.

★House of the Vettii

The very interesting House of the Vettii in the Vicolo di Mercurio has well-preserved ornamental paintings and fine frescoes in the triclinium. The peristylium (partly rebuilt) still has its original marble decoration and has been replanted. The kitchen still contains its cooking utensils.

South-west of the House of the Vettii is the House of the Labyrinth (Casa del Labirinto), with two atria.

★House of the Faun

Opposite this, to the south, is the House of the Faun (Casa del Fauno; entrance from the Via di Nola), the most palatial mansion in Pompeii, taking up a whole insula (80 × 35 m (263 × 125 ft)). By the impluvium is a copy of the statuette of a faun which was discovered here. The famous mosaic of "Alexander's Battle" was found in the room with red columns.

★Forum Baths

In the Via delle Terme, the westerly continuation of the Via di Nola (the western part of which is also called the Via di Fortuna), are the Forum Baths (Terme del Foro), smaller and more modest than the Stabian Baths but also occupying a whole insula. On the south side of the baths is a modern bar.

House of the Tragic Poet

To the north of the Baths is the elegant and richly appointed House of the Tragic Poet (Casa del Poeta tragico), on the threshold of which is a mosaic of a chained dog with the inscription "Cave canem" ("Beware of the dog").

Wall paintings in the Villa dei Misteri

Adjoining the House of the Tragic Poet on the west is the House of Pansa (98 × 38 m (322 × 138 ft)), one of the largest and most regularly planned houses in Pompeii.

House of Pansa

On the north side of the House of the Tragic Poet is a fuller's workshop, to the left of which are the House of the Large Fountain and the House of the Small Fountain, with the beautiful fountains after which they are named. From the latter house the Vicolo di Mercurio runs west to the House of Sallust, where can be seen good paintings. From here Via Consolare runs north-west to the Porta Ercolano, which probably dates from the Augustan period.

House of Sallust

★Street of Tombs

Outside the gate lies a suburban district of which only the main street has been excavated. This Street of Tombs is, from the scenic point of view, the most attractive part of Pompeii. Lined with imposing monuments to distinguished citizens, it ranks with the Via Appia outside Rome as the most impressive surviving example of the Roman practice of erecting tombs along public roads.

At the north-west end of the street is the large Villa of Diomedes, with an extensive garden enclosed by a portico 33 m (108 ft) long each way. In the centre of the garden is a basin and six columns which belonged to a pavilion. In an underground passage (cryptoporticus) were found the bodies of 18 women and children. Near the garden door (now walled up) was the body of a man, presumably the owner of the house, with a key in his hand and a slave beside him carrying money and valuables.

★Villa of Diomedes

200 m north-west of the Villa of Diomedes, outside the main excavation area, is the magnificent Villa of the Mysteries (Villa dei Misteri; reached

★Villa of the Mysteries

from the main entrance to the excavations on a road which runs past the station (500 m) and continues for another 700 m), with the finest surviving ancient wall paintings, preserved in all the brilliance of their original colouring. The most remarkable of these is a frieze 17 m (56 ft) long in the large triclinium with almost life-size figures, dating from the pre-Augustan period (probably based on models of the 3rd c. BC), which depicts scenes from the Dionysiac mysteries.

Pontine Islands   G–H14

Region: Latium/Lazio
Province: Latina (LT). Population: 4000

Ferries — Boat services from Formia to Ponza and Ventotene; from Anzio to Ponza and from Naples via Ventotene to Ponza; hydrofoils from Anzio, Formia and Terracina.

Location — The Pontine Islands (Italian Isole Ponziane) lie off the coast of southern Latium; they form the boundary of the Gulf of Gaeta (Golfo di Gaeta) and the Tyrrhenian Sea. They are of volcanic origin and are frequently shaken by minor earth tremors.
  The inhabitants live mainly from vine-growing and fishing; in recent years there has also been a developing tourist trade on the two main islands of Ponza and Ventotene.

Islands

Ponza — The north-western group of islands consists of the almost uninhabited islands of Palmarola and Zannone (known to the Romans as Palmaria and Sinonia) and Gavi and the well-cultivated main island of Ponza, a crater ridge 7.5 km (4³/₄ mi.) long, rising to a height of 284 m (937 ft) at the southern end in Monte della Guardia, and fringed by picturesque coves and cliffs. Below the north side of the hill is a bay forming a sheltered harbour, with the villages of Ponza (hotels) and Santa Maria.
  The south-eastern group consists of the islands of Ventotene, part of a former crater (3 km (2 mi.) long by 1 km (¹/₂ mi.) across), with a village of the same name, and Santo Stefano, a granite island with a former prison.

★Portofino   D7

Region: Liguria
Province: Genova (GE)
Altitude: 3 m (10 ft). Population: 600

Location — Portofino, some 30 km (19 mi.) south-east of Genova, is picturesquely situated in a narrow cove at the south-eastern tip of the promontory of the same name.

Resort — The village owes its popularity with visitors to its beautiful setting, its agreeable climate and its luxuriant Mediterranean vegetation.

Sights

The houses of the former fishing village line the bay, and the slopes are covered with pines and olive trees. To the south, above the harbour, is the

Portofino, a picturesque natural harbour

church of San Giorgio, from which there is a beautiful view of Portofino. There are even more extensive views from the platform beside the Fortezza di San Giorgio, to the east, extending north-west to Capo Mele and the Maritime Alps.

★Surroundings

There is a very attractive boat trip (1½ hours) under the precipitous south side of the promontory to San Fruttuoso, a former abbey which appears in the records as early as 984, with an early Gothic church and a cloister, picturesquely situated in a small rocky cove. Offshore, 17 m (56 ft) below sea-level, is a bronze figure of Christ, the so-called Christo degli Abissi, 2.5 m (8¼ ft) high (1954) on a concrete base weighing 80 metric tons.

San Fruttuoso

From San Fruttuoso there is a pleasant walk (2 hours), steep in the first section, to the Semàforo Vecchio (610 m (2013 ft)), the highest point on the Portofino promontory, which thrusts out squarely into the sea for 4–5 km (2½–3 mi.), affording views which extend in clear weather as far as Corsica. From here it is half an hour's walk to the Portofino Vetta (450 m (1485 ft)), the view from which is famous. To the north-west can be seen the coastline from Camogli to Genoa and beyond this Capo Berta, above which, best seen in the morning light, are the snow-covered Cottian Alps; to the southeast are Rapallo, Chiavari and Sestri Levante, the islands off Portovenere and the Apuan Alps. Here too is the aerial tower, 117 m (386 ft) high, of the Genoa television transmitter.

Portofino Vetta

On the west side of the Portofino promontory the picturesquely situated little port of Camogli has a beautiful parish church and the ruined Castello Dragone.

Camogli

Region: Toscana. Province: Firenze (FI)
Altitude: 61 m (201 ft). Population: 162,000

Location
The Tuscan town of Prato lies on the River Bisenzio, about half-way between Florence and Pistoia. The centre is surrounded by town walls.
On account of its important woollen industry, already known in the Middle Ages, Prato is also known as the "Italian Manchester".

Access
The town centre is closed to cars.

★Prato Cathedral

Exterior
In the Piazza del Duomo, in the northern part of the town, stands the cathedral, begun in the 12th c. in Tuscan Romanesque style and remodelled in Gothic style in 1317–20, with a Lombard tower (13th–14th c.).
On the façade (1385–1457) is a pulpit by Donatello and Michelozzo, with reliefs of dancing children (1434–38; originals replaced by copies). Above the main entrance is a terracotta relief by Andrea della Robbia of the Madonna with SS. Stephen and Lawrence (1489).

Interior
The interior is decorated with green-white marble as in Pisan examples. The Cappella del Sacro Cingolo ("Holy Belt") has interesting wall paintings by Agnolo Gaddi (scenes from the life of the Virgin, particularly the Assumption of the Virgin Mary and the role the belt plays in it). In the choir are frescos by Filippo Lippi (St John the Baptist and St Stephen). In the nave is a rich marble pulpit with reliefs by Mino da Fiesole and Antonio Rossellino (1473).

The pulpit on the outside of Prato cathedral

To the left of the cathedral is the Museo dell'Opera del Duomo (Cathedral Museum), containing altarpieces and the shrine of the Holy Belt, including the original reliefs (dancing children) from the outer pulpit of the cathedral.

Cathedral Museum

Town centre

From the Piazza del Duomo Via Mazzoni runs south to the Piazza del Comune in the centre of the town. At the south-west corner of the square stands the Palazzo Pretorio (13th–14th c.) which houses the Galleria Comunale, with pictures by Florentine masters of the 14th and 15th c., including Filippo Lippi.

Palazzo Pretorio (Galleria Comunale)

Opposite the Palazzo Pretorio is the Palazzo Comunale which was restored in the 19th c.

Palazzo Comunale

The Palazzo, south of the Piazza del Comune, was the residence of the merchant and banker Francesco di Marco Datini (1330–1410). After Datini's death the façade was decorated with frescos, depicting scenes from his life. There are only a few sinopes left.

Palazzo Datini

In the west of the town centre, in Piazza San Domenico, is the church of San Domenico (1283–1322) with an unfinished façade. Particularly notable is the richly decorated portal of the south transept. Inside there is a large painted crucifix (c. 1400).

San Domenico

Through the 15th c. cloister we reach the Museo di Pittura Murale (Wall Painting Museum), with frescos, sinopes (13–17th c.) including documents showing fresco techniques and several restoration methods.

Museo di Pittura Murale

From the Piazza del Comune, Via Ricasoli runs south to the Piazza San Francesco on the left side of which is the 13th c. church of San Francesco. In the beautiful cloister to the right of the church we find the entrance to the chapter-house, which has fine wall paintings of the school of Giotto (Gerini, 14th c.).

San Francesco

In the adjoining square to the east, on the left, is the church of Santa Maria delle Carceri, a good example of a church on a Greek cross plan with a dome. It contains a fine high altar by Sangallo (1515) and terracotta medallions of the Evangelists by Andrea della Robbia.

★Santa Maria delle Carceri

To the south of Santa Maria delle Carceri the Castello dell'Imperatore, a crenellated castle built in the reign of the Emperor Frederick II (1237–48), has two 10th c. towers.

Castello dell'Imperatore

★Centro per l'Arte Contemporanea Luigi Pecci

In 1988 the Centro per l'Arte Contemporanea Luigi Pecci (Museum of Contemporary Art) was opened in Prato. The museum, on the plan of a rectangular "U", is in the south of the old town, in Via della Repubblica (corner of Via delle Fonti di Mezzana). The building was financed by the Associazione Luigi Pecci which was founded by the industrialist Enrico Pecci who died in 1988. The house, with an adjoining research centre, is to be a forum for painting, sculpture, design, video and other forms of creative expression. At the opening of the "U" is an arena with steps for seating. The arena, in the form of a Greek amphitheatre, accommodates 600 to 800 persons.

Prócida/Isola di Prócida

See Ilschia.

Rapallo D7

Region: Liguria. Province: Genova (GE)
Altitude: 2 m (7 ft). Population: 27,000

Location

Rapallo, the largest resort on the Riviera di Levante lies tucked away in the Bay of Rapallo or Golfo Tigullio, some 33 km (20 mi.) south-east of Genoa.

Sights

Old town

The houses in the town are built along the bay. A number of streets run parallel to this bay, others run uphill. The town's busiest square is the Piazza Cavour, in which are the old parish church with a façade of 1857, and a leaning tower of 1753. To the north lies the large Piazza delle Nazione, with the municipal museum and the town hall. The tower of the "Commune Rapallese" (1459) is the town's symbol. The municipal museum displays locally-produced pillow lace.

Castello

On the south-east side of the fishing harbour, beyond the mouth of the Torrente San Francesco, is a medieval Castello, now an exhibition centre. To the west of it lies the magnificent Promenade des Lungomare Vittoro Veneto, lined with palm trees, hotels and cafés.

Municipal park
Lace Museum

On the eastern edge of the town is the Parco Communale Casale, with the Villa Tigullio which houses the Museo del Pizzo a Tombolo (pillow lace).

Rapallo, a Riviera resort rich in tradition

Surroundings

North of Rapallo is the pilgrimage church of the Madonna di Montallegro, high up on the hillside (612 m (202 ft); also reached by cableway, 10 minutes). From the top there are far-ranging views of the Gulf of Rapallo.

Madonna di Montallegro
11 km (7 mi.) N

See entry.

Portofino

From Rapallo a coastal road leads south to the pretty holiday resort of Santa Margherita Ligura (3 km (2 mi.)).

★**Santa Margherita Ligura**

Ravenna   G7

Region: Emilia-Romagna. Province: Ravenna (RA)
Altitude: 3 m (10 ft). Population: 137,000

Ravenna, a provincial capital and the see of an archbishop, lies in the south-east corner of the North Italian plain, here traversed by numerous drainage canals. Originally a seaport, it is now connected with the sea by a canal 10 km (6 mi.) long linking it with Porto Corsini.

Location

Town

With its important early medieval buildings, Ravenna is one of the most interesting towns in Italy, and visitors get a vivid impression of early medieval art.

The town centre is closed to cars.

Access

In the time of the Etruscans and Romans Ravenna was a lagoon town like Venice. Augustus made the port of Portus Classis, 5 km (3 mi.) from the town, the base of the Roman Adriatic fleet. Ravenna's heyday began, how-ever, when the Western Roman Emperor Honorius moved his court from Milan to the natural fortress of Ravenna, protected by the surrounding marshes, in 402. While the rest of Italy was being devastated during the Great Migrations, an active programme of building was carried out here under Honorius and his sister Galla Placidia (Regent 425–450), and the art of mosaic-working flourished. After the fall of the Western Roman Empire the Herulian Odoacer was proclaimed king by the Germanic mercenary troops and ruled the whole of Italy from Ravenna (476–493). After his murder the Ostrogothic king Theodoric the Great, who had been brought up in Constantinople (493–526), brought further splendour to the town, building several churches for the Arian Church, to which the Ostrogoths belonged, as well as a royal palace. In 539, under Justinian (527-565), the Byzantine general Belisarius drove out the Ostrogoths. Thereafter Ravenna became the seat of a Byzantine governor (Exarch) and, favoured by the emperor, enjoyed a third period of prosperity, which introduced Byzantine art to the West. In 751, however, the Lombards put an end to the Exarchate. From 1297 to 1441 Ravenna was ruled by the Ghibelline Polenta family, for a period thereafter belonged to the Venetians and from 1509 to 1859 was incorporated in the States of the Church.

History

Sights

In the centre of the town is the Piazza del Popolo, with the Palazzo Comunale (Town Hall, 1681). In front of the Town Hall are two granite columns erected by the Venetians in 1483. In the square stands the Palazzo Veneziano, a portico of eight granite columns, with Theodoric's mono-gram on four of the capitals.

Piazza del Popolo

A short distance south-west of the Piazza del Popolo is the Cathedral of Sant'Orso, built 1734–43 on the site of the oldest church in Ravenna,

Cathedral

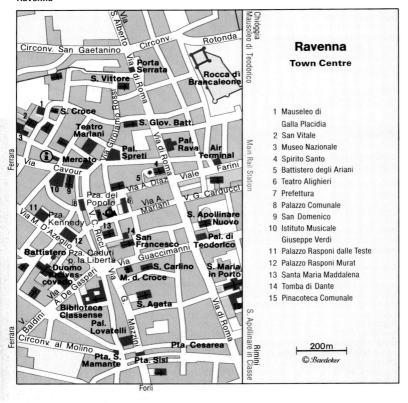

Ravenna

Town Centre

1 Mauseleo di
  Galla Placidia
2 San Vitale
3 Museo Nazionale
4 Spirito Santo
5 Battistero degli Ariani
6 Teatro Alighieri
7 Prefettura
8 Palazzo Comunale
9 San Domenico
10 Istituto Musicale
  Giuseppe Verdi
11 Palazzo Rasponi dalle Teste
12 Palazzo Rasponi Murat
13 Santa Maria Maddalena
14 Tomba di Dante
15 Pinacoteca Comunale

200m

© Baedeker

founded by St Ursus (d. 396); the campanile (10th c.) dates from this earlier church. In the nave, on the right, the 6th c. pulpit was reconstructed from
the separate marble slabs, decorated with animal figures, of which it was
originally composed. In the second chapel on the right and in the south
transept are Early Christian marble sarcophagi.

★Baptistery of the
Orthodox

Immediately north of the cathedral is the Baptistery of the Orthodox or
Neoniana, an octagonal 5th c. brick structure. The mosaics in the dome
(some of which have been restored) are among the oldest in Ravenna. The
font is 16th c. but the parapet is ancient.

Archbishop's
Palace

Behind the cathedral, to the south-east, stands the Archbishop's Palace
(Arcivescovado), on the first floor of which, on the left, is the Museo
Arcivescovile (Archbishop's Museum), with the so-called throne of
Archbishop Maximilian, actually 6th c. Egyptian work, with ivory reliefs.

San Francesco

Farther east of the Palazzo is the modern Piazza dei Caduti per la Libertà,
from which several streets lead off. To the east of the square is the Franciscan church of San Francesco, founded in the 5th c., with a Romanesque
tower (10th c.).

To the north of the church can be seen Dante's Tomb (Tomba di Dante). The exterior is Neo-Classical (1780); in the interior is a sarcophagus containing the remains of the poet, who died in exile in Ravenna in 1321 at the age of 56. The Museo Dantesco contains exhibits relating to Dante's life and work.

Dante's tomb

★★San Vitale

500 m north-west of the Piazza del Popolo is the church of San Vitale, an externally unadorned octagonal structure on a centralised plan (diameter 35 m (115 ft) with an octagonal dome, begun in 526 during the reign of Theodoric and consecrated in 547. The interior, which has been freed from later additions with the exception of the Baroque frescoes in the dome, is divided by eight piers into a central space and a surrounding ambulatory. The principal interest lies in its mosaics in Byzantine style. The 6th c. mosaics in the choir apse (below, left and right) depict Justinian and his wife Theodora, who are accompanied by their suite (next to the emperor is Archbishop Maximilian); above is Christ on a sphere flanked by St Vitalis (on the left) and St Ecclesius (on the right). The altar is of translucent alabaster.

Beyond San Vitale is the mausoleum of Galla Placidia (c. 440), in the form of a Latin cross, with a barrel-vaulted roof and a dome over the crossing. The interior is decorated with beautiful mosaics (5th c.) on a dark blue ground – a cross, the symbols of the Evangelists, figures of the Apostles, above the door Christ as the Good Shepherd. To the rear and in the two lateral arms of the cross are marble sarcophagi, said to be those of Galla Placidia, her second husband Constantius III (d. 421) and her son Valentinian III (d. 455).

★Mausoleum of Galla Placidia

To the west, adjoining San Vitale, is the interesting Museo Nazionale, with inscriptions, sculpture, carved ivories and other valuable objects.

Museo Nazionale

Superb mosaics in the Mausoleum of Galla Placidia

Ravenna

★Sant'Apollinare
Nuovo

In the busy Via di Roma, on the east side of the town, is the church of Sant'Apollinare Nuovo, a basilica built by Theodoric after 500 as an Arian cathedral and converted into a Roman Catholic church in 560. The porch and the apse date from the 16th and 18th c. The interior of the church contains 24 marble columns from Constantinople. The walls of the nave have interesting 6th c. mosaics: on the left-hand wall the Roman port of Classis, with ships; on the right-hand wall the town of Ravenna, with its churches and Theodoric's palace, and saints in Byzantine costumes; above the friezes prophets; and above the windows interesting compositions from the New Testament – on the left the sayings and miracles of Christ (who is shown beardless), on the right scenes from the Passion (with a bearded Christ).

A little way south of Sant'Apollinare, at the corner of Via Alberoni, are remains of the so-called Palace of Theodoric (richly articulated façade, with a central projection).

Santa Maria in
Porto

Farther south stands the large Renaissance church of Santa Maria in Porto (16th c.; façade 1784). The adjoining Logetta Lombardesco and the Renaissance cloister house the Pinacoteca Comunale (Picture Gallery).

San Giovanni
Evangelista

North-east of Sant'Apollinare, in the area around the station, which suffered heavy damage during the Second World War and has been completely redeveloped since then, is the church of San Giovanni Evangelista (fine campanile), founded by Galla Placidia in 424 and rebuilt in its original form after severe war damage.

Baptistery of the
Arians

A short distance west (entered from Via Paolo Costa) are the Basilica of the Santo Spirito, built in the reign of Theodoric, and the former Baptistery of the Arians (later Santa Maria in Cosmedin), with 6th c. mosaics (Baptism of Christ), heavily restored, in the dome.

★Tomb of
Theodoric

750 m east of the Porta Serrata (at the north end of the Via di Roma) is the Tomb of Theodoric, built about 520, probably on the order of Theodoric himself. This is a monumental two-storey rotunda built in square blocks of Istrian limestone and roofed with a single huge block 11 m (36 ft) in diameter. The tomb is reminiscent of Syrian rather than Roman models. The ornamentation shows clear Germanic influence. The lower floor is a barrel-vaulted chamber in the form of a Greek cross, on the upper floor is an antique porphyry sarcophagus.

★★Sant'Apollinare in Classe

5 km (3 mi.) S

South of Ravenna, on the road to Rimini, stands the fine church of Sant' Apollinare in Classe, the only preserved building of the town of Classis, with a porch and a round campanile. The church, begun about 535 on a site just outside the ancient port of Classis, was consecrated in 549; it was restored in 1779 and freed from encroaching buildings in 1904. The spacious interior contains 24 Byzantine marble columns. On the walls are medallions with portraits of bishops and archbishops of Ravenna (18th c.). In the aisles are marble sarcophagi of archbishops of the 5th–8th c. The 12th c. crypt has an ancient bronze window-grating. The mosaics in the apse and on the triumphal arch date from the 6th–7th c. (restored). In the apse is a Christ as the Good Shepherd, below the church's patron with followers (shown as sheep); above the triumphal arch Christ as the pantocrater, surrounded by sheep symbolising the twelve Apostles.

Near the church are excavations (Zona Archeologica di Classe).

5 km (3 mi.) south-east of Sant'Apollinare are the remains of the Pineta di Classe, a once famous pinewood which has been much reduced by felling and fire. A short way to the west is "Mirabilandia", opened in 1992, the largest leisure park in Italy, with over 30 attractions.

Tomb of Theodoric

Sant'Apollinare in Classe, near the old Roman harbour

Surroundings

Marina di Ravenna
11 km (7 mi.) NE

North-east of Ravenna, on the Adriatic coast, is the seaside resort of Marina di Ravenna.

Beyond the Canale Candiano (ferry) is Porto Corsini, the port of Ravenna.

Reggio di Calabria   K19

Region: Calabria. Province: Reggio di Calabria (RC)
Altitude: 31 m (102 ft). Population: 177,000

Location

Reggio di Calabria (to distinguish it from Reggio nell'Emilia), "Reggio Calabria" for short, lies in the south-west of Italy, on the east side of the Strait of Messina. There are numerous shipping links between Reggio di Calabria and Messina.

History

The old port, the Greek Rhegion (founded in 743 BC) or Roman Rhegium, is the principal town of Calabria, the capital of the province and the see of an archbishop.

It was destroyed by an earthquake in 1783, and again suffered heavy damage in 1908. Thereafter it was rebuilt and recovered all its former economic importance. Reggio is the world's principal centre for the production of oil of bergamot, used in making perfumes.

Sights

Piazza Italia

The town's centre is the Piazza Italia, near the sea, in which are the Prefecture, the Palazzo Provinciale, and the Town Hall.

Cathedral

Along the south-east side of the square runs the Corso Garibaldi, the busy main street of the town, 2 km (1¼ mi.) long. Along this street to the south-west is the Piazza del Duomo, with the imposing cathedral, in Romanesque-Byzantine style, rebuilt in 1908.

Farther south-west are the gardens of the Villa Comunale.

Castello Aragonese

From the 15th c. Castello Aragonese to the north-east of the cathedral there are magnificent views.

There are also fine views from Via Reggio Campi, 500 m farther east.

★National Museum

From the Piazza Italia the Corso Garibaldi runs north-east past the Tempio della Vittoria, a war memorial (1933), to the National Museum, with prehistoric, medieval and modern sculpture and early Italic and Greek archaeological material, including the "Heroes of Riace", two bronze statues (5th c. BC) which were found in the sea in 1972 near the town of Riace.

Harbour

From the National Museum the Viale Genoese Zerbi runs north, passing close to a large bathing station, and crosses the Torrente Annunziata to reach the harbour (ferry services to Messina).

★Lungomare Giacomo Matteotti

Running south-west from the National Museum the Lungomare Giacomo Matteotti, a beautiful seafront promenade some 3 km (2 mi.) long, affords fine views of the coast of Sicily. In the southern section of the seaside promenade can be seen remains of Greek town walls and Roman baths of which the mosaic pavement is partly preserved.

Surroundings

Scilla

24 km (15 mi.) north of Reggio di Calabria lies the charming little town of Scilla (population 6000; destroyed by an earthquake in 1908), the ancient

Scylla, dominated by a picturesque castle. The rocks of Scylla, made famous in Homer's Odyssey, and Charybdis are described in ancient poems as a danger to shipping.

9 km (5½ mi.) south-west of Scilla lies the little town of Villa San Giovanni (population 12,000), from where ferries leave to cross the 4 km (3 mi.) of the Messina Strait to Sicily. A bridge across the strait is planned.

Villa San Giovanni

Reggio di Calabria to Aspromonte (c. 43 km (27 mi.))

An interesting trip can be made to the Aspromonte, which in ancient times was counted as part of the Sila range. The best point of approach is Gambarie di Aspromonte (1310 m (4323 ft)), a holiday resort (also popular with winter sport enthusiasts) 24 km (15 mi.) north-east of Reggio (chair-lift to the Puntone di Scirocco, 1660 m (5478 ft), to the south-east).

Gambarie di Aspromonte

From Gambarie di Aspromonte 3.5 km (2¼ mi.) south on SS183, then 15 km (9¼ mi.) east on a moderately good mountain road through pine and beech forests, to Montalto (Monte Cocuzza, 1955 m (6452 ft)), the highest point in the Aspromonte. On the summit is a statue of Christ: magnificent views of the sea and of Calabria and Sicily.

Montalto

Reggio nell'Emilia   E6

Region: Emilia-Romagna. Province: Reggio nell'Emilia (RE)
Altitude: 58 m (191 ft). Population: 130,000

The provincial capital of Reggio nell'Emilia lies on the Via Emilia near the southern edge of the north Italian plain.
    The town was known in Roman times as Regium Lepidi; the poet Lodovico Ariosto was born here in 1474 (d. 1533).

Location

The town centre is closed to cars.

Access

Sights

In the centre is the Piazza Cesare Battisti, with the 13th c. crenellated Palazzo del Capitano del Popolo. The square lies on the line of the ancient Via Aemilia, which traverses the town under the name of Via Emilia a San Pietro (to the east) and Via Emilia a Santo Stefano (to the west).

A little way south is the large Piazza Prampolini on the east side of which stands the cathedral (13th c., rebuilt in 15th–16th c.). Behind the unfinished Renaissance façade is the original Romanesque structure, with remains of frescos and sculpture (on the façade and in the interior) by Prospero Spani (d. 1584), a pupil of Michelangelo's and Bartolomeo Spani, both natives of Reggio.

Cathedral

To the south-east of the cathedral stands the 16th c. church of San Prospero, on the site of an earlier Romanesque building. On the façade (rebuilt 1748) are six marble lions from the original building. The church has frescos, including a "Last Judgment" by Camillo Procaccini (1585–89), choir-stalls of 1546 with intarsio decoration, and a copy of the "Birth of Christ" (1528) by Correggio. Adjoining the church is a fine octagonal campanile.

San Prospero

To the north of Piazza Cesare Battisti in the Piazza Cavour is the large Municipal Theatre (1857). Near the square can be found the Municipal Museum (Musei Civici), with an 18th c. natural history collection, a paleo-

Musei Civici

ethnological collection, works of art of several periods and a picture collection. A palace to the west of the Piazza Cesare Battisti houses the Galleria Parmeggiani, with folk costumes, goldsmith's work and sculpture.

★Madonna della Ghiaira

In the western part of the town, in the broad Corso Garibaldi, is the church of the Madonna della Ghiaira, a Baroque church built 1597–1619, on a Greek cross plan with a dome over the crossing. The interior, notable for the beauty of its proportions, has charming stucco decoration and frescos.

Surroundings

San Polo d'Enza

Near San Polo d'Enza, some 20 km (13 mi.) south-west of Reggio, lie the ruins of four castles which were once owned by the influential Margravine of Tussin (1045–1115). The most famous is Canossa, where in 1077 the excommunicated Emperor Henry IV came as a penitent and humbled himself before Pope Gregory VII. Today little remains of this historically important castle.

Castelnovo ne' Monti

44 km (27 mi.) south-west of Reggio nell'Emilia is Castelnovo ne' Monti (700 m (2310 ft)), a small town on the north-west slopes of the conspicuous rocky peak of the Pietra di Bismantova (1047 m (3455 ft)), from the top of which there are magnificent views of the Apennines. A road (5 km (3 mi.)) ascends the hill; then it is 15 minutes' walk to the top.

Rimini   G7

Region: Emilia-Romagna. Province: Forlì (FO)
Altitude: 7 m (23 ft). Population: 130,000

Location

Rimini lies on the Adriatic in the south-east corner of the North Italian plain, at the meeting-place of two important ancient roads, the Via Aemilia and the Via Flaminia, some 150 km (93 mi.) south of Venice.

It is one of the most favoured seaside resorts and has a beach 20 km (12 mi.) long ("Riviera del Sole").

History

The ancient Ariminum became a Roman colony in 268 BC, commanding the road into northern Italy. In the 13th c. it fell into the hands of the Malatesta family, and in 1528 was incorported in the States of the Church.

Old town

Museo delle Arti Primitive

In the centre of the old town is the Piazza Cavour, in which are the Palazzo Comunale (Town Hall, 1562), the Palazzo dell'Arengo (begun 1204), in Romanesque and Gothic style. Worth visiting is the Castello on the Piazza Malatesta (15th c.), which now houses the Museo delle Culture Extra-europa. A market is held on this square on Wednesdays and Saturdays.

Ponte di Tiberio

From Piazza Cavour the broad Corso di Augusto runs north-west to the Ponte di Tiberio, a Roman bridge completed in AD 20, during the reign of Tiberius.

Tempio Malatestiano

South-east of Piazza Cavour stands the Tempio Malatestiano, a 13th c. Gothic structure remodelled in Early Renaissance style in 1447–60. The façade was designed by Leon Battista Alberti, who drew his inspiration from the Arch of Augustus, and it was the first structure to be based on ancient models at the very beginning of the Renaissance. The interior is finely decorated with frescos by Piero della Francesca, depicting Sigismondo Malatesta kneeling before St Sigismondo. There is also a painted cross attributed to Giotto.

At the south-east end of the Corso di Augusto rises the Arch of Augustus (Arco d'Augusto), a triumphal arch built in 27 BC (the oldest one known) to commemorate the construction of the Via Flaminia.

★Arco d'Augusto

Resort

To the north-east of the old town, beyond the railway, extends the resort of Rimini, with numerous villas, hotels and pensioni. The adjoining districts of Rivabella, Viserba and Torre Pedrere are also popular resorts.

Near Viserba the miniature village "Italia in Miniatura" is worth visiting. There are more than 200 attractions, miniature imitations. among which mountains, lakes, castles and famous squares (e.g. the Campo dei Miracoli of Pisa).
  3 km (2 mi.) south-east, on the road to Riccione, is Miramare, also a bathing resort, with a large airport.

Italia in Miniatura

Between Rimini and Riccione is another attraction, the amusement park "Fiabilandia", with a great choice (Show Boat, King Kong, Fort Apache, water games, Baby Park, railway, theatre, etc.).

Fiabilandia

Surroundings

8 km (5 mi.) south-east of Rimini is Riccione (12 m (40 ft); population 32,000), one of Italy's most popular holiday resorts, with thermal springs.

Riccione

The small spa and seaside resort of Misano Adriatico is situated about 4 km (2½ mi.) south-east of Riccione.

Misano Adriatico

Another 4 km (2½ mi.) down the coast is Cattolica (10 m (33 ft); population 16,000), a seaside resort since the mid 19th c., particularly in favour with

Cattolica

Parasols on the beach at Rimini

Riviera

German visitors. There are many villas, boulevards and fine shops. The beach, 2 km (1¼ mi.) long, has good facilities for visitors. The town offers a rich choice for active holidays: sailing, wind-surfing, water-skiing, crazy golf, tennis, riding, bowling, etc. There are concerts and other events.

Gradara

On a hill 8 km (5 mi.) south of Cattolica the little town of Gradara (142 m (469 ft)) has a completely preserved circuit of walls and towers and a very interesting castle.

Cesenatico

20 km (12 mi.) north-west of Rimini is Cesenatico (4 m (13 ft); population 20,000), an old fishing village. The little town is traversed by a harbour canal, part of which is now a floating maritime museum, the Museo della Marineria, consisting of old fishing boats with painted sails.

Cervia

8 km (5 mi.) north-west of Cesenatico is Cervia (3 m (10 ft); population 25,000), one of the most elegant seaside resorts in Romagna, the northern part of the Emilia-Romagna. The town has a broad beach of fine sand and modern thermal baths. For hundreds of years the town was the centre of salt production, and – according to experts – the salt content of the water in the baths is equal to that of the Dead Sea. The old town with the cathedral and bishop's palace was founded in the 18th c.

Milano Marittima

Beyond the canal harbour is the suburb of Milano Marittima, beautifully situated on the edge of a pinewood, with an excellent beach and thermal (Fango) baths.

★San Leo

32 km (20 mi.) SW

Leave Rimini on SS258, which runs up the broad valley of the Marecchia and in 16 km (10 mi.) passes below the little town of Verucchio (333 m (1099 ft); population 6000), with a Malatesta castle (magnificent views), lying off the road to the left. In another 3 km (2 mi.) a road goes off on the left to San Marino (frontier in 500 m), from which it is possible to return, making an attractive round trip.

The main road continues up the valley to (4 km (2½ mi.)) the little village of Villa Nuova, where a road branches off up a side valley, climbs steeply and comes in another 9 km (5½ mi.) to San Leo (583 m (1924 ft); population 3000), situated on a conical hill, with a massive castle (picture gallery), a Romanesque cathedral and a 9th c. parish church.

San Marino

See entry.

Riviera   B–D6–8

Region: Liguria
Provinces: Genova (GE), Imperia (IM), La Spezia (SP) and Savona (SV)

Location

The Riviera ("coast") is the narrow coastal strip which extends along the Mediterranean from Marseilles to La Spezia. The Italian Riviera, between Ventimiglia and La Spezia, is one of the most beautiful scenic stretches in Italy, with precipitous cliffs, forested hills, old-world little port towns and ruined watch-towers standing above the brilliant blue sea. The hills shelter it from the rough north winds, and with its southern exposure it benefits to the full from the power of the sun and the warmth of the sea. Mild winters and warm summers promote the growth of luxuriant southern vegetation. During winter and spring many visitors seek relaxation in the resorts, to which even larger numbers come in summer for sea-bathing.

★Riviera di Levante

The Italian Riviera is divided by the Gulf of Genoa into two parts. To the east is the Riviera di Levante (from Genoa to La Spezia) with a mild but somewhat variable climate and large areas of forest, the south-eastern part of which, beyond Sestri Levante, still preserves its original character. The towns and villages have narrow streets and tall houses huddled on the narrow coastal plains, and side valleys. In this section there are relatively few luxury hotels outside the main centres.

To the west of the Gulf of Genoa is the Riviera di Ponente (From Genoa to Ventimiglia), with a more equable climate than the Riviera di Levante. The coastal plain is wider, accommodating many large resorts with numerous first-class hotels and (for the most part) excellent beaches.

★Riviera di Ponente

The western part of the Riviera di Ponente, between Alassio and the French frontier, is known as the Riviera dei Fiori on account of its large-scale flower-growing industry.

Riviera dei Fiori

Along the Riviera di Ponente (c. 165 km (102 mi.))

The road runs west from the station, past the Old Harbour, and comes to:

6 km (3³/₄ mi.): Cornigliano Ligure (10 m (33 ft)), a busy suburb of Genoa, with a new industrial area extending some 800 m into the sea on reclaimed land. Beyond the town a good road goes off on the left to Genoa's Cristoforo Colombo Airport. To the right, on a high conical hill, is the church of the Madonna del Gazzo (421 m(1389 ft)).

Cornigliano Ligure

5 km (3 mi.): Pegli (6 m (20 ft)), a popular resort for holidays and weekends throughout the year, with beautiful parks and villas. Near the station is the Villa Durazzo-Pallavicini (1837), with an archaeological museum (Museo Civico di Archeologia Ligure) and a park extending up the hillside, with various water features, grottoes, an underground lake and a medieval-style castle. In the Villa Doria, also near the station, is the Genoa Naval and Maritime Museum, with mementoes of Columbus.

Pegli

5 km (3 mi.): Voltri (5 m (17 ft)), Genoa's last industrial suburb, with the attractive large park of the Villa Galliera. At the upper end of the park is the pilgrimage church of the Madonna delle Grazie (fine views).

Voltri

Beyond Voltri the road leaves the extensive built-up area of Genoa.

7 km (4¹/₂ mi.): Arenzano (6 m (20 ft)), a charmingly situated resort (good beach) with an old castle and a beautiful park around the Villa La Torre. The road then runs inland past a promontory covered with woodland and macchia and returns to the coast.

Arenzano

12 km (7¹/₂ mi.): Varazze (5 m (17 ft); population 15,000), a summer and winter resort, prettily situated amidst orange-groves, with a beach 2 km (1¹/₄ mi.) long.

Varazze

4 km (2¹/₂ mi.): Celle Ligure (44 m (145 ft)), an attractive resort above which is a fine old pinewood.

Celle Ligure

4 km (2¹/₂ mi.): Albisola Marina (19 m (63 ft)), a popular resort with a beach of fine sand. 1 km (³/₄ mi.) north is the little town of Albisola Superiore, with the Villa Gavotti, formerly called the Villa delle Rovere, in which Pope Julius II (1503–13) was born.

Albisola Marina

Beyond Albisola Marina the road comes in another 3 km (2 mi.) to the town of Savona (10 m (33 ft); population 75,000), a provincial capital situated on the River Letimbro, with an important harbour (export of cars) and a variety of industry (large steel rolling-mill). On the harbour quay stands the Torre Pancaldo, named after the navigator of that name. In Via Paleocapa is the church of San Giovanni Battista (16th and 18th c.), with paintings by Savonese artists of the 17th and 18th c. A little way south the

Savona

Pinacoteca Civica houses pictures, sculpture and majolica. Close by is the cathedral (1604; façade 1886) with a fine painting "The Ascension" by Ludovico Brea (c. 1500).

Vado Ligure

6 km (4 mi.): Vado Ligure (12 m (40 ft); population 9000), an industrial town at the junction of the old Roman Via Aurelia with the beginning of the Via Iulia Augusta. The SS1 (Via Aurelia) skirts Capo Vado (lighthouse; fine view back towards Savona), an attractive stretch of road which for part of the way has been hewn out of the rock. Beyond the cape the rocky islet of Bergeggi, crowned by a Roman tower, can be seen on the left.

Noli

10 km (6 mi.): Noli (4 m (13 ft)), a charmingly situated little fishing town and seaside resort with a picturesque old town, remains of town walls, old towers, a castle and the late Romanesque church of San Paragorio (12th c.). It is the birthplace of Antonio da Noli (1415–62), who discovered the Cape Verde islands. Events and celebrations are held throughout the year.

Finale Ligure

Beyond Noli the road goes through a tunnel (114m (376 ft) long) under Capo Noli and continues along the high overhanging cliffs of the Malpasso to (9 km (5½ mi.)) Finale Ligure (3 m (10 ft); population 14,000), a prettily situated resort, with the Castelfranco (1342) above the town and the fine Baroque church of San Giovanni Battista. Near the station is an early Christian Capuchin church. 2 km (1½ mi.) north-west is the walled village of Finalborgo, with a beautiful Romanesque-Baroque parish church. In the monastery of St Catherina (15th c.) is an archaeological museum containing material discovered locally. Still farther north-west in Perti is Castel Gavone with a fine keep. In the vicinity are limestone caves. Beyond Finale the road cuts across the Caprazoppa promontory.

Pietra Ligure

In 6 km (3¾ mi.) we reach Pietra Ligure (3 m (10ft)), a resort (sandy beach) with an interesting church and a ruined castle on an isolated crag. On the

Piazza Vittorio Emanuele II in Finale Ligure

hillside are the buildings of the Pietranuova sanatorium (sun and sea-air cures).

4 km (2¹/₂ mi.): Loana (4 m (13 ft); population 13,000), a popular resort with a former Doria palace (1578), now the Town Hall. On the hillside is the former monastery of Monte Carmello. About 6 km (3³/₄ mi.) farther is the Grotta di Toirano (tour with guide, 1¹/₂ hours). In the forecourt is the Museo Prehistorico (prehistoric history). View of the Ligurian Alps and Monte Carmo (1389 m (4560 ft)). **Loana**

Beyond Loana there is an attractive view, to the right, of the Ligurian Alps, with Monte Carmo (1389 m (4584 ft)).

10 km (6 mi.): Albenga (5 m (17 ft); population 22,000), with a picturesque old town centre, town walls and many towers which belonged to noble families. Other features of interest are the Romanesque cathedral (11–14th c.; lower part of façade 5th c.) with three Romanesque-Gothic naves; the small early Romanesque church of Santa Maria in Fontibus (13th c.); the Museo Ingauno e Battistero (5th c. baptistery, Liguria's most important early Christian work) and a Roman shipping museum. Near the Via Aurelia is the Ponte Lungo, a medieval bridge 147 m (482 ft) long over the former course of the River Centa. Beyond Albenga the rocky islet of Gallinara (90 m (297 ft)), with the ruins of a 6th c. Benedictine abbey, can be seen. **Albenga**

7 km (4¹/₂ mi.): Alassio (5 m 17 ft); population 14,000), a large and very popular resort with a beach of fine sand more than 3 km (2 mi.) long. On the seafront promenade stands an old watch-tower. Above stands the church of Santa Croce (11th and 12th c.). **Alassio**

The road continues along the precipitous coast, high above the sea.

6 km (4 mi.): Capo Mele (lighthouse), with a fine view of Alassio to the rear. Then on through Marina di Andora and round Capo Cervo. **Capo Mele**

7 km (4¹/₂ mi.): Cervo (66 m (218 ft)), a picturesquely situated hillside village. The road then passes through the resort of San Bartolomeo al Mare (26 m (86 ft)). **Cervo**

3 km (2 mi.): Diano Marina (4 m (13 ft). 2 km (1¹/₄ mi.) north-west is the walled village of Diano Castello (135 m (446 ft)). **Diano Castello**

Beyond Diano Marina the road winds its way gently uphill to Capo Berta, from which there is a magnificent view to the rear, extending as far as Capo Mele.

6 km (3³/₄ mi.): Imperia (10 m(33 ft); population 42,000), a provincial capital, comprising the districts of Oneglia (to east) and Porto Maurizio (to west), separated by the broad stony bed of the River Impero. Porto Maurizio is picturesquely situated on the slopes of a promontory with the imposing cathedral of San Maurizio (1781–1832).
The naval museum (Museo Navale Internazionale del Ponente Ligure) and the municipal picture gallery (Pinacoteca Civica) are worth a visit. **Imperia**

18 km (11 miles: Arma di Taggia (10 m (33 ft)), a resort with a beautiful beach, situated at the mouth of the River Argentina, or Fiumara di Taggia. 3 km (2 mi.) up the valley is the picturesque little town of Taggia (39 m (129 ft), with old patrician houses. In the church of the Dominican convent are pictures of the early Ligurian school. **Arma di Taggia**

8 km (5 mi.): San Remo. See entry. San Remo

6 km (3³/₄ mi.): Ospedaletti (30 m (99 ft), a popular resort, with an attractive Casino and a beautiful palm-shaded avenue, the Corso Regina Margherita. **Ospedaletti**

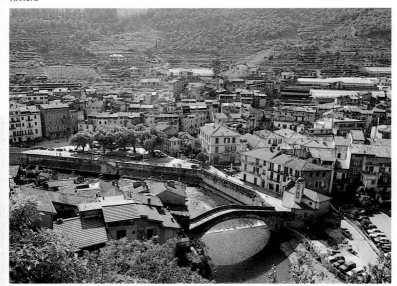

View from Dolceacqua castle

Beyond Ospedaletti the road continues along the steep and rocky coast, through beautiful scenery. To the left by the shore, is a fine park (private property). At the mouth of the Val del Sasso, are the Vallone Gardens, laid out by a German gardener named Ludwig Winter (d. 1912), also private property and not open to the public.

Bordighera

6 km (3¾ mi.): Bordighera. See entry.

Albintimilium

Farther on, shortly before Ventimiglia, is the entrance (on the right) to the remains of the Roman town of Albintimilium, with a theatre (2nd c. AD).

Ventimiglia

5 km (3 mi.): Ventimiglia (9 m (30 ft); population 27,000), the frontier town, situated at the mouth of the River Roia, with an important flower market. In the new town, to the east of the river, are the Town Hall and the palm-shaded Giardino Pubblico; in the picturesque walled old town, on the hill west of the river, are the Romanesque cathedral, with an adjoining baptistery, and the 11th c. church of San Michele (columns with Roman inscriptions). From the Piazzale del Capo, a little way south of the cathedral, there are magnificent views, extending westwards as far as Cap Ferrat.

From Ventimiglia there is a rewarding trip to the Giardino Hanbury with a variety of rare plants (about 6 km (3¾ mi.) west in Mortola Inferiore), laid out by the Englishman Thomas Hanbury.

A kilometre (¾ mi.) farther west, near the French frontier, are the Balzi Rossi, caves hewn from rock, which were inhabited in prehistoric times (skeletons, etc. in the museum near the Barma Grande).

From Ventimiglia an attractive excursion can be made up the beautiful Nervia valley to the little town of Dolceacqua (50 m (165 ft)), picturesquely situated on a hillside, with an old bridge 10 m (33 ft) high, borne on pointed arches, and a ruined castle which was the ancestral home of the Doria family of Genoa. 4 km (2½ mi.) farther on is the village of Isolabona (ruined castle), and 2 km (1¼ mi.) beyond this in a side valley is the hill village of Apricale, clinging picturesquely to a steep hillside. From here it is another 8 km (5 mi.) to Baiardo (see San Remo, Surroundings).

Inland from the Riviera Ponente, with its crowds of summer visitors, are many quiet little villages well off the beaten tourist track which are well worth visiting not only for the beauty of their setting, on hilltops or precipitous slopes, but also for the picture they give of typical Italian hill settlements. Characteristic examples of such villages can be seen on the road from San Remo via Ceriana to Baiardo (25 km (16 mi.)) or on the road from Ventimiglia via Dolceacqua to Apricale (13 km (8 mi.). It is also possible to take in these places on the way from San Remo to Ventimiglia (additional distance 29 km (18 mi.).

Inland

Along the Riviera di Levante (c. 115 km (71 mi.))

Leave Genoa by way of Corso G. Marconi and then travel east along Corso Italia.

8 km (5 mi.): Quinto al Mare (20 m (66 ft)) is a suburb of Genoa surrounded by orange-groves and palms, with fine villas and the Aquarium der Lega Navale Italiana (underwater flora and fauna of Liguria). To the north-east is Monte Moro (fort; 412 m (1352 ft)) with wonderful views, especially early in the day.

Quinto al Mare

2 km (1¼ mi.): Nervi (27 m (89 ft)), the oldest winter resort (rocky beach) on the Riviera di Levante, in a sheltered situation amid olive-, orange- and lemon-groves, with a seafront promenade 1.8 km (1 mi.) long hewn from the rock. On the east side of the Viale delle Palme lies the Parco Municipale, with many exotic plants and the Galleria d'Arte Moderna; open Tue.–Sun. To the east, in a beautiful park in Sant'Ilario Basso, is the Museo di Ville Luxoro, with applied art, pictures and furniture. Open Tue.–Sat.

Nervi

11 km (7 mi.) beyond Nervi is Recco (5 m (17 ft); population 11,000), from which there is an attractive detour to Uscio (361 m (1191 ft)), 11 km (7 mi.) north. From Uscio it is possible to return to Genoa-Apparizione on a beautiful panoramic road (20 km (12 mi.).

Recco

4 km (2½ mi.): Ruta (290 m (957 ft)), a straggling villa suburb on the saddle between the coastal hills and the Portofino promontory, projecting squarely into the sea from some 4–5 km (2½–3 mi.), with scenery which is among the finest on the Riviera.

Ruta

7 km (4½ mi.): Rapallo. See entry.

Rapallo

6 km (3¾ mi.): Zoagli (30 m (99 ft)), with many villas on the slopes of the hillside, panoramic road to Sant'Ambrogio (3 km (2 miles)).

Zoagli

6 km (3¾ mi.): Chiavari (3 m (10 ft); population 30,000), a seaside resort situated in a fertile plain at the mouth of the Entella. Near the station, at the end of a beautiful avenue of palms, stands the cathedral (1613; pillared portico added 1841). Morning markets are held on the Piazza Mazzini in the town centre, dominated by the Palace of Justice (1886); to the rear is the old castellated citadel tower (1537).

Chiavari

2 km (1¼ mi.): Lavagna (5 m (17 ft); population 13,000), a resort with a large yacht harbour (1976).

Lavagna

Beyond Lavagna the road runs close to the shore.

6 km (3¾ mi.): Sestri Levante (4 m (13 ft); population 20,000), a seaside and winter resort in a picturesque setting on the saddle of the Isola promont–

Sestri Levante

Sestri Levante with Monte di Portofino and Chiavari

ory (70 m (231 ft)), between two small bays. From the beautiful seafront promenade in the flat bay to the west there are extensive views of the Gulf of Rapallo, also called Golfo Tigullio. From the square beside the harbour, at the south end of the bay, there is a road to the tip of the promontory, which is crowned by the Castelli Gualino, imitations of medieval castles. There is also a pleasant walk (1 hour) south-east to the Telegrafo, a signal station on the southern spur of the pine-clad Monte Castello (265 m (875 ft); views).

Beyond Sestri Levante the Via Aurelia runs inland bypassing a stretch of rocky coast more than 60 km (37 mi.) long, some of the places on which – such as the picturesque fishing villages of the Cinqueterre – can be reached only by the railway, running through tunnels for much of its course.

Passo del Bracco — 18 km (11 mi.): Passo del Bracco (615 m (2030 ft)). On an isolated crag by the roadside is the small aerial of the Savona television station (view).

La Baracca — 2 km (1¼ mi.): La Baracca (589 m (1944 ft)).

Levanto — From La Baracca a scenic road (SS332) winds its way down (15 km (9 mi.) south), mostly through pine forests, to the little town, frequented by visitors both in summer and in winter, of Levanto (11 m (36 ft)), with remains of its medieval town walls and castle. The former oratorium near the church of Sant'Andrea now houses a local museum (Museo Permanente della Cultura Materiale). The Torre dell'Orologio (clock-tower) is the only one of the original seven towers of the medieval town-wall to have survived.

Passo della Foce — 35 km (22 mi.): Passo della Foce (241 m (795 ft)), with views of the bay of La Spezia and the Apulian Alps.

La Spezia — 6km/3¾ miles: La Spezia (see entry).

Rome

The principal gates are the Porta del Popolo, the Porta Pinciana, the Porta Salaria and the Porta Pia on the north; the Porta San Lorenzo and the Porta Maggiore on the east; the Porta San Giovanni, the Porta San Sebastiano and the Porta San Paolo on the south; and the Porta San Pancrazio on the west.

Cultural centre

Already known in ancient times as the Eternal City (Roma aeterna), Rome was for a millennium and a half the cultural centre of Europe and the scene of great historical events. It was the first city of world stature, capital of the Roman Empire, and thereafter the home of the Popes with their world-wide spiritual authority. In the heyday of the Roman Empire, at the beginning of the 2nd c. AD, the city had a population of over a million. Rome was the birthplace of the Roman Catholic Church, one of the most powerful single religious communities in the history of the world, and it was here that about AD 1200 Innocent III established a secular Papal state which subsisted until 1870 and was succeeded in 1929 by the new sovereign state of the Vatican City. Present-day Rome is a creation of its long past, and its attraction and interest to visitors are enhanced by an awareness of that past.

After the devastation suffered by Rome during the period of the Great Migrations and its vicissitudes in subsequent centuries, the population in the 14th c. was barely 20,000 and at the beginning of the 16th c. only 55,000. In 1832 it was 148,000 and in 1870 at the end of Papal rule it was 221,000. By 1921 it had risen to 660,000. After the First World War, and still more after the Second World War, the population began to grow on a massive scale, bringing it to its present figure of nearly 3 million.

History

Ancient city

The ancient city was traditionally founded on April 21st 753 BC; but there must have been a Latin settlement of some consequence before then on this convenient site near the mouth of the Tiber. The oldest part of the town consisted of the Palatine and Quirinal hills and between them the Forum at the foot of the Capitol.

After the destruction of the town by the Gauls (c. 387 BC) the development began which was to make Rome capital of the Empire – a development reflected in its architecture. Important temples and secular buildings were built; in 312 the first aqueduct and the first paved road, the Via Appia, were constructed, and the characteristic Roman technique of building vaulted structures of rubble bound with mortar was evolved. The city developed still further in the time of Augustus (27 BC–AD 14), who "found Rome of brick and left it of marble" and extended the built-up area on to the Campus Martius, and again after the great fire in the time of Nero (54–68) which destroyed most of Rome. The zenith of its development was reached in the 2nd c. AD.

Medieval Rome

The development of medieval Rome was shaped by Christianity, which came to Rome in the mid 1st c. and thereafter, in spite of successive persecutions, particularly during the 3rd c. and in 303 during the reign of Diocletion (the final wave of persecution), demonstrated its ability to withstand the declining authority of paganism. In 313 Constantine the Great granted freedom of religious exercise. The old religion received a final blow in 408, when the Emperor Honorius decreed the confiscation of all its property. The old temples were destroyed and their columns and other materials used in the building of Christian churches (basilicas); later whole temples were converted for use as churches. The number of churches increased rapidly. There were 25 parish churches (titoli) and five patriarchal churches. The patriarchal churches – of which the Pope himself was priest and to which all the faithful belonged – were San Giovanni in Laterano, San Pietro in Vaticano, San Paolo fuori le Mura, San Lorenzo fuori le Mura and Sant Maria Maggiore. In addition to these five churches there were two others which enjoyed particular veneration, Santa Croce in Gerusalemme and San Sebastiano, above the catacombs on the Via Appia. These were the Seven Churches of Rome, visited by pilgrims from all over the Western world down to the present day.

In political terms, however, Rome's importance declined. Constantine's decision in 330 to transfer the Imperial residence to Byzantium and Milan reduced Rome to the status of a provincial town. The Campagna reverted to wasteland, and malaria spread inland from the coastal regions. The stormy years of the Great Migrations, in particular the sack of Rome by Alaric's Goths and again in 455 by Gaiseric's Vandals, brought a further decline. Only the tradition of the great battles and victories of the Christian faith, which were indissolubly linked with Rome, preserved the city from extinction.

The conversion of ancient Rome into Christian Rome made the Papacy the supreme spiritual power in the West. Particularly powerful representatives of Papal authority were popes Leo the Great (440–61) and Gregory the Great (590–604). The secular power of the popes and their authority over Rome began to develop in the 8th c., when the foundations of the States of the Church were laid by the grant of territory to the Pope by the Lombard king Luitprand (727) and the Frankish king Pipin (755). On Christmas Day 800 Leo III (795–816) crowned Charlemagne Emperor and thus re-established the secular empire which was to preserve for a millennium at least the name of the old Roman Empire. *Papacy*

In subsequent centuries Rome was ravaged by enemy attacks, the struggle between the Empire and the Papacy and strife between the great noble families. It suffered a further blow with the exile of the popes to Avignon (1309–77), during which Cola di Rienzo tried to establish a republic on the ancient Roman model (1347). The population now fell to barely 20,000.

The Renaissance, breathing fresh life into learning and art throughout Italy, established itself at the Papal court and brought a new flowering to Rome. Tuscan architects, sculptors and painters had already been summoned to Rome in considerable numbers during the 15th c., but it was in the following century that the great Renaissance popes Julius II (1503–13) and Leo X (1513–21) made the city the real centre of the High Renaissance. From here Bramante (1444–1514), Michelangelo (1474–1564) and Raphael (1483–1520) set the artistic pattern of the whole 16th c. (Cinquecento). Leonardo da Vinci (1452–1519) also worked in Rome in 1513–15. Among noted architects of this period were Baldassare Peruzzi (1481–1536) and Antonio da Sangallo the Younger (1483–1546). *Renaissance*

After the occupation and sacking of Rome by Charles V's forces in 1527 ("Sacco di Roma"), which drove away almost all the city's artists, recovery was slow. In 1546 Michelangelo built the Palazzo Farnese, the plan of which was to have enormous influence on the palaces of the Baroque period. The reign of Pope Sixtus V (1585–90), for whom Domenico Fontana designed a whole series of fine buildings, saw the beginning of the vigorous and powerful Baroque style of the 17th c. The architects of this period – in particular the Neapolitan Lorenzo Bernini (1598–1680), his like-minded contemporary Francesco Borromini (1599–1667), Carlo Maderna (1556–1629) and Carlo Rainaldi (1611–91) – created the magnificent churches and palaces, with their impressive command of space and picturesque effect, which still largely determine the architectural character of the older parts of Rome. In the field of painting Caravaggio (c. 1573–1610), the most gifted artist of the Early Baroque, was the leader of the naturalistic school; the chief representatives of the opposite trend, the "Eclectics" of Bologna, were Annibale Carracci (1560–1609) and his pupils Guido Reni (1575–1642), Domenichino (1581–1641) and Guercino (1591–1666). In the following century Antonio Canova (1757–1822) produced the first works of monumental sculpture in Neo-Classical style. *Early Baroque*

In the 18th and 19th centuries the economic importance and artistic achievement of Rome both declined. Nevertheless the city continued to *18th and 19th centuries* attract increasing numbers of artists and connoisseurs from many lands in quest of the Classical art of antiquity, particularly after the publication of Johann Joachim Winckelmann's history of Greek art, written in Rome about 1760. A revival of the city's life and art came only with its incorporation in the new kingdom of Italy in 1870, which gave Rome the status of a national capital and royal residence. This was the period of the "Third Rome" ("Terza Roma"). New and imposing public buildings were erected, usually aiming at a kind of ancient Roman monumentality (Banca d'Italia, Ministry of Finance, Palace of Justice, National Monument) but employing overcharged Renaissance and Baroque forms. It was only in the 20th c. that this style gave place to simpler and more straightforward structures.

20th century

The 20th century created the "Fourth Rome" ("Quarta Roma"). A development plan initiated in 1931 provided for the opening up of overcrowded slum areas, the disengagement and restoration of ancient buildings (the Theatre of Marcellus, Trajan's Market and Trajan's Column, the Imperial Fora and the Arch of Constantine, the Mausoleum of Augustus, Castle Sant'Angelo, etc.), the construction of large new avenues (Via dei Fori Imperiali, Corso del Rinascimento, Via Regina Elena, the Via della Conciliazione between the Ponte Sant'Angelo and St Peter's Square, etc.) and the creation of public parks and gardens and well-planned modern suburbs. Notable among recent developments are the University City, the Air Ministry building, the Via del Mare to Lido di Ostia, the new ring road, the EUR exhibition area, the Termini Station and the new underground railway system (Metropolitana). In 1960 Rome was host to the 17th Olympic Games, for which the Olympic Village, a number of major sporting facilities and new link roads (including the Strada Olimpia from the EUR to the Foro Italico) were constructed. In consequence of chronic financial difficulties the 1965 development plan has been only very partially carried out, and many buildings are still awaiting the urgent renovation they require.

In March 1957 the treaties establishing the European Economic Community and the European Coal and Steel Community (the Rome treaties) were signed in Rome. In 1968 economic leaders and experts from more than 30 countries formed the "Club of Rome". Archbishop Karol Woityla from Krakau was crowned Pope (John Paul II) in 1978; he was severely wounded in an assassination attempt in 1981. During the football World Cup held in Italy in 1990 many buildings in Rome were restored and new building projects undertaken. In 1993 there were spectacular bomb attacks in Rome and other cities, causing deaths and damage to many buildings including the Lateran basilica and the church of San Giorgio.

Piazza Venezia

The busiest traffic intersection in Rome is the Piazza Venezia, at the south end of the Via del Corso.

Palazzo Venezia

Museo di Palazzo Venezia

On the west side of the square is the Palazzo Venezia, originally a fortress-like building erected about 1455, from 1564 the Venetian and from 1797 the Austro-Hungarian embassy to the Vatican, from 1926 to 1943 Mussolini's official residence and now a museum. It has a fine arcade (unfinished) in the inner courtyard. In the east wing the Museo di Palazzo Venezia, houses tapestries, pictures, busts, applied art, printing, porcelain and glass of various centuries, nations and cultures.

★National Monument to Victor Emmanuel II

On the south side of the Piazza Venezia stands the huge National Monument to Victor Emmanuel II, in white Brescia marble, begun in 1885 to the

National Monument to Victor Emmanuel II, known disrespectfully as the "Rome Dentures"

design of Count Giuseppe Sacconi as a symbol of the new y united Italy and inaugurated in 1911. This is the largest and most magnificent monument in Italy, 70 m (231 ft) high. At the top of several flights of steps is the Altare della Patria, the Tomb of the Unknown Soldier, and above this are an equestrian statue of Victor Emmanuel II in gilded bronze, 12 m (40 ft) high, and a massive colonnade (panoramic view from the top).

In the eastern part of the monument are the Museo Centra e del Risorgimento and the Museo Sacrario delle Bandiere e Cimeli della Marina Militare (Flag Museum).

Museums

Capitol

Behind the National Monument, to the south, rises the Capitol (Italian Campidoglio or Monte Capitolino), the smallest but historically the most important of Rome's hills. On the north side of the hill (50 m (165 ft)), approached by a long flight of steps, is the church of Santa Maria in Aracoeli ("on the Altar of Heaven"), on the site of the Capitoline Temple of Juno. It contains 22 ancient columns and has a gilded 16th c ceiling; in the north aisle is a carved wooden image of the Infant Christ (the "Santo Bambino"), which is the subject of particular veneration at Christmas.

Santa Maria in Aracoeli

The Capitoline Museum (Museo Capitolino), adjoining the church on the south, contains the municipal collection of ancient sculpture. Particularly notable items are the "Dying Gaul" (in the Sala del Galata Morente on the upper floor), a copy of a Greek bronze statue, and (in a side room of the Galleria) the Capitoline Venus, a variant of the Cnidian Aphrodite of Praxiteles.

Museo Capitolino

Piazza del Campidoglio

The Capitoline Museum forms the north side of the Piazza del Campidoglio, which is approached from the west by a staircase of shallow steps designed by Michelangelo, and by the winding Via delle Tre Pile. The square itself, also designed by Michelangelo and constructed from 1547 onwards, is one of the most finely conceived of Renaissance squares. Here from 1538 until 1981 stood the equestrian statue of the Emperor Marcus Aurelius; restoration of the statue was completed in 1990. The original is now housed in the Capitoline Museum and is to remain there; a copy now stands in front of the Town Hall but its colouring differs somewhat from the greenish-gold of the original.

Palazzo dei Senatori

On the south-east side of the square is the Palazzo dei Senatori, the official residence of the Mayor and the City Council of Rome, with a façade of 1598. Designed by Michelangelo (1541–54) it stands on the site of the Roman Tabularium (78 BC), which was built to house the state archives of Rome (*tabula* = document).

Palazzo dei Conservatori

On the south-west side of the Capitol square, partly built on the substructures (of dressed tufa blocks) of the Temple of Jupiter, is the Palazzo dei Conservatori (1568), originally the seat of the city council, which houses a collection of major importance. Notable items are the "Boy with a Thorn" ("Il Spinario", 1st c. BC), in the Sala dei Trionfi di Mario, and the "Capitoline She-Wolf", an Etruscan work of the 5th c. BC (in the adjoining Sala della Lupa). On the 2nd floor the Pinacoteca Capitolina has a fine collection of pictures, including works by Titian, Tintoretto, Caravaggio, Lorenzo Lotto and Veronese.

Museo Nuovo

The adjoining Palazzo Caffarelli houses the Museo Nuovo, with Greek sculpture of the 5th c. BC, sarcophagi, urns, etc.

Tarpeian Rock

At the south-west corner of the Palazzo dei Conservatori is the Tarpeian Rock (Rupe Tarpea), from which in Roman times condemned prisoners were hurled to their death.

Ancient Rome

★★Forum Romanum

From the Via del Campidoglio, between the Palazzo dei Conservatori and the Palazzo Senatorio, there is a magnificent view of the remains of the Forum Romanum (Foro Romano) and the massive brick walls of the Palatine, crowned by pines and holm-oaks, with the Arch of Titus and the Colosseum to the rear.

In due course the whole of this area is to be turned into an "archaeological park".

The area of low ground, south-east of the Capitol, between the Palatine and the Esquiline, was drained in the 6th c. BC by the construction of the Cloaca Maxima, with its outlet into the Tiber, and thereafter was occupied by markets and other trading activities and became the meeting-place of popular assemblies and courts of law. Caesar set in train a large-scale extension of the Forum, and his plans were carried through by Augustus. Under Augustus and his successors the old buildings of the Republican period were restored and rebuilt and the Forum was embellished with splendid new buildings, triumphal arches, columns and statues, resplendent in rare marbles and gilded bronze.

The destruction of the Forum began in the 6th c. Columns and other architectural elements were torn out of the ancient buildings and used in the construction of churches or other new buildings, and the marble that

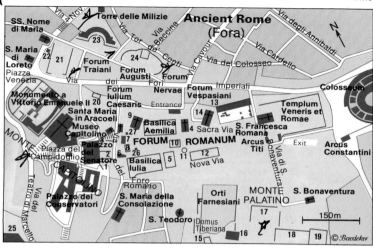

Ancient Rome (Fora)

SS. Nome di Maria
Torre delle Milizie
Via A. Nov.
Via Tor de' Conti
Via de' Baccina
Via Cavour
Via Cardello
Via del Colosseo
Via degli Annibaldi
S. Maria di Loreto
Piazza Venezia
23
22 21
Forum Traiani
24
Forum Augusti
Via dei Fori
Forum Nervae
Forum Imperiali
Colosseum
Monumento a Vittorio Emanuele II
20
Forum Iulium
Caesaris
Entrance
Forum Vespasiani
13
Templum Veneris et Romae
Santa Maria in Aracoeli
9
Basilica Aemilia
14
4 Sacra Via
S. Francesca Romana
Museo Capitolino
3
27
7
FORUM
10 ROMANUM
Arcus Titi
Exit
Arcus Constantini
MONTE CAPITOLINO
Palazzo del Senatore
Piazza del Campidoglio
2
6
1
Basilica Iulia
5
11
12
Nova Via
Via di S. Bonaventura
Via del Teatro di Marcello
Palazzo dei Conservatori
Foro Romano
S. Maria della Consolazione
Orti Farnesiani
MONTE PALATINO
S. Bonaventura
S. Teodoro
Domus Tiberiana
17
150m
25
15
16
18 19
© Baedeker

1 Portico of the Twelve Gods (Porticus Deorum Consentium)
2 Temple of Vespasian (Templum Vespasiani)
3 Temple of Concordia (Templum Concordiae)
4 Temple of Faustina (Templum Divae Faustinae et Divi Antonini)
5 Temple of Castor and Pollux (Templum Dioscurorum)
6 Temple of Saturn (Templum Saturni)
7 Arch of Septimus Severus (Arcus Septimii Severi)
8 Rostra (orator's platform)
9 Curia Julia (Church of Sant'Andriano)

10 Temple of Caesar (Templum Divi Julii)
11 Temple of Vesta (Aedes Vestae)
12 House of Vestal Virgins (Atrium Vestae)
13 Basilica of Maxentius or of Constantine (Basilica Maxentii/Constantini)
14 Church of Santi Cosma e Damiano
15 Temple of Cybele (Domus Cybelae)
16 House of Livia (Domus Liviae)
17 Palace of Flavians (Domus Flaviorum)

18 Palace of Augustus (Domus Augustiana)
19 Stadium (Hippodromus)
20 Temple of Venus Genetrix (Templum Veneris Genetricis)
21 Basilica Ulpia
22 Trajan's Column (Columna Traini)
23 Trajan's Market (Mercati Traiani)
24 Temple of Mars Ultor (Templum Martis Ultoris)
25 Theatre of Marcellus (Theatrum Marcelli)
26 Column of Phocas
27 Lapis Niger

still remained was burned to produce lime. The systematic clearance of the Forum and Palatine began only in 1871.

Below the Tabularium, separated from the rest of the Forum excavations by the modern Via del Foro, are the remains of three ancient shrines – the Portico of the Twelve Gods, dating from the last days of the pagan faith (restored as late as AD 367); the Temple of Vespasian (AD 81), of which three columns survive; and the Temple of Concordia, originally built in 366 BC and splendidly restored by Tiberius.

Temple of Vespasian

Beyond the Via del Foro is the enclosed area containing the main part of the Forum (entrance from the Via dei Fori Imperiali, on the north side). Immediately left of the entrance is the Temple of Faustina (AD 141), of which the portico and part of the cella survive; it is now the church of San Lorenzo in Miranda. To the right of the entrance are the remains of the Basilica Aemilia, a portico built in 179 BC to provide additional accommodation for traders.

★Temple of Faustina

Opposite this, on the far side of the Sacra Via, the oldest street in Rome, which climbed up to the Capitol as the Clivus Capitolinus, stands the

★Temple of Castor and Pollux

385

Basilica Iulia originally built by Julius Caesar in 46 BC and to the east of this the Temple of Castor and Pollux with three fine Corinthian columns of Greek marble dating from the Augustan period which are one of the most characteristic landmarks of Rome. North-west of the Basilica Iulia are the eight granite columns of the portico of the Temple of Saturn, which contained the city treasury (Aerarium publicum), and the imposing marble Arch of Septimius Severus.

★ Arch of
Septimius Severus

The marble triumphal Arch of Septimius Severus (23 m (76 ft) high, 25 m (82 ft) wide), was erected in AD 203 in honour of the victories over the Parthians won by the emperor and his sons Caracalla and Geta.

Rostra

To the left of the Arch of Septimius Severus are the Rostra, the orators' tribune erected in the time of Augustus and named after the ships' prows (rostra) which stood here and bounded the Forum proper, paved with limestone slabs. In front of the Rostra, on a high brick pedestal, we find the Column of Phocas, commemorating the emperor of that name, a centurion who had himself crowned emperor in Constantinople about 600. To the right of the Rostra, under a protective roof, is the Lapis Niger, a piece of black marble on a square pillar bearing a mutilated inscription in an early form of Latin (4th c. BC?), which was believed in Cicero's time to be the tomb of Romulus.

Curia Iulia

Beyond it, to the north, is the Curia Iulia or Senate House, originally built by Julius Caesar and restored about AD 303. In this are temporarily displayed two marble slabs, the Anaglypha Traiani, with fine reliefs.

Temple of Vesta

At the north-east corner of the Temple of Castor and Pollux is the substructure of the Temple of Caesar, erected by Augustus in 29 BC on the spot on which Caesar's body was burned in 44 BC after his murder. To the south of this can be seen one of the most sacred shrines of ancient Rome, the Temple of Vesta, dedicated to the virgin goddess of the domestic hearth. Beyond it is the Atrium Vestae, the house of the vestal virgins, with a rectangular courtyard containing three cisterns for storing rain-water (since the vestal virgins were forbidden to use water from the ordinary piped supply).

To the east of this are the three massive arches of the Basilica of Maxentius (access from the Via dei Fori Imperiali; see below), with the church of Santi Cosma e Damiano to the left.

★ Arch of Titus

Adjoining the Basilica of Maxentius to the south-east is the site of the Temple of Venus and Rome, erected by the Emperor Hadrian in AD 135, which is now occupied by the church of Santa Francesca Romana. A little way south stands the Arch of Titus (Arco di Tito), erected to commemorate the capture of Jerusalem (AD 70), with fine reliefs under the arch (triumphal procession with Jewish prisoners, the table with the show-bread, the seven-branched candlestick and trumpets from the temples of Jerusalem).

Palatine Hill

Above the south side of the Forum rises the Palatine Hill (Monte Palatino, 51 m (168 ft), the site of the earliest settlement ("Roma Quadrata"). In late antiquity visitors to the Palatine were shown the hut occupied by Romulus and the cave of the she-wolf which suckled Romulus and Remus. Augustus, who was born on the Palatine, built on the hill the great imperial palace, the Palatium, which gave its name to all later palaces; successive emperors enlarged and embellished the structures on the hill. From the 4th c. the Palatine decayed along with the rest of Rome, and by the 10th c. the ruins of the Imperial palaces gave place to gardens, convents and defensive towers. Systematic excavation began in 1871.

Under the Farnese Gardens (Orti Farnesiani), which occupy the highest part of the Palatine, to the north-west, are the remains of the Palace of Tiberius. The terraces on the north-west side afford magnificent views of the Forum, the Colosseum, the Capitol and the city from the Lateran to the Janiculum. At the other end of the gardens a flight of steps leads down to the brick substructures of the Temple of Cybele (191 BC) and the House of Livia (mother of Tiberius and later wife of Augustus), which contains wall paintings.

Orti Farnesiani

To the east of the Farnese Gardens is the site of the Palace of the Flavians, which dates from the time of Domitian, the greatest builder on the Palatine (c. AD 92), with the throne room in which the emperor gave audiences, the basilica in which he dispensed justice and (beyond a square garden) a large dining-room. To the south are the substructures of the Palace of Augustus and the so-called Stadium, a garden in the shape of a racecourse.

Palace of the Flavians

From the north-east corner of the Stadium steps lead up to the ruins of the Palace of Severus and the Belvedere, a terrace affording magnificent views. From here can be seen the whole area of the Circus Maximus, Rome's "largest circus", with seating for 185,000 spectators. Along its south side runs the Via del Circo Massimo.

Via dei Fori Imperiali

From the Piazza Venezia the Via dei Fori Imperiali, flanked by gardens, runs past the Imperial Fora to the Colosseum. The massive growth of the city in late Republican and Imperial times made it necessary to erect new buildings to house markets and courts, and the first of a series of new forums was built by Julius Caesar. He was followed by Augustus and his successors Trajan, Nero and Vespasian, each of whom created a new forum in an area previously occupied by a maze of narrow streets and embellished it with a temple as the central feature, colonnades, law courts and a profusion of monuments and works of art. From 1925 onwards the remains were systematically cleared (good views from outside).

At the near end of the Via dei Fori Imperiali, on the right, is the Foro di Cesare (Caesar's Forum), with its colonnade and the high substructure of the Temple of Venus Genetrix (the mythical mother of the Iulians), completed only in AD 113 by Trajan, of which three columns have survived.

Caesar's Forum

To the north is the Foro di Traiano (Trajan's Forum; entrance from Trajan's Market), built AD 107–118, the largest and most magnificent of the Imperial Fora, made up of four elements – the unexcavated Forum proper, in front of the massive semicircle of Trajan's Market, the partly excavated Basilica Ulpia, an unexcavated temple and two libraries of which nothing is now left. Here too stands the 38 m (125 ft) high Trajan's Column (Colonna Traiana), cleaned and restored in the 1980s, which originally held, concealed in the base, a golden urn containing the emperor's ashes. Around the column runs a spiral band of carvings 200 m (656 ft) long with scenes from Trajan's Dacian Wars (AD 101–106). The column, formerly crowned by a statue of Trajan, now bears a figure of the Apostle Peter set up in 1587. Inside there is a spiral staircase of 185 steps.

★Trajan's Forum

★Trajan's Column

On the north-east side of Trajan's Forum is Trajan's Market (Mercati Traianei; excavated 1926–30), a two-storeyed semicircular structure in brick, 60 m (197 ft) long. Between this and an inner semicircle faced with marble lay a paved street flanked by shops, and above this, to the rear, rose a range of multi-storeyed buildings.

★Trajan's Market

Immediately south-east of Trajan's Forum is the Foro di Augusto (Forum of Augustus), with the Temple of Mars Ultor (Avenging Mars), built by Augustus in fulfilment of a vow made at the battle of Philippi (42 BC) in which he defeated the army of Caesar's murderers.

Forum of Augustus

Trajan's Market

Nerva's Forum	Farther south-east is the Foro di Nerva (Nerva's Forum), which preserves two fine Corinthian columns and a section of the entablature on its south-east side. Adjoining Nerva's Forum is the unexcavated Forum Vespasiani (Vespasian's Forum), which had a Temple of Peace erected after the destruction of Jerusalem. Here too, on the south side of the Via dei Fori Imperiali, is the entrance to the church of Santi Cosma e Damiano, founded in the 6th c. on a site in the Forum Romanum. On the triumphal arch in the upper church and in the apse are 6th c. mosaics which are perhaps the finest in Rome. In a room to the right of the entrance is a gigantic Neapolitan crib, an 18th c. work.
★Basilica of Maxentius	Farther along the Via dei Fori Imperiali, on the right, we come to the entrance to the massive Basilica of Maxentius, which was enlarged by his conqueror Constantine and is therefore also known as the Basilica of Constantine. Its massive barrel vaulting served as a model for many later architects. In summer concerts are given in the basilica.
Santa Francesca Romana	At the south-east corner of the basilica of Maxentius, built partly on the site of the Temple of Venus and Rome, is the church of Santa Francesca Romana (patron saint of motorists), originally built in the 10th c. but subsequently much altered, with a handsome Baroque façade (1615) and a richly appointed interior.

★★Colosseum

Near the south-east end of the Via dei Fori Imperiali and the Forum Romanum stands the Colosseum or Flavian Amphitheatre, one of the world's most celebrated buildings.

With its monumental proportions and severely disciplined structure the Colosseum has long been the symbol of the greatness of Rome. Originally

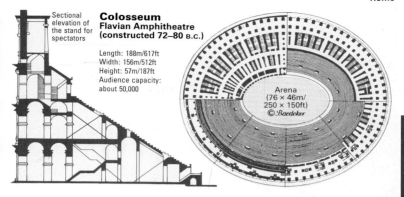

Sectional elevation of the stand for spectators

Colosseum
Flavian Amphitheatre
(constructed 72–80 B.C.)

Length: 188m/617ft
Width: 156m/512ft
Height: 57m/187ft
Audience capacity: about 50,000

Arena
(76 × 46m/
250 × 150ft)
© Baedeker

built by Vespasian (AD 72 onwards) with three storeys, it was heightened to four storeys by Titus and inaugurated in AD 80 with gladiatorial contests and other shows lasting 100 days and involving 1000 gladiators and 5000 animals. It is elliptical in plan, measuring 188 × 156 m (617 × 561 ft) and standing 57 m (187 ft) high. The exterior is constructed of travertine blocks; the interior also incorporates tufa and brick. The north-east part still preserves its original four storeys, the three lower storeys being in the form of arcades, the pillars of which have semi-columns of the Doric, Ionic and Corinthian orders, while the solid wall of the fourth storey has windows set between Corinthian pilasters.

There are four main entrances, each with a triple opening; those at the ends were reserved for the emperor, while those on the sides were used for the processional entry of the gladiators and other participants. The spectators (some 40,000–50,000) entered through the lower arcades, which were numbered, and found their way to their seats by the appropriate staircases. The seats in the lowest row (podium) were occupied by the emperor, senators and vestal virgins. The arena, measuring 76 × 46 m (249 × 151 ft), had extensive substructures accommodating hoists and other stage machinery, cages for wild beasts, etc. The bloody gladiatorial contests were abolished by the Emperor Honorius in 404; the fights with wild beasts continued until the time of the Gothic ruler Theodoric the Great.

During the Middle Ages some sections of the walls collapsed during earthquakes, and further damage was caused by the use of parts of the structure by Roman nobles as fortresses and by its later use as a quarry of building materials. Finally Pope Benedict XIV (1740–58) consecrated the remains to the Passion of Christ, in commemoration of the blood of the martyrs which had flowed in the Colosseum, and set up a bronze cross (re-erected in 1926). Restoration work on the Colosseum was started in 1992 and will last for several years.

South-west of the Colosseum stands the Arch of Constantine, a triumphal arch of white marble with a triple opening, erected by the Senate to commemorate Constantine's victory over Maxentius in the battle of the Milvian Bridge (AD 312). Rome's best preserved triumphal arch incorporates architectural elements and sculpture (now exposed to damage from air pollution) from earlier monuments.

★Arch of Constantine

Via di San Gregorio

From the Arch of Constantine an imposing avenue, the Via di San Gregorio (the ancient Via Triumphalis), runs south between the Caelian Hill and the

Santi Giovanni e Paolo

Colosseum or Flavian Amphitheatre

The arena of the Colosseum

Arch of Constantine

Palatine. 350 m along this street a side street branches off on the left to the church of Santi Giovanni e Paolo (originally founded *c.* 400 but several times rebuilt), with very early frescos.

Farther along Via di San Gregorio, also on the left, is the church of San Gregorio Magno, founded by Pope Gregory I in 575 in his family palace and completely rebuilt in the 17th and 18th c.

San Gregorio Magno

Via di San Gregorio joins the Piazza di Porta Capena, at the east end of the Circus Maximus. On the south side of the square stands the Axum Obelisk (3rd–4th c.), brought here from Ethiopia in 1937.

Piazza di Porta Capena

Beyond the obelisk, extending along Viale Aventino rises the massive FAO Building, erected in 1948 to house the Food and Agriculture Organisation, with the Lubin Memorial Library. In the south-west wing is part of the Ministry of Posts.

FAO Building

From the east corner of the FAO Building the Viale Guido Baccelli runs through the Parco di Porta Capena, which contains some ancient remains, to the Baths of Caracalla (Terme di Caracalla; Latin Thermae Antonianae; during the summer performances of opera), a gigantic bathing establishment (330 m (1083 ft) square, with an area of 10.9 ha (27 acres) built by Caracalla in AD 216. The baths proper, in the centre of the courtyard, include a hot bath (caldarium), a pool for cold dips (frigidarium), etc. In spite of the loss of their rich marble decoration and their columns, and the collapse of the roof, the Baths still display the architectural skill of their builders and give some impression of public baths during the Imperial period.

★Terme di Caracalla

From Piazza di Porta Capena the Via delle Terme di Caracalla runs south-east to the Piazzale Numa Pompilio and then south into the Via Cristoforo

Sepolcro degli Scipioni

Colombo, a fine modern highway built for the 1960 Olympic Games. Alternatively it is possible to bear south-east along Via di Porta San Sebastiano to the Tomb of the Scipios (Sepolcro degli Scipioni), built in 312 BC (still preserving the original sarcophagi).

Close by is the Columbarium of Pomponius Hylas or of the Freedmen of Ocatavia (Nero's wife), a subterranean tomb with good stucco decoration and painting.

Arco di Druso

Via di Porta San Sebastiano ends at the so-called Arch of Drusus (Arco di Druso; probably in fact dating from the time of Trajan). Immediately beyond it, in the Aurelian Walls, is the crenellated Porta San Sebastiano, the ancient Porta Appia, from which the Via Appia Antica runs south to the Catacombs.

Lateran

The Lateran Palace (Palazzo del Laterano) was for many centuries the residence of the popes; adjoining it is the Lateran Basilica. Via di San Giovanni in Laterano runs south-east from the Colosseum to the Lateran district.

★San Clemente

In Via di San Giovanni in Laterano, built over an ancient temple of Mithras, is the church of San Clemente (1108), a good example of an early Christian basilica. The nave is flanked by aisles, but there is no transept; fine marble choir screens, flanked by two ambos; in front of the main entrance is an atrium, with a fountain for ablutions; there are wall paintings (8th–11th c.) in the old lower church.

Santo Stefano Rotondo

The Lateran can be also reached from the Colosseum by going south along Via Claudia and from there north-east through the Via di Santo Stefano Rotondo. To the south of this street, on the Caelian, stands the church of Santo Stefano Rotondo (460–480), a round church, also built over a temple of Mithras, with 56 columns in the interior and an open timber roof structure. Excavations under the church brought to light remains of a barracks (Castra Peregrinorum) for soldiers passing through and a mithraeum of the 3rd c. AD, with frescoes and sculptures.

Obelisk

Via di San Giovanni joins the Piazza di San Giovanni in Laterano, in the centre of which rises a red granite Egyptian obelisk (15th c. BC), set up here in 1588; it is the largest of its kind, standing 32 m (106 ft) high, not counting the base.

★Baptistery

In the south-west corner of the square is the Baptistery of San Giovanni in Fonte, the oldest baptistery in Rome (432–440) and the model for all later buildings of the same kind.

★San Giovanni in Laterano

On the south side of the square stands the church of San Giovanni in Laterano, built by Constantine the Great in the 4th c. in a palace belonging to the Laterani, one of the five patriarchal churches of Rome, "mother and head of all churches". It was much altered between the 10th and 15th c., and its present Baroque form including the two bell-towers dates from the mid 16th c.; the massive Late Baroque façade, with its conspicuous attic storey and its crown of statues, dates from 1735; the new choir was added in 1885. Of the five doorways the central one has ancient bronze doors from the Curia Iulia (Main entrance: Via Vittorio Emanuele Filberto; side entrance: Piazza San Giovanni in Laterano 4).

Interior

The present interior, with five aisles, was designed by Francesco Borromini (16th–17th c.); the magnificent timber ceiling in the nave is by Daniele da Volterra (1564–72); the richly inlaid pavement is 15th c.

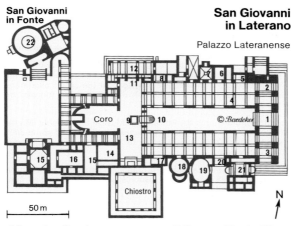

**San Giovanni
in Fonte**

San Giovanni
in Laterano

Palazzo Lateranense

1 Bronze doors (Roman)
2 Holy Door
3 Statue of Constantine the
Great
4 Frescoes by Giotto (Boniface VIII)
5 Orsini Chapel
6 Torlonia Chapel
7 Massimo Chapel
8 St John's Chapel
9 Papal altar
10 Tomb of Pope Martin V (crypt)
11 Baroque organ
12 Side door

13 Monument of Pope Leo XIII.
Entrance to Portico of Leo XIII
14 Choir chapel
15 Sacristies
16 Chapterhouse
17 St Hilary's Chapel.
Entrance to cloister
18 Chapel of St Francis of Assisi
(monument of 1927)
19 Santorio Chapel
20 Chapel of Assumption
21 Corsini Chapel
22 Baptistery

The ancient columns in the nave were joined in pairs by Borromini to form piers; the large statues of the Apostles in niches were added after 1700.

Four steps lead up into the transept, in the centre cf which is the Altare Papale, at which only the Pope or his representative can celebrate Mass. The tabernacle dates from 1369. Among the relics preserved here are the heads of the Apostles Peter and Paul.

Altare Papale

The choir is richly decorated with marble. In the apse are mosaics (much restored) dating from 1290.

In the south aisle, to the rear of the first pier of the nave, is a fresco (Pope Boniface VIII proclaiming the first jubilee year, 1300) attributed to Giotto but much restored. There are numerous monuments in the church.

A door beside the last chapel in the north aisle leads into the early 13th c. Cloister (Chiostro), which has numerous twisted colonnettes with mosaic decoration.

Cloister

Adjoining the north side of the Lateran Church is the Lateran Palace, built in 1586 on the site of an earlier palace, occupied by the popes from the time of Constantine onwards, which was burned down in 1308. At present it is occupied by the Vicariate of the city of Rome.

Lateran Palace

Opposite the Lateran Palace to the north-east, in a 16th c. building, is the Scala Santa, a flight of 28 marble steps (now covered with wood for protection) which is believed to be the staircase ascended by Christ in Pilate's palace in Jerusalem and which the faithful climb only on their

Scala Santa

knees. At the top, beyond a grille, is the chapel known as the Sancta Sanctorum, with 13th c. mosaics.

Porta San Giovanni

Close by, on the south side of Piazza di Porta San Giovanni, stands the 16th c. Porta San Giovanni, from which the Via Appia Nuova runs south-east.

Santa Croce in Gerusalemme

From Piazza di Porta San Giovanni the Viale Carlo Felice runs east to the church of Santa Croce in Gerusalemme, one of the seven pilgrimage churches of Rome (rebuilt 1743), which may have been founded by St Helena.

Museum of Musical Instruments

To the north of the church the Museum of Musical Instruments (Museo Nazionale degli Strumenti Musicali) houses a collection of some 3000 instruments dating from ancient times to 1800, including the famous 17th c. Barberini Harp.

Porta Maggiore

Farther north towers the massive Porta Maggiore, originally an arch carrying the Acqua Claudia (Aqueduct of Claudius) over the Roman road, later a gate in the Aurelian Walls.

Termini Station district

Domus Aurea di Nerone

North-east of the Colosseum, in the Parco Traiano on the Esquiline Hill, are the remains of Nero's Golden House or Domus Aurea di Nerone, a palace complex with numerous magnificent State apartments, planned with a lavish disregard for expense but which was left unfinished. Trajan later used it as the substructure of his Baths. The palace contains much fine painting, which Raphael took as his model for the Loggias in the Vatican.

Museo Nazionale d'Arte Orientale

Some 500 m north-east of Nero's Golden House is the Museo Nazionale d'Arte Orientale, which contains fine art from Asia.

★San Pietro in Vincoli

North of the Parco Traiano stands the church of San Pietro in Vincoli, an aisled basilica with 20 ancient columns, originally built in 442 to house the chains (vincula) of St Peter and completely rebuilt and enlarged in the 15th c. In the south transept is the powerful figure of Moses by Michelangelo (1513–16), created for the unfinished tomb of Pope Julius II, a symbol of strength controlled by super-human will-power. The second altar in the north aisle has 7th c. mosaic decoration; adjoining it is the tomb of Cardinal Nicolaus Cusanus (d. 1464). On the high altar are the chains of St Peter.

★Santa Maria Maggiore

A little way north of San Pietro in Vincoli is Via Cavour, which branches off the Via dei Fori Imperiali and runs north-east to the Piazza dell'Esquilino. On the south-east side of this square is the imposing church of Santa Maria Maggiore, one of Rome's five patriarchal churches and the largest of its 80 or so churches dedicated to the Virgin. Founded in the 5th c., it was rebuilt in the 16th and 17th c.; the main front with its loggia dates from 1743. The tower (1377) is the highest in Rome (75 m (248 ft)). From the porch (13th c. mosaics), with its five doorways, four entrances lead into the church; the fifth, the Porta Santa (to the left), is opened only in Holy Years.

Interior

The aisled interior is splendidly decorated. The pavement of the nave dates from the 12th c., the magnificent ceiling, richly gilded with the first gold

Mosaic in the apse of Santa Maria Maggiore

brought from America, from 1493 to 1498. Above the architrave, borne on 40 Ionic columns, as well as on the triumphal arch, are 5th c. mosaics. In the apse are mosaics by J. Torriti (1295).

In the south transept the magnificent Sistine Chapel, or Chapel of the Holy Sacrament, has a domed roof; the chapel was built in 1585 in the reign of Sixtus V. In the north aisle is the Borghese Chapel (1611), also domed, with an image of the Virgin, believed to be miraculous, on the high altar.

300 m north-west of Santa Maria Maggiore stands the church of Santa Pudenziana, with a 12th c. tower, which legend claims to be the oldest church in Rome. The apse contains mosaics (Christ with Apostles, 401–417) which are among the finest in Rome.

Santa Pudenziana

Just south of Santa Maria Maggiore, concealed among buildings, is the church of Santa Prassede, built in 822 in honour of St Praxedis and several times restored, most recently in 1869. It has a beautiful interior, with fine 9th c. mosaics on the triumphal arch, in the apse and in the chapel of San Zeno (south aisle).

Santa Prassede

Termini Station

At the north-east end of Via Cavour we come to the large Piazza dei Cinquecento. On the south-east side of this square is the Termini Station (Stazione Centrale Roma-Termini), completed in 1950, an imposing structure of distinctive design, making much use of glass and steel, which was a landmark in the development of modern railway architecture. In the concourse is the entrance to the Metropolitana line (partly underground, partly above ground). The Metropolitana Line A runs from the Stazione Termini to Via Ottaviano (near the Vatican) or by way of Cinecittà to Via Anagnina; the Metropolitana Line B runs by way of the Porta di San Paolo to the EUR district (Via Laurentina) or north-eastwards in the direction of Rebibbia.

Terme di Diocleziano

The north side of the Piazza dei Cinquecento and the area to the north are occupied by the Baths of Diocletian (Terme di Diocleziano), built AD 298–305, which were no less magnificent than the Baths of Caracalla and measure 350 m (1148 ft) each way. Michelangelo was commissioned by Pope Pius IV to convert the Baths into a Carthusian monastery, and transformed the large vaulted tepidarium (warm bath) into the church of Santa Maria degli Angeli (1563–66). Since 1885 the monastic buildings have housed the Baths Museum. The great semicircle described by the outer wall now forms the Piazza della Repubblica, with a fountain. In a rotunda at the west end is the round church of San Bernardo, consecrated 1600.

★Museo
Nazionale
Romano o delle
Terme

The Museo Nazionale Romano o delle Terme (Roman National Museum or Baths Museum), founded 1886, contains material discovered on state property in and around Rome and has developed into the most important collection of antiquities in Rome, except for the museums of the Vatican.

The old rooms around the south transept of Santa Maria degli Angeli, the actual rooms of the Baths, contain the largest collection in Italy of Roman sarcophagi and mosaics. Particularly notable items in the new rooms are the "Niobe Wounded", a Greek original of the 5th c. BC; the "Maiden of Anzio", an original work of the early Hellenistic period; the headless and armless "Venus of Cyrene" (4th c. BC); a "Kneeling Youth" (ephebe) from Subiaco (3rd c. BC); a bronze "Defeated Pugilist" (3rd c. BC); and a copy of Myron's "Discobolus" (5th c. BC). In the Small Cloister (Piccolo Chiostro), behind glass walls, is the Ludovisi Collection (temporarily closed). Notable items here are the so-called Ludovisi Throne (5th c. BC); the "Galatian and his Wife", a Roman copy of the Galatian who, when threatened by enemies, killed his wife and himself, "Ares Resting" (Ares Ludovisi), the Ludovisi Juno and the Head of a sleeping Fury, the so-called Ludovisi Medusa.

The Baths of Diocletian

The Large Cloister (Grande Chiostro), completed in 1565, with a fountain in the centre, contains marble sculpture, architectural elements, sarcophagi, mosaics and inscriptions.

On the first floor of the Museum can be seen a collection of mosaics, stucco work and frescos, including wall paintings from the Villa of Livia in Prima Porta (only partially open, owing to building works).

At present the museum to be known as the Palazzo Massimo alle Terme is being constructed on the Piazza dei Cinquecento. When completed it will house some of the many exhibits owned by the National Museum.

Palazzo Massimo alle Terme

Via XX Settembre

A little way north of the Museo delle Terme is the Via XX Settembre commemorating September 20th 1870, when Italian troops marched into Rome after the withdrawal of the French. In this street which leads to the north-eastern districts of the city, to the north of San Bernardo, is the church of Santa Maria della Vittoria, a sumptuous Baroque church designed by Carlo Aderna (1608–20), which contains (fourth chapel on left) one of the great masterpieces of High Baroque style, Bernini's "Ecstasy of Teresa" (1647).

Santa Maria della Vittoria

Opposite the church is the imposing Acqua Felice Fountain (by Domenico Fontana, 1585–87), with marble sculpture. Farther along, on the right, the Ministry of Finance (1870–77) can be seen.

Acqua Felice Fountain

Via XX Settembre ends at the Porta Pia in the old town walls (designed by Michelangelo, 1561–65).

Immediately outside the Porta Pia, on the right-hand side of Via Nomentana, which continues the line of Via XX Settembre to the north-east, is the Ministry of Public Works.

Porta Pia

San Lorenzo fuori le Mura

North-east of the Stazione Termini stands the Basilica San Lorenzo fuori le Mura, one of the five patriarchal churches of Rome, originally founded by Constantine the Great. It was entirely remodelled in the 6th and again in the 13th c., partly destroyed during the Second World War, but restored after the war. The floor of the nave and choir dates from the 12th–13th c., the baldacchino over the high altar from 1148. The triumphal arch has 6th c. mosaics. Adjoining the church is a picturesque Romanesque cloister.

Beside the church is a large cemetery, the Campo Verano.

To the west of Piazza San Lorenzo is the University City (Città Universitaria), a large complex of buildings set amid gardens established here in the 1930s, with the Biblioteca Alessandrina, the University Library. Today the university has become too small for the number of students.

University City

Farther south, in the Castro Pretorio, is the National Library (Biblioteca Nazionale Centrale Vittorio Emanuele II), built 1971–75. This contains some 3 million volumes, 1883 incunabula, 6169 manuscripts and 30,000 autographs, and consists of a long ten-storey book-stack, an office block, a low building housing the catalogue and reading rooms, and a low conference building.

National Library

A kilometre (³/₄ mi.) farther on, also on right, lies the beautiful park of the Villa Torlonia, a good example of Romantic landscape gardening. Under the ground are Jewish catacombs. In the park is the early 19th c. Palazzo Torlonia, Mussolini's residence from 1925 to 1944, the cellars of which (no admission) contain one of Italy's largest private collections of antiquities, with over 600 works of art.

Villa Torlonia

Rome

Sant'Agnese fuori le Mura

Another 2 km (1¼ miles) out is the church of Sant'Agnese fuori le Mura, founded by Constantine the Great to house the tomb of St Agnes and rebuilt in the 7th and 15th c. and again in 1856. The apse contains mosaics dating from the 7th c. Under the church are catacombs, some still in their original state (before AD 300).

Adjoining Sant'Agnese is the round church of Santa Costanza, built as a mausoleum for Constantine's daughter, with fine 4th c. mosaics.

From Sant'Agnese Via Nomentana continues north-east to the Quartiere Monte Sacro, a large suburban area which has grown up since the last war on and around Mons Sacer.

To the south-west on Monte Antenne Campeggio an Islamic culture centre and mosque are being built.

Palazzo Colonna

From the north side of the Piazza Venezia it is a short distance east along Via Cesare Battisti to the elongated Piazza Santi Apostoli, with the Palazzo Colonna, begun about 1417 by Pope Martin V (Colonna) and much altered in the 17th and 18th c. The richly decorated rooms on the first floor contain a collection of pictures, the Palazzo Colonna (entrance in Via della Pilotta) including works by da Cortona, Veronese, Tintoretto, Van Dyck and Ricci.

Santi Apostoli

On the north side of the Palazzo Colonna is the church of the Santi Apostoli (1702), with a porch dating from 1475. At the end of the north aisle is the tomb of Pope Clement XIV (by Canova, 1789).

Universitas Gregoriana

North-east of the church, in Piazza Pilotta, stands the Universitas Gregoriana or Pontifical University, founded in 1553; the present buildings date from 1930.

Torre delle Milizie

From the Palazzo Colonna Via IV Novembre runs south to the medieval Torre delle Milizie or Torre di Nerone and the Via Magnanapoli. By the Torre delle Milizie is the entrance to Trajan's Market and Forum.

Via Nazionale

From the Torre delle Milizie Via Nazionale, one of Rome's main traffic arteries, runs north-east, past the Banca d'Italia (on the right), the Palazzo Rospigliosi (1603: ceiling paintings by Guido Reni) and the Palazzo delle Esposizioni (1880–83), to the Piazza della Repubblica. Beside the Palazzo delle Esposizioni (on the left) is the mouth of the tunnel (348 m (1142 ft) long) driven under the Quirinal in 1902, providing a link with the Piazza di Spagna.

Quirinal

From the Via Magnanapoli Via XXIV Maggio runs past the church of San Silvestro al Quirinale (1524: on the left) and the west wing of the Palazzo Rospigliosi to the Piazza del Quirinale, on the Quirinal Hill.

★Horse-Tamers

In the centre of the square are the two famous marble statues of the "Horse-Tamers" (Dioscuri), fine examples of the classical style of sculpture of the Imperial period, based on Greek models of the 5th c. BC.

Palazzo del Quirinale

On the east side of the Piazza del Quirinale are the Palazzo della Consulta (built 1732–34: no admission), with a beautiful staircase, and the Palazzo del Quirinale, an imposing palace built on the summit of the Quirinal Hill. Begun in 1574 as a summer residence for the Pope, it was enlarged and altered in later centuries. From 1870 to 1946 it was a royal palace, and it is now the official residence of the President of Italy, although he does not in fact live here. It is set in a beautiful park.

★Sant'Andrea al Quirinale

To the east of the Quirinal Palace stands the church of Sant'Andrea al Quirinale (by Bernini, 1658–70), one of the most harmonious creations of Roman Baroque architecture, on an oval ground-plan.

Still farther east, at the junction of Via del Quirinale with Via Quattro Fontane, are the Quattro Fontane (Four Fountains). To the right is the little church of San Carlo alle Quattro Fontane or San Carlino, a complex Baroque building by Borromini, who died in 1667 prior to its completion.

Quattro Fontane

Palazzo Barberini

In the northern part of Via Quattro Fontane, on the right, is the Palazzo Barberini, an imposing Baroque structure begun in 1626 by Carlo Maderna and completed in 1633 by Borromini and Bernini. It now houses the Galleria Nazionale d'Arte Antica, with works by Italian and foreign artists of the 13th–16th c., including Hans Holbein the Younger's "Portrait of Henry VIII", El Greco's "Baptism of Christ" and "Nativity", and Raphael's "La Fornarina". In the principal room is a fine ceiling painting depicting the "Triumph of the Barberini Family" by Pietro da Corona, a masterpiece of Baroque monumental painting (1633–39). 17th and 18th c. pictures from the Palazzo Corsini are also of interest.

Galleria Nazionale d'Arte Antica

Adjoining to the north-west in the centre of the busy, elongated Piazza Barberini can be seen the beautiful Fontana del Tritone (by Bernini, 1640), with a figure of a triton blowing a conch.

★Fontana del Tritone

From the north end of the Piazza Barberini the famous Via Vittorio Veneto (Via Veneto for short), a wide tree-lined avenue, climbs in an S-shaped curve to the Porta Pinciana, a distance of almost 1 km (1/2 mi.).

Via Vittorio Veneto

A little way along the lower part, on the right, underneath the Capuchin church of Santa Maria della Concezione (1626) with fiine altar-pieces are five mortuary chapels, the walls of which are covered with the bones of more than 4000 Capuchins.

Santa Maria della Concezione ★Mortuary Chapels

The Via Veneto, the 500 m stretch between Via Ludovisi and the Porta Pinciana, was closed to vehicles for a time but is now again the scene of busy traffic coming from both directions. At one time it was the territory of the "dolce vita" and formed the backcloth for Fellini's famous film of that name. Elegant shops and street cafés are once again making it a favourite rendezvous for locals and visitors alike.

Via Veneto

Villa Borghese

Beyond the Porta Pinciana is the beautiful park of the Villa Borghese, laid out by Cardinal Scipio Borghese in the 17th c., which was purchased by the State in 1902 and thrown open to the public under the name of Villa Umberto I. At the south end of the park is a large underground car park. Scattered about in the grounds, planted with chestnut trees, holm-oaks and beautiful umbrella pines, are a variety of ornamental buildings, fountains and monuments. In the southern section of the park is a *galoppatoio* (race-track).

To the east is the Casino Borghese, built about 1615 and richly decorated with marble and frescos at the end of the 18th c. Notable features in the interior are a figure of Pauline Borghese, Napoleon's sister, as Venus (1807), a masterpiece by Canova, and several youthful works by Bernini, including "David with his Sling" and "Apollo and Daphne".

Casino Borghese Museo e Galleria

On the upper floor of the Casino the Galleria Borghese, one of Rome's finest picture galleries, has masterpieces by Raphael ("Entombment"), Titian ("Sacred and Profane Love"), Caravaggio ("David", "Madonna dei Palafrenieri"), Correggio ("Danaë"), works by painters of the Roman Baroque school, as well as by Rubens, Lucas Cranach, Domenichino, Veronese and Andrea del Sarto.

In the northern part of the park of the Villa Borghese is a Zoo, established by Karl Hagenbeck in 1911.

Zoo

Villa Borghese: the park

★Galleria
Nazionale d'Arte
Moderna

To the west of this, in Viale delle Belle Arti, the Galleria Nazionale d'Arte Moderna contains the largest collection of modern art in Italy, covering the period from the beginning of the 19th c. to the present day, with Italian Neo-Classical artists and Neo-Impressionists, other European Impressionists and Expressionists, contemporary painting and sculpture.

★Villa Giulia
Museo Nazionale
Etrusco

Nearby is the Villa Giulia, built for Pope Julius III by Vignola (1550–55), with beautiful stucco-work and painting by Taddeo Zuccaro. The villa now houses the large State collection of Etruscan antiquities from the province of Rome, outstanding among which are the Cista Ficoroni (3rd c. BC), a cylindrical toilet casket with finely engraved scenes from the story of the Argonauts, the Apollo of Veii, a painted terracotta statue dating from about 500 BC, and a terracotta sarcophagus from Cerveteri with the reclining figures of a man and his wife (6th c. BC).

Piazza di Spagna

Column of the
Immacolata

From the Piazza Barberini the busy Via del Tritone runs west to join the Via del Corso. Going along this street and in 200 m turning right along Via Due Macelli, we come to the Piazza di Spagna, under the south side of the Pincio. It is named after the large Palazzo di Spagna, which has been the residence of the Spanish Embassy to the Holy See since the 17th c. In front of the palace rises the Column of the Immacolata, erected to commemorate the proclamation of the dogma of the Immaculate Conception by Pope Pius IX in 1854.

La Barcaccia

On the south side of the square is the Palazzo di Propaganda Fide, a centre and college for the propagation of the Roman Catholic faith (missionary

400

archives). In the centre of the square is La Barcaccia, a low fountain in the shape of a boat (by Bernini, 1629).

From here the famous Spanish Steps (Scalinata della Trinità dei Monti), a magnificent Baroque staircase, with 137 steps, alternating with ramps, designed by Francesco de Sanctis (1723–26), usually gay with flowers, climb up to the twin-towered French church of the Santiss ma Trinità dei Monti, founded in 1495, on the Pincio. A little way north of the church is the 16th c. Villa Medici, which came into the hands of the Medici family in the 17th c. and has been occupied since 1803 by the French Academy of Art.

★Spanish Steps
Santissima Trinità dei Monti

To the west and north-west of the Piazza di Spagna are a number of busy streets, including Via dei Condotti, Via del Babuino and Via Margutta, with elegant shops and boutiques.

Shop

Farther north, above the east side of the Piazza del Popolo, is the Pincio, a beautiful park laid out in 1809–14 on the hill of that name (50 m (165 ft)), the most northerly of Rome's hills, with numerous busts and monuments commemorating famous Italians and a monumental piece of sculpture, 11 m (36ft) high, by Giacomo Manzù (1975). From the terrace on the west side of the park there is a famous prospect of Rome, with an impressive view of St Peter's. A bridge links it with the Villa Borghese park.

Pincio

Via del Corso

The Via del Corso, which runs north-west from the Piazza Venezia to the Piazza del Popolo, flanked by numerous Baroque palaces, has long been Rome's principal street (1.5 km (1 mi.) long but only 12 m (39 ft) wide).

The first building on the left-hand side is the 17th c. Palazzo Bonaparte, and just beyond this another 17th c. mansion, the Palazzo Doria, has a handsome pillared courtyard. On the first floor of the latter is the Galleria Doria Pamphili, which contains Velázquez's famous portrait of Pope Innocent X (Pamphili), a masterpiece notable equally for its sharp delineation of character and its brilliance of colour (1650). The gallery has also fine works by Raphael, Titian, Tintoretto, Correggio, Caravaggio ("Rest on the Flight into Egypt") and Claude Lorrain.

★Galleria Doria Pamphili

Beyond the Palazzo Doria a short street, Via Lata, on the left, runs from the Corso, leading to the Palazzo Sciarra, into the Piazza del Collegio Romano, on the right-hand side of which we come to the Collegio Romano (by Bartolomeo Ammannati and Giuseppe Valeriani, 1583–85), a Jesuit college until 1870 and now a State school.

Collegio Romano

In a small square to the west of the Collegio Romano stands the church of Santa Maria sopra Minerva, built before 800 on the site of Domitian's temple of Minerva and rebuilt in 1280. It is Rome's only medieval church in the Gothic style. In front of the high altar, to the left, is Michelangelo's statue of the Risen Christ with the Cross (1521). The altar itself contains the relics of St Catherine of Siena (1347–80). The Cappella Caraffa, in the south transept, has frescoes by Filippino Lippi (1489). There are numerous fine monuments; to the left of the choir is the tombstone of the Dominican Fra Giovanni Angelico (1387–1455).

Santa Maria sopra Minerva

★★Pantheon

North-west of Santa Maria sopra Minerva, in the Piazza della Rotonda, the centre of the old town, is the Pantheon, the best preserved building of ancient Rome.

The Pantheon was built in 27 BC by Marcus Vipsanius Agrippa, Augustus's friend and general, and several times rebuilt or restored, notably by Hadrian

in 120–126. After the extinction of paganism the Eastern Emperor Phocas presented it to Pope Boniface IV, who consecrated it in 609 as the church of Santa Maria ad Martyres, popularly called Santa Maria Rotonda. The portico has sixteen ancient granite columns 12.5 m (41 ft) high, and the entrance still preserves its two massive ancient bronze-clad doors. The huge dome of the rotunda, lit only by a round aperture 9 m (29 ft) in diameter (the "Eye"), ranks as the supreme achievement of Roman interior architecture. The overwhelming effect of the building depends on the consummate harmony of its proportions no less than on its huge dimensions: its height (43.2 m (143 ft)) is the same as its diameter, and the hemisphere of the dome is the same height as its vertical walls. The figures of the gods which once stood in the seven principal niches and the rest of the valuable furnishings of the Pantheon have been removed to other places in the course of the centuries. In the second niche on the right is the tomb of King Victor Emmanuel II (d. 1878); opposite this is the tomb of Umberto I (assassinated 1900); and to the right is the tomb of Raphael (1483–1520).

From the Pantheon Via del Seminario runs east, past the Ministry of Posts, to the Baroque church of Sant'Ignazio (by O. Grassi, 1626–50), built on the model of the Gesù in honour of the founder of the Jesuit order, Ignatius of Loyola (1491–1556), who was canonised in 1622. It has a famous ceiling painting by Andrea Pozzo, a masterpiece of perspective, best seen from the middle of the nave. Sant'Ignazio

Facing Sant'Ignazio, to the north, is the Exchange. The north front, on Piazza di Pietra, has eleven Corinthian columns, 12.9 m (43 ft) high, probably from a temple built in honour of the Emperor Hadrian (AD 76–138). Exchange

★Column of Marcus Aurelius

To the east of Sant'Ignazio, on east side of the Via del Corso, is the 17th c. Palazzo Sciarra-Colonna. A little way north, off the west side of the Corso, the busy Piazza Colonna was named after the Column of Marcus Aurelius (Colonna di Marco Aurelio: 29.5 m (97 ft) high) which stands in the centre of the square. Like Trajan's column, it is covered with reliefs (originally painted) depicting Marcus Aurelius's campaigns against the Marcomanni and other Germanic tribes. The column is topped by a bronze statue of the Apostle Paul which was erected by Pope Sixtus V.

On the east side of the Piazza Colonna (and of the Corso) is the Galleria Colonna, with a Y-shaped arcade. The Palazzo Wedekind, on the west side of the square, has a portico of sixteen Ionic columns from the Etruscan city of Veii (Veio). On the north side is the Palazzo Chigi (begun 1562, completed by Carlo Maderna), which now houses the Italian Cabinet offices. Galleria Colonna

Adjoining the Piazza Colonna on the west is the Piazza di Montecitorio, on an eminence formed by an accumulation of rubble. In the centre of this square rises a 26 m (86 ft) high Egyptian obelisk (6th c. BC). The north side of the square is occupied by the Italian Parliament Building, also known as the Palazzo Montecitorio. Originally built by Bernini in 1650 for the Ludovisi family, it was converted for the use of the Papal courts in 1694 by Carlo Fontana and again altered in 1871 to house the new Italian Parliament. Piazza di
Montecitorio
Obelisk

Some 250 m east of the Piazza Colonna is the popular Fontana di Trevi, built against the south end of the Palazzo Poli. The most monumental of Rome's Baroque fountains, it was the work of Niccolo Salvi, based on designs by Bernini (1735–62). In the central niche is a figure of Neptune, flanked by ★Fontana di Trevi

◀ *The Spanish Steps*

Detail from the Column of Marcus Aurelius

figures of Health and Fertility; in front is a large basin, some 20 m (66 ft) across. It is an old custom when leaving Rome to throw a coin backwards over your head into the basin in order to ensure that you will return.

Facing the Trevi Fountain, to the south-east, is the church of Santi Vincenzo ed Anastasio, with a Baroque façade of 1650.

Museo Nazionale delle Paste Alimentari A short way from the Fontana di Trevi, on the Piazza Scandenberg, lies the Museo Nazionale delle Paste Alimentari, which provides details of the making and preparation of pasta.

Palazzo Ruspoli San Carlo al Corso 350 m north of the Piazza Colonna, on the left-hand side of the Via del Corso, is the Palazzo Ruspoli (begun 1556), with a fine staircase of about 1650. Beyond this, to the right, there is a charming glimpse along Via Condotti to the Spanish Steps. Farther north again, on the left, stands the church of San Carlo al Corso, a fine Baroque structure (17th c.).

Mausoleo di Augusto

A little way north-west of San Carlo is the Mausoleum of Augustus (Mausoleo di Augusto), a monumental rotunda, 89 m (292 ft) in diameter at the base and originally 44 m (145 ft) high, built by Augustus in 28 BC as a burial place for himself and his family, which also contained the remains of some of his successors down to Nerva (AD 96–98). From the 11th c. it served several purposes, but in 1936 it was restored to its original condition.

★Ara Pacis Augustae Between the Mausoleum and the Tiber, in a glass hall in Via di Ripetta, is the Ara Pacis Augustae, an altar dedicated to the goddess of peace, re-erected here in 1938. Built on the Campus Martius in 13–9 BC, after Augustus's return from Spain and Gaul, it is decorated with fine plant ornaments, including acanthus, ivy and laurel, and noble carved friezes depicting a Roman procession.

The famous Fontana di Trevi

At Via del Corso 17 is the Goethe Museum, with pictures, manuscripts, books, etc., in a house where Goethe lived during his stay in Rome (1786–88).

Goethe Museum

Piazza del Popolo

The Via del Corso runs into the oval Piazza del Popolo, laid out in its present form in 1816–20. On the north side stands the Porta del Popolo (1565 and 1655), the old north gate of Rome.

In the centre of the square, at the point of intersection of three streets from the south, the Via di Pipetta, Via del Corso and Via del Babuino, rises an Egyptian obelisk (24 m (79 ft) high; including base and cross 36 m (119 ft)) erected by Pope Sixtus V in 1589.

Obelisk

On the south side of the square are two domed churches, Santa Maria in Monte Santo to the east and Santa Maria dei Miracoli to the west, both begun by Rainaldi in 1662 and completed by Bernini and Carlo Fontana in 1675 and 1679 respectively.

Churches

Adjoining the Porta del Popolo is the church of Santa Maria del Popolo, built in 1472–77, with a new choir by Bramante (1505–09) and a Baroque interior (remodelled in 1655). It contains numerous works of art, in particular 15th c. monuments. In the chapel to the left of the choir are two magnificent pictures by Caravaggio ("Conversion of Paul", "Crucifixion of Peter"). In the Augustinian convent which formerly stood here Luther stayed during his visit to Rome in 1510–11.

★Santa Maria del Popolo

On the east side of the church of Santa Maria del Popolo is an entrance to the Pincio park.

Piazza Venezia to the Tiber

★Gesù church

From the Piazza Venezia it is a short distance west along Via del Plesbiscito to the Piazza del Gesù, where stands the Gesù (il Gesù), the principal church of the Jesuit order and one of the richest and most sumptuous churches in Rome, the model for all the other splendid Jesuit churches and a magnificent example of Baroque architecture. It has a wide, high nave, with the aisles converted into chapels. In the north transept is the splendid Altar of St Ignatius (1696–1700), under which is a gilded bronze sarcophagus containing the remains of St Ignatius of Loyola (1491–1556).

Corso Vittorio Emanuele II

Largo di Torre Argentina

From the far side of the Piazza del Gesù the busy Corso Vittorio Emanuele II, driven through the medieval town from 1870 onwards to provide a link between the Piazza Venezia and the Vatican City, continues west. A short distance along this street, on the left, is the Largo di Torre Argentina. In this low-lying square, in front of the Teatro Argentina, are the remains (excavated 1927–30) of four temples (Templi di età repubblicana: 3rd c. BC), which – unlike those in the Forum – have preserved much of their original form.

★Fontana delle Tartarughe

A short distance south of the Largo di Torre Argentina, in the little Piazza Mattei, is the Tortoise Fountain (Fontana delle Tartarughe), a charming bronze group by Taddeo Landini (1585).

Sant'Andrea della Valle

Farther along the Corso Vittorio Emanuele II, beyond the Largo di Torre Argentina, stands the domed church of Sant'Andrea della Valle, begun by F. Grimaldi and G. della Porta in 1591, completed by Carlo Maderna in 1625, with a richly decorated façade of 1665 and a sumptuous interior. Particularly notable are the fine frescos by Domenichino (1624–28) in the pendentives under the dome and on the vaulting of the apse. There are also some interesting paintings and statues in the side-chapels.

Palazzo Massimo alle Colonne

Farther along the Corso, on the right, is the Palazzo Massimo alle Colonne, one of the finest Renaissance buildings in Rome (by Baldassare Peruzzi, 1532–36), with a curved façade adapted to a bend in the old street and a picturesque double courtyard.

Museo Barracco

Beyond this, on the left of the Piazza di San Pantaleo, we find the Piccola Farnesina (1523), a Renaissance palace which houses the Museo Barracco, with a fine collection of ancient sculpture, including Greek, Assyrian, Egyptian and Etruscan tombstones.

Museo di Roma

On the opposite side, in the Palazzo Braschi (1972), is the interesting Museo di Roma, illustrating the history of Rome in recent centuries, with a railway coach which belonged to Pope Pius IX, two State carriages, terracotta figures, majolica, carpets and costumes.

★Piazza Navona

North of the Palazzo Braschi we come to an elongated square, the busy Piazza Navona (pedestrians only), the most characteristic of Rome's 17th c. squares. Its shape (240 × 65 m (787 × 213 ft)) reflects the fact that it occupies the site of the Stadium of Domitian, as its official name of Circo Agonale (Greek *agon* = contest, fight) also indicates. It is embellished with three fountains, one at the north end erected in 1878, the other two by Bernini *c.* 1650; the finest is the centre one, with magnificent vigorous figures representing the rivers Danube, Ganges, Nile and Plate and an ancient obelisk.

Sant'Agnese in Agonale

Opposite, on the west side of the square, is the church of Sant'Agnese in Agonale (by Borromini and Rainaldi, 1652–73), an imposing Baroque church on a centralised plan, with a sumptuous interior.

North-west of the Piazza Navona is the church of Santa Maria dell'Anima (1500–14), old church of the German-speaking Catholics.

Santa Maria dell'Anima

Immediately north-west of this the church of Santa Maria della Pace, built in 1480, has a beautiful semicircular porch added in 1657. Above the first chapel on the right are figures of Sibyls painted by Raphael (1514), and in the octagonal dome are other fine 16th c. frescos. The cloister is by Bramante (1504).

Santa Maria della Pace

The Palazzo Altemps, not far from the Piazza Navona, was opened as an archaeological musuem in 1997. A total of 160 works of art are displayed in 33 rooms and include the "Ludovisi Throne", a Greek altar from the 5th c. BC on which the birth of Venus is depicted.

Palazzo Altemps (Museum)

To the east of Piazza Navona, in the Corso del Rinascimento, stands the Palazzo Madama (1642), the seat of the Italian Senate since 1871.

Palazzo Madama

On its north side is the French national church, San Luigi dei Francesi (consecrated 1589). In the fifth chapel can be seen three notable pictures by Caravaggio depicting scenes from the life of St Matthew.

San Luigi dei Francesi

In a little square just north of San Luigi the church of Sant'Agostino (by Giacomo da Pietrasanta, 1469–83), one of the first domed churches to be built in Rome, has a notable interior; on the third pillar on the left is a fresco by Raphael of the prophet Isaiah (1512), in the first chapel on the left Caravaggio's "Madonna dei Pellegrini" (1605).

Sant'Agostino

★Piazza della Cancelleria

Just beyond the Piazza di San Pantaleo, on the left of the Corso Vittorio Emanuele II, in the elongated Piazza della Cancelleria, is the Palazzo della Cancelleria, the Papal Chancery, one of the noblest Renaissance buildings in Rome (1486–1511), in a style suggesting Florentine influence; particularly notable is the fine arcaded courtyard.

From the Piazza della Cancelleria a street runs south by way of the Campo dei Fiori to the Piazza Farnese, in which are two fountains with ancient basins. On the south-west side of the square we come to the Palazzo Farnese, one of the most typical of Rome's old palaces, now occupied by the French embassy. Built for Cardinal Alexander Farnese, later Pope Paul III, it was begun in 1514 by Antonio da Sangalio the Younger and continued from 1546 onwards by Michelangelo. On the vaulting of the principal room on the first floor are mythological paintings by Annibale Carracci and others (1597–1604).

★Palazzo Farnese

South-east of the Palazzo Farnese is the Palazzo Spada (c. 1540), the seat of the Italian Council of State. At the end of the second courtyard is a colonnade by Borromini which achieves an effect of depth by a skilful and typically Baroque use of perspective. On the first floor (entrance in the inner courtyard), is the Galleria Spada, a picture gallery notable particularly for works of the 17th c. Bologna School (Guercino, Reni, etc.).

Palazzo Spada

Galleria Spada

Farther along the Corso Vittorio Emanuele II, on the right beyond the Palazzo della Cancelleria, stands the Chiesa Nuova or Santa Maria in Vallicella, built between 1575 and 1605 for the Oratorian order founded by St Philip Neri in 1575.

Chiesa Nuova

To the left of the church is the Oratorio dei Filippini, with a curved façade, one of Borromini's finest buildings (1637–50); it is now used for concerts and lectures. The name of the order and the word "oratorio" are both derived from the spiritual exercises and musical performances instituted by St Philip Neri in oratories.

★Oratorio dei Filippini

The Corso Vittorio Emanuele II ends at the Tiber bridge, the Ponte Vittorio Emanuele (1911).

Ponte Vittorio Emanuele

Sights in the south-west

To get from the Piazza Venezia to the Avertine, we go south, passing the National Monument, through Via del Teatro di Marcello. On the left there is a flight of steps which leads up to Santa Maria in Aracoeli and the Campidoglio.

Theatre of Marcellus

Beyond this, on the right, is the Theatre of Marcellus (Teatro di Marcello), built by Augustus in 17–13 BC and named after his nephew Marcellus, who had died young in 23 BC. The curved outer wall of the auditorium, which could seat an audience of 13,000–14,000, originally had three storeys, but the top storey was destroyed during the Middle Ages, when the theatre was converted into a fortress and residence for the Orsini family. In front of the theatre, to the right, stand three re-erected columns from a temple of Apollo.

San Nicola in Carcere

Farther along the street, on the right, is the church of San Nicola in Carcere, with fragments of three ancient temples.

★Temple of Fortuna Virilis

Via del Teatro di Marcello joins the spacious Piazza Bocca della Verità, at the east end of the Ponte Palatino. On the north side of the square is the well-preserved so-called Temple of Fortuna Virilis or Tempio di Portuno, a tufa building in the Ionic style (1st c. BC).

To the south of this is another smaller circular temple which has been known since medieval times as the Temple of Vesta, with nineteen (formerly twenty) Corinthian columns.

★Ianus Quadrifons

San Giorgio in Velabro

At the east end of the Piazza Bocca della Verità rises the so-called Ianus Quadrifons ("four-sided Janus") or Arco di Giano, a triumphal arch with four façades which probably dates from the time of Constantine. Here too is the ancient church of San Giorgio in Velabro, which contains sixteen ancient columns. Adjoining the church is the richly decorated Arco degli Argentari or Arch of the Money-Changers (AD 204).

Santa Maria in Cosmedin

On the south side of the Piazza Bocca della Verità we find the church of Santa Maria in Cosmedin, originally built at some time before the 6th c. on the foundations of a temple of Hercules and of a market hall (to which the marble columns on the entrance wall belonged), and rebuilt in the 11th–12th c. In the porch is the Bocca della Verità ("Mouth of Truth"), an antique marble disc with the mask of a Triton, into whose mouth according to medieval belief, the Romans used to insert their right hand when taking an oath. The church has a fine interior (aisled), with ancient columns and a 12th c. mosaic pavement and two marble pulpits.

Pons Aemilius

On the north side of the Ponte Palatino, in the middle of the Tiber, is a pier belonging to the old Pons Aemilius, originally built in 181 BC but frequently damaged and finally abandoned after its destruction by flood-water in 1598; hence its Italian name of Ponte Rotto, the "Broken Bridge". On the south side of the Ponte Palatino, in a niche in the embankment wall, can be seen (provided the water level is not too high) the threefold arch at the mouth of the ancient Cloaca Maxima, the drain, which continued in use until the 20th c.

Aventine

Immediately south of the Piazza Bocca della Verità is the Aventine (Monte Aventino, 46 m (152 ft)), on which the plebeians lived in the earliest days of Rome. Later the hill was occupied by convents and vineyards, and it is only in quite recent times that it has been more intensively built up and has developed into a pleasant residential area.

On the west side of the Aventine, in Via di Santa Sabina, which runs parallel with the Tiber above the Lungotevere Aventino on the embankment, is the church of Santa Sabina, originally built between 423 and 435 and subsequently much altered. This was the place of origin of the Dominican order (1215), and since its restoration in 1914–19 and 1936–38 it presents an excellent example of an Early Christian basilica. The cypress-wood door of the principal entrance is decorated with fine 5th c. reliefs, including (above, left) one of the earliest known representations of the Crucifixion. The fine interior has 24 ancient marble columns. In the nave is the schola cantorum (choir), rebuilt during the last restoration. The cloister dates from the 13th century.

★Santa Sabina

South-west of Santa Sabina the church of Sant'Alassio, which is referred to in the 7th c. with a dedication to St Boniface, was completely rebuilt in the 13th and 18th centuries.

Sant'Alassio

Farther south-west, in a little square, is the entrance to the Villa del Priorato di Malta, residence of the Grand Master of the order of the Knights of Malta, founded in 1070. The round aperture above the keyhole of the park gate affords a famous view of the dome of St Peter's, glimpsed at the end of the main avenue. There is also a beautiful view from the gardens (admission only by special arrangement). In the church of Santa Maria Aventina, reached from the gardens, are the tombs of knights of the order.

Priorato di Malta

Immediately south of the priory is the International Benedictine Seminary, with the church of Sant'Anselmo (consecrated 1900).

Sant'Anselmo

Porta San Paolo

From here Via di Porta Lavernale and its continuation lead south into the broad Via della Marmorata, at the south end of which, in the Aurelian Walls, is the Porta San Paolo, the ancient Porta Ostiensis. To the right of the gate rises the Pyramid of Cestius, 27 m (89 ft) high, a brick structure faced with marble blocks, built about 12 BC as the tomb of Gaius Cestius, a member of the priestly college of the Epulones.

Pyramid of Cestius

Immediately south-west, beyond the pyramid but still inside the Aurelian Walls, lies the Protestant Cemetery, or more precisely the Cimiterio degli Stranieri Acattolici (entrance on the north side), the cemetery for British, Germans, Scandinavians, Americans and orthodox Russians, in which Shelley and Keats are buried.

Protestant Cemetery

To the west of the cemetery is Monte Testaccio, an isolated mound rising to a height of 35 m (116 ft) above the Tiber and about 850 m (2789 ft) in circumference, composed entirely of fragments of the large earthenware jars in which wine and olives were shipped to Rome and discharged at a nearby quay on the banks of the Tiber. The hill is honeycombed with cellars, some of them connected with taverns. In addition to the modest little houses, which have been there for a long time, modern dwellings and bars have now appeared on Monte Testaccio.

Monte Testaccio

★San Paolo fuori le Mura

2 km (1¹/₄ m.) south of the Porta San Paolo, on the Via Ostiense, the road to Ostia and Lido di Ostia, stands the church of San Paolo fuori le Mura, one of Rome's five patriarchal churches, founded by Constantine the Great in 324 over the tomb of the Apostle Paul, rebuilt in 386 as an aisled basilica, destroyed by fire in 1823 with the exception of the choir and thereafter

San Paolo fuori le Mura

rebuilt on the original plan (1854), with the support of many Christian nations. The bronze door of the main entrance is by A. Maraini (1930–31).

Interior

The interior is imposing (120 m (394 ft) long, 60 m (197 ft) wide, 23 m (76 ft) high). There are double aisles on each side, separated by 80 granite columns. The church has a rich coffered stucco ceiling, partly gilded, with sumptuous marble decoration. Above the columns are portraits of all the popes from Peter to Paul VI. There is beautiful mosaic (440–61, restored) on the triumphal arch and in the apse. The destroyed 13th c. mosaic from the apse was replaced in the 19th c. by a copy. Above the high altar is a Gothic tabernacle (1285) and to the right a fine paschal candlestick (c. 1180). In the south aisle, near the entrance, is a bronze door ("sacred door") of 1070, damaged in the fire but later restored.

Cloister

On the south side of the church is a cloister, built between 1204 and 1241 by members of the Vassaletti family, famous mosaic artists. It belonged to a Benedictine monastery and with the varying forms of its columns and the colourful pattern of the stones, it ranks as one of the most beautiful cloisters in Rome.

Trastevere, Janiculum and Castel Sant'Angelo

Isola Tiberina

To the rear of the Theatre of Marcellus is the Ponte Fabricio, the oldest of Rome's present-day bridges, built in 62 BC, by which one reaches Tiber Island (Isola Tiberina), with the church of San Bartolomeo, perhaps occupying the site of a temple of Aesculapius. The story goes that in the year 300 BC, after consulting an oracle, the Romans brought to Rome a snake belonging to the god Aesculapius. As they arrived the snake escaped from the ship and swam to the island in the Tiber, where the Temple of Aesulapius then took shape.

Trastevere

From Tiber Island the Ponte Cestio leads into the densely populated district of Trastevere, on the right bank of the Tiber. In the time of Augustus it was a suburb of Rome (Regio Transtiberina), with numerous villas; later, when the Aurelian Walls were built, it was incorporated in the city proper. Later still it became the haunt of freed slaves and prostitutes. In the 19th and 20th c. it was a working-class district with a vigorous and down-to-earth character of its own; then from about 1970 a programme of slum clearance and redevelopment was begun, unfit houses being pulled down and replaced. It is now noted for its many little restaurants, but visitors should be on their guard against pick-pockets and beggars, particularly after dark.

Some 300 m south of the Ponte Cestio is the church of Santa Cecilia in Trastevere, which is supposed to occupy the site of a house in which the patron saint of music (martyred *c.* 230) lived. The church, founded before 500 but much rebuilt and restored in later centuries, is preceded by a spacious court and has a 12th c. campanile. On the high altar is a beautiful tabernacle of 1283; the apse has 9th c. mosaics. In the crypt can be seen the saint's sepulchral chapel, well restored. | Santa Cecilia in Trastevere

Some 500 m from the church of Santa Cecilia, near the Ponte Sublicio, is the Porta Portese, where a flea-market is held on Sunday mornings. | Porta Portese

500 m north-west of Santa Cecilia stands the church of Santa Maria in Trastevere, one of the oldest churches in Rome, founded in the 3rd c. and rebuilt in the 12th c., with a porch added in 1702. It has a picturesque interior, with 22 ancient columns, a richly decorated ceiling (1617) and fine 12th and 13th c. mosaics. | Santa Maria in Trastevere

Close by the church, in Piazza Sant'Egidio, is a Folk Museum (Museo de Folclore e dei Poeti Romaneschi). | Folk Museum

500 m north of Santa Maria in Trastevere, on the banks of the Tiber beyond the Porta Settimiana, we come to the Villa Farnesina, a Renaissance palace surrounded by gardens which was built by B. Peruzzi in 1509–11 for the Pope's banker Agostino Chigi and decorated with frescoes by Raphael and other artists – scenes from the story of Amor and Psyche (1515–18) designed by Raphael and executed by his pupils, and Galates borne over the sea in a shell, by Raphael himself (1514). From 1580 to 1731 the villa belonged to the Farnese family; it is now State-owned, and also houses the Gabinetto Nazionale delle Stampe (prints and engravings; admission only by special arrangement). | ★Villa Farnesina

Immediately west, opposite the villa is the Palazzo Corsini, occupied from 1668 to 1689 by Queen Christina of Sweden (daughter of Gustavus Adolphus, who became a Catholic) and rebuilt in 1729–32 for Cardinal Neri Corsini, with pillared courtyards and a beautiful view of the gardens. It now houses the Accademia Nazionale dei Lincèi, which has a large library. | Palazzo Corsini

San Pietro in Montorio

From the south side of the Porta Settimiana the Via Garibaldi runs south-west and then winds its way up the long ridge of the Janiculum (Monte Gianicolo), with extensive views. At the foot of the ascent is the church of San Pietro in Montorio, a Renaissance church (15th c.) founded on the spot on which, according to a medieval legend, the Apostle Peter was crucified; it has a fine interior. In the adjoining cloister is the influential Tempietto, a small round pillared temple by Bramante (1502). From the square in front of the church a magnificent view can be enjoyed.

Via Garibaldi then continues uphill to the Fontana Paolo, an elaborate fountain built for Pope Paul V in 1612 by Giovanni Fontana and Carlo | Fontana Paolo

Maderna as the terminal point of the restored Aqua Traiana (aqueduct), and ends at the Porta San Pancrazio, on the summit of the Janiculum (84 m (277 ft)).

Villa Doria Pamphili

To the west is the entrance to the Villa Doria Pamphili, a large park laid out by Algardi after 1644 for Prince Camillo Pamphili; it is now municipal property and open to the public.

Villa Sciarra

Some 500 m south of the Porta San Pancrazio is the Villa Sciarra, a public park with a luxuriant growth of southern vegetation and a lookout pavilion.

★Passeggiata del Gianicolo

To the north of the Fontana Paolo is a gate which marks the south entrance to the Passeggiata del Gianicolo, a broad avenue which runs along the ridge of the Janiculum through an attractive park. In the Piazzale Garibaldi is an equestrian statue (by Gallori, 1895) of Giuseppe Garibaldi (1807–82). Beyond this, on the left, is a monument (1912) to his first wife Anita Garibaldi. Nearby is a cannon, usually fired at noon. Farther on, to the right, stands a marble beacon (Italian "faro"; erected 1911) which at night flashes its green, white and red lights over Rome. The views of Rome and the Campagna from the Passeggiata del Gianicolo, which are particularly fine towards sunset, have an extraordinary variety and beauty.

Sant'Onofrio

At the northern end of the Janiculum is the church of Sant'Onofrio (begun 1439), with 15th–16th c. frescos; view. In the adjoining convent is the small Museo Tassiano, with relics and mementoes of the poet Torquato Tasso (1544–95) who died here.

Ponte Sant'Angelo

At the end of the Corso Vittorio Emanuele II the Ponte Vittorio Emanuele crosses to the right bank of the Tiber a little way downstream from the Castel Sant'Angelo. Just above it the imposing Ponte Sant'Angelo makes straight for the Castel Sant'Angelo. This bridge, for long the only road access to the Vatican, was originally built in AD 136 by the Emperor Hadrian and called the Pons Aelius after his family name. The ten colossal figures of angels which now adorn it were designed by Bernini, executed by various sculptors and set up on the bridge in 1668.

★Castel Sant'Angelo

At the end of the Ponte Sant'Angelo, rising above the right bank of the Tiber, is the Castel Sant'Angelo or Mausoleo di Adriano, built by Hadrian in AD 130 as a mausoleum for himself and his successors and completed by Antoninus Pius in 139. The rotunda, built on a square substructure, originally faced with marble contains the tomb chambers (open to the public) in which the Roman emperors down to Caracalla (d. AD 217) were buried. From the 6th c. onwards it was used by the rulers of Rome as a fortress, and in 1379 passed into the hands of the popes. During the Middle Ages it was transformed into a defensive bridgehead, with outer works and a covered passage leading to the Vatican.

Museum

Between 1870 and 1901 the building was used as a barracks and a prison; thereafter it was restored and fitted out as a museum, with a collection of weapons, models illustrating the history of the structure, several chapels, the treasury and the library. From the upper terrace there is a magnificent view. On the highest point is a bronze statue of the Archangel Michael (1752), recalling a vision of Pope Gregory the Great (590) to which the Castel Sant'Angelo owes its name.

Castel Sant'Angelo, on the right bank of the Tiber

To the east of the Castel Sant'Angelo is the massive Palazzo di Giustizia (Law Courts; by Calderini, 1910). Via della Conciliazione (Street of Reconciliation) leads from the Castel Sant'Angelo to the Vatican.

Vatican City

Vatican City (Stato della Città del Vaticano; SCV; Santa Sede = Holy Throne) lies on the right bank of the Tiber. It was established as a substitute for the Papal States or States of the Church which had been abolished in 1870. Under the Lateran treaties of February 11th 1929 the Italian government under Mussolini recognised the sovereignty of the Pope in international relations and his jurisdiction over the territory of the Vatican City, comprising St Peter's Church, St Peter's Square, the Vatican and the Vatican gardens, with a total area of 44 ha (109 acres), and populated by about 400 inhabitants.

Stato della Città del Vaticano

The Pope ("Holy Father"), at present the Pole Karol Wojtyla, John Paul II, elected 1978, supreme head of the Roman Catholic Church (over 700 million adherents), has legislative, executive and judicial powers. In external affairs he is represented by the Cardinal Secretary of State, while the administration (Curia) is headed by a Governor responsible only to the Pope.

Governatorato

The Pope's bodyguard consists of the Swiss Guards who are Roman Catholic citizens of Switzerland aged between 19 and 25, unmarried (minimum height 1.78 m; period of service 2–20 years), with a present strength of 100 (4 officers, 23 non-commissioned officers, 70 halberdiers, 2 drummers and 1 chaplain).

Swiss Guards

The Vatican City has its own currency (1 Vatican lira = 1 Italian lira), postal service (issuing stamps which are valid throughout Rome), telephone and

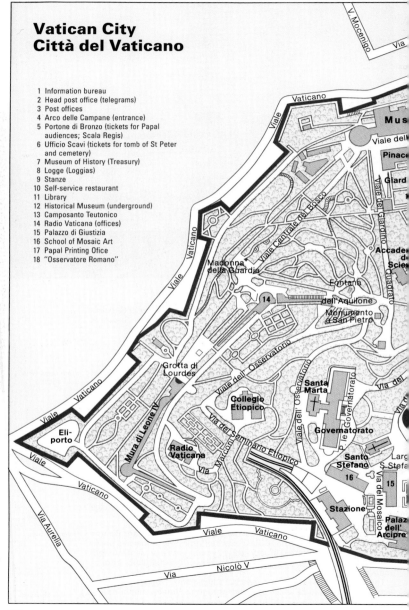

Vatican City
Città del Vaticano

1 Information bureau
2 Head post office (telegrams)
3 Post offices
4 Arco delle Campane (entrance)
5 Portone di Bronzo (tickets for Papal audiences; Scala Regis)
6 Ufficio Scavi (tickets for tomb of St Peter and cemetery)
7 Museum of History (Treasury)
8 Logge (Loggias)
9 Stanze
10 Self-service restaurant
11 Library
12 Historical Museum (underground)
13 Camposanto Teutonico
14 Radio Vaticana (offices)
15 Palazzo di Giustizia
16 School of Mosaic Art
17 Papal Printing Ofice
18 "Osservatore Romano"

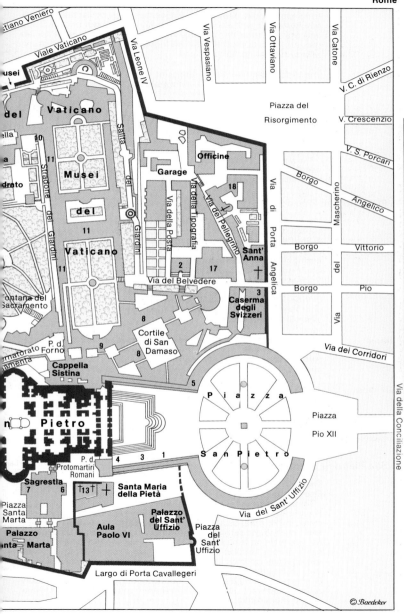

Rome

Via Sebastiano Veniero

Viale Vaticano

Via Leone IV

Via Vespasiano

Via Ottaviano

Via Catone

V.C. di Rienzo

V. Crescenzio

V. S. Porcari

Piazza del Risorgimento

Borgo Angelico

...usei

del Vaticano

Musei

del

Vaticano

...ella

...a

...drato

10

11

11

11

Salita del

Stradone del Giardini

Via dei Giardini

Garage

Officine

Via della Posta

Via della Tipografia

Via del Pellegrino

18

Sant' Anna

2

17

Via del Belvedere

Via di Porta Angelica

Borgo Mascherino

Borgo del

Borgo

Vittorio

Pio

Via

...ontana del Sacramento

3

Caserma degli Svizzeri

8

Cortile di San Damaso

8

P. d. Forno

...matorato

...amenta

9

Cappella Sistina

Via dei Corridori

Via dei Corridori

5

P i a z z a

Piazza Pio XII

Via della Conciliazione

n

Pietro

S a n   P i e t r o

P. d. Protomartiri Romani

4

3

1

Sagrestla

7

6

13

Santa Maria della Pietà

Piazza Santa Marta

Palazzo del Sant' Uffizio

Via del Sant' Uffizio

Palazzo ...nta Marta

Aula Paolo VI

Palazzo del Sant' Uffizio

Piazza del Sant' Uffizio

Largo di Porta Cavallegeri

© Baedeker

telegraph services, newspapers and journals (in particular the "Osservatore Romano"), with a circulation of 60,000–70,000), radio station (Radio Vaticana; transmissions on medium and short waves in some 35 languages), a fleet of about 100 vehicles (registration letters SCV) and its own railway station and helicopter pad.

Vatican flag

The Vatican flag has vertical stripes of yellow and white, with two crossed keys under the Papal tiara (triple crown) on a white ground. Papal possessions outside the Vatican City include the three basilicas of San Giovanni in Laterano, San Paolo fuori le Mura and Santa Maria Maggiore, the Papal administrative offices and the Pope's summer residence at Castel Gandolfo. These places enjoy extra-territorial status and are not subject to Italian law.

The territory of Vatican City, with the exception of certain permitted areas (St Peter's, the museums, the Camposanto Teutonico, etc.) can be entered only with special permission.

★★ Piazza di San Pietro

Vatican City can be reached by way of the Ponte Vittorio Emanuele and the Via della Conciliazione which runs west to end in St Peter's Square (Piazza di San Pietro), a magnificent creation by Bernini (1656–67), 340 m (1116 ft) long, up to 240 m (787 ft) wide, which enhance the effect of the most imposing church in Christendom. On either side of the oval are semicircular colonnades, formed by 284 columns and 88 pillars of the Doric order in four rows, surmounted by balustrades with 140 colossal statues of saints. In the centre of the square is an Egyptian obelisk 25.5 m (84 ft) high, hewn in the reign of Caligula (AD 37–41) and set up here in 1586; it has stood until 1586 in a circus. On either side of the obelisk are two fine fountains 14 m (46 ft) high (1613, 1675).

Forecourt

On the west side of the central oval is a forecourt, with a broad staircase. On the south side of this forecourt are the Vatican Information Office (Ufficio Informazioni Pellegrini e Turisti; bus tours of Vatican museums) and a post office (Ufficio Postale; sale of Vatican City stamps).

Audience Hall

To the rear, farther south, is the large Audience Hall (Aula Paolo VI; entrance beside Palazzo del Sant'Uffizio) built by P. L. Nervi (1964–71), with seating for 6300 or standing room for up to 12,000.

Arco delle Campagne

To the left of St Peter's Church is the Arco delle Campagne, the main entrance to the Vatican City (Swiss Guards).

★★ San Pietro in Vaticano

The west side of St Peter's Square is occupied by St Peter's Church (San Pietro in Vaticano), on the site of an Early Christian basilica.

The original church was built by Constantine the Great at the request of Pope Sylvester I (314–336) over the tomb of the Apostle Peter and consecrated in 326. It was a basilica with double aisles and a pillared forecourt, later enlarged and surrounded by chapels and convents. At Christmas in the year 800 Charlemagne received the Roman imperial crown from the hands of Pope Leo III in front of the high altar, and many emperors were subsequently crowned here. In the course of time the church fell into a state of dilapidation and was replaced by the present building, begun by Bramante in 1506 in the reign of Pope Julius II. The new church was conceived by Bramante in the form of a Greek cross (i.e. with arms of equal length) with a central dome.

St Peter's Square

Pietà by Michelangelo in St Peter's

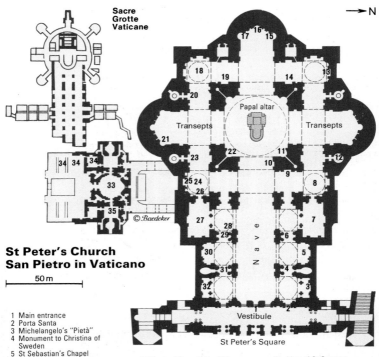

Sacre
Grotte
Vaticane

→ N

Papal altar

Transepts   Transepts

© Baedeker

**St Peter's Church
San Pietro in Vaticano**

50 m

1 Main entrance
2 Porta Santa
3 Michelangelo's "Pietà"
4 Monument to Christina of
  Sweden
5 St Sebastian's Chapel
6 Monument to Margravine
  Mathilda of Tuscany
7 Chapel of the Sacrament
8 Gregorian Chapel
9 Altar of St Jerome
10 Statue of St Peter
11 Entrance to Vatican Sacred
   Grotto
12 Entrance to Dome
13 Altar to Archangel Michael
14 Altar of St Peter (restoring
   Tabitha to life)

15 Tomb of Pope Urban VIII
16 Cathedral Petri (by Bernini)
17 Tomb of Pope Paul III
18 Chapel of the Column
19 Altar of St Peter (healing
   the lame man)
20 Tomb of Pope Alexander VII
21 Altar of the Crucifixion of
   St Peter
22 Statue of St Andrew
23 Tomb of Pope Pius VIII
24 Clementine Chapel

25 Altar of St Gregory
26 Monument to Pope Pius VII
27 Choir Chapel
28 Tomb of Pope Innocent VIII
29 Monument to Pope Pius VII
30 Chapel of the Presentation
31 Monument to Maria Sobieska
32 Baptistery
33 Sacristy
34 Museo Storico Artistico
   (Treasury)
35 Canons' Sacristy

Exterior

After his death in 1514 the work was directed by Raphael (1515–20), Antonio da Sangallo (1520–46) and other masters, and finally (1547) by Michelangelo, who designed the mighty dome, 132 m (436 ft) high (1586–93). In 1605 the centralised plan favoured by Bramante and Michelangelo was replaced by a Latin-cross plan with a nave. The nave and the Baroque façade (completed 1614; 112 m (368 ft) wide, 44 m (145 ft) high) were the work of Carlo Maderna. The effect of the dome as conceived by Michelangelo is thus entirely lost except from a distance. From the loggia above the central doorway the Pope gives his benediction "urbi et orbi" (to the city and the world) on solemn occasions (Easter, Christmas).

Portico

The portico of St Peter's is 71 m (233 ft) wide and 20 m (66 ft) high. The bronze doors of the large central doorway were the work of the Florentine sculptor Antonio Filarete (1433–45). The door on the left (Door of Death; 1964) has bronze reliefs by Giacomo Manzù (life of John XXIII, etc.). The door on the right (the Seven Sacraments) is by Messina (1965).

To the right of this is the Porta Santa, which is opened in Holy Years (every 25 years; plenary indulgence for all pilgrims to Rome).

Porta Santa

The interior (appropriate dress required) is of overwhelming effect, with its huge dimensions (186 m (610 ft long, with space for a congregation of 60,000). The effect is increased as the visitor realises the beauty of the individual features and the symmetry and harmony of the proportions. In the pavement, beginning at the central doorway, are marked the lengths of other great cathedrals: St Paul's London, 158.1 m (519 ft), Florence 149.28 m (490 ft), Rheims 138.69 m (455 ft), Milan and Cologne 134.94 m (443 ft) (Milan is actually 148 m (486 ft) wide), San Petronio, Bologna, 132.54 m (435 ft), Seville and Notre Dame, Paris, 130 m (427 ft). The total length of St Peter's, including the portico, is 211.5 m (694 ft), its width 114.7 m (376 ft) (across the transepts 152 m (499 ft), its area 16,160 sq. m (Milan 11,700, St Paul's 7875, St Sophia in Istanbul 6890, Berlin Cathedral 6270, Cologne 6166 sq. m).

Interior

In the nave, in which the second Vatican Council met in 1962–65, is a seated figure of St Peter in bronze (4th pillar on right), probably dating from the 13th c., whose right foot has been worn smooth by the kisses of the faithful. The huge dome which soars above the Papal altar and the crypt containing the tomb of St Peter has a diameter of 42 m (138 ft) and an internal height of 123.4 m (405 ft) (external height including cross 132.5 m (435 ft). It is borne on four huge piers, each with a circumference of 71 m (233 ft).

Nave

Above the Papal altar is a bronze canopy or baldacchino, 29 m (96 ft) high, with four richly gilded spiral columns and a fantastic superstructure (by Bernini, 1633). In front of the altar, enclosed by a balustrade with 95 sanctuary lamps which are always lit, is the confessio, a devotional area over St Peter's tomb, to which a double marble staircase leads down.

Papal altar

In the first chapel in the south aisle, protected by a glass screen, is Michelangelo's Pietà, a profoundly sensitive work created by the young Michelangelo at the age of 25 (1499, damaged by a vandal in 1972, skilfully restored 1973).

Pietà

Throughout the church are numerous Papal tombs, some of them of great magnificence; particularly impressive are those of Urban VIII and Paul III (both in the apse) and Innocent VIII (2nd pillar on left).

Papal tombs

From the north aisle we enter the Sacristy (1776–84) and the interesting Museo Storico-Artistico or Tesoro di San Pietro (Treasury of St Peter), with a cross which belonged to the Emperor Justin II (d. 578), sarcophagi of the consul Iunius Bassus (d. 359) and Pope Sixtus IV (d. 1484).

Museo Storico-Artistico

Also in the north aisle (ticket office beyond the first chapel) is the entrance to the dome (steps or lift to roof), then easy steps to the galleries round the dome (at heights of 53 m (175 ft) and 73 m (241 ft), from which there are astonishing views of the interior of the church. On the inner wall of the dome is a frieze 2 m (6½ ft) high with the inscription, in blue mosaic letters on a gold ground, "Tu es Petrus et super hanc petram aedificabo ecclesiam meam et tibi dabo claves regni caelorum" ("Thou art Peter, and upon this rock I will build my church and I will give unto thee the keys of the kingdom of heaven": Matt. 16, 18–19). From the colonnade on the lantern of the dome (123.5 m (405 ft) above floor level) there are far-ranging views and a glimpse of the Vatican Gardens.

Dome

From the space under the dome a staircase leads down to the interesting Sacre Grotte Vaticane, lying between the floor of the present church and

Sacre Grotte Vaticane

that of the original basilica, 3.5 m (11 ft) below. The 16th c. chambers beneath the dome contain numerous monuments from the old basilica, together with the plain stone sarcophagi of Pius XII (d. 1958), John XXIII (d. 1963), Paul VI (d. 1978) and John Paul (d. 1978). In the older parts, under the nave, are numerous Papal tombs and Early Christian sarcophagi.

Excavations

With a special permit it is possible to see the excavations (scavi) beneath St Peter's. Archaeologists have excavated the old cemetery on the Vatican hill, including what is supposed to be the tomb of St Peter and foundations of the old basilica of Constantine.

*Vatican Palace

To the right of St Peter's, occupying an area of some 5.5 ha (13½ acres) stands the Vatican Palace (Palazzi Vaticani), originally built in the 6th c. but the Pope's permanent residence only since the 14th c., when it replaced the Lateran, and much enlarged and altered since then. The rooms in which the Pope lives and works are on the upper floors of the square building on the right-hand side of St Peter's Square. Among the principal features of the palace are the Stanze, the Sistine Chapel, the Logge di Raffaello, the former Garden-House or Belvedere, the Vatican Library and the Vatican collections, with major works of ancient art and valuable pictures. Altogether there are some 1400 rooms, chapels and other apartments.

Portone di Bronzo

The Portone di Bronzo (Swiss guard; access only to office which issues tickets for Papal audiences), at the end of the right-hand colonnade in St Peter's Square, is the entrance to the Papal apartments, which form only a small part of the whole palace.

Scala Regia

The corridor straight ahead leads to the Scala Regia, remodelled by Bernini in 1663–66. In spite of the limited space, which contracts towards the top, an imposing effect was achieved by the skilful arrangement of the columns and decoration.

To the right is the Scala di Pio IX (19th c.), leading to the Cortile di San Damaso.

Entrance to the State apartments

The entrance to the State apartments – i.e. to the museums, the Library, the Borgia apartments, the Stanze, the Sistine Chapel, etc. – is on the north side of the palace, 800 m from St Peter's Square. There are regular bus services from spring until autumn to and from the Information Office, going through the Vatican Gardens; departure from upper entrance to museums. Pedestrians should go north along Via di Porta Angelica to the Piazza del Risorgimento, then west along the Vatican walls and round the bastion on Via Leone IV into Viale Vaticano.

**Vatican Museums

From the entrance to the Vatican Museums (Musei Vaticani), with statues of Raphael and Michelangelo, visitors make their way up on a curving staircase or by lift to the vestibule (ticket-offices, information, sales counters, cloakroom, lavatories, etc.). The tour is for the most part a one-way route marked by coloured arrows, with video-electronic surveillance (total length 7 km (4 mi.)). Half-way round there is an exit at the Sistine Chapel (no admission).

Collection of antiquities

From the vestibule we go east (left) through the Atrio dei Quattro Cancelli and up the Scala Simonetti to reach the Vatican collection of antiquities, the largest in the world, with several thousand pieces of sculpture. The origins of the collection go back to the Renaissance period (16th c.). The collection

Vatican Museums
Musei Vaticani

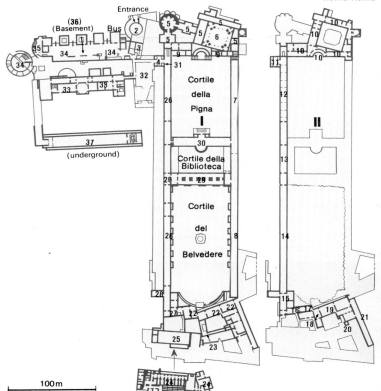

1 Lift
2 Stairs
3 Vestibule (tickets, information)
4 Atrio dei Quattro Cancelli
5 Museo Pio-Clementino
6 Cortile Ottagono
7 Museo Chiaramonti
8 Galleria Lapidaria
9 Museo Gregoriano Egizio (Egyptian Museum)
10 Museo Gregoriano Etrusco (Etruscan Museum)
11 Sala della Biga
12 Galleria dei Candelabri
13 Galleria degli Arazzi (Tapestry Gallery)

14 Galleria delle Carte Geografiche (Map Gallery)
15 Pius V's Chapel
16 Sala Sobieski
17 Sala dell'Immacolata
18 Urban VIII's Chapel
19 Stanze di Raffaello
20 Nicholas V's Chapel (Beato Angelico)
21 Logge di Raffaello (Loggias of Raphael)
22 Appartamento Borgia
23 Salette Borgia
24 Collezione d'Arte Religiosa Moderna (Museum of Modern Religious Art)

25 Sistine Chapel
26 Vatican Library
27 Museo Sacro della Biblioteca
28 Sala delle Nozze Aldobrandine
29 Salone Sistino
30 Braccio Nuovo
31 Museo Profano della Biblioteca
32 Cortile della Pinacoteca
33 Pinacoteca (Picture Gallery)
34 Museo Gregoriano Profano (Museum of Secular Art)
35 Museo Pio Cristiano
36 Museo Missionario Etnologico
37 Museo Storico (Historical Museum)

as we see it today, however, really began in the time of Clement XIV (1769–74). The main part of the collection, the Museo Pio-Clementino, is named after him and his successor Pius VI. Pius VII added the Museo Chiaramonti and the Braccio Nuovo, Gregory XVI (1831–46) the Egyptian and Etruscan museums. Most of the items were found in and around Rome, and the enormous quantity of sculpture to be seen here and in the other museums in Rome gives some idea of the extraordinary wealth of art in the public buildings and private houses of ancient Rome and bears witness of the Roman interest in the culture of Greece. There are very few Greek originals, but numerous copies of famous works of art, made by either Greek or Roman sculptors, as well as specially Roman works of art, have survived into modern times, often little the worse for their burial under the accumulated rubbish of the centuries. Although the restorations and retouching practised in the past may sometimes give an erroneous impression, here as nowhere else we can get a general impression of the whole range of ancient creative art.

Museo Pio-Clementino

We come first to the Museo Pio-Clementino. Particularly notable are:

In the Sala a Croce Greca the porphyry sarcophagi of St Helena and Constantia, mother and daughter of Constantine the Great (4th c. AD).

In the Sala Rotonda the bust of Zeus from Otricoli (4th c. BC).

In the Sala delle Muse the famous Belvedere Torso, a seated figure of a powerful muscled man (by Apollonius of Athens, 1st c. BC) and a series of portrait herms and statues of muses.

In the Sala degli Animali many figures of animals in white and coloured marble.

In the Galleria delle Statue the Apollo Sauroctonus (the Lizard-Killer), a copy of the 4th c. BC work.

In the Sala dei Busti busts.

In the Gabinetto delle Maschere (cabinet of masks) the famous Venus of Cnidos, an imitation of the Cnidian Aphrodite of Praxiteles.

"Parnassus", in the Stanze di Raffaello

In the Cortile Ottagono the famous group of Laocoön and his two sons being killed by two snakes, a masterpiece (probably 1st c. AD) by Agesandrus, Polydorus and Athenodorus of Rhodos (restored 1957–60).

In the Gabinetto dell'Apoxyomenos the Apoxyomenus, a youth scraping the oil and dust of the palaestra from his arms with a strigil, a Roman copy of the original by Lysippus (4th c. BC).

Beyond this is the Museo Chiaramonti, a corridor mostly containing Roman copies of ancient sculpture. In the adjoining Galleria Lapidaria (shut off by a grating: admission by special arrangement) 5000 inscriptions.

Museo Chiaramonti

Adjoining the south side of the Museo Pio-Clementino the Egyptian Museum (Museo Gregoriano Egizio) consists of ten rooms containing Egyptian sculpture, mostly found in and around Rome, including mummies, papyri, etc.

Egyptian Museum

On the floor above (reached by way of the "Staircase of the Assyrian Reliefs" from the Sala a Croce Greca) we come to the Etruscan Museum (Museo Gregoriano Etrusco), the rooms of which contain Etruscan antiquities recovered by excavation or received by gift, including sarcophagi, small items and a collection of Greek vases.

Etruscan Museum

In the west wing of the upper floor (to the right of the Assyrian Staircase) the Sala della Biga, a circular domed hall with a view of the Vatican Gardens, contains the two-horse chariot from which the room takes its name (only the body of the chariot and part of the right-hand horse are ancient) and two Discus-Throwers, one of them after an original by Myron (5th c. BC; head modern).

Sala della Biga

In the corridor to the south are the Galleria dei Candelabri, the Galleria degli Arazzi (tapestries of the 16th-18th c.) and the Galleria delle Carte Geografiche, with maps and views of towns painted on the walls (1580–83).

Galleria delle Carte Geografiche

At the end of the corridor is the Chapel of Pius V (tapestries, fine decorations).

In the south wing of the upper floor, above the Appartamento Borgia, are the Stanze di Raffaello, a suite of three rooms and a larger hall, the private apartments of Pope Julius II, with paintings by the 25-year-old Raphael, his teacher Perugino and his pupils (1509–20). The finest paintings are: in the Stanza dell'Incendio di Borgo, the "Fire in the Borgo" (showing the façade of the original St Peter's Church); in the Stanza della Segnatura, the most famous of the rooms, named after the Papal court (the Segnatura di Grazia) which met here weekly, the "Disputa" (the glorification of the Christian faith) and "The School of Athens" (an assembly of scholars, with Plato and Aristotle in the middle); in the Stanza d'Eliodoro "Heliodorus driven out of the Temple in Jerusalem by a Heavenly Horseman" and "The Mass of Bolsena"; and in the Sala di Constantino frescos by Giulio Romano and others, some of them based on sketches by Raphael, including "The Victory of Constantine the Great" over his rival Maxentius at Ponte Molle (AD 312).

★Stanze di Raffaello

From the Sala di Constantino we go diagonally across the Sala dei Palafrenieri which adjoins it on the south into the Chapel of Nicholas V, with frescoes by Fra Angelico (scenes from the lives of SS Lawrence and Stephen, 1447–50).

Chapel of Nicholas V

Returning across the Sala dei Palafrenieri, we enter the Loggias around the Cortile di San Damaso, the west wing of which has stucco decoration and ceiling paintings of Biblical scenes ("Raphael's Bible") by pupils of Raphael, including Giovanni da Udine (1517–19).

★Loggias of Raphael

From the Loggia we go down the staircase in the Borgia Tower to the Appartamento Borgia at the south end of the ground floor: six rooms

★Appartamento Borgia

occupied by Pope Alexander VI Borgia with brilliantly coloured wall paintings executed under the direction of Pinturicchio (1492–95). Particularly fine is the fourth room, the Sala della Via dei Santi.

Museum of Modern Religious Art

The rooms house part of the Museum of Modern Religious Art (Collezione d'Arte Religiosa Moderna, established 1973), most of which is accommodated in 55 rooms under the Sistine Chapel, including works by Barlach, Rodin, Klee, Dix, Picasso, Chagall, Dali, Moore, de Pisis, etc.

★★ Sistine Chapel

We now come to the Sistine Chapel (Cappella Sistina), the Papal domestic chapel, built in 1474–81 in the reign of Sixtus IV, and which is the meeting-place of the Conclave which elects a new Pope. The chapel (40.5 × 13.2 m (133 × 43 ft) and over 20 m (66 ft) high) owes its fame to the magnificent frescos which cover its walls and ceiling. The paintings on the upper part of the side walls (Old Testament scenes on one side, New Testament scenes on the other) were the work of the best Florentine and Umbrian painters of the day – Perugino, Pinturicchio, Botticelli, Ghirlandaio, Roselli, Signorelli (1481–84), restored 1965–74.

Ceiling paintings

The ceiling paintings by Michelangelo (1508–12), ranking among the most powerful master-works of world art, depict the story of the Creation, the Fall and its consequences, with the superhuman figures of seven prophets and five sibyls at the foot of the vaulting. Almost 30 years later (1534–41) Michelangelo painted the huge fresco of the Last Judgment on the altar wall, with more than a hundred figures dipicted with lively vigour.

There is an exit here to St Peter's (no readmission).

★ Vatican Library

From the Sistine Chapel we continue north into the Vatican Library (Biblioteca Apostolica Vaticana), founded by Pope Nicholas V about 1450, which now contains some 800,000 books, 80,000 manuscripts, 10,000 incunabula and over 100,000 engravings and woodcuts. The 70 m (230 ft) long room was built by Domenico Fontana. Glass cabinets house some especially valuable books.

Museo Sacro

At the south end of the library is the Museo Sacro, with material excavated in the catacombs, reliquaries, carved ivories, glass, enamel-work and textiles. One of the oldest items is a 3rd c. tunic.

Sala delle Nozze Aldobrandini

In the Sala delle Nozze Aldobrandini are ancient paintings, including scenes from the "Odyssey" and the Aldobrandini Marriage, one of the finest surviving ancient wall paintings, probably an Augustan copy of a Greek original of the 4th c. BC.

★ Salone Sistino

We know come to the south cross-wing in which is the Salone Sistino, originally the main hall.

Braccio Nuovo

To the right is the north cross-wing, the Braccio Nuovo ("new arm"), a hall 70 m (230 ft) long containing numerous statues. Notable among them are a statue of Augustus found at Prima Porta; a colossal group representing the Nile surrounded by 16 playing children (symbolising the 16 cubits which the river rises when in flood); and a Doryphorus (spear-bearer) after Polycletus.

Museo Profano della Biblioteca

From here we continue through a series of frescoed rooms belonging to the Library to the Museo Profano (ancient small sculpture, etc.), which we leave at the Atrio dei Quattro Cancelli.

Secret Archives of the Vatican

Associated with the Library are the famous Secret Archives of the Vatican, with a school of palaeography.

★★ Pinacoteca Vaticana

From the Cortile della Pinacoteca we reach the Picture Gallery (Pinacoteca Vaticana), in a building erected in 1927–32, with 15 rooms which give an excellent survey of Italian painting from the 13th to the 17th c.

Room I: Byzantine and early Italian paintings.
Room II: Giotto and his school.
Room II: Fra Filippo Lippi, Fra Angelico, Benozzo Gozzoli.
Room IV: frescoes by Melozzo da Forli (heads of Apostles), etc.
Roome V and VI: Lucas Cranach the Elder ("Pietà"), Crivelli, Giotto.
Room VII: Perugino and Umbrian painters of the 15th c.
Room VIII: dedicated to Raphael: "Madonna of Foligno" (1512; in the background the town of Foligno), "Transfiguration" (1517–20, his last great work; restored 1972–76) and tapestries (arazzi) of scenes from the lives of the Apostles (woven in Brussels 1516–19 from cartocns by Raphael).
Room IX: pictures by various 16th c. masters including Leonardo da Vinci.
Room X: Titian ("Madonna in Glory"), Caravaggio, Guido Freni, Fra Bartolomeo and Veronese.
Room XI: Renaissance and Baroque masters.
Room XII: 17th c. (Baroque).
Rooms XIII and XIV: 17th and 18th c. pictures.
Room XV: portraits of popes.
Rooms XVI–XVIII: contemporary painting.

A new building (1970) parallel to the Pinacoteca on the north houses the former Lateran museum.

The Museo Gregoriano Profano contains Greek and Roman sculpture, either in the original or in copies, and ancient sarcophagi. In the second side room on the right is a figure of Niobe which may be an original from a group by the School of Scopas (4th c. BC). ★Museo Gregoriano Profano

The Museo Pio Cristiano has early Christian sarcophagi (mostly 4th–5th c.), sculpture and inscriptions. Museo Pio Cristiano

The Museo Missionario Etnologico (on the lower floor) gives an excellent survey of the missionary activities of the Roman Catholic Church and the ethnology, prehistory and natural history of the mission lands. Museo Missionario Etnologico

From here a passage leads to the Museo Storico (historical museum, opened 1973), situated underground to the south of the Pinacoteca, which contains vehicles and relics of the military forces of the former Papal States. Museo Storico

To the south of the Arco delle Campagne (the main visitor's entrance to Vatican City, to the left of St Peter's) is the Camposanto Teutonico, the old German cemetery. The church, originally 15th c., was restored in 1973. To the rear is a priests' college and a collection of ancient finds. Camposanto Teutonico

The Vatican Gardens include the area of St Peter's, a number of administrative buildings, churches, and the Casina di Pio IV (seat of the Papal Academy of Science); they extend as far as the station and the Vatican Museums. Open Mon.–Tue., Thu.–Sat.; closed religious holidays. Tickets from the tourist office in Piazza di San Pietro. Giardini Vaticani

Vatican to the Foro Italico

From the Piazza del Risorgimento a broad traffic artery, beginning as the Via Ottaviano, runs north to the Piazza Maresciallo Giardino, from which Via di Villa Madama continues north-west to Villa Madama, on the eastern slopes of Monte Mario. The villa was built in 1516–27 for Cardinal Giulio de' Medici from designs by Raphael. It is now an administrative building of the Italian government; fine views of the town. Villa Madama

On Monte Mario (139 m (459 ft)), the Italian zero meridian, marked by the Torre del Primo Meridiano, are a public park (view) and an observatory. On Monte Mario the south-east slopes are the headquarters of the Italian radio and televi-sion corporation RAI (Radiotelevisione Italiana). Higher up, to the west, is the church of the Madonna del Rosario, with a fine viewpoint.

★Foro Italico

From the Piazza Maresciallo Giardino the Lungotevere Maresciallo Cadorna runs alongside the Tiber to the Piazza De Bisis, where the Ponte Duca d'Aosta (1939) provides a link with the Via Flaminia. On the west side of the square, marked by a monolith 17 m (56 ft) high, is the entrance to the Foro Italico or Campo della Farnesina, a sports centre built shortly before and after the Second World War in which the principal events in the 1960 Summer Olympic Games were held. Notable features of the centre are the Swimming Pool, the Swimming Stadium, the Stadio dei Marmi, sur-rounded by 60 statues of athletes in Carrara marble and the Stadio Olimpico (1953), where the 1990 World Cup football final was held. On the north side of the complex is the Ministry of Foreign Affairs (Ministerio degli Affari Esteri). Higher up, on the slopes of the Monti della Farnesina, is the French Military Cemetery.

Ponte Milvio

East of the Foro Italico the Ponte Milvio or Ponte Molle, the Roman Pons Milvius, originally built to carry the Via Flaminia over the Tiber, was rebuilt in stone and improved in the 19th c. Only the four central arches are of Roman origin.

Stadio Flaminio

South of the Tiber are the Stadio Flaminio (1959), the circular Palazzetto dello Sport (1957) and the Olympic Village, built in 1960 and now occupied by government employees and their families.

Esposizione Universale di Roma (EUR)

On the southern outskirts of the city, 7 km (4 mi.) from the Piazza Venezia on the road to Lido di Ostia and Anzio, straddling the Via Cristoforo Colombo, is the extensive area (420 ha (1037 acres), well provided with open spaces) of the Esposizione Universale di Roma or EUR for short (Metropolitana from Termini Station). This was the site elected for a great international exhibition to be held in 1942 but cancelled because of the Second World War, and numbers of grandiose buildings were erected, most of them completed only after 1945 and now occupied by government departments, offices of various kinds and museums, including a residential area. The sports facilities in this area were provided for the 1960 Olympics. These include the large Centro Sportivo delle Tre Fontane (several facilities); to the south on higher ground the circular Palazzo dello Sport (1960) and 750 m west of this is the Velodromo Olimpico (1960), a cycle-racing track.

Palazzo della
Civiltà del Lavoro

At the north-west corner of the area, near the Magliana Metro station, is the striking Palazzo della Civiltà del Lavoro, 68 m (224 ft) high. Some distance south-west is the large domed church of Santi Pietro e Paolo.

Palazzo dei
Congressi

From the Palazzo della Civiltà the broad Viale della Civiltà del Lavoro runs east to the Palazzo dei Congressi, to the north-east of which is a large amusement park.

Museo Nazionale
delle Arti e
Tradizioni Popolari

100 m west of the Palazzo dei Congressi, in Piazza Marconi, we find the Museo Nazionale delle Arti e Tradizioni Popolari, with departments of folk art and folk traditions. The costume exhibits give an impression of the traditions of the various regions in Italy.

Museo Preistorico
ed Etnografico
Luigi Pigorini

Farther south is the Museo Preistorico ed Etnografico Luigi Pigorini, with material illustrating the prehistory of Latium and ethnographical collec-tions from Ethiopia, Oceania, South America and other countries.

Museo dell'Alto
Medioevo

The above building also houses the Museo dell'Alto Medioevo (Museum of the Early Medieval Period), with material of that period.

Farther east again is the Museo della Civiltà Romana, an impressive collection of material illustrating the development and the greatness of the Roman Empire, as well as the architectural development in Republican and Imperial times; a particularly notable feature (Room 37) is the model of Rome as it was in the 4th c. AD.

★Museo della Civiltà Romana

Some 500 m north-east of the latter museum, on the spot where St Peter is supposed to have been beheaded, is the Trappist Abbazia delle Tre Fontane (Abbey of the Three Fountains), with three churches (13th and 16th c.).

Abbazia delle Tre Fontane

8 km (5 mi.) south of the EUR, on SS148 near Castel de Decima, a large Latin cemetery of the 9th–7th c. BC was discovered in 1974, containing princely graves with rich burial goods.

Latin cemetery

Surroundings

South-west of Rome, on the coast, is the little town and resort of Fiumicino (population 15,000), founded only in 1825. (Take the Via Ostiense; the old road, the Via Portuense, is 4 km (2½ mi.) shorter, but hilly and winding.) Near the town are the excavations of the old port of Rome.

Fiumicino
32 km (20 mi.) SW

Just before the town, to the right, is the large Leonardo da Vinci Airport. (There is a rail link between the airport and the Stazione Termini station in the city (30 minutes)).

Leonardo da Vinci Airport

The place of the ancient port of Rome, has been taken by Civitavecchia (11 m (36 ft); population 49,000). The only feature of interest in the town, which was almost completely destroyed during the Second World War and was rebuilt after the war in modern style, is the fortress, begun by Bramante and Michelangelo. In early 1995 Civitavecchia was the scene of the "miracle" of the "weeping Madonna" in the church of Sant Agostino in nearby Partano.

Civitavecchia
75 km (47 mi.) NW

★Via Appia Antica

A trip along the Via Appia Antica, starting from the Porta San Sebastiano, is very rewarding. It is planned to establish an "archaeological park" here. The road, constructed in 312 BC, originally ran from Rome via Terracina to Capua and was later extended to Benevento and Brindisi. Alongside the road can be seen the remains of the rows of tombs which lined the roads outside the city, together with the well-preserved or restored individual tombs of wealthy Romans, which combine with the huge arches of Roman aqueducts such as the Aqua Marcia and the Aqua Claudia, at varying distances from the road, to make up the particular charm of the Roman Campagna.

The catacombs were originally the officially recognised burial-places of both Christians and pagans, known by the Greek name of coemeteria ("place of rest"). Until the early 9th c. the cemeteries containing the remains of martyrs were much venerated, and many relics were removed and deposited in churches. Thereafter the cemeteries were abandoned and neglected. The present name is derived from a burial-place of this kind at a spot called Catacumba, near San Sebastiano.
   The scientific exploration of the catacombs began at the end of the 16th c. Recent research has shown that the catacombs were used only for burial and for Masses for the dead, not as places of refuge for persecuted Christians or for ordinary religious services. The arrangement of the catacombs is very simple – narrow passages with long recesses, hewn from the walls in several tiers, for the reception of bodies, the individual recesses being closed by tablets of marble or terracotta. The style of decoration (painting,

★Catacombs

Via Appia Antica

more rarely sculpture) reflects that of the pagan art of the period. The decorative themes are mainly symbolic – the sacrificial lamb, the fish (Greek ichthys, which consists of the initial letters of the Greek phrase "Jesus Christ, Son of God, Saviour). There are also early representations of the Last Supper and the Virgin Mary. The older inscriptions give only the name of the dead person.

Domine Quo Vadis

Some 800 m from the Porta San Sebastiano, on the left of the road at the point where the Via Ardeatina branches off on the right, is the little church of Domine Quo Vadis, so named from the legend that Peter, fleeing from Rome to escape martyrdom, met Christ here and asked "Domine, quo vadis?" ("Master, where are you going?") and received the answer "Venio iterum crucifigi" ("I come to be crucified a second time"); whereupon Peter, ashamed of his weakness, returned to Rome. In the church is a copy of Christ's footprint.

★Catacombs of St Calixtus

1 km (³/₄ mi.) farther on, at a clump of cypresses on the right (Via Appia Antica 110), is the entrance to the Catacombs of St Calixtus (Catacombe di San Callisto), the most interesting of these Early Christian underground burial-places which encircle Rome.

Notable features of the Catacombs of St Calixtus, which extend over a considerable area on several levels, are the Cubiculum Pontificium, containing the tombs of a number of 3rd c. popes (Urban I, Pontianus, Anterus, Fabianus, Lucius, Eutychianus); the empty tomb of St Cecilia; the tomb chamber of Pope Eusebius (309–311); and the tomb of Pope Cornelius (251–253), in what was originally the separate Cemetery of Lucina.

Catacomb of Praetextus

A short distance beyond the Catacombs of St Calixtus, near the point where the Via Appia Pignatelli branches off the Via Appia Antica on the left, is the Catacomb of Praetextus (martyred in the time of Diocletian), with the tomb chamber of the 2nd c. martyr Januarius. Admission by appointment only.

500 m from the Catacombs of St Calixtus, on the right of the Via Appia
Antica, is the church of San Sebastiano, one of Rome's seven pilgrimage
churches, built in the 4th c. on a spot thought to have been the temporary
resting-place ("Ad Catacumbas") of the bodies of the Apostles Peter and
Paul. The church was rebuilt in the 17th c. with a portico of ancient
columns.

San Sebastiano

In the first chapel on the right is a stone with what is believed to be the
footprint of Christ. On the left is St Sebastian's Chapel, the sacristy with
sarcophagi, and the entrance to the impressive Catacombs of St Sebastian.
   Under the centre of the church is an assembly room (triclia) for memorial services, with numerous inscriptions dating from the 3rd and 4th c.
scratched on the walls. The invocations to the Apostles Peter and Paul
seem to confirm the tradition that during the Valerian persecution in the
year 258 the remains of the two Apostles were brought here or hereabouts
from the Vatican and the Via Ostiense for safety. There are also tomb
chambers on several levels dating from the 1st c., with paintings, stucco
decoration and inscriptions. Behind the apse steps lead down to the
Platonia, with the tomb of the martyr Quirinus. To the left of this is a cell
with the inscription "Domus Petri" and 4th c. wall paintings.

Catacombs of
St Sebastian

Just before San Sebastiano the Vicolo delle Sette Chiese branches off on
the right. 650 m along this are the Fosse Ardeatine, with a mausoleum,
commemorating the 335 Italians who were shot here by the Germans in
March 1944 in reprisal for a bomb attack.

Fosse Ardeatine

300 m farther on are the extensive Catacombs of Domitilla, with Early
Christian inscriptions and wall paintings, and the 4th c. Basilica of St
Petronilla (restored in the 19th c.).

Catacombs of
Domitilla

Continuing along the Via Appia, we come to a large gateway on the left,
near which is the Circus of Maxentius, constructed in AD 311, which was
used for chariot races (482 m (1581 ft) long, 79 m (259 ft) across).

Circus of
Maxentius

Just beyond this, also on the left, is the Tomb of Caecilia Metella, the best-
known ruin in the Campagna, a circular structure 20 m (66 ft) in diameter
faced with travertine, with a marble frieze adorned with wreaths of flowers
and ox-skulls. In the 13th c. it was used as a fortified tower by the Caetani
family and equipped with battlements.
   Beyond this point the original paving of the Via Appia is visible in several
places. The road runs south-east, with beautiful views of the Alban Hills
straight ahead and the arches of the Aqua Marcia and Aqua Claudia on the
left. On both sides are the remains of numerous tombs, including two tumuli
from which there are extensive views of the Campagna.

★Tomb of Caecilia
Metella

Some 2.5 km (1½ mi.) beyond the Tomb of Caecilia Metella, near the farm
of Santa Maria Nuova, are the extensive remains of a large villa of the time
of Hadrian, the Villa dei Quintili or Roma Vecchia.

Villa dei Quintili

1.25 km (¾ mi.) farther on, at Casale Rotondo, is a large tomb of the 1st c. AD.

Casale Rotondo

Rome to Frascati and Albano (35 km (22 mi.))

Leave Rome by way of Porta San Giovanni and the Via Appia Nuova, and
very shortly turn left into the Via Tuscolana (SS215).

10 km (6 mi.): Cinecittà, a large complex of film studios where many Italian
films have been made.

Cinecittà

1 km (¾ mi.): road on the right (10 km (6 mi.) to Grottaferrata (329 m (1086 ft);
population 52,000), a little town in the Alban Hills, with a fortress-like

Grottaferrata

monastery of Greek Basilian monks and an old church, almost entirely rebuilt in 1754; in the chapel of St Nilus in the south aisle are fine frescos by Domenichino (1609–10).

Frascati

10 km (6 mi.): Frascati (see entry).

Ponte Squarciarelli

3 km (2 mi.) beyond Frascati on the road to Albano one reaches the Ponte Squarciarelli, where roads go off on the right to Grottaferrata (2 km (1¼ mi.)), on the left to Rocca di Papa and Monte Cavo (11 km (7 mi.)) and straight ahead to Albano.

Marino

3 km (2 mi.): Marino (355 m (1172 ft); population 31,000), picturesquely situated on a spur of the Alban Hills.

★Nemi

1 km (¾ mi.) farther on the Via dei Laghi (17 km (11 mi.)), branches off on the left, runs high above the Lago Albano and comes in 9 km (5½ mi.) to side roads to the Lago di Nemi and the village of Nemi (521 m (1719 ft)), above the Lago di Nemi (318 m (1049 ft); area 1.7 sq. km (½ sq. mi.); perimeter 5.5 km (3½ mi.), greatest depth 34 m (112 ft)), a crater lake surrounded by tufa cliffs 200 m (660 ft) high. In the village is the Shipping Museum, with reduced scale models of the two State galleys of the Emperor Caligula which were discovered during drainage of the lake in 1928–31 and were burned by German forces in 1944.

Velletri

The road continues through wooded country to Velletri (cathedral with crypt and museum, and a beautiful medieval crucifix).

★Lago Albano

The Lago Albano (293 m (967 ft); perimeter 10km/6 miles; greatest depth 170 m (558 ft)), above which lay the Latin federal capital of Alba Longa, destroyed at an early stage by the Romans, is of volcanic origin, and is drained by an ancient tunnel (emissario; guided visit) said to have been constructed by the Romans in the 4th c. BC.

The road to Albano continues beyond the turn-off, running high above the west side of the Lago Albano.

Castel Gandolfo

3 km (2 mi.): Castel Gandolfo (426 m (1405 ft); population 6000), the summer residence of the Pope, beautifully situated above the Lago Albano. In the centre of the little town is the Piazza del Plesbiscito, with the parish church of San Tommaso (by Bernini, 1661), built on a centralised plan, and the Pope's Summer Palace (by Carlo Maderna, 1629), containing the Papal observatory (established 1578; in the Vatican until 1935). Together with the adjacent Villa Barberini it was made part of the Vatican City State in 1929. In the grounds of the palace is an audience hall which can accommodate 8000 people. From Castel Gandolfo there is a funicular down to the lake.

From here Albano can be reached either on foot along the scenically attractive Galleria di Sopra, flanked by evergreen oaks (3.5 km (2¼ mi.)), or by car on the Galleria di Sotto, which is 1 km (¾ mi.) shorter but relatively featureless.

Albano Laziale

2 km (1¼ mi.): Albano Laziale (384 m (1267 ft); population 28,000) lies on the high west side of Lago Albano. It has been the see of a bishop since 460 and is a resort much favoured by the people of Rome in summer for its beautiful setting. In the south-eastern outskirts of the town, on the right-hand side of the Via Appia, is a cube-shaped tomb of the late Republican period known (without any justification) as the Tomb of the Horatii and Curiatii. On the north-west side of the town, in the garden of a house at Via Saffi 86, are the remains of a large underground cistern known as il Cisternone, dating from the time of Septimius Severus and built for his mercenaries. Farther north-west, between the convent of San Paolo and a Capuchin convent, the remains of an amphitheatre, also dating from the reign of Septimius (3rd c. AD) can be seen through a gate.

Rome to Terracina over the Agro Pontino
(125 km (78 mi.))

Leave Rome by the Porta San Paolo or by the Porta Ardeatina and then take the Via Pontina (SS148), which gives a good impression of the land reclaimed from the former Pontine Marshes. After passing through the EUR the road runs through the Roman Campagna.

31 km (19 mi.): a road on the right (1 km (³/₄ mi.)) leads to the little town of Pomezia (89 m (194 ft); population 30,000), founded in 1939.

15 km (9 mi.): the Via Pontina enters the Agro Pontino, an area of some 800 sq. km (309 sq. mi.) criss-crossed by countless canals and water channels. This low-lying area between the Monti Lepini and the sea, fringed by lines of dunes, degenerated after the abandonment of the Roman drainage system into marshland (the Pontine Marshes). From 1928 onwards the land was drained and brought into cultivation.

26 km (16 mi.): Latina (21 m (69 ft); population 96,000) was founded in 1932 and known until the Second World War as Littoria, with concentric rings of streets round a large central square, the Piazza del Popolo; it is the provincial capital.

From Latina it is 23 km (14 mi.) to Sabaudia (12 m (40 ft); population 13,000) and then 27 km (17 mi.) on the coast road to Terracina.

Pontine Marshes

Pomezia

Agro Pontino

Latina

Terracina

Rome to Lido di Ostia, Anzio and Terracina
(145 km (90 mi.))

Leave Rome by the Porta San Paolo and the Via Ostiense, and shortly before the church of San Paolo fuori le Mura bear right into SS8 (the "Via del Mare", of motorway standard), which runs close to the Tiber for most of the way.

8 km (5 mi.): road on the right (motorway standard) over the Tiber to the Leonardo da Vinci Airport.

16 km (10 mi.): road to the excavations of ancient Ostia (see entry).

4 km (2¹/₂ mi.): Lido di Ostia (see Ostia).

The road to Anzio runs along the south-east side of Lido di Ostia, past the end of a road from Rome running through the area once occupied by an international exhibition, and then skirts the beautiful Pineta di Castel Fusano, 4 km (2¹/₂ mi.) long, in which the paving of the ancient Via Severiana has been brought to light. It then follows the coast, passing close to the excavations of ancient Lavinium.

20 km (12 mi.): the road reaches Tor Vaianica (3 m (10 ft)), a small bathing resort.

11 km (7 mi.): road (sharp left) to Ardea (8 km (5 mi.)), with the Museo Manzù, devoted to the work of the famous sculptor.

6 km (3³/₄ mi.): Lavinio Lido di Ernea (20 m (66 ft)) is a seaside resort on the territory of Anzio.

8 km (5 mi.): Anzio (10 m (33 ft); population 28,000), a seaside resort, is situated at the end of a small promontory. It was the birthplace of the emperors Caligula and Nero. On the east side of the town is the new harbour built by Pope Innocent XII in 1698. To the west of the pier (view extending to Capo Circeo and the Pontine Islands) is Nero's harbour, now

Leonardo da Vinci Airport

Ostia

Lido di Ostia

Pineta di Castel Fusano

Tor Vaianica

Ardea

Lavinio

Anzio

silted up, with remains of the old breakwater. There are attractive boat trips along the coast, which is littered with ancient remains. Below the lighthouse the promontory is riddled with ancient passages, the "Grotte di Nerone", which led to a large imperial villa. To the north-west is the Arco Muto, an artificial archway in the rock.

The road to Terracina continues past villas and bathing beaches.

Nettuno

3 km (2 mi.): Nettuno (11 m (36 ft); population 30,000), another seaside resort which was the scene of heavy fighting in January 1944, when American forces landed here while British forces landed in Anzio. In the northern outskirts of the town is the largest American military cemetery in Italy (7500 graves). Also in Nettuno is the tomb of Maria Goretti (1890–1902), who was canonised in 1950.

Torre d'Astura

12 km (7 mi.): a narrow side road on right goes to the Torre d'Astura, 2 km (1¼ mi.) south on an islet linked to the mainland by a bridge. The tower is the only remnant of a castle of the Frangipani family in which Conradin of Swabia vainly sought shelter after the battle of Tagliacozzo in 1268.

Lago di Caprolace

Shortly after this the main road returns to the coast and then runs inland in a wide bend between the Lago di Fogliano on the left and the little Lago dei Monaci on the right. Beyond this it skirts the Lago di Caprolace (4 km (2½ mi.) long).

Lago di Sabaudia

28 km (17 mi.): a road on the left goes to Sabaudia (3 km (2 mi.)), along the north side of the Lago di Sabaudia, a much indented lake 7 km (4¼ mi.) long.
Beyond the turning for Sabaudia the coast road runs between the west side of the Lago di Sabaudia and the sea.

Monte Circeo

7 km (4¼ mi.): the road crosses the Emissario Romano, an ancient channel from the Lago di Sabaudia, which was used as a harbour in Roman times. Beyond this is Monte Circeo, the Roman Promontorium Circaeum, the traditional site of the palace of the Homeric enchantress Circe. The promontory is an isolated outlier of the Apennines which has been joined to the mainland by alluvial deposits (rich flora; national park).

Circe's Cave

Beyond the bridge over the Emissario, on the hillside to the right, is the massive Torre Paola, from which a footpath (sometimes closed) ascends to Circe's Cave (no entry); the walk takes half an hour.
The road continues along the north side of the promontory.

San Felice

5 km (3 mi.): take the road on the right (2 km (1¼ mi.)) to the village of San Felice (89 m (294 ft); population 8000), in a commanding situation on the north-east slope of Monte Circeo, with an old castle which belonged to the Caetani family (beautiful view from the tower). Above the village is a wall of polygonal cyclopean masonry known as the Cittadella Vecchia, a relic of the town of Cercei or Circei. From here a narrow and winding hill road climbs (3.5 km (2¼ mi.) west) to the Semáforo (448 m (1478 ft); military area), from which there are superb views south-west as far as Ischia, Capri and Vesuvius, and south to the Pontine Islands. From the Semáforo there is a rewarding climb (1 hour) to the summit of the hill (541 m (1785 ft)), from which the dome of St Peter's can be seen in clear weather.
Beyond the turn-off the main road continues, keeping close to the coast all the way.

Terracina

15 km (9 mi.): Terracina. The town is magnificently situated at the foot of high limestone crags, on the boundary between central and southern Italy. In the upper town which rises above the main road to the north stands the 12th c. cathedral of San Cesareo, incorporating a temple of Roma and Augustus, with a portico borne on eleven ancient columns and a fine

campanile (view). The church has a notable interior, with remains of a mosaic pavement, a magnificent pulpit and a richly ornamented Easter candlestick, all 13th c. Cosmatesque work.

From the cathedral a strada panoramica leads (3 km (2 mi.)) to the summit of Monte Sant'Angelo or Monte Teodorico (228 m (752 ft)), from which there are splendid views, extending in fine weather as far as Vesuvius. On a projecting spur of rock is a terrace, partly supported on arcades with the remains of an imposing temple of Jupiter Anxur (1st c. BC).

Monte Sant'Angelo

  On the eastern outskirts of the town is the Taglio di Pisco Montano, a notable example of Roman road-building, where the rock face was cut away to lower the course of the Via Appia by some 40 m (131 ft).

Salerno   J14

Region: Campania. Province: Salerno (SA)
Altitude: 4 m (13 ft). Population: 156,000

Salerno, capital of the province of the same name, lies some 50 km (31 mi.) south-east of Naples at the north end of the Gulf of Salerno, where the hills of the Sorrento peninsula fall steeply down to the Tyrrhenian Sea.

Location

The old town, rising up the slopes of the hill on the site of the ancient Salernum. It had the oldest medical school in Europe, which flourished from the 11th c. until it was closed down by Murat, Napoleon's brother-in-law, in 1812.

Medical school

Harbour and town centre

Along the seafront to the east of the harbour, now used only by local shipping (trips to Capri, Amalfi and Positano), extends the Lungomare Trieste, a fine promenade lined by imposing modern buildings and affording extensive views. Parallel to the Lungomare Trieste is Via Roma, which with its continuation to the south-east, the Corso Giuseppe Garibaldi, is the town's principal traffic artery. At the west end of Via Roma we come to the Piazza Amendola, bounded on the east by the Palazzo di Città (Town Hall) and on the south-west by the Prefecture. Behind the Prefecture are the beautiful Public Gardens (Villa Comunale), on the west side of which is the Teatro Verdi.

Half-way along Via Roma stands the Palazzo di Provincia. From here Via del Duomo runs north, crossing the picturesque Via dei Mercanti, to the cathedral of San Matteo, built about 1080 in the time of Robert Guiscard and restored in 1768 and after 1945. A flight of steps leads up to an atrium with 28 ancient columns from Paestum and fourteen ancient sarcophagi. The magnificent bronze doors were made in Constantinople in 1099.

★Cathedral

  Above the doorway is a large half-length mosaic of St Matthew, of the Norman period.

In the nave are two ambos (12th c.) with rich Cosmatesque mosaic decoration, and near the right-hand one is an Easter candlestick decorated in similar style. At the end of the north aisle is the splendid tomb of Margaret of Anjou (d. 1412).

Interior

  The pavement of the choir and the choir screens are decorated with mosaics. In the chapel to the right of the high altar is the tomb of Pope Gregory VII, who died in Salerno in 1085; in the apse of the chapel is a mosaic figure of the Archangel Matthew (1260).

  In the richly decorated crypt under the altar lie the remains of the Evangelist Matthew, brought here from Paestum.

Salerno

View of Salerno container port

Cathedral Museum	In the Cathedral Museum is a 12th c. altar frontal, with ivory reliefs of Biblical scenes.
Museo Provinciale in Salerno	A little way east of the cathedral, in Via San Benedetto, is the interesting Provincial Museum, with antiquities, including an over-life-size bronze head of Apollo of the 1st c. BC and pictures.
Castello di Arechi	From the cathedral it is a 45-minute walk to the old Lombard Castello di Arechi (263 m (868 ft)) on the hill north-west of the town. The castle was strengthened by Robert Guiscard in the 11th c. From here there are extensive views.

Cava de' Tirreni

Near Salerno, surrounded by hills, is the attractively situated little town of Cava de' Tirreni (180 m (594 ft); population 50,000), a popular holiday resort. On the hills around the town are dotted slender round towers, many of which are still used to trap wild pigeons in October, the birds being attracted by small white stones thrown from the towers and are then caught in nets.

★ Monte San Liberatore	2.5 km (1½ mi.) south-east of Cava lies Alessia (270 m (891 ft)), from which it is a 45-minute walk up Monte San Liberatore (466 m (1538 ft)), perhaps the finest viewpoint in the Gulf of Salerno.
★ La Trinità della Cava	3.5 km (2 mi.) south-west of Cava, on Corpo di Cava, stands the Benedictine abbey of La Trinità della Cava, founded in 1011. The present buildings date from the late 18th c. The church contains marble and mosaic altars, tombs of the earliest abbots and a 12th c. marble pulpit. Other notable features are the chapter-house (16th c.), the Romanesque cloister (small museum), the old crypt, a picture gallery and the archives.

Velia

In addition to Pompeii, Herculaneum and Paestum (see entries) there is
the interesting Roman site of Velia (south of Salerno and Paestum), once
a popular resort of the Roman aristocracy, which has the remains of a
number of villas and town gates. 5 km (17 ft) beneath the Roman city were
found remains of the Greek town of Elea, including some fine pieces of
statuary and the notable Porta Rosa (4th c. BC), a masterpiece of Greek
architecture. The Greek town was founded in 536 BC by Phocaeans who
had been driven out of their original settlement at Alalia on Corsica.
Between c. 540 and 460 BC this was the home of the famous Eleatic school
of philosophy led by Xenophanes, Parmenides and Zeno; the town also
had a noted school of medicine. At that time Elea probably had a population of 40,000, and its walls had a total length of 6 km (3½ mi.), later
extended to 7 km (4½ mi.). The excavation of the ancient city (under which
earlier remains dating from the 8th c. were found) is still in progress
(museum exhibits in various buildings).

On a hill to the north of the site excavations have brought to light the
foundations of a temple of the 5th c. BC, which was destroyed during the
construction of the medieval castle, together with remains of a square
tower of the 4th c. BC, three smaller temples, a sacrificial altar, several
dwelling houses (2nd c. BC) and the road from the acropolis to the harbour.

Avellino

About 30 km (19 mi.) north of Salerno lies Avellino (348 m (1148 ft); population 57,000), capital of the province of the same name and the see of an
archbishop. The town has food and textile industries and is a trade centre
for agricultural produce.

Palinuro

Along the bays of Naples and Salerno in particular are numerous
seaside resorts, some of them very elegant and fashionable. Further south
is the resort of Palinuro (53 m (174 ft)), with excellent facilities for all kinds
of water sports (diving centre). To the west of the town is the Grotta
Azzurra (Blue Grotto), which is accessible only by boat.

80 km (50 mi.) SE

2.5 km (1½ mi.) south-west lies Capo Palinuro (203 m (670 ft); lighthouse),
the south side of which falls sheer down to the sea. Here, too, are several
caves accessible only from the sea.

Capo Palinuro

★Grotta di Pertosa

From the A3 motorway east of Salerno an attractive detour can be made
by way of the little town of Auletta (280 m (924 ft)), below the north side of
the Monti Alburni (1742 m (749 ft)), to the stalactitic Grotta di Pertosa, a
cave system 2250 m (7425 ft) long. The caves were inhabited from the end
of the Neolithic period.

★Certosa di San Lorenzo

Another detour can be made off the A3 motorway in southern Campania.
Just outside Padula (699 m (2307 ft); population 6000) stands the Certosa
di San Lorenzo, founded in 1308, a massive building dating mostly from
the 17th and 18th c., with three beautifully arcaded courtyards and a large
external staircase by Vanvitelli.

70 km (44 mi.) SE

★★San Gimignano   F9

Region: Toscana. Province: Siena (SI)
Altitude: 324 m (1069 ft). Population: 7500

Location

The little town of San Gimignano lies on a hill, visible from afar, some 35 km (22 mi.) north-west of Siena and 50 km (31 mi.) south-west of Florence.
San Gimignano is one of the most attractive little towns in Tuscany, still preserving a picturesque medieval aspect with its circuit of walls and its towers.

History

In the 13th and 14th c. San Gimignano was an independent city, but in 1353 it became subject to Florence. Until then it was involved in the strifes between the house of Ardinghelli (Guelf) and the house of Salvucci (Ghibelline). The rivalry led to the erection of the towers (originally 56). The remaining thirteen towers and the walls surrounding the town give it a medieval aspect.

Sights

Palazzo del Popolo (Pinacoteca Civica)

The central feature of San Gimignano is the Piazza della Cisterna with a beautiful fountain surrounded by tall towers. Adjoining this square, on the north-west is another square, the Piazza del Duomo, on the south side of which is the Palazzo del Popolo, built in 1288–1323 as the Palazzo Nuovo del Podestà, with the tallest tower in the town, the 54 m (178 ft) Torre Grossa ("Big Tower"; views). The palace houses the Town Hall (Palazzo Comunale) and the Pinacoteca Civica (Municipal Museum), with a large collection of pictures; particularly notable is a large fresco, "Maestà" (Madonna Enthroned), by Lippo Memmi (1317).

★Cathedral

On the west side of the Piazza del Duomo is the cathedral, usually called the Collegiata, a Romanesque structure with three aisles, dating from the 12th c. and enlarged in 1456 by Giuliano da Maiano on the plan of a Latin cross. In the course of time the façade has been remodelled several times but it has remained without any external decoration.
The inside of the façade is decorated with frescoes (1456) by Benozzo Gozzoli depicting the martyrdom of St Sebastian, and there are two wooden statues, the Annunciation, by Jacopo della Quercia (1421).
In the south aisle are monumental 14th c. frescoes by Barna da Siena consisting of three rows with scenes from the New Testament. At the end of the south aisle is the Cappella di Santa Fina (the town's patron saint), a Renaissance masterpiece by Giuliano and Benedetto da Maiano (1468).
On the altar is a carved altar-piece bearing a sarcophagus which contained the remains of Santa Fina until 1738. Beyond can be seen the Madonna with Child flanked by two angels.
The side arcades have fine frescos by Domenico Ghirlandaio (1475) depicting the life and death of Santa Fina.

Palazzo del Podestà

Facing the cathedral is the Palazzo del Podestà (13th–14th c.). The tall Torre dell'Orologio (51m/168ft) marks the height which privately built towers were not allowed to exceed.

Museo d'Arte Sacra

Adjoining the cathedral is the Museo d'Arte Sacra (Museum of Religious Art), which contains 14th–15th c. sculpture and robes.

Museo Etrusco

The same building houses the Museo Etrusco, with a small collection of Etruscan urns, vases, coins, etc.

Rocca

A little way west of the cathedral, by the town walls, is the ruined Rocca, from which there is a fine view of the town's towers and of the surrounding area.

The distinctive silhouette of San Gimignano

At the north-west end of the town stands the church of Sant'Agostino. Particularly notable in the choir chapel are the frescos by Benozzo Gozzoli (1465), depicting in seventeen scenes the life of St Augustine (354–430), a famous Church Father.

Sant'Agostino

To the south, outside the Porta San Giovanni, stands the Museo di Arti e Mestieri (Museum of Art and Handicrafts), with exhibits dating from the Middle Ages to the present day.

Museo di Arti e Mestieri

San Marino   G8

Repubblica di San Marino. Area: 61 sq. km (24 sq. mi.)
Altitude: 640 m (2112 ft). Population: 22,400 (country); 4200 (town)

San Marino, capital of the little republic of the same name (Repubblica di San Marino), lies some 23 km (14 mi) south-west of Rimini on the eastern fringe of the Apennines. The territory is bounded by the Italian region of Emilia-Romagna to the north and the Marche to the south, and is one of the smallest states in Europe.

Location

State flag

   With its magnificent situation on Monte Titano (745 m (2486 ft)), its three castles crowning the triple peaks of the hill and its picturesque old houses and streets, it attracts large numbers of summer visitors, particularly from the seaside resorts around Rimini.

Legend has it that San Marino was founded in AD 301 by St Marinus, a stone-mason from the Dalmatian town of Rab who fled here during the

History

Diocletian persecutions. The present republic developed out of a settlement which grew up around a convent mentioned in the records in 885. It received the constitution which is still in force in 1263, was recognised by Pope Urban IV in 1631 and has since maintained its independence, from 1897, under the protection of Italy under the terms of a treaty of friendship which was renewed in 1953.

Constitution

Legislative power rests with the 60 members of the Consiglio Grande e Generale, executive power with the ten deputies of the Congresso di Stato and the two Capitani reggenti, who change every six months. Old medieval costumes are worn at the ceremonial change-over on April 1st and October 1st and on San Marino's National Day September 3rd.

Città di San Marino

The old town (Centro Storico) is surrounded by town walls. On the south-west side of the town is the 15th c. Porta San Francesco or Porta del Loco. Just inside the town walls, on the right, stands the church of San Francesco (14th c.), which houses the Pinacoteca, with notable pictures by Matteo Loves and others. North-west of the church is a memorial stone commemorating Garibaldi who marched through the town.

In the centre of the old town is the Piazza della Libertà, the town's attractive main square, on the north-west side of which is the Neo-Gothic Palazzo del Governo or Palazzo Pubblico (1894), with a sumptuously appointed interior, particularly notable features being the Hall of the Grand Council, the Audience Chamber and the Voting Chamber which contains a painting of St Marinus, the state's patron, by Guernico. From the roof of the palace there are magnificent views.

A little way north of the main square is the Neo-Classical Basilica di San Marino (1836), with a richly decorated interior; the remains of the saint are preserved in the high altar. To the right of the basilica is the chapel of San Pietro, which claims to possess the stone beds of St Marinus and his companion St Leo.

Fortress on Monte Titano

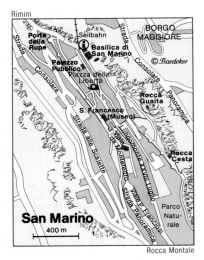

North-west of the main square is the lower station of a funicular, situated on the Strada Panoramica which encircles the town. To the right is the State Tourist Office (Ufficio di Stato per il Turismo).

The funicular leads to Borgo Maggiore, with three museums: the Firearms Museum, the Postal Museum, with stamps and coins and the Garibaldi Museum. Once a week there is a market in the Borgo.

Borgo Maggiore

From the Basilica di San Marino a road runs south-east to the three peaks of Monte Titano with their three castles: first the 11th c. Rocca or Guaita, with coloured panels depicting the history of the castle; then the 13th c. Cesta or Fratta, on the highest peak (745 m (2459 ft)), commanding extensive views, with a museum of arms and armour; and finally the 13th c. Montale, at the foot of which is a park; in the eastern part of the park can be seen the Kursaal (Palazzo dei Congressi).

★Rocche

★San Remo   B8

Region: Liguria. Province: Imperia (IM)
Altitude: 11 m (36 ft). Population: 56,000

San Remo (Sanremo), Italy's largest and oldest winter health resort, lies on the "Riviera dei Fiori", in a bay enclosed by a semicircle of hills. From San Remo it is only about 20 km (12 mi.) to the Italian-French frontier.

Location

Thanks to its sheltered situation San Remo has a mild and equable climate in winter, and in summer it is a lively and popular resort, with a beach which is partly artificial. Here olive groves have given place to glasshouses in which carnations and roses are grown for export.

Town

Every year in February the Italian Popular Song Festival takes place here.

Festival di San Remo

Sights

San Remo is divided into two clearly separated sections – the Old Town and the New Town. On a steep hill between the short valleys of the Torrente San Francesco and Torrenta San Romolo is the Old Town, a huddle of medieval houses with arcades and pointed windows, built in narrow lanes ("carrugi") linked by arches as a protection against earthquake.

★Old Town

Through the Piazza Eroi Sanremesi is the New Town lying at the foot of the hill. Its main traffic artery is the Corso Matteotti, a long street lined with shops. At its west end stands the Casino Municipale, with gaming rooms, a theatre and other facilities.

New Town

The Romanesque-Gothic cathedral was built in the 13th c. By the north door is a relief showing the paschal lamb between palms, by the south door a Madonna between saints. The late medieval bell-tower was given a new dome in the Baroque period, and was rebuilt after the Second World War. Inside are a large crucifix above the high altar and a painting of San Siro (1550).

San Siro

The Corso Imperatrice is a promenade shaded by palms in the west of the bay. At its far end is the beautiful Parco Marsaglia with an auditorium (theatre, concerts).

Parco Marsaglia

Corso Garibaldi forms the eastward continuation of Corso Matteotti, with a covered flower market (Mercato dei Fiori), where auctions are held early every morning.

Flower market

San Remo

The modern promenade in San Remo

Harbour	The harbour lies between the east and west bays. The Forte Santa Tecia dates from the Genoese period. To the east of the fort lies the old fishing harbour which is also used by pleasure craft. The modern yacht harbour with its 1 km ($\frac{1}{2}$ mi.) long breakwater can accommodate over 800 boats.
★Villa Nobel	Alfred Nobel, famous as the discoverer of dynamite, lived and died (1896) in this villa on Corso Felice Cavalotti. Since 1973 it has served as a cultural centre; there is also a small Nobel Museum.
Civico Museo Archeologico	At the top of Corso Felice Cavalotti lies the Palazzo Borea D'Olmo, an impressive 15th c. palace with a Baroque façade. It houses an archaeological museum, with finds from Palaeolithic and Bronze and Iron Age settlements in the San Remo region.

Surroundings

Baiardo	Another rewarding excursion is to Baiardo (25 km (16 mi.) north-west; 900 m (2970 ft)), situated on a hill, with a beautiful parish church and the ruins of another church (16th c.) destroyed by an earthquake in 1887. From a nearby terrace there are magnificent views of the mountains. From Baiardo the trip can be continued via Apricale to Ventimiglia.
Bussana Vecchia	9 km (6 mi.) east of San Remo is Bussana Vecchia (201 m (663 ft)), a hill village, which was destroyed in 1887 by an earthquake. At present it is occupied by painters and other artists.

Sardinia C–D 13–18

Region: Sardegna
Provinces: Cagliari (CA), Nuoro (NU), Oristano (OR) and Sassari (SS)
Area: 24,090 sq. km (9299 sq. mi.). Population: 1,500,000

Regular services (carrying cars) from Civitavecchia to Golfo Aranci, Olbia   Ferries
and Cagliari, from Genoa to Porto Torres, Olbia resp. Arbatax and Cagliari,
from Livorno to Porto Torres, Olbia and Cagliari and from Naples to
Cagliari.

Cagliari International Airport, 4 km (2¹/₂ mi.) west of the town; airports for   Air travel
domestic services at Olbia and Alghero.

The island of Sardinia lies in the Mediterranean, to the west of the Italian
mainland. It is separated from the south tip of the neighbouring French
island of Corsica by the narrow Strait of Bonifacio.
    The island forms the autonomous region of Sardinia, made up of the
four provinces of Cagliari, Nuoro, Oristano and Sassari.

Geologically the island is a remnant of a rump mountain range composed   Geography
of gneisses, granites and schists, overlaid by a band of limestone running
from north to south and partly covered with recent volcanic deposits. The
only plain of any size, the Campidano, lies between the Iglesiente uplands
with their rich mineral resources to the south-west and the rest of the
island, a hilly region with gentler slopes in the west and more rugged
country in the east, rising in Gennargentu to a height of 1834 m (6052 ft)
and falling steeply down to the sea in the sheer cliffs on the east coast.

The summers on the island are hot and dry; the winters bring heavy rain.   Climate

The population, which from the late Middle Ages until the beginning of   Population
this century was decimated by malaria, is concentrated in the coastal
areas.
    For many years Sardinia has been economically backward and
underdeveloped. In the 1960s more than half the population obtained
their subsistence from agriculture. Efforts to achieve a better balance,
especially in the field of petro-chemicals, have met with only limited
success. Recently, hopes have been pinned more on the growth of
small industries and tourism. As a result, less than 14 per cent of the
workforce now obtains a living from agriculture.

More than half the population obtain their subsistence from agriculture.   Agriculture
Corn, vine, olives, citrus fruits, vegetables and tobacco are grown in the
Campidano plain, in the coastal areas and in the fertile valleys of the
numerous rivers. The upland regions are mainly devoted to pastoral farming (sheep, goats and cattle). In the coastal regions fishing (tunny, ancho-   Fishing
vies, spiny lobsters) also makes a contribution to the economy.

Mining was already an important activity in ancient times. The main min-   Mining
ing area is the Iglesiente, where zinc, lead, manganese and barytes are
worked (now declining considerably). Around Carbonia there is opencast
coal-mining. At present the Sardinian mining has entered a state of crisis
which results in unemployment and migration.

Recent development has led to the establishment of various industries.   Industry
The building of the new oil harbour nearby Cagliari is the base for new
petro-chemical industry. Mining in the Iglesiente has created new industrial areas such as Sulcis in Portovesme. Other new developments can be
seen in Tortoli and Arbatax, with paper-processing industries on the east
coast and inland, at Ottana, a centre for the production of synthetic fibres.

The extraction of magnesium and cooking salt from sea-water is also an   Salt
industry of some significance.

In recent years tourism has developed into an important element of the   Tourism
island's economy. In addition to the established tourist areas around
Alghero and Santa Teresa a very modern holiday resort has been developed on the Costa Smeralda.

441

Sardinia

Gigantic tomb of Coddu'Ecchiu

History

Evidence of the earliest inhabitants of Sardinia is provided by the remains of numerous prehistoric settlements, in particular the nuraghi (singular nuraghe), massive towers characteristic of the island culture of the Bronze and Iron Ages which show a striking similarity to the talayots of the Balearics. Like the talayots, they no doubt served as fortresses, watch-towers and burial-places, and can be dated to the period between 1500 and 500 BC.

From the 9th c. onwards Phoenicians and later Carthaginians settled on the coasts. In 238 BC the island was occupied by the Romans, attracted by its rich deposits of minerals. About AD 455 it fell into the hands of the Vandals and later became subject to Byzantium. Between the 8th and 10th c. it was frequently ravaged by Saracen raids; but these piratical activities were repressed by Pisa and Genoa following an appeal by the Pope, who rewarded them with the grant of the territory. The traditional system of rule by four giudici (judges) in the districts of Torre, Gallura, Cagliari and Arborea was, however, maintained. In 1297 Sardinia was granted by the Pope to the crown of Aragon. Under the treaty of Utrecht in 1713 it was assigned to Austria, and in 1718 was exchanged with Sicily and passed to the dukes of Savoy as the kingdom of Sardinia. In 1948 it was given the status of an autonomous region within the Republic of Italy.

Culture

Thanks to the ruggedness and remoteness of much of the island its old customs and traditions are still vigorously alive. The Sardinian language is a Romance tongue which has developed independently of mainland Italian and preserves certain archaic features.

Island tour (720 km (446 mi.))

The first section of the tour leads from Cagliari to Sassari. Leave Cagliari on SS131, which runs north-west.

Monastir

20 km (12 mi.): Monastir (83 m (274 ft)), a village of Oriental aspect on the slopes of a volcanic hill, with rock-cut tombs. 5.5 km (3¹/₂ mi.) south-west

at San Sperate is an open-air museum of modern sculpture. Beyond Monastir the road follows the east edge of the Campidano plain.

23 km (14 mi.): Sanluri (135 m (446 ft); population 8000), with a 14th c. castle containing a "Risorgimento" museum.

Sanluri

Excursion:
24 km (15 mi.) north-east of Sanluri is the village of Barumini, near which (1 km (1/2 mi.) west, to the left of the road to Tuili) is the largest nuraghic village in Sardinia, Su Nuraxi, with 396 houses and a massive central structure with several towers.

★★Su Nuraxi

Excursion:
From Sanluri SS197 runs west to the wooded Costa Verde, a coastal region now being developed as a popular holiday area, with new roads, hotels and sports facilities.

Costa Verde

9 km (5½ mi.): Sardara (163 m (538 ft)). By the little church of Santa Anastasia is an underground spring sanctuary of nuraghic type. 3 km (2 mi.) west is a small spa with thermal springs (50 and 68°C (122 and 154°F)).

Sardara

36 km (22 mi.): Santa Giusta (10 m (33 ft)), on the north side of a marshy lake, the Stagno di Santa Giusta, with a 12th c. church in Pisan style.

Santa Giusta

3 km (2 mi.): Oristano (9 m (30 ft); population 30,000), which is noted for its pottery. It still preserves a number of towers belonging to its medieval defences. Notable are the 18th c. cathedral, on the site of an earlier building of the 13th–14th c. and the Archaeological Museum, with finds from the ancient city of Tharros, which lay to the north-west of the Gulf of Oristano. Beautiful traditional costumes can often be seen here on market days. A popular attraction is the Sariglia, an equestrian tournament dating back to the 16th c., which is held at Shrovetide every year (on the Sunday and the Tuesday).

Oristano

Excursion:
An interesting trip can be made to the nature reserve of San Vero Milis, 21 km (13 mi.) north-west. This is a marshy area, and numerous flamingoes can be seen here in September and October.

San Vero Milis

16 km (10 mi.): Bauladu (29 m (96 ft)), on the north edge of the Campidano plain. The road then continues up the Bobolica valley.

Bauladu

Excursion:
5 km (3 mi.) farther on SS131d. branches off. Running diagonally across the

Nuoro

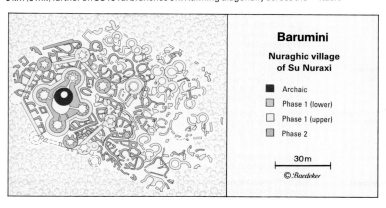

Barumini

Nuraghic village of Su Nuraxi

■ Archaic

▨ Phase 1 (lower)

□ Phase 1 (upper)

▥ Phase 2

30 m

© *Baedeker*

The main tower of Su Nuraxi

island this is the quickest and shortest route from Cagliari or Oristano to Olbia (309 km (192 mi.) and 182 km (113 mi.) respectively). In 50 km (36 mi.) it bypasses the provincial capital of Nuoro (546 m (1802 ft); population 37,000), charmingly situated on a hillside, between limestone hills of Alpine type to the south and the peak of Ortobene (995 m (3284 ft); view) to the east. Beautiful local costumes are worn on the feast of the Saviour (last Sunday in August). Nuoro was the birthplace of the writer Grazia Deledda (1893–1936; Nobel prize 1926). At the south-east end of the town is the 19th c. neo-classical cathedral. Worth visiting is the Civico Museo Speleo-Archeologico, where finds from caves and prehistoric material can be seen, including menhirs.

1.5 km (1 mi.) north-east are the pilgrimage church of Nostra Signora della Solitudine (view) and, beyond the Colle di San Onofrio (594 m (1960 ft); view), the Sardinian Museum of Costume, housed in over 20 buildings in the style of Sardinian peasants' houses. Around the town are several nuraghi.

Mamoiada Fonni

From Nuoro there is a beautiful drive south to the villages of Mamoiada (644 m (2125 ft); costumes) and Fonni (1000 m (3300 ft); population 5000), the highest village on the island. In the surrounding area are numerous nuraghi and "fairies' houses".

★Gennargentu massif

Fonni is the starting point for the ascent (4 hours, with guide), of Bruncu Spina (1829 m (6036 ft); panoramic views), the northern peak of the Gennargentu massif, from which the southern peak, Punta la Marmora (1834 m (6052 ft)), can be climbed (45 minutes).

Losa

Shortly after the turning on the road Nuoro to Olbia, we see on the left the well-preserved nuraghe of Losa, with a number of subsidiary structures.

Abbasanta

2 km (1¼ mi.): Abbasanta (315 m (1040 ft)), the largest livestock market in Sardinia, on the southern edge of the Abbasanta plain, an area of black basalt

rock. 10 km (6 mi.) south-east is the Tirso Dam, which has impounded the water of the island's principal river to form Lago Omodeo, 22 km (14 mi.) long and up to 5 km (3 mi.) wide.

16 km (10 mi.): Macomer (563 m (1858 ft); population 11,000), situated on a high plateau of basalts and trachytes on the slopes of the Catena del Marghine, with beautiful far-ranging views. In front of the church of Macomer are three Roman milestones found in the area.

Macomer

Some of the best preserved nuraghi in Sardinia can be seen in the immediate surroundings of the town. Particularly fine is the nuraghe of Santa Barbara (648 m (2138 ft); 45 minutes north), a conical structure on a high square base.

Excursion:
3 km (2 mi.) beyond Macomer SS129 bis goes off on the left to the village of Suni (23 km (14 mi.): extensive views) and, 6 km (3³/₄ mi.) beyond this, the little port of Bosa (10 m (33 ft); population 8000), with the castle of Serravalle (1112). 16 km (10 mi.) south of Suni lies Cuglieri (479 m (1581 ft); population 5000), on the lower slopes of Monte Ferru (1050 m (3465 ft)), an extinct volcano.

Bosa

2 km (1¹/₄ mi.): on the left of the road is the almost completely preserved nuraghe of Succoronis (Muradu).

★Succoronis

27 km (17 mi.): road on right (1 km (³/₄ mi.) south-east) to the three-storey nuraghe of Santu Antipe, 16 m (53 ft) high.

Santu Antipe

Excursion:
5 km (3 mi.): Bonnanaro (405 m (1337 ft)), where a road goes off on the left (4 km (2¹/₂ mi.) south-west) to the richly ornamented church of San Pietro di Sorres (Pisan period, 12th c.). Beyond Bonnanaro the road runs through the beautiful wooded uplands of Logudoro.

Bonnanaro

Excursion:
21 km (13 mi.): SS597, the direct road from Sassari to Olbia. goes off. 2 km (1¹/₄ mi.) along this road is the former abbey church of the Santissima Trinità di Saccargia, the finest example of Pisan architecture in Sardinia, with 13th c. frescoes.

★Santissima Trinità di Saccargia

15 km (9 mi.): Sassari (see entry).

For the next section of the tour from Sassari to Olbia or La Maddalena, there are alternative routes – either by the direct road on SS597 (101 km (63 mi.)) or the more interesting SS127.

Sassari

14 km (9 mi.) (600 m (1980 ft); population 6000), renowned for its beautiful costumes. From the ruined Malaspina castle and the nearby Cappella di Bona-ria there are beautiful views. The road continues through the wooded Aglona district.

Osilo

Excursion:
39 km (24 mi.): turn-off, a road through beautiful scenery, via the village of Sedini (16th c. church), picturesquely situated above gorges, to the little port town of Castelsardo (114 m (376 ft); population 5000), in a magnificent situation on a promontory which falls sheer down to the Golfo dell'Asinara. This is the principal basketwork centre in Sardinia. In the parish church is a beautiful 15th c. Madonna, a masterpiece of the Sardinian-Spanish school of painting. From the ruined castle there are fine views.

Castelsardo

Some 4 km (2¹/₂ mi.) beyond the turning for Castelsardo, at Perfugas (just off SS127), a fortified village of the nuraghic period and a spring sanctuary have been excavated.

26 km (16 mi.): Tempio Pausania (566 m (1868 ft); population 13,000), formerly chief town of the district of Gallura, situated below the north face of the jagged Monti di Limbara (cork industry).

Tempio Pausania

Sardinia

Calangianus
10 km (6 mi.): Calangianus (518 m (1709 ft); population 6000), an old town surrounded by forest, with a pretty parish church.

Olbia
35 km (22 mi.): Olbia (15 m (50 ft); population 33,000), formerly known as Terranova Pausania, lying at the west end of the deeply indented Gulf of Olbia. A causeway 1.5 km (1 mi.) long carrying the road and the railway which links the town with the little Isola Bianca, where the ships from Civitavecchia come in.

Beside the town railway station is the 11th c. church of San Simplicio, in Pisan style, with a collection of Roman inscriptions (particularly milestones), and a sarcophagus with a decoration of garlands. From the church and from the harbour there are fine views of the bay and the massive offshore island of Tavolara (up to 555 m (1832 ft); area 6 sq. km (2^1/$_4$ sq. mi.).

Excursion:

★Costa Smeralda
To the north of Olbia, extending along the shores of a large peninsula, is the beautiful Costa Smeralda (Emerald Coast), whose beaches of fine sand are being developed as a holiday area by the construction of new roads and the provision of tourist facilities. The roads to the various resorts branch off SS125, which runs north from Olbia to Palau.

Golfo di Marinella
6 km (3^3/$_4$ mi.): road (8 km (5 mi.)) to the Golfo di Marinella.

Porto Cervo
1 km (^{1}/$_2$ mi.): coast road via Cala di Volpe (15 km (9 mi.)) and Romazzino (17 km (11 mi.)) to Porto Cervo (30 km (19 mi.)), the chief place on the Costa Smeralda.

Baia Sardinia
3 km 2 mi.) north, beyond Capo Ferro, is the bay of Liscia di Vacca, and 5 km (3 mi.) farther on Baia Sardinia (51 m (168 ft); population 4000), with numerous hotels.

At the south end of the Costa Smeralda lies the holiday centre of Portisco.

Arzachena
17 km (11 mi.) north on SS125 is Arzachena.

Palau
12 km (7 mi.): Palau (5 m (17ft)).

La Maddalena
From Palau there is a boat service several times daily (30 minutes) to La Maddalena (19 m (63 ft); population 11,000), a port on the island of the same name (157 m (518 ft); area 20 sq. km (7 sq. mi.), which together with the neighbouring islands was strongly fortified until the Second World War, commanding the Strait of Bonifacio between Sardinia and Corsica.

★Caprera
The island is traversed by a panoramic road 7 km (4^1/$_4$ mi.) long which is carried by a swing bridge over the Passo della Moneta, a strait fully 500 m (1640 ft) wide, on to the neighbouring island of Caprera ("Goat Island", up to 212 m (700 ft); area 15.75 sq. km (6 sq. mi). 1.5 km (1 mi.) east of the bridge is a house once occupied by Garibaldi, who died here on June 2nd 1882 (collection of mementoes). In front of the house stands a monument to Garibaldi, behind it an olive-grove containing his tomb, which attracts visitors from all over Italy, particularly on the anniversary of his death.

The third section of the Sardinian tour, from Olbia to Cagliari, is on SS125, which runs south-east past a number of salt-water lagoons. Thereafter the road continues at varying distances from the coast.

Siniscola
57 km (35 mi.): Siniscola (42 m (139 ft); population 9000), at the west end of a large coastal plain, renowned for its beautiful costumes.

From Peniscola a panoramic road (edges not guarded) runs along the rocky ridge of Monte Albo (1127 m (3719 ft)), through a region well stocked with wildlife, to Bitti (549 m (1812 ft); population 6000).

6 km (3³/₄ mi.) north-east of Siniscola is the developing resort of La Caletta.   **La Caletta**
From Siniscola it is possible to return to Cagliari either by taking the shorter
but less interesting road via Nuoro and Oristano or by continuing on the
coast road.

36 km (22 mi.): Orosei (19 m (63 ft); population 5000), on the right bank of   **Orosei**
the River Cedrino, with a ruined castle.

21 km (13 mi.): Dorgali (387 m (1277 ft); population 8000), a little town   **Dorgali**
(costumes), situated on the slopes of Monte Bardia (882 m (2911 ft)). Notable
is the Museo Civico Archeologico.

In the surrounding area are a number of beautiful stalactitic caves (Grotta   Stalactitic caves
Toddeitu, Grotta del Bue Marino and Grotta Ispinigoli) and the rock-cut
tombs, the so-called domus de janas. 11 km (7 mi.) north-west of Dorgali
is the nuraghic village of Serra Orrios.

Excursion:
2 km (1¹/₄ mi.): side road (7 km (4¹/₄ mi.)) which winds its way down to the   **Cala Gonone**
little port of Cala Gonone (25 m (83 ft)).

Beyond Dorgali the road passes through beautiful montainous country.

61 km (38 mi.): Tortoli (15 m (50 ft); population 8000), at the beginning of an   **Arbatax**
extensive plain. 5 km (3 mi.) east is the attractively situated little port of
Arbatax (population 1000), formerly also known as Tortoli Marina, which
ships the agricul-tural produce and minerals of the Ogliastra region. Nearby
are picturesque red porphyry cliffs.

Excursion:
From Tortoli there is a very attractive trip, first on SS198 through the   **Lanusei**
Ogliastra uplands, with hills of crystalline limestone, sometimes in curiously contorted shapes, to Lanusei (595 m (1964 ft); population 5000),
prettily situated amid vineyards, Seui (800 m (2640 ft)) and the Cantoniera
di Santa Lucia; then on SS128 and SS131 to Cagliari.

Beyond Tortoli SS125 follows a winding course through the south-eastern
part of the Ogliastra region.

10 km (6 mi.): Bari Sardo (50 m (166 ft)), from which there is a view of   **Bari Sardo**
the Gennargentu massif. The road continues, with many bends, through
lonely hill country.

121 km (75 mi.): Quartu Sant'Elena (6 m (20 ft); population 42,000), a thriv-   **Quartu Sant'Elena**
ing town, in an area which produces the famous white wine, Malvasia.
On the feast of St Helena (May 21st) there is a picturesque procession of
richly decked teams of oxen. The parish church has a large altarpiece,
probably by Antioco Mainas (16th c.).

8 km (5 mi.): Cagliari (se entry).   Cagliari

Sassari   C14

Region: Sardegna. Province: Sassari (SS)
Altitude: 225 m (743 ft). Population: 120,000

Sassari, Sardinia's second largest town, the capital of the province of the   Location
same name, lies on a limestone plateau, in the north-west of the island,
some 15 km (9 mi.) south of the Golfo dell'Asinara.
   Sassari is an archiepiscopal see and a university town as well as an
important commercial and administrative centre. Two well-known festivals

are celebrated in Sassari, the Cavalcata Sarda (riding competitions and procession with historical costumes) in May and the Festa dei Candelieri on August 14th.

Sights

The hub of the town's traffic is the palm-shaded Piazza Cavallino de Honestis, immediately south-east of which is the large Piazza d'Italia, with a monument to Victor Emmanuel II and a modern Prefecture.

Museo G. A. Sanna

From the Piazza d'Italia the tree-lined Via Roma runs south-east to the Museo G. A. Sanna, with the collections assembled by Giovanni Antonio Sanna, a member of the Italian Parliament, containing prehistoric, Punic and Roman antiquities and pictures of the 14th–19th c. by Sardinian, Italian and foreign artists.

San Nicola

North-west of the Piazza Cavallino de Honestis, reached by way of Piazza Azuni, is the Corso Vittorio Emanuele, Sassari's principal street. From this we turn left along Via del Duomo to reach the cathedral of San Nicola, with a Baroque façade and a restored interior.

East of this in Via Santa Catarina is the fine Palazzo del Duca, now the Town Hall.

Santa Maria di Betlem

To the west of the cathedral, in the spacious Piazza Santa Maria, stands the church of Santa Maria di Betlem, rebuilt in modern style but still preserving its Romanesque façade of the Pisan period. The interior has been remodelled in Gothic style.

Fonte Rosello

On the north side of the town is the pretty Fonte Rosello, with a Baroque well-house of 1605.

Surroundings

Porto Torres
19 km (12 mi.) NW

A pleasant drive through the coastal district of Nura leads to the little industrial town of Porto Torres (10 m (33 ft); population 21,000), the port of Sassari, situated in the Golfo dell'Asinara. On the east side of the town is the church of San Gavino (11th–13th c.; fortified in the 18th c.), a basilica in Pisan Romanesque style. In the interior are 22 ancient columns and six pillars, and in the crypt several Roman sarcophagi of the 3rd–4th c. To the west of the harbour a seven-arched Roman bridge spans the little Rio Turritano, and near this are the remains of a large Temple of Fortuna, popularly known as the "Palazzo Re Barbaro".

Stintino

North-west of Porto Torres we come to the fishing village of Stintino (9 m (30 ft)), and 5 km (3 mi.) beyond this is the Punta del Falcone, the north-west tip of Sardinia. Lying off the promontory to the north are the little Isola Piana (24 m (79 ft)) and the long indented Isola Asinara (up to 408 m (1346 ft) high; area 52 sq. km (18 sq. mi.)).

★Alghero
37 km (23 mi.) SW

Another very attractive trip is to the charmingly situated town and seaside resort of Alghero, whose inhabitants still speak a Catalan dialect (7 m (23 ft); population 38,000). Features of interest are the cathedral (1510; Spanish Gothic doorway), the church of San Francesco (cloister), the picturesque Spanish bastions and towers and many old houses.

★Grotta di Nettuno

14 km (9 mi.) west of Alghero (also reached by motorboat), on the west side of the precipitous Capo Caccia is a beautiful stalactitic cave, the Grotta di Nettuno.

★Selinunte   G20

Region: Sicilia. Province: Trapani (TP)
Altitude: 74 m (244 ft)

The ruins of Selinunte lie on both banks of the little river Modione (Greek   Location
Selinon) and Gorgo di Cottoni, near the south-west coast of Sicily, some
15 km (9 mi.) south of Castelvetrano and 70 km (45 mi.) north-west of
Agrigento.

Selinus, the most westerly Greek colony in Sicily, was founded about   History
650 BC on a hill near the sea, and later extended on to the plateau to the north.
A sacred precinct was established on the hill to the east during the 6th c. BC.
In 409 BC the flourishing city was conquered and destroyed by the Carthaginians, and a new fortified town built on the western hill from 407 onwards
was in turn destroyed by them in 250 BC, during the first Punic War.
   The importance of the ancient city is attested by the extent and scale of
the ruins, in particular the massive remains of eight Doric temples (6th–
5th c. BC), which probably collapsed as a result of earthquakes between the
5th and 8th c. AD and were then gradually covered with blown sand. Since
1925 restoration and further excavation has been carried on steadily: two
temples have been re-erected, and others are to follow.

Ancient city

On the western hill are the remains of the Acropolis (450 m (1476 ft) long   ★Acropolis
and up to 350 m (1148 ft) across), formerly surrounded by walls and traversed by two principal streets, one running north–south, the other east–west.
In the south–east section are the remains of the small Temple A and the foundations of the very similar Temple O. Immediately north on the east–west
street is the tiny Temple B, of which no columns remain erect, and to the
north of this, on top of the hill, is Temple C (columns re-erected in 1925 and
1929), the oldest on the Acropolis and together with Temple E the most
striking features of the site. Farther north again is the rather later Temple D.

On the northern edge of the Acropolis are the excavated remains of the Greek   Defensive walls
defensive walls (restored in 407 BC, an excellent example of the highly
developed Greek art of fortification. Beyond this point, on the Manuiza
plateau to the north of the Acropolis, extends the town proper, of which only
a few remains have been preserved.

Following the east–west street westward from the Acropolis, we cross the   Temple of
River Modione, at the mouth of which the west harbour was situated, and   Demeter
come to the hill of Manicalunga. On the slopes of this hill, in the sacred

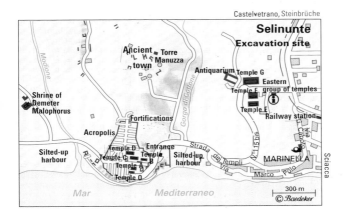

precinct, lie the remains of the Temple of Demeter, dedicated to Demeter Malophoros (the "Fruit-Bringer"). At the north corner of the precinct is the little shrine of Zeus Meilichios ("the Forgiving").

Necropolis

To the west of the Temple of Demeter is a necropolis extending for some 2 km (1¼ mi.).

Temple E

From the Acropolis a road 1.5 km (1 mi.) long runs east over the Gorgo di Cotone to the eastern hill, with the remains of three large temples which even in their present state of ruin are overwhelmingly impressive. To the south is Temple E, dedicated to Hera, which was re-erected in 1959, with 38 columns. To the north are Temple F and Temple G (113 m (371 ft) long), probably dedicated to Apollo, which, with the Temple of Zeus at Agrigento and the Artemision at Ephesus, ranks as the largest of all Greek temples.

Sicily   G–K 19–22

Region: Sicilia
Provinces: Agrigento (AG), Caltanissetta (CL), Catania (CT), Enna (EN), Messina (ME), Palermo (PA), Ragusa (RG), Siracusa (SR) and Trapani (TR)
Area: 25,708 sq. km (9923 sq. mi.). Population: 5,000,000

Ferries

Regular services (carrying cars) from Reggio Calabria and Villa S. Giovanni to Messina, from Genoa and Livorno to Palermo, from Naples to Palermo and Catania resp. Syracuse.

Air travel

Sicily's International Airport is close by Catania; airports for internal flights are near Palermo and Comiso and about 12 km (7½ mi.) south of Trapani.

Location

Sicily, the largest Italian island, lies south-west of the Italian peninsula in the Mediterranean.
It is an autonomous region with its capital at Palermo.

Landscape

Sicily is an almost entirely mountainous island, bearing the marks of vigorous volcanic activity. Its most notable landmark is the massive snow-covered cone of Etna (3343 m (11,032 ft)), Europe's largest active volcano, which rises above the east coast, visible from afar.

Population

The main concentration of population, including most of the large towns, are on the fertile and well-watered coastal plains.

Agriculture

Sicily's productive and rapidly developing agriculture gives it a leading place among the farming regions of Italy. Intensive vegetable growing (tomatoes, cucumbers, early potatoes, etc.), fruit orchards (citrus fruits, almonds, olives) and wine production, particularly at the western tip of the island around Marsala, predominate in the fertile coastal areas; the dry and hilly interior is suitable only for extensive arable cultivation (wheat alternating with beans) and some pastoral farming (sheep, goats). The traditional feudal system and the often inefficient working of the land by small tenant farmers, which is its legacy, stand in the way of the more rapid development which the potential of the land would permit.

Fishing

Significant contributions to the economy are also made by the coastal fisheries (tuna, anchovies, cuttlefish, swordfish) and the extraction of salt in the Trapani area.

Industry

Sicily has little industry. The only industrial activities of any consequence are petro-chemical (around Syracuse and Gela), the mining of potash, which has superseded the once considerable sulphur-workings, and the working of asphalt (around Ragusa) and marble. In recent years, however, there has been a significant development of industry which has helped to

Sicilian countryside at the foot of Etna

reduce the drift of population to the highly industrialised states of northern Europe.

Sicily's magnificent scenery and its beautiful beaches, particularly on the north and east coast, its great range of ancient remains, including the best preserved Greek temples to be found anywhere, and the very remarkable art and architecture of its Norman rulers, have long made the island one of the great Meccas of travellers and tourists. In recent times tourism has become an important factor of the economy.

Tourism

Circuit of Sicily (*c.* 930 km (577 mi.))

The first part of the circuit, from Messina to Palermo, is partly on the A 20 motorway and partly on SS113 (the "Settentrionale Sicula"), following the coast of the Tyrrhenian Sea through scenery of great beauty and variety. The road runs north-west from Messina through garden suburbs, crosses the Colle San Rizzo pass (465 m (1533 ft); motorway tunnel) in the wooded Monti Peloritani (1374 m (4534 ft)) and descends to the sea.

37 km (23 mi.): Milazzo/Isole Eolie motorway exit. 6 km (3³/₄ mi.) north is Milazzo (30 m (100 ft); population 31,000), with good beaches and boat services to the Lipari Islands. The town, founded by the Greeks in 716 BC, has a Norman castle. 7 km (4¹/₄ mi.) farther north we come to the Capo di Milazzo.

Milazzo

12 km (7 mi.) along SS113 lies the spa (sulphureous water) of Castroreale Terme.

Castroreale Terme

Excursion:
The SS185 goes off on the left 3 km (2 mi.) farther on and follows a winding course to the little town of Novara di Sicilia (675 m (2228 ft)), 20 km (12 mi.) inland; then over the Portella Mandrazzi (1125 m (3713 ft)) to the ridge

Novara di Sicilia

of the Monti Peloritani; on, with a magnificent view of Etna, to Francavilla di Sicilia (675 m (2228 ft)); and from here another 22 km (14 mi.), passing close to the Gola dell'Alcantara, to Giardini, below Taormina (see entry).

Tyndaris

Excursion:
Farther along SS113, 12 km (7 mi.) beyond the exit for Milazzo, a road branches off on the right, passes the monastery of the Madonna del Tindari, traverses the village of Tindari and comes in 2 km (1¼ mi.) to the remains of Tyndaris, the last Greek colony in Sicily, founded by Dionysius I in 396 BC and probably destroyed by the Saracens. Here can be seen remains of the town walls, a theatre, a Roman basilica and mosaic floors, including the notable Museum, the "Antiquarium".

Patti

29 km (18 mi.) beyond Milazzo/Isole Eolie on the motorway is the exit for Patti (157 m (518 ft); population 13,000), with large monasteries and a cathedral which occupies the site of an earlier castle and contains the tomb of Adelasia of Montferrat (d. 1118), wife of King Roger I of Sicily. When building the motorway between Patti and the railway station remains of a late Roman villa, rich in mosaics, were uncovered. The site is open to visitors.

Capo Calavà

9 km (5½ mi.): tunnel through the precipitous Capo Calavà, and beyond this a fine view of the fertile coastal area, with Capo d'Orlando (93 m (307 ft)) reaching far out to sea.

Capo d'Orlando

24 km (15 mi.): exit for Capo d'Orlando (12 m (40 ft); population 11,000), a little town which is also a seaside resort.

Randazzo

Excursion:
From Capo d'Orlando SS116 runs south via Naso (497 m (1640 ft)) and over the Portella dello Zoppo (1264 m (4171 ft)), a pass on the ridge of the Monti Nebrodi (1847 m (6095 ft)), to Randazzo (764 m (2521 ft); population 12,000),

Remains of the ancient town of Tyndaris

which, with its old houses built of dark-coloured lava blocks, still preserves much of its medieval character.

At the east end of the main street, Via Umberto I, stands the church of Santa Maria (1217–39), with columns which are hewn from black lava. From here the picturesque Via degli Archi runs west to the church of San Nicolò (originally Norman, remodelled in the 16th c., badly damaged during the Second World War), which contains a statue of St Nicholas by Antonio Gagini (1523). Beyond the church, to the north-west, is the Palazzo Finocchiaro (1509), with a fine façade. At the west end of Via Umberto I the church of San Martino, has a 14th c. campanile and a rich treasury; nearly opposite is a tower of the old ducal palace.

From Capo d'Orlando we continue on SS113 over the fertile coastal plain, the Piana del Capo, and then through the Bosco di Caronia, the largest forest in Sicily (mainly scrub).

Bosco di Caronia

Excursion:
49 km (30 mi.): SS117 branches off and runs south via Mistretta (900 m (2970 ft); population 7000) and over the Portella del Contrasto (1107 m (3653 ft)), a pass on the ridge of the Monti Nebrodi, to Nicosia (46 km (29 mi.); alt. 720 m (2376 ft); population 16,000), with the 14th c. cathedral of San Nicolà, the 18th c. church of Santa Maria Maggiore (marble reredos 8 m (26 ft) high by Antonio Gagini, 1512) and a castle.

Nicosia

Beyond the mentioned junction the coast road skirts the foot of the Madonie hills (Pizzo Carbonaro, 1979 m (65311 ft)).

Madonie hills

37 km (3 mi.): Cefalù (see entry).
Beyond Cefalù we take the motorway.

Cefalù

15 km (9 mi.): junction with the A 19 motorway to Enna and Catania. 2 km (1¼ mi.) south on A 19 is the Buonfornello exit, from which we continue on SS113. A short distance along this, on the right, are the remains of the Greek city of Himera, founded in 648 BC and destroyed by the Carthaginians in 409 BC (Doric temple of c. 480 BC; temple of 6th c. BC; Antiquarium).

Himera

13 km (8 mi.): exit for Termini Imerese (77 m (254 ft); population 26,000), finely situated on a promontory. In the lower town is the spa establishment (warm radioactive saline springs, 42°C (108°F)), in the upper town the cathedral and the Belvedere park. The Museo Civico contains archaeological finds of several periods.

Termini Imerese

10 km (6 mi.) south, on a rocky crag above the Fiume San Leonardo, perches the little town of Caccamo (521 m (1719 ft); population 9000), with a well-preserved 12th c. castle, containing the notable "Room of Conspiracy".

Caccamo

4 km (2½ mi.): exit for Trabia (population 6000), on the coast, with a battlemented castle.

Trabia

16 km (10 mi.): exit for Casteldaccia.

Casteldaccia

Excursion:
From Casteldaccia we continue on the coast road to Santa Flavia, where a road goes off on the right via Porticello and Sant'Elia to Capo Zafferano (14 km (9 mi.): 225 m (743 ft); lighthouse). From this road a side road (1.5 km (1 mi.)) winds steeply up to the remains of Soluntum (or Solus; Italian Solunto), a Phoenician settlement and later a Roman town, situated on the south-east slopes of Monte Catalfano (376 m (1241 ft)). Particularly notable is the re-erected part of a peristyle belonging to a building known as the Gymnasium, the remains of a theatre and the Antiquarium. From the top of

Soluntum

the hill there are magnificent views westward of Palermo Bay and eastward, on clear days as far as Etna.

Bagheria

3 km (2 mi.) beyond Trabia on the motorway take the exit for Bagheria (80 m (264 ft); population 42,000), notable for its numerous Baroque villas (18th c.). At the end of the Corso Butera, the town's main street, is the Villa Butera (1658; "Certosa", with wax figures in Carthusian habits). A little way east the Villa Palagonia (1715) has an extraordinary collection of grotesque sculptured figures. Still farther east stands the Villa Valguarnera (1721; view from the terrace and from the nearby hill of Montagnola).

Palermo

12 km (7 mi.): exit for Palermo (see entry).

The next part of the circuit, from Palermo to Trapani, can be done either direct on the A 29 and A 29d motorways or on the coast road (SS187), passing through the little port of Castellammare del Golfo and Erice. Longer, but well worth the extra distance, is the route via SS186 and SS113. For this route leave Palermo by the Porta Nuova and the Corso Calatafimi.

★★Monreale

8 km (5 mi.): Monreale (300 m (990 ft); population 25,000), the see of an archbishop, beautifully situated above the Conca d'Oro.

Cathedral

On the left-hand side of the main street is the cathedral with its two towers, the finest example of Norman architecture in Sicily. 102 m (335 ft) long by 40 m (131 ft) wide, in the form of a basilica, it boasts a beautiful choir with interlaced pointed arches of dark grey lava which preserves the structure of a Byzantine church. The main doorway has a fine bronze door by Bonanno Pisano, with reliefs from scriptural history and inscriptions in early Italian (1186). The left-hand doorway, below a porch of 1569, has a bronze door by Barisanus of Trani (1179). In the interior are eighteen ancient columns with fine capitals, and its walls are covered with magnificent mosaics, completed in 1882, which cover an area of 6340 sq. m (68,245 sq. ft) (the largest area of mosaics in Sicily), with scenes from the Old Testament and the life of Christ and the Apostles. In the south transept are the sarcophagi of William I and II, son and grandson of Roger II. In the south aisle is the 16th c. Cappella di San Benedetto (marble reliefs), in the north aisle the Cappella del Crocifisso (1690), with fine wood-carvings of the Passion on the side doors. It is well worth while making the ascent to the roof of the cathedral for the view it affords.

Mosaics

Cloister

To the right of the cathedral stands the former Benedictine monastery. Of the original building nothing is left but the cloister (Chiostro di Santa Maria Nuova), the largest and finest in the Italian Romanesque style, with 216 columns. The cloister is overshadowed on the south side by a ruined wall of the original monastery.

Partinico

21 km (13 mi.) beyond Monreale on SS186 lies Partinico (175 m (578 ft); population 25,000), dominated by an ancient tower. From here we continue on SS113.

Alcamo

20 km (12 mi.): Alcamo (56 m (185 ft); population 45,000), a town founded by the Arabs. In the main street is the 17th c. cathedral, with a 14th c. campanile. Inside can be seen paintings by Borreman (1736–37) and sculpture by Antonio Gagini and his pupils. In the churches of Santa Chiara and the Badia Nuova are stucco figures by Giacomo Serpotta. There is also a 14th c. castle. Above the town rises Monte Bonifato (825 m (2723 ft); view); the climb takes two hours.

★Segesta

15 km (9 mi.): road to the remains (about 3 km (2 mi.) west) of the ancient city of Segesta or Egesta (318 m (1049 ft)), one of the oldest towns in Sicily,

Monreale: some of the magnificent mosaics ...

... and the impressive cloister

founded by the Elymians in pre-Greek times. It was almost incessantly at war with its Greek neighbours; later it became Carthaginian and then Roman, and was finally destroyed by the Saracens. From the end of the access road a stepped path leads up to the temple, standing in majestic solitude on a levelled ridge of hill below the west side of the ancient city. Begun in 430 BC but left unfinished, it is one of the best preserved temples in Sicily (61 m (200 ft) long by 26 m (85 ft) across), with 36 Doric columns still supporting the entablature and gable.

From the end of the access road a track winds up to the site of the ancient city, situated 1.5 km 1 (mi.) south-east on Monte Barbaro (415 m (1370 ft)), with remains of fortifications, houses (mosaic pavements) and a theatre hewn from the rock (3rd–2nd c. BC).

Calatafimi

3 km (2 mi.) beyond the turning for Segesta is Calatafimi (350 m (1155 ft); population 8000), with a castle on a hill to the west of the town.

Monument to Garibaldi

Excursion:
1 km (¹/₂ mi.): minor road (3 km (2 mi.) south-west) to the Ossario, a conspicuous monument to Garibaldi erected in 1892 to commemorate his first victory over numerically superior Bourbon forces on May 15th 1860.

Trapani

1 km (¹/₂ mi.): the road forks. SS113, to the right, leads to Trapani (35 km (22 mi.); SS188A, to the left, runs via Salemi (10 km (6 mi.); 442 m (1459 ft); population 13,000), with a castle built in the time of Frederick II in which Garibaldi proclaimed his dictatorship of Sicily in 1860 (commemorative column), to Castelvetrano (another 26 km (16 mi.)).

The third part of the circuit of Sicily, from Trapani to Syracuse, is on SS115.

Marsala

32 km (20 mi.): Marsala (see entry).

Mazara del Vallo

19 km (12 mi.): Mazara del Vallo (8 m (26 ft); population 46,000), with an 11th c. cathedral (remodelled in the 17th and 20th c.) founded by Count Roger and the 17th c. Norman-style church of San Nicolò Regale.

Campobello di Mazara

15 km (9 mi.): Campobello di Mazara (110 m (363 ft); population 12,000). 3 km (2 mi.) south-west are the ancient quarries known as the Rocche di Cusa or Cave di Campobello which supplied the building material for Selinus or Selinunte (closed 409 BC).

Castelvetrano

8 km (5 mi.): Castelvetrano (190 m (627 ft); population 32,000), with the churches of San Giovanni (statue of John the Baptist by Antonio Gagini (1512) in the choir); San Domenico (stucco figures by Antonio Ferraro, 1574–80 and marble Madonna by Domenico Gagini); and the 16th c. Chiesa Madre (Renaissance doorway).

3.5 km (2¹/₄ mi.) west of the town is the restored Norman church of the Santissima Trinità della Delia (12th c.), in Byzantine style on a centralised plan.

9 km (5¹/₂ mi.): road on right to the ruins of Selinunte.

Sciacca

37 km (23 mi.): Sciacca or Sciacca Terme (60 m (198 ft); population 38,000), with the spa and holiday centre of Sciaccamare.

At the west entrance to the town is the Porta San Salvatore. Just beyond it, to the right, stands the church of Santa Margherita (1342, remodelled in the 16th c.), the northern doorway of which is in marble (1486), and to the left the Chiesa del Carmine. North-east of the Porta San Salvatore, in Corso Vittorio Emanuele, is the Gothic Casa Steripinto, with a façade of faceted stones. Nearby is the cathedral, with a Madonna by Francesco Laurana (1467, in the fourth chapel on right). Farther east are the Giardino Comunale (view) and the Terme Selinuntine, the spa establishment (sulphur baths), on the site of the ancient baths. Higher up, on the line of the town walls, are the remains of the castle of Count Luna (1380).

Segesta: the amphitheatre

Excursion:

7 km (4¹/₄ mi.): road on left into the picturesque valley of Cava d'Ispica, the rock walls of which contain numerous caves used as dwellings and tombs in the Byzantine period.

★ Cava d'Ispica

32 km (20 mi.): Noto (158 m (521 ft); population 24,000), a small town, laid out in terraces. It was built from 1703 onwards to replace the older town, 11 km (7 mi.) south-east, which was destroyed by an earthquake in 1693.

Noto

On the town's main street, the Corso Vittorio Emanuele, which traverses it from west to east, are three monumental squares. In the first of these, the Piazza Ercole (officially the Piazza XVI Maggio), are the Baroque church of San Domenico (18th c.) and an ancient statue of Hercules. In the second, the Piazza del Municipio, stand the cathedral, with an imposing Baroque façade, the Palazzo Ducezio (Town Hall) and the church of San Salvatore. In the third, the Piazza Immacolata, we find the church of the Immacolata (or San Francesco) and the monastery of San Salvatore. To the north is the Chiesa del Crocifisso, with a Madonna by Francesco Laurana (1471).

9 km (5¹/₂ mi.) beyond Noto, on SS115, is Avola (40 m (132 ft); population 31,000). The road then crosses the River Cassibile, the ancient Kakyparis, where Demosthenes and his 6000 Athenians were compelled to surrender to the Syracusans in 413 BC. Upstream, in the rock faces of the Cave Grande, is a Siculan necropolis.

Avola

23 km (14 mi.): Syracuse (see entry).

Syracuse

The last part of the circuit of Sicily, from Syracuse to Messina, is on SS114 (the "Orientale Sicula"; from Catania also the A 18 motorway), running close to the sea for most of the way.

14 km (9 mi.) from Syracuse the road forks. Straight ahead is the old and more interesting road via Lentini (53 m (175 ft); population 31,000); to the right the new road, SS114, is 8 km (5 mi.) shorter and much faster.

Lentini

Sicily

Augusta	SS114 passes large oil refineries and comes in 7 km (4¼ mi.) to the turning for Augusta, the principal Italian naval base in Sicily (14 m (46 ft); population 40,000).
Catania	63 km (39 mi.): Catania (see entry).
Aci Castello	9 km (5½ mi.) beyond Catania on SS114 lies the little town of Aci Castello, dominated by a picturesque ruined castle on a high crag (15 m (50 ft); population 15,000).
Scogli de' Ciclopi	Just beyond the town can be seen the seven Scogli de' Ciclopi (Cyclops' Islands) or Faraglioni, traditionally the rocks which the blinded Cyclops hurled after Odysseus' ship ("Odyssey"). On the largest of the islands, the Isola d'Aci, is a marine biological station.
Acireale	7 km (4¼ mi.): Acireale (Sicilian Iaci; 161 m (531 ft); population 50,000). On the near side of the town to the right of the road, are the Terme di Santa Venera (warm radioactive water containing iodine, sulphur and salt). Here begins the town's main street, the Corso Vittorio Emanuele, with the church of San Sebastiano (Baroque façade) on the right, beyond this, in the Piazza del Duomo, are the cathedral, the Town Hall and the church of Santi Pietro e Paolo. From the municipal park at the north end of the town there are fine views.
Mascali	18 km (11 mi.): Mascali, a little town which formerly lay farther west but was destroyed by lava in 1928 and rebuilt on its present site.
Taormina	15 km (9 mi.): Taormina (see entry).
Messina	48 km (30 mi.): Messina (see entry).
Monte San Calogero	Excursion: From the Porta San Salvatore a road runs 7.5 km (4½ mi.) north-east to the limestone hill of Monte San Calogero (388 m (1280 ft)), with the Santuario San Calogero on its summit (monastery; view). Below the monastery are caves with vapour baths (Le Stufe: temperature 34–40°C (93–104°F)).
Caltabellotta	Excursion: 20 km (12 mi.) north-east of Sciacca is the little town of Caltabellotta (839 m (2802 ft); population 5500), dominated by its castle, which has a cathedral dating from the Norman period.
Eraclea Minoa	Excursion: 23 km (14 mi.) farther along SS115 a road goes off on the right to the remains (6 km (3¾ mi.) south-west on Capo Bianco) of the ancient city of Eraclea Minoa, destroyed in the 1st c. BC. Notable features are a theatre (3rd c. BC) and the remains of the town walls.
Porto Empedocle	41 km (25 mi.): Porto Empedocle, the port of Agrigento.
Agrigento	6 km (3¾ mi.): road on left to Agrigento, running between the temples of Zeus and Hera and then winding its way up to the town (see entry).
Palma di Montechiaro	32 km (20 mi.): Palma di Montechiaro (165 m (545 ft); population 22,000), with a fine Baroque church. On the hill beyond it, to the right, is the 14th c. Castello di Montechiaro (286 m (944 ft)).
Licata	20 km (12 mi.): Licata (12 m (40 ft); population 42,000), beautifully situated on the sloping hillside at the mouth of the river Salso, an expanding port which is the principal commercial town on the south coast of Sicily (export of sulphur). The Museo Civico contains numerous archaeological finds, particularly from graves. Farther up, to the west, is the 16th c. Castel San Angelo (restored).

11 km (7 mi.): on the coast, to the right, is the 15th c. Castello di Falconara (restored).

Falconara

22 km (14 mi.): Gela (45 m (149 ft); population 77,000), a port which was formerly called Terranova di Sicilia (oil refineries), also frequented as a seaside resort.

Gela

To the west of the town are the extensive cemeteries of the ancient city, founded by Dorian settlers in 689 BC, and the Zona Archeologica di Capo Soprano, with the imposing remains of Greek defensive walls of the 5th–4th c. BC (200 m (656 ft) long, built of regular stone blocks in the lower part and sun-dried bricks in the upper part, the earliest known use of such bricks) and Greek baths of the 4th c. BC. At the east end of the town is the Museo Regionale Archeologico; adjoining are the most recent excavations (houses and shops of the 4th c. BC). South of the museum, on the Molino e Vento (Windmill) hill, the Acropolis, is the municipal park, with the remains of two Doric temples (6th and 5th c. BC).

33 km (20 mi.) beyond Gela on SS115 is Vittoria (168 m (554 ft); population 53,000), the principal centre of the Sicilian wine trade. In the main square are the Neo-Classical Teatro Vittorio Emanuele and the church of the Madonna delle Grazie (18th c.).

Vittoria

8 km (5 mi.): Comiso (209 m (690 ft); population 29,000), with two 18th c. domed churches, the Chiesa Madre and the Chiesa della Santissima Annunziata, a 14th c. castle and a beautiful Fountain of Diana in the Piazza Municipio.

Comiso

17 km (11 mi.): Ragusa (562 m (1855 ft); population 67,000), a provincial capital, picturesquely situated above the gorge of the River Irminio, with a Baroque cathedral (18th c.) and the splendid Baroque church of San Giorgio (18th c.) in the old part of the town, Ibla, to the east (steep winding streets). The Museo Archeologico Ibleo contains finds of the surroundings of Ragusa.

Ragusa

From the bypass to the south of the town there are fine views. Around the town are deposits of bituminous limestone, large asphalt pits. In recent years oil has been worked here.

15 km (9 mi.) beyond Ragusa, on SS115, is Modica (296 m (977 ft); population 50,000), a flourishing town rising up the slopes on both sides of the Modica valley. In the lower town, at the top of a flight of steps, is the church of San Pietro (18th c.); the massive church of San Giorgio (18th c.) stands in the upper town.

Modica

See entry.

Selinunte

Siena

F9

Region: Toscana. Province: Siena (SI)
Altitude: 322 m (1063 ft). Population: 64,000

The provincial capital of Siena lies 70 km (43 mi.) east of Florence in the Tuscan hills. From this area comes the brown pigment known as burnt sienna.

Location

The town has a university and is the see of an archbishop. It is one of the great art centres, with a profusion of fine architecture and numerous churches and palaces.

The town centre is closed to cars, but access to the hotels is permitted.

Access

In Roman times Saena Iulia was a place of no importance, but under the Franks it became the residence of a count. After the death of Countess Matilda of Tuscany in 1115 the town asserted its independence. Thereafter it was governed by the Ghibelline nobility, and this brought it into sharp

History

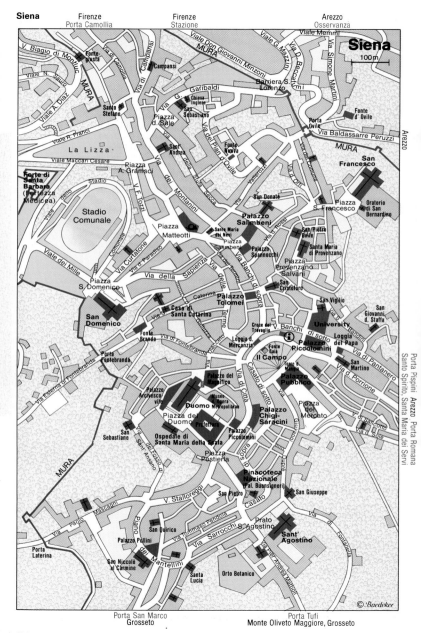

Siena

Firenze
Porta Camollia

Firenze
Stazione

Arezzo
Osservanza

Siena

100m

V. Biagio di Montluc
Fonte
giusta
Campansi
Viale N. Sauro
MURA
Viale A. Diaz
V. di Camollia
Via di Camollia
Garibaldi
Chiesa
Inglese
Viale Don Giovanni Minzoni
MURA
Viale G. Mazzini
Via D. Beccafumi
Viale G. Mazzini
Viale Memmi
Barriera S.
Lorenzo
Simone Martini
Viale R. Franci
Santo
Stefano
Via G.
San
Sebastiano
Piazza
d. Sale
Porta
Ovile
Fonte
d'Ovile
La Lizza
Viale Maccari Cesare
Sant'
Andrea
Via dei Pian d'Ovile
Fonte
Nuova
Via Baldassarre Peruzzi
MURA
Arezzo
Forte di
Santa
Barbara
(Fortezza
Medicea)
detto
Stadio
V.E. Iozzi
Via della Sapienza
Via dei Montanini
Vanterozzi
Via del Comune
San Donato
Via di Città
San
Francesco
Piazza
S. Francesco
Oratorio
di San
Bernardino
Stadio
Comunale
Piazza
Matteotti
Palazzo
Salimbeni
Santa Maria
dei Neri
Piazza
Salimbeni
Via di Rossi
San Pietro
Ovile
Santa Maria
di Provenzano
Via Curtatone
Via di Paradiso
Palazzo
Spannocchi
Piazza
Provenzano
Salvani
Piazza
S. Domenico
Via delle Terme
San
Cristoforo
Viale dei Mille
Via Fieravecchia
Via Banchi di sopra
San Vigilio
San
Giovanni
d. Staffa
Via delle
Caterina
Casa di
Santa Caterina
Palazzo
Tolomei
Università
San Domenico
Fonte
Branda
Via di Fontebranda
Croce del
Travaglio
V. Banchi
di sotto
Palazzo
Piccolomini
Loggia
del Papa
Porta
Fontebranda
Loggia d.
Mercanzia
Fonte
Gaia
Il Campo
San
Martino
Via di Pantaneto
Via Esterna di Fontebranda
Casato di sotto
Torre d.
Mangia
Palazzo
Pubblico
Via di Porrione
Palazzo del
Magnifico
Piazza
del
Mercato
Palazzo
Arcivescovile
Museo
dell'Opera
Metropolitana
Via del salicotto
Duomo
Via di Città
Palazzo
Chigi-
Saracini
Via d. Sole
Piazza del
Duomo
Prefettura
Palazzo
Piccolomini
MURA
San
Sebastiano
Ospedale di
Santa Maria della Scala
Via del Fosso di
Sant'Agelo
Piazza
Postierla
Via del Casato di sopra
Via del Porrione
Pinacoteca
Nazionale
(Pal. Buonsignori)
San Pietro
San Giuseppe
V. Stalloreggi
Casato
Prato
S. Agostino
Via
di
Fontanella
San Quirico
Via Tommaso Pendola
Via Sarrocchi
Sant'
Agostino
Via Paolo
Via dei Mantellini
Palazzo
Pollini
San Niccolò
al Carmine
Santa
Lucia
Orto Botanico
Via Pier Andrea Mattioli
Via Mascagni
Piano
Porta
Laterina

Porta Pispini Arezzo Porta Romana
Santo Spirito, Santa Maria dei Servi

© Baedeker

conflict with Florence, a stronghold of the Guelfs. The two towns were constantly at war. After the fall of the Hohenstaufens (1270) Charles of Anjou succeeded in establishing his influence in Siena and incorporated it in the Guelf federation of Tuscan towns. In 1348 the town was ravaged by the plague. After a period of internal strife Siena was governed by tyrants, among them Pandolfo Petrucci (1487 onwards). In 1555 Siena was occupied by the Spaniards, and in 1559 it was ceded to Duke Cosimo I of Tuscany.

The heyday of Sienese art was in the 13th and 14th c. The cathedral and many of the palaces are magnificent examples of Gothic architecture. The availability of good brickmaking clay in the area favoured the use of brick in building. The delicate, graceful Sienese painting of the 13th and 14th c. (Duccio, Simone Martini, Ambrogio and Pietro Lorenzetti) surpassed the early painting of Florence. Jacopo della Quercia (1374–1438) was one of the founders of Renaissance sculpture, and his influence can still be detected in the work of Michelangelo.

Art

Sights

In the centre of Siena a spacious semicircular area, the Piazza del Campo extends in front of the massive Town Hall, the uniform architecture making it one of the finest squares in Italy. The "Palio delle Contrade" is held on July 2nd and August 16th. The Palio is a picturesque procession in medieval costumes and a horse-race; the price for the winners being a banner (Latin pallium) bearing the image of the Madonna.

★★Piazza del Campo

On the north side of the square stands a copy of the marble fountain, the Fonte Gaia (1419), a masterpiece by Jacopo della Quercia, the original of which can be seen in the Museo Civico (see below).

Fonte Gaia

View of the Piazza del Campo from the tower of the Palazzo Pubblico

Siena

Palazzo Pubblico	Along the south side of the Campo extends the Palazzo Pubblico, a huge Gothic building of travertine and brick (1297–1310); the top floor of the lower side wing was added in 1680. At its side is the Torre del Mangia, built 1338–48 (102 m (337 ft) high; 412 steps), from the top of which there are fine views. Below this is the Cappella di Piazza, a loggia built after the great plague of 1348, with a Renaissance upper storey added in 1468.

The interior of the Palazzo Pubblico is notable for the numerous frescoes of the Sienese school which reflect the views and attitudes of the proud citizens of Siena in the 14th and 15th c.; particularly interesting is the painting by Ambrogio Lorenzetti in the Sala della Pace, "Good and Bad Government" (1337–43), with a contemporary view of the city.

Museo Civico	On the first and second floors the Museo Civico houses drawings, paintings and other documents of the history of the town.

On the third floor is a loggia in which the original sculpture from the Fonte Gaia has been assembled.

Loggia della Mercanzia	From the north-west side of the Campo, steps lead up to the Loggia della Mercanzia (1428–44), the old commercial tribunal, near the so-called Croce del Travaglio ("Cross of Work"). There the three principal streets of the town meet: to the north the Banchi di Sopra, to the east the Banchi di Sotto and to the south-west the Via di Città.
Palazzo Chigi-Saracini	In Via di Città stands the Palazzo Chigi-Saracini (14th c.), now occupied by the Accademia Musicale Chigiana (Music Academy; concerts). The building also contains pictures by Botticelli, Pinturicchio, Sodoma and Spinello Aretina (visit by appointment).
★Palazzo Piccolomini	In Banchi di Sotto is the University and opposite it, on the right, the Palazzo Piccolomini, one of the finest Early Renaissance palaces in Siena, built for Nanni Piccolomini, father of Pope Pius II after 1469 and now the repository of the extensive State Archives.
Logge del Papa	Situated in the nearby Piazza Piccolomini, the elegant Logge del Papa was built for Pius II in 1462.
★Baptistery of San Giovanni	From Via di Città the Via dei Pellegrini runs west past the Palazzo del Magnifico (1508), on the left, to the little Piazza San Giovanni, on the south-west side of which is the choir of the cathedral, which occupies the highest point in the town. Beneath the cathedral is the Baptistery of San Giovanni, with a beautiful but unfinished Gothic façade of 1382. The interior contains a fine font by Jacopo della Quercia (1427–30), with bronze reliefs by Donatello and other artists.
Palazzo Arcivescovile	From the Piazza San Giovanni we go to the Archbishop's Palace (Palazzo Arcivescovile), which contains the famous "Madonna del Latte" ("Nursing Madonna"), a panel ascribed to Ambrogio Lorenzetti.
★★Cathedral	From the Archbishop's Palace it is only a few steps to the Piazza del Duomo, which lies on the highest point of the town. Here stands the cathedral of Santa Maria Assunta. It was begun in the mid 12th c., and by 1264 it had been completed as far as the dome; about 1317 the choir was extended eastwards over the baptistery. In 1339 the citizens of Siena resolved to carry out a rebuilding that would have made the cathedral the largest and finest in Italy; but this project was abandoned as a result of structural defects and the great plague in 1348. The present cathedral has a total length of 89 m (292 ft) and a width of 24 m (79 ft) (across the transepts 54 m (177 ft)). The façade, in red, black and white marble, was not completed until 1380; the rich sculptural decoration consists largely of reproductions dating from 1869, and the mosaics were added in 1877. The campanile dates from the late 13th c.

Sienna Cathedral ▶

The "Palio delle Contrade"

On July 2nd and more especially on August 16th every year Siena is full of life, for it is then that the "Palio delle Contrade", a horse-race combined with a popular festival, is held on the Piazza del Campo. *Contrade*, (singular: *contrada*) is the name given to the town quarters of Siena, a division which can be traced back to the Middle Ages. Of the seventeen contrade ten participate in the competition which is held in honour of the Holy Virgin. The winning contrada receives the "palio", a banner with a picture of the Virgin Mary. Which ten contrade shall take part in the race is decided by drawing lots.

The actual race lasts only a few minutes. During the morning the most beautiful part of the festivities, the colourful procession, can be witnessed. Those taking part are dressed in historical costumes. Accompanied by the banging of drums and waving of flags, the procession moves through the Piazzo del Duomo to the festively decorated "Campo". The people watch the spectacle from the windows, balconies, even the roofs of the surrounding houses. At the head of the historic procession rides a standard-bearer, proudly swinging the black and white flag which is the emblem of Siena. He is followed by the musicians and standard-bearers of the towns and castles which once formed part of the old city state of Siena. Then come representatives of the ten contrade which will take part in the race, each dressed in the colours of his particular part of town. Each group has a drummer, several standard-bearers, a leader, four pages, a knight on a parade horse and the "barbaresco", holding the racehorse by the reins. Those contrade which are not taking part in the race are also represented. The procession is completed by a triumphal coach with gilt and coloured decoration. This coach houses the "palio", the banner which will be awarded to the winner, the "Martinella" bell and four representatives of the "biccherna", the medieval tax authority.

The Palio, the most famous of Siena's folk festivals, can be traced back to about 1310, when its introduction was officially confirmed in a document issued by the town's General Assembly. At first there was only the one Palio, celebrated on August 16th in honour of the Assumption of the Virgin Mary. From the middle of the 12th century the independent town, governed by the Ghibelline nobility, was in conflict with Florence, a stronghold of the Guelphs. In 1260 the Sienese were victorious over the Florentines at Montaperti. After that the Palio became more important, even politically so. It served to pay homage to the Virgin Mary and at the same time to emphasise the town's independence. The other Palio, held on July 2nd, was not officially recognised until 1656 and it is held in honour of the Madonna of Provenzano. The result is that the religious ceremony for the Palio of August 16th is held in Siena cathedral, while that for the July 2nd race is celebrated in the church of Santa Maria in Provenzano, which houses the Madonna di Provenzano, fragments of a *pietà* owned by the Sienese Ghibelline leader Provenzano Salvari.

On the day prior to the Palio (from the Latin *pallium* = cloak or coverlet) a qualifying heat is run. For the actual race wooden grandstands are erected on the Piazza del Campo. Each contrada leads its horse into a church for it to be blessed.

Early in the afternoon the ceremonial entry into the Piazza del Campo takes place. The race is started by a tape stretched across the route. The riders do not have to hail from Siena; each of the quarters can sign one up from anywhere in Italy. Each rider must be top class but not normally a jockey, light in weight but strong and competitive by nature. During the race the riders are "armed" with a bullwhip which they employ with gusto to frighten the opponent's horse and to drive their own on mercilessly. They give their all to come first in the race. The wildness of the Palio, in which basic fighting instincts come to the fore, also infects the audience. For the inhabitants of Siena it has a communicative effect and strengthens local patriotism. It is said that the best thing the losers can do is flee the scene immediately to avoid the wrath of their disappointed supporters. The winner of the race, on the other hand, returns to his quarter to be fêted amid much noise and jubilation. The aim of the subsequent banquet is either to drown one's sorrows or to celebrate victory. While for centuries the Palio was a very expensive matter for the people of the town, today the event brings money in from the many visitors that are attracted to the spectacle.

The writer Kasimir Edschmid summarised his impressions of the event as follows: "During the days of the Palio festival the good people of Siena give vent to their innermost feelings in expressing everything this proud town has ever experienced in its history in the way of fighting traditions, ambition, old disputes, honour and glory, defeats and triumphs. The Palio is the horse race in which the seventeen quarters of the town, the "contrade" of Siena, compete one against the other and in which the riders of the various contrade, the "fantini", bitterly fight it out on the town's most magnificent square".

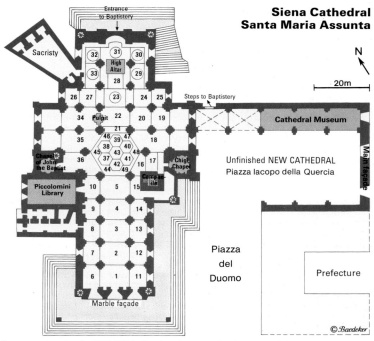

**Siena Cathedral
Santa Maria Assunta**

Scenes represented on the PAVEMENT (various dates between 1372 and 1562: partly imitations and copies – originals in Cathedral Museum)

1 Hermes Trismegistus
2 Coats of arms of Siena (centre), Pisa, Lucca, Florence, Arezzo, Orvieto, Rome, Perugia, Viterbo, Massa, Grosseto, Volterra and Pistoia
3 Imperial Altar
4 Fortune
5 Wheel of Fortune; for philosophers
6–15 Sibyls
16 Seven Ages of Man

17 Faith, Hope, Charity, Religion
18 Jephthah defeats the Ammonites
19 Death of Absalom
20 Emperor Sigismund
21 Moses draws water from the rock
22 Dance round the Golden Calf
23 David and Goliath
24 Moses
25 Samson defeats the Philistines

26, 27 Joshua
28 Abraham's Sacrifice
29 Wisdom
30 Moderation
31 Compassion
32 Justice
33 Strength
34 Judith and Holofernes
35 Massacre of the Innocents
36 Fall of Herod
37–49 Ahab and Elijah

Interior

The interior, with its regularly alternating courses of black and white marble, at first produces a rather strange effect. A unique feature is the marble pavement, with its beautiful graffito figures and scenes, mostly from the Old Testament, carried out to designs of famous artists. (Some of them are copies; originals in the Cathedral Museum.) Along the cornice in the nave are numerous terracotta busts of Popes (15th c.). In the north aisle is a masterpiece of decorative sculpture, the entrance wall of the Cathedral Library by Marrina, a fine sculptor of the Sienese High Renaissance.

In the north transept, decorated with frescos by Pinturicchio, the Cappella di San Giovanni Battista has a beautiful doorway by this artist and a bronze statue of John the Baptist by Donatello (1457). A particularly notable feature is the white marble pulpit, with fine reliefs of New Testament scenes by Nicola Pisano (1266–68).

From the north aisle we enter the famous Cathedral Library (Libreria Piccolomini), one of the finest and best preserved creations of the Early Renaissance. It was built in 1492 for Cardinal Francesco Piccolomini (later Pope Pius III) in honour of his kinsman Aeneas Sylvius Piccolomini (Pope Pius II, 1458–64) and decorated by Pinturicchio and his pupils with brilliantly coloured frescos depicting scenes from the life of Aeneas Sylvius (1502–09).

★Piccolomini Library

Opposite the south-east side of the cathedral, three long buildings belonging to the New Cathedral, house the Cathedral Museum (Museo dell'Opera Metropolitana), with material illustrating the constructional history of the cathedral, pictures by Sienese masters, including Duccio di Buonisegna's "Maestà", a picture of a Madonna enthroned with angels and saints painted in 1308–11 for the high altar of the cathedral, the "Birth of the Virgin", a wooden "Crucifixion" and embroidered vestments (14th–18th c.).

Cathedral Museum

Opposite the façade of the cathedral are the church and hospital of Santa Maria della Scala (13th–14th c.), with frescos depicting the work of the hospital in the 15th c.

Santa Maria della Scala

From the Piazza del Duomo the Via del Capitano runs south-east past the Prefecture, the former Palazzo Reale (on the left), and the Palazzo del Capitano del Popolo (on the right) to the little Piazza di Postierla, from which Via di San Pietro leads to the Palazzo Buonsignori, a 14th c. brick building now housing the Pinacoteca Nazionale, with an important and representative collection of works of the Sienese school from the 12th to the 16th c. Represented in the gallery are works by Guido da Siena, Duccio di Buoninsegna, Ambrogio Lorenzetti, Pietro Lorenzetti, Giovanni de Paolo, Pinturicchio and the Lombard artist Giovanni Antonio Bazzi, surnamed Il Sodoma.

★Pinacoteca Nazionale

Sights in the north-east

In Via Banchi di Sopra, going north from the Loggia di Mercanzia, stands the Early Gothic Palazzo Tolomei (on the left). Beyond this, in Piazza Salimbeni, are the battlemented Palazzo Salimbeni and, on the south side, the Palazzo Spannocchi, a fine Early Renaissance building by the Florentine Giuliano da Maiano (begun 1470).

Palaces

To the east, on the edge of the town, is the church of San Francesco (1326–1475), founded by the Franciscans, with a façade of 1913. In the north transept is a fine fresco by Pietro Lorenzetti ("Crucifixion"; c. 1330).

San Francesco

Adjoining the church of San Francesco is an Oratory built in the 15th c. on the spot where the Franciscan St Bernard of Siena used to preach. The upper floor of the little church has particularly fine frescos by Sodoma and Early Renaissance ceiling decoration.

Oratorio di San Bernardino

North-west of the Palazzo Tolomei is situated the Museo Archeologico Nazionale (National Archaeological Museum). The collections consist of finds, mainly from the surroundings of the town, particularly of the Etruscan period, including urns, bronze work and a remarkable variety of coins.

Museo Archeologico

On the west side of the town is the fortress-like church of San Domenico, a rough brick structure in the Gothic style (1226–1465) with a crenellated campanile. In the north-west wall of the nave is the entrance to the domed chapel containing the oldest picture of St Catherine of Siena (1347–80), a

San Domenico

fresco painted by Andrea Vanni (c. 1400). On the high altar in the choir are a ciborium and two candelabra by Benedetto da Maiano (1475).

Fonte Branda

Below the hill of San Domenico the Fonte Branda, a fountain which is mentioned in the records as early as 1081, has a colonnade of three arches built over it in 1246.

Santuario Cateriniano

A little way east of the fountain, in Via Santa Caterina, is the Sanctuary of St Catherine. St Catherine of Siena (1347–80), the daughter of a dyer named Benincasa, prevailed on Pope Gregory XI to return from Avignon to Rome in 1377. The best known of her visions was her "mystic marriage" to the Infant Christ, a favourite theme with painters. The fine Renaissance doorway has the Latin inscription "Sponsae Kristi Catherinae Domus" ("House of Catherine, Bride of Christ").

Forte di Santa Barbara

From San Domenico we can go either north-west along the Viale dei Mille, past the Stadium, or north round the Stadium to a beautiful park, the Passeggio della Lizza, with a monument to Garibaldi (1896). At the west end of the park is the entrance to the Forte di Santa Barbara, a fortress built by Duke Cosimo I in 1560, which is now used for open-air performances. In the cellar of the first bastion (on the left) is the Enoteca Italica, a permanent wine exhibition.

Fontegiusta

A short distance north of the Lizza park is the little church of Fontegiusta (1484), with a high altar by Marrina, one of the finest examples of High Renaissance work of its kind (1519).

Santa Maria dei Servi

In the south-east of the old town is the church of Santa Maria dei Servi (13th–15th c.), with a fine campanile. The interior contains several pictures by artists of the Sienese school, including the famous fresco "Child Murder at Bethlehem" (c. 1330) by Pietro Lorenzetti.

Porta Romana

A little way south is the Porta Romana in the town wall, a massive town gate of 1327.

Colle di Val d'Elsa

23 km (14 mi.) NW

North-west of Siena on SS2 is Colle di Val d'Elsa (population 16,000), situated above the River Elsa. The little town consists of an industrial lower town, Colle Basso (137 m (452 ft)), and the old upper town or Colle Alta (223 m (736 ft)), with medieval palaces and a 17th c. cathedral.

From Colle di Val d'Elsa it is possible either to drive to Volterra, 27 km (17 mi.) west, or to go north to Poggibonsi and then west to the interesting town of San Gimignano (20 km (12 mi.)); see entry.

★Monte Oliveto Maggiore

35 km (22 mi.) SE

Another very interesting excursion is to the large monastery of Monte Oliveto Maggiore (273 m (901 ft)). One of the most renowned monasteries of the Olivetans (a branch of the Benedictines), it was founded in 1313 by Bernardo Tolomei. A visit to the monastery is most rewarding. In the cloister are fine frescos with scenes from the life of St Benedict by Luca Signorelli (1497–98) and Sodoma (1505).

Abbazia di San Galgano

33 km (20 mi.) SW

South-west of Siena is the abbey of San Galgano (Abbazia di San Galgano), the ruins of which are an excellent example of Cistercian Gothic in Italy. The ruins of the church, built in 1224 to 1288, have an overwhelming effect.

★Sorrento   J14

Region: Campania. Province: Napoli (NA)
Altitude: 50 m (165 ft). Population: 17,000

The little town of Sorrento (in the local dialect Surriento), the ancient   Location
Surrentum, is situated amid lemon and orange-groves on the south side
of the Bay of Naples, on the edge of tufa cliffs 50 m (165 ft) high rising
precipitously from the sea.
  Sorrento is the see of an archbishop.

Sights

The two harbours, Marina Grande and Marina Piccolo, extend along the
steep coast. From the Villa Comunale, a terrace above the Marina Grande,
there are far-ranging views of the Gulf of Naples. Sorrento's main street is
the Corso Italia. In Piazza Tasso, near the town's centre, stands a marble
statue of the poet Torquato Tasso (1544–95), who was born in Sorrento.
From here a road runs down to Marina Piccolo, where the boats come in.

In the new part of Sorrento the Museo Correale, founded in 1924, contains   Museo Correale
a death mask of Torquato Tasso and some special editions of his works,
pictures, interarsia work, furniture and porcelain, including the so-called
"basis of Sorrento", reliefs from Augustan times and the remains of a medieval choir screen.

Some time ago this new Archaeological Museum was opened in the Villa   Museo
Florentino. On display are finds uncovered in Massa Lubrense (see below)   Archeologico
and at other sites.

Harbour and coastline of sunny Sorrento

Piano di Sorrento To the east of Sorrento extends the fertile Piano di Sorrento, in Roman times a favourite residence of the great and the wealthy and still a popular holiday resort which attracts visitors from far and wide.

Sorrento to Positano

Massa Lubrense From Sorrento the road runs south-west to the little town of Massa Lubrense or Massalubrense (120 m (396 ft); population 11,000), with the Castello di Santa Maria (224 m (409 ft)) rearing above it.

Punta della From here it is a 2 hours' walk to the Punta della Campanella, at the
Campanella farthest tip of the peninsula of Sorrento opposite the island of Capri.

Sant'Agata Beyond Massa Lubrense the road skirts Monte San Nicola and comes in another 5 km (3 mi.) to Sant'Agata sui due Golfi (391 m (1290 ft)), a pleasant little summer resort below the Deserto. On a hill 1 km ($\frac{1}{2}$ mi.) north-west is the Deserto (455 m (1502 ft)), a former monastery which is now an orphanage. From the roof there are fine views of the bays of Naples and Salerno.

Nastro Azurro From Sant'Agata it is another 13 km (8 mi.) on a beautiful road (the stretch to Colli San Pietro being known as the "Nastro Azurro" or the "Blue Ribbon") which passes close to the conspicuous chapel of Sant'Angelo (462 m (1525 ft); view), to the left of the road, before coming to Positano.

La Spezia   D7

Region: Liguria. Province: La Spezia (SP)
Altitude: 3 m (10 ft). Population: 113,000

Location The provincial capital of La Spezia lies between Genoa and Pisa on the wide Golfo della Spezia, one of the largest and safest natural harbours in the Mediterranean, extending 9 km (5$\frac{1}{2}$ mi.) into the coast and 7 km (4$\frac{1}{2}$ mi.) wide. It is some 70 km (43 mi.) north-west to Genoa and about 45 km (28 mi.) south-east to Pisa.

Sights

Museums The main street of La Spezia is the Corso Cavour, where, at No. 251, are the Biblioteca Civica (some 80,000 volumes), the Musei Civici (local history, natural history) and the Museo Archeologico Lunense (Roman antiquities and finds from Luni).

The Corso Cavour runs south-east into Via D. Chiodo, which is lined with orange trees, and near which is the Giardino Pubblico, with fine palms and yuccas. From here Viale Mazzini and Viale Italia run north-east, separated by a line of palms and flanked on the seaward side by the Passeggiata Morin, from which there are beautiful views of the bay and the Apuan Alps with the shimmering white spoil heaps of Carrara.

Cathedral Via Chiodo leads north-east to the Piazza G. Verdi, with modern office blocks, and beyond this the Piazza Italia, in which stands the new Town Hall. On a terrace above the square rises the new cathedral (1976).

North-west of Piazza Verdi, running along the hillside, is Via XXVII Marzo, with the 14th c. Castello San Giorgio.

Shipping Museum At the south-west end of Via Chiodo is the Piazza Chiodo and farther on, beyond a canal, the main entrance to the Naval Arsenal, the basic features of which were outlined by Napoleon. The interesting Shipping Museum at the entrance contains models illustrating the history of seafaring from the origins to the present day and also charts and navigation apparatus.

La Spezia, a trading port and naval base

Surroundings

There is a very attractive drive around the north side of the town on the Giro della Foce, which follows the slopes of Monte Castellazzo (285 m (941 ft)) to the Passo della Foce (241 m (795 ft)), with views of the Gulf of Spezia and the Apuan Alps.

Passo della Foce

The coast road is also very beautiful. 11 km (7 mi.) west we come to Riomaggiore, the first village in the Cinqueterre (see entry).

Riomaggiore

10 km (6 mi.) south on the west side of the gulf is Portovénere (10 m (33 ft); population 5000), an old-world little port picturesquely situated on the Bocchette, the narrow strait, only 150 m wide, between the Costa dell'Olivo promontory and the island of Palmaria. From the little church of San Pietro (1277) at the southern tip of the promontory there are charming views of the precipitous cliffs of the Cinqueterre to the north-west and the bay of Lerici to the east. Above the church are a Genoese castle and the parish church of San Lorenzo.

Portovénere

South-west of La Spezia lies the little port of Lérici (10 m (33 ft); population 14,000), which in the Middle Ages, together with Portovénere, was the principal port on the Gulf of Spezia. Beside the church of San Rocco is an unusual Romanesque campanile. On a projecting tongue of land stands a well-preserved 13th c. castle, now a museum. From Lérici there is a pleasant drive, passing a number of pretty coves and the fishing village of Fiascherino, to the picturesquely situated village of Tellaro (4 km (2½ mi.) south-east).

Lérici
11 km (7 mi.) SW

East of La Spezia is Sarzana (21 m (69 ft); population 20,000), founded in 1202 as the successor to the ancient Etruscan city of Luni (of which sparse remains can be seen 7 km (4½ mi.) south-east). The town has remains of its 15th c. walls, the Cittadella, and a white marble cathedral in Italian Gothic style

Sarzana
16 km (10 mi.) E

Portovénere, a favourite spot for outings

(13th c.; completed in 1474), containing a painted crucifix from Luni (by Guillelmus, 1138), the earliest dated panel painting in Italy. To the north of the town stands the picturesque castle of Sarzanello (121 m (399ft); view).

Spoleto   G10

Region: Umbria. Province: Perugia (PG)
Altitude: 305–453 m (1007–1495 ft). Population: 38,000

Location   Spoleto is situated in the Central Italian region of Umbria above the left bank of the River Tessino, which here emerges from a narrow valley in the Umbrian Apennines into the plain of Umbria. Spoleto is the see of an archbishop.

Sights in the Old Town

Teatro Romano   On the Piazza della Libertà are the remains of a Roman theatre (1st c. BC, which could accommodate 3000 spectators. Near the amphitheatre lies the entrance to the Spoleto Archaeological Museum.

Arco di Druso   A narrow, steep lane leads up to the Baroque church of Sant'Ansano (18th c.), built on the site of a Roman temple. The Arch of Drusus (Arco di Druso), made of large stone blocks in AD 24, once formed the entrance to the Roman forum, the present Piazza del Mercato (market place).

Via del Palazzo   On the lane going off the Piazza del Mercato near the Baroque wall-fountain are medieval workshops and shops (botteghe) which now house delicatessens and handicraft shops.

Spoleto: cathedral and the Piazzo del Duomo ▶

Spoleto

Palazzo Comunale

Between Via Saffi and Via dei Munizipio lies the Palazzo Comunale (13th c.; entrance in Via del Munizipio), with the town's picture collection occupying a few rooms. Opposite the Palazzo Comunale are the remains of a small Roman temple (basilica). On Via Saffi, to the north behind the Palazzo Comunale, in the courtyard of the Bishop's Palace, is hidden the pretty Romanesque church of Sant'Eufemia (12th c.), the choir of which can be seen from the Piazza del Duomo.

★Cathedral

On the east side of the Bishop's Palace a wide stepped ramp leads down to the long Piazza del Duomo, to the rear of which stands the cathedral of Santa Maria Assunta with its magnificent façade. Destroyed by Emperor Frederick I (Barbarosa) in 1155, it was rebuilt in 1175. The porch was added in 1491. The upper part of the façade is dominated by a large mosaic showing Christ with Mary and John (1207).

The interior was remodelled in the Baroque style in 1638. The choir contains frescos by Filippo Lippi (1467–69), depicting in particular scenes from the life of Mary. On the left side of the south transept is the tomb of Filippo Lippi (1412–69).

Rocca

On the east side of the Town Hall lies the tree-shaded Piazza Campello. From here Via della Rocca runs to the Rocca, built in the 14th c. as the residence of the Papal governor and now a prison. The castle has two fine courtyards surrounded by a rectangular wall with towers. Below the Rocca Via del Ponte leads to the Porta Rocca, outside which are remains of the old town walls (on the left).

Porta Rocca

★Ponte delle Torri

Continuing past these above the deep ravine of the Tessino, we come to the imposing Ponte delle Torri, an aqueduct and viaduct (pedestrians only) linking the town with Monte Luco (804 m (2653 ft)). Built of freestone, with ten arches (230 m (755 ft) long, 81 m (67 ft) high), it was constructed in the 14th c., probably on the foundations of an earlier Roman aqueduct.

San Gregorio Maggiore

In the large Piazza Garibaldi in the northern part of the town the Romanesque church of San Gregorio Maggiore, consecrated in 1146, has a 16th c. porch and an interesting interior with old frescos.

Roman Bridge

From Piazza Garibaldi the Porta Garibaldi leads into the Piazza della Vittoria (gardens). Immediately east of the gate are the remains of a Roman Bridge, the Ponte Sanguinario (24 m (79 ft) long, 10 m (33 ft) high), to which visitors can descend.

San Salvatore

From the Porta Garibaldi we cross the Tessino and 100 m beyond the bridge turn right along the river and then left up the hill to reach the church of San Salvatore (also known as il Crocifisso), on a terrace in the Camposanto, which was originally built at the end of the 4th c. within the remains of a Roman temple.

San Ponziano

A short distance south is the 13th c. church of San Ponziano.

Surroundings

★San Pietro

From the east end of the Ponte delle Torri a road follows the edge of the Tessino ravine (1 km (¹⁄₂ mi.)) to the church of San Pietro (388 m (1280 ft)), founded in the 5th c. and rebuilt in the 14th c., with 11–12th c. reliefs on the façade (the four upper scenes are later).

★Monteluco
8 km (5 mi.) SE

Another road from the east end of the Ponte delle Torri winds its way up the wooded hillside to Monteluco (804 m (2653 ft)), from which there are magnificent views.

Below the summit is a Franciscan friary.

Spoleto to Ascoli Piceno (125 km (78 mi.))

From Spoleto there is an attractive drive to Ascoli Piceno. The road passes through beautiful upland country, much of it forest-covered and comes in 49 km (30 mi.) to Norcia (604 m (1993 ft); population 5000), the Roman Nursia a little walled town below the west side of the Monti Sibillini which was the birthplace of St Benedict and his sister Scholastica. In the main square are the Town Hall, the 14th c. church of San Benedetto, built over the remains of the house in which St Benedict was born, and the Prefecture, in a castellated 16th c. building, the Castellina (beautiful courtyard).

Norcia

The road continues east from Norcia, climbs up to the crest of the ridge, coming in 19 km (12 mi.) to the Forca Canapine (1543 m (5092 ft)), a pass on the boundary between Umbria and the Marche, with magnificent views of the Gran Sasso d'Italia to the south-east and the Monti Sibillini to the north-east.

It then descends with many bends, into the beautiful valley of the Tronto and comes in 20 km (12 mi.) to Arquata del Tronto (777 m (2564 ft)), with a 13th c. castle. This is the starting point for the ascent (4½ hours, with guide) of Monte Vettore (2476 m (8171 ft)), the highest peak in the Monti Sibillini which are snow-covered until well into the summer (winter sports). It is possible also to drive to the Forca della Presta (1540 m (5082 ft)), 13.5 km (8½ mi.) north-west (first part of road dust-free), climb to the Rifugio Zilioli (2215 m (7310 ft); 3½ hours) and continue from there to the summit (1 hour).

Arquata del Tronto

The road continues down the Tronto valley, which at times narrows into a gorge, and comes in another 13 km (8 mi.) to Acquasanta Terme (411 m (1356 ft)), a spa which was already frequented in Roman times (ad Aquas), with warm sulphur springs.

Acquasanta Terme

12 km (7 mi.) beyond Acquasanta we join the road from Macerata and follow it for another 8 km (5 mi.) down the valley to Ascoli Piceno.

Ascoli Piceno

Subiaco H12

Region: Lazio. Province: Roma (ROMA)
Altitude: 408 m (1346 ft). Population: 9000

The little town of Subiaco, 70 km (43 mi.) east of Rome, is situated on a hill above the Aniene valley, dominated by an 11th c. castle.

Location

The Roman Sublaquem grew up on the site of a large villa belonging to Nero, who narrowly escaped being struck by lightning while dining here. The main features of interest of the town, which still preserves its medieval aspect, are the famous Benedictine monasteries near by.

Town

2 km (1¼ mi.) south-east of the town centre on the road to Ienne, situated above the River Aniene (on the right), is the large monastery of Santa Scolastica, with a fine campanile from 1052, founded by St Benedict about 510 and later named after his sister. In 1052 a second monastery was built here, and later rebuilt in Gothic style and in 1235 a third, with a Romanesque cloister with mosaic decoration. The present buildings are modern. The church of Santa Scolastica, founded in 975, was completely remodelled in the 18th c. In 1464 two German printers, Arnold Pannartz and Konrad Schweinheim, stayed in the monastery and produced what are probably the earliest Italian printed books.

Monastery of Santa Scolastica

1.5 km (1 mi.) farther east, above the road to Ienne (on the left), is the monastery of San Benedetto or Sacro Speco (640 m (2112 ft)), built against a sheer cliff in a magnificent lonely mountain setting. Both the upper and the lower church are decorated with frescos. The lower church has 13th c.

★Monastery of San Benedetto

475

frescos in Roman style while the frescos of the upper church dating from the 14th–15th c. are in Sienese and Umbrian style. The chapel adjoining the upper church contains a unique early picture of St Francis, who, according to legend, while he was staying in the monastery about 1223 transformed the thorns grown by St Benedict into the roses which still flourish in the monastery garden. In the cave in which St Benedict lived as a hermit until he moved to Montecassino in 529 is a statue of the saint by a pupil of Bernini.

Surroundings

Vallepietra
21 km (13 mi.) E

The road continues down the Aniene valley beyond the monastery of San Benedetto (9 km (5½ mi.)) to the beautifully situated little town of Ienne (834 m (2752 ft)). 12 km (7 mi.) from here along the Simbrivio valley lies the village of Vallepietra (825 m (2723 ft)), in a cirque on the south-east side of Monte Autore.

Monte Autore

From Vallepietra it is a climb of 1½–2 hours to the Santuario della Santissima Trinità (12th c. frescos; festival on Sunday after Whitsun), situated at an altitude of 1337 m (4412 ft) below a vertical rock face 300 m (990 ft) high. From here it is another 2½–3 hours' climb (with guide) to the summit of Monte Autore (1853 m (6115 ft)), the second highest peak in the wooded Monte Simbruini (2156 m (7115 ft)); magnificent panoramic views from the top.

Sulmona H11

Region: Abruzzo. Province: L'Aquila (AQ)
Altitude: 375 m (1230 ft). Population: 25,000

Location

Sulmona lies in a fertile valley between the Gran Sasso massif to the north and the Maiella group, with the Morrone hills in the foreground, to the east. It was the Roman Sulmo, birthplace of Ovid, who was much attached to his "cool home country, abounding in water".
Sulmona is the see of an archbishop.

Sights

Palazzo
dell'Annunziata

At the north end of the town stands the cathedral of San Panfilo, with a Romanesque crypt and a Gothic doorway. From here Viale Roosevelt and the Corso Ovidio, Sulmona's principal street lead to the 15th c. Palazzo dell'Annunziata, which has a Gothic doorway and Renaissance elements. The church, founded in 1320 was rebuilt in 1710 after earthquake damage. The palace houses the Museo Civico which contains a 15th c. wooden tabernacle painted by Giovanni da Sulmona. Farther along the Corso Ovidio is a Romanesque doorway, all that remains of the church of San Francesco della Scarpa, destroyed by an earthquake. Opposite is a beautiful Renaissance fountain (1474), fed by an aqueduct constructed in 1256, with 21 arches still standing. It is an interesting example of medieval constructional techniques.

Sulmona to Pescara (80 km (50 mi.))

There are alternative routes from Sulmona to Pescara: either down the Pescara valley via Popoli (population 5000; castle of the counts of Cantelmi), with a detour to the abbey of San Clemente a Casauria, founded by the Emperor Ludwig II in 871 (12th c. church; museum); or along the lower slopes of the Maiella group (Monte Amaro, 2795 m (9224 ft)) via Campo di Giove (1064 m (3511 ft); from here ascent of Monte Amaro, 10–12 hours) and Caramanico Terme (sulphur springs; ascent to Monte Amaro, 6–9 hours) and thereafter down into the Pescara valley.

Sulmona to Villetta Barrea (60 km (37 mi.))

There is a very fine drive from Sulmona through the wild Sagittario gorge and the rocky gateway of La Foce to Scanno (1050 m (3465 ft); population 3000), a delightfully situated hill village (traditional costumes), and from there past the Fonti di Pantano and down the Sangro valley to Velletta Barrea, a village at the west end of the Lago di Barrea, an artificial lake 5 km 3 mi.) long (entrance to Abruzzi National Park).

Syracuse K21

Region: Sicilia. Province: Siracusa (SR)
Altitude: 17 m (56 ft). Population: 118,000

Syracuse, capital of its province, is situated partly on an island off the east coast of Sicily, separated by a narrow channel from the Sicilian mainland, on which are the modern town and the principal remains of the ancient city. The bay of Porto Grande, which cuts deep inland to the south of the town, is perhaps Italy's largest and best natural harbour.

The town's situation, its beautiful surroundings and the monuments and relics of its splendid past make Syracuse one of the most fascinating places in Sicily.

Syracuse (Greek Syrakusa, Latin Syracusae) was founded on the island of Ortygia in the second half of the 8th c. BC by settlers from Corinth, and rapidly rose to prosperity. From the 5th c. onwards it was ruled mostly by tyrants, the first of whom were Gelo (485–478) and Hiero (478–467). Some of Greece's greatest poets, including Aeschylus and Pindar, lived at Hiero's court. In 415 BC Syracuse was drawn into the conflict between Athens and Sparta, but an Athenian expedition against the city (415) ended in the total annihilation of the Athenian army and fleet in 413. During the struggle with Carthage, Syracuse rose during the reigns of Dionysius I (406–357) and his successors to become the most powerful Greek city, with a perimeter, according to Strabo, of 180 stadia (33 km (20 mi.)) and a population of half a million. Among the eminent men who lived in Syracuse during this period was the mathematician and physicist Archimedes.

After the first Punic War, in which Syracuse was allied with Rome, the city went over to the Carthaginian side. Thereupon it was besieged and captured by the Romans (212 BC). Thereafter Syracuse shared the destinies of the rest of Sicily but never recovered its earlier importance.

Syracuse is the see of an archbishop.

Location

Resort

History

Old town

The old town, with its narrow winding streets and its old houses and palaces – many of them with attractive balconies – lies on an island.

The town's centre is the Piazza Archimede, which is surrounded by old palaces. On the west side of the square is the Banca d'Italia, with a 15th c. courtyard, and a little way north-east the Palazzo Montalto (1397), with magnificent Gothic windows.

Piazza Archimede

From here Via Dione runs north to the Temple of Apollo (6th c. BC), which was also dedicated to Artemis (the Roman Diana). The oldest Doric temple in Sicily, it was excavated in 1933 and has recently been partly re-erected.

Temple of Apollo

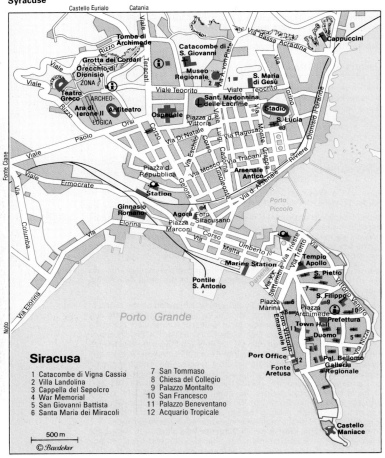

Siracusa

1 Catacombe di Vigna Cassia
2 Villa Landolina
3 Cappella del Sepolcro
4 War Memorial
5 San Giovanni Battista
6 Santa Maria dei Miracoli
7 San Tommaso
8 Chiesa del Collegio
9 Palazzo Montalto
10 San Francesco
11 Palazzo Beneventano
12 Acquario Tropicale

500 m

© Baedeker

★Cathedral	South-west of Piazza Archimede is the elongated Piazza del Duomo, with the Palazzo del Senato (Town Hall, 17th c.) and next to it the cathedral, built in the 7th c. on the site of a temple of Athena of the 5th c. BC, enlarged in the 17th c. and provided with a fine Baroque façade between 1728 and 1757. Notable features in the interior are a Romanesque marble font (13th c.) and a picture by Antonello da Messina.
Fonte Arethusa	From the south end of the Piazza del Duomo Via Picherale continues south to the semicircular basin of the Fountain of Arethusa (Fonte Arethusa) with its papyrus plants. The legend of the nymph Arethusa, pursued by the river god Alpheus from Olympia to here, reflects the idea that the Peloponnesian river Alpheus continues flowing under the sea and emerged at this point.
★Foro Italico	To the north of the Fountain extends the Foro Italico, a fine seafront promenade with view of the harbour and of Etna. At the south end of the

Syracuse: the Baroque façade of the Cathedral

Foro, in a small park, is the entrance to the Acquario Tropicale, with rare fishes from tropical seas.

Acquario Tropicale

At the north end of the Foro are the Porta Marina, with Hispano-Mauresque ornaments (15th c.), and the church of Santa Maria dei Miracoli (1501).

Porta Marina

A little way east of the Fountain of Arethusa, at the south end of Via Roma, which runs down from Piazza Archimede, is the Palazzo Bellomo (15th c.), with the Galleria Regionale, which contains medieval and Renaissance collections, and a picture gallery with the famous "Propagation" by Antonello Da Messina (1474).

Palazzo Bellomo
Galleria Regionale

The Castello Maniace, a Hohenstaufen stronghold built about 1239 at the southern tip of the island, has a fine gateway; there is a good view from the south bastion.

Castello Maniace

New town

At the north end of the island, west of the Temple of Apollo, is the Piazza Pancali, from which there is a bridge over the canal (Darsena) to the new town on the mainland, with the railway station (Stazione Centrale) and the impressive remains of the ancient city. The Corso Umberto I, the main street of the modern town, runs west from the bridge to the large Foro Siracusano on which remains of the ancient agora can be seen. To the west are the remains of the Ginnasio Romano (Gymnasium), once surrounded by colonnades.

Foro Siracusano

★★Parco Archeologico della Neapoli

1 km (½ mi.) north-west of the Foro Siracusano, to the left of the Corso Gelone (the Catania road, SS114), is the Parco Archeologico della Neapoli, with

Syracuse

the Amphitheatre (probably 3rd c.; 140 m (459 ft) long, 119 m (390 ft) across), in the part of the Roman town known as Neapolis. 100 m (328 ft) west of this is the Altar of Hierro II (Ara di Ierone II), a gigantic altar 198 m (650 ft) long by 22.5 m (74 ft) broad which originally rose in two tiers to a height of 10.5 m (34½ ft). Here probably was performed the annual sacrifice of 450 oxen.

★Latomia del Paradiso

Opposite the altar is the entrance to the Latomia del Paradiso, an ancient quarry 30–40 m (98–144 ft) deep, now covered with a luxuriant growth of vegetation, which was used, like other latomie, as a prison for offenders who were condemned to stone-breaking and also for confinement of prisoners of war.

★Ear of Dionysius

Keeping left immediately inside the entrance archway along the garden wall, we come to the so-called Ear of Dionysius, an S-shaped cave hewn from the rock, 65 m (213 ft) deep, 23 m (76 ft) in height and 5–11 m (16–36 ft) wide, contracting towards the top, in which sound is considerably amplified without any recurring echo. It has borne its present name since the 16th c., reflecting the belief that the tyrant Dionysius was thus able to overhear even the whispered remarks of state prisoners confined in the quarry. Farther to the right, under the west wall of the quarry, is the Grotta del Cordari, named after the ropemakers who carried on their trade there.

Latomia di Santa Venera

Immediately east is the Latomia di Santa Venera, with a particularly lush growth of vegetation.

Necropoli Grotticelli

From the Latomia di Santa Venera a stony path leads to the Necropoli Grotticelli, a necropolis with Greek (5th–4th c.), Hellenistic, Roman and Byzantine tombs.

★★Teatro Greco

Immediately west of the Latomia del Paradiso is the Greek Theatre (Teatro Greco, 5th c. BC), with a semicircular auditorium hewn from the rock, the largest in the Greek world (diameter 138.5 m (454 ft). Two tunnels under the auditorium give access to the orchestra (diameter 24 m (79 ft). In this theatre Aeschylus (d. 456 BC) directed the performance of his "Persian" (c. 472 BC), and it is still used for the performance of classical plays (in spring, in alternate, even-numbered years). From the top of the theatre there is a magnificent view at sunset of the town, the harbour and the sea.

Nymphaeum

In the rock face above the theatre is the so-called Nymphaeum, a cave which was the terminal point of an ancient aqueduct.

Streets of Tombs

From the left-hand side the Streets of Tombs (Via dei Sepolcri), hewn from the rock, runs up in a curve for some 150 m with numerous cavities and tomb chambers of the late Roman period.

San Giovanni alle Catacombe

500 m north-east of the Amphitheatre, to the right of the Catania road (SS114), stands the little church of San Giovanni alle Catacombe, the western part of the early medieval cathedral, of which nothing is left but the west front of the present church, with a conspicuous round window, and the 15th c. porch.

★Catacombe di San Giovanni

From the church a flight of steps leads down to the cruciform Crypt of St Marcian (4th c., with remains of frescos) and the adjoining Catacombs (Catacombe di San Giovanni), which are among the most imposing known, far larger than the catacombs of Rome.

★Latomia dei Cappuccini

From the catacombs, going north-east along Via Augusto von Platen, with the entrance to the Catacombs of Vigna Cassia, and then 500 m east along Via Bassa Acradina, past the Old Cemetery, we come to a Capuchin monastery and beside it the Latomia dei Cappuccini, one of the ancient quarries, in which the 7000 Athenian prisoners taken in 414 BC were probably confined.

Greek Theatre in the Parco Archeologico

A little way south-east of San Giovanni alle Catacombe is the Villa Landolina. In the garden of the villa stands the Museo Nuovo Archeologico, one
of the most important archaeological museums in Italy, with a large
collection of antiquities, mostly of Sicilian origin, ranging in date from
prehistoric to early Christian times. Particularly notable items are the
sarcophagus of Valerius and Adelfia (4th c. AD) from the catacombs of San
Giovanni, with carvings of scenes from the Old and New Testaments, and
the Landolina Venus (Venus Anadyomene), with a dolphin by her side, a
copy (2nd c. AD) of a fine Hellenistic work.

★★Museo Nuovo
Archeologico

West of the Archaeological Museum stands the Papyrus Museum, descri-
bing the use of papyrus in ancient times.

Papyrus Museum

South of the Archaeological Museum is the Santuario della Madonna delle
Lacrime, dedicated by Pope John Paul II in 1994, at the spot where, in 1953,
a statuette of the Madonna is said to have wept real tears on several
occasions.

Santuario della
Madonna delle
Lacrime

★Fort of Euryelos

North-west of the Foro Siracusano, at the west end of the outlying district
of ancient Syracuse, Epipolae, on higher ground, is the Fort of Euryelos
(Castello Eurialo), built between 402 and 397 BC at the meeting of the north
and south edges of the plateau, one of the best preserved works of fortification (view).

8 km (5 mi.) NW

Fountain of Cyane

A pleasant outing from Syracuse is a boat trip (3–4 hours there and back)
from the harbour up the little River Ciane (on a hill to the left two columns of

Syracuse harbour

the Olympieion, a temple of Zeus of the 6th c. BC, between tall stands of papyrus, to the Fountain of Cyane (Fonte Ciane or Testa della Pisma), the "azure spring" into which the nymph of that name was metamorphosed for opposing Pluto when he was abducting Proserpina.

Syracuse to the Necropoli Pantalica (c. 70 km (43 mi.))

Palazzolo Acreide

33 km (20 mi.) west is the interesting town of Palazzolo Acreide, the ancient Akrai (Latin Paceolum, Arabic el-Akrat), which was founded by settlers from Syracuse in 664 BC. On the nearby hill of Acremonte, the site of the ancient city, is a Cinta Archeologica containing the remains of the late Greek theatre (seating for 600), to the west of this the Bouleuterion (Council Chamber), to the south-east latomie (gorges) containing Greek and early Christian tombs, and two tomb chambers known as the Templi Ferali (funerary temples).

Santoni reliefs

From here it is a 15 minutes' walk to the valley of Contrada dei Santicelli, near the large Cemetery of Acrocoro della Torre, to the reliefs (mutilated in the 19th c.) of the so-called Santoni, crudely carved cult images in niches in the rock. Most of them represent a seated goddess, presumably Cybele, with Hermes beside her. On the far side of the valley is Monte Pineta, with many small tomb chambers.

★Necropoli di Pantalica

34 km (21 mi.) north-east of Palazzolo Acreide via Ferla is the Necropoli di Pantalica, the cemetery of the Siculan town (13th–8th c. BC) on the hill to the north with thousands of tomb chambers hewn from the rock faces in the Anapo valley. During the Middle Ages the tombs were used as dwellings. Jewellery and ornaments found in the tombs are displayed in the Archaeological Museum in Syracuse.

★★Taormina

Region: Sicilia. Province: Messina (ME)
Altitude: 204 m (673 ft). Population: 10,000

The little town of Taormina, the ancient Tauromenium, enjoys a magnificent situation on a terrace high above the Ionian Sea on the east coast of Sicily. A ruined castle on a rocky crag and the little hill town of Castelmola tower above it. Taormina is one of the most beautiful places in the whole of Sicily.

Location

The centre of the northern part of the town is the Piazza Vittorio Emanuele. The scenic road which winds its way up to Taormina from the coast, Via L. Pirandello, terminates at the Porta Messina, to the north of the square. A little way north-east the church of San Pancrazio, occupies the cella of a Greek temple. In the Piazza Vittorio Emanuele stand the Gothic Palazzo Corvaia (15th c., with a fine façade) and the little church of Santa Caterina. Near the church of Santa Caterina are the remains of a Roman odeon, built in Imperial times. In the vicinity of the Piazza Vittorio Emanuele is a congress centre, the Palazzo del Congressi.

Piazza Vittorio Emanuele

From the Piazza Vittorio Emanuele the Via del Teatro Greco runs south-east of the Greek Theatre, which was reconstructed in Roman style in the 2nd c. AD. With a diameter at the top of 109m/358ft, it is the largest theatre in Sicily after the one in Syracuse. It is renowned for its excellent acoustics (performances of classical plays). The view from the top of the theatre of the precipitous east coast of Sicily, with the gigantic cone of Etna, snow-covered for most of the year, and of the Calabrian coast is one of the most breathtaking in Italy.

★ Teatro Greco

From the Piazza Vittorio Emanuele the town's main street, Corso Umberto, flanked by fine old houses, runs south-west to the Piazza IX Aprile (view) with the church of San Giuseppe and the deconsecrated church of Sant'Agostino.

Piazza IX Aprile

It then passes the Palazzo Ciampoli (on the right), and joins the Piazza del Duomo, where stands a beautiful 12th c. fountain. In the small cathedral (13th–16th c.) are a number of fine altarpieces and, to the right of the high altar, a 15th c. Madonna.

Cathedral

On the hillside north of the Piazza del Duomo are the ruins of the Gothic Badia Vecchia (14th c.). To the south, on the edge of the terrace, a finely situated Dominican monastery is now the Hotel San Domenico Palace (fine cloister); from the tower of the church (destroyed in 1943) there is a beautiful view.

San Domenico

To the west of the Piazza del Duomo, beyond the Porta Catania or Porta del Tocco, is the Palazzo Duca di Santo Stefano (1330), its vaulting supported on a massive granite column. The palace contains modern sculpture.

Palazzo Duca di Santo Stefano

Below the former Dominican monastery, Via Roma (fine views) runs east to the municipal gardens (Villa Comunale), in a commanding situation, from which Via Bagnoli Croce continues to the Belvedere (magnificent views). From here we can return on Via Luigi Pirandello, passing below the Greek Theatre, to the Porta Messina.

Villa Comunale

Surroundings

From the west end of the town near the Badia Vecchia, a road winds steeply uphill, with sharp bends, to the chapel of the Madonna della Rocca (2 km (1¼ mi.)), from which it is a few minutes' climb to the Castello di Taormina on Monte Tauro (398 m (1313 ft)).

**Castello di
Taormina**

Taormina: Greek Theatre with Etna in the background

Castelmola

Even more attractive is the further stretch of road (3 km (2 mi.)) to the village of Castelmola (529 m (1746 ft)), perched on a precipitous crag, which commands panoramic views from its various lookout terraces, but particularly from its highest point near the ruined castle.

From Castelmola it is a 2 to 3 hours' climb to Monte Venere (884 m (2917 ft)), from the top of which there are magnificent views.

★★Etna

A very rewarding excursion from Taormina is the ascent of Etna (see entry), or the circuit of the mountain by rail.

Taranto   M14–15

Region: Puglia. Province: Taranto (TA)
Altitude: 15 m (50 ft). Population: 245,000

Location

Taranto, the capital of the Apulian province and the see of an archbishop, lies on the Mare Grande, the northern bay of the Gulf of Taranto, on the south coast of Italy.

Town

The old town is built on a low rocky island between the Mare Grande and the Mare Piccolo, which runs deep inland on the north-east side of the town. From here a bridge leads to the Borgo, an industrial suburb (large steelworks) to the north-west, which in turn is linked by a swing bridge with the new town, situated on a peninsula, to the south of the old town.

Economy

The port is also a considerable industrial and commercial town, which ranks with La Spezia as one of Italy's two principal naval bases. Taranto is renowned for its honey and fruit. Fishing and the culture of oysters and shellfish also make a contribution to the town's economy.

The town (Greek Taras, Latin Tarentum) was founded by Spartan settlers in 708 BC, and by the 4th c. BC was the most powerful city in Magna Graecia. In the time of Augustus it still had a predominantly Greek population, but thereafter it was Romanised. In AD 494 it was occupied by the Ostrogoths, and in 540 came under Byzantine rule. Taranto was destroyed by the Saracens in 927 but was rebuilt, and in 1063 was incorporated by Robert Guiscard in the Norman kingdom of southern Italy. Thereafter Taranto shared the destinies of the kingdom of Naples.

History

Old Town

In the centre of the Old Town (Città Vecchia), a rectangle of narrow lanes traversed by four parallel longitudinal streets, stands the cathedral of San Cataldo (originally built in the 11th c.; rebuilt in the 18th c., with the exception of the dome and campanile), on the site of the ancient acropolis. The dome shows Byzantine influences. The interior contains columns with ancient and early medieval capitals. To the right of the choir is the richly decorated Baroque chapel of San Cataldo, with the tomb of the town's patron saint. The crypt has Byzantine frescos.

Cathedral

At the south-east corner of the old town stands the Castello Aragonese (15th–16th c.).

Castello Aragonese

New Town

From the old town the Ponte Girevole leads over the Canale Navigabile, one of the few places in the Mediterranean where the ebb and flow of the tide can be observed, into the New Town (Città Nuova), with its wide parallel streets. 100 m beyond the bridge is the palm-shaded square known as Villa Garibaldi, on the east side stands the imposing Palazzo degli Uffici (1896).

On the north side of the square the National Museum (Museo Nazionale), one of the most important museums in southern Italy, houses prehistoric antiquities, a collection of vases (fine decoration, including scenes from mythology), old jewellery and a collection of coins.

★National Museum

To the south, on the Mare Grande, is an avenue of palms, the Lungomare Vittorio Emanuele III, with the modern premises of the Prefecture and the Head Post Office.

Lungomare Vittorio Emanuele III

To the north of the National Museum, on the Mare Piccolo, the Institute of Oceanography (Istituto Talassografico; visitors admitted) has the municipal park, the Villa Comunale Peripato, on its east side.

Institute of Oceanography

Tarquinia   F11

Region: Lazio. Province: Viterbo (VT)
Altitude: 133 m (439 ft). Population: 13,000

The town of Tarquinia, founded in the early medieval period on the territory of ancient Tarquinii, occupies a commanding situation on a limestone plateau above the River Marta, 5 km (3 mi.) from the Tyrrhenian Sea and some 20 km (12 mi.) north of Civitavecchia.

Location

Sights

★Museo Nazionale Tarquiniense	The main square of Tarquinia is the Piazza Cavour, at the west end of the town. In this square a magnificent palace, part of it in Gothic style and part of it Romanesque, with a beautiful pillared courtyard, the Palazzo Vitelleschi (1436–39), now houses the Museo Nazionale Tarquiniense, an important collection of Etruscan antiquities of the 6th–2nd c. BC. The collection includes sarcophagi, vases, jewellery, glass, carved ivories, coins and fragments of large decorative reliefs. Note particularly the terra-cotta statues of two winged horses (4th/3rd c. BC) and the magnificent wall-paintings from the Tomba del Triclino (480–450 BC).
Cathedral	Nearby is the modernised cathedral with 16th c. frescoes by Antonio da Viterbo in the chancel. The picturesque quarters in the north of the town with their churches, towers and old houses, built around the Palazzo dei Priori, and the church of San Pancrazio, have preserved medieval features.
Santa Maria di Castello	At the north-west tip of the town, near the remains of the Castello, the church of Santa Maria di Castello (1121–1208) has a three-naved basilica and is both externally and internally embellished with Cosmatesque decoration.
San Francesco	On higher ground in the east of the town stands the fine Romanesque and Gothic church of San Francesco (13th c.).

★★Tarquinii

On a stony hill 3 km (2 mi.) east of Tarquinia are the meagre remains of ancient Tarquinii, the most notable of the twelve cities of the Etruscan federation. The town, originally surrounded by a wall 8 km (5 mi.) long, was devastated by the Saracens in the 13th c. and razed to the ground in 1307 by the inhabitants of the neighbouring town of Corneto.

Around the old town, particularly on the hill of Monterozzi (157 m (518 ft)) to the south, extends the necropolis (discovered in 1823), one of the best preserved of Etruscan cemeteries. A tour of the tombs takes anything from 1½ to 5 hours. The splendid painted decoration of the tombs (hewn from rock) gives a picture of the culture, art and religion of the Etruscans.

Surroundings

Tuscania 25 km (16 mi.) NE	There is an interesting trip north-eastwards from Tarquinia on the Viterbo road to the little town of Tuscania (166 m (548 ft); population 8000) which is still surrounded by medieval walls and towers. The ancient Tuscana, it was known until 1911 as Toscanella. A severe earthquake of February 6th 1971 destroyed the old town and damaged the churches outside the town. The houses have been rebuilt or restored, and the town has regained its former appearance.
★San Pietro	To the east of the town, on the Viterbo road, is the Romanesque church of San Pietro (8th–12th c.), with a richly decorated façade, a fine interior and an ancient crypt.
★Santa Maria Maggiore	Nearby, in the valley, the fine church of Santa Maria Maggiore (1050–1206), has an old pulpit and a fresco of the Last Judgment (14th c.) on the wall of the choir.
★Museo Nazionale Etrusco	North of Tuscania is the 15th c. church of Santa Maria del Riposo. The adjoining monastery houses the Museo Nazionale Etrusco (Etruscan National Museum).

During the last years several Etruscan necropolises have been discovered in the surroundings of Tuscania.

From 1979 to 1987 the French artist Niki de Saint Phalle built the "Park of the Tarot" near the village of Capalbio. The 22 huge concrete sculptures depict the symbols of the tarot cards.

Capalbio
30 km (19 mi.) N

Terni   G10

Region: Umbria. Province: Terni (TR)
Altitude: 130 m (429 ft). Population: 110,000

Terni, the capital of the Umbrian province of the same name, lies in the fertile valley of the Nera some 100 km (62 mi.) north of Rome.
    Terni is a rising industrial town which since its rebuilding after severe destruction in the Second World War has a predominantly modern aspect.

Location

Sights

The heart of the town comprises the Piazza della Repubblica in which stands the Town Hall and the Piazza Europa, with the massive Palazzo Spada (16th c.). To the south-west, in the Piazza del Duomo, is the cathedral (13th–17th c.), with a crypt of the 10th c. A short distance south of the cathedral are the outer walls of an amphitheatre (1st c. AD). Beyond the cathedral and the amphitheatre extends the municipal park, from where there is an attractive view of the Nera valley.

Cathedral

The nearby Palazzo Fabrizi contains the Picture Gallery (Pinacoteca), with pictures by Benozzo Gozzoli (Wedding of St Catherine, 15th c.), Niccolò Alunno, Giovanni Spagna, Domenico Alfani, Francesco Melanzio, Arrigo Fiammingo, Gerolamo Troppa and other artists.

Palazzo Fabrizi

In the south of the town is the church of San Salvatore, the town's oldest building, probably erected in early Christian times (5th c.) on the site of a Roman building. The church is a rotunda with a cylindrical dome, a vestibule and the Manassei Chapel, which is decorated with frescos by an Umbrian painter (14th c.).

San Salvatore

In the north of the town the interesting church of San Francesco has notable frescos (c. 1400) in the Cappella Paradisi (on the right of the choir), with scenes from the "Divine Comedy". The bell-tower (1445) was designed by Angelo de Orvieta.

San Francesco

Surroundings

East of Terni beyond the industrial suburb of Papigno, to the right of the Ferentillo road (SS209), are the Cascate delle Marmore, the falls formed by the River Velino at its confluence with the Nera. The falls were created by a Roman consul in 271 BC to prevent further marshiness of the area (coloured illuminations between May and August). The falls plunge down vertically in three leaps, a total drop of 165 m (545 ft). The best view is from the Cascate tram stop. From here it is possible to cross the Nera on a natural bridge and climb up on a steep path and flights of steps to a series of lookout terraces, joining the road from Terni to Rieti after some 45 minutes' walk.

★**Cascate delle Marmore**
7 km (4½ mi) E

There is also a very attractive drive to the beautiful Lago di Piediluco (368 m (1214 ft); boat trips available; not suitable for bathing), on the north side of which is the charmingly situated village of Piediluco (377 m (1244 ft)), towered over by a ruined castle.

★**Lago di Piediluco**
14 km (9 mi.) E

Tivoli

★**Narni**
13 km (8 mi.) SW

South-west of Terni, commandingly situated on a high crag on the left bank of the Nera, which here forces its way out of the Terni basin through a narrow ravine, is the little medieval town of Narni (240 m (792 ft); population 21,000). In the centre of the town stands the cathedral, which is mainly 11th c., with a porch of 1497 and a fine interior. In the nearby Piazza Priora are the beautiful Loggia dei Priori (14th c.) and the Palazzo del Podestà which now houses the municipal offices. Below the town, on the line of the ancient Via Flaminia, are the ruins of the so-called Bridge of Augustus.

Tivoli   G12

Region: Lazio. Province: Roma (ROMA)
Altitude: 225 m (738 ft). Population: 52,000

Location

The town of Tivoli, the ancient Tibur, lies 30 km (19 mi.) east of Rome in the Sabine Hills, magnificently situated on a limestone ridge extending south from Monte Gennaro (1271 m (4194 ft); cableway), above the ravine carved by the River Aniene. In Roman Imperial times it was a favourite resort of the great Roman nobles, including Maecenas and the Emperor Augustus himself.

Sights

★Villa d'Este

At the Porta Santa Croce, the south-west entrance to the town, is the spacious Largo Garibaldi. A short way north of this, in the little Piazza Trento, is the entrance to the Villa d'Este (son et lumière shows in summer), one of the classic creations of the Renaissance period, designed by Pirro Ligorio for Cardinal Ippolito d'Este (1549). It was owned by Archduke Francis Ferdinand of Austria-Este, who was assassinated at Sarajevo in 1914. From the villa and from the beautiful gardens, laid out in terraces with magnificent fountains and cascades and what are said to be the tallest cypresses in Italy, there are attractive views of the Roman Campagna.

Cathedral

In the north of the town stands the cathedral of San Lorenzo, originally Romanesque but rebuilt in 1635. In the side chapels are the remarkable group "Descent from the Cross" (13th c.) and a triptych depicting the Saviour between the Virgin and St John (12th c.).

488

Villa d'Este . . .

. . . and Villa Adriana (Villa of Hadrian)

Todi

★Temple of Vesta

Going east from the cathedral along Via San Valerio to the Piazza Rivarola and turning left along the Via della Sibilla, we come to the Temple of Vesta (Tempio di Vesta), a circular structure with Corinthian columns (2nd c. BC) which stands on a crag in the grounds of a hotel. Close by is the so-called Temple of Sibyl (Tempio di Sibilla) and also the exit from the park of the Villa Gregoriana.

★Villa Gregoriana

To the east of Piazza Rivarola the Ponte Gregoriana spans the gorge of the Aniene, and beyond the bridge is the main entrance to the park of the Villa Gregoriana. The waters of this river are diverted through the Traforo Gregoriano, a double tunnel (270 m (886 ft) and 300 m (984 ft) long) driven through the west side of Monte Catillo in 1826–35 to prevent the floods which had repeatedly devastated the town. The water emerging from the tunnel forms magnificent waterfalls with a total drop of 160 m (528 ft) (volume reduced at night to supply a power station). At the end of the tunnels is the Grande Cascata (108 m (356 ft), of which there are fine views from the upper and middle terraces. Also in the park are the Sirens' Grotto and, at the end of a gallery, the Grotto of Neptune, through which the main channel of the Aniene formerly flowed. From the entrance to the gallery a path zigzags up to the exit near the two temples.

★Via delle Cascatelle

From the entrance to the Villa Gregoriana the Via Quintilio Varo runs around the outside of the park and then along the right bank of the Aniene, past an arch in honour of the Virgin erected in 1955, to the Via delle Cascatelle, which affords beautiful views of the waterfalls and the town, particularly from the Belvedere lookout terrace and the church of Sant'Antonio.

★★Villa of Hadrian

6 km (3³/₄ mi.) SW

South-west of Tivoli, to the right of the Via Tiburtina, is the Villa of Hadrian (Villa Adriana), a magnificent complex of buildings and gardens covering an area of 75 ha (185 acres). It dates from the later years of the widely travelled emperor (d. AD 138), who sought to reproduce here some of the great buildings of Greece and Egypt. Near the houses temples, a library and a museum were erected. Many of the works of art to be seen in the museums of Rome came from here. The chief charm of the villa lies in its scenic beauty. There is a model of the whole complex in a building at the car park. Since 1870 the area has been progressively excavated. Many of the art treasures discovered are on display in museums in Rome. The Imperial Palace lies in the north of the park, adjoining a library courtyard with some interesting mosaics. Also to be seen are a pillared courtyard, baths, a nymphaeum and a museum.

Todi	**G10**

Region: Umbria. Province: Perugia (PG)
Altitude: 410 m (1353 ft). Population: 17,000

Location

Todi, the ancient Umbrian city of Tuder, lies in the south of the central Italian region of Umbria, some 40 km (25 mi.) south of Perugia. The town occupies a triangular site still partly surrounded by its rings of Etruscan, Roman and medieval walls, on a ridge above the Tiber valley. An American study carried out in 1990 selected Todi as the town enjoying the best quality of life anywhere in the world.

Sights

In the centre of the town is the Piazza del Popolo surrounded by medieval palaces. On the north side of the square, approached by a flight of steps, stands the Late Romanesque cathedral (12th–16th c.), with beautiful choir-stalls of 1530.

★Piazza del Popolo
Cathedral

On the south side of the square is the Palazzo dei Priori or Palazzo del Podestà (13th–14th c.), with an eagle (1339), the arms of Todi, on its façade. On the east side of the square are the 13th c. Palazzo del Popolo and Palazzo del Capitano, linked by a later flight of steps. Both palaces have picture collections, etc. (closed at present). Between the Piazza del Popolo and the Tempio di San Fortunato there are picturesque old streets to be explored.

South of the Piazza del Popolo, in the Piazza della Repubblica, is the fine Gothic church, the Tempio di San Fortunato (13th–14th c.), approached by a flight of steps with a landing half way up. The façade (unfinished) has a beautiful central doorway (c. 1320). In the fourth chapel on the right is a fresco of the Madonna by Masolino da Panicale (1432) and there are also some beautiful choir-stalls. In the crypt (on the left) is the tomb of the monk Jacopone da Todi (1230–1306), supposed author of the solemn Passion hymn "Stabat Mater dolorosa".

Tempio di San Fortunato

To the west of the church lies the picturesque oldest part of the town, above which, to the west, are the ruins of the old Rocca, from where there is a fine view of the pilgrimage church of Santa Maria della Consolazione (see below).

On a terrace outside the town walls is the pilgrimage church of Santa Maria della Consolazione, a domed church notable for its nobility and beauty, one of the finest creations of Renaissance architecture by Cola di Matteuccio da Caprarola, started in 1508 and completed in 1607.

★Santa Maria della Consolazione

Trani   L13

Region: Puglia. Province: Bari (BA)
Altitude: 7 m (23 ft). Population: 46,000

The little port of Trani, the ancient Turenum, lies on the Adriatic coast between Bari (30 km (19 mi.) south-east) and Barletta (10 km 6 mi.) north-west). Trani is the see of an archbishop.

Location

Sights

To the north-west of the harbour, by the sea, stands the cathedral (1150–1250), one of the finest Romanesque churches in Apulia, which shows Norman influences. It has a Romanesque west doorway (13th c. carvings) and beautiful bronze doors (c. 1180) by the bronze founder Barisano da Trani. The 32 sections are decorated with figures of Christ, the Virgin, Apostles and Saints. The campanile (reconstructed) is almost detached from the nave.

★Cathedral

The impressive interior of the cathedral, the only example of an Apulian church with double columns, was restored to its original Romanesque form in 1952–55. From the side aisles there is access to the Crypt of St Nicholas the Pilgrim (d. 1094), begun about 1100 and decorated with fine capitals. The lower church, the Chiesa dei Santa Maria della Scala (7th c.), a rectangular space with an ambulatory, contains the Crypt of St Leucius (c. 670) under the transept. St Leucius was the first bishop of Brindisi (7th c.).

Trani

Hohenstaufen
Castello

To the west of the cathedral is the castle (1233–49) of Frederick II.

Church of
Ognissanti

On the west side of the harbour we find the Gothic Palace of Simone Caccetta (15th c.) and a little way south of this the church of Ognissanti, with a deep porch, which was formerly a Templars' hospice; above the doorway are Romanesque carvings of the Annunciation and the Tree of Life.

Municipal gardens

East of the harbour, by the Baroque church of San Domenico, are the municipal gardens (Villa Comunale), with three Roman milestones from the Via Traiana which ran from Benevento by way of Canosa, Ruvo, Bari and Egnazia to Brindisi. From the west end of the gardens a view of the harbour and the cathedral can be enjoyed.

Molfetta

15 km (9 mi.) SE

In Molfetta (population 65,000), near the harbour, stands the Duomo Vecchio (7th–8th c.), a Romanesque building, which is considered to be the most important example of a domed church in Apulia.

Ruvo di Puglia

22 km (14 mi.) SE

South-east of Trani is Ruvo di Puglia (260 m (858 ft); population 25,000), with a Norman cathedral (12th–13th c.), which has a fine doorway. The Palazzo Iatta contains a fine collection of vases (6th–3rd c. BC) found here.

Trapani   G19

Region: Sicilia. Province: Trapani (TP)
Altitude: 3 m (10 ft). Population: 73,000

Location

Trapani, capital of the province of the same name, lies on a sickle-shaped peninsula on the north-west coast of Sicily.

In antiquity it was named Drepanon (= sickle) and was the port of the ancient city of Eryx, lying inland to the north-east. It is still a port of some consequence, shipping salt, wine and tunny meat.

Sights

Corsa Vittorio
Emanuele

The main street is the Corso Vittorio Emanuele; in its eastern half are the 17th c. cathedral of San Lorenzo and the Chiesa del Collegio (1636), which was elaborately adorned with marble and stucco in the 18th c. At the east end of the Corso is the Old Town Hall (17th c.: now the registry office), with a magnificent Baroque façade. To the south-east the former church of Sant'Agostino, with a beautiful rose window, once belonged to the Templars; it is now a concert and lecture hall. Farther east is the church of Santa Maria di Gesù (15th c.).

Torre di Ligny

From the Old Town Hall the Via Torrearsa runs south to the harbour, skirted by an attractive seafront promenade. At the north end of the peninsula, on a spit of land, stands the Torre di Ligny, which houses a museum (prehistoric material). In the north-east of Trapani extend the Villa Margherita public gardens, opposite which is the busy Piazza Vittorio Emanuele.

Santuario
dell'Annunziata

From the Piazza Vittorio Emanuele the wide Via Fardella runs east into the Borgo Annunziata quarter. In this district is the Santuario dell'Annunziata (1315–32; most of it restored in 1760), with a 14th c. Madonna (in the

Cappella della Madonna di Trapani), richly decked with jewellery and other votive gifts, which is venerated as miraculous (candle procession on August 16th).

The old monastic buildings, with a beautiful cloister, house the Museo Regionale with pictures, including one by Titian depicting St Francis of Assisi with stigmata, sculpture, decorative art (coral carvings), prehistoric and classical antiquities.

Museo Regionale Pepoli

Erice

There is a rewarding drive (north-east) on a road with numerous steep bends (also accessible by cableway) to Erice (751 m (2473 ft); population 27,000), magnificently situated on an isolated hill. Known until 1934 as Monte San Giuliano, this was the ancient Eryx, much venerated in antiquity, particularly by seamen, as the hill of Venus Erycina. The Elymians built a walled town here, of which a few traces remain. The Chiesa Matrice at the Porta Trapani, the west entrance to the town, was restored in 1865 and only the west porch (15th c.) and campanile (1312) are old. In the third chapel on the right stands a beautiful statue of the Madonna by Francesco Laurana (1469). In Piazza Umberto I stands the Town Hall (library, museum). At the east end of the town are the municipal gardens, with a number of medieval towers, and the Castello di Venere (12th–13th c.), built on the site of a temple of Venus (inside remains of the Tempio di Venere), from which there are magnificent views. To the southwest Trapani and the Isole Egadi can be seen and occasionally, Cap Bon (175 km (109 mi.) on the African coast. To the south the view frequently extends to the island of Pantelleria and to the east sometimes as far as the summit of Etna, 210 km (130 mi.) away.

15 km (9 mi.) NE

Isole Egadi

A pleasant trip from Trapani is by boat (daily) or hydrofoil (several times daily) to the Isole Egadi, situated off the Sicilian coast, the main tunny-fishing area.

The boats call at the islands of Favignana (314 m (1036 ft); area 19.75 sq. km (7½ sq. mi.), the largest island of the archipelago, Levanzo (278 m (917 ft); 7 sq. km (2¾ sq. mi.) and Marettimo (686 m (2264 ft); 12.25 sq. km (4¾ sq. mi.)).

★Gibellina

A new village has been built on the site of Gibellina which was destroyed by an earthquake in 1968.

The buildings were erected from plans drawn by well known Italian architects. Numerous sculptures, some created by foreign artists adorn the houses.

55 km (35 mi.) S

Tremiti Islands

K11

Region: Puglia. Province: Foggia (FG)
Area: 3.06 sq. km (1 sq. mi.). Population: 350

Regular services from Manfredonia or Rodi Garganico, Termoli and Ortona to San Nicole, from there to San Domino as required.

Ferries

The Tremiti Islands (Italian Isole Tremiti) lie some 20 km (12 mi.) north of the Monte Gargano promontory in the Adriatic.

Location

The beautiful rocky limestone archipelago has preserved its traditional character unspoiled. The precipitous coasts with their numerous inlets and sea caves offer ideal conditions for scuba diving.

The islands

Isola San Domino

The most westerly and scenically most attractive of the three major islands is San Domino (up to 16 m (53 ft); area 2 sq. km (1³/₄ sq. mi.)), an island with large areas of pine-forest which was used as a place of exile until 1943 and is now becoming an increasingly popular tourist resort. The largest place on the island, San Domino, lies above the east coast. There are a number of interesting caves accessible only from the sea, such as the Grotta delle Viole and the Grotta del Bue Marino, both with a beautiful play of light.

Isola San Nicola

North-east of San Domino is the smaller island of San Nicola (up to 75 m (248 ft); area 50 ha (124 acres)), on which is the little walled village of San Nicola, capital of the archipelago, with a castle (rebuilt in the 15th c.), the church of Santa Maria (1045), situated on a hill, and the remains of a 9th c. abbey with a beautiful Renaissance doorway and parts of a Romanesque mosaic pavement (11th–12th c.).

Il Cretaccio

To the north, between San Domino and San Nicola, are the island of Il Cretaccio and a number of isolated stacks.

Isola Caprara

The most northerly of the three larger islands is the almost uninhabited island of Caprara or Capraia (up to 53 m (175 ft); area 50 ha (124 acres)).

Trento   F3

Region: Trentino-Alto Adige. Province: Trento (TN)
Altitude: 193 m (637 ft). Population: 100,000

Location

Trento, capital of the province of the same name and of the region of Trentino-Alto Adige, lies on the left bank of the Adige in a valley enclosed by high limestone hills.
It is the see of an archbishop.

Town

The town forms part of the southern part of the territory of Tirol which was transferred from Austria to Italy in 1919. With its numerous towers and palaces, many of them with painted façades, it is a town of distinctly Italian character.

History

The town (the Roman Tridentum) was a place of some importance from an early period by virtue of its commanding situation at the junction of the trading route from Venice up the Val Sugana with the road over the Brenner, and was strongly fortified. From 1027 to 1803 it was the residence of a prince-bishop directly subject to the emperor. From 1545 to 1563 it was the meeting-place of the Council of Trent, which laid down the pattern of the Counter-Reformation.

Treaty of Saint-Germain

Between 1814 and 1918 it belonged to Austria, and after the peace treaty of Saint-Germain to Italy. In 1948 (the "Gruber-De Gaspari-Agreement") the province of Trento was combined with the province of Bolzano (which included the German-speaking Alto Adige or South Tirol) to form the autonomous region of Trentino-Alto Adige.

Sights

★Cathedral

In the centre of the town is the Piazza del Duomo, which has a beautiful Neptune Fountain (1768). The cathedral (11th–12th c.), on the south side of

494

the square, was remodelled internally at the beginning of the 13th c. as a pillared basilica in Lombard Romanesque style; the central dome was entirely renewed in 1887–89. The Council of Trent met in the church from 1545 to 1563. The interior has 13th–14th c. frescoes and numerous bishops' tombs (mostly 14th and 15th c.). Under the cathedral are the remains of an early Christian church (6th c.), with a fine mosaic floor.

On the east side of the square is the Palazzo Pretorio, with the Torre Grande (Clock-Tower). The palace houses the Diocesan Museum, with a notable treasury and 16th c. Flemish tapestries. Diocesan Museum

In the choir of the Renaissance church of Santa Maria Maggiore (1520–23) north-west of the cathedral are a beautiful organ gallery (1534) and a picture of 1563 with likenesses of the members of the Council of Trent, which sometimes met here. Santa Maria Maggiore

From the Piazza del Duomo the wide Via Belenzani runs north. This, the finest street in the town, has a series of fine palaces with remains of painting on the façades. Near the north end of the street, on the right, is the 16th c. Palazzo Municipale, with the 15th c. Casa Geremia opposite. Palazzo Municipale

Trento

Trento – Austrian until 1918

Trento: the Castello del Buonconsiglio

Via Belenzani joins the main street of the town, Via Manci, which has also a number of fine palaces, as well as the beautiful Baroque church of San Fancesco Saverio. Farther north in front of the station is the Giardino Pubblico, with a monument to Dante (1896) 17.6 m (58 ft) high, and a monument to Alois Negrelli (1799–1858), an early advocate of the Suez Canal. On the west side of the gardens stands the 12th c. church of San Lorenzo (restored). *Giardino Pubblico*

On the north-east side of the town is the Castello del Buonconsiglio, former residence of the prince-bishop, from 1811 to 1918 a barracks and since then a museum. The 13th c. Castelvecchio, built around the oldest part, the massive round tower, was remodelled in Venetian Gothic style from 1475 onwards. The Magno Palazzo, a magnificent Renaissance building with arcaded courtyards and frescoes by Romanino and Dosso Dossi was built in 1528–35, and a linking wing added in 1686. The Castello houses the Museo Provinciale d'Arte; among its exhibits are pictures of the months in the Torre dell'Aquila by an unknown 15th c. painter, sculptures, period furniture, archaeological and ethonological collections. The building also houses the Museo del Risorgimento, with relics of the struggle for the liberation of Italy, including mementos of the "irredentists" (supporters of the reunion of the Trentino with Italy) Cesare Battisti, Chiesa and Filzi, who were executed by the Austrians for treason in 1916. *Castello del Buonconsiglio*

On the Doss Trento (307 m (1013 ft)) on the right bank of the Adige, is the conspicuous mausoleum of Cesare Battisti (1875–1916), from which there are fine views of Trento and the Adige valley. *Mausoleum of Cesare Battisti*

Surroundings

For an attractive drive to Monte Bondone leave Trento on the Riva road, going north-west, and in 3 km (2 mi.) turn left into a road which winds its way south-west via the village of Sardagna (571 m (1884 ft), also reached by cableway from the banks of the Adige) and Candriai (1025 m (3383 ft)), to the hotel settlement of Vaneze (1300 m (4290 ft)), beautifully situated on the slopes of Monte Bondone and popular both as a summer and winter sports resort. **Monte Bondone**
   The highest peak in the range, Palon (2098 m (6923 ft)), can be climbed in 2 hours, or can be reached by means of two chair-lifts (via Vason, 1650 m (5445 ft)).
   There are other chair-lifts on the north side of Monte Bondone (e.g. Montesel, 1739 m (5739 ft)).

Paganella

Another rewarding drive is from Trento to Paganella. The road goes first to Fai della Paganella, about 18 km (11 mi.) north-west (1030 m (3399 ft)), then there is a twin chair-lift from Santel to Paganella (2125 m (7013 ft)), with magnificent views, particularly of the nearby Brenta group.

Rovereto

South of Trento is Rovereto (204 m (6763 ft); population 33,000). In the centre of the town is the Piazza Rosmini, and a little way north of this the fine Renaissance palace now occupied by the Savings Bank, with an arcaded court-yard (restored in its original style 1902–05). Nearby is the Museo Civico, with a geological collection. In the Castello (14th–15th c.), on higher ground, is a War Museum, with a collection of First World War mementoes. To the south of the old town stands a conspicuous circular *25 km (16 mi.) S* building, the Sacrario di Castel Dante (306 m (1010 ft); view), in which more than 20,000 dead of the First World War are buried. Above it is a gigantic bell (over 2.6 metric tons), cast in 1965 to commemorate the dead of all nations, which is rung every evening at 8.30 or 9.30pm.

Treviso   G4

Region: Veneto. Province: Treviso (TV)
Altitude: 15 m (50 ft). Population: 83,000

Location
Treviso, capital of the province of the same name, lies in the Veneto plain, some 20 km (12 mi.) north of Venice.

Town
The ancient town of Treviso was the Roman Tarvisium, later the seat of a Lombard duchy, and in the late Middle Ages a colony of German "Venetian" merchants.

Sights

Town walls
It is a historic town of narrow streets, many of them lined with arcades, and it is still surrounded by well-preserved 15th c. walls and a circuit of canals or moats.

Piazza dei Signori
In the centre of the town is the picturesque Piazza dei Signori, with the Palazzo dei Trecento (after 1217), once the seat of the Great Council of the town, and the Palazzo del Podestà with the tall Torre del Comune. The Palazzo Pretorio, a Renaissance palace, houses the town council.

Treviso: fish market

From the Piazza dei Signori Via Calmaggiore, the main street of the town, flanked by fine 15th and 16th c. houses, runs north-west to the Piazza del Duomo. The cathedral of San Pietro, with five domes, was built in the 15th and 16th c. on the site of an earlier Romanesque church, with a crypt dating from the 11th and 12th c.; the porch was added in 1836. The interior contains pictures by Titian ("Annunciation", 1517) and Paris Bordone, and fine frescos by Pordenone (1519–20). The Cappella del Sacramento is decorated with fine sculptures by Pietro and Tullio Lombardo and L. Bregno.

To the left of the cathedral stands the Romanesque Baptistery (11th–12th c.), with 13th c. frescoes and a fine font.

From the cathedral Via Canova and Via Cavour lead north-west to the Museo Civico Luigi Bailo, with an archaeological collection and an excellent picture gallery, which contains frescos by Tommaso da Modena and Girolamo da Treviso, and pictures by Bellini, Lotto, Pisanello, Titian and many other artists.

In Via San Nicolò, at the south-west corner of the old town, the Dominican church of San Nicolò, a spacious Gothic church built in brick (13th–14th c.), has round piers and an unusual vaulted timber roof (restored). In the interior are a "Madonna Enthroned" by Fra Marco Pensaben and Savoldo (1521; on the high altar) and the tomb of Senator Agostino Oningo (d. 1490) by Pietro and Tullio Lombardi.

In the chapterhouse of the former Dominican monastery are frescoes by Tommaso da Modena (1352).

In Viale San Antonio, in the north of the town, lies the church of San Francesco. Pietro Alighieri, a son of Dante, is buried there (d. 1364). Inside, note the frescos and sculpture of St Sebastian.

At the north-east corner of Treviso is the fine Porta San Tommaso (1518). The northern rampart walk which begins here affords beautiful views of the Alps.

*Cathedral

Museo Civico
Luigi Bailo

San Nicolò

San Francesco

Porta San
Tommaso

Trieste   H4

Region: Friuli-Venezia Giulia. Province: Trieste (TS)
Altitude: 54 m (178 ft). Population: 231,000

The port of Trieste, capital of the region of Friuli-Venezia Giulia, lies on the Gulf of Trieste, framed by the precipitous slopes of a limestone plateau, in the north-east corner of the Adriatic.

Location

Trieste is an important port in the Adriatic. With a greatly increased capacity since its reconstruction after war damage, it has gained considerably in importance compared with the pre-war period as a transhipment point for goods from Central Europe and the Danube region (particularly Austria).

An annual Trade Fair is held in Trieste.

Economy

Trieste, the Roman Tergeste, was held by Austria from 1382 until 1919. It was made a free port by the Emperor Charles VI in 1719, and from the end of the 18th c., after the construction of an artificial harbour, it captured the trade with the Near East which had been dominated by Venice for more than 500 years. As the last harbour of any size left to Austria Trieste developed into the leading commercial town in the Adriatic, particularly after the construction of the Semmering railway line (1854) and the new port installations to the north of the town (1867–83). After the First World War the town, mainly inhabited by Italians, was assigned to Italy and thus lost its hinterland; but the consequent decline in trade was made good by the large-scale development of industry. Under the Allied treaty with Italy

History

in 1947 the territory immediately bordering on Trieste, with a predominantly Slav population, was ceded to Yugoslavia and the town itself (in Serbo-Croat Trst) together with part of the Istrian peninsula became a free state under the United Nations, divided into two zones. On the basis of a later treaty between Italy and Yugoslavia (October 5th 1954) Zone A and the town of Trieste were returned to Italian administration (and finally incorporated in Italy in 1963), while Zone B was assigned to Yugoslavia. Since 1962 Trieste has been the capital of the Friuli-Venezia Giulia region.

Harbour

On the west side of the town lies the harbour, which has no natural anchorage and is exposed to strong north-east winds (the bora) blowing down from the plateau. To the north the Punta Franco Vecchio (Old Free Port) has four piers and a long breakwater. To the south, beyond the Campo Marzio station, are the Punta Franco Nuovo (New Free Port) and the industrial zone, with a number of large shipyards.

Town centre

Piazza dell'Unità d'Italia

The largest square in the older part of the town is the Piazza dell'Unità d'Italia, on the Old Harbour. On its north side is the Palazzo del Governo (1904), on the south side the massive palazzo (1882–83) of Lloyd Triestino, a shipping line founded in 1836 as the Austrian Lloyd company, and on the east side the Town Hall (Palazzo del Municipio; 1876).

Old Exchange

A little way north-east of the Town Hall, in Piazza della Borsa, is the Old Exchange (Borsa Vecchia), a Neo-Classical building of 1806.

Teatro Verdi
Molo Audace

North-east of the Piazza dell'Unità d'Italia, along the quay, stands the Teatro Verdi, with the Theatre Museum. From the pier opposite the theatre, on the left, the Molo Audace, there are good views of the town and the harbour.

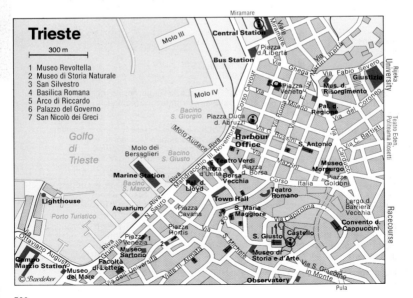

Trieste

1 Museo Revoltella
2 Museo di Storia Naturale
3 San Silvestro
4 Basilica Romana
5 Arco di Riccardo
6 Palazzo del Governo
7 San Nicolò dei Greci

In the Old Harbour of Trieste

Farther along the quay, on the right, is the Greek church of San Nicolò dei Greci, and farther north again is the Canale Grande (1756), the harbour formerly used by sailing ships.

Canale Grande

From the Old Exchange the Corso Italia, the town's principal traffic artery, lined with modern buildings, runs east to the busy Piazza Goldoni, which is linked with the industrial suburbs to the south by a tunnel 347 m (1139 ft) long under the castle hill and another tunnel 1 km (1/2 mi.) long.

Corso Italia

South-east of the Town Hall is the broad Via del Teatro Romano, at the east end of which towers the Grattacielo ("Skyscraper"). To the right of this is the Roman Theatre (Teatro Romano; 2nd c. AD), which was excavated in 1938. Some of the fine marble statues from the stage of the theatre are now in the Museum of History and Art.

Teatro Romano

Castle hill

To the south-west of the Roman Theatre is the castle hill. Half-way up the hill, on the right, is the small Protestant church of San Silvestro (11th c.), and opposite it, on the left, the Jesuit church of Santa Maria Maggiore (1627–82), with a Baroque interior.

Close by stands the so-called Arco di Riccardo, a gateway which probably dates from the 1st c. BC.

Arco di Ricardo

From the Arco di Ricardo it is only a few steps to the Museo di Storia e d'Arte, in Via Cattedrale 15, which contains antiquities of varying provenance, including Roman and medieval vases, sculptures and grave-inscriptions.

Museo di Storia e d'Arte

In the Orto Lapidario is the tomb (c. 1830) of the German classical scholar Johann Joachim Winckelmann (1717–68), who was murdered in Trieste.

Orto Lapidario

The magnificent Palazzo del Municipio

★Cattedrale di San Giusto

At the end of Via Cattedrale stands the cathedral of San Giusto, on the site of an Augustan temple. It was formed in the 14th c. by the joining up of two churches (6th–11th c.) and a baptistery: to the right San Giusto and to the left Santa Maria, their lateral aisles combined to make the central aisle or nave of the cathedral. Fragments of Roman work can be seen in the doorway and campanile (enlarged in 1337). In the lateral apses are fine mosaics (7th and 12th c.).

To the left of the cathedral is a column of 1560. Beyond it are the remains of a Roman forum (2nd c.), the so-called Tempio Capitolino (1st c.) and an Italian war memorial of 1934.

★Castle, Museum

On top of the castle hill the Castello (15th–17th c.) contains the interesting Castle Museum, with medieval weapons, furniture, tapestries, etc. From the Castello and from the Parco delle Rimembranza on the north side of the castle hill there are fine views of the town and the sea.

Sights in the south

Piazza Venezia Marine Station Fish Market Aquarium

On the pier to the south of the Piazza dell'Unità d'Italia is the Marine Station, and farther along the quay the Pescheria (Fish Market), with an interesting Aquarium.

Beyond this lies the Piazza Venezia.

Museo Civico Revoltella

At the corner of the square is the Museo Civico Revoltella, one of Italy's major museums of modern art, with more than a thousand paintings, 800 sculptures as well as prints and drawings. It covers six floors and 40 rooms.

Museo di Storia Naturale

Beyond the Museo Civico Revoltella is the Piazza A. Hortis. On the south-east side of the square are the Museum of Natural History (Museo di Storia Naturale) and the Municipal Library.

Nearby is the Museo Sartorio, which contains ceramics, majolica, porce-   Museo Sartorio
lain and pictures, typical equipment of Trieste's villas at the end of the 19th
century. At present only the furnished living-rooms on the first floor are
open to visitors.

To the south of the harbour the Museum of the Sea (Museo del Mare) has   Museo del Mare
numerous ship models of all times, particularly sailing ships.

Sights in the north

At the end of the canal (Canale Grande) we come to the Neo-Classical   Sant'Antonio
church of Sant'Antonio (1849), Trieste's largest church. To the right of this
is the Serbian Orthodox church of San Spiridione.

A short distance to the east of Sant'Antonio the Via G. Carducci runs north-   Piazza Oberdan
west from near the castle hill to the Piazza Oberdan, the main square of   Museo Civico del
the newer part of the town. In this square is the Museo Civico del   Risorgimento
Risorgimento.
   From the Piazza Oberdan we can go north by tram to the Piazza Scorcola,
with the lower station of an electric funicular to Villa Opicina.
   From the Piazza Oberdan the Via Fabio Severo leads past the massive
Palazzo di Giustizia to the university, built in 1939–50.

Surroundings

Reached by road from Piazza Oberdan or by funicular from Piazza Scorcola   **Villa Opicina**
is the villa suburb of Villa Opicina (348 m (1148 ft)). From the obelisk at Villa   9 km (5½ mi.) NE
Opicina there are magnificent views of Trieste and the sea. A footpath
runs north-west from the obelisk to the viewpoints of Villa Opicina (397 m
(1310 ft)) and Vedetta d'Italia (335 m (1100 ft)), from which there are extensive prospects in all directions.

3 km (2 mi.) north of Villa Opicina is the Grotta Gigante, a stalactitic cave   **Grotta Gigante**
with a huge chamber approx. 130 m (430 ft) long and 100 m (330 ft) high;
at the entrance is a museum.

Trieste to Montefalcone (c. 20 km (12 mi.))

2.5 km (1½ mi.) north-west of Trieste, above Barcola (5 m (17 ft)) rises the   **Victory Beacon**
68 m (224 ft) high Victory Beacon, erected in 1927, from which there are
beautiful views (open throughout the day).

3.5 km (2¼ mi.) farther north-west, on a crag above the sea, stands the   ★**Castello di**
Castello di Miramare, built in 1855–60 for Archduke Maximilian of Austria,   **Miramare**
later briefly emperor of Mexico. Now owned by the State, it houses a
historical museum (closed Mondays). From the terrace and the park
(bronze statue of Maximilian) there are magnificent views of the sea, here
protected as a nature reserve, the Parco Marino di Miramare, with the interesting flora and fauna of the northern Adriatic.

7 km (4½ mi.) along the coast of the Gulf of Trieste is the little port and   **Duino**
seaside resort of Duino, where Rainer Maria Rilke (1875–1926) wrote his
"Duino Elegies". The Castel Nuovo (destroyed 1916, rebuilt 1929 onwards:
no admission) and the picturesque ruins of the Castel Vecchio are magnificently situated on a projecting crag (fine views).
   Near the castle is the International Centre of Theoretical Physics.

From Duino the Rilke Promenade leads along the coast of the "Riviera   Sentiero Rilke
Triestina" to Sistiana in the south. For many years this path was unusable,
but has recently been repaired.

The splendid Castello di Miramare

San Giovanni al Timavo	Beyond Duino the village of San Giovanni al Timavo (4 m (13 ft)) has a 15th c. Gothic church, San Giovanni in Tuba, containing the remains of a mosaic pavement belonging to an earlier basilica of the 5th–6th c.
	At San Giovanni the River Timavo, with an abundant flow of water, emerges after an underground course of 40 km (25 mi.) from the caves of Skocjan in the former Yugoslavia, and soon afterwards flows into the sea.
Monfalcone	7 km (4½ mi.) from Duino is Monfalcone (6 m (20 ft); population 30,000), a port and industrial town in the foothills of the karstic plateau. Continuing on SS305 we come to the military cemetery of Redipuglia, finely situated on the slopes of Monte Sei Busi (118 m (389 ft)), with the graves of 100,000 men who fell in the First World War.

Turin   B5

Region: Piemonte. Province: Torino (TO)
Altitude: 230 m (759 ft). Population: 1,035,000

Location	Turin, capital of the north Italian region of Piedmont and the province of the same name, lies on the left bank of the Po in a fertile plain, at the confluence of the Rivers Dora Riparia and Po.
Town	The regularity of the city's layout is an inheritance from Roman times; its present aspect was largely shaped by the architects of the Baroque period, chief among whom were Guarino Guarini (1624–83) of Modena and the Sicilian Filippo Juvarra (1678–1736). Many of the long straight streets of Turin are lined with arcades. Turin is the see of an archbishop.
Economy	The city's varied range of industry includes a number of large firms, among them the Fiat and Lancia car plants, factories manufacturing

engines and rolling-stock, an electricity corporation, plants producing man-made fibres (Snia, Viscosa), woollen and cotton mills, etc. Turin is also renowned for its vermouths (Martini & Rossi, Cinzano), its chocolate and the sweets called caramelle.

Taurasia, capital of a Celto-Ligurian tribe, the Taurini, became a Roman colony in the time of Augustus under the name of Augusta Taurinorum. In the Frankish period it was the seat of a marquis, but the town did not really begin to develop until it passed in 1418 to the main branch of the counts of Savoy. During the War of the Spanish Succession it was besieged by the French but was relieved in 1706 by Prince Eugene of Savoy and Prince Leopold of Anhalt-Dessau. In 1720 it became capital of the Kingdom of Sardinia and Piedmont, and after the French occupation (1798–1814) became the centre of the Italian striving towards unity. From 1861 to 1865 it was capital of the Kingdom of Italy. The house of Savoy kept its royal status until 1945. | History

Piazza Castello

The central feature of the older part of the town is the Piazza Castello, in the middle of which stands the massive Palazzo Madama. The core of the structure is a 13th c. castle built on the remains of the Roman east gate which was enlarged in the 15th c. and embellished by Filippo Juvarra in 1718 with the handsome west front, a fine example of Piedmontese Baroque architecture, and the magnificent double staircase. | ★Palazzo Madama

The palace now houses the Museo Civico d'Arte Antica (ground floor and second floor), with a valuable collection of sculpture in stone and wood, stained glass; pictures and applied art (Duc de Berry's Book of Hours, with Dutch miniatures of c. 1400). On the first floor are the state apartments, richly appointed in 18th c. style. | Museo Civico d'Arte Antica

On the north side of the Piazza Castello is the courtyard of the Royal Palace, to the left of which can be seen the Baroque church of San Lorenzo (1668–80) by Guarini, with an unusual and boldly designed dome. The former Royal Palace (Palazzo Reale) is a plain brick building (1646–58), with the Appartamento di Madama Felicità and 26 sumptuously decorated state apartments (Reali Appartamenti). In the right wing is the Prefecture, with the entrance (first door on left) to the former Royal Armoury, containing one of the largest collections of arms and armour in Europe; there are many complete suits of armour and other items dating from the 15th–19th c., including the field armour of Prince Eugene of Savoy. | San Lorenzo, Palazzo Reale

Beyond the Palazzo Reale are the Royal Gardens (Giardini Reali) at the corner of which (on Corso Regina Margherita) is the Museo di Antichità. The museum contains artefacts from prehistory to the late Roman period. | Museo di Antichità

Adjoining the palace on the north-west is the Cathedral of San Giovanni Battista (1492–98; tower completed 1720). Behind the high altar is the Chapel of the Holy Shroud (Cappella della Santa Sindone), a circular structure by Guarini (1668–94). | Cathedral

An urn above the altar contains the Santa Sindone or Santo Sudario, the linen cloth in which according to legend the body of Christ was wrapped after his descent from the Cross; however, scientific research has proved that the linen cloth dates from the Middle Ages. The original is rarely displayed; however, there is a full-size replica in the north aisle of the cathedral. | ★Holy Shroud
  Beside the cathedral are the remains of a Roman theatre (1st c. AD).

On the south side of the square in which the cathedral stands is the Palazzo Chiablese, with the Film Museum (Museo Nazionale del Cinema). | Film Museum

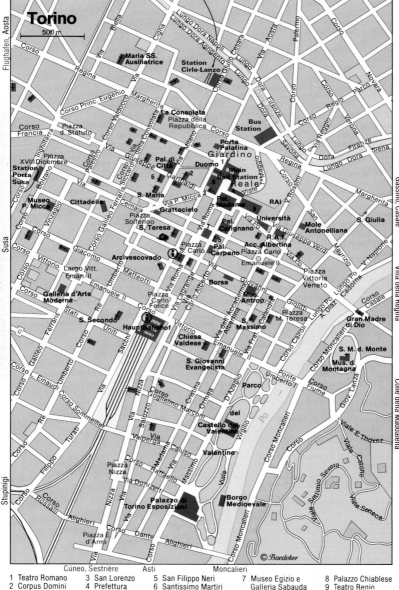

Milan

Torino

500 m

© Baedeker

1 Teatro Romano	3 San Lorenzo	5 San Filippo Neri	7 Museo Egizio e	8 Palazzo Chiablese
2 Corpus Domini	4 Prefettura	6 Santissimo Martiri	Galleria Sabauda	9 Teatro Regio

Panorama of Turin

Porta Palatina

The Porta Palatina (1st c. AD), north-west of the cathedral, the north gate of the Roman town, has two brick towers.

Museo Nazionale del Risorgimento Italiano

Just south of Piazza Castello is the Palazzo Carignano (by Guarini, 1679–85), meeting place of the Sardinian parliament from 1848 to 1859 and of the Italian parliament from 1861 to 1864. The establishment of the Kingdom of Italy was proclaimed here on March 14th 1861. The building now houses, in 30 rooms on the first floor, the Museo Nazionale del Risorgimento Italiano, the largest museum of its kind, with mementoes and relics of the campaign for Italian unity and of the two world wars.

Citadel
Artillery Museum

Via P. Micca runs from the Piazza Castello (south-west) to Piazza Solferino, where stands a 14-storey building. From the square Via Cernaia leads to the Artillery Museum, which is housed in the old gatehouse of the Citadel, demolished in 1857, and in which can be seen weapons of many different periods.

At the north-west of Via Cernaia stands the 18-storey office (1967) of RAI, the Italian radio and television corporation (studios also in Via Rossini), and also the Porta Susa Station.

Santi Martiri

To the north of the Piazza Solferino is the church of Santi Martiri, a splendid Baroque building by Pellegrini (1577).

Palazzo di Città

North of the church is the narrow Via Garibaldi, part of the old Roman main street (decumanus). The Palazzo di Città (Town Hall), on the right-hand side, was built by Francesco Lanfranchi in 1658–65.

Santuario della Consolata

500 m farther north-west, in Via della Consolata, is the Santuario della Consolata, a church in which the Madonna was honoured ever since the 4th c. The present Baroque pilgrimage church (1679–1705) by Guarini was

sumptuously rebuilt in 1903–04. Inside there are marble statues, including one of Queen Maria Theresia. Beside the Santuario is a beautiful Romanesque 11th c. campanile.

★★Palazzo dell'Accademia delle Scienze

Opposite the Palazzo Carignano, to the south-west, is the Palazzo dell'Accademia delle Scienze, built by Guarini (1679) as a Jesuit college and made over to the Academy of Sciences in 1758.

Egyptian Museum   The Palace houses the Egyptian Museum, one of the finest collections of Egyptian antiquities in the world, with numerous statues of pharaohs of the New Kingdom, including Rameses II, papyruses and two tomb chambers from Thebes.

Galleria Sabauda   The palace also contains the Galleria Sabauda, a richly stocked picture gallery. The collection includes pictures by the Piedmontese artists Macrino d'Alba and Defendente Ferrari, the Lombards Gaudenzio Ferrari and Sodoma, the Venetians Mantegna ("Madonna with Saints"), Paolo Veronese, Tintoretto, Tiepolo and Canaletto, the Emilians Guido Reni and Guercino, the Tuscans Beato Angelico ("Angels in Adoration", etc.), Lorenzo di Credi and Piero Pollaiuolo ("Tobias with the Archangel Raphael"), numerous Dutch and Flemish paintings, including works by Jan van Eyck, Roger van der Weyden, Hans Memling (portraits), Van Dyck, and Rembrandt (a youthful work, "Old Man Asleep"). One room is devoted to the Gualino Collection, with pictures by Botticelli and Veronese.

San Felippo Neri   East of the Academy of Sciences in Via Maria Vittoria the church of San Filippo Neri was begun in 1675 and rebuilt by Juvarra in 1714; the porch was added in 1835. The church has a fine interior.

Monument to Cavour   Via Maria Vittoria runs from the church south-east to the Piazza Carlo Emanuele II, where there is a marble monument (1873) to Camillo Cavour (1810–61), a native of Turin, the great statesman who achieved Italian unity, and the church of Santa Croce, designed by Juvarra in 1718.

Via Roma

The main traffic artery of the city centre is the monumental Via Roma, with uniform modern stone façades and arcades, which runs from Piazza Castello to the main station. At the near end, on the right, is the Torre (1934), an office 87 m (286 ft) high.

Piazza San Carlo   The Piazza San Carlo, a symmetrically designed square halfway along, was laid out in 1638. On the south side are the church of Santa Cristina (1637: to the east), with a façade by Juvarra (1718), and the church of San Carlo (1619), with a façade in similar style (1836). In the centre of the square stands an imposing equestrian statue of Duke Emmanuel Philibert (1838).

Central Station   At the south end of Via Roma lies the Piazza Carlo Felice, with the Central Station (Stazione di Porta Nuova).

★Galleria d'Arte Moderna   In front of this, at right angles to Via Roma, is the Corso Vittorio Emanuele II, a 3.5 km (2¼ mi.) long avenue leading to the west. At its intersection with the broad Corso Galileo Ferraris can be seen a conspicuous monument to Victor Emmanuel, 38 m (125 ft) high (1899). A little way south of the monument along Corso G. Ferraris, on the right, is the Galleria d'Arte Moderna (1942), one of the finest collections of modern art in Italy. Here can be seen pictures by the Italian artists Modigliani, De Chirico, Carrà, De Pisis and Guttuso, as well as by foreign artists such as Renoir, Utrillo, Paul Klee, Max Ernst, Chagall and others.

Mole Antonelliana

From Piazza Castello the arcaded Via Po runs south-east, passing close to the Accademia Albertina di Belle Arti (collection of pictures), to the Piazza Vittorio Veneto, a square in Neo-Classical style on the banks of the Po (1830). A short distance north of Via Po, in the Via Montebello, rises the huge Mole Antonelliana, begun by Alessandro Antonelli in 1863 as a synagogue, with a tall spire added in 1878–80 (167 m (551 ft) high, with a lift to 85 m (281 ft); fine views from the top).

To the east is the massive building of the University (1968).

Sights on the right bank of the Po

From Piazza Vittorio Veneto the Ponte Vittorio Emanuele I crosses the Po to the church of the Grande Madre di Dio (1818–31), which was modelled on the Pantheon in Rome and which was erected in thanksgiving for the return of Victor Emmanuel I in 1814.

Gran Madre di Dio

From the Gran Madre di Dio church we go south along Corso Moncalieri and almost immediately turn left into Via Maresciallo Giardino to reach the Monte dei Cappuccini, a wooded hill rising above the river (45 m (149 ft)). On top of the hill are a Capuchin monastery founded in 1583, the church of Santa Maria del Monte and the interesting Museo Nazionale della Montagna Duca degli Abruzzi, with Alpine maps, photographs, reliefs, models, etc.

Monte dei Cappuccini

From the hill there is a magnificent view of Turin and the chain of the Alps.

South-west of the Monte dei Cappuccini, beyond the Ponte Umberto I, is the large Parco del Valentino on the left bank of the Po, together with the Botanic Gardens (established 1729) and the fine Renaissance Castello del Valentino (1630–60). The latter was lavishly furnished and for many years was the focal point of Turin society. Inside is a banqueting hall with ornamental plasterwork and frescoes by the Binchi family of artists from Lugano. Towards the south end of the park stands the impressive equestrian statue of Duke Amadeo of Aosta (king of Spain 1870–73), erected in 1902.

★Parco del Valentino

To the south-east, on the banks of the river, are the Borgo and Castello Medioevale, a medieval village and castle built for an exhibition in 1884.

Borgo and Castello Medioevale

At the south end of the park stands the Palazzo di Torino Esposizioni (1948–52), in which the popular Motor Show and Industrial Vehicle Show are held.

Palazzo di Torino Esposizioni

Still farther south, at Corso dell'Unità d'Italia 40, is the Motor Museum (Museo dell'Automobile Carlo Biscaretti di Ruffia), opened in 1960, which provides a comprehensive survey of the development of the motor car, with many veteran and vintage cars.

★Motor Museum

In the south of the town, beyond the large Piazza d'Armi, is the Stadio Comunale, with the Marathon Tower, two open-air swimming pools and an indoor pool.

Stadio Comunale

Farther south, in the suburb of Lingotto, is the original factory of the Fiat company which was closed in 1982; the building is to be preserved as an example of early industrial architecture. In the meantime a services industry centre has been set up there. In 1997 Fiat moved its head office back to Lingotto.

Lingotto

Surroundings

10 km (6 mi.) north-east of Turin, reached on a road which follows the Po to the suburb of Sassi (218 m (719 ft)) and then winds its way up to the top of

★**Basilica di Superga**

Turin

The Baroque Basilica di Superga

the hill (or rack railway from Sassi, 16 minutes), is the Basilica di Superga (672 m (2218 ft)), on the second highest hill in the Colli Torinesi. This large and conspicuous church, built on a centralised plan with a dome 75 m (248 ft) high flanked by 60 m (198 ft) high towers, the masterpiece of the great Baroque architect Juvarra, was erected in 1717–31 to commemorate Prince Eugene's victory in 1706 and served as the mausoleum of the royal house of Savoy from 1730 to 1849 (tombs in crypt). From the terrace in front of the church, in clear weather, there is a prospect of the Alps; from the forecourt there is a view of Turin.

Colle della Maddalena

Another attractive excursion (10 km (6 mi.)) is to the Colle della Maddalena (715 m (2360 ft)), the highest of the Colli Torinesi, crowned by the Faro della Vittoria, a beacon in the form of a bronze statue (by E. Rubino, 1928) of the goddess of victory carrying a torch, 18.5 m (61 ft) high; from the top there are fine panoramic views.

Turin to Montgenèvre via Sestriere (115 km (71 mi.))

Turin is a good base for some magnificent drives into the mountains. Particularly fine is the road to Sestriere and the Montgenèvre pass. Leave Turin by way of the Fiat works at Mirafiori and follow the SS23.

Stupinigi

11 km (7 mi.): Stupinigi (244 m (805 ft), a magnificent Baroque castle (by Filippo Juvarra, 1729–33), set in a large park which now houses the Museo d'Arte e dell'Ammobigliamento.

Pinerolo

27 km (17 mi.): Pinerolo (376 m (1241 ft); population 36,000), a beautifully situated town with an 11th c. cathedral. In the church of San Maurizio is a burial vault of the house of Savoy. Beyond this stands the church of the Madonna delle Grazie, from which there is a fine view of Monviso (3841 m (12,675 ft)).

From Pinerolo a detour (15 km (9 mi.) south-west) can be made to the little town of Torre Pellice (516 m (1703 ft)), a popular summer resort prettily situated in the Pellice valley, a stronghold of the Waldensians, Protestants who fled from France during the Albigensian wars (1209–29) and sought refuge in the Piedmontese valleys on the east side of the Cottian Alps, where they were able to maintain themselves in spite of frequent persecution. There are now some 25,000 Waldensians, most of them still French-speaking, in the Pellice valley and the lower Chisone valley. **Torre Pellice**

Beyond Pinerolo the road to Montgenèvre ascends the Chisone valley, towards the main chain of the Cottian Alps.

18 km (11 mi.): Perosa Argentina (614 m (2026 ft); population 5000), a little industrial town mainly populated by Waldensians. The road then traverses a gorge and before reaching Fenestrelle passes the large Agnelli Sanatorium, on a hill to the right (1700 m (5610 ft); road, 6.5 km (4 mi.), and cableway). **Perosa Argentina**

16 km (10 mi.): Fenestrelle (1154 m (3808 ft)), a village with imposing fortifi-cations extending up to the 18th c. fort of San Carlo, linked by 4000 steps. **Fenestrelle**

22 km (14 mi.): Sestriere (2033 m (6709 ft)), on the saddle between the Chisone valley and the valley of the Dora Riparia. This is one of Europe's largest winter sports resorts, also popular in summer. Cableways to Monte Fraitève (2690 m (8877 ft)) to the north-west, Monte Sises (2658 m (8771 ft); upper station 2597 m (8570 ft)) to the south-east, Monte Banchetta (2552 m 8421 ft)) to the east; chairlift, many ski lifts. **Sestriere**

Beyond Sestriere the road descends into the valley of the Dora Riparia.

11 km (7 mi.): Cesana Torinese (1354 m (4468 ft)), where it joins the road from Turin via Susa. Chairlift to Sagna Longa (2002 m (6607 ft)) and Colle Bercia (Monti della Luna, 2203 m (7270 ft)). Beyond Cesana the road continues to climb. **Cesana Torinese**

6 km (3³/₄ mi.): Claviere or Clavières (1760 m (5808 ft)), a resort favoured by winter sports enthusiasts; chairlift to La Cloche (1960 m (6468 ft)). **Claviere**

Soon after Claviere the road comes to the French frontier.

2 km (1¹/₄ mi.): Col de Montgenèvre (1854 m (6118 ft); winter sports, chair-lifts to 2600 m (8580 ft)), formerly an important Alpine pass providing the shortest route between the Po valley and southern France, used by Julius Caesar and in the Middle Ages by the Emperor Barbarossa among many others. **Col de Montgenèvre**

Turin to the Montgenèvre pass via Susa (95 km (59 mi.))

Leave Turin on SS25, going west. In 13 km (8 mi.) the road comes to Rivoli (390 m (1287 ft); population 5000), an old-world town situated between morainic hills, once a favourite residence of the house of Savoy, with a Baroque palace (by Juvarra, 1712), of which only a third was completed (419 m (1383 ft)). **Rivoli**

Beyond Rivoli the road enters the Cottian Alps and ascends the Val di Susa, the valley of the Dora Riparia. At the mouth of the valley, on a hill to the left, is the Sacra di San Michele abbey (11th–13th c.: alt. 962 m (3175 ft)).

40 km (25 mi.): Susa (503 m (1660 ft); population 7000), an old town, beauti-fully situated between high mountains, which controlled the Montgenèvre and Mont Cenis roads. On the west side of the picturesque old town, on the **Susa**

right bank of the Dora, rises a marble triumphal arch (13.5 m (44¹/₂ ft) high) erected in 8 BC in honour of the Emperor Augustus by the prefect Cottius, after whom the Cottian Alps are named. North-east of the arch stands the cathedral of San Giusto (11th–13th c.), with a beautiful campanile.

At Susa the road forks: Montgenèvre to the left, Mont Cenis straight ahead.

The road to Mont Cenis (SS25), constructed by Napoleon in 1803–10, runs uphill, with numerous curves and sharp bends.

10 km (6 mi.): Molaretto (Italian customs).

Passo del Paradiso 9 km (5¹/₂ mi.): Passo del Paradiso, which since 1947 has marked the French-Italian frontier.

4 km (2¹/₂ mi.): to the left the Lac du Mont Cenis, in a beautiful setting (1913 m (6313 ft)).

Col du Mont Cenis 4 km (2¹/₂ mi.): Mont Cenis pass (Col du Mont Cenis, 2084 m (6877 ft)), on the old French-Italian frontier.

Beyond Susa the Montgenèvre road (SS24) passes through a gorge formed by the Dora Riparia.

Exiles 12 km (7 mi.): Exiles (on left), a picturesque village dominated by a massive fortress (17th c.); fine views.

Sauze d'Oulx 11 km (7 mi.): Oulx (1100 m (3630 ft)), 5 km (3 mi.) east of which is the winter sports resort of Sauze d'Oulx (1510 m (4983 ft)); chair-lifts, including to Sportinia (2170 m (7161 ft)), to the south.

Bardonecchia 14 km (9 mi.) north-west of Sauze d'Oulx is the village of Bardonecchia, a popular resort both in summer and winter (1312 m (4330 ft); population 3000). It lies near the entrance to the Galleria del Fréjus, the first Alpine tunnel (1861–70), leading to the French town of Modane (Mont Cenis rail tunnel, 13.6 km (8¹/₂ mi.) long; road tunnel 12.3 km (7¹/₂ mi.) long). From Bardonecchia there are a number of chair-lifts, including one via Granges Hyppolites (1520 m (5016 ft): change lifts) up Colomion (2054 m (6778 ft)).

Cesana Torinese 11 km (7 mi.): Cesana Torinese, where the road from Turin via Sestriere comes in.

Montgenèvre pass 8 km (5 mi.): Montgenèvre pass (1854 m (6118 ft)).

Turin to the Santuario d'Oropa (c. 100 km (62 mi.))

Biella 86 km (53 mi.) north-east of Turin, beautifully situated in the foothills of the Alps on the River Cervo, is the industrial town of Biella (420 m (1386 ft); population 52,000). In the lower town are the cathedral (originally built 1402, rebuilt 1772, façade 1825), and adjoining an early Romanesque baptistery (9th–10th c.) and the Town Hall. In the south-west part of the lower town stands the beautiful Renaissance church of San Sebastiano (1604; façade 1882). To the west, above the lower town (funicular), is the picturesque upper town or Piazzo, from which there are fine views.

Santuario della Madonna d'Oropa From Biella an interesting excursion on SS144 (13 km (8 miles)), goes north, with beautiful views, past the little spa of Oropa Bagni (1060 m (3498 ft)) to the magnificent Santuario della Madonna d'Oropa (1180 m (3894 ft)), the most popular place of pilgrimage in Piedmont, said to have been founded by St Eusebius in 369. From here a cableway runs up to the Rifugio Mucrone (1820 m (6006 ft)), near the Lago di Mucrone, and then to Monte Mucrone (2335 m (7706 ft); cableway, station 2189 m (7224 ft)). From the Rifugio Mucrone there is another cableway up Monte Camino

(2391 m (7890 ft); mountain hut); from which there are superb views, including Monte Rosa and the Matterhorn.

Through the Monferrato (c. 155 km (96 mi.))

There is an attractive drive through the Monferrato uplands, famous for their wine.

The road comes to Alba (34 km (21 mi.); alt. 172 m (568 ft); population 31,000), which has a Gothic cathedral (beautiful choir-stalls of 1512), fine churches and medieval towers. It then continues through the vine-growing Langhe region, where the much sought-after white truffles are harvested in autumn, and down the valley of the Bormida, on the edge of the Ligurian Apennines, to Savona, on the Riviera dei Fiori.

Alba

Turin to Genoa via Acqui Terme (c. 185 km (115 mi.))

Another interesting drive leads from Turin via Acqui Terme to Genoa. Leave on SS29 (the Alessandria road), which runs through Poirino (249 m (822ft).

56 km (35 mi.): Asti (see entry).

Asti

9 km (5½ mi.): Piano d'Isola (130 m (429 ft)). The road now leaves the Tanaro valley and traverses a densely populated upland region (vine-growing).

Piano d'Isola

20 km (12 mi.): Nizza Monferrato (138 m (455 ft); population 10,000), a little vine-growing town on the River Belbo. The road runs over a hill and enters the wide valley of the Bormida.

Nizza Monferrato

19 km (12 mi.): Acqui Terme (164 m (541 ft); population 22,000), a spa and centre of the wine trade on the left bank of the Bormida, with a cathedral consecrated in 1067, and the church of San Pietro (c. 1015). The mineral springs, containing salt and sulphur, are recommended for the treatment of rheumatic conditions. The hottest spring (La Bollente, 75°C (167°F) is in the Nuove Terme, in the town. From here the Corso Bagni leads over the river (beyond the bridge, on the right, remains of an ancient aqueduct) and past a large thermal swimming pool (6500 sq. m) to the Antiche Terme.
  Beyond Acqui the road continues for a short distance along the Bormida valley and then climbs into the Ligurian Apennines, goes over a hill and descends into the Orba valley.

Acqui Terme

24 km (15 mi.): Ovada (186 m (614 ft)), at the junction of the Stura and the Orba.

Ovada

17 km (11 mi.): Campo Ligure (342 m (1129 ft); population 4000), a pictures-que little town and summer resort with a tower which belonged to a 13th c. castle. There is an interesting museum with local filigree work.

Campo Ligure

8 km (5 mi.): Passo del Turchino (532 m (1756 ft): short tunnel), from which the road runs down into the pleasant valley of the Leiro.

Passo del Turchino

28 km (17 mi.): Genoa (see entry).

Genoa

Tuscany

E–F 7–10

Region: Toscana
Provinces: Firenze (FI), Arezzo (AR), Grosseto (GR), Livorno (LI), Lucca
  (LU), Massa-Carrara (MS), Pisa (PI), Pistoia (PT), Siena (SI)
Area: 22,992 sq. km (8875 sq. mi.). Population: 3,580,600

Tuscany

Location
Tuscany is a Central Italian region. It extends from the ridge of the Tuscan or Etruscan Apennines over the Tuscan uplands, with their gently rounded hills and their clumps of slender cypresses, to the Maremma along the Tyrrhenian coast, and beyond this to Elba and a number of smaller islands off the Tuscan coast.

The capital of Tuscany is Florence.

Economy
Most of the inhabitants of Tuscany live in the catchment areas of the industrial conurbations in the Arno valley, between Florence and Livorno and from there north along the coast to Carrara. In this area are concentrated a multiplicity of enterprises, mostly of small and medium size, covering an extraordinary range of crafts and industries. The major industries are the working of minerals (iron, lignite, mercury) and marble, but other important activities are engineering, shipbuilding, pharmaceuticals, glass and crystal manufacture, textiles and various forms of applied and decorative art.

Winemaking
In the upland areas the predominant activity is agriculture, together with the various industries concerned with the processing of its produce. A leading place among these is taken by the winemaking industry. Tuscany is the home of the famous dry dark red wine, Chianti, which is found here in excellent quality. Corn and olives are also grown in large quantities, and in the Arno valley and along the coast there is much market gardening and flower-growing.

Tourism
A major contribution to the economy is also made by the tourist trade, particularly in the great art centres of Florence, Siena and Pisa, the numerous spas (Montecatini Terme, Bagni di Lucca, etc.) and the resorts on the coast.

Etruria
The present territory of Tuscany coincides broadly with that of ancient Etruria, occupied by the numerous city states of the Etruscans which flourished between the 9th and 5th c. BC, forming a kind of federation (the league of twelve towns), which varied in membership and nature from time to time, and extending their power and influence into Campania and the Po valley. Since the surviving documents in the Etruscan language are confined to inscriptions of a funerary or votive nature or relating to the ownership of property, they tell us little about the advanced culture of the Etruscans, the origins of which are still obscure. Much more informative are the objects recovered from their tombs, which usually imitate the form of houses, and their sculpture and tomb painting, predominantly depicting scenes from everyday life, which bear witness to a high standard of art and craftsmanship, particularly of the goldsmiths.

Etruscan cities
The Etruscan cities usually occupied strong defensive positions, preferably on isolated rocky plateaux with good views of the surrounding area. Outside the cities lay the extensive necropolises. As the massive circular tombs of this period show, the Etruscans were familiar with the principle of the false dome and the barrel vault. They were a seafaring people who carried on an active trade with the other peoples of the Mediterranean but were also – if Greek accounts are to be believed – much given to piracy.

Later history
The power of the Etruscans began to decline in the 5th c., and by the beginning of the 4th c. the decline was irremediable. More and more of their territory fell into the hands of the Romans, and by about 300 BC the whole of Etruria was under Roman control.

After the fall of Rome Tuscany was successively ruled by the Ostrogoths, the Byzantines, the Lombards and the Franks, and in the 11th c. it became part of the county of Tuscia. In the 13th c. Florence, now steadily increasing in strength, succeeded in establishing its dominance over the rival cities in the region, particularly Siena and Pisa, and after the defeat of these two towns in the 15th c. asserted its position as the intellectual and political

centre of the Duchy of Tuscany, which became a Grand Duchy under
Cosimo I Medici.

In later centuries the region suffered from the effects of the War of
the Spanish Succession, from epidemics of plague and from crippling
taxation. Under the Treaty of Vienna in 1735 Tuscany passed to Francis
Stephen of Lorraine, husband of the Empress Maria Theresa. On October
1st 1800, as the kingdom of Etruria, it was assigned to Duke Luigi of Parma,
but in 1807 it was incorporated in the French Empire and ruled by
Napoleon's sister Elisa Bachiocchi, who took the title of duchess of
Tuscany. Her successor Ferdinand II and his son Leopold II of Austria came
into violent conflict with nationalist and anti-Austrian forces in the country, and in 1859 Leopold, finding himself without any support, abdicated
under protest. In 1860, following a referendum, Tuscany was formally
annexed by the kingdom of Sardinia and Piedmont, the nucleus of the
later united kingdom of Italy.

Every visitor to Tuscany will of course want to visit the great art cities of   Art centres
Florence, Pisa and Siena.

There is also much of interest to see along the Via Aurelia, which runs   Via Aurelia
south from Pisa via Livorno to Grosseto, now keeping close to the coast,
now a little way inland.

Populonia

On the way down it is well worth making a detour from the rather featureless port and industrial town of Piombino (19 m (63 ft); population 40,000)
to the village of Populonia (179 m (591 ft)), situated high above the sea on
the north side of a promontory, formerly an island, 14 km (9 mi.) north
of Piombino. This was the Etruscan port of Pupluna, with remains of its
circuit of walls and an interesting Etruscan necropolis on the coast below
the village. The Etruscan Museum (Museo Etrusco) contains numerous
finds from the necropolis.

Grosseto

The provincial capital of Grosseto (12 m (40 ft); population 70,000) is the
economic centre of the strip of coastal territory known as the Maremma.
The town was founded in the Middle Ages round a small castle which was
erected to protect the Via Aurelia, the old Roman road from Pisa to Rome.
The main square of the town, which is still surrounded by a wall with
six bastions, is the Piazza Dante, on the north side of which stand the
Town Hall and the cathedral (begun 1294; façade restored 1840–45). In the
north transept of the cathedral is an "Assumption" by Matteo di Giovanni
(15th c.). A little way north of the cathedral is the interesting Museo d'Arte
Sacra e d'Arte della Maremma which contains prehistoric finds, particularly from the Etruscan and Roman period. The museum also has a collection
of sacral art.

6 km (3³/₄ mi.) north-east of Grosseto we come to the sulphur springs of   ★**Rusellae**
Bagno Roselle (25 m (83 ft)). Nearby are the remains of Rusellae (184 m
(607 ft)), one of the twelve principal cities of the Etruscan federation, with
sections of its circuit of walls still standing, a number of Etruscan houses
and a Roman amphitheatre.

Some 20 km (12 mi.) north-west of Grosseto, on higher ground, is Vetulo-   ★**Vetulonia**
nia (344 m (1135 ft)), now part of the community of Castiglione della
Pescaia. Under the name of Vatluna it belonged to the Etruscan federation.
To the north-east and the west of the former town are Etruscan necropolises. The principal part of the finds of the tombs can be seen in the
museums of Grosseto and Florence.

Etruscan life

Etruscan culture, which flourished from the 8th to the 4th century BC, especially in Toscana (Tuscany, the land of the Tuscans), remains obscure to this day. Whether the Etruscan people descended from the original inhabitants of central Italy or whether they immigrated from Asia Minor has long been a matter of disagreement among experts. Either seems possible, because there is little – apart from brief and formal inscriptions of a funerary or votive nature – in the way of surviving documents, and what there is has so far defied all attempts to decipher it. Moreover, not much remains of their secular dwellings and temples, so there is scanty evidence from that source to provide details of the daily lives of the people named "Tusci" by the Romans.

However, there are other sources which reflect the quality of Etruscan life. These are the many relics of their various death-cults which provide a serenely idealised portrayal of life on earth. For his journey into the next world the deceased was buried with those possessions which he had loved and prized in life – artistic ceramics, objects in bronze and precious metals and much more besides – so as not to lack these in the afterlife.

Their cemeteries resemble real towns with houses, streets and squares. They are composed partly of round burial mounds or walled tombs,

partly of rows of dwelling-like chambers hewn out of the soft volcanic rock. The wall-paintings which decorate many of the chambers contain portrayals of dancing, festivities or hunting expeditions; the dynamic movement in these paintings expresses true *joi de vivre* such as is not found in any other death-cults. The best examples of such art can be found in the graves at Tarquinia.

Often the mortal remains are interred in sarcophagi or terracotta urns, the lids of which contain a recumbent figure of the deceased. It is interesting to note that the containers and lids appear to be "mass-produced" with the aid of a pre-prepared mould, and only the portrait-like head is made individually and then added.

Abbadia San Salvatore

About 60 km (37 mi.) south-east of Siena is the old town of Abbadia San
Salvatore (812 m (2680 ft); population 8000). The Abbazia di San Salvatore
(Abbey of the Saviour), to which the little old town owes its name, is
one of the oldest abbeys in Tuscany, of which only the church is left. The
notable crypt contains columns with partly richly decorated capitals.

There is an attractive road from Abbadia San Salvatore (14 km (9 mi.))
to the top of Monte Amiata (1738 m (5735 ft)), an extinct and craterless
volcano. From the summit, with a mountain hut and an iron cross 22 m
(73 ft) high, there are magnificent views.
   The drive round Monte Amiata from Abbadia San Salvatore (65 km
(40 mi.)) is also very rewarding.

★**Monte Amiata**

Strada del Vino

The Strada del Vino (Wine Road) was opened in 1933. It leads from Cecina
through the interior to Piombino and links the well-known tiny villages
scattered along this stretch of country.

Udine   H3

Region: Friuli-Venezia Giulia. Province: Udine (UD)
Altitude: 114 m (374 ft). Population: 100,000

Udine, capital of the province of the same name, lies at the east end of the
north Italian plain in the flood-plain of the River Tagliamento. The town is
about 40 km (25 mi.) from the Adriatic coast and about 20 km (12 mi.) from
the frontier of the former Yugoslavia.
   It is the see of an archbishop and a university town. Udine is the economic centre of the Friulan plain and popular with shoppers.

Location

Udine, the Roman Utina, was from 1238 to 1752 the residence of the
Patriarchs of Aquileia (south of Udine on the Adriatic coast), to whom the
Emperor Otto II had granted the castle in 983. The town came under
Venetian control in 1420. Two of the old town gates, Porta Aquileia and
Porta Villalta, have been preserved.

History

Sights

The town contains many old noble palaces, some of them with rather
faded painting on their façades. The principal square, at the foot of the
castle hill, is the Piazza della Libertà, in which stands the Palazzo del
Comune (Loggia del Lionello), in the style of the Doge's Palace in Venice
(1457, restored 1876).

Palazzo del
Comune

Opposite the Palazzo del Comune is the Porticato di San Giovanni or
Loggia di San Giovanni (1533), a triumphal arch surrounded by arches on
slender columns, the entrance of St John's chapel, now a war memorial.
Inside there is a victory column by Raimondo d'Aronco. The adjoining
clock-tower resembles the one in Venice.
   On the south side of the Piazza della Libertà is a tall column bearing the
lion of St Mark, and on the north side a statue of the Goddess of Peace,
commemorating the peace of Campoformio (1797) between France and
Austria, in which Venice came under Austrian control. The Palazzo
d'Aronco on the Piazza del Libertà is now the Town Hall.

Porticato di San
Giovanni

On the castle hill, north of the Piazza della Libertà, is the 16th c. Castello,
which suffered severe damage from an earthquake in 1976, but has since

Castello

Udine

Udine: Loggia del Lionello

Museums	been restored. In the Hall of Honour, in the centre of the main building, the members of the parliament of Friuli once met. The Castello now houses the Museo Civico and the Galleria d'Arte Antica. The Art Museum contains pictures and sculpture of the 15th c. up to modern times, including pictures by Carpaccio, Giovanni Battista Tiepolo, Bicci di Lorenzo, Ghirlandaio, Caravaggio and Canova. From the Watch Tower of the castle there are fine views of the Alps.
Cathedral	A short distance south-east of the Piazza della Libertà, in the Piazza del Duomo, stands the cathedral, a Gothic structure of 1236, remodelled in the 18th c. It has a hexagonal campanile. Above the main doorway is a lunette, the reliefs of which depict the crucifixion of Christ. The interior is decorated with stucco and frescos by Giovanni Battista Tiepolo.
Oratorio della Purità	Behind the cathedral is the little Oratorio della Purità, with frescos by Giovanni Battista Tiepolo and his son Giovanni Domenico Tiepolo.
Archbishop's Palace	North of the cathedral is the Archbishop's Palace, with notable frescos by Giovanni Battista Tiepolo (1726–30) and Giovanni da Udine (1487–1584).
Tempio Ossario dei Caduti	In the west of the town, the newer part, is the Piazzale XXVI Luglio. In its centre is a sculpture of 1969, a memorial to the resistance fighters who fought Fascism in the Second World War. In the same square stands the Tempio Ossario dei Caduti d'Italia, a domed structure of 1931 and a mausoleum for 22,000 Italians who died in the First World War.
Galleria d'Arte Moderna	The Gallery of Modern Art, in Piazzale Paolo Diacono on the northern edge of the town, is also worth a visit.

Umbria · G8–9

Region: Umbria. Provinces: Perugia (PG) and Terni (TR)
Area: 8456 sq. km (3265 sq. mi.). Population: 825,000

The Central Italian region of Umbria extends on both sides of the Tiber, whose wide valley is flanked by the foothills of the Apennines. Umbria is bounded on the west by Tuscany, on the east by the Marche and on the south by Latium. The political region of Umbria, with its capital Perugia, takes in the two provinces of Perugia and Terni.

Location

The spacious countryside of Umbria, with its easily accessible hills and its fertile lowlands, has been from time immemorial a prosperous farming region (corn, olives, wine, sugar-beet, tobacco, market gardening; sheep and pigs). Umbria is one of the regions where truffles can be found.

Only around the towns of Terni, Narni and Foligno, where power is supplied by large hydro-electric stations, has there been any considerable development of industry (chemicals, metal-working). Textile manufacture and the production of craft articles have become established in the Perugia and Spoleto areas. Tourism is also important in the region.

Economy

In ancient times this was the homeland of the Umbrians, and there was also some Etruscan settlement in the region. In 295 BC it came under Roman control, and in the reign of Augustus was combined with Etruria to form the sixth region (Regio VI) of the Empire. After the fall of Rome and the subsequent Gothic wars it became part of the Lombard duchy of Spoleto and of the States of the Church. During the Middle Ages, rent by bitter conflicts between the various towns – which enjoyed a large measure of independence – and the ruling families, the region fell into a decline, until the Church succeeded in establishing its authority in the 16th c.

History

View of the Umbrian town of Todi

521

Lake Trasimene

In 1860, after a plebiscite, Umbria and its capital Perugia became part of the united kingdom of Italy. In September 1997 a heavy earthquake hit the Umbrian region, causing damage to numerous historic buildings.

Sights

Umbria has a number of towns which stand high among Italy's tourist attractions, in particular Perugia, Assisi and Orvieto (see entries) and a number of smaller historic towns e.g. Spoleto, Città di Castello, Todi (see entries) and Montefalco (see Foligno, Surroundings). Scenically charming are Lake Trasimene (see below) in the west and the south-east of Umbria bordering on the Appenines which is easily reached from Terni (see entry).

Lake Trasimene

To the west of Perugia is Lake Trasimene (Lago Trasimeno). The lake, at an altitude of 259 m (855 ft), is the largest in the Italian peninsula (area 128 sq. km (49 sq. mi.), circumference about 50 km (31 mi.); greatest depth 7 m (23 ft)) though it is subject to considerable variation of level.

Lake Trasimene is famous as the scene of the second Punic War, a battle between Carthaginians and Romans, in which Hannibal defeated the Roman consul Gaius Flaminius in 217 BC.

On a promontory on the north side of the lake is the ancient little town of Passignano sul Trasimento (289 m (954 ft)), with an old castle; on another promontory rising above the west side of the lake is Castiglione del Lago (304 m (1003 ft)), with the ducal castle of the Cornia family.

Urbino   G8

Region: Marche. Province: Pesaro e Urbino (PS)
Altitude: 485 m (1601 ft). Population: 15,500

The town of Urbino lies on a steep-sided hill in the north of the Central Italian region of Marche, some 35 km (22 mi.) west of Pesaro and about 70 km (43 mi.) south of Rimini.

Location

Urbino is the see of an archbishop.

Urbino was the Roman Urvinum Metaurense. In 1213 it came into the hands of the Montefeltro family, which acquired the ducal title in the 15th c. The court of Duke Federico di Montefeltro (1444–82), a discriminating patron of art and learning, was recognised to be the most splendid of its day. From 1508 to 1631 the duchy was held by the Della Rovere family; thereafter it was incorporated in the States of the Church.

History

In the 15th c. the painters Paolo Uccello, Piero della Francesca, Melozzo da Forli and Giovanni Santi (Raphael's father) worked in Urbino. The great architect Bramante (1444–1514) was born near the town, and probably worked for Luciano de Laurana. Raphael (1483–1520) and the Baroque painter Federigo Barocci (c. 1537–1612) were natives of Urbino. It was here that Count Baldassare Castiglione (1478–1529) wrote his "Il Librodel Cortegiano", a manual for courtiers.

Art

In the centre of the town is the Piazza della Repubblica, the market square. From here Via Vittorio Veneto leads up to the Piazza Duca Federico, on the north side of which stands the cathedral, rebuilt in 1801 after the destruction of an earlier church by an earthquake in 1789. It contains a number of fine paintings, including in particular works by Federigo Barocci. In the third chapel in the crypt (entered from outside the church, under the arcades to the left) is a marble figure of the dead Christ by Giovanni Bandini.

Cathedral

To the right of the cathedral is the Museo del Duomo "Albani", which contains 14th c. frescos, ceramics, sacral objects and chasubles, 14th–17th c. pictures and a bronze paschal candelabra.

Cathedral Museum

Urbino: Palazzo Ducale

Varese

★★ Palazzo Ducale	The Palazzo Ducale, opposite the cathedral, built by the Dalmatian architect Luciano da Laurana from 1465 onwards, is the most perfectly preserved example of an Italian princely residence of the period. Notable features are the colonnaded courtyard (c. 1470) and the staircase.
★ Galleria Nazionale delle Marche	The magnificent state apartments on the first and second floors now house the Galleria Nazionale delle Marche (National Gallery of the Marche), a rich picture gallery, with Raphael's "Mute" and pictures by Paolo Uccello ("Miracle of the Communion"), Piero della Francesca, Titian, Barocci, Gentileschi and Simone de Magistris. There are also tapestries and sculpture.
San Domenico	Opposite the Ducal Palace can be seen the church of San Domenico (14th–5th c.), with a fine doorway by Maso di Bartolomeo (1449–54). A little way south is the university founded in 1671, with a coat of arms above the doorway.
Casa Natale di Raffaello	From the Piazza della Repubblica Via Raffaello climbs up towards the north-west. At the near end, on the right, is the church of San Francesco (14th c.), with a porch and a fine campanile. On the left (No. 57) is Raphael's Birthplace (Casa Natale di Raffaello; plaque and museum); Raphael lived here until the age of fourteen.
Raphael Monument	Via Raffaello meets the spacious, park-like Piazzale Roma, with a monument to Raphael (1897). From the adjoining bastion, Pian del Monte, there are excellent views, extending as far as San Marino.
Oratorio di San Giuseppe	South-west of the Piazza della Repubblica, at the end of the short Via Barocci, the Oratorio di San Giuseppe has a life-size Nativity group by Federico Brandano. Nearby in the Oratorio di San Giovanni are paintings by Lorenzo and Jacopo Salimbeni (1416).

Surroundings

★**Furlo Gorge** 20 km (12 mi.) SE	There is a rewarding drive to the Furlo Gorge (Gola del Furlo), enclosed by sheer rock faces. At the narrowest point is the Galleria Romana del Furlo or Forulus (177 m (584 ft)), a tunnel 37 m (121 ft) long carrying the Via Flaminia through the rock. It bears an inscription recording that it was cut by the Emperor Vespasian in AD 76. Adjoining is the older Galleria Piccola del Furlo 8 m (26 ft) long (3rd c. BC).

Varese   C4

	Region: Lombardia. Province: Varese (VA) Altitude: 383 m (1264 ft). Population: 88,000
Location	The provincial capital of Varese is attractively situated on hills along the southern edge of the Alps near the Lago di Varese, with the Campo dei Fiori looming above it. The town, a centre of shoe manufacture, lies some 20 km (12 mi.) west of Como and some 50 km (31 mi.) north-west of the Lombardian city of Milan.

Sights

	The hub of the town's traffic is the Piazza Monte Grappa, with monumental modern buildings and a tower. From here the main street of Varese, the

The romantic Furlo Gorge near Urbino

arcaded Corso Matteotti, leads to the Piazza del Podestà. A little way east stands the church of San Vittore, built in its present form to the design of Pellegrino Tibaldi (1580–1615), with a Neo-Classical façade (1795) and a campanile (1617–1773) 72 m (238 ft) high. Behind it is a baptistery (1185–87).

A short distance west of Piazza Monte Grappa, on the left-hand side of Via Luigi Sacco, the Palazzo Ducale or Palazzo Estense, built for Duke Francesco III of Este in 1766–73 and used as a summer residence until 1780, is now the Town Hall.

Palazzo Ducale

Behind the palace is the Giardino Pubblico (formerly the palace grounds), beautifully laid out in traditional Italian style. In the southern part of the gardens is the Villa Mirabello, in which are the municipal museums. Of particular interest are the Museo del Risorgimento, with records of Garibaldi and the movement for a united Italy, and the fine Museo Archeologico, with prehistoric and Roman antiquities, including material from pile dwellings on the Lago di Varese and from Roman tombs.

Museums

1.5 km (1 mi.) west of the Palazzo Ducale is the Colle dei Campigli (453 m (1495 ft)), on which are the Kursaal and the Grand Hotel Palace. From the top there are magnificent views of the Lago di Varese and the western Alps, with Monte Rosa.

Colle dei Campigli

Surroundings

A little way west of the town we come to the Lago di Varese. Near the east end of the lake, above the village of Gazzada, is the Villa Cagnola, bequeathed to the Vatican by Count Cagnola, with valuable furniture and tapestries. From the large park there are magnificent views of the lake and the Alps.

Villa Cagnola

Sacro Monte

8 km (5 mi.) W
The road runs north-west to Sant'Ambrogio Olona and from there up the Sacro Monte (880 m (2904 ft)), on the summit of which is a pilgrimage chapel (view).

Campo dei Fiori

10 km (6 mi.) NW
Another rewarding trip is to take the road which runs up from Sant' Ambrogio Olona to the Campo dei Fiori (1032 m (3406 ft); panoramic views).

Continue on foot (20 minutes) to the summit of Monte Tre Croci (1083 m (3574 ft), from where there is a famous view embracing six lakes, the Lombard plain and part of the chain of the Alps.

Sibrium

9 km (5½ mi.) S
South of Varese, in the forest near the village of Castelseprio, are the remains of the Lombard fort of Sibrium, with a restored castle. In the adjoining church of Santa Maria Foris Portas (7th or 8th c.) frescos dating from the 7th resp. 8th–9th c. were exposed in 1944.

Castiglione Olona

10 km (6 mi.) S
A little way west of SS233 (the Milan road), is the old-world village of Castiglione Olona (307 m (1013 ft)). In the Gothic collegiate church are fine frescoes by Tuscan masters, among them a Virgin Mary by Masolino da Panicale, a pupil of Giotto. The frescoes in the baptistery (1435) depict scenes from the life of John the Baptist, also by Masolino. Inside the notable Chiesa di Villa (1430–41) is the tomb of Count Guido Castiglioni.

Venetia   E–G 3–5

Region: Veneto
Provinces: Venezia (VE), Belluno (BL), Padova (PD), Rovigo (RO), Trevisio (TV), Verona (VR) and Vicenza (VI)
Area: 18,365 sq. km (7091 sq. mi.). Population: 4,400,000

Location
The region of Venetia (Veneto), the territory of the old Republic of Venice, lies in the north-east of the North Italian plain, extending northward from the lower course of the Po to the Venetian Alps and bounded on the west by Lake Garda and the River Mincio, on the east by the Adriatic coast, a strip of former marshland now occupied by numerous lagoons.

Administrative regions
The area is now divided into three administrative regions: in the east Friuli-Venezia Giulia (see Friuli); in the north Trentino-Alto Adige (see Alto Adige); and between these two, extending towards the Po and the Adriatic, the region of Veneto (formerly Venezia Euganea), the heartland of the old territory of Venetia.

Economy
The region of Veneto is notable for its scenic variety and economic diversity. The population is concentrated mainly in the larger cities of the Po plain, which has a highly developed agriculture (grain, particularly maize and rice, vines, fruit, vegetables, cattle-farming), with the associated processing industries (canning, manufacture of foodstuffs).

Large companies have settled here as there is much general industrial development (textiles, building materials, metalworking, chemicals, petrochemicals, shipbuilding), promoted by an abundant supply of power (hydro-electric schemes in the Alps, natural gas in the Po plain). The region is also famous for its applied and decorative art, in particular the glass-blowing and lace-making of the Venice area. Tourism is an additional source of income. The "Villas in Veneto" are a special feature of this region. See Baedeker Special, page 310-11.

Sights

In northern Venetia, on the River Piave, is the provincial capital of Belluno (389 m (1265 ft); population 36,000) which dates back to pre-Roman times. The cathedral, built from 1517 onwards and restored in 1873, has two beautiful altarpieces in the south aisle; from the campanile, 68 m (223 ft) high, there are fine views. Also in this square are the Palazzo dei Rettori (1496), a fine Early Renaissance building which now houses the Prefecture, and the Gothic church of Santo Stefano (1468), with an adjoining cloister. The Museo Civico, with pictures and bronzes, is worth visiting.

Belluno

12 km (7 mi.) south-east is a winter sports area on the Nevegal (chair-lift to Rifugio Cadore, 1600 m (5280 ft); Alpine garden).

Nevegal

There is an attractive road from Belluno (30 km (19 mi.) north-west) through the magnificent gorge on the River Cordevole known as the Canal d'Agordo (15km/9 miles long) to the little town of Agordo (611 m (2021 ft); population 4000), ringed by high mountains, a popular walking and climbing centre. In the main square is the picturesque Palazzo Crotta di Manzoni (17th–18th c.).

Agordo

From Agordo it is another 18 km (11 mi.) north to the south end of the Lago D'Alleghe (966 m (3188 ft)), a lake 2 km (1¼ mi.) long formed by a landslide in 1771.

Lago D'Alleghe

On the east side of the lake lies the village of Alleghe (979 m (3231 ft)), a popular summer resort and climbing centre. From here there is a pleasant walk on a bridle path which goes east (3 hours) to the sombre Lago Coldai (2146 m (7082 ft)); then another 20 minutes over the Coldai pass (2190 m (7227 ft)) to the Rifugio Coldai (2150 m (7095 ft)), magnificently situated on the northern slopes of the massive Monte Civetta (3218 m (10,619 ft)), which can be climbed from here in 6 hours (guide necessary).

Alleghe

3 km (2 mi.) north-west is the village of Caprile (1023 m (376 ft)), from which an excursion can be made up the Pettorina valley to the villages of Rocca Piétore (3 km (2 mi.); 1143 m (3772 ft)) and Sottoguda (7 km (4½ mi.); 1252 m (4132 ft)). From here it is possible in summer to continue for another 7 km (4½ mi.) on the old road through the gorge of Serrai di Sottoguda to the Malga Ciapela (1428 m (4712 ft); cableway via the Forcella Serauta 2270 m (7491 ft) to the Punta di Rocca 3270 m (10,791 ft)) and the Pian di Lobbia (1841 m (6075 ft)); then 2 km (1¼ mi.) to the Fedaia pass (2047 m (6756 ft)) and another 3 km (2 mi.)along the Lago di Fedaia to the Rifugio Marmolada; chair-lift to Marmolada glacier and road to Canazei.

Caprile

18 km (11 mi.) north-east of Belluno, at the mouth of the Zoldo valley, is the little town of Longarone (468 m (1544 ft)), which was destroyed on October 9th 1963, together with four neighbouring villages, by a flood wave 100 m (330 ft) high when a landslide on Monte Toc caused the Lago di Vajont to overflow. Some 2000 people, including 1700 in Longarone, lost their lives in the disaster; the town is being rebuilt on the slopes to the west.

Longarone

From Longarone a road climbs up (sharp bends, tunnels), passing through the wild Vajont gorge (4 km (2½ mi.) long; galleries through rock), to the Lago di Vajont, a reservoir formed by a dam 265 m (765 ft) high, now largely drained, and then over the Passo di Sant'Osvaldo (827 m (2729 ft)) to the summer resort of Cimolais (652 m (2152 ft)).

Cimolais

Venetia

Pieve di Cadore

25 km (16 mi.) north-east of Longarone up the Piave valley, which becomes steadily narrower, is Pieve di Cadore (878 m (2897 ft)), chief town of the upper Piave region and a popular health and winter sports resort, beautifully situated high above the River Piave, here dammed to form a lake 8 km (5 mi.) long. In the main square is a monument to Titian, who was born here; his birthplace (museum) is in a little square with a fountain. The parish church has a Madonna with Saints by Titian.

Bassano del Grappa

In the west of the region of Veneto, some 40 km (25 mi.) north of Padova, lies Bassano del Grappa (122 m (403 ft); population 39,000) where an old wooden bridge leads over the River Brenta. The town is noted as the home of the Da Ponte family, the most important member of which was Jacopo da Ponto, called Bassano. The Museo Civico and the cathedral contain works by this painter.

Museo della Grappa

The town at the foot of Mount Grappa is the capital of the Italian brandy-making region. In an old patrician house by the Ponte Vecchio is the Museo della Grappa, a Brandy Museum (with a shop) portraying the history of distillation.

Asolo

It is worth making a detour to Asolo, lying on a hillside north of Bassano del Grappa. Well-known personalities who have stayed here include Eleonora Duse and the poet Robert Browning.

Rovigo

In the south of the Veneto region, on the Naviglio Adigetto, lies the provincial capital of Rovigo (7 m (23 ft); population 53,000). In the centre of the town in the elongated Piazza Vittorio Emanuele are a tall column bearing the lion of St Mark, the Palazzo del Municipio or Loggia dei Notai (Town Hall, with tower) and the Pinacoteca dei Concordi (picture gallery, with paintings of the Venetian school). To the west is the cathedral (17th c.; restored) and to the north of this two towers and the remains of the old castle. In the east of the town is the pilgrimage church of "La Rotonda" (1600).

Bassano del Grappa on the Brenta

Venetia: magnificent park on Portogruaro

At the east end of the region of Venetia is Portogruaro (5 m (16ft); population   **Portogruaro** 25,000), with fine old arcaded houses, a Gothic Town Hall (14th–16th c.) and a Romanesque, leaning tower (the campanile of the cathedral). The Museo Nazionale Concordiese contains Roman and Early Christian remains from Concordia Sagittaria, the Roman military station of Concordia, 2 km (1¼ mi.) downstream, which preserves a Roman bridge and an early medieval baptistery.

28 km (16 mi.) north-west of Portogruaro, in the Friul-Venezia Giulia   **Pordenone** region, is the old provincial capital of Pordenone (24 m (79 ft); population 51,000), birthplace of the painter Giovanni de Sacchis, known as Pordenone (1484–1539). There are pictures by this artist in the Late Gothic cathedral (15th c.) and in the Pinacoteca Civica. The Town Hall was built between 1291 and 1365. The Palazzo Amalteo, a little to the north, houses a natural history museum.

Cortina d'Ampezzo, Dolomites, Lake Garda, Padua, Venice, Verona,   Other sights Vicenza; see entries.

Venice   G5

Region: Veneto. Province: Venezia (VE)
Altitude: 1 m (3ft). Population: 306,000

The description of Venice in this guide book is concise as there is a comprehensive guide to Venice in the Baedeker series.

Venice, capital of the Veneto region and the province of Venezia, lies at the   Location very head of the Adriatic, 4 km (2½ mi.) from the mainland (rail and road

Venice

causeway) in the Laguna Veneta, a salt-water lagoon 55 km (34 mi.) long and up to 12 km (7½ mi.) wide which is separated from the Adriatic by a series of narrow spits of land (*lidi*). There are more than 30 larger and smaller islands in the lagoon.

Architecture

The town is built on 118 small islands and traversed by something like 100 canals (canale, rio), which are spanned by almost 400 bridges, mostly stone-built. Its 15,000 houses, built on piles, form a close-packed huddle of narrow streets and lanes (calle, salizzada, etc.), often no more than 1.5 m (5 ft) wide, filled with bustling activity. There is only one piazza; smaller squares are called campo or campiello. The quays or embankments are called riva or fondamenta.

Transport

In the inner city boats play an important part in public transportation (see Piazzale Roma landing-stage).

Industry

In the past Venice's industry was confined to craft products (particularly glass and lace), boatbuilding, etc., but there has been a considerable development of large-scale industry since the First World War in the suburban district of Mestre. The port is one of Italy's largest, with an annual turnover of some 24 million metric tons. The industrial port is Porto di Maghera, Mestre; the Bacino della Stazione Marittima, south-west of the Piazzale Roma, also handles freight traffic.

History

In ancient times the Venice area was occupied by an Illyrian tribe, the Veneti, who formed a defensive alliance with Rome in the 3rd c. BC and rapidly became Romanised. In AD 451, the inhabitants of the coastal region fled to the safety of the islands in the lagoon, and in 697 they joined to form a naval confederation under a doge (from Latin *dux*, "leader"). In 811 Rivus Altus (Rialto) – i.e. present-day Venice – became the seat of government. In 829 the remains of the Evangelist Mark were brought to Venice from Alexandria, and thereafter Mark became the patron saint of the Venetian republic, which took his name and used his lion as its emblem. The young state prospered as the main channel and entrepôt for trade between Western Europe and the East, occupied the east coast of the Adriatic, conquered Constantinople in 1204 and established itself on the coasts of Greece and Asia Minor. The so-called "Hundred Years' War" with Genoa was decided by the Venetian naval victory off Chioggia in 1380, and in the 15th c. the republic reached the peak of its power, controlling the whole of the eastern Mediterranean and extending its conquests on the Italian mainland as far as Verona, Bergamo and Brescia ("terra ferma"). In the 15th and 16th c. Venice achieved its finest cultural flowering.

Towards the end of the 15th c., however, the advance of the Turks and the discovery of America and the new sea routes to India brought the beginnings of decline. In the 16th c. the Venetian possessions on the mainland of Italy involved the republic in the conflicts between Austria and Spain on the one hand and France on the other, and the struggle against the Turks ended in 1718 with the loss of all Venice's possessions in the East. In 1797 the French put an end to the city's independence, and under the treaty of Campoformio in that year it was assigned provisionally to Austria. In 1815 it formally became part of Austria, and remained so until it joined the new Kingdom of Italy in 1866.

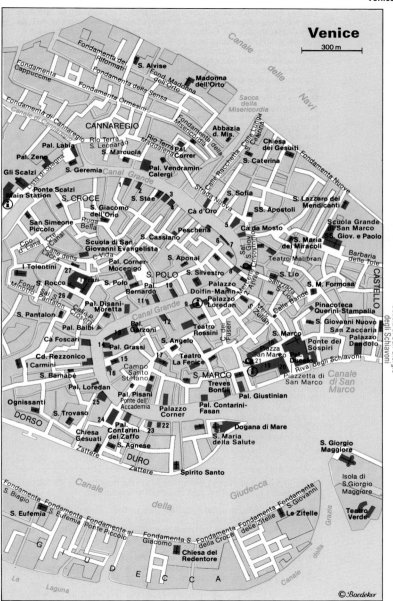

Venice

300 m

Fondamenta dei Riformati
Fondamenta Cappuccine
S. Alvise
Fond. Madonna dell'Orto
Madonna dell'Orto
Fondamenta della Sensa
Fondamenta Ormesini
Fondamenta di Cannaregio
Canale di Cannaregio
CANNAREGIO
Rio Terrà S. Leonardo
Rio Terrà Maddalena
Pal. Labia
Fondamenta della Misericordia
Sacca della Misericordia
Canale delle Navi
Abbazia d. Mis.
Chiesa dei Gesuiti
S. Marcuola
Correr
S. Caterina
Pal. Zena
Calle Racchetta
Calle Lunga
Calle Caselli
Fondamenta Nuove
Pal. Vendramin-Calergi
Gli Scalzi
S. Geremia
Canal Grande
Lista di Spagna
Ponte Scalzi
Main Station
S. CROCE
S. Giacomo dell'Orio
Ruga Bella
1
S. Stae
2
3
4
Strada Nuova
S. Sofia
Cà d'Oro
5
SS. Apostoli
S. Lazzaro dei Mendicanti
San Simeone Piccolo
Cpo d'Lana
Cre Canal
Calle della Lacca
Pescheria
S. Cassiano
Scuola di San Giovanni Evangelista
C Vida
6
7
Ca da Mosto
Teatro Malibran
S. Maria dei Miracoli
Scuola Grande SS. Giov. e Paolo
S. Aponal
Barbaria delle Tole
I Tolentini
Pal. Corner-Mocenigo
S. Silvestro
8
S. Lio
CASTELLO
27
Frari
S. Rocco
S. POLO
Pal. S. Polo
10
Palazzo Dolfin-Manin
Salizzada S. Lio
S. M. Formosa
Fond. Minotto
Sal. S Pantalon
26
Pal. Disani-Moretta
Pal. Bernardo
11
9
Palazzo Loredan
Pinacoteca Querini-Stampalia
S. Pantalon
Calle P Crosera
Canal Grande
12
S. Giovanni Nuovo
Pal. Balbi
Pal. Garzoni
Teatro Rossini
S. Zaccaria
Ca Foscari
13
S. Angelo
S. Marco
Palazzo Dandolo
Cd. Rezzonico
14
Pal. Grassi
17
Teatro La Fenice
Piazza San Marco
Ponte del Sospiri
I Carmini
15
Campo Santo Stefano
21
19
Pal. Ducale
Riva degli Schiavoni
S. Barnabè
16
S. MARCO
20
Piazzetta di San Marco
Canale di San Marco
Pal. Loredan
Treves Bontili
Pal. Pisani
Ponte dell'Accademia
Pal. Giustinian
Ognissanti
25
Palazzo Corner
Pal. Contarini-Fasan
DORSO
S. Trovaso
24
Pal. Contarini del Zaffo
23
22
Dogana di Mare
S. Maria della Salute
S. Giorgio Maggiore
Chiesa Gesuati
S. Agnese
DURO
Zattere
Spirito Santo
Isola di S.Giorgio Maggiore
Zattere
Canale
della
Giudecca
Teatro Verde
Fondamenta S. Biagio
Fondamenta della
Fondamenta al Ponte Piccolo
S. Eufemia
S. Eufemia
G
U
D
E
C
A
Fondamenta S. Giacomo
Fondamenta della Croce
Chiesa del Redentore
Fondamenta delle Zitelle
Le Zitelle
Fondamenta S.Giovanni
Grazia
della
Canale
La Laguna

Scuola di San Giorgio degli Schiavoni

© Baedeker

Art

Venice occupies a special place in the history of art through its relations with the Greek Empire of the East. St Mark's Church is Byzantine in style, as are its earliest mosaics. Gothic, which reached Venice only in the 14th c., took on a different aspect here from the rest of Italy, displaying a lively fantasy and a wealth of decoration and colour. The Early Renaissance style came in the second half of the 15th c., producing buildings which cannot compare with those of Tuscany in harmony of proportions, since the façades seek above all to achieve a picturesque effect. Some of the Venetian churches, in particular Santi Giovanni e Paolo and the Frari church, are notable for their numerous fine tomb monuments. The leading architects of the period were Mauro Coducci, Antonio Rizzo and Pietro Lombardi, who were also sculptors, together with the Florentine Jacopo Sansovino, who brought the High Renaissance to Venice, and Andrea Palladio, whose influence was felt even by such vigorous exponents of the Baroque style as Vincenzo Scamozzi (1552–1616) and Baldassare Longhena (1604–82).

The sculptors working in Venice included Alessandro Leopardi (d. 1522) and, slightly later, Alessandro Vittoria (1525–1608). Among 15th c. painters were Vivarini and Jacopo Bellini (Mantegna's father-in-law), both from Murano, and Carlo Crivelli, a native of Venice. Jacopo's son Giovanni Bellini (c. 1430–1516), with his skill in composition and his love of colour, was the precursor of the great period of Venetian painting. Among his contemporaries were his elder brother Gentile Bellini (c. 1429–1507), Vittorio Carpaccio (c. 1455 to after 1523) and Cima da Congliano (c. 1459–1518). His greatest pupils were Girogione (c. 1477–1510, born in Castelfranco), Palma il Vecchio from Bergamo (c. 1480–1528) and the greatest of them all, Titian (Tiziano Vecellio, c. 1490–1576, born in Pieve di Cadore), who lavished his skill and vigorous imagination equally on representations of the Renaissance delight in life and on highly charged religious scenes, and enjoyed high favour as a portrait painter with the Italian princes as well as with Charles V and Philip II of Spain. The contemporaries of these three great masters included such artists as Sebastiano del Piombo, Lorenzo Lotto, Bonifazio dei Pitati, Pordenone and Paris Bordone.

The tradition was carried on by a younger generation which included Paolo Veronese (Caliari, 1528–88, born in Verona), the Bassano family and Palma il Giovane. A fresh lead was given by Jacopo Tintoretto (Robusti, 1518–94), whose works, combining vigorous light and colour with the expression of profound spiritual emotion, mark the high point of Venetian Baroque painting.

In the 18th c. the two Canalettos (Antonio Canal and his pupil Bernardo Bellotto) and the talented Francesco Guardi (1712–93) excelled in the painting of townscapes, Pietro Longhi (1702–85) in the depiction of contemporary manners. The last great Venetian painter, heir to a brilliant tradition of 300 years, was the decorative painter Giovanni Battista Tiepolo (1696–1770), notable for the glowing colour and spatial effect of his wall and ceiling paintings.

Piazzale Roma

At the end of the causeway from Mestre, on the mainland, is the Piazzale Roma, with a large parking area and multi-storey garage.

Boat services

A short distance north of the Piazzale Roma, on the Canale di Santa Chiara, is the landing-stage for the city boat services.

From the landing-stage there are motor-boats (motoscafi) to St Mark's Square. The trip along the Grand Canal takes 25 minutes, the more direct route by the Rio Nuovo 10 minutes.

There are also motor-launches (vaporetti) which ply along the Grand Canal to St Mark's Square (30 minutes), taking another 15 minutes to reach the Lido or San Giorgio Maggiore.

Canal Grande, the "main street" of Venice ▶

The famous gondolas (gondole) take about an hour to reach St Mark's Square.

Stazione di Santa
Lucia

Opposite, on the north side of the Canale di Santa Chiara, is the modern Stazione Santa Lucia (main station). In the street running from the station, the Lista di Spagna, are most of the hotels in the western part of the city.

★★Grand Canal

The Grand Canal (Canal Grande: 3.8km (2¹/₃mi.) long, with an average breadth of 70 m (230 ft) and depth of 5 m (16ft), Venice's principal traffic artery, starts from the station and traverses the city from north-west to south-east in a reversed S-curve; it gives an overwhelming impression of the wealth and splendour of Venice in its heyday with a continuous succession of great palaces of the princely Venetian merchants. Every style of architecture from the 12th to the early 18th c. is represented along the Grand Canal. Particularly charming is the Venetian Gothic style with its fantastic arcades; and the Early Renaissance buildings are scarcely less splendid. The posts (pali) in front of the steps leading into the palaces, painted in their owner's heraldic colours, serve to protect the gondolas lying at their moorings.

★★Piazza San Marco

From the Riva degli Schiavoni we cross the Piazzetta and walk past the Doge's Palace into St Mark's Square (Piazza di San Marco, or the "Piazza" for short), the hub of the city's life and one of the world's finest squares, giving striking evidence of Venice's past greatness and still serving as a setting for great occasions (concerts, etc.). The square, 175 m (574 ft) long and up to 82 m (269 ft) wide, is paved with slabs of trachyte and marble and lined on three sides by tall arcades housing shops and cafés. The square is particularly beautiful on bright moonlit nights. The innumerable pigeons (colombi, piccioni) are regularly fed.

Procuratie

On the north and south sides of the square are the Procuratie, formerly the administrative offices of the procurators, the highest officials of the Republic.

Procuratie Vecchie

The Procuratie Vecchie on the north side were built from 1514 onwards, and are a fine example of Venetian Early Renaissance. The façade is decorated with arcades on the ground and top floor.

Museo
Archeologico

The Procuratie Nuove on the south side were begun in 1584 by Vincenzo Scamozzi and used from the time of Napoleon I as a royal palace. The former residence of the procurators now houses the archaeological museum (Museo Archeologico). Its entrance is at the Libreria Marciana (Piazzeta No. 17). The museum provides a unique comparison of the ancient archaeological finds with the art of the Renaissance. Here the observer will notice the influence of ancient art on the artists of the Renaissance.

★Museo Correr

Along the west end of the square is the Ala Napoleonica, a linking wing added in 1810 on Napoleon's request, which houses the Museo Correr, with an excellent collection illustrating the history and culture of Venice, including pictures by old masters.

★★Campanile di
San Marco

At the south-east corner of St Mark's Square rises the Campanile of St Mark (Campanile di San Marco), a 96.8 m (319¹/₂ft) high bell-tower rebuilt in 1905–12 after the collapse of the original campanile in 1902; from the top (lift) there are fine views. The Loggetta on the east side of the campanile (by Jacopo Sansovino, 1540) was originally the meeting-place of the Venetian nobles.

Campanile di San Marco, the symbol of Venice ▶

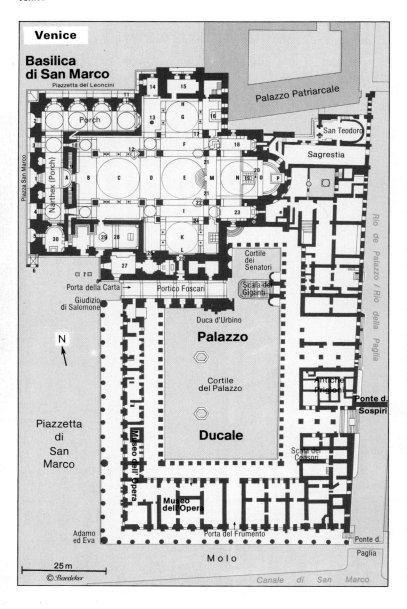

Venice

Basilica di San Marco

Piazzetta dei Leoncini

Palazzo Patriarcale

Porch

San Teodoro

Sagrestia

Piazza San Marco

Narthex (Porch)

Palazzo Patriarcale

Cortile dei Senatori

Scala dei Giganti

Porta della Carta

Portico Foscari

Giudizio di Salomone

Duca d'Urbino

Palazzo

N

Cortile del Palazzo

Antiche Prigioni

Ponte d. Sospiri

Piazzetta di San Marco

Ducale

Museo dell' Opera

Scala dei Censori

Museo dell'Opera

Adamo ed Eva

Porta del Frumento

Ponte d. Paglia

Rio de Palazzo / Rio della Paglia

Molo

25 m

© Baedeker

Canale di San Marco

Near the mouth of the Canal Grande is the church of Santa Maria della Salute

Almost opposite the campanile, at the east end of the Procuratie Vecchie, Torre dell'Orologio
is the Clock Tower (Torre dell'Orologio, 1496–99); on the platform are two
bronze moors (1497) which strike the bell every hour.

At the foot of the Clock Tower an arched gateway leads into the Merceria
(shopping street).

★★Basilica di San Marco

St Mark's Church (Basilica di San Marco), dedicated to the Evangelist Mark,
whose remains are in the high altar, was begun in 829, rebuilt after a fire
in 976 and remodelled in the 11th c. in Byzantine style with an Oriental

1 Main portal	17 Altare di San Pietro	**MOSAICS**
2–5 Portal recesses	18 Cappella di San Pietro	A Arch of Paradise
6 Pietra del Bando	19 High Altar	B Arch of the Apocalypse
7 Pilastri Acritani	20 Pala d'Oro	C Scenes of Pentecost
8 Sculpture of the Tetrarchs	21 Iconostasis	D Scenes from the Passion
9 Stairs up to the Museo	22 Reliquary	E The Ascension
Marciano	23 Cappella di San Clemente	F St Michael with sword
10 Porta di San Pietro	24 Altare di San Giacomo	G St John
11 Porta dei Fiori	25 Passage to the Doges'	H Mary's family tree
12 Capitello del Crocifisso	Palace	I The Washing of the Feet,
(Capital of the Cross)	26 Entrance to the Treasury	Temptation in the Wilderness
13 Romanesque stoup with	27 Tesoro (Treasury), with	K St Leonard
angels (12th c.)	goldsmiths' work, etc.	L Four miracles of Jesus
14 Cappella della Madonna dei	28 Battistero (Baptistery)	M St Peter, The Resurrection,
Mascoli	29 Font dating from 1546	etc.
15 Cappella di Sant'Isidoro	30 Cappella Zen, named	N Choir mosaics
16 Cappella della Madonna	after Cardinal G. B. Zen	O Lamb of God
Nicopeia	(d. 1501)	P Christ in Majesty, with Saints

lavishness of decoration. 76.5 m (251 ft) long by 51.75 m (170 ft) wide, it has the form of a Greek cross, with five domes. Externally and internally it is adorned with ancient marble columns, mostly from the East. Until 1981 there stood above the main doorway four bronze horses from Constantinople, 1.6 m (5¼ft) high, the only surviving example of the four-horse team of an ancient quadriga. They have been replaced by copies and the originals are in the Museo di San Marco. Two of the original horses are in Roman style (4th c.), the remaining two are in Greek style (4th–3rd c. BC).

Interior

The interior of St Mark's is notable for the beauty of its lines and the picturesque and constantly changing vistas which it affords. The vaulting is decorated with mosaics, most of them dating back to 1160–1200, depicting scenes from the lives of the Virgin and Christ (Passion and Ascension).

Pala d'Oro

On the high altar the Pala d'Oro is a masterpiece of enamel work set with jewels, originally an altar frontal made in Constantinople (best side to rear). Its completion took about five centuries.

Treasury

In the south transept is the valuable Treasury (Tresoro) filled with precious objects the Venetians brought back from Constantinople after its conquest in 1204.

Cappella Zen

In the Cappella Zen can be seen the fine tomb of Cardinal Giambattista Zen (d. 1501).

Museo di San Marco

From the gallery (entrance at main doorway, on the left) there is access to the outer gallery and the bronze horses. Adjoining the gallery the Museo di San Marco, the Church Museum, houses 15th c. tapestries, Byzantine sculpture (12th c.) and pictures.

Mosaics in St Mark's Church

★Piazzetta di San Marco

On the south-east side of St Mark's Square, extending to the Canale di San
Marco, is the Piazzetta di San Marco. Near the water's edge, on the Molo,
where the gondoliers wait for custom, are two granite columns from Syria
or Constantinople, erected here in 1180, topped by a figure of St Theodore
(copy, original in Palazzo Ducale), Venice's earlier patron saint, and the
winged lion of St Mark.

On the west side of the square is the Library (Libreria Marciana), Jacopo
Sansovino's finest work (1536–53). The building houses the celebrated
Library of St Mark (Biblioteca Nazionale Marziana; tour by appointment).
The ceiling painting in the vestibule is by Titian (1560), and part of the
ceiling of the Hall of Honour was painted by Veronese; the walls have
portraits of philosophers, including works by Tintoretto.

Libreria Marciana
(Library)

   The rooms contain manuscripts, illuminated books, etc. The original
Library of St Mark is now housed in the former Mint (Zecca; 1536), which
is connected to the exhibition rooms.

In the Castello quarter to the north, in the Renaissance Palazzo Ducale, is
the Diocesan Museum (Museo Diocesano). The treasures of the museum
include liturgical vessels and silver work.

Museo Diocesano

★★Doge's Palace

The east side of the Piazzetta is occupied by the Doge's Palace (Palazzo
Ducale), said to have been the residence of the Doges since about 814. The
oldest part of the present building is the 71 m (233 ft) long south wing on
the Molo (1309–40); the 75 m (246 ft) long west wing facing on to the
Piazzetta was added in 1424–38).

   The main feature of the building is the upper part of the battlemented
façade, decorated with coloured marble in a lozenge pattern.

The Doge's Palace, the most famous secular building in Venice

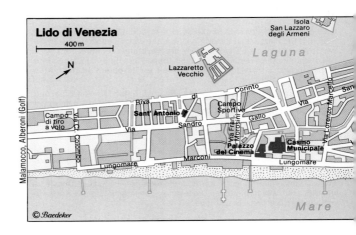

Around the ground floor runs a beautiful arcade with free-standing columns, and above this is the Loggia, with elegant pointed arches and quatrefoil decoration in Venetian Gothic style. Large windows and a Gothic balcony on each side give relief to the marble block above this.

Loggia

The Gothic Porta delle Carta leads into the magnificent Cortile dei Senatori, a courtyard which shows a picturesque mingling of Late Gothic and Early Renaissance styles.

Interior

The interior of the palace is reached from the courtyard by way of the Scala dei Giganti and the Scala d'Oro, which lead to the upper floors, with the State Apartments, redecorated after damage by fire in 1574 and 1577. Notable features of these rooms – magnificent examples of the Late Renaissance and Baroque periods – are the richly decorated and gilded ceilings and the numerous pictures (by Titian, Paolo Veronese, Tintoretto and other artists) glorifying Venice and its doges in historical scenes and allegories.

Museo dell'Opera

The Museo dell'Opera on the ground floor of the Doge's Palace houses original items of the decoration of the palace which had to be replaced by copies.

Sala del Maggior Consiglio

On the second floor the Sala del Maggior Consiglio (54 m (177 ft) long) has scenes from the history of Venice on its walls. On the frieze are 76 portraits of doges ranging in date from 804 to 1559, and on the entrance wall is Tintoretto's "Paradise", the largest oil painting in the world (24.65 m by 7.45 m (81 ft by 24½ ft) high). From the balcony of the Sala there are magnificent views of the lagoon, the islands of San Giorgio Maggiore and Giudecca, and the Lido.

Doge's Private Apartments

In the east wing are the Doge's Private Apartments (Appartamento Ducale), which escaped damage in the fire.

Sala del Senato

On the third floor are the large Sala del Senato, the meeting-place of the Senate, with pictures by Tintoretto, Palma il Giovane and other artists, and the Sala d'Armi, the armoury of the Republic, with a fine collection of weapons.

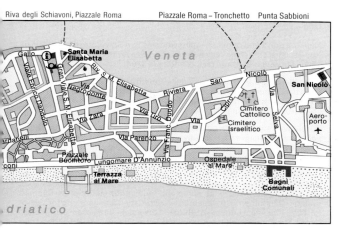

Riva degli Schiavoni, Piazzale Roma Piazzale Roma – Tronchetto Punta Sabbioni

From the first floor of the palace visitors can enter the Prigioni, dark and   Prigioni
dismal cellars with which are associated a torture chamber and place of
execution.

From the Doge's Palace the Molo runs east to the Ponte della Paglia   ★Bridge of Sighs
("Straw Bridge"), from which there is a good view, to the left, of the Bridge
of Sighs (Ponte dei Sospiri), built about 1595 to link the palace with the
Prigioni (erected 1571–97), its name recalling the sighs of the criminals led
over the bridge to the place of execution.

★Riva degli Schiavoni

From the Ponte della Paglia we go straight ahead and come to the Riva
degli Schiavoni, a busy and lively promenade 500 m long with several
landing-stages for boats serving the city and the lagoon (including services
to the Lido), and fine views of the passenger vessels in the harbour.

Beyond the second bridge the Sottoportico San Zaccaria, on left, leads to   San Zaccaria
the nearby church of San Zaccaria (15th c.), which contains (to the left, on
the second altar) a "Madonna Enthroned" by Giovanni Bellini (1505).

North-east of San Zaccaria is the Scuola di San Giorgio degli Schiavoni, the   Scuola di San
house of the brotherhood of the Dalmatian merchants, the "Schiavoni". In   Giorgio degli
the beginning of the 16th c. Vittore Carpaccio decorated t with cycles of   Schiavoni
pictures, which today are among the greatest art treasures of the city.

On the continuation of the Riva degli Schiavoni are the Giardini Pubblici   Giardini Pubblici
(landing-stage for motor-launches), a beautiful municipal park with the
Paradiso café-restaurant and the galleries used for the Biennale d'Arte, the
international art exhibition held every other year from June to September.

Surroundings of the Merceria

The narrow Merceria (Marzaria), which leaves the north-east corner of St
Mark's Square, by the Clock-Tower, and runs north-west under various
names (Merceria San Zuliàn, etc.) is the city's principal shopping street,

providing a direct link between St Mark's Square and the Rialto Bridge (500 m).

San Salvatore | Near the north end of the shopping street is San Salvatore, the finest High Renaissance church in Venice (by Giorgio Spavento and Tullio Lombardi, 1506–34), with a Baroque façade added in 1704.

Santa Maria Formosa | From Merceria San Zuliàn, beyond the church of San Giuliano (San Zuliàn), Calle della Guerra and Calle delle Bande lead to the church of Santa Maria Formosa, which contains in the second chapel to the right of high altar a "St Barbara" by Palma Vecchio.

Palazzo Querini-Stampalia | A little way south of the church is the Palazzo Querini-Stampalia, with a collection of pictures by Venetian artists of the 14th–18th c., including works by Donato Veneziano, Palma the Younger, Giovanni Bellini, Lorenzo di Credi, Palma the Elder, Pietro Longhi, Alessandro Longhi and Tiepolo.

★★Statue of Colleoni | From Santa Maria Formosa we go along Calle Lunga and turn into the street on left (Calle Cicogna) to reach the Campo Santi Giovanni e Paolo, with the church of the same name and the famous statue of Bartolomeo Colleoni (Monumento di Colleoni), a mercenary leader working for Venice (d. 1475), the finest equestrian statue of the Italian Renaissance, modelled by the Florentine sculptor Andrea del Verrochio in 1481–88 and cast by Alessandro Leopardi in 1496. The statue depicts the ideal of a proud and mighty condottiere.

Santi Giovanni e Paolo | The former Dominican church of Santi Giovanni e Paolo (San Zanipolo), a Gothic brick-built structure (1246–30) is the burial-place of many doges, and contains numerous handsome monuments (the finest being that of Doge Andrea Vendramin, on the north side of the choir).

To the left of the church stands the Scuola di San Marco (now a hospital), with a richly decorated Renaissance façade (1485–95).

★Santa Maria dei Miracoli | A little way west the church of Santa Maria dei Miracoli, an elegant Early Renaissance building by Pietro and Tullio Lombardi (1481–89), is entirely clad in marble both externally and internally. The church is dedicated to a miraculous picture of the Virgin.

Sights in the south-west

Campo Francesco Morosini | From the south-west corner of St Mark's Square we go along a busy shopping street, the Salizzada San Moisè, with the Baroque church of the same name, and its continuation Calle Larga XXII Marzo, passing the Baroque church of Santa Maria Zobenigo, to reach the large Campo Francesco Morosini.

★Teatro La Fenice | On our way to the square we pass (to the east) the Teatro La Fenice (1790–1792), the largest theatre in Venice (1500 seats).

Palazzo Pisani | To the south of the Campo Francesco Morosini the Palazzo Pisani a Santo Stefano (now the Conservatoire) is a good example of a wealthy merchant's mansion of the Baroque period.

★★Gallerie dell'Accademia

To the south-west of the Palazzo Pisani is the Ponte dell'Accademia, which leads to the Accademia di Belle Arti with the Gallerie dell'Accademia, in premises once occupied by the convent of Santa Maria della Carità. The academy's picture gallery contains more than 800 pictures, mainly by Venetian artists and including some works of the highest quality, which give an excellent survey of the achievement of the Venetian schools.

Among the outstanding works in the collection are the brilliantly coloured pictures of Venetian life by Gentile Bellini (in Room XX) and Vittore Carpaccio (including nine scenes from the legend of St Ursula, Room XXI); beautiful religious paintings by Giovanni Bellini (particularly in Rooms IV and V); and masterpieces by Giorgione (including "The Storm", the finest work in the collection, Room V); Titian ("Presentation of the Virgin", Room XXIV; "Lamentation", his last picture, completed by Palma il Giovane, Room X); Paris Bordone ("Presentation of the Ring", Room VI); Jacopo Tintoretto (particularly the large pictures from the Scuola di San Marco in Room X and other works in Rooms VI and XI) and Paolo Veronese ("Jesus in the House of Levi", 12.3 × 5.7 m (40 × 19 ft), one of the artist's finest works, Room X).

The collection also includes notable pictures by Mantegna ("St George", Room IV), Cima de Conegliano, Pietro Longhi, Francesco Guardi, Sebastiano Ricci, Palma Vecchio, Piero della Francesca, Lotto, Tiepolo, Antonia Canaletto, Alvise, Bartolomeo and Antonio Vivarini.

★★I Frari

From the Accademia landing-stage we can take the motor-launch north to the next landing place, San Tomà. A short distance north-west is the former Franciscan church of I Frari or Santa Maria Gloriosa dei Frari, a brick-built Gothic basilica (1338) with a tall campanile, the largest and most beautiful church in Venice after St Mark's. Like Santi Giovanni e Paolo, it is the burial-place of many famous Venetians. On the high altar is Titian's "Assumption", the finest work of his early period (1516–18). In the north aisle, beside the tomb of Bishop Jacopo Pesaro, is Titian's "Madonna of the House of Pesaro" (1519–26).

The adjoining monastery houses the State Archives of Venice, one of the finest collections of the kind in the world.

From the Franciscan church it is only a few steps to the Scuola di San Rocco (1524–60), an impressive structure built in white marble. The school is famous for its large wall and ceiling paintings by Tintoretto (16th c.), depicting scenes from the New Testament. ★Scuola di San Rocco

Opposite, on the north, the church of San Rocco has a façade of 1771 and some fine pictures by Tintoretto. San Rocco

From here we cross the Campo San Stin to reach the Scuola di San Giovanni Evangelista, with an outer courtyard in the style of Pietro Lombardo (1481) and a staircase by Moro Coducci (d. 1504). Scuola di San Giovanni Evangelista

Isola della Giudecca

On the long island of Giudecca, lying to the south of the main part of the city and separated from it by the Canale della Giudecca (300 m (984 ft) wide), is the conspicuous church of the Redentore, formerly belonging to the Franciscans. Built in 1577–92, by Palladio; after his death it was completed by his pupils. It has two slender round towers to the rear of the central dome and a harmoniously proportioned interior. On the high altar are marble reliefs by Giuseppe Mazza and bronze statues by Girolamo Campagna. Il Redentore

★★Isola di San Giorgio Maggiore

East of La Giudecca lies the little island of San Giorgio Maggiore, with the prominent monastic church of the same name, a domed structure begun by Palladio in 1565 and completed in 1610. It has fine Baroque choir-stalls and contains several pictures by Tintoretto. From the 60 m (198 ft) high campanile (entrance from choir) there is the finest view in Venice.

Venice

Fondazione
Giorgio Cini

The former monastic buildings (beautiful staircase by Longhena, two cloisters) have been occupied since 1951 by the Fondazione Giorgio Cini, which is concerned with the promotion of research on the cultural history of Venice. There is also an international art and culture centre with 30 rooms, a theatre and an open-air theatre.

★Lido di Venezia

From the Riva degli Schiavoni it is a 15 minutes' trip by motor-launch to the Lido, the northern part of the spit of land known as the Malamocco which borders the east side of the lagoon. The Lido was once Italy's most famous seaside resort, with numerous hotels, pensions and summer villas.

From the Santa Maria Elisabetta landing-stage the Gran Viale Santa Maria Elisabetta runs across the spit to the Hôtel des Bains. South of the hotel is the Lungomare G. Marconi, a large square in which are the Casino Municipale and the Palazzo del Cinema (1937–52), the scene of the Biennale film festival. On the Lido there are also numerous sporting facilities (golf-course, tennis courts, riding).

Lido di Iesolo

From the Lido there is a motor-boat service (and also a car ferry) to the Punta Sabbioni, from which a road runs 20 km (12 mi.) north to the large resort of Lido di Iesolo (2 m (7 ft); population 6000)). With its beautiful broad beach Lido di Iesolo ranks with Rimini, Riccione and the Venice Lido as one of the most popular resorts on the Adriatic.

★Murano

From the Fondamente Nuovo, the seaside promenade on the north side of Venice there is a motor-launch service (landing-stage near the church of the Gesuiti: 10 minutes), passing the cemetery island of San Michele, to the little town of Murano (population 8000), on the island of the same name, which has been the main centre of the Venetian glass industry since the end of the 13th c. A few minutes from the Colonna landing-stage is the church of San Pietro Martire (15th c., restored 1511), which has a beautiful Madonna by Giovanni Bellini (1488) in the south aisle. Beyond this, on the far side of the main canal, stands the cathedral of Santi Maria e Donata (12th c.), with fine columns of Greek marble, a mosaic pavement and a Byzantine mosaic in the apse. Near the cathedral is the Town Hall, with the Museo dell'Arte Vetraria (products of the local glass-making industry, which had its heyday in the 15th and 16th c.). Now each glass-blowing workshop has a shop where Murano glass can be bought.

★Torcello

8 km (5 mi.) NE

Another very attractive boat trip is to the picturesque little fishing town of Burano (population 5500), centre of the Venetian lace-making industry, and the island of Torcello, with the ancient little town of the same name. Torcello has a beautiful cathedral (Santa Maria Assunta, 7th–11th c.), with fine mosaics (13th–15th c.) and a campanile, from the top of which there are far-ranging views. Near the octagonal church of Santa Fosca (11th c.) the 14th c. Palazzo dei Consigli houses the Museo dell'Estuario, with pictures, sculptures and objects d'art of several centuries.

★Chioggia

45 km (28 mi.) S

Near the south end of the Venice lagoon (on SS309, the Strada Romea, from Marghera) lies the interesting island town of Chioggia (2 m (7ft); population 50,000), formerly the centre of Venetian salt production, destroyed

Torcello: Romanesque Cathedral of Santa Maria Assunta

by the Genoese in 1379 and now a large fishing port. With its narrow streets of old houses, picturesque in decay, its canals and its bustling life and activity, it is a popular resort of artists. In the main street the Corso del Popolo, are the cathedral (rebuilt by Longhena), with a 64 m (211 ft) high campanile (14th c.), and the little Gothic church of San Martino (1392).

A bridge 800 m (2625 ft) long leads from the old town of Chioggia to Sottomarina (2 m (7 ft)), a popular bathing resort.

Sottomarina

20 km (12 mi.) south-east of Sottomarina is the lagoon island of Albarella, a tourist resort with many facilities, including a tennis and riding centre, an 18-hole golf course, and a yacht harbour.

Albarella

Verona

F5

Region: Veneto. Province: Verona (VR)
Altitude: 59 m (195 ft). Population: 255,000

Verona, capital of the province of the same name, lies at the point where the River Adige emerges from the Alps into the north Italian plain. The main part of the town is situated below the Alpine foothills of the Altipiano dei Lessini on a peninsula enclosed on two sides by the rapidly flowing Adige and linked with the districts on the left bank by ten bridges.
   Verona, a city rich in art and architecture, lies about 80 km (50 mi.) from Venice and the Adriatic.

Location

It is also a considerable commercial centre, handling the produce (particularly fruit and vegetables) of the province's fertile irrigated soil.

Economy

Verona, which still preserved the name of the prehistoric settlement on this site, became a Roman colony in 89 BC and thereafter developed into a town

History

Verona

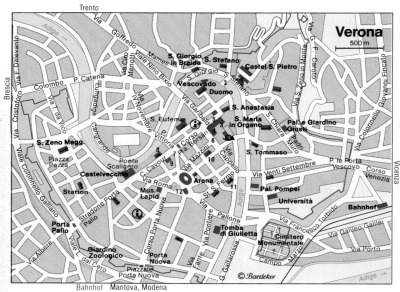

1 Teatro Romano / Museo Archeologico
2 Ponte della Pietra
3 Arche Scaligere
4 Palazzo della Regione

5 Loggia del Consiglio
6 Piazza delle Erbe
7 Porta dei Borsari
8 San Lorenzo

9 Palazzo Bevilacqua
10 Santa Maria della Scala
11 San Fermo Maggiore
12 Rathaus

of considerable importance, as the remains of the amphitheatre and other buildings testify. In the 6th c. the Ostrogothic king Theodoric (d. 626) made it one of his royal residences, together with Pavia and Ravenna. During the Frankish period Charlemagne's son Pepin reigned here as king of Italy, and later the Saxon and Hohenstaufen emperors found the town, situated at the end of the road over the Brenner, a convenient base from which to control Italy. From the middle of the 13th c. Verona was ruled by the Ghibelline family of Della Scala (the Scaligers), but in 1387 they were expelled by the Viscontis. In 1405 the town passed into the hands of Venice.

During the Austrian period (1814–66) Verona became a fortress town, forming with Peschiera, Mantova and Legnago the famous defensive "quadrilaterial". In 1866 it was incorporated in the united Kingdom of Italy.

Art

Verona is notable for its fine Romanesque churches (11th c.), but is was also a considerable artistic centre in the Renaissance period, particularly in the field of architecture. Its leading architects were the Dominican monk Fra Giocondo (c. 1433–1515) and Michele Sammichele (1484–1559). Sammichele sought to embellish his works of fortifications by the use of classical architectural forms, erected numerous splendid buildings and built the bastioned town walls (1530 onwards).

Old town

Piazza delle Erbe

The central feature of the old town is the elongated Piazza delle Erbe, one of the most picturesque squares in Italy, on the site of the Roman forum (now a fruit and vegetable market). In the centre of the square is the Berlina (16th c.), a canopy borne on four columns, formerly used for the

Verona and the River Adige

election of the Signori and the Podestà. To the north of it is the Market Fountain (1368), with the "Madonna Verona", an ancient marble statue (restored). At the north end of the square the Marble Column bears the lion of St Mark, the emblem of Venetian authority. At the north-east corner stands the Casa Mazzanti, originally built by the Scaligers; like many houses in the town, it is adorned with Renaissance frescoes. On the north side of the square is the Baroque Palazzzo Maffei (1668), and to the left of this the Torre del Gardello (1370). The Casa dei Mercanti at the corner of Via Pellicciai was rebuilt in 1878 in its original form (1301). Opposite rises the 84m/277ft high Torre del Lamberti, with a medieval bell, "E Rengo", used as a storm warning (lift to the top; view).

The short street to the left of the Torre del Comune runs east into the Piazza dei Signori (a name recalling the rule of the Scaligers), surrounded by palaces. In the centre is a monument to Dante (1865). Recent excavations have uncovered Roman mosaics and other remains. ★Piazza dei Signori

The Palazzo della Ragione (Town Hall), on the south side of the square, was begun in 1193 but much altered in later centuries; the main front is Renaissance (1524). In the courtyard are a Gothic grand staircase (1446–50) and the entrance to the Torre del Comune.

Also in the square are a battlemented tower and the Palazzo dei Tribunali, formerly the Palazzo del Capitano with a Renaissance doorway by Michele Sammichele, converted in 1530–31 from a Scaliger Palace. On the east side of the square we find the Palazzo del Governo (Prefecture), originally another Scaliger palace, rebuilt in the 16th c. (doorway by Sammichele, 1532).

On the north side of the Piazza dei Signori stands the Loggia del Consiglio, one of the finest Early Renaissance buildings in Italy (by Fra Giocondo, 1486–93), crowned by statues of famous citizens of Verona in antiquity. ★Loggia del Consiglio

Piazza dei Signori

★Santa Maria Antica

The passage between the Prefecture and the Tribunal leads to the church of Santa Maria Antica (12th c.), with a Romanesque campanile. Adjoining it are the imposing Gothic Tombs of the Scaligers (Arche Scaligere), with the ladder (scala) which was the heraldic emblem of the family frequently recurring in the elaborate wrought-iron railings. Above the church door are the sarcophagus and a copy of an equestrian statue of Cangrande della Scala (d. 1329); to the left are seen the mural monument of Giovanni (d. 1359) and the sarcophagus of Mastino I (d. 1277). Within the railings, under a canopy, are the sarcophagi and equestrian statues of Mastino II (d. 1351) and Cansignorio (d. 1375).

Sant'Anastasia

To the north of the tombs, at the end of the Corso Sant'Anastasia, on the Adige, is the Dominican church of Sant'Anastasia, a brick-built Gothic structure (1290–1323, 1422–81) with a magnificent interior (richly decorated altars of the 15th–18th c., frescos, etc.). The nearby Palazzo Forti houses the Galleria d'Arte Moderna.

Cathedral

From here it is a short distance north-west to the cathedral, a 12th c. Romanesque basilica with a 15th c. Gothic nave. Adjoining it is a campanile on a Romanesque base, designed by Sammichele but not completed until 1927. On the beautiful main doorway of the cathedral are figures of Charlemagne's two paladins Roland and Oliver (c. 1139–53). Within the church, on the first altar on the left, is an "Assumption" by Titian (1525), at the end of the south aisle the Gothic tomb of St Agatha (1353). Note also the red marble pillars and marble choir-screen.

To the left of the cathedral is a Romanesque cloister (1123), with an Early Christian mosaic pavement on a lower level.

Ponte Garibaldi

From the cathedral we continue towards the river and cross the Ponte Garibaldi to the left bank.

Verona: the cathedral façade ▶

Verona

Detail from the Church of Sant'Anastasia   *The famous "Juliet" Balcony*

Porta dei Borsari	On to the right bank of the Adige, we go upstream along the Lungadige Panvinio (views) and then turn left past the church of Sant'Eufemia into the Corso Porta Borsari, which begins at the Piazza delle Erbe. At its west end is the Porta dei Borsari, one of the Roman city gates (1st c. AD; restored in 265).

Corso Cavour to the Amphitheatre

Castelvecchio	Farther west the Corso Cavour, once the main street of Verona, is flanked by fine old palaces. On the left (No. 19) is the imposing Palazzo Bevilacqua (by Sammichele, 1530), with the Romanesque church of San Lorenzo (c. 1110) opposite. At the end of the Corso Cavour, on the banks of the Adige, stands the Castelvecchio, built by the Scaligers in 1354–55; from the platform of the main tower (completed 1375) there are extensive views. The castle now houses the Civico Museo d'Arte, which contains Veronese sculpture, applied art and an excellent picture gallery with works of the 15th–16th c. Veronese school.
Ponte Scaligero	Below the castle the Adige is spanned by the fine Ponte Scaligero (14th c.; restored 1949–51 after wartime destruction).
Piazza Brà	To the south of Corso Cavour and linked with it by a number of streets is the spacious Piazza Brà (from Latin pratum, "meadow"). On the north side of the square, near the end of Via Mazzini, is the Palazzo Malfatti, by Sammichele. Opposite it stands an equestrian statue of Victor Emmanuel II (1883).
★★Amphitheatre	The Roman Amphitheatre (Arena), one of the largest of its kind, on the east side of the square, was built in the reign of Diocletian (c. AD 290). Of the outer wall only four arches on the north side have survived. With its 44 rows

The Arena now serves as an open-air theatre

of seating it can accommodate some 22,000 spectators; from the top rows there are fine views. The overall length of the structure was 152 m (499 ft), its height 32 m (16ft). In July and August a famous operatic festival is held in the Arena.

On the south side of the Piazza Brà is the Palazzo Municipale or Town Hall (1836–38, semicircular extension built after 1945). To the right the long building of the Gran Guardi was the old guard-house (1614), and adjoining this the Portoni della Brà, an old gateway and tower. Beyond this are the Museo Lapidario Maffeiano (Lapidarium) and the Teatro Filarmonico (opera).

Palazzo Municipale

From the Piazza delle Erbe Via Cappello, with the so-called Casa di Giuletta (Gothic, 13th c. – Juliet's House with her balcony), and its continuation Via Leoni (on left, the Roman Porta del Leoni) runs south-east to the church of San Fermo Maggiore, with a Romanesque lower church (11th–12th c.; 14th c. wooden crucifix) and a Gothic upper church (13th–14th c.), its façade beautifully decorated with marble. It contains a number of notable monuments and pictures by Pisanello and others.
Immediately beyond the church is the Ponte delle Navi.

★San Fermo Maggiore

In the Campo di Fiera, near the Adige in the southern part of the town, visitors are shown, in a cloister built in 1899, a medieval trough which purports to be the coffin of Juliet Capulet (Tomba di Giuletta), Shakespeare's heroine. On Via Cappello stands the Casa di Giuletta, a 13th c. building said to be Juliet's residence, with the famous balcony.

Tomba di Giuletta

Casa di Giuletta

Corsa di Porta Nuova to the Basilica of San Zeno

Passing through the Portoni della Brà, we follow the wide Corso di Porta Nuova to the Porta Nuova (by Sammichele), beyond which is the principal railway station, the Stazione di Porta Nuova.

Porta Nuova

From the Porta Nuova we follow the tree-lined avenue inside the old walls, past the zoo and come to the magnificent Porta Palio (by Sammichele, 16th c.).

Porta Palio

From here we go east along the wide Stradone di Porta Palio and then turn left into Via Aurelio Saffi to reach the former Franciscan church of San Bernardino (15th c.), with a large arcaded courtyard (gravestones, remains of frescoes). The Cappella Pellegrini (begun by Sammichele before 1554) has fine Renaissance decoration.

San Bernardino

Verona

★San Zeno
Maggiore

To the north of San Bernardino is the large Basilica of San Zeno Maggiore (11th–12th c.), perhaps the finest Romanesque building in northern Italy, with a beautiful main front flanked by a slender Romanesque campanile (1045–1178) and the battlemented defensive tower (14th c.) of a former Benedictine abbey. The bronze doors have Romanesque reliefs with Biblical and other scenes. The interior boasts an unusual timber roof (14th c.) and beautiful Romanesque capitals, and in the aisles are frescoes of the 13th–15th c. In the choir can be seen a marble figure, ascribed to the 14th c., of St Zeno, bishop of Verona (d. 380), whose reliquary is in the crypt. On the high altar is a "Madonna with Saints" by Mantegna (1456–59) and on the north side of the church an elegant Romanesque cloister.

Sights on the left bank of the Adige

Giardino Giusti

Beyond the Ponte delle Navi, going north-east through the Interrato dell'Acqua Morta and then turning right into Via Carducci, we come to the Palazzo Giusti (1580) and the Giardino Giusti, with beautiful old cypresses (delightful views from the terrace).

Santa Maria in
Organo

Farther north is the church of Santa Maria in Organo, originally founded in the Lombard period and rebuilt in Renaissance style in 1481, with an unfinished façade designed by Sammichele (1592). The choir has fine stalls by Fra Giovanni da Verona (1519).

Roman Theatre

Beyond the Roman bridge, the Ponte della Pietra, on the hillside, below the commandingly situated Castel San Pietro, is the Roman Theatre (Teatro Romano), with remains of the stage wall; built in the reign of Augustus, it was excavated between 1904 and 1939.

Archaeological
Museum

Near the theatre in the former Convento di San Girolamo, the Archaeological Museum (Museo Archeologico) contains prehistoric and Roman material.

Santo Stefano

A little way north of the Roman theatre stands the Romanesque church of Santo Stefano, a very ancient building (originally 5th–8th c.) with two ambulatories round the choir (8th c. capitals); the choir itself contains an episcopal throne of 1000. The façade bears interesting inscriptions.

★San Giorgio in
Braida

Farther west the 16th c. church of San Giorgio in Braida has a beautiful dome by Sammichele. The altarpieces are by masters of the Veronese and Brescian schools. On the high altar is "The Martyrdom of St George" by Veronese. In a side chapel is a notable Madonna by Girolamo dai Libri.

Surroundings

In the countryside around Verona are a number of beautiful villas, especially in the north and west towards Lake Garda. These include the Villa Sarego Boccoli near Pedemonte, designed by Palladio and modelled on houses from the ancient world; it was never completed.

Villafranca di
Verona
16 km (10 mi.) SW

South-west of Verona, on the River Tione, is Villafranca di Verona (54 m (178 ft); population 25,000), with a ruined castle, part of the "Serraglio", the frontier fortifications of Verona, which extend to Valeggio, 9 km (5½ mi.) west. In 1859 an armistice agreement was made in Villafranca between France and Austria.

In Valeggio is the well-tended park of Sigurtà.

East of Verona is the little medieval town of Soave (40 m (´32 ft); population 6000), renowned for its white wine, with battlemented town walls and towers and fine palaces.

★**Soave**
15km (9 mi.) E

Giazza

Another attractive excursion from Verona (north) is to the beautiful uplands of Monti Lessini and Giazza (758 m (2501 ft)), the only one of the "Tredici Comuni" (Thirteen Communes) inhabited by the descendants of settlers from Bavaria and Tirol, and where German is still spoken.

45 km (28 mi.) N

See entry.

Lake Garda

★★Vesuvius   J14

Region: Campania. Province: Napoli (NA)

Rearing abruptly out of the plain some 15 km (9 mi.) south-east of Naples on the shores of the bay of Naples, Vesuvius has been since the 17th c. the only volcano on the European mainland which is still intermittently active.

Location

The height of Vesuvius has varied over time, since every eruption of any violence alters the shape of the summit; at present it is 1281 m (4227 ft) high. The crater now has a circumference of 1.4 km (1 mi.), a maximum diameter of 600 m (1969 ft) and a depth of 216 m (709 ft); before the last major eruption in 1944 the circumference was 3.4 km (2 mi.).

North-east of the main crater, and separated from it by the deep valley known as the Atrio del Cavallo, is Monte Somma (1132 m (3736 ft)), a relic of the caldera of an older volcano which had a diameter of 4 km (2½ mi.).

Monte Somma

Vesuvius first emerged in the Quaternary in the form of an island. In antiquity it was regarded as extinct until the violent eruption on August 24th in the year AD 79 which destroyed Pompeii, Herculaneum, Stabiae and a number of smaller places.

Eruptions

Between that date and 1139 there were 15 eruptions, after which the volcano appeared to be quiescent, and woodland and scrub spread right up to the rim of the crater. In 1631, however, it came back to life with a fearsome eruption. The last eruption was on March 10th 1944, when the funicular from Ercolano (then known as Resina) up the mountain was destroyed. Since then Vesuvius – as is normally the case for a few years after a major eruption – has remained inactive apart from a number of fumaroles.

The ash cone and the more recent lava flows are almost devoid of vegetation, but the older weathered lavas form a fertile soil for the growth of oaks and chestnuts at medium heights and of fruit and vines (Lacrima Christi wine) below 500 m (1640 ft).

Ascent of Vesuvius

For the ascent of Vesuvius, leave the Naples-Salerno motorway at the Ercolano exit and take the Strada del Vesuvio, which winds its way uphill between lava flows. In 7 km (4½ m.) it comes to the Albergo Eremo, where a short side road goes off to the Observatory, founded in 1845, with a museum.

In another 3 km (2 mi.) the road forks. To the left is a road running up the north side of Vesuvius to the Colle Margherita (3 km (2 mi.)), from which it is a 20 minutes' climb on foot to the rim of the crater. The road continues straight ahead and in 1.5 km (1 mi.) comes to the lower station of a chair-lift (753 m (2485 ft)) which goes up to the upper station (1158 m (3821 ft)); at present the chair-lift is not in operation. At the top there is a fascinating one-hour walk around the crater and magnificent views.

Toll road

Another road (toll payable) runs from Torre Annunziata, a village to the south-west of the volcano. The route first leads north-east for 2 km (1¼ mi.) to Boscotrecase, then 10 km (6 mi.) north-west, past the Nuova Casa Bianca restaurant and up the south-east slopes of Vesuvius with numerous bends. Some time ago the area around the crater was designated a protected area.

★Viareggio   E8

Region: Toscana. Province: Lucca (LU)
Altitude: 2 m (7 ft). Population: 58,000

Location

The seaside resort of Viareggio lies on the Gulf of Genoa, some 55 km (34 mi.) south-east of La Spezia and about 25 km (16 mi.) west of Lucca.
Viareggio is renowned for its carnival. Thousands of masked revellers accompanied by decorated vehicles join the colourful parade on the wide seafront promenade.

Town

Thanks to its long sandy beach Viareggio is one of the most important resorts on the west coast of Italy. The town has a rectangular network of streets. There is much tourist traffic in the area which extends along the through road up to the beach. The promenade is lined with buildings in the Art Nouveau and Art Deco styles.

Pineta del Ponente

In the northern part of the town is the large Pineta del Ponente, a park with tall umbrella pines. Farther south the Burlamacca-canal extends to the yachting harbour.
There is a pleasant walk along the pier which extends several hundred metres into the sea. Beyond the canal begins the Riviera di Levante.

Carnival in Viareggio

Torre del Lago Puccini

6 km (3¾ mi.) S

East of Viareggio, near the Lago Massaciuccoli, is the town of Torre del Lago Puccini (2 m (7 ft)). The composer Giacomo Puccini (1858–1924) lived here in the Villa Puccini, and he and his wife (d. 1930) are buried in the park. The villa is open to the public. In the open-air theatre near Torre del Lago Puccini performances of Puccini operas are given in summer.

Vicenza: Basilica Palladiana

Vicenza F4

Region: Veneto. Province: Vicenza (VI)
Altitude: 40 m (131 ft). Population: 107,000

The provincial capital of Vicenza lies north-west of Padua on the edge of the fertile Po plain on both sides of the River Bacchiglione. It is included in the UNESCO list of sites of major historical importance, and is famous for its goldsmiths' work and the "baccalà", a tasty fish dish. — Location

The ancient Vicetia (Vicentia) was a Roman town in AD 49. In the early Middle Ages it was the seat of the Duke of Lombard, then of a Frankish count, and later became part of the community of Verona. In the 12th c. the bishops took it over, then Vicenza became engaged in struggles against Emperor Frederick I (Barbarossa) for its independence. In 1404 it finally became part of the Venetian Republic. — History

The old town, still partly enclosed by its walls, is renowned for its numerous palaces of the 15th–18th c., most notably those built by the Vicenza-born Andrea Palladio (1508–80), the last great master of the High Renaissance, whose grand style, based on his study of ancient architecture, provided a model for the whole of the Western world. His principal successors were Vincenzo Scamozzi (1552–1616) and Ottone Calderari (1730–1803). The leading painter of the 15th c. Vicenza school was Bartolomeo Montagna (c. 1450–1523), a native of Orzinuovi, whose works can be seen in the picture gallery of the Museo Civico and in several churches in the town. — Art

Sights

★Piazza dei Signori	In the heart of the old town is the Piazza dei Signori, the site of the old Roman forum, with two columns dating from the Venetian period and the slender Torre di Piazza, 82 m (271 ft), built in 1174 for defensive purposes.
Loggia del Capitano	At the north-west corner of the square the Loggia del Capitano (now part of the Town Hall), was formerly the residence of the Venetian governor; it was begun by Palladio in 1571 but only half finished.
	To the right is the Palazzo del Monte di Pietà, flanking the Baroque façade of the church of San Vincenzo (1617).
★★Basilica Palladiana	On the south-east side of the square stands the Basilica Palladiana (1549–1614), Palladio's masterpiece, with open colonnades of two storeys (lower part Doric and upper part Ionic), a very impressive combination. The basilica was not built as a church but as a meeting-place for the Grand Council. On the first floor is a hall 52 m (172 ft) long with a wooden vaulted roof. In front of the west end of the basilica is a marble statue of Palladio (1859). The basilica houses the Museo Palladiano, with models, designs and other work by Palladio.
Cathedral	From the Basilica Palladiana Via Garibaldi runs south-west to the Piazza del Duomo, on the north-side of which stands the cathedral, a Gothic structure with a façade of white and red marble (15th c.) and a fine interior. Under the cathedral are the foundations of three earlier churches. On the south-west side of the Piazza del Duomo the Bishop's Palace has a Neo-Classical façade of 1819. In the courtyard, on the right, is an elegant Early Renaissance Hall by Bernardino da Milano (1494).
Corso Andrea Palladio	A little way north-west of the Piazza dei Signori is the main street of Vicenza, the Corso Andrea Palladio, lined with palaces. Half-way along this street we find the fine Palazzo del Comune (formerly Palazzo Trissino, by Vincenzo Scamozzi, 1592–1662) and 100 m north-east of this the Gothic Palazzo Da Schio, known as the Cà d'Oro.
Santo Stefano	A little way north is the Baroque church of Santo Stefano (by Guarini, early 18th c.), which has a "Madonna Enthroned" by Palma il Vecchio in the north transept.
Santa Corona	From here Via Santo Stefano runs north-east to the Gothic church of Santa Corona (13th c.), which has a "Baptism of Christ" by Giovanni Bellini (c. 1501; fifth altar on left). On the third altar, on the right, is an "Adoration of the Kings".
Museo Civico	At the north-east end of the Corso Andrea Palladio, in the Palazzo Ciericati, one of Palladio's finest buildings, is the Museo Civico. On the ground floor are archaeological collections, on the first floor a picture gallery containing major works by painters of the Vicenza school (Bartolomeo Montagna, Giovanni Buonconsiglio, etc.), Venetian masters (Carpaccio, Veronese, Tintoretto, Tiepolo) and others.
★Teatro Olimpico	Opposite the museum is the Teatro Olimpico (damaged by an earthquake shock in 1976), which was begun by Palladio in 1580 and completed by Vincenzo Scamozzi in 1584. Built of wood and stucco, this is a Renaissance adaption of the ancient type of theatre. The auditorium, with seating for 1000, rises in semi-oval tiers; the magnificent stage wall offers vistas through three openings of streets contrived to secure the effect of perspective.
San Lorenzo	From the middle section of the Corso Andrea Palladio the Via Fogazzaro (at No. 16, on the right, the Palazzo Valmarana) runs north-west to the church of San Lorenzo, a brick-built Romanesque and Gothic structure (1280–1344) with a slender campanile and a beautiful main doorway; fine interior with a fresco by Bartolomeo Mantagna (Beheading of St Paul, c. 1500).

The Teatro Olimpico, Palladio's final work

At the south-west end of the Corso Andrea Palladio are a number of fine palaces, including the Palazzo Bonin (No. 13, on the north side) and the Palazzo Zileri Dal Verme (No. 36, on the south side).

Porta Castello

The Corso ends in the Piazza Castello, in which is the Porta Castello. To the left, on the shorter side of the square, the unfinished Palazzo Porto-Breganze, was probably designed by Palladio and built by Vincenzo Scamozzi about 1600.

In the south-west of Vicenza stands the Chiesa dei Santi Felice e Fortunato, which was rebuilt in the 10th–12th c. in its present form, with notable floor mosaics (4th–5th c.) from an earlier building. The church has a 12th c. leaning tower (campanile).

Chiesa dei Santi Felice e Fortunato

Surroundings

From the Villa Roi, on the southern outskirts of the town, the Portici di Monte Berico (1746), a series of arcades, lead up to the Basilica di Monte Berico. This pilgrimage church was built by the Bologna architect C. Borella in 1668; it has a centralised plan modelled on the Rotonda (see below). In the chapel to the right of the high altar is a "Lamentation" by Bartolomeo Montagna (1500), in the refectory a large picture by Bartolomeo Montagna ("Banquet of St Gregory Magnus").

Basilica di Monte Berico
2 km (1¼ mi.) S

From the square in front of the church there are magnificent views of the city and the Pre-Alps, including Monte Pasubio and Monte Grappa.

At the bend in the Portici a road runs east, and 2 minutes along this a footpath goes off on the right and leads past the Villa Valmarana (with mythological frescoes by Giovanni Battista, 1757) to reach in 10 minutes the famous Rotonda, a square structure crowned by a dome which was begun by Palladio about 1550 and completed by Scamozzi in 1606. (The Villa Valmarana and the Rotonda can also be reached by road from the Strada della Riviera Berica, which skirts the east side of Monte Berico.)

★La Rotonda
2 km (1¼ mi.) SE

Viterbo: façade of the Palazzo dei Papi

Viterbo

G11

Region: Lazio. Province: Viterbo (VT)
Altitude: 327 m (1073 ft). Population: 58,000

Location

The provincial capital of Viterbo is situated at the foot of the Monti Cimini, some 80 km (50 mi.) north-west of Rome.

Noted in the past as the "city of beautiful women and beautiful fountains", it still preserves its old Lombard walls, fine historic buildings and picturesque old-world nooks and crannies. It suffered much damage during the last war, but this has now been repaired.

History

The town was presented to the Pope by Pepin the Short in the 8th c. At the end of the 11th c. it became a free city, but in 1396 was again incorporated in the States of the Church.

Sights

Town Hall

The central feature of the town is the Piazza del Plebiscito, on the west side of which stands the Palazzo dei Priori (begun 1247; porch 15th c.), now the Town Hall. In the courtyard, from which there is an attractive view of the western part of the town, is an elegant 17th c. fountain.

Piazza della Morte

From the Piazza del Plebiscito Via di San Lorenzo runs south to the little Piazza del Gesù, with the church of San Silvestro, and the Piazza della Morte, which has another charming fountain, the Fontana a Fuso.

★San Lorenzo

Continuing west past the 15th c. Palazzo Farnese (on right), we come to the Piazza San Lorenzo, with the fine Cathedral of San Lorenzo, a Romanesque basilica with a Gothic campanile; the façade was renewed in 1570.

To the right of the cathedral stands the Palazzo dei Papi (1266), with a Gothic loggia, which has been the Bishop's Palace since the 15th c. In its huge hall various conclaves met for the election of a pope in the 13th c.

★ Palazzo dei Papi

South-east of the Piazza della Morte lies the picturesque San Pellegrino quarter, which has preserved many medieval houses, particularly in the Piazza San Pellegrino, with the Case degli Alessandri.

★ San Pellegrino

From the Piazza del Plesbiscito the busy Via Cavour runs south-east to the Piazza Fontana Grande, with the town's largest and most beautiful fountain, the Fontana Grande, completed in 1279.

★ Fontana Grande

From the square Via Garibaldi continues east to the Porta Romana (1653). To the left of the gate is the church of San Sisto, a Lombard building of the 9th c. with a fine apse which was increased in height in the 12th c.

San Sisto

Going north from the Porta Romana outside the town walls, we come to the former monastic church of Santa Maria della Verità (12th c.; restored after 1945), with a beautiful cloister. The Cappella Mazzatosta is decorated with fine frescos by Lorenzo da Viterbo. The monastic buildings now house the Museo Civico, with Etruscan sarcophagi, archaeological finds, medieval pictures, etc.

Santa Maria della Verità

Museo Civico

In the north-east of Viterbo, inside the town walls, is the church of Santa Rosa (rebuilt from 1840 onwards), with the mummified body of St Rosa (d. 1261). Every year on September 3rd, the eve of her feast-day, the saint's statue is borne on a 30m/100ft high tower from the Porta Romana to the church – a ceremony first introduced in 1664.

Santa Rosa

North-west of Santa Rosa, in the Piazza San Francesco, the Gothic church of San Francesco contains the tombs of Pope Clement IV (d. 1268) in the north aisle (on the right) and of Pope Hadrian V (d. 1276) in the south aisle (on the left).

San Francesco

Adjoining the Piazza San Francesco on the west is the Piazza della Rocca, with a fountain which is ascribed to Vignola and the remains of the Rocca (1457), which suffered severe destruction during the Second World War. It now houses the Museo Archeologico Nazionale.
   Still farther west, outside the Porta Fiorentina (1768), lies the beautiful Giardino Pubblico.

Rocca
(Museum)

Surroundings

3 km (2 mi.) north-east of Viterbo, in the suburb of La Quercia, is the pilgrimage church of the Madonna della Quercia (1470–1525), a fine Renaissance building with an interesting interior. In the adjoining Dominican monastery are two beautiful cloisters with fountains of 1508 and 1633.

La Quercia

On the road coming from Viterbo and running eastward is the village of Bagnaia (441 m (1455 ft)), with the Villa Lante, once the summer residence of the ducal family of that name. In the park are beautiful fountains.

Bagnaia
5 km (3 mi.) E

North of Viterbo is Ferento, originally an Etruscan settlement, the inhabitants of which formed an alliance with the Romans in the 3rd c. BC (Ferentum). Here can be seen the restored remains of a Roman theatre (1st c. AD), now used for theatrical performances.

Ferento
9 km (5½ mi.) N

West of Viterbo we come to the little spa establishment of Bagni di Viterbo (258 m (851 ft)).
   1 km (¾ mi.) north-east of Bagni di Viterbo, on a flat-topped hill of travertine with a fine view of Viterbo and the Monti Cimini, is the sulphur spring

Bagni di Viterbo
5 km (3 mi.) W

In the Bomarzo "Park of Monsters"

known as the Bullicame (298 m (983 ft)), a pool of clear blue water surrounded by a low wall, constantly effervescing with bubbles of gas. The water of the spring, which is mentioned by Dante ("Inferno", XIV, 79), is still used for medicinal bathing.

Bomarzo
23 km (14 mi.) NE

One trip which will appeal to children as well as to adults is to the little town of Bomarzo (263 m (868 ft)), picturesquely situated on a high crag above the Tiber valley north-east of Viterbo. In the town is a palace of the Orsini family (16th c.), now the Town Hall. From the terrace in front of the church there is a superb view of the Tiber valley.

★Parco dei Mostri

Outside the town, on the slopes of the hill, is the Parco dei Mostri ("Park of Monsters"), a beautiful terraced park with a whole series of monstrous and grotesque beasts, hewn from the rock in the 16th c. by Turkish prisoners of war.

Caprarola
25 km (15 mi.) SE

In Caprarola the visitor will be impressed by the Villa Farnese (1570), a pentagonal building with a round inner courtyard. The elegant spiral staircase inside, designed by Vignola, is decorated with open-air scenes by Antonio Tempesta. Some rooms are decorated in typical Italian Late Renaissance style.

Volterra   E9

Region: Toscana. Province: Pisa (PI)
Altitude: 555 m (1832 ft). Population: 14,000

Location

Volterra lies on a hill in the Tuscan uplands, about 50 km (31 mi.) off the Maremma coast, and 65 km (40 mi.) south-east of Pisa.

Voltera: cathedral and campanile

The town is noted for its alabaster industry, which provides employment for about a third of the population; many articles on sale.

Alabaster

Volterra was one of the twelve cities of the Etruscan confederation, under the name of Velathri. In the 3rd c. BC it became the Roman municipium of Volaterrae. A free city during the medieval period, it passed under Florentine control in 1361.

History

Sights

The central feature of the town is the Piazza dei Priori, surrounded by medieval palaces. On the west side of the square the fine Palazzo dei Priori (1208–54), now the Town Hall, has Renaissance coats cf arms and two lions on the façade. On the first floor is the frescoed Sala del Consiglio.

★Piazza dei Priori

Opposite the Town Hall is the Palazzo Pretorio (13th c.), with the Torre del Podestà integrated in the building.

Palazzo Pretorio

Behind the Town Hall, to the west, stands the cathedral, consecrated in 1120 and enlarged in Pisan style in 1254, with a fine interior, including a fresco ("The Three Kings") by Gozzoli.

★Cathedral

Opposite it is the Baptistery of San Giovanni, an octagonal structure on a centralised plan (1283), with a font by A. Sansovino (1502).

Baptistery

From the cathedral it is only a few steps to the Museo d'Arte Sacra (Diocesan Museum), with sacral requisites, valuable chasubles, etc.

Museo Diocesano d'Arte Sacra

A little way south, in the circuit of Etruscan town walls, is the Arco Etrusco or Porta dell'Arco, a town-gate with supports of the 4th–3rd c. BC; from the top there are extensive views.

Arco Etrusco

Volterra

Le Balze, Pisa

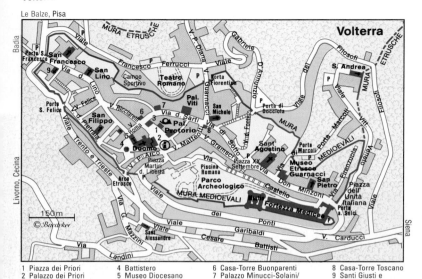

1 Piazza dei Priori
2 Palazzo dei Priori
3 Bishop's Palace

4 Battistero
5 Museo Diocesano
   d'Arte Sacra

6 Casa-Torre Buonparenti
7 Palazzo Minucci-Solaini/
   Museo Civico

8 Casa-Torre Toscano
9 Santi Giusti e
   Clemente

Palazzo Minucci-Solaini	Near the Piazza dei Priori stands the Palazzo Minucci-Solaini, which houses the Pinacoteca (picture collection), with works by Ghirlandaio, Signorelli and other painters. The same palace contains the Municipal Museum (Museo Civico).
Casa-Torre Buonparenti	West of the museum, at the crossing of Via Roma and Via Ricciarelli, is the Casa-Torre Buonparenti, a 13th c. residential tower.
Museo Etrusco Guarnacci	In the eastern part of the old town, at Via Minzoni 15, the Museo Etrusco Guarnacci houses a rich assemblage of Etruscan material from the town and surrounding area. Particularly notable is its collection of over 600 ash-urns, mostly of alabaster, dating from the Etruscan period (6th–1st c. BC), with curiously foreshortened figures of the dead persons on the lids.
Citadel	South-east of the museum is the Citadel (Fortezza Medicea, now a prison), a massive Renaissance structure. It consists of the Rocca Vecchia (the old castle; 14th c.) to the east and the Rocca Nuova (the new castle; 15th c.) to the west. The round tower in the middle of the new castle is called "Maschio" ("Little Man") and the tower of the old castle is known as the "Femmina" ("Little Woman").
Parco Archeologico	At the west end of the Citadel extends the Archaeological Park. In 1926 the remains of an ancient acropolis with the foundations of two temples (2nd c. BC) and a cistern have been excavated here.
Mura Etrusche	Leaving the Piazza dei Priori on Via Ricciarelli, we continue past the church of San Lino and San Francesco to the Porta San Francesco; a little north are the remains of the Etruscan town walls (Mura Etrusche).
Teatro Romano	From the Porta San Francesco we follow the Via Volterrana and in 100 m turn right into Viale Francesco Ferrucci, which runs along the north side of

Rocca Vecchia

the town walls to the Roman Theatre (Teatro Romano) dating from the 1st c. AD, which has been excavated from 1951 onwards.

San Girolamo

North-east of the town stands the monastic church of San Girolamo, notable for its pictures and its terracotta altarpieces by Giovanni della Robbia.

1 km (³/₄ mi.) NE

★Balze

Very impressive is the Balze, north-west of the town, an inhospitable area, almost devoid of vegetation, formed by landslides and erosion, which engulfed the Etruscan necropolises, a section of the ancient walls and the medieval church.

Tour to Massa Marittima (*c.* 85 km (53 mi.))

Take the road which runs 10 km (6 mi.) south-west to Saline di Volterra, noted for its salt-works, which supply the whole of Tuscany, then south over the bare uplands of the Colline Metallifere (Poggio di Montieri, 1051 m (3468 ft)) and via the little town of Pomarance (25 km (16 mi.); 367 m (1211 ft); population 8000) to Larderello (10 km (6 mi.); 390 m (1287 ft), lying off the main road on the slopes of Monte Cerboli (691 m (2280 ft)). The volcanic water vapour which issues from the ground in jets (*soffioni*) deposits the boric acid and other chemicals which it contains in underground reservoirs (*lagoni*) and supplies the motive power for the turbines of an electric power station. The columns of steam can be seen from a long distance away.

Larderello

563

The Etruscan Porta dell'Arco (Arco Etrusco)

Volterra: Roman Theatre

The Balze, formed by landslides and erosion

Massa Marittima

From Larderello the road continues past ancient mines (copper pyrites and argentiferous galena) and comes in 34 km (21 mi.) to Massa Marittima (380 m (1254 ft); population 10,000), one of the principal towns in the Maremma. The main square of the town is the fine Piazza Garibaldi, with the principal public buildings. The Cathedral of San Cerbone (11th–13th c.), a Romanesque-Gothic structure in Pisan style, has a notable font by Giroldo da Como (1267) and in the crypt the reliquary of San Cerbone by Goro di Gregorio da Siena (1324). In the Romanesque Palazzo Comunale (13th c.) is a five-part altarpiece by Ambrogio Lorenzetti (c. 1330). The Palazzo Pretorio (13th c.) houses the Museo Archeologico, with numerous finds of Etruscan tombs. Other features of interest are the Pinacoteca ("Maestà" by Lorenzetti) and the massive ruins of the 14th c. Fortezza dei Senesi in the "Città Nuova".

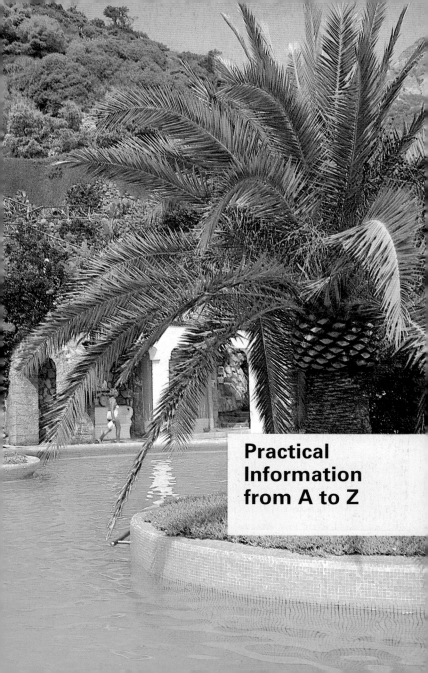

**Practical
Information
from A to Z**

Accommodation

See Hotels, Youth Hostels, Camping and Caravanning.

Air Travel

Airports
Italy is linked with the international network of air services by a number of airports. The most important international airport is the Leonardo da Vinci Airport at Rome/Fiumicino.

Alitalia
The national airline, Alitalia, flies both international and domestic routes. It has desks at all Italian and the principal foreign airports.

Meridiana
The Italian company Meridiana flies services to Sardinia.

Concessions
For children under 2 years of age accompanied by an adult and not occupying a seat there is a reduction of 90 per cent on the adult fare; for children between 2 and 12 the reduction is 50 per cent; for young people between 12 and 22 it is 25 per cent. There are also reductions for adults at weekends.

Airline addresses in Rome
Alitalia
Via Bissolati 11–13, I-00187 Roma; tel. (06) 65621, 65643

British Airways
Via Bissolati 54, I-00187 Roma; tel. (06) 479991, 485480

Canadian Airlines
Via Carlo Veneziana 58, I-00187 Roma; tel. (06) 6591300

Meridiana
Via Barberini 37, I-00187 Roma; tel. (06) 47804222, 478041

TWA
Via Barberini 67, I-00187 Roma; tel. (06) 47211

Banks

See Currency

Bus Services

Bus services play a major part in public transport, particularly in the more thinly populated upland and rural regions. They are run by the Italian State Railways and by a number of private companies.

Information about bus services can be obtained from ENIT offices (see Information) and from Italian State Railways (see Railways).

Business Hours

NB
Shops, smaller museums and in particular churches do not always keep strictly to advertised opening times. Hours are also prone to alteration at short notice.

◄ *Holidaymakers on Ischia*

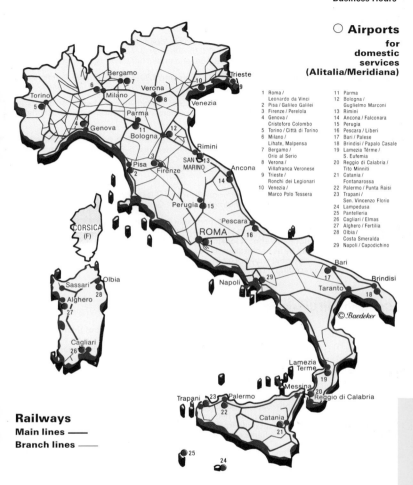

○ **Airports**

**for
domestic
services
(Alitalia/Meridiana)**

1 Roma /
   Leonardo da Vinci
2 Pisa / Galileo Galilei
3 Firenze / Perelola
4 Genova /
   Cristoforo Colombo
5 Torino / Città di Torino
6 Milano /
   Lihate, Malpensa
7 Bergamo /
   Orio al Serio
8 Verona /
   Villafranca Veronese
9 Trieste /
   Ronchi dei Legionari
10 Venezia /
   Marco Polo Tessera

11 Parma
12 Bologna /
   Guglielmo Marconi
13 Rimini
14 Ancona / Falconara
15 Perugia
16 Pescara / Liberi
17 Bari / Palese
18 Brindisi / Papalo Casale
19 Lamezia Térme /
   S. Eufemia
20 Reggio di Calabria /
   Tito Minniti
21 Catania /
   Fontanarossa
22 Palermo / Punta Raisi
23 Trapani /
   Sen. Vincenzo Florio
24 Lampedusa
25 Pantelleria
26 Cagliari / Elmas
27 Alghero / Fertilia
28 Olbia /
   Costa Smeralda
29 Napoli / Capodichino

© *Baedeker*

Railways
Main lines ——
Branch lines ——

Food shops: 8.30am–1pm and 3–7.30pm (in southern Italy 7.30am–
1.30pm and 5.30–8pm).

   Other shops: Mon.–Sat. 8.30/9/9.30/10am–12.30/1pm and 3.30/4/4.30–
7/7.30pm.

   Saturday is normally a working day with shops remaining open until
7.30pm. Large stores and shops in centres of tourism generally stay open
throughout the lunch break. Closed one half-day a week and on Sundays.

   During the season shops in centres of tourism tend to stay open later in
the evenings as well as on Sundays and public holidays (mornings only).
The statutory rest day varies from place to place and season to season
with shops closing on Monday mornings or Saturday/Wednesday after-
noons in addition to Sunday.

Shops

Banks	Usually open Mon.–Fri. 8/8.30am–1.30pm and 2.30/3–4pm. Closed from late morning on the eve of public holidays. Larger branches open Sat. morning.
Petrol stations	Motorway filling stations remain open round the clock. Otherwise Mon.–Fri. 7am–noon and 1.30–10pm or 3–7.30pm, Sat. am only. Most filling stations are closed Sun. and public holidays, even in larger towns.
Chemist shops	Summer: Mon.–Fri. 9am–12.30pm and 3.30–7.30pm. Closed Sundays and alternate Wednesdays/Saturdays.
Post Offices	Open: Mon.–Fri. 8.30am–2pm, Sat. 8.30am–noon. Main post offices in larger towns: 8.30am–6pm. Post offices at airports and at main post offices are manned 24 hours a day.
Museums	Museums normally open Tue.–Sat. 8am–1/2pm or 9am–7pm for larger museums, Sun. 9am–1pm (sometimes also 5–8pm). Open-air museums: 9am to 1 hour before sunset. For specified local exhibitions check exact opening times with the local tourist office or ENIT.
Restaurants	Most are open from noon–3pm and 7–11pm (though in summer many remain open until midnight or later). Generally closed one day a week.
Churches	One or two churches of particular importance are open throughout the day. Most however are open only during services and for a short period before and after. If looking round a church while a service is in progress, try to be as unobtrusive as possible and avoid disturbing those at worship. Note that works of art in churches are generally covered during the week preceding Easter Sunday as a sign of mourning.

Camping and Caravanning

	Italy has large numbers of good camping sites, most of them in the Alto Adige, in the Aosta valley, on the North Italian lakes and on the coasts of the Adriatic, Tyrrhenian and Ligurian Seas. Sites on the coast are generally more expensive, with relatively few short-term places available. During the main holiday season it is advisable to reserve a place in advance if you plan to stay for some time at a particular site.
Off site	Off-site camping on public land is not permitted with the exception of overnight roadside parking by trailer or motor caravans (unless prohibited by local or regional bye-laws). Permission to camp on private property should be obtained from the owner. For reasons of security, however, it is advisable whenever possible to make use of an official camp site.
Information	Lists of camping sites can be obtained from ENIT offices (see Information) or from the Italian camping organisation: Federazione Italiana del Campeggio e del Caravanning Via Vittorio Emanuele II I-50041 Calenzano/Firenze tel. (055) 882391

Car Rental

	Anyone renting a car in Italy must be at least 18 years of age and hold a valid national driving licence. The international car rental firms have offices at airports and in the larger towns and resorts in Italy, and there are numerous small local firms (listed in the telephone directory under the heading "noleggio").

Consulates

See Embassies and Consulates

Currency

The unit of currency is the Italian *lira* (plural *lire*).

There are banknotes for 1000, 2000, 5000, 10,000, 20,000, 50,000, 100,000 and 500,000 lire and coins in denominations of 20, 50, 100, 200, 500 and 1000 lire.

£1 sterling = 2500 lire	1000 lire = £0.40	Exchange rates
$1 (US) = 1600 lire	1000 lire = $0.62	(subject to variation)

On January 1st 1999 the euro became the official currency of Italy, and the Italian lira became a denomination of the euro. Italian lira notes and coins continue to be legal tender during a transitional period. Euro bank notes and coins are likely to be introduced by January 1st 2002. — Euro

There are no restrictions on the import of lire and foreign currency into Italy; but since there may sometimes be a strict control on the export of currency it is advisable to declare any large amount on the appropriate form (Modulo V2), obtainable at the frontier when entering the country.
    Unless declared on entry, only lire and foreign currency up to a value equivalent to 20,000,000 lire may be exported — Currency regulations

There is no limit on the amount of money which can be taken into Italy in the form of Eurocheques or traveller's cheques (best for security). The maximum drawable on a single Eurocheque is 300,000 lire; a charge is made for each cheque. Bancomat machines, found in most Italian towns, are the most convenient source of obtaining currency. Here again there is a limit of 300,000 lire and a charge for each transaction.
    Many stores, shops and filling stations in Italy now accept Eurocheque cards. — Eurocheques / Bancomat

Most international credit cards are accepted by banks, the larger hotels and better restaurants, car rental firms and many shops. — Credit cards

Since rates of exchange tend to be more favourable in Italy itself than in the UK, it is best to take only a small amount in lire to cover immediate expenses. Facilities for changing money (cambio) are found in the large hotels as well as at banks (for opening times see Business Hours), stations, airports and at the frontier. Travel agencies also operate their own bureaux de change. Commission charges vary and should be compared. Retain all receipts (ricevute) and other documentation. — Changing money

Customs Regulations

In theory there is now no limit to the amount of goods that can be taken from one EU country to another provided they have been purchased tax paid in an EU country, are for personal use and not intended for resale. However, customs authorities have issued guidelines to the maximum amounts considered reasonable for persons over 17 years of age. These are: 10 litres of spirits or strong liqueurs, 20 litres fortified wine (port, sherry, etc.) 90 litres of table wine (of which not more than 60 litres may be sparkling wine), 110 litres of beer, 800 cigarettes or 400 cigarillos or 200 cigars). There is no limit on perfume or toilet water.

Entry from non-EU countries

For those coming from a country outside the EU or who have arrived from an EU country without having passed through custom control with all their baggage, the allowances for goods obtained anywhere outside the EU for persons over the age of 17 are: 1 litre spirits or 2 litres of fortified wine or 3 litres table wine, plus a further 2 litres table wine; 60cc perfume, 250cc toilet water; 200 cigarettes or 100 cigarillos or 50 cigars.

Duty-free goods

The allowances for goods purchased "duty-free" from airports, on aircraft and ferries are the same as for entry from non-EU countries above.

Electricity

Electricity supplies in Italy are normally 220 volts AC.
An adaptor is required for British and American-type plugs.

Embassies and Consulates

United Kingdom

Embassy:
Via XX Settembre 80A
I-00187 Roma (Rome)
tel. (06) 4825441, 4825551

Consulates:
Viale Colombo
I60 0-90455 Cagliari
tel. (070) 828628

Palazzo Castelbarco
Lungarno Corsini 2
I-50123 Firenze (Florence)
tel. (055) 212594, 284133, 287449

Piazza della Vittoria 15–16
I-16121 Genova (Genoa)
tel. (010) 564833

Via San Paolo 7
I-20121 Milano (Milan)
tel. (02) 723001

Via Francesco Crispi 122
I-80122 Napoli (Naples)
tel. (081) 663511

Via Saluzzo 60
I-10125, Torino (Turin)
tel. (011) 6509202

Vicolo delle Ville 16
I-34100 Trieste
tel. (040) 30 28 84

Accademia 1051, Dorsoduro
P.O. Box 679
I-30100 Venezia (Venice)
tel. (041) 5227207, 5227408

Embassy: USA
Via Vittorio Veneto 119A
I-00187 Roma (Rome); tel. (06) 46741

Consulates:
Lungarno Amerigo Vespucci 38
I-50100 Firenze (Florence)
tel. (055) 2398276

Banca d'America e d'Italia Building
Piazza Portello 6
I-16124 Genova (Genoa)
tel. (010) 584492

Via Principe Amedeo 2/10
I-20121 Milano (Milan)
tel. (02) 02290351

Piazza della Repubblica
I-80122 Napoli (Naples)
tel. (081) 5838111

Via Vaccarini 1
I-90143 Palermo
tel. (091) 6110020

Embassy (Consular Section):   Canada
Via Zara 30
I-00198 Roma (Rome)
tel. (06) 06445981

Consulate:
Via Vittor Pisani 19
I-20124 Milano (Milan); tel. (02) 67581

Emergencies

It is advisable always to carry a few suitable lire coins and telephone   NB
tokens (*gettoni*) or a phonecard for use in case of emergency.

Police emergencies/accident rescue (soccorso pubblico di emergenza):   Emergency
dial 113.   services
Police (carabinieri): dial 112
Fire (vigili del fuoco): dial 115
   Emergency numbers are also listed on page 1 of local telephone direc-
tories (elenco telefonico).

See Medical Assistance   Medical

For the ACI (Automobile Club Italiano) breakdown service dial 116   Breakdown
(throughout Italy).   service
   If help cannot be obtained locally drivers covered by the Automobile
Association emergency service can telephone the AA Continental Emergency Centre in Boulogne (tel. 0033 21872121) or, by arrangement with
the Dutch motoring club ANWB, ANWB's English-speaking emergency
service at Mendrisio on the Swiss-Italian border (tel. 0041 91468861).

Events

| General | Many Italian festivals retain their ancient form and survive largely unchanged, with traditional costumes, dances and crafts preserved. Religious events such as the processions during Holy Week (Settimana Santa) and Corpus Christi frequently take on the character of folk festivals.

Patron saint and church consecration day celebrations play an important part in the life of almost every town.

From time to time cities and towns with major museums have cultural weeks or "Porte Aperte" (open days) with free admission to museums, galleries, etc. |
|---|---|
| Dates | Movable dates should always be checked, either by contacting ENIT (see Information) before leaving home, or on the spot. |

A selection of the principal festivals and cultural events:

February	San Remo: Italian Festival of Popular Song (Festival della Canzone Italiana)
February/March	Viareggio, San Remo, Pisa, Turin and other places on the Riviera: Carnival
Venice: Carnevale Veneziana
March	Milan–San Remo road race (cycling)
Many places: St Joseph's Day celebrations (San Giuseppe, March 19th) with, in Siena, a street festival and market around St Joseph's Church
Palm Sunday	Many places but especially Rome and Florence: Blessing of Palms, processions
Maundy Thursday	Many places: Washing of Feet (in Rome, papal Mass in San Giovanni in Laterano)
Good Friday	Many places: Good Friday processions (in Rome a "Way of the Cross" around the Coliseum). In 1995, for the first time, women from Italy and Switzerland were allowed to carry the $1^{1}/_{2}$ m (5 ft) high wooden cross.
Taranto: Mystery procession
Many places in Sicily: Mystery plays and Good Friday processions (continuing over a period of 22 hours in Trapani and Caltanisetta)
Easter Saturday	Many places: Lighting of the Sacred Fire
Easter Day	Rome: Papal blessing "Urbe et Orbi" (St Peter's)
Sicily: Easter processions in many places
Cesenatico: Vele di Pasqua (regatta for catamarans)
Florence: Scoppio del Carro (Burning of the Cart) between the Cathedral and the Baptistery. Costume procession.
March–June	Volterra: Spring music festival (classical music)
April 1st	San Marino: Investiture of the Capitani Reggenti, a dignified ceremony held twice yearly (April 1st and October 1st) ever since 1244
End April/ beginning May	Bolzano: Traditional flower festival (Festa Tradizionale dei Fiori: goes back over 100 years)
Verona: Spring Festival
May	Cesenatico: A Maggio Cesenatico piú buona (gastronomic week)
Cocullo: Procession of the Serpents (Processione dei Serpari, in which a snake-swathed statue of St Domenico is carried through the streets)
Sassari (Sardinia): Calvalcata Sarda (cavalcade of riders in historic costume commemorating victory over the Saracens)
Assisi: Calendimaggio (colourful three-day festival held at the beginning of May; historical parade, theatre, concerts and inter-district contests)

Verdi's "Aida" performed in the amphitheatre at Verona

Naples: San Gennaro (feast day of the city's patron saint) — First Sunday in May

Camogli: Festival of San Rocco (patron saint) with Sagra del Pesca (fishermen's festival) — Second Sunday in May

Gubbio: Corsa dei Ceri (very popular folk festival named after the Candle Race in which candles weighing 50 kg or more are carried through the steep streets of the Old Town to the church of St Ubaldus, Gubbio's patron saint). — May 15th

Brescia–Rome: Mille Miglia (veteran car rally from Brescia via Florence to Rome) — Mid May

Bolzano: Mostra Assaggio Vini (in Maretsch Castle; towards the end of May)

Florence: Maggio Musicale Fiorentino (concerts, opera, musicals, ballet; also films) — Mid May–beginning of June

Gubbio: Palio della Balestra (Piazza della Signoria; crossbow shooting, costume procession) — Last Sunday in May

Ferrara: Palio di Ferrara (traditional races) — End of May

Cremona: Cremona Festival (classical concerts in the Teatro Ponchielli) — May/June

Loreto Aprutino: Tradizione del bue di San Zopito (a festively adorned ox and cherub are borne through the streets) — Whit Monday

Events

June	Campobasso: Sagra dei Misteri (consecration celebrations)
	Scarperia/Mugello: Motomondiale (motor racing)
	Many places: Infiorita (folk festival marking Corpus Christi, streets carpeted with flowers)
	Pisa: Festa di San Rainieri (with historic Arno regatta, 16th c. costumes, rowing competitions)
	Florence: Calcio storico in costume (costume football match in the Piazza della Signoria)
Mid June–end of July	Ravenna: Ravenna Festival (concerts, opera and ballet)
June 29th	Syracuse: Festi di San Paolo
End of June/beginning of July	Spoleto: Festival dei Due Mondi (Two Worlds Festival), an international festival of music, ballet, drama and film
June–October	Venice: Biennale d'Arte di Venezia (one of the principal international exhibitions of contemporary art, inaugurated in 1895)
July	Bolzano: Bolzano Danza (ballet)
	Perugia: Umbria Jazz (ten-day festival featuring leading exponents of modern jazz)
	Piombino: Historic procession, archery tournament, fisherman's festival (fish fried in pans 3 m (10 ft) in diameter)
	Ravello: Festival Musicale di Ravello (in the gardens of the Villa Rufolo)
	Turin: Teatro Regio (ballet)
July 2nd and August 16th	Siena: Palio delle Contrade (world-famous horse race in the Piazza del Campo preceded by costumed procession; see Baedeker Special p. 464)

Costumes and pageantry echo Italy's glittering history

Venice: Festa del Redentore (Feast of the Redeemer; commemorates deliverance from the plague in 1576; procession of boats from San Marco to Giudecca Island) — July 15th and 16th

Fiuggi: International folk festival — End of July
Levanto: Festa del mare (parade of boats, fireworks and nocturnal costume procession in honour of San Giacomo, patron saint of fisherfolk)

Torre del Lago: Festival Puccini (festival of opera with works by Puccini) — July/August
Forte dei Marmi: Concerti Musica Jazz (jazz concerts)
Rosignano Marittimo: cultural festival (Castello Pasquini)

Verona: Festival of opera (in the Roman amphitheatre) — July–September
Volterra: Estate Musica (summer programme of music, classical, jazz, etc.)

Fiuggi: Festival of classical music — August
Pescara: Festa di Sant'Andrea (procession to the sea)
Villafranca in Lunigiana: Mostra mercato medioevale (traditional craft fair)

Ascoli Piceno: Giostra della Quintana (costume parade and equestrian tournament) — First Sunday in August
La Spezia: Festival by the sea including a regatta (the "Palio di Golfo") and a folk festival

Many places: Assunzione (processions celebrating the ascension of the Virgin) — August 15th

Pesaro: Rossini Opera Festival — Mid to end of August

Marina di Massa: Spettacola pirotecnico di fine estate (fireworks to mark the passing of summer) — End of August
Ravenna: Ravenna Jazz (the longest-established jazz festival in Italy)
San Daniele del Friuli: Aria di Festa (four-day festival celebrating the famous San Daniele ham and Friuli wine)

Bolzano: Giro Cicloturistico delle Dolomiti (cycle race in the Dolomites) — End of August/beginning of September
Marina di Carrara: Tutta in fiera (beer and feasting)

Venice: International Film Festival (the most important of its kind after Cannes and the Berlinale) — August/September
Stresa: Settimane Musicale (four weeks or thereabouts devoted to music)

Cefalù: Cefalù incontri (drama, concerts, films) — August–October

San Vicenzo: beer festival and concerts on the Piazza — September
Trento: Autunno Trentino (autumn festival)
Viterbo: Trasporto della Macchina di Santa Rosa (procession of the mortal remains of the town's patron saint; a 30 m (100 ft) long iron and papier mâché tower weighing some 4 tons is borne through the steep streets and alleyways at a run).

Venice: Regatta Storica (spectacular regatta for gondolas on the Grand Canal; magnificent medieval costumes and historic craft) — 1st Sunday in September

Foligno: Quintana (torch-light procession followed next day by an equestrian tournament; Renaissance costumes) — 2nd Sunday in September

Perugia and elsewhere: Sagra Musicale Umbra (Umbria Music Festival, one of the region's most prestigious cultural events) — 2nd half of September

Naples: Festival in honour of San Gennaro, the city's patron saint — September 19th

Farmhouse Holidays

Beginning of October	Asti: Palio degli Asini (donkey races between the various districts of the town) San Remo: Car rally organised by the San Remo Automobile Club)
Mid October	Casola Valsenio: Festa dei frutti dimenticati (festival, inaugurated in 1984, in praise of traditional but now neglected fruits such as pomegranates, medlars, etc.) Merano: Grape and wine fest; costume processions with folk music and concerts on the spa promenade
November 24th–December 23rd	Bolzano: Mercatino di Natale (Christmas market)
December 13th	In many Italian towns: Nativity plays
December 25th	Rome: Papal blessing "Urbi et Orbi" in many languages
December 31st	Bolzano: Corsa Internazionale di San Silvestro (New Year's Eve race through the Old Town)

Farmhouse Holidays

General
The Italian term "agriturismo" is best translated "farmhouse holidays". These range from modest rural cottages to luxurious country houses. Prices vary accordingly.

Farmhouse holidays in the Alto Adige
A list of farmhouse accommodation in the Alto Adige is available from the tourist office in Bolzano or from the local farmers' association (Brennerstr. 7c, I-39100 Bolzano, tel. (0471) 999308).

Further information
Further information can be obtained from ENIT (see Information) or from: Agriturist, Corso Vittorio Emanuele II 101
I-00186 Roma, tel. (06) 6852342.

Food and Drink

General

Gastronomically Italy takes a high place among the countries of Europe. Its cuisine is notable both for its variety and its excellence.

Italian cuisine
Apart from the numerous pasta dishes, served in infinite variety and with a wide range of different sauces or dressings, the Italian menu includes many excellent fish dishes. Much use is made of olive oil in cooking. The famous Italian pizza was originally made of bread dough spread with tomatoes and herbs and is a simple but tasty alternative to ordinary bread; the numerous variations with cheese, salami, ham, mushrooms, artichoke hearts, etc., developed later with increasing prosperity, particularly in northern Italy and under the influence of tourism.

Drinks
The standard drinks with all meals are wine and mineral water. Beer is found everywhere, both the light Italian beer and foreign brands (birra estera), particularly German, Danish and Dutch.

Mealtimes
Lunch is usually served in Italian restaurants from noon onwards, though in Rome and the southern parts of the country it tends to be taken considerably later. Dinner is seldom eaten before 7, and 8 o'clock is widely regarded as the "normal" time.

Breakfast is a meal of little consequence to the Italians. The hotels, however, have mostly adapted to northern European habits and provide bread, butter and jam – plus eggs, sausage or cheese if required – to accompany the morning cup of coffee (usually *cappuccino*, with foaming hot milk).

Lunch usually consists of several courses. Spaghetti and other forms of pasta (and in the north, rice dishes) are merely a substitute for soup – hence the term *primo*, "first course". They are often preceded by an *antipasti* (hors d'œuvre). The pasta is followed by the *secondo* (second course), a meat or fish dish, and this in turn is often followed by cheese and fruit or a sweet of some kind. Lunch always ends with a cup of *espresso* (strong black coffee), which some connoisseurs prefer *corretto* – "corrected" by the addition of grappa (Italian brandy) or cognac.

The evening meal is usually also a substantial one.

Reading an Italian menu (lista, carta)

Table-setting *coperto*; spoon *cucchiaio*; teaspoon *cucchiaino*; knife *coltello*; fork *forchetta*; plate *piatto*; glass *bicchiere*; cup *tazza*; napkin *tovagliolo*; corkscrew *cavatappi*.

Breakfast *prima colazione*; lunch *pranzo*; dinner *cena*.

Hors d'œuvre (*antipasti*): anchovies, sardines, olives, artichokes, mushrooms, radishes, sausage, ham, eggs, salads of seafood or with mayonnaise, etc.

Brodo broth; *consommé* consommé, clear soup; *minestra* soup with pasta, vegetables, etc.; *minestrone* thick vegetable soup; *stracciatella* broth with beaten eggs; *zuppa* (*di pesce*, etc.) (fish, etc.) soup.

Mouth-watering selection at the local delicatessen

The invention of pasta

The Italians may well feel offended – rumour now has it that pasta, supposed to have been invented in Italy, was in fact first cooked in China and not on the stove of an Italian mamma. One of Marco Polo's sailors, Spaghetti by name, is said to have discovered it there and brought it back to Italy on the backs of elephants in 1295.

You can believe this version or not, as you wish; the historical problem is not who it was who first threw a few scraps of moist dough, which we would now call dumplings, *gnocchi*, into a pan of boiling water. And nobody will dispute the fact that it was the Italians who turned the making of pasta into a fine art and cultivated it like no other nation on earth. A decisive factor in the making of pasta was the discovery that flour paste does not go bad after a few days if it is dried in the sun. Grains of wheat do admittedly keep quite well, but this is somewhat impractical because turning them into an easily digestible dish is time-consuming and laborious. Semolina, flour and dough tend to go off and even today can be kept only for a certain length of time under suitable conditions. It was not until dried pasta was invented that the prepared food could be kept without any problems, produced on an industrial scale and be sold all over the world as a popular dish.

The quality of Italian pasta results from the unique formula of the ingredients: semolina, water and nothing else. Only for "Sunday best" egg-pasta are fresh eggs used instead of water. By law, the dried pasta sold in Italy has to be made from semolina and water. The hard (durum) grains of wheat used in Italian pasta come mainly from Apulia, Sicily and Canada, and Italian mills sell semolina in varying qualities and price ranges (400 to 1000 lira per kilo). The most expensive is the Canadian, which has a high albumen content and is an intensive shade of yellow. As a rule, the main pasta manufacturers use a mixture from various sources.

The criteria which the pasta industry applies when buying in and making up its semolina mixes are limited to certain analytical factors: protein value (as high as possible) and shade of yellow (as intensive as possible). As in the case of wine, however, quite apart from the analytical quality, there can be marked differences of taste in various wheats. So that this is ultimately reflected in the taste of the pasta the product has to be carefully monitored from the seed stage onwards.

The semolina delivered by the mill is susceptible to attack by insects and mildew and so must be processed within a few days. It is mixed with water in kneading machines until the dough attains a moisture content of 30 per cent. The temperature of the water used plays a decisive part in determining the subsequent character of the pasta; it varies from manufacturer to manufacturer and from one form of pasta to another, and may be anything between 10°C and 55°C. The mass of dough is worked until it is homogeneous and then pressed onto moulds. Depending on the kind of pasta, the dough is either pressed through fine sieves and cut into lengths by rotating blades (e.g., spaghetti, macaroni) or else cut or stamped out from a sheet of pasta (tagliatelle, lasagne). A decisive factor in determining the nature of the resultant pasta is the material used to line the holes through which the dough is forced. In traditional firms this lining is of bronze, which produces a rustic pasta with a rough surface, while in modern industrial plants mainly teflon is used, which results in a smoother type of pasta.

The water content of the finished pasta is around 30 per cent. To reduce it to the legal maximum of 12·5 per cent macaroni and similar types must be dried at once. Formerly this was done by laying the pasta out in the sun or in drying rooms – a lengthy process which could take up to three weeks. While small firms still lay their fresh pasta out on trays in drying cabinets or hang it on rails and thus allow the water to evaporate in temperatures of 30 to 50°C, computer-controlled drying plants of large concerns accomplish this in two to five hours at temperatures of between 85 and 110°C. This is really more akin to baking than drying and has a permanent effect on the taste. Pasta manufacturers who are very concerned about the individual taste of their product may leave their spaghetti to dry for up to 36 hours and do not exceed temperatures of 60 to 70°C.

However, the trend nowadays towards drying at high temperatures does have its advantages; for example, the noodles are more suitable for boiling and the colour is deeper. Moreover, the high heat destroys undesirable enzymes and improves the taste. On the other hand, any qualitative short-comings may be disguised by the place of origin and type of wheat used, which may also produce subtle differences in taste. Thanks largely to improved technology, really bad pasta is very rare, and the products of market leaders in this field are guaranteed to meet constantly high standards. Ten years ago there were 238 industrial pasta manufacturing firms in Italy; today only 170 are still in business. The price war and monopolistic trends in this sector are no less harsh than in other branches of the food industry.

The "big boys" of the pasta business include Barilla, Buitoni, Voiello, Agnesi, De Cecco, Corticella and Delvedere. With its headquarters in Palma Barilla is the undisputed market leader with 35 per cent. In second place with only six per cent is Nestlé (Buitoni and Pezullo), followed by De Cecco with a five per cent market share.

Business mergers do not appear to have had any deleterious effect on the demand for Italian pasta. Today pasta supplies about one-fifth of the calorie requirements of the Italian population and a few years ago, particularly in the north of Italy, consumption per capita again increased; on average, it is now about 24 kg (53 lb) per person per annum, whereas in other European countries it is between 4 and 6 kg (9 and 13 lb) per person.

The fact that Italians have not grown tired of pasta is due in no small part to the many varieties now available, the almost unlimited ways of preparing it and – last but not least – the cooking skills of the Italian housewife. In short, Italy without pasta would be a bleak culinary desert. It would still be interesting to know for certain whether the thin noodle that we know as spaghetti was invented in China or Italy, or would it?

© Merum

Food and Drink

Pasta	*Pasta* or *farinacei:* *Agnelotti* a kind of ravioli with meat filling; *cannelloni* large rolls of pasta; *capellini* long thread-like spaghetti; *cappeletti* "little hats", a form of ravioli with various fillings; *fettucine* egg noodles; *gnocchi* a form of ravioli; *lasagne* broad strips of pasta, often green; *maccheroni* macaroni; *panzotti* small packets of pasta with cheese and spinach filling; *pasta asciutta* the general term for all kinds of pasta; *ravioli* ravioli; *rigatoni* short macaroni; *spaghetti* spaghetti; *vermicelli* vermicelli (thread-like spaghetti).
Risotto	*Risotto* risotto; *riso* rice.
Polenta	*Polenta* boiled maize flour (solid when cold).
Eggs	*Uova* eggs; *alla coque, al guscio* soft-boiled; *sode* hard-boiled; *al piatto, al tegame* fried; *frittata* omelette.
Bread	*Pane* bread; *panini* rolls; *grissini* thin sticks of rusk-like bread.
Fish and seafood	Italy has a wide range of different kinds of fish *(pesce)* and seafood *(frutti di mare):* *Acciughe* anchovies; *anguilla* eel; *aragosta* lobster; *aringa* herring; *baccalà* dried cod; *calamari* cuttlefish; *carpa, carpone* carp; *cefalo* mullet; *cernia* grouper; *cozze* mussels; *datteri* clams; *dentice* dentex; *fritto misto mare* mixed fried fish; *gamberetti* shrimps; *gambero* crayfish; *gambero di mare* lobster; *gamberoni* prawns; *granchio* crab; *luccio* pike; *merluzzo* hake; *moscardino* curled octopus; *muscoli* mussels; *nasello* hake; *orata* gilthead bream; *ostriche* oysters; *pescatrice* angler fish; *pesce persico* perch; *pesce spada* swordfish; *pesce ragno* greater weever; *polpo* octopus; *razza* skate; *riccio marino* sea-urchin; *rombo* turbot; *salmone* salmon; *sarde* pilchards; *sardine* sardines; *scampi* scampi; *sogliola* sole; *sgombro* mackerel; *spigola* bass; *storione* sturgeon; *tonno* tunny; *triglia* red mullet; *trota* trout; *vongole* palourdes; *zuppa di pesce* fish soup.
Snails	*Lumache* snails.
Meat	*Carne* meat. Animals/kinds of meat: *Abbacchio* spring lamb; *agnello* lamb; *bue* ox/beef; *capretto* kid; *coniglio* rabbit; *maiale* pig/pork; *manzo* bullock/beef; *montone* ram/mutton; *porchetto, porcello* sucking pig; *vitello* calf/veal; *vitellone* older calf/young beef. Cuts of meat: *Animelle* sweetbreads; *cervello* brain; *bistecca* steak; *coda* tail; *coscia* haunch, leg; *cuore* heart; *costoletta, costata* cutlet; *fegato* liver; *filetto* fillet; *lingua* tongue; *lombata* loin; *ossobuco* shin of veal; *paillard* veal fillet; *petto* breast; *piccata* sliced veal; *piede, piedino* foot; *polmone* lung; *rognoni* kidneys; *scaloppa* scallop, schnitzel; *spezzatino* veal goulash; *testa, testina* head; *trippa* tripe; *zampone* pig's trotter. Methods of cooking: *Arrosto* roast; *bollito* boiled; *bolliti misti* mixed boiled meats; *cibrero* ragout; *ben cotto* well done; *ai ferri* grilled; *al girarrosto* roasted on the spit; *alla griglia* grilled; *all'inglese* underdone; *lesso* boiled; *pasticcio* pie; *polpette* rissoles, meat balls; *al sangue* rare; *stracotto, stufato, stufatino* steamed, stewed.
Sausage	*Salame* slicing sausage; *salsiccia* small sausage.
Ham	*Prosciutto* ham; *crudo* raw; *cotto* boiled; *coppa* cured shoulder of pork; *pancetta* stomach of pork.
Cold meat	*Affettato* cold meat.

Selvaggina game: *camoscio* chamois; *capriolo* roebuck; *cervo* venison; *cinghiale* wild boar; *fagiano* pheasant; *faraona* guineafowl; *lepre* hare; *pernice, starna* partridge; *piccione* pigeon; *tordo* thrush.

Game

Pollame poultry: *anitra* duck; *gallinaccio, dindo, tacchino* turkey; *oca* goose.

Poultry

Verdure, legumi vegetables; *guarnizioni* garnishings.
Asparagi asparagus; *barbaforte* horse-radish; *brocoli* broccoli; *carciofi* artichokes; *cardoni* cardoons; *cavolfiore* cauliflower; *cavolo* cabbage; *cavolini di Bruxelles* Brussels sprouts; *cipolle* onions; *crudezze* raw vege-table salads; *fagioli haricot* beans; *fagiolini* French beans; *fave* broad beans; *finocchio* fennel; *funghi* mushrooms; *lenticchie* lentils; *melanzana* aubergine; *patate* potatoes; *peperoni* sweet peppers; *piselli* peas; *pomodori* tomatoes; *rafano* horse-radish; *ravanelli* radishes; *sedano* celery; *spinaci* spinach; *zucchini* courgettes.
  Insalata salad.

Vegetables and garnishings

Salsa al burro butter sauce; *salsa alle noci* walnut sauce (made from ground almonds and cream); *salsa napoletana* tomato sauce; *salsa bolognese* tomato sauce with meat; *salsa verde* parsley sauce with oil, egg, spices and capers; *maionese* mayonnaise; *pesto alla genovese* green basil sauce with pine nuts, parmesan cheese and garlic.

Sauces

Aceto vinegar; *aglio* garlic; *burro* butter; *mostarda* candied fruit in mustard sauce; *olio* oil; *pepe* pepper; *sale* salt; *senape* mustard; *sugo* gravy, juice.

Condiments

Dessert, dolce dessert. *Bavarese* a mousse of cream and egg; *budino* pudding, mousse; *cassata* sponge cake or ice-cream with candied fruits; *frittata* omelette; *gelato* ice; *macedonia* fruit salad; *panettone* cake with dried fruit; *torta* flan, tart; *zabaglione* egg-flip with marsala.

Desserts

Frutta fruit. *Anguria, cocomero* water-melon; *arancia* orange; *ciliege* cherries; *fichi* figs; *fragole* strawberries; *frutta secca* dried fruit; *lamponi* raspberries; *limone* lemon; *mandorle* almonds; *mela* apple; *melone* melon; *nespola* medlar; *noci* walnuts; *pera* pear; *pesca* peach; *pistacchi* pistachios; *pompelmo* grapefruit; *popone* melon; *prugna* plum; *uva* grapes; *uva seccha, passa* raisins.

Fruit

Formaggio cheese. Bel Paese (soft); Brancolino (goat's-milk); Gorgonzola (blue-veined); Mozzarella (moist curd cheese); Parmigiano (parmesan); Provolone (mellow, soft, sometimes smoked); Pecomo (ewe's-milk); Ricotta (soft, unsalted); Romano (ewe's-milk); Stracchino (with mould but without blue veins).

Cheese

Table wine (*vino da pasto*) is served in carafes.
Nero, rosso red; *bianco* white; *secco* dry; *asciutto* very dry; *abboccato, amabile* slightly sweet; *dolce, pastoso* sweet; *vino del paese* local wine; *un litro* a litre; *mezzo litro* half a litre; *un quarto* a quarter litre; *un bicchiere* a glass. Older wines and wines of high quality are served in the normal way in corked and labelled bottles.

Table wine

Other popular drinks *(bevande)* are *birra* beer, *acqua minerale* mineral water, *aranciata* orangeade, *limonata* lemonade, *succo (di . . .)* fruit juice and *spremuta (di . . .)* freshly pressed fruit juice.

Beer, soft drinks

Wine

The Wine-growing regions and wines of Italy

1 Piedmont, Aosta valley, Liguria.
  Barbera d'Asti: ruby-red, dry. Barbera d'Alba: ruby-red, dry. Barbera del Monferrato: deep red. dry to slightly sweet, semi-sparkling. Nebbiolo

The wine revolution

Chianti, that's right – until a few years ago the wines of Italy were synonymous with holiday memories, carefree drinking sessions, sun and Mediterranean hospitality. Holiday wines, pizza wines, garden party wines, Little more was expected of them. One picked up a bottle of *nostrano* and got into the Italian mood with the help of large glassfuls of the stuff. Whether the red liquid was Chianti, Dolcetto or Valpolicella was incidental, as long as it tasted all right, was strong and did not cost too much. In the context of the holiday as a whole it played a minor and interchangeable role.

By the end of the 1970s Italy was producing well over 8 billion litres of wine a year. But little was imbibed again after returning home and holiday memories of cypresses and olive trees, white beaches and old town walls, or the hospitality of Giovanni and Maria had begun to fade. Then, in the early 1980s, a development took place in Tuscany and Piemonte which gave those wines which until then had ranked as "outsiders" an enormous boost by raising both the quality and the prices. The reason behind this development lay with the wine consumption of the Italians themselves, which suddenly fell. From the traditional 100 to 120 litres per head per annum it dropped down to a meagre 55 litres in the 1980s and the Italian wine industry faced a serious crisis. From a "wine deficit" of 2 billion litres shortly after the end of the Second World War they were faced thirty years later with a wine surplus of a similar size, and as late as 1984 Italy destroyed 2·5 billion litres by distillation. It was the despairing search for new markets which led the Italians to discover the "great wines" and to improve their own wines year by year. As the demand for ordinary cheap vino became less and less they began to develop a sector of the industry which until then had been almost the monopoly of the French. Within a few years a dusty old wine called Barolo developed into a modern, expensive red wine which proved a hit with wine-dealers inside and outside Italy. Abruptly torn from a hundred years' slumber, Brunello di Montalcino, a wine which until then had been bottled only in small quantities by three or four producers, received rapturous acclaim in the press and was offered for sale in considerable quantities by over 100 wine-merchants.

The once cheap and sparkling Tuscan Chianti Classico in the raffia-covered bottle became one of Italy's best-known wines. 7000 hectares (17,000 acres) of vineyards were needed to produce some 30 million bottles. Chianti Classico is one of the most outstanding examples of the "wonderful transformation" in recent years of what had been some rather banal Italian wines.

The wondrous thing about the Italian "wine revolution", however, is not the fact that the quality rapidly improved as such but the short time span required for this to happen and the way in which Italian wine acquired a completely new image, especially abroad. Barely fifteen years have passed since the beginning of the "revolution". Apart from the astounding entrepreneurial flexibility of the Italians this change *all'italiana* hides few secrets: drastically reduced output per acre, a massive investment by wine-lovers who filled their cellars and a (sometimes) almost excessively uncompromising use of the most modern ecological knowledge. No country in Europe is more richly blessed with areas of land ideally suited to the cultivation of quality grapes than Italy.

Wine can be produced from the southernmost islands with their African climate to high up in the Alpine valleys in the north. In all, a million hectares (two and a half million acres) of vineyards are cultivated by a similar number of growers. Even more astounding than the richness of the wine-producing lands of Italy is the large choice of native species of grapes.

The staggering diversity found in the world of Italian wine, made even more so by typical Italian individualism, is at the same time one of its greatest problems. 270 guaranteed marks of origin (DOC and DOCG) have been granted to date, but even this is not enough: these marks are often only collectively applied to groups of completely different kinds of wine. Theoretically speaking, one would have to memorise the names of 1144 different wines in order to possess a complete picture of the official Italian world of wine.

One would have thought that Italian wine-producers would have been satisfied with this already confusingly large list, but no, there is scarcely a single grower who can control his vanity enough not to add to it by means of one or more creations of his own, mostly in the *vino da tavola* range. In Italy there are more than 40,000 bottlers with at least 200,000 labels – the confusion for the average wine-drinker is beyond compare. And there is little chance for the non-connoisseur quickly to learn his way around and to be able to choose a wine on the spot and be sure he has not made a mistake.

When in doubt, stick to well-known names and as a rule of thumb remember the maxim "an expensive wine is not necessarily good, a cheap one never can be!"

A certain guarantee of quality is provided by the DOC or DOCG stamp. Under Italian law, wines in this category must undergo an examination by analysis and taste before being bottled. However, ordinary table wines can be sold without any such checks; the producer's name is the only guarantee of quality.

From a legal point of view, the *vina da tavola* (table wines) fall into the lowest category quality-wise. In the early 1980s, however, in an attempt to improve their image vis-à-vis the DOC wines, a large number of producers began to bring their best wines on to the market as table wines. The highly-praised *super vino da tavola* freed the producers from any legal restrictions while enabling them to realise their wildest wine fantasies. Often these table wines are fortified by adding French grapes to local blends. In 1992 a new wine law came into force which differentiated between various qualities in such a way as to take the wind out of the sails of the new fashion for table wine and was able to prevent a further escalation of the creative chaos.

However, the Italian "wine revolution" is not over by any means. The success of the avant-gardists is infectious and is encouraging many growers to try out their own new ideas. The Italian wine-connoisseur has consequently become accustomed to being able to try something new almost every day. Admittedly it is not a simple matter for the non-expert to find his way through this maze, but on the other hand the Italian wine scene is taking good care to ensure that even longstanding fans of Italy will never be bored!

d'Alba: deep ruby-red, dry or slightly sweet, sparkling. Moscato d'Asti (various kinds): straw-coloured to golden yellow, sweet. Barolo: garnet-red, dry, full and fragrant. Gattinara: garnet-red, dry. Carema: garnet-red, soft, velvety and full-bodied. Barbaresco: garnet-red, dry

2 Lombardy.
Moscato dell'Oltrepò Pavese: light yellow, aromatic. Barbera dell' Oltrepò Pavese: ruby-red, dry. Pinot dell'Oltrepò Pavese: greenish-yellow, dry, aromatic. Riesling dell'Oltrepò Pavese: light yellow, dry. Valtellina (Veltliner): deep red, dry to very dry

3 Alto Adige, Trentino.
Santa Maddalena: ruby-red to garnet-red, full, velvety. Lagarina: deep red, full, soft, velvety. Terlaner: greenish-yellow to golden . yellow, dry, fresh. Cabernet: ruby-red, dry, full. Teroldego: light red to ruby-red, dry

4 Veneto.
Valpolicella: ruby-red to garnet-red, dry to semi-sweet, full-bodied, well rounded. Bardolino: light red, dry, well rounded. Soave: straw-coloured to greenish-yellow, dry, well rounded

5 Friuli-Venezia Giulia.
Grave del Friuli: red and white, made from different varieties of grape. Isonzo: white, several kinds made from Tokay, Malvasia, Riesling or Weissburgunder grapes; red, several kinds made from Merlot or Cabernet grapes.

6 Emilia-Romagna.
Lambrusco: ruby-red, sparkling; several kinds, dry to sweet. Albano di Romagna: straw-coloured to golden yellow, dry to semi-sweet. Sangiovese di Romagna: ruby-red, dry, well rounded

7 Tuscany.
Chianti: ruby-red to garnet-red, dry, well rounded. Vernaccia di San Gimignano: light yellow, dry, well rounded

8 Umbria, Latium.
Colli Albani: straw-coloured, dry to slightly sweet. Frascati: straw-coloured, soft, velvety, semi-sweet to sweet (several varieties). Est Est Est (Montefiascone): straw-coloured, full, slightly sweet. Orvieto: light yellow to straw-coloured, dry

9 Marche, Abruzzi.
Verdicchio dei Castelli di Iesi:. straw-coloured, dry, well rounded. Montepulciano d'Abruzzo: deep ruby-red, dry, soft. Bianchello del Metauro: straw-coloured, dry, fresh

10 Campania, Apulia, Calabria, Basilicata.
Ischia: red and white, several kinds. San Severo: straw-coloured, fresh and well rounded; ruby-red, dry, full-bodied. Locorotondo: greenish-yellow to straw-coloured, dry, pleasant. Rossa Barletta: ruby-red, dry, well rounded

11 Sardinia.
Cannonau: ruby-red, dry to slightly sweet, pleasant. Monica di Sardegna: light ruby-red, dry, aromatic. Nuragus: light straw- coloured, dry

12 Sicily.
Etna: red and white, several kinds. Marsala: the famous dessert wine, amber-yellow, full-bodied, dry or sweet

Categories and labelling of Italian wines

General

Wines can vary widely in quality and those dispensed from a carafe in a pizzeria or trattoria are unlikely to be very distinguished. Better by far to select a bottled wine, consulting the label carefully. By law Italian wines must be classified in one of several categories some of which are very strictly controlled.

Vino di Tavola

Table wines of unspecified origin: no restrictions on where produced; subject neither to chemical analysis nor checks on taste.

Wine-Growing Regions of Italy

Table wines labelled with geographical origin: otherwise no restrictions on where produced; subject neither to chemical analysis nor checks on taste.

Vino da Tavola con indicazione geografica

Denominazione di Origine Controllata: must be produced within a precisely defined area and satisfy certain other requirements; chemical analysis and checks on taste are compulsory before the wine can be marketed.

DOC

Denominazione di Origine Controllata e Garantita: wines so labelled undergo a further production test in addition to meeting the requirements for DOC wines. The numbered stripe on the bottle neck is a guarantee of origin.

DOCG

Vino Spumante di Qualità: sparkling wine (spumante) without a guarantee of origin.

VSQ

VSQPRD   Vino Spumante di Qualità prodotta in Regioni determinate: sparkling wine of controlled origin, subject to the same requirements as DOC wines.

Getting to Italy

By car

It is a long way from Britain or northern Europe to Italy. Motorists will be well advised, therefore, to use motorways and trunk roads wherever possible. The quickest route from the Channel is via Calais, Basle and the St Gotthard tunnel, but there are many alternative routes via France or Germany and Switzerland. The road journey can be shortened by using the car sleeper services which operate in summer from Boulogne, Brussels and Paris to Milan.

Motorways are free in Holland, Belgium and Germany, but are subject to tolls in France and Italy. Drivers using the Swiss motorways must pay a flat-rate tax and display a vignette on the windscreen. The vignette can be bought from motoring organisations in the UK or at the Swiss frontier.

By bus

In addition to numerous package tours by coach from Britain to Italy there are various regular bus services. Euroways run services from London to Aosta, Bologna, Brindisi, Florence, Genoa, Milan, Rome, Turin and Venice, and National Express Eurolines have services from London to Aosta, Bologna, Florence, Milan, Rome, Turin and Venice.

Information

Eurolines UK Ltd
52 Grosvenor Gardens
London SW1
tel. (0171) 7308235

National Express Eurolines
Victoria Coach Station
London SW1
Central Reservation number: (0990) 143219

By rail

British Rail can issue tickets from main stations in Britain to main stations in Italy, covering the Channel crossing and sleeping cars (first class, second class or couchettes) from the continental port. Advance booking is advisable.

Information

European Rail Travel Centre
P.O. Box 303
Victoria Station
London SW1V 1JY
Tel. (0990) 848848

By air

There are regular direct flights from London to Bologna, Genoa, Milan, Naples, Pisa, Rome, Turin and Venice; from Manchester to Milan and Rome; and from Birmingham and Glasgow to Milan. There are connections from Milan and Rome to other Italian airports as well as numerous charter flights from Britain, particularly during the main holiday season.

Help for Visitors with Disabilities

Information
in the UK

The principal UK sources of information and advice on travel by the disabled are: the Royal Association for Disability and Rehabilitation (RADAR), 12 City Forum, 250 City Road, London EC1V 8AS (0171) 2503222; the Spinal Injuries Association, 76 St James's Lane, London N10 3DF, tel. (0181) 4442121.

Information about rail and air travel facilities for the disabled (including any reductions) is available from travel agencies.

Accommodation brochures issued by local tourist offices (see Information) include details of facilities for people with disabilities.

Accommodation in Italy

Hotels

The hotels in the higher categories in large towns and holiday centres offer the usual international standards of comfort and amenity, but in remoter areas the accommodation available will often be of a more modest standard. In the larger towns and in spas and seaside resorts there are numerous *pensioni* (pensions, guesthouses).

Italian hotels (*alberghi, singular albergo*) are officially classified in five categories: categoria di lusso, di prima, di seconda, di terza and di quarta categoria (luxury and I, II, III and IV). The range is from the 5-star luxury hotel to the one-star hotel of more modest pretensions.
   In this guide the luxury hotels are indicated by the letter L and a red star before the name. The categories of other hotels are shown by the Roman figures I, II, III and IV. In terms of stars the equivalence is as follows:

Categories

★★★★★	L
★★★★	I
★★★	II
★★	III
★	IV

For most hotels the number of beds is indicated (e.g. 40 b.); for some the number of rooms is given (e.g. 20 r.). SP indicates that the hotel has a swimming pool, CP an indoor pool. Area dialling codes are given in the margin.

Hotel tariffs vary considerably according to season, and are substantially higher in large towns and popular holiday areas than in the rest of the country.

Tariffs

Lists of hotels in particular towns or areas can be obtained, before leaving home, from the Italian State Tourist Office (ENIT: see Information) or, in Italy, from local tourist information offices.

Terme Bristol Buja, Via Monteortone 2, tel. 8669390, fax 667910, I, 236 b, SP
Terme La Residence, Via Monte Ceva 8, tel. 8668333, fax 8668396, I, 177 b, SP
President, Via Montirone 31, tel. 8 66 82 88, fax 667909, I, 182 b, SP
Grand Hôtel Trieste e Victoria, Via Pietro d'Abano 1, tel. 8669101, fax 8669779, I, 160 b, SP
Metropole, Via Valerio Flacco 99, tel. 8600777, fax 8600935, I, 160 b, CP, SP
Quisisana, Viale delle Terme 67, tel. 8600099, fax 8600039, I, 158 b, SP
Ritz, Via Monteortone 19, tel. 8669990, fax 667549, I, 219 b, SP
Terme Mioni Pezzato, Via Marzia 34, tel. 8668377, fax 8669338, I, 264 b, SP
Harry's Hotel Terme, Via Marzia 50, tel. 667011, fax 8668500, II, 91 b, SP
Terme Hotel Smeraldo, Via Flavio Busonera 174, tel. 8669555, fax 8669752, II, 108 b, SP

Abano Terme (049)

Giardino, Via 1° Maggio 63, II, tel. 778106, fax 776444, 73 b
Kappa Due, Via del Laghetto 15, tel. 778609, fax 776337, II, 24 b

Abbadia San Salvatore (0577)

Antiche Terme, Viale Donati, tel. 322101, fax 324909, I, 137 b
Nuove Terme, Piazza Italia 1, tel. 322106, fax 324909, II, 133 b, SP

Acqui Terme (0144)

Hotels

Agrigento
(0922)
Villa Athena (18th c. villa, beautifully situated opposite the Concordia Temple; basic comforts), Via dei Templi, tel. 596288, fax 402180, II, 40 r, SP

Alassio
(0182)
★Spiaggia Grand Hôtel, Via Roma 78, tel. 643403, fax 640279, L, 169 b, SP
Diana Grand Hôtel, Via Garibaldi 110, tel. 642701, fax 640304, I, 142 b, CP
Lido, Via IV Novembre 9, tel. 643141, fax 660198, II, 91 b
Nuovo Suisse, Via Mazzini 119, tel. 640192, fax 660267, II, 87 b
Arcobaleno, Via Massabò 6, tel. and fax 642589, III, 25 b

Alberobello
(080)
Dei Trulli (typical Trulli: circular white building with tiled roof), Via Cadore 32, tel. 9323555, fax 9323560, I, 54 b, SP

Alghero
(079)
Villa Las Tronas (former summer residence of the Italian kings; Moorish-style villa on a small rocky peninsula with beach), Lungomare Valencia 1, tel. 981818, fax 981044, I, 55 b, SP
Carlos V, Lungomare Valencia 24, tel. 979501, fax 980298, I, 220 b, SP
Calabona, Calabona, tel. 975728, fax 981046, II, 222 b, SP
El Faro (on Capo Cacchia, 13 km (8 mi.) north-west; Mediterranean-style hotel, all rooms with balconies and sea views), tel. 942010, fax 942030, I, 207 b, SP

Amalfi
(089)
Santa Caterina (lovely antique furniture, terraces and gardens; elevator to sea), Via Statale Amalfitana Postana, tel. 871012, fax 871351, I, 68 r, SP
Cappuccini Convento, (12th c. former monastery; sea view; elevator), Via Annunziata 46, tel. 871877, fax 871886, I, 54 r
Luna Convento (13th c. former monastery; breakfast room in Byzantine cloister; Wagner and Ibsen stayed here), Via P. Comite 33, tel. 871002, fax 871333, I, 45 r, SP
Dei Cavalieri (view of the Gulf), Via M. Comite 26, tel. 831333, fax 831354, II, 60 r

Ancona
(071)
Grand Hôtel Passetto, Via Thaon de Revel 1, tel. 31307, fax 32856, I, 74 b, CP
Grand Hôtel Palace, Lungomare Vanvitelli 24, tel. 201813, fax 2074832, I, 68 b
Fortuna, Piazza Fratelli Rosselli 15, tel. 42663, fax 42662, II, 99 b

Aosta
(0165)
Europe, Piazza Narbone 8, tel. 236363, fax 40566, I, 131 b
Hostellerie du Cheval Blanc, Via Clavalité 20, tel. 239140, fax 239150, I, 127 b, SP
Valle d'Aosta, Corso Ivrea 146, tel. 41845, fax 236660, I, 208 b
Ambassador, Via Duca degli Abruzzi 2, tel. 42230, fax 236851, II, 82 b
Turin, Via Torino 14, tel. 44593, fax 361377, II, 90 b

Arezzo
(0575)
Etrusco, Via Fleming 39, tel. 984067, fax 382131, I, 160 b
Minerva, Via Fiorentina 4, tel. 370390, fax 302415, II, 262 b
Continentale, Piazza Guido Monaco 7, tel. 20251, fax 350485, II, 137 b

Ascoli Piceno
(0736)
Gioli, Viale De Gasperi 14, tel. and fax 255550, I, 77 b
Marche, Viale Kennedy 34, tel. 45575, fax 342812, I, 60 b

Assisi
(075)
Subasio (near the Basilica of St Francis of Assisi; ★view from the terrace), Via Frate Elia 2, tel. 812206, fax 816691, I, 115 b
Fontebella, Via Fontebella 25, tel. 812883, fax 812941, I, 74 b
Giotto, Via Fontebella 41, tel. 812209, fax 816479, I, 110 b
Le Silve, Via Armenzano 82, in Armenzano, tel. 8019000, fax 8019005, I, 26 b, SP
Dei Priori, Corso Mazzini 15, tel. 812237, fax 816804, II, 62 b
La Terrazza, Via Fratelli Canonichetti, tel. 812368, fax 816142, II, 40 b
San Francesco, Via San Francesco 48, tel. 812281, fax 816237, II, 78 b
Umbra (central, but in a quiet spot), Vicolo degli Archi 6, tel. 812240, fax 813653, II, 48 b

Salera, Via Monsignor Marello 19, tel. 410169, fax 30039, I, 100 b
Aleramo, Via E. Filiberto 13, tel. 595661, fax 5945661, I, 75 b
Lis, Via Fratelli Rosselli 10, tel. 595051, fax 353845, I, 49 b
Rainero, Via Cavour 85, tel. 353866, fax 594985, II, 85 b
On a hill outside Asti (SS 10, 4 km (2¹/₂ mi.)): Hasta, a country house hotel,
Valle Benedetta 25, tel. 213312, fax 219580, I, 26 r

Asti
(0141)

Bernabo, Bagni Caldi Ponte a Serraglio, tel. 805215, II, 10 b
Bridge, Piazza di Ponte a Serraglio 5/A, tel. and fax 805324, II, 20 b

Bagni di Lucca
(0583)

Des Geneys Splendid, Viale Einaudi 21, tel. 99001, fax 999295, I, 57 r
Park Hotel Rosa Serennella, Viale della Vittoria 37, tel. 902087, fax 999848,
II, 33 r

Bardonecchia
(0122)

Palace, Via Lombardi 13, tel. 5216551, fax 5211499, I, 200 r
Villa Romanazzi Carducci (in a lovely park), Via Capruzzi 326, tel. 5227400,
fax 5560297, I, 193 b, SP
Grand Hôtel Ambasciatori, Via Omodeo 51, tel. 5010077, fax 5021678, I,
177 r, SP

Bari
(080)

Itaca, Viale Regina Elena 30, tel. 37741, fax 347786, I, 27 r, SP
Artù, Piazza Castello 67, tel. 332121, fax 332214, II, 32 r

Barletta
(0883)

★ Grand Hôtel Villa Serbelloni (magnificent palace in lakeside park setting;
terrace restaurant in summer), Via Roma 1, tel. 950216, fax 951529, L, 93
r, SP

Belvedere (★sea view), Via Valassina 31, tel. 950410, fax 950102, I, 50 b, SP
Du Lac (★sea view; roof garden terrace), Piazza Mazzini 32, tel. 950320,
fax 951624, I, 48 r

Bellagio
(031)

In Bellaria:
Elizabeth, Via Rovereto 11, tel. 344119, fax 345680, I, 82 b, SP
Ermitage, Via Ala 11, tel. 347633, fax 343083, I, 100 b, SP
Miramare, Lungomare C. Colombo 37, tel. 344131, fax 347316, 96 b, SP

In Igea Marina:
Agostini, Viale Pinzon 68, tel. 331510, fax 330085, II, 94 b
Arizona, Viale Pinzon 216, tel. 331043, II, 176 b

Bellaria-
Igea Marina
(0541)

Villa Carpenada, Via Mier 158, tel. 948343, fax 948345, I, 40 b
Mirella, Via Don Minzoni 6, tel. 941860, fax 942126, II, 25 b

Belluno
(0437)

Grand Hôtel Italiano, Viale Principe di Napoli 137, tel. 24111, fax 21758, II,
71 r

Benevento
(0824)

Cappello d'Oro e del Moro, Viale Papa Giovanni XXIII 12, tel. 232503, fax
242946, I, 238 b
Excelsior San Marco, Piazza della Repubblica 6, tel. 366111, fax 223201, I,
297 b
Pantheon, Via Borgo Palazzo 154, tel. 308111, fax 308308, I, 172 b
Starhotel Cristallo Palace, Via Betty Ambiveri 35, tel. 311211, fax 312031,
I, 164 b
Il Gourmet (comfortable rooms, good food), Via S. Vigilio 1, tel. and fax
256110, II, 19 b

Bergamo
(035)

Grand Hôtel Baglioni, Via dell'Indipendenza 8, tel. 225445, fax 234840, I,
240 b
Royal Hotel Carlton, Via Montebello 8, tel. 249361, fax 249724, I, 462 b
Corona d'Oro (good location in the historic town centre), Via Oberdan 12,
tel. 236456, fax 262679, I, 62 b
Grand Hôtel Elite, Via Aurelio Saffi 36, tel. 6491432, fax 6492426, I, 268 b
Tre Vecchi, Via dell'Indipendenza 47, tel. 231991, fax 224143, I, 191 b
Dei Commercianti (in the pedestrian precinct adjacent to the cathedral),
Via de Pignattari 11, tel. 233052, fax 224733, II, 35 r
Maxim, Via Ferrirese 152, tel. 323235, fax 320535, II, 65 b

Bologna
(051)

Hotels

Bolsena
(0761)
Columbus Hotel sul Lago, Viale Colesanti 27, tel. 799009, fax 798172, II, 78 b

Bolzano
(0471)
Parkhotel Laurin (old palazzo, centrally situated; Park and Belle Epoque restaurants, Laurin Bar), Laurinstr. 4, tel. 311000, fax 311148, I, 184 b, SP
Mondschein, Piavestr. 15, tel. 975642, fax 975577, I, 130 b
Stiegl (with garden restaurant), Brennerstr. 11, tel. 976222, fax 981141, I, 100 b, SP
Reichrieglerhof, Reichrieglerweg 9, tel. 285742, fax 266345, II, 18 b, SP
Magdalenerhof, Rentscher Str. 48/A, tel. 978267, fax 981076, II, 45 b
Parkhotel Werth, Pfarrhofstr. 19, tel. 250103, fax 251514, II, 50 b
Pircher, Meraner Str. 52, tel. 917513, fax 202433, II, 44 b

Bordighera
(0184)
Grand Hôtel Cap Ampelio, Via Virgilio 5, tel. 264333, fax 264244, I, 160 b, SP
Grand Hôtel del Mare, Via Portico della Punta 34, tel. 262201, fax 262394, I, 216 b, SP
Centrohotel, Piazza Stazione 10, tel. and fax 265265, II, 67 b
Villa Elisa, Via Romana 70, tel. 261313, fax 261942, II, 65 b, SP

Bormio
(0342)
Baita dei Pini, Via Don Peccedi 15, tel. 904346, fax 904700, I, 90 b
Palace, Via Milano 54, tel. 903131, fax 903366, I, 154 b, CP
Posta, Via Roma 66, tel. 904753, fax 904484, I, 95 b, CP
Astoria, Via Roma 73, tel. 910900, fax 905253, II, 80 b
Olimpia, Via Funivia 39, tel. and fax 901510, III, 53 b

Brescia
(030)
★Vittoria, Via X Giornate 20, tel. 280061, fax 280065, L, 103 b
Ambasciatori, Via Crocefissa di Rosa 90/92, tel. 399114, fax 381883, I, 101 b
Alabarda, Via Labirinto 6, tel. 3541377, fax 3541300, II, 41 b

Bressanone
(0472)
Dominik, Unterdrittelgasse 13, tel. 830144, fax 836554, I, 45 b, CP
★Elefante (rich in history; built in 1550 to house the attendants of an elephant, a present to the Habsburg Emperor Ferdinand from the King of Portugal), Weßlahnstr. 4, tel. 832750, fax 836579, I, 72 b, SP
Temlhof, Elvaser Str. 76, tel. 836658, fax 835539, II, 100 b, CP, SP
Goldene Krone, Stadelgasse 4, tel. 835154, fax 835014, II, 62 b
Senoner-Unterdrittel, Rienzdamm 22, tel. 832525, fax 832436, II, 41 b

Brindisi
(0831)
Majestic, Corso Umberto I 151, tel. 222941, fax 524071, I, 68 r
Mediterraneo, Viale Aldo Moro 70, tel. 582811, fax 587858, II, 65 r

Cagliari
(070)
Mediterraneo, Lungomare C. Colombo 46, tel. 301271, fax 301274, I, 284 b
Panorama, Viale Armando Diaz 231, tel. 307691, fax 305413, I, 227 b, SP
Calamosca sul Mare, Viale Calamosca 50, tel. 371628, fax 370346, II, 115 b
Italia, Via Sardegna 31, tel. 660410, fax 650240, II, 175 b

Caltanissetta
(0934)
San Michele, Via Fasci Siciliani, tel. 553750, fax 598791, I, 122 r, SP
Plaza, Via Berengario Gaetani 5, tel. and fax 583877, II, 21 r

Campobasso
(0874)
Roxy, Piazza Savoia 7, tel. and fax 411541, II, 153 b
Skanderbeg, Via Navelli 31B, tel. 413341, fax 416430, II, 136 b

Capri
(081)
In Anacapri: ★Europa Palace (with Beauty Farm; terrace), Via Capodimonte 2, tel. 8 373800, fax 8373191, L, 90 r, SP
In Capri: ★Grand Hôtel Quisisana (Capri's most elegant hotel), Via Camerelle 2, tel. 8370788, fax 8376080, L, 135 r, SP
Punta Tragara (Le Corbusier-designed; beautifully situated high above the sea; tasteful décor; garden with tropical plants), Via Tragara 57, tel. 8370844, fax 8377790, I, 10 r, SP
Luna, Viale Matteotti 3, tel. 8370433, fax 8377459, I, 50 r, SP
Villa Brunella (lovely terrace), Via Tragara 24, tel. 8370122, fax 8370430, II, SP
Villa Sarah (among vineyards), Via Tiberio 3a, tel. 8377817, fax 8377215, 20 r

Jolly, Viale Vittorio Veneto 9, tel. 325222, fax 354522, I, 103 r
Europa, Via Roma 19, tel. 325400, fax 245805, II, 58 r

Caserta
(0823)

Forum Palace, Via Casilina, km 136.5, tel. 301211, fax 302116, I, 191 b, SP
Rocca, Via Sferracavalli 105, tel. 311213, fax 25427, II, 55 b, SP

Cassino
(0776)

Castelvecchio, Via Pio XI, tel. 9360308, fax 9360579, II, 40 b
Culla el Lago, tel. 9360047, fax 9360425, II, 57 b

Castel Gandolfi
(06)

La Medusa, Via Passeggiata Archeologica 5, tel. 8723383, fax 8717009, I,
54 r, SP
Stabia (roof garden restaurant with sea view), Corso V Emanuele 101, tel.
and fax 8722577, I, 92 r

Castellammare
di Stábia
(081)

Hotel Villagio Pedraladda, Via Zirulia 50, tel. 470383, fax 470499, II, 240 b,
SP
Riviera, Lungomare Anglona 1, tel. 470143, fax 471312, II, 58 b

Castelsardo
(079)

Duca della Corgna, Via B. Buozzi 143, tel. 953238, fax 9652446, II, 25 b
Miralago, Piazza Mazzini 6, tel. 951157, fax 951924, II, 38 b

Castiglione
del Lago
(075)

Excelsior, Piazza Verga 39, tel. 537071, fax 537015, I, 167 r

Catania
(095)

Guglielmo, Via A. Tedeschi 1, tel. 741922, fax 722181, I, 72 b
Grand Hôtel, Piazza Matteotti, tel. 701256, fax 741621, II, 158 b

Catanzaro
(0961)

Caravelle, Via Padova 6, tel. 962416, fax 962417, I, 70 b, SP
Waldorf Palace, Via Gran Bretagna 10, tel. 951210, fax 954932, I, 228 b
Belsoggiorno, Viale Carducci 88, tel. and fax 963133, II, 68 b
Europa Monetti, Via Curiel 39, tel. 954159, fax 958176, II, 105 b, SP
Ines, Via del Prete 107, tel. and fax 954775, II, 68 b, SP
Ambassador, Via Forli 8, tel. 953420, III, 76 b, SP

Cattolica
(0541)

Carlton Riviera (elegant ambience), in Capo Plaia, tel. 420004, fax 420264,
II, 281 b, SP
In Caldura: Kalura (wide range of sports facilities), tel. 412354, fax 423122,
II, 117 b, SP
In Mezzaforno: Baia del Capitano (pleasant smaller hotel amid olive
groves; stylish atmosphere, good sports facilities), tel. 420005, fax
420163, II, 64 b, SP

Cefalù
(0921)

Riviera, Via Colla 55, tel. 990541, I, 104 b
San Michele, Via Monte Tabor 26, tel. 990017, fax 993111, I, 98 b, SP

Celle Ligure
(019)

★Grand Hôtel Villa d'Este (★foyer with antique furnishings, magnificent
park, terrace; tennis, golf, horse-riding nearby), Via Regina 40, tel. 3481,
fax 348844, L, 151 r, SP, CP
Regina Olga, Via Regina 18, tel. 510171, fax 340604, I, 80 r, SP
Miralago, tel. 510125, fax 248126, II, 42 b

Cernobbio
(031)

Grand Hôtel Cervia, Lungomare Grazia Deledda 9, tel. 970500, fax 972086,
I, 92 b
Beau Rivage, Lungomare Grazia Deledda 116, tel. 971010, fax 971746, II,
72 b, SP
Conchiglia, Lungomare Grazia Deledda 46, tel. 970436, fax 71370, II, 100 b,
SP

Cervia
(0544)

Britannia, Viale Carducci 129, tel. 672500, fax 81799, I, 83 b, SP
Pino, Via A. Garibaldi 7, tel. 80645, fax 84788, I, 111 b
Miramare, Viale Carducci 2, tel. 80006, fax 874785, II, 57 b, SP
Torino, Viale Carducci 55, tel. 80044, fax 672510, II, 87 b, SP

Cesenatico
(0547)

Hotels

Chianciano Terme (0578)	Alexander Palme, Viale B Buozzi 76, tel. and fax 64010, I, 95 b, SP Ambasciatori, Viale della Libertà 512, tel. and fax 64371, I, 177 b, SP Grand Hotel Excelsior, Viale S. Agnese 6, tel. 64351, fax 63214, I, 144 b, SP Michelangelo, Via delle Piane 146, tel. 64004, fax 64080, I, 122 b, SP Bosco, Via C. Marchesi 83, tel. 64307, II, 87 b, SP Carlton Elite, Viale U. Foscolo 21, tel. 6 43 95, fax 64440, II, 84 b, SP Cristallo, Viale Lombardia 35, tel. 64051, fax 64052, II, 172 b, SP
Chieti (0871)	Dangiò, Strada Solferino 20, in Tricalle, tel. 347356, fax 346984, I, 62 b Abruzzo, Via Asinio Herio 26, tel. 420141, fax 42042, II, 113 b
Chioggia (041)	Grande Italia, Piazza Vigo 1, tel. 400515, fax 400185, II, 93 b Bristol, Lungomare Adriatico 46, tel. 5540389, fax 5541813, I, 120 b Ritz, Lungomare Adriatico 48, tel. 491700, fax 493900, I, 150 b, SP Pineta, Via Lungomare Adriatico 16, tel. 401388, fax 401829, II, 149 r
Chiusi (0578)	In Querce al Pino, 6 km (3¾ mi.) from Chiusi: Ismaele, tel. 274077, fax 274069, II, 84 b, SP
Città di Castello (075)	Tiferno, Piazza Raffaello Sanzio 13, tel. 8550331, fax 8521196, I, 74 b Delle Terme, Via Fontecchio 4, tel. 8520614, fax 8557236, II, 201 b, SP
Cividale dei Friuli (0432)	Roma (informal atmosphere), Piazza A. Picco 3, tel. 731871, fax 701033, II, 91 b Locanda al Castello (former Jesuit monastery; rustic; garden setting), Via del Castello 18, tel. 733242, fax 700901, 20 b
Civitavecchia (0766)	Sunbay Park, with Dépendance Sunbay (annexe), Via Aurelia sud km 68.75, tel. and fax 22801, I, 164 b, SP
Como (031)	Barchetta Excelsior, Piazza Cavour 1, tel. 3221, fax 302622, I, 175 b Como, Via Mentana 28, tel. 266173, fax 266020, I, 149 b Firenze, Piazza Volta 16, tel. 300333, fax 300101, II, 81 b
Cortina d'Ampezzo (0436)	★Miramonti Majestic Grand Hotel, Via Peziè 103, tel. 4201, fax 867019, L, 198 b, SP Cortina, Corso Italia 92, tel. 4221, fax 860760, I, 78 b De la Poste, Piazza Roma 14, tel. 4271, fax 868435, I, 134 b Parc Hotel Victoria, Corso Italia 1, tel. 3246, fax 4734, I, 71 b Menardi (former coaching inn), Via Majon 110, tel. 2400, fax 862183, II, 87 b Trieste, Via Majon 28, tel. 2245, fax 868173, II, 52 b In Pocol: Sport Hotel Tofana, tel. 3281, fax 868074, II, 125 b
Cortona (0575)	San Michele (15th c. palazzo), Via Guelfa 15, tel. 604348, fax 630147, I, 66 b
Cosenza (0984)	Royal, Via Molinella 24/E, tel. 412165, fax 411777, I, 84 b Centrale, Via del Tigrai 3, tel. 73681, fax 75750, II, 83 b
Costa Smeralda (0789)	★Cala Di Volpe (fashionable hotel in the island style with towers, terraces, arcades and footways; harbour), tel. 976111, fax 976617, L, 263 b, SP ★Pitrizza (built of local stone), Liscia di Vacca, tel. 930111, fax 930611, L, 102 b, SP In Porto Cervo: ★Romazzino (rooms with private terrace), tel. 977111, fax 96292, L, 186 b, SP Le Ginestre (small villas in park), tel. 92030, fax 94087, I, 156 b, SP Valdiola, tel. 96215, fax 96652, II, 66 b, SP
Courmayeur (0165)	Les Jumeaux, Strada Regionale 35 (annexe, Strada delle Volpi 17B), tel. 846796, fax 844122, 201 b Palace Bron (terrace with ★panoramic view), Plan Gorret 41, tel. 846742, fax 844015, I, 52 b Pavillon, Strada Regionale 62, tel. 846120, fax 846122, I, 104 b, SP Cresta et Duc, Via Circonvallazione 7, tel. 842585, fax 842591, II, 77 b

Continental (middle-of-the-range 1950s-style hotel with excellent restaurant; periphery of town centre), Piazza Libertà 26, tel. and fax 434141, I, 114 b
Cremona
(0372)

Principe, Piazza Duccio Galimberti 5, tel. 693355, fax 67562, I, 74 b
Royal Superga, Via Pascal 3, tel. 693223, fax 699101, II, 60 b
Cuneo
(0171)

Rizzi, Viale Carducci 9, tel. 531617, fax 536135, I, 76 b
Mina, Corso Italia 56, tel. 531098, fax 536327, II, 71 b
Darfo Boario
Terme
(0364)

Residence Oliveto, Lungolago C. Battisti-Via Tito Malaguti 4/6, tel. 9911919, fax 9911224, I, 117 r, SP, CP
Piccola Vela, Viale Dal Molin 36, tel. and fax 9914666, 80 b, SP
Piroscafo, Via Porto Vecchio 11, tel. 9141128, fax 9912586, II, 62 b
Desenzano
del Garda
(030)

Bellevue e Méditerranée, Via Generale Ardoino 2/4, tel. and fax 402693, I, 130 b, SP
Diana Majestic, Via degli Oleandri 15, tel. 495445, fax 494039, I, 156 b, SP
Gabriella, Via dei Gerani 9, tel. 403131, fax 405055, II, 88 b, SP
Golfo e Palme, Viale Torino 12, tel. 495096, fax 494304, II, 77 b
Diano Marina
(0183)

Grande Albergo Sicilia, Piazza Colaianni 7, tel. 500850, fax 500488, II, 70 r
Enna
(0935)

Cavallino, Via Forlivese 185, tel. 634411, fax 634440, I, 160 b
Vittoria, Corso Garibaldi 23, tel. 21508, fax 29136, I, 79 b
Faenza
(0546)

Elisabeth Due, Piazzale Amendola 2, tel. 823146, fax 823147, II, 32 r
Corallo, Via Leonardo da Vinci 3, tel. 804200, fax 803637, II, 22 r
Fano
(0721)

★Duchessa Isabella (15th c. palazzo; ★lounges with coffered ceilings), Via Palestro 68/70, tel. 202121, fax 202638, L, 56 b
Ripagrande, Via Ripagrande 21, tel. 765250, fax 764377, I, 97 b
Touring, Viale Cavour 11, tel. 206200, fax 212000, II, 84 b
Ferrara
(0532)

Finale Ligure
(019)
Boncardo, Corso Europa 4, tel. 601751, fax 680419, I, 90 b
Grand Hôtel Moroni, Via San Pietro 38, tel. 692222, fax 680330, I, 173 b
Astoria, Via Calvisio 92, tel. 601635/6, fax 601480, II, 108 b
Internazionale, Via Concezione 3, tel. 692054, fax 692053, II, 62 b
Park Hotel Castello, Via Caviglia 26, tel. 691320, fax 692775, II, 33 b

In Fiuggi Fonte: ★Grand Hôtel Palazzo della Fonte, Via dei Villini 7, tel. 5081, fax 506752, L, 303 b, SP
Vallombrosa, Via Valle del Silenzio 1/2, tel. 515531, fax 506646, I, 147 b
Villa Igea, Corso Nuova Italia 32, tel. 515435, fax 515438, I, 50 b, SP
Fiuggi Terme, Via Prenestina 9, tel. 515212, fax 506566, II, 103 b, SP
Mondial Park, Via Sant'Emiliano 82, tel. 515848, fax 506671, II, 64 b, SP
Fiuggi
(0775)

★Excelsior (beside the Arno), Piazza Ognissanti 3, tel. 264201, fax 210278, L, 312 b
★Grand Hotel, Piazza Ognissanti 1, tel. 288781, fax 217400, L, 202 b
★Regency (Florentine aristocrat's villa with rooms in the English style), Piazza M. Azeglio 3, tel. 245247, fax 2346735, L, 66 b
★Villa Cora (Neo-Classical villa in its own gardens, built by Baron Oppenheim in 1865; dining-room originally a salon decorated in Arab style), Viale Machiavelli 18, tel. 2298451, fax 229086, L, 92 b, SP
★Villa Medici (city centre), Via il Prato 42, tel. 2381331, fax 2381336, L, 198 b, SP
Baglioni (roof garden restaurant with ★magnificent view), Piazza Unità Italiana 6, tel. 23580, fax 2358895, I, 357 b
Brunelleschi (built by Italo Gamberini; near the cathedral; small private museum), Piazza Santa Elisabetta 3, tel. 562068, fax 219653, I, 166 b
Florence
(055)

Hotels

Plaza & Lucchesi (beside the Arno 10 minutes' walk from the city centre), Lungarno della Zecca Vecchia 38, tel. 264141, fax 2480921, I, 172 b

Kraft (near the theatre; roof garden restaurant with ★fine view), Via Solferino 2, tel. 284273, fax 2398267, I, 120 b, SP

Mona Lisa (old palazzo in a lovely garden; elegant ambience), Borgo Pinti 27, tel. 2479751, fax 2479755, I, 43 b

Montebello Splendid (elegant 14th c. villa; city centre), Via Montebello 60, tel. 2398051, fax 211867, I, 80 b

Torre di Bellosguardo (12th c. palazzo; tranquil setting; ★view of the city), Via Roti Michelozzi 2, tel. 2298145, fax 229008, I, 30 b, SP

Villa Belvedere (★view of Florence), Via Castelli 3, tel. 222501, fax 223163, I, 50 b, SP, tennis

Villa Carlotta (patrician villa near the Palazzo Pitti and Boboli Gardens), Via Michele di Lando 3, tel. 2336134, fax 2336147, I, 46 b

Auto Park Hotel, Via Valdegola 1, tel. 431771, fax 4221557, II, 198 b

Hermitage (★terrace with view of the Ponte Vecchio, Palazzo Pitti, cathedral dome, etc.), Vicolo Marzio 1, tel. 287216, fax 212208, II, 15 b

Villa Le Rondini, Via Bolognese Vecchia (at Trespiano 7 km (4¹/₂ mi.)), tel. 400081, fax 268212, II, 57 b, SP

Ariston, Via Fiesolana 40, tel. 2476693, fax 2476980, III, 46 b

In Candeli: ★Villa la Massa (16th c. building; excellent restaurant), Via La Massa 6, tel. 6510101, fax 6510109, L, 74 b, SP

In Fiesole: ★Villa San Michele (former 15th c. Franciscan monastery in lovely setting; splendidly furnished rooms, delightful garden), Via Doccia 4, tel. 59451, fax 598734, L, 54 b, SP

Foggia (0881)	Cicolella, Viale XXIX Maggio 60, tel. 688890, fax 678984, I, 93 r White House, Via Monte Sabotino 24, tel. 721644, fax 721646, I, 37 r President, Viale degli Aviatori 130, tel. 618010, fax 617930, II, 129 r
Foligno (0742)	Poledrini, Viale Mezzati 3, tel. and fax 341041, II, 89 b Villa Roncalli, Viale Roma, tel. 391091, fax 671001, III, 10 r
Forlì (0543)	Michelangelo, Via Buonarotti 4/6, tel. 400233, fax 400615, I, 20 r Masini, Corso Garibaldi 28, tel. 28072, fax 21915, II, 42 r
Frascati (06)	Villa Tuscolana, Via del Tuscolo, tel. 9417450, fax 9424747, II, 154 b Flora, Viale Vittorio Veneto 8–10, tel. 9416110, fax 9420198, II, 60 b
Frosinone (0775)	Cesari, Via L. Refice 331, tel. 291581, fax 293322, I, 107 b Astor, Via Casilina Nord 20, tel. 270131, fax 270135, II, 84 b
Gabbice Mare (0541)	Alexander, Via Panoramica 35, tel. 954166, fax 960144, I, 82 b, SP Cavalluccio Marino, Via V. Veneto III, tel. 950053, fax 954402, III, 35 r Grand Hotel Michelacci, Piazza Giardini Unità d'Italia, tel. 954361, fax 954544, I, 96 b, SP Venus, Via Panoramica 29, tel. 962601, fax 952220, I, 75 b, SP
Gaeta (0771)	Aenea's Landing, Via Flacca, km 23.6, tel. 741713, fax 741356, II, 30 b Il Ninfeo, Via Flacca, km 22, tel. 742291, fax 740736, II, 94 b, SP Serapo, in Serapo, tel. 741403, fax 741507, II, 249 b, SP
Garda (045)	Eurotel, Via Marconi 18, tel. 6270333, fax 7256640, I, 207 b, SP Park Hotel Oasi, Via della Pace, tel. 7256690, fax 7256705, I, 244 b, SP Sport Hotel Olimpo, tel. 7256444, fax 7256797, I, 148 b, SP Flora, Via Giorgione 27, tel. 7255348, II, 104 b, SP Imperial, Via Pascoli 4, tel. 7255382, fax 7256311, II, 81 b, SP
Gardone Riviera (0365)	Fasano Grand Hôtel, Corso Zanardelli 160, tel. 290220, fax 290221, I, 136 b, SP Grand Hôtel, Corso Zanardelli 84, tel. 20261, fax 22695, I, 303 b, SP Villa Principe, Corso Zanardelli 160, tel. 290220, fax 290221, I, 24 b., SP Villa Fiordaliso, Via Zanardelli 150, tel. 20158, fax 290011, II, 14 b

Bristol Palace, Via XX Settembre 35, tel. 592541, fax 561756, I, 235 b   Genoa
Savoja Majestic, Via Arsenale di Terra 5, tel. 261641, fax 261883, I, 195 b   (010)
Starhotel President, Piazza delle Americhe 6, Corte Lambruschini 4, tel.
    5727, fax 5531820, I, 384 b
Alexander, Via Bersaglieri d'Italia 19, tel. 261371, fax 265257, II, 54 b
Crespi, Via A. Doria 10, tel. 261723, fax 261724, II, 82 b
Helvetia, Piazza Della Nunziata 1, tel. 205839, fax 2470627, II, 45 b
Nuovo Astoria, Piazza Brignole 4, tel. 873316, fax 8317326, II, 123 b
Metropoli, Piazza Fontana Marose, tel. 2468888, fax 2468686, II, 45 r
Bel Soggiorno, Via XX Settembre 19/2, tel. 542880, fax 581418, III, 30 b

Palace, Corso Italia 63, tel. 82166, fax 31658, II, 70 r   Gorizia
                                                           (0481)

Grand Hôtel Astoria, largo San Grisogono 2, tel. 83550, fax 83355, I, 118 r   Grado
    SP   (0431)

Bastiani Grand Hôtel, Piazza Gioberti 64, tel. 20047, fax 29321, I, 92 b   Grosseto
Leon d'Oro, Via San Martino 46, tel. 22128, fax 22578, III, 53 b   (0564)

Park Hotel Ai Cappuccini, Via Tifernate, tel. 9234, fax 9220303, I, 189 b   Gubbio
Sporting, Via del Botagnone, tel. 9220705, fax 9220555, I, 104 b   (075)
San Marco, Via Perugina 5, tel. 9220234, fax 9273716, II, 111 b

Puntaquattroventi, Via Marittima 59, tel. 7773041, fax 7773757, II, 37 r   Herculaneum
                                                                           (081)

Centro, Piazza Unità Nazionale 4, Oneglia, tel. 273771, fax 273772, II, 36 b   Imperia
Corallo, Corso Garibaldi 29, Porto Maurizio, tel. and fax 666264, II, 77 b   (0183)
Croce di Malta, Via Scarincio 148, Porto Maurizio, tel. 667020/1, fax 63687,
    II, 73 b

Stefania Terme, Casamicciola Terme, Piazzetta Nizzola 16, tel. 994130, fax   Ischia
    994295, IV, 30 r   (081)
Grand Hôtel Excelsior, Via Emanuele Gianturco 19, Ischia Porto, tel.
    991522, fax 984100, I, 72 r, SP, CP
Grand Hôtel Punta Molino Terme, Lungomare Cristoforo Colombo 25, tel.
    991544, I, 82 r, SP, CP
Bristol Hotel Terme, Via Venanzio Marone 10, tel. 992181, fax 993201, II,
    61 r, SP

Grand Hôtel Europa, on the SS 17, Isernia North exit, tel. 411450, fax   Isernia
    413243, I, 80 b   (0865)
Sayonara, Via G. Berta 131, tel. 50992, II, 41 b

★La Posta Vecchia (old coaching inn converted into a luxury hotel by Jean   Ladispoli
    Paul Getty, the American oil millionaire; Renaissance-style suites and   (06)
    magnificent terrace overlooking the sea), in Palo Laziale, 35 km (22 mi.)
    or so north-west of Rome, tel. 9949501, fax 9949507, L, 24 b, CP

Splendid, Piazza Badaro 4, tel. 690325, fax 690894, I, 81 b, SP   Laigueglia
Mediterraneo, Via Andrea Doria 18, tel. 690240, fax 499739, II, 65 b   (0182)

Grand Hôtel del Parco, Corso Federico II 74, tel. 413248, fax 65938, I, 64 b   L'Aquila
Duca degli Abruzzi (restaurant with panoramic view), Viale Giovanni XXIII   (0862)
    10, tel. 28341, fax 61588, II, 230 b
Le Cannelle, Via Trancredi da Pentima, tel. 411194, fax 412453, II, 274 b, SP

Ghironi, Via Tino 62, tel. 504141, fax 524724, I, 92 b   La Spezia
Firenze, Via Paleocapa 7, tel. 713210, fax 714930, II, 110 b   (0187)
Genova, Via Fratelli Rosselli 84, tel. 732972, fax 732923, II, 44 b

Admiral, Via dei Devoto 89, tel. 306072, II, 51 b, SP   Lavagna
Tigullio, Via Matteotti 3, tel. 392965, fax 390277, II, 72 b   (0185)

Hotels

Lecce (0832)	President, Via Salandra 6, tel. 311881, fax 372283, I, 281 b Tiziano, Superstrada Lecce-Brindisi, tel. and fax 247180, I, 351 b
Lecco (0341)	Don Abbondio, Piazza Era 10, tel. 362563, fax 366315, II, 35 b Giordano, Lungo Lago Cadoma 20, tel. 367160, fax 283634, II, 26 b
Levanto (0187)	Carla, Via Martiri della Libertà 28, tel. 808275, fax 808261, II, 69 b Stella d'Italia, Corso Italia 26, tel. 808109, fax 809044, II, 74 b
Lido Adriano (0544)	Grand Hôtel Adriano/Club Hotel Adriano (beach hotel complex; garden restaurant, local and international cuisine), Viale Petrarca 402, tel. 495446, fax 495164, SP and other sports facilities.
Lido di Jesolo (0421)	Amalfi, Via Verde 43, tel. 971631, fax 370246, I, 145 b, SP Beau Rivage Pineta, Piazza Europa 6, tel. 961074, fax 961075, I, 110 b Park Hotel Brasilia, Via Levantina 11, tel. 380851, fax 92244, I, 67 b, SP Alexander, Piazza Nember 20/21, tel. 971714, fax 370699, II, 148 b, SP Dainese, Viale Oriente 140, tel. 961023, fax 961335, III, 56 b, SP
Lido di Ostia (06)	Satellite Palace, Via delle Antille 49, tel. 5693841, fax 5695994, I, 519 b La Riva, Piazzale Magellano 22, tel. 5622231, fax 5621667, II, 24 b
Lido di Savio (0544)	Palace Lido (modern, beautifully maintained hotel in quiet position by the sea; mini club for children; wide range of sports facilities), Via Marradi 12, tel. 940223, fax 949298, II, 140 b, SP Asiago Beach (modern hotel in quiet location right by the sea; dining-room with panoramic view; large terrace overlooking the sea), Viale Romagna 217, tel. 949187, fax 979110, II, 72 b, plenty of opportunities for sports, SP Tropicana (another modern hotel in a quiet position right by the sea; garden), Viale Adriatico 32, tel. 949195, II, 78 b, SP Bahamas (modern hotel in quiet situation a few yards from the sea), Via Cesena 8, tel. and fax 949190, II, 69 b Hotel Club Bikini (own sports facilities and more near by; beauty treatments), Via Casola 2, tel. 949286, fax 949239, II, 160 b, SP Delle Rose (modern hotel in quiet position by the sea; tennis courts, horse-riding and golf course near by; Mirabilandia aqua park), Viale Marradi 1, tel. 949020, fax 939709, III, 76 b
Lignano Sabbiadoro (0431)	Atlantic, Lungomare Trieste 160, tel. 71101, fax 71103, I, 112 b, SP Bristol, Lungomare Trieste 132, tel. 73131, fax 720420, I, 107 b Conca Verde, Via Carinzia 28, tel. 71765, fax 720380, II, 105 b Los Nidos (holiday village), tel. 71508, 70077, fax 720450, I, 600 chalets
Lipari Islands (090)	On Lipari: Meligunis (spacious rooms; terrace with sea view), Via Marte 7, tel. 9812426, fax 9880149, I, 64 b Carasco (*sea view; panoramic vista from the terrace), Porto delle Genti, tel. 9811605, fax 9811828, I, 163 b, SP Gattopardo Park (18th c. villa with hotel chalets in a lovely garden setting), Viale Diana, tel. 9811035, fax 9880207, II, 99 b
Livigno (0342)	Intermonti, Via Gerus 17, tel. 970003, fax 970231, I, 346 b, SP Golf Hotel Parè, Via Gerus 1/3, tel. 970263, fax 997435, I, 79 b, SP Bucaneve, Via SS 301 6, tel. 996201, fax 997588, II, 72 b, SP
Livorno (0586)	Palazzo, Viale Italia 195, tel. 805371, fax 803206, I, 207 b Granduca, Piazza Micheli 16, tel. 891024, fax 891153, II, 102 b
Loano (019)	Garden Lido, Lungomare N. Sauro 9, tel. 669666, fax 668552, I, 160 b, SP Villa Beatrice, Via S. Erasmo 6, tel. 668244, fax 668245, II, 54 b, SP
Lodi (0371)	Lodi, Via Grandi 7, tel. 35678, I, 178 b Anelli, Viale Vignati 7, tel. 421354, fax 422156, II, 29 r

Orlando da Nino, Via Villa Costantina 89, tel. and fax 978501, IV, 20 r

Loreto
(071)

★Principessa Elisa (with annexe), Strada Statale del Brennero N. 1952,
  tel. 379737, fax 379091, L, 19 b, SP
Napoleon, Viale Europa 536, tel. 316516, fax 418398, I, 92 b
Celide, Viale Giusti 25, tel. 954106, fax 954304, II, 93 b

Lucca
(0583)

Pietra di Luna, Lungomare Capone 24, tel. 877500, fax 877483, I, 96 r
Panorama (★terrace), Via S. Tecla 8, tel. 877202, fax 877998, II, 76 r, SP

Maiori
(089)

Park Hotel Querceto (service on terrace in summer), in Campiano 17/19
  (5 km (2 mi.)), tel. 7400344, fax 7400848, I, 40 b
Villa Smeralda, Via Panoramica 23, tel. 7400230, fax 6570161, III, 42 b

Malcesine
(045)

San Lorenzo (in the pedestrian precinct; antique furnishing, spacious
  rooms), Piazza Concordia 14, tel. 220500, fax 327194, I, 71 b
Broletto, Via Accademia 8, tel. 326784, fax 221297, I, 16 r

Mantua
(0376)

Park Hotel Ravenna, Viale delle Nazioni 181, tel. 531743, fax 530430, I,
  289 b, SP
Bermuda, Viale della Pace 363, tel. 530560, fax 531643, II, 30 b

Marina di
Ravenna

Cap 3000, Via Trapani 161, tel. 989055, fax 989634, II, 86 b, SP
Villa Favorita, Via Favorita 27, tel. 989100, fax 980264, III, 87 b, SP

Marsala
(0923)

Delfino (★view of the sea and Isle of Capri), Via Nastro d'Oro 2, tel. 8789261,
  fax 8089074, I, 67 r, SP
Bellavista, Via Partenope 26, tel. 8789181, fax 8089341, II, 33 r

Massa
Lubrense
(081)

Il Sole (in the town centre), Via della Libertà 43, tel. 901971, fax 901959, II,
  95 b

Massa Marittima
(0566)

De Nicola, Via Nazionale 158, tel. 385111, fax 385113, II, 151 b

Matera
(0835)

Grand Hôtel Victoria, Lungolago Castelli 7–11, tel. 32003, fax 32992, I,
  104 b, SP
Bellavista, Via IV Novembre 21, tel. 32136, fax 31793, II, 88 b, SP

Menaggio
(0344)

Palace, Cavourstr. 2/4, tel. 211300, fax 234181, I, 200 b, SP
Parc Hotel Mignon (with annexe), Grabmayrstr. 5, tel. 230353, fax 230644,
  I, 80 b, SP
Kur-Hotel Schloß Rundegg, Schennastr. 2, tel. 234100, fax 237200, I, 58 b,
  SP
Castel Freiberg (medieval castle, on a hill; quiet location, elegant rooms),
  Freiberg, Labers-Str. 13, tel. 244196, fax 244488, I, 66 b, SP, CP
Aurora, Passerpromenade 38, tel. 211800, fax 211113, I, 53 b
Bavaria, Kirchsteig 15, tel. 236375, fax 236371, I, 84 b
Villa Tivoli, Giuseppe-Verdi-Str. 72, tel. 446282, fax 446849, I, 41 b
Isabella, Piavestr. 58, tel. 234700, fax 211360, II, 48 b
Schloß Labers (among vineyards; welcoming rooms, al fresco service in
  summer), Labers 25, tel. 234484, fax 234146, II, 53 b, SP
Zima, Winkelweg 83, tel. 230408, fax 236469, II, 42 b, SP

Merano
(0473)

Royal Palace, Via T. Cannizzaro 224, tel. 6503, fax 2921075, I, 174 b
Paradis, Via Consolare Pompea 441, tel. 310682, fax 312043, II, 164 b

Messina
(090)

★Four Seasons, Via Gesù 8, tel. 77088, fax 77085000, L, 201 b
★Palace, Piazza della Repubblica 20, tel. 63361, fax 654485, L, 321 b
★Duca di Milano, Piazza della Republicca 13, tel. 62841, fax 6555966, L,
  110 b

Milan
(02)

Hotels

Grand Hôtel et de Milan, Via Manzoni 29, tel. 723141, fax 86460861, L, 189 b

De la Ville (close to cathedral, La Scala and Galleria Vittorio Emanuele; all rooms with bath en suite), Via Hoepli 6, tel. 867651, fax 866609, I, 198 b

Diana Majestic (in earlier days the first ladies' swimming baths in Italy, known as the Diana Baths, were opened here; Art Deco features; comfortable rooms), Viale Piave 42, tel. 29513404, fax 211072, I, 151 b

Excelsior Gallia (opposite the station; 1930s building, tasteful décor, very good food), Piazza Duca D'Aosta 9, tel. 67851, fax 66713239, I, 397 b

Hilton International, Via Galvani 12, tel. 69831, fax 66710618, I, 461 b

Ramada Grand Hôtel Milano (at Milan's Exhibition Centre, 4 km (2¹/₂ mi.) from the city centre; shuttle service to the airport), Via Washington 66, tel. 480089 81, 48521, fax 48008991, I, 312 r, 11 suites.

Spadari al Duomo, Via Spadari 11, tel. 72002371, fax 861184, I, 85 b

Casa Svizzera, Via San Raffaele 3, tel. 8692246, fax 72004690, II, 79 b

Europeo, Via Canonica 38, tel. 3314751, fax 33105410, II, 55 b

Marconi, Via F. Filzi 3, tel. 66985561, fax 6690738, II, 98 b

Pasteur, Via Guinizelle 22, tel. 2870031, fax 26110285, II, 186 b

Milano Marittima (0544)	Acapulco, VI Traversa 19, tel. 992396, fax 993833, I, 90 b, SP Aurelia, Viale II Giugno 34, tel. 975451, fax 972773, I, 181 b, SP Bellevue Beach, XIX Traversa 9/10, tel. 994233, fax 994336, I, 124 b Deanna Golf Hotel, Viale Matteotti 131, tel. 991365, fax 994251, I, 136 b Mare e Pineta, Viale Dante 40, tel. 992262, fax 992739, I, 368 b, SP Imperiale (modern hotel by the beach), Piazzale Torino 1, tel. 992282, fax 992283, I, SP
Modena (059)	Canalgrande (Neo-Classical building, comfortable rooms, gardens), Corso Canal Grande 6, tel. 217160, fax 221674, I, 79 r Central Park, Viale Vittorio Veneto 10, tel. 225858, fax 225141, I, 48 r Centrale, Via Rismondo 55, tel. 218808, fax 238201, II, 41 r Eden, Via Emilia Ovest 666, tel. 335660, fax 820108, II, 51 r
Montecatini Terme (0572)	★Grand Hôtel Bellavista Palace & Golf, Viale Fedeli 2, tel. 78122, fax 73352, L, 199 b, SP ★Grand Hotel La Pace (★palatial hotel with comfortable rooms in a large park; Health Center with baths, massage, etc.), Via della Torretta 1/A, tel. 75801, fax 78451, L, 278 b, SP, tennis Ambasciatori Grand Hôtel Cristallo, Viale IV Novembre 12, tel. 73301, fax 911876, I, 120 b, SP Belvedere, Viale Fedeli 10, tel. 70251, fax 70252, II, 180 b, CP Cappelli Croce di Savoia, Viale Bicchierai 139, tel. 71151, fax 70153, II, 102 b, SP Brasile, Viale Bicchierai 53, tel. 70362, III, 57 b
Montegrotto Terme (049)	Augustus Terme, Viale Stazione 150, tel. 793200, fax 72242, I, 180 b Caesar Terme, Via Aureliana, tel. 793655, fax 8910616, I, 235 b, SP International Hotel Bertha, Largo Traiano 1, tel. 8911700, fax 8911771, I, 195 b, SP Bellavista, Via dei Colli 5, tel. 793333, fax 793772, II, 108 b, SP Olimpia Terme, Viale Stazione 25, tel. 793499, fax 8911100, II, 157 b Terme delle Nazioni, Via Mezzavia 20, tel. 8911690, fax 8911783, II, 159 b Terme Vulcania, Viale Stazione 6, tel. 793299, fax 793451, III, 110 b, SP
Montepulciano (0578)	Granducato, Via delle Lettere 62, tel. 758597, fax 758610, II, 25 b Marzocco, Piazza Savonarola 18, tel. 757262, fax 757530, II, 16 b
Monterosso al Mare (0187)	Palme, Via IV Novembre 18, tel. 829037, fax 829081, I, 96 b Porto Roca, Via Carone 1, tel. 817502, fax 817692, I, 43 r
Naples (081)	★Excelsior (traditional seaside Grand Hôtel; restaurants, bars), Via Partenope 48, tel. 764 0111, fax 7649743, L, 252 b

★Vesuvio (by the sea; Caruso died here), Via Partenope 45, tel. 7640044, fax 5890380, I, 292 b

Jolly Ambassador (centrally situated; restaurant with ★panoramic view of the city, Gulf of Naples and Vesuvius), Via Medina 70, tel. 416000, fax 5518010, I, 501 b

Majestic (convenient location in fashionable shopping district), Largo Vasto a Chiaia 68, tel. and fax 416500, I, 213 b

Parker's (roof garden restaurant with view), Corso Vittorio Emanuele 135, tel. 7612474, fax 663527, I, 73 r

Royal (★overlooking the Castel dell'Ovo), Via Partenope 38, tel. 7644800, fax 7645707, I, 492 b, SP

Santa Lucia (views of the Gulf of Naples and Castel dell'Ovo), Via Partenope 46, tel. 7640666, fax 7648580, 219 b

Belvedere (★view of the city and Gulf), Via Tito Angelini 51, tel. 5788169, fax 5785417, II, 27 r

Astor, Viale delle Palme 16, tel. 3728325, fax 3728486, I, 83 b	Nervi
Esperia, Via Al Cismon 1, tel. 3726071, fax 321777, II, 35 b	(010)
Capo Noli, Via Aurelia 52, tel. 748751/2, fax 748753, II, 103 b	Noli
El Sito, Via La Malfa 2, tel. 748107, fax 7485871, II, 14 r	(019)

Italia, Via Solaroli 10, tel. 399316, fax 399310, I, 111 b — Novara (0321)
La Rotonda, Bordo Massimo d'Azeglio 4/6, tel. 399246, fax 623695, I, 43 b
Parmigiano, Via dei Cattaneo 4, tel. 623231, II, 72 b

Grazia Deledda, Via Lamarmora 175, tel. 31257, fax 34017, I, 108 b — Nuoro (0784)
Sandalia, Via Einaudi, tel. 38353, fax 38353, II, 94 b

Martini, Via G. D'Annunzio, tel. 26066, fax 26418, I, 66 r — Olbia (0789)
Centrale, Corso Umberto I 85, tel. 23017, fax 26464, II, 28 r

Mistral, Via Martiri di Belfiore, tel. 212585, fax 210058, I, 252 b, SP — Oristano (0783)
Ca.Ma., Via Vittorio Veneto 119, tel. 74374, fax 74375, II, 90 b

Aquila Bianca, Via Garibaldi 13, tel. 341246, fax 342273, I, 71 b — Orvieto (0763)
La Badia (lovely hotel in what was once a Roman-Lombard monastery; large park; rural atmosphere), La Badia 8, Orvieto Scalo, tel. 90359, fax 92796, I, 49 b, SP, tennis
Maitani, Via Maitani 5, tel. and fax 342011, I, 40 r

Le Rocce del Capo, Lungomare Colombo 203, tel. 699733, II, 43 b, SP — Ospedaletti (0184)

Donatello, Via del Santo 102/104, tel. 8750634, fax 8750829, I, 94 b — Padua (049)
Le Padovanelle, Via Chilesotti 2 (at Ponte di Brenta 5 km (2 mi.)), tel. 625622, fax 625320, I, 80 b, SP
Leon Bianco (one of the city's oldest hotels; terrace with ★fine view), Piazzetta Pedrocchi 12, tel. 8750814, fax 8756184, II, 42 b
Majestic Toscanelli (comfortable hotel in the heart of the city; good food), Piazzetta dell'Arco 2, tel. 663244, fax 8760025, II, 70 b

Le Palme, Via Sterpinia (at Laura 5 km (2 m.)), tel. 850125, fax 851507, I, 50 r, SP — Paestum (0828)
Schuhmann, Via Laura Mare (at Laura 5 km (2 mi.)), tel. 851151, fax 851183, I, 36 r
Villa Rita, in the archaeological zone, Via Principe di Piemonte, tel. 811081, fax 722555, IV, 12 r

★Villa Igiea Grand Hôtel (exceptional comfort, excellent service; bar, veranda, garden), Via Belmonte 43, tel. 543744, fax 547654, L, 218 b — Palermo (091)
Astoria Palace, Via Montepellegrino 62, tel. 6371820, fax 6372178, I, 625 b
Jolly Hotel del Foro Italico, Foro Italico 22, tel. 6165090, fax 6161441, I, 469 b, SP
Cristal Palace, Via Roma 477, tel. 6112580/1, fax 6112589, II, 155 b

Hotels

Sole Grande Albergo, Corso Vittorio Emanuele 291, tel. 581811, fax 6110183, II, 257 b

Palinuro
(0974)
King's Residence (★coastal or sea view), Piano Faracchio, tel. 931324, fax 931418, I, 36 r, SP

Parma
(0521)
Grand Hôtel Baglioni, Viale Piacenza 14 (Parco Ducale), tel. 292929, fax 292828, I, 332 b
Verdi, Via Pasini 18 (Parco Ducale), tel. 293539/49, fax 293559, I, 31 b
Park Hotel Toscanini, Viale A. Toscanini 4 (central), tel. 289141, fax 283143, I, 72 b
Daniel, Via Gramsci 16, tel. 995147/8, fax 292606, II, 56 b

Passignano sul Trasimeno
(075)
Lido, Via Roma 1, tel. 827219, fax 827251, II, 100 b
Villa Paradiso, Via Fratelli Rosselli 5, tel. 829191, fax 827229, II, 212 b

Pavia
(0382)
Ariston, Via A. Scopoli 10, tel. 34334, fax 25667, II, 75 b
Moderno, Viale Vittorio Emanuele 41, tel. 303401, fax 25225, I, 92 b
Rosengarten (with annexe), Piazzale Policlinico 21, tel. 526312, fax 525186, II, 134 b

Perugia
(075)
★Brufani (Perugia's oldest and most elegant hotel), Piazza Italia 12, tel. 57325 41, fax 5720210, L, 47 b
Locanda della Posta (former palazzo in the heart of the historic town centre), Corso Vannucci 97, tel. 5728925, fax 5722413, I, 67 b
Giò Arte e Vini, Via R. Andreotto, tel. and fax 5731100, I, 184 b, SP
Grifone, Via S. Pellico 1, tel. 5837616, fax 5837619, I, 80 b
La Rosetta, Piazza Italia 19, tel. and fax 5720841, I, 162 b
Perugia Plaza, Via Palermo 88, tel. 34643, fax 30863, I, 208 b, SP
Palace Hotel Bellavista, Piazza Italia 12, tel. 5720741, fax 5729092, II, 131 b

Pesaro
(0721)
Vittoria, Piazzale della Libertà, tel. 34343, fax 65204, I, 27 r, SP
Bristol, Piazzale della Libertà 7, tel. 30355, fax 33893, I, 27 r
Spiaggia (modern hotel, refined atmosphere), Viale Trieste 76, tel. 32516, fax 35419, II, 74 r, SP
Atlantic, Viale Trieste 365, tel. 370333, fax 370373, II, 49 r
Nettuno, Viale Trieste 367, tel. and fax 400440, II, 65 r, SP

Pescara
(085)
Carlton, Viale della Riviera 35, tel. 373125, fax 4213922, I, 101 b
Esplanade, Piazza 1° Maggio 46, tel. 292141, fax 4217540, I, 280 b

Peschiera del Garda
(045)
La Fortuna, Via Venezia 26, tel. 7550111, fax 7550111, I, 84 b
Residence Puccini, Via Puccini 2, tel. 6401428, fax 6401419, II, 64 b
Vecchia Viola, Via Milano 5–7, tel. 551666, fax 6400063, II, 20 r

Piacenza
(0523)
Grande Albergo Roma, Via Cittadella 14, tel. 323201, fax 339548, I, 90 r
Florida, Via Colombo 29, tel. 592600, fax 592672, II, 50 r

Pietra Ligure
(019)
Paco (relatively quiet, on the hill), Via Crispi 63, tel. 615615, 615715, fax 615716, I, 84 b, SP
Royal (well-run hotel; terrace), Via Bado 129, tel. 616192, fax 616195, I, 174 b
Capri, Via della Repubblica 132, tel. 612716, fax 616216, II, 38 r

Piombino
(0565)
Centrale, Piazza Verdi 2, tel. 220188, fax 220220, I, 66 b
Collodi, Via Collodi 7, tel. 224272, fax 224382, II, 46 b

Pisa
(050)
Cavalieri (brick building in the city centre opposite the station), Piazza della Stazione 2, tel. 43290, fax 502242, I, 143 b
D'Azeglio, Piazza Vittorio Emanuele 18b, tel. 500310, fax 28017, I, 46 b
Grand Hôtel Duomo, Via S. Maria 94, tel. 561894, fax 560418, I, 167 b
Terminus e Plaza, Via Colombo 45, tel. and fax 500303, II, 91 b
Villa Primavera, Via Bonanno 3, tel. 23537, fax 27020, III, 21 b

Milano, Viale Pacinotti 10, tel. 975700, fax 32657, II, 19 r
Pistoia
(0573)

Forum, Via Roma 99, tel. 8501170, fax 8506132, II, 19 r
Villa Laura, Via della Salle 13, tel. 8631024, fax 8504893, II, 38 b
Bristol, Piazza Vittorio Veneto 1–3, tel. 8503005, fax 8631625, II, 50 r
Pompei
(081)

Villa Ottoboni, Piazzetta Ottoboni 2, tel. 208891, fax 208148, I, 93 r
Palace Hotel Moderno, Viale Martelli 1, tel. 28215, fax 520315, II, 107 r
Pordenone
(0434)

★Il Pellicano (4.5 km (2³/₄ mi.)) south-west on scenic road at Cala dei Santi;
has played host to many a distinguished guest), tel. 833801, fax 833418,
L, 32 r, SP
Porto Ercole
(0564)

Airone, in San Giovanni (next to the San Giovanni thermal complex),
tel. 929111, I, 200 b, 2 SP, tennis, moorings
Le Picchiaie Residence (★view of the Gulf of Portoferraio), in Monte Orello,
I, 200 b, 2 SP, tennis, golf and riding-school near by
Portoferraio
(0565)

Splendido (once belonged to Count Spinola; now an exceptionally luxuri-
ous hotel), Viale Baratta 13, tel. 269551, fax 269514, I, 119 b, SP, tennis
courts
Piccolo, Via Duca degli Abruzzi 31, tel. 269015, fax 269621, I, 46 b
Portofino
(0185)
Potenza
(0971)

Grande Albergo, Corso 18 Agosto, tel. and fax 41 02 20, I, 108 b
Tourist, Via Vescovado 4, tel. 25955, fax 21437, II, 131 b
Prato
(0574)

Art Hotel Museo, Viale Repubblica, tel. 5787, fax 578880, I, 110 r, SP
Flora, Via Cairoli 31, tel. 33521, fax 606591, II, 31 r

Mediterraneo Palace, Via Roma 189, tel. 621944, fax 623799, I, 91 r
Montreal, Corso Italia 70, tel. and fax 621133, II, 54 r
Ragusa
(0932)

Astoria, Via Gramsci 4, tel. 273533, fax 274093, I, 34 b
Eurotel, Via Aurelia Ponente 22, tel. 60981, fax 50635, I, 106 b, SP
Rosabianca, Lungomare V. Veneto 42, tel. 50390, 52262, fax 65035, I, 27 b
Vittoria, Via San Filippo Neri 11, tel. 231030, fax 66250, II, 59 b
Rapello
(0185)

Bisanzio (in the historic town centre; quiet rooms overlooking garden), Via
Salara 30, tel. 217111, fax 32539, I, 63 b
Argentario (central; pleasant atmosphere), Via di Roma 45, tel. 35555, fax
35147, II, 54 b
Diana, Via Rossi 47, tel. 39164, fax 30001, II, 33 r
Centrale Byron, Via IV Novembre 14, tel. 33479, II, 88 b
Ravenna
(0544)

Excelsior, Via Vittorio Veneto 66, tel. 812211, fax 893084, I, 84 r
Ascioti, Via San Francesco da Paola 18, tel. 897041, fax 26063, I, 50 r
Reggio Calabria
(0965)

Grand Hôtel Astoria, Viale L. Nobile 2, tel. 435245, fax 453365, I, 112 r
Posta (in the heart of the Old Town; Rococo-style furnishings), Piazza Del
Monte 2, tel. 432944, fax 452602, I, 34 r
Reggio nell'
Emilia
(0522)

★Grand Hôtel des Bains, Viale Gramsci 56, tel. 601650, fax 606350, L, 126
b, SP
Atlantic, Lungomare della Libertà 15, tel. 601155, fax 606402, I, 121 b
Corallo, Viale Gramsci 113, tel. 600807, fax 606400, I, 155 b, SP
Lungomare, Lungomare della Libertà 7, tel. 69 28 80, fax 692354, I, 116 b,
SP
Dory, Viale Puccini 4, tel. 642896, fax 644588, II, 46 r
Arizona, Via d'Annunzio 22, tel. 644422, fax 644108, II, 105 b, SP
Riccione
(0541)

Miramonti, Piazza Oberdan 7, tel. 201333, fax 205790, I, 52 b
Cavour, Piazza Cavour 10, tel. 485252, fax 484072, II, 70 b
Rieti
(0746)

603

Hotels

Rimini (0541)	★Grand Hotel, Piazzale Indipendenza 2, Parco Federico Fellini, tel. 56000, fax 566866, L, 230 b Imperiale, Viale Vespucci 16, tel. 52255, fax 28806, I, 120 b, SP Milton (very high standard, superbly successful design; has its own bicycles), Viale Capellini 1, tel. 54600, fax 54698, I, 75 r, SP Parco dei Principi, Viale Regina Elena 98, tel. 380055, fax 393327, I, 124 b, SP Residenza Grand Hotel Dépendance, Parco Indipendenza, tel. 56000, fax 566866, I, 86 b, SP Brown, Via Pola 29, tel. 55495, fax 710011, II, 52 b, SP Corallo, Viale Vespucci 46, tel. 390732, fax 391808, II, 148 b, SP Villa Adriatica, Viale Vespucci 3, tel. 54599, fax 26962, II, 146 b Atlas, Viale Regina Elena 74, tel. 380561, III, 122 b, SP
Riva del Garda (0464)	Du Lac et du Parc (at the little harbour), Viale Rovereto 44, tel. 551500, fax 555200, I, 457 b, CP, SP Grand Hôtel Riva (with roof garden restaurant), Piazza Garibaldi 10, tel. 521800, fax 552293, I, 167 b International Hotel Liberty, Viale Carducci 3/5, tel. 553581, fax 551144, I, 126 b, CP Astoria, Viale Trento 9, tel. 552658, fax 521222, II, 179 b, SP Luise, Viale Rovereto 9, tel. 552796, fax 554250, II, 117 b, SP
Rome (06)	Rome has more than 200 hotels covering every price category. The reservation service HR operated by city hoteliers offers a convenient way of booking in advance, tel. (06) 6991000.
Near the main railway station	★Le Grand Hôtel et de Rome (Ciga Hotel Group), Via Vittorio Emanuele Orlando 3, tel. 47901, fax 4747307, L, 328 b Atlantico, Via Cavour 23, tel. and fax 485951, I, 145 b Genova, Via Cavour 33, tel. 476951, fax 4827580, I, 175 b Massimo D'Azeglio, Via Cavour 18, tel. 4880646, fax 4827386, I, 312 b Mediterraneo, Via Cavour 15, tel. 4884051, fax 4744105, I, 466 b Napoleon (near Santa Maria Maggiore), Piazza Vittorio Emanuele 105, tel. 4467264, fax 4467282, I, 141 b Palatino, Via Cavour 213, tel. 4814927, fax 4740726, I, 380 b Quirinale (hotel and restaurant with terrace, bar; garden), Via Nazionale 7, tel. 47 07, fax 4820099, I, 340 b Aretusa, Via Gaeta 14, tel. 4440011, fax 4441377, II, 101 b Diana, Via Principe Amedeo 4, tel. 4827541, fax 486998, II, 322 b Globus, Viale Ippocrate 119, tel. 4457001, fax 4941062, II, 174 b Medici, Via Flavia 96, tel. 4827319, fax 4740767, II, 136 b San Marco, Via Villafranca 1, tel. 490437, fax 4958303, II, 138 b San Remo, Via M. D'Azeglio 36, tel. 4881741, fax 4817669, II, 113 b Siracusa, Via Marsala 50, tel. 4460396, fax 4441377, II, 197 b Tirreno, Via San Martino ai Monti 18, tel. 4880778, fax 4884095, II, 77 b Torino, Via Principe Amedeo 8, tel. 4814741, fax 4882247, II, 177 b
Between the Quirinale and the Villa Borghese	★Bernini Bristol, Piazza Barberini 23, tel. 4883051, fax 4824266, L, 222 b ★Excelsior, Via Vittorio Veneto 125, tel. 4708, fax 4826205, L, 616 b ★Hassler Villa Medici (at the Spanish Steps; ★roof garden restaurant with magnificent view over Old Rome; bar piano), Piazza Trinità de' Monti 6, tel. 6782651, 699340, fax 6789991, L, 190 b Flora, Via Vittorio Veneto 191, tel. 489929, fax 4820359, I, 264 b Imperiale, Via Vittorio Veneto 24, tel. 4826351, fax 4826352, I, 169 b Parco dei Principi (opposite the Villa Borghese), Via G. Frescobaldi 5, tel. 8841071, 854421, fax 8845104, I, 366 b, SP Savoia, Via Ludovisi 15, tel. 4744141, fax 4746812, I, 230 b Victoria (near the Via Veneto; roof garden), Via Campania 41, tel. 473931, fax 4871890, I, 160 b
In the Old City	Colonna Palace (elegant breakfast room; roof terrace), Piazza Montecitorio 12, tel. 6781341, fax 6794496, I, 165 b

D'Inghilterra (Liszt and Mendelssohn were among the hotel's many distinguished guests), Via Bocca de Leone 14, tel. 69981, fax 69922243, I, 185 b

Forum (former palazzo opposite the Foro Romanum; roof garden), Via Tor de' Conti 25, tel. 6792446, fax 6786479, I, 151 b

Raphael (smallish hotel near the Piazza Navona; terrace with ★panoramic view), Largo Febo 2, tel. 682831, fax 6878993, I, 132 b

Sole al Pantheon (opposite the Pantheon; Jean-Paul Sartre was a regular visitor), Via del Pantheon 63, tel. 6780441, fax 69940689, I, 52 b

Piccolo, Via dei Chiavari 32, tel. 68802560, III, 25 b

★Lord Byron (near the Villa Borghese; excellent Relais Le Jardin restaurant), Via G. De Notaris 5, tel. 3220404, fax 3220405, L, 73 b — North city

★Aldrovandi, Via U. Aldrovandi 15, tel. 3223993, fax 3221435, I, 212 b

Borromini, Via Lisbona 7, tel. 8841321, fax 8417550, I, 147 b

Ritz, Via Chellini 41, tel. 803751, fax 8072916, I, 265 b

Porta Maggiore, Piazza Porta Maggiore 25, tel. 7027927, fax 7027936, II, 378 b — East city

San Giusto, Piazza Bologna 58, tel. 44244598, fax 44244583, I, 123 b

Sheraton Roma, Viale del Pattinaggio, tel. 54 53, fax 5940689, I, 1067 b — South city

EUR Motel, Via Pontina 416, tel. 5074152, fax 507051, II, 38 b

Piccadilly, Via Magna Grecia 122, at the Porta S. Giovanni, tel. 70474858, fax 70476686, II, 91 b

★Cavalieri Hilton (in a ★park on Monte Maria; fine view from La Pergola roof restaurant; health club with gym and Turkish bath, etc.), Via Cadiolo 101, tel. 35091, fax 35092241, L, 837 b, SP — Right bank of the Tiber

Giulio Cesare (elegant hotel, once the home of Countess Solari), Via degli Scipione 287, tel. 3210751, fax 3211736, I, 145 b

Holiday Inn EUR, Viale Castello della Magliana 65, tel. 65581, fax 6557005, I, 538 b, SP

Jolly Leonardo da Vinci (in the quiet Prati district not far from the Vatican and the Piazza del Popolo), Via dei Gracchi 324, tel. 32499, fax 3610138, L, 501 b

Imperator, Via Aurelia 619, tel. 66418041, fax 66415373, II, 79 b

Marc'Aurelio, Via Gregorio XI 141, tel. 6637630, fax 6525269, II, 220 b

Olympic, Via Properzio 2/a, tel. 6896650, fax 68308255, II, 100 b

Golf Hotel (discreet elegance; Albarelax fitness centre; bar piano), Albarella Island, Via Po di Levante 1, tel. 367811, fax 330628, I, 22 r, CP, golf, horse-riding, tennis — Rosolina (0426)

Rovereto, Corso Rosmini 82/d, tel. 435222, 439644, fax 423777, II, 49 r — Rovereto (0464)

Leon d'Oro, Via Tacchi 2, tel. 437333, II, 64 b

Villa Regina Margherita, Viale Regina Margherita 6, tel. 365040, fax 31301, I, 43 b — Rovigo (0425)

Jolly, Lungomare Trieste 1, tel. 225222, fax 237571, I, 104 r, SP — Salerno (089)

Plaza, Piazza Vittorio Veneto 42, tel. 224477, fax 237311, II, 42 r

Grand Hotel et de Milan, Via Dante 1, tel. 572241, fax 573884, I, 188 b — Salsomaggiore Terme (0524)

Excelsior, Viale Berenini 3, tel. 575641, fax 573888, I, 84 b

Grand Hôtel Porro, Viale Porro 10, tel. 578221, fax 577878, I, 151 b, SP

Regina, Largo Roma 3, tel. 571611, fax 576941, I, 149 b

Ritz, Via Milite Ignoto 5, tel. 577744, fax 574410, II, 54 b

Golf Hotel Castello Formentini (delightful hotel; rooms furnished with ancestral antiques; breakfast on terrace overlooking the garden; cellar restaurant with open fire), Via Oslavia 2, tel. 884051, fax 884052, I, SP, golf course, tennis — San Floriano del Collio (0481)

Hotels

San Gimignano (0577)	Relais Santa Chiara, Via Matteotti 15, in Santa Chiara, tel. 940701, fax 942096, I, 65 b Villa San Paolo (★view of San Gimignano's towers and surrounding countryside), Strada per Certaldo, in Casini, tel. 955100, fax 955113, I, 25 b Bel Soggiorno (lovely 13th c. building in centre of town), Via San Giovanni 91, tel. and fax 940375, II, 44 b L'Antico Pozzo (15th c. building, rich in atmosphere), Via San Matteo 87, tel. 942014, fax 942117, II, 32 b La Cisterna (former monastery), Piazza della Cisterna 24, tel. 940328, fax 942080, II, 92 b
San Marino (0549)	Grand Hôtel San Marino, Viale Antonio Onofri 31, tel. 992400, fax 992951, I, 56 r Titano (terrace restaurant with ★view), Contrada del Collegio 21, tel. 991006, fax 991375, I, 46 r
San Pellegrino Terme (0345)	Terme, Via B. Villa 26, tel. 21125, fax 23497, I, 87 b Bigio, Via Matteotti 2, tel. 21058, fax 23463, II, 96 b
San Remo (0184)	★Royal (spacious rooms, garden with subtropical plants), Corso Imperatrice 80, tel. 5391, fax 661445, L, 295 b, SP Astoria West End, Corso Matuzia 8, tel. 667701, fax 663318, I, 224 b, SP Grand Hôtel Londra, Corso Matuzia 2, tel. 668000, fax 668073, I, 284 b Miramare Continental Palace (and Dépendance Miramare), Corso Matuzia 9, tel. 667601, fax 667655, I, 109 b, SP Ariston Montecarlo, Corso Mazzini 507, tel. 513655, fax 510702, II, 86 b Bobby Executive, Corso Marconi 208, tel. 60255, fax 60296, II, 164 b
San Vincenzo (0565)	Park Hotel I Lecci (modern hotel; restaurant, La Campigiana, serves Maremma specialities in addition to international cuisine; park), Via della Principessa 116, tel. 704111, fax 703224, I, 148 b, SP, wide range of sporting facilities
Sàssari (079)	Grazia Deledda, Viale Dante 47, tel. 271235, fax 280884, I, 206 b Leonardo da Vinci, Via Roma 79, tel. and fax 280744, II, 214 b Marini Due, Via Pietro Nenni 2, tel. 277282, fax 280300, II, 98 b
Savona (019)	Mare, Via Nizza 89, tel. 264065, fax 263277, II, 78 b Motel Agip, Via Nizza 62, tel. 861961, fax 861632, II, 120 b
Sciacca (0925)	Grande Albergo delle Terme, Lungomare Nuove Terme N° 1, tel. 23133, fax 21746, II, 72 r, SP
Sestriere (0122)	Grand Hôtel Principi di Piemonte (comfortable rooms, luxury suites; boutiques, disco), Via Sauze 3/6, tel. 7941, fax 70270, I, 174 b Grand Hôtel Sestriere, Via Assietta 1, tel. 76476, fax 76700, I, 194 b Miramonti, Via Cesana 3, tel. 755333, fax 755375, II, 60 b
Sestri Levante (0185)	★Grand Hôtel dei Castelli, Via alla Penisola, tel. 487220, fax 44767, L, 55 b Due Mari, Vico del Coro 18, tel. 42695, fax 42698, II, 48 b Helvetia, Via Cappuccini 43, tel. 41175, fax 47216, II, 45 b
Siena (0577)	Certosìa di Maggiano (14th c. charterhouse; antique furnishings), Via di Certosa 82, tel. 288180, fax 288189, I, 35 b, SP Park (former palazzo; ★view of Siena Old City and Tuscan countryside), Via Marciano 18, tel. 44803, fax 49020, I, 137 b, SP ★Villa Patrizia (patrician villa in delightful park), Via Fiorentina 58, tel. and fax 50431, I, 64 b, SP ★Garden, Via Custoza 2, tel. 47056, fax 46050, II, 107 b, SP; also annexe, 145 b, SP ★Villa Cortine Palace (Neo-Classical villa; park with palm trees), Via Grotte 12, tel. 9905890, fax 916390, L, 100 b, SP

★Grand Hôtel Terme, Viale Marconi 7, tel. 916261, fax 916568, I, 113 b
Du Lac (with annexe), Via XXV Aprile 58/60, tel. 919047, fax 9196472, II, 65
   b, SP

   Sirmione
   (030)

Della Posta, Piazza Garibaldi 19, tel. 510404, fax 510210, I, 64 b

   Sondrio
   (0342)

Locando del Lupo (guest house; built in the 18th c. by the princes Meli
   Lupi; furniture and paintings of the 17th c. Italian school; Italian food and
   Parma specialities), Via Garibaldi 64, tel. 597100, fax 597066, 45 r

   Soragna
   (0524)

Excelsior Grand Hôtel Vittoria (on a cliff-top overlooking the Gulf of
   Naples; garden and winter-garden; terrace with ★sea view; spacious
   rooms), Piazza Tasso 34, tel. 8071044, fax 8771206, I, 137 b, SP
Sorrento Palace, Via S. Antonio 13, tel. 8784141, fax 8782933, I, 786 b, SP
Grand Hôtel Cesare Augusto, Via degli Aranci 108, tel. 8782700, fax
   8071029, I, 240 b, SP
Ambasciatori, Via Califano 18, tel. 8782025, fax 8071021, I, 198 b, SP
Imperial Hotel Tramontano, Via Vittorio Veneto 1, tel. 8782588, fax
   8072344, I, 195 b, SP
Tirrenia, Via Capo 1, tel. 87813 36, fax 8772100, II, 115 b
Desirée, Via Capo 31/bis, tel. and fax 87815 63, III, 37 b

   Sorrento
   (081)

Ritz, Lungomare Adriatico 48, tel. 491700, fax 493900, I, 150 b, SP
Bristol, Lungomare Adriatico 46, tel. 5540389, fax 5541813, I, 120 b
Park, Via Lungomare Adriatico Sud, tel. 4965032, fax 490111, II, 82 b

   Sottomarina
   (041)

In Fiorelle:
La Playa, tel. 549496–8, fax 54106, II, 76 b, SP
Parkhotel Fiorelle (quiet location, ★garden; own vegetable garden producing delicious home grown vegetables), Via Fiorelle 12, tel. 54092, fax
   549246, II, 49 b

   Sperlonga
   (0771)

Albornoz Palace, Viale G. Matteotti, tel. 221221, fax 221600, I, 192 b
Dei Duchi, Viale Matteotti 4, tel. 44541, fax 44543, I, 97 b
Gattapone (tastefully furnished rooms, ★panoramic view), Via del Ponte 6,
   tel. 223447, fax 223448, I, 16 b
Motel Agip, on the SS Flaminia, km 127, tel. 49368, fax 29293, II, 112 b

   Spoleto
   (0743)

Royal, Lungomare Kennedy 125, tel. 745074, fax 745075, I, 188 b, SP
Delle Palme, Via Aurelia 39, tel. and fax 7451 61, II, 63 b
La Torre, Via Alla Torre 23, tel. 745390, fax 746487, II, 38 b
Riviera, Via Berninzoni 18, tel. 745320, fax 747782, II, 85 b

   Spotorno
   (019)

★Des Iles Borromées, Lungolago Umberto I 67, tel. 938938, fax 32405, L,
   304 b
La Palma, Lungolago Umberto I 33, tel. 32401, fax 32404, I, 237 b, SP
Regina Palace, Corso Umberto I 27, tel. 933777, fax 933776, I, 307 b, SP
Du Parc, Via Gignous 1, tel. 30335, fax 33596, II, 39 b
Verbano (charming small hotel, terrace; Toscanini stayed here), on the
   Isola dei Pescatori, Via Ugo Ara 2, tel. 30408, fax 33129, II, 24 b

   Stresa
   (0323)

Roma, Via F. Petrarca 38, tel. 85239, fax 822288, III, 56 b

   Subiaco
   (0774)

Armando's, Via Montenero 15, tel. 210787, fax 210783, II, 35 b

   Sulmona
   (0864)

Palace, Viale Scala Greca 201, tel. 491566, fax 756612, I, 262 b
Fontane Bianche, Via Mazzarò 1, tel. 790611, fax 790571, II, 308 b, SP
Relax, Viale Epidpoli 159, tel. 740122, fax 740933, II, 80 b, SP
Grand Hotel, Viale Mazzini 12, tel. 464600, fax 464611, L

   Syracuse
   (0931)

Hotels

Taormina (0942)	★San Domenico Palace (former 15th c. monastery on the periphery of the Old Town), Piazza San Domenico 5, tel. 23701, fax 625506, L, 177 b Excelsior Palace (built on the foundations of an old palazzo, ★view of Etna; period furniture; restaurant serves Sicilian and international specialities), Via Toselli 8, tel. 23975, fax 23978, I, 166 b, SP in splendid garden with ancient trees Grand Hôtel Miramare (well-kept, elegant, quiet hotel; hillside location with ★view of Bay of Mazzaro), Via Guardiola Vecchia 27, tel. 23401, fax 626223, 128 b, SP Villa Fiorita, Via L. Pirandello 39, tel. 24122, fax 625967, II, 48 b, SP Villa Ducale, Via L. da Vinci 60, tel. 28153, fax 28710, II, 12 r Villa Esperia, Via Nazionale 244, tel. 23377, fax 21105, II, 77 b, SP
Taranto (099)	Delfino, Viale Virgilio 66, tel. 7323232, fax 7304654, I, 288 b, SP Mar Grande Park, Viale Virgilio 90, tel. 7351713, fax 369494, II, 155 b
Tarquinia (0766)	Tarconte, Via Tuscia 19, tel. 856141, fax 856585, II, 100 b Grand Hôtel Helios, Via Porto Clementino, tel. 864618, fax 88295, I, 190 b, SP Velca Mare, Via degli Argonauti 1, tel. 864380, fax 864024, II, 40 b
Tempio Pausania (079)	Delle Sorgenti, Via delle Fonti 6, tel. 671516, fax 630033, II, 53 b Petit Hotel, Piazza A. De Gasperi 9/11, tel. 631134, fax 631176, II, 81 b
Teramo (0861)	Sporting, Via De Gasperi 41, tel. 414723, fax 414723, I, 105 b Abruzzi, Viale Mazzini 18, tel. 241043, fax 242704, II, 79 b
Terni (0744)	Garden, Via Bramante 4/6, tel. 300041, fax 300414, 206 b, SP Allegretti, Strada dello Staino 7/b, tel. 426747, fax 401246, II, 99 b
Terracina (0773)	Il Guscio, Via Bad Homburg 16, tel. 730236, II, 51 b, SP River, Via Pontina, km 106, tel. 730681, fax 763838, II, 186 b, SP
Tivoli (0774)	Torre Sant'Angelo, Via Quintilio Varo, tel. and fax 322533, I, 74 b Il Padovano, Via Tiburtina 170, tel. 530807, III, 32 b Grand Hôtel Duca d'Este, Via Tiburtina Valeria 330, tel. 3883, fax 3885101, I, 359 b, SP
Todi (075)	Bramante (in a former 14th c. convent), Via Orvietana 48, tel. 88948381, fax 8948074, I, 85 b, SP Villa Luisa, Via A. Cortesi 147, tel. 8948571, fax 8948472, II, 75 b
Torbole (0464)	Clubhotel La Vela, Via Strada Grande 2, tel. 505940, fax 505968, I, 70 b, Caravel, Via Coize 2, tel. 505724, fax 505935, II, 144 b, SP
Tortoli (0782)	Victoria, Via Mons. Virgilio, tel. 623457, fax 624116, II, 110 b
Toscolano-Maderno (0365)	Maderno, Via Statale 12, tel. 641070, fax 644277, II, 33 r, SP Milano, Lungolago Zanardelli 12, tel. 540595, fax 641223, II, 38 r
Trani (0883)	Royal, Via De Robertis 29, tel. 588777, fax 582224, II, 42 r Trani, Corso Imbriani 137, tel. 588010, fax 587625, III, 50 r
Trapani (0923)	Crystal, Via S. Giovanni Bosco 12, tel. 20000, fax 25555, I, 151 b Cavallino Bianco, Lungomare Dante Alighieri, tel. 21549, fax 873002, III, 75 b
Tremiti Islands (0882)	Isola San Domino: Kyrie, tel. 663241, fax 663415, I, 64 r, SP Gabbiano, tel. 663410, fax 663428, II, 40 r

Vicolo Grand Hôtel Trento, Via Alfieri 1/3, tel. 271000, fax 271001, I, 153 b   Trento
America, Via Torre Verde 50, tel. 983010, fax 230603, II, 80 b   (0461)
Everest, Corso degli Alpini 16, tel. 825300, fax 824527, II, 221 b

Cà del Galletto, Via Santa Bona Vecchia 30, tel. 432550, fax 432510, I, 95 b   Treviso
Carlton, Largo Porta Altinia 15, tel. 411661, fax 411620, II, 149 b   (0422)

San Guisto, Via C. Belli 3, tel. 762661, 7606585, II, 62 r   Trieste
Duchi d'Aosta (large and very beautiful hotel in the centre of Trieste;   (040)
    modern day comfort and excellent food), Piazza Unità d'Italia 2, tel. 7351,
    fax 366092, I, 104 b
Abbazia, Via della Geppa 20, tel. 369464, fax 369769, II, 35 b
Colombia, Via della Geppa 18, tel. 369191, fax 369644, II, 59 b

City, Via F. Juvarra 25, tel. 540546, fax 548188, I, 73 b   Turin
Concord, Via Lagrange 47, tel. 5177656, fax 5176305, I, 243 b   (011)
Jolly Hotel Principi di Piemonte, Via Piero Gobetti 15, tel. 5629693, fax
    5620270, I, 206 b
Turin Palace, Via Sacchi 8, tel. 5625511, fax 5612187, I, 227 b
Villa Sassi (quiet location in a park; excellent food), Via Traforo del Pino 47,
    tel. 8980556, fax 8980095, I, 35 b
Astoria, Via XX Settembre 4, tel. 5620653, 5 62 58 66, II, 104 b
Giotto, Via Giotto 27, tel. 6637172, fax 6637173, II, 80 b

Ambassador Palace, Via Carducci 46, tel. 503777, fax 503711, I, 87 r   Udine
La' di Moret, Viale Tricesimo 276, tel. and fax 545096, II, 46 r, SP   (0432)
President, Via Duino 8, tel. 509905, fax 507287, II, 67 r

Bonconte, Via della Mura 28, tel. 2463, fax 4782, I, 23 r   Urbino
     (0722)

Cristallo, Via Cilea 4, tel. 97264, fax 96392, I, 83 b   Varazze
Savoy, Via Marconi 4, tel. 934626, fax 932480, I, 90 b   (019)
Royal, Via Cavour 25, tel. 931166, 96664, I, 31 r, SP

Royal Victoria, Piazza San Gorgio 5, tel. 815111, fax 830722, I, 43 r   Varenna
Du Lac, Via del Prestino 4, tel. 830238, fax 831081, II, 18 r   (0341)

Palace (★park), Via L. Manara 11, tel. 312600, fax 312870, I, 189 b, SP,   Varese
    billiard room, tennis   (0332)
City (opposite the station), Via Medaglie d'Oro 35, tel. 281304, fax 232882,
    I, 83 b

★Danieli (former 15th c. doge's palace on the embankment near St Mark's   Venice
    Square; ★view from the Terrazza Danieli restaurant), Riva degli Schiavoni   (041)
    Castello 4196, tel. 5226480, fax 5200208, L, 423 b, SP
★Gritti Palace Ciga Hotel (15th c. palazzo with terrace on the Grand Canal;
    cookery courses – Mediterranean, vegetarian cuisine, etc.), San Marco
    2467, tel. 794611, fax 5200942, L, 163 b
Bauer Grünwald & Grand Hôtel (Grand Canal terrace), Campo Santa Maria
    del Criglio, San Marco 1459, Campo San Moisè, tel. 5207022, fax
    5207557, I, 411 b
Cipriani (five minutes by vaporetto from St Mark's Square; ★restaurants,
    terrace bars and gardens), Isola della Giudecca 10, tel. 5207744, fax
    5203930, I, 189 b, SP, tennis
Metropole (collection of fans, antique furniture), Riva degli Schiavoni 4149
    Castello, tel. 5205044, fax 5223679, I, 74 r
Saturnia e International (14th c. palazzo close to St Mark's Square), Via
    XXII Marzo 2398, tel. 5208377, fax 5207131, I, 184 b
Accademia Villa Maravege (B&B hotel in 17th c. palazzo with lovely garden;
    quiet location near the Grand Canal and Accademia art gallery), Fonda-
    menta Bollani 1058, Dorsoduro, tel. 5210188, fax 5239152, II, 46 b

Information

On Lido: ★Excelsior (high class seaside hotel in the style of a Moorish palace), Lungomare G. Marconi 41, tel. 5260201, fax 5267276, L, 408 b, SP, tennis
Belvedere, Piazzale Santa Maria Elisabetta 4, tel. 5260115, fax 5261486, II, 57 b

Ventimiglia
(0184)
Kaly, Corso Trento e Trieste 44, tel. 295218, fax 295118, II, 27 r
Al Mare, Vico Pescatori 7, tel. 299025, III, 45 b

Verbania
(0323)
In Intra: Ancora, Corso Mameli 65, tel. 53951, fax 53978
In Pallanza: Europalace Residence, Viale delle Magnolie 16, tel. 556441, fax 556442, I, 88 b
Majestic (★situated right on the lakeside, with its own bathing beach), Via Vittorio Veneto 32, tel. 504305, fax 556379, I, 212 b, CP
Belvedere, Viale Magnolie 6, tel. 503202, fax 504466, II, 83 b

Vercelli
(0161)
Il Giardinetto, Via Sereno 3, tel. 257230, fax 259311, II, 16 b

Verona
(045)
★Gabbia d'Oro (14th c. palazzo in the pedestrian precinct; roof terrace with ★view of the Old Town), Corso Porta Borsari 4/A, tel. 8003060, fax 590293, L, 54 b
Due Torri Hotel Baglioni, Piazza Sant'Anastasia 4, tel. 595044, fax 8004130, I, 158 b
San Marco, Via Longhena 42, tel. 569011, fax 572299, I, 91 b
Giulietta e Romeo, Via Tre Marchetti 3, tel. 8003554, fax 8010862, II, 56 b

Viareggio
(0584)
Astor, Viale Carducci 54, tel. 50301, fax 55181, I, 114 b, SP
Excelsior, Viale Carducci 88, tel. 50726, fax 50729, I, 154 b
Grand Hôtel & Royal, Viale Carducci 44, tel. 45151, fax 31438, II, 202 b
Bonelli, Via Regia 96, tel. 961282, fax 961264, III, 37 b

Vicenza
(0444)
Forte Agip (4 km (2 mi.)), Via Scaligeri 64, tel. 564711, I, 258 b
Viest, Strada Pelosa 241, tel. 582677, I, 122 b
Continental, Viale Trissino 89, tel. 505476, fax 513319, II, 69 b

Vieste
(0884)
★Pizzomunno Vieste Palace (beauty treatment, bar piano, garden), tel. 708741, fax 707325, L, 183 r, SP

Viterbo
(0761)
Balletti Park (with annexe), Via F. Molini, tel. and fax 344777, I, 80 b, SP
Leon d'Oro, Via della Cava 36, tel. 344444–7, fax 344447, II, 58 b
Tuscia, Via Cairoli 41, tel. 344400, 345976, II, 40 r

Volterra
(0588)
San Lino, Via San Lino 26, tel. 85250, fax 80620, I, 82 b, SP
Villa Nencini (outside the walls, ★fine view; comfortable rooms in the extension), Borgo S. Stefano 55, tel. 86386, fax 80601, II, 27 b, SP

Information

Italian Government Travel Office (ENIT)
Ente Nazionale Italiano per il Turismo (ENIT)
Via Marghera 2, I-00185 Roma
tel. (06) 49771, fax 4463379 and 4469907
Information Office: Via Marghera 2/6,
tel. (06) 4971222 and 4971282

In United Kingdom
Italian State Tourist Office
1 Princes Street, London W1R 8AY
tel. (0171) 4081254

In USA
Italian Government Travel Office
500 North Michigan Avenue, Suite 2240
Chicago IL 60611; tel. (312) 6440990

630 Fifth Avenue, Suite 1565
New York NY 10111; tel. (212) 2454822

12400 Wilshire Boulevard, Suite 550
Los Angeles CA 90025; tel. (310) 8201898

Italian Government Travel Office   In Canada
Store 56, Plaza, 1 Place Ville Marie, Suite 1914
Montréal H3B 3M9; tel. (514) 8667667–9

There are ENIT offices at the main frontier crossings and at Rome, Milan   Information
and Naples airports.   within Italy
   Within Italy tourist information is provided by the Regional Tourist
Offices (Assessorati Regionali per il Turismo) in regional capitals, provincial tourist offices (Enti Provinciali per il Turismo, EPT), and spa adminis-
trations and local tourist offices (Aziende Autonome di Soggiorno, Cura e
Turismo, AA and Azienda Autonoma Soggiorno e Turismo, AAST). In
small towns information can be obtained from the local Pro Loco organisation.
   Offices promoting tourism (Aziende di Promozione Turistica, APT) are
found in ever increasing numbers in the larger towns; tourist information
is also distributed by bureaux of the Uffici Assistenza Turistica and Uffici
di Informazioni e Accoglienza Turistica (IAT).

Insurance

Visitors are strongly advised to ensure that they have adequate holiday   General
insurance including loss or damage to luggage, loss of currency and
jewellery.

British citizens, like nationals of other European Union countries, are   Health insurance
entitled to obtain medical care under the Italian health services on the
same basis as Italians. Before leaving home they should apply to their
local social security office for a form E111, which certifies their entitlement
to insurance cover. If possible this should be presented to the local health
office (Unità Sanitaria Locale) before seeking treatment. It is nevertheless
advisable, even for EU nationals, to take out short-term health insurance
(available, for example, under the AA's Five Star Europe service) providing full cover and possibly avoiding bureaucratic delays. Nationals of
non-EU countries should certainly have insurance cover.

Visitors travelling by car should ensure that their insurance is compre-   Vehicles
hensive and covers use of the vehicle in Italy.
   See also Travel Documents.

Medical Assistance

The emergency number throughout Italy is 113.   Emergency
                                                                                  Number

The "pronto soccorso" first aid service, with doctor in attendance, is avail-   First Aid
able at airports, railway stations and all hospitals. In many resorts and
tourist centres an emergency medical service known as the "Guardia
Medica Turistica" operates during the tourist season.

For routine treatment other than emergencies, visitors should apply to one   Non-emergency
of the local health units ("Unita Sanitaria Locale") attached to a hospital.   treatment

See Insurance.   Health insurance

Motoring in Italy

Roads
The Italian road system is extensive, well laid out and well maintained. It consists of motorways, national highways (trunk roads), provincial roads and secondary roads.

Motorways
Practically all towns of any size are served by motorways (*autostrade,* numbered and prefixed with the letter S), which are mostly toll roads. Among the motorways of most importance to visitors are those from Varese or Como via Milan, Genoa and Pisa to Livorno or Florence; from Milan via Parma, Bologna and Florence to Rome, and from there to Naples; and from Bologna to Ravenna or via Rimini, Ancona, Pescara and Bari to Taranto. The motorway from the Brenner (Austrian-Italian frontier) via Bolzano, Trento and Verona links up with the Milan-Bologna motorway at Modena. There is also an important west/east link from Milan via Verona, Padua and Venice to Trieste.

National highways
Motorways apart, many important trunk routes are served by national highways (*strade statali*), the majority being good roads, well maintained. A new system of numbering, just a number or a number prefixed by a single letter S, has now replaced the old "SS plus number". Several of these highways also have names (e.g. Via Aurelia, Via Emilia), often more commonly used than the number.

Provincial roads
The provincial roads (*strade provinciali, strade di grande comunicazione*), which are unnumbered, are also of good quality.

Secondary roads
Local connections are provided by the secondary roads (*strade secondaria*).

Road signs
Road signs and markings are in line with international standards. Among the more important signs likely to be encountered are:

Deviazone	Diversion
Rallentare	Slow
Sbarrato	Closed to traffic
Senso unico	One-way street
Tenere la destra	Keep right
Tutte direzioni	All directions
Zona tutelata INIZIO	Entering no parking zone

Traffic lights
Traffic lights change straight from red to green, then to green and amber and finally red again. Also unique to Italy are the large permanently red traffic lights at crossroads. Traffic is controlled by directional arrows which must always be obeyed.

Rule of the road
As in the rest of continental Europe, traffic goes on the right, with overtaking on the left.

Seat belts
All occupants of a car must wear seat belts. Children under 4 must be in special children's seats.

Alcohol
Driving under the influence of alcohol is strictly prohibited.

Speed limits
The speed limit in built-up areas is 50 k.p.h. (31 m.p.h.) for all types of vehicle.
Outside built-up areas speed limits are as follows:
On single carriageways 90 k.p.h. (56 m.p.h.), on dual carriageways with crash barriers 110 k.p.h. (68 m.p.h.), and on motorways 130 k.p.h. (80 m.p.h.)

Cars with trailers 70 k.p.h. (43 m.p.h.) and on motorways 80 k.p.h. (50 m.p.h.).

Caravans over 3.5 metric tons 80 k.p.h. (50 m.p.h.), on motorways 100 k.p.h. (62 m.p.h.).

Motor cycles below 150 cc are prohibited on motorways, as are sidecars; motor cycles of 150 cc to 349 cc on motorways 110 k.p.h. (68 m.p.h.), 350 cc or above 130 k.p.h. (80 m.p.h.).

Fog or restricted visibility (below 100 m (330 ft) 50 k.p.h. (31 m.p.h.).

Penalties for exceeding the speed limit are severe, as they are for any failure to observe traffic regulations.

Maximum lengths

Single-axle trailers: trailer only (including tow-bar) 6.5 m (21 ft), length overall (vehicle and trailer) 14 m (46 ft).

Twin-axle trailer or caravan: trailer only (including tow-bar) 8 m (26 ft), length overall (vehicle and trailer/caravan) 15.5 m (51 ft).

Priority

Traffic on main roads has priority over side roads only if the main road has the priority sign (a white or yellow square, corner downwards, in a red or black and white frame); otherwise, even at roundabouts, traffic coming from the right has priority. On narrow mountain roads the ascending vehicle has priority. Vehicles on rails always have priority.

Overtaking

Drivers moving from one lane to another before and after overtaking must give warning of their intention by the use of their direction indicators. Outside built-up areas the horn must also be sounded before overtaking.

Ban on use of horn

In towns of any size the use of the horn is prohibited. The ban is indicated by a sign showing a horn with a bar through it or by the words *zona di silenzio*.

Lights

On roads or streets with good lighting only sidelights may be used. In tunnels and galleries dipped headlights must be used.

Petrol

See entry

Breakdowns

For breakdown assistance, see Emergencies.

In the event of a breakdown on a motorway it is not permitted to have the car towed away by another private car; on ordinary roads, however, this is permissible.

Motoring organisations

See entry

Motoring Organisations

Touring Club Italiano (TCI)

Head office:
Corso Italia 10
I-20122 Milano (Milan)
tel. (02) 85261

Automobile Club d'Italia (ACI)

Head office:
Via Marsala 8
I-00185 Roma (Rome)
tel. (06) 4998251

The ACI and TCI have offices in all provincial capitals, in major tourist centres and at the main frontier crossing points.

Petrol

General

Petrol prices in Italy continue to be somewhat above the European average. Credit cards are not accepted except at some motorway filling stations.

Post and Telephone

Lead-free petrol	Lead-free petrol ("benzina senza piombo" or "benzina verde", 95 octane) is now available throughout the country as are leaded petrol (97 octane), diesel and gasoline.
Spare petrol	It is prohibited, on safety grounds, to carry a reserve supply of petrol or to fill a can with petrol at a filling station.
Opening times	See Business Hours

Post and Telephone

Opening times	See Business Hours
Post-boxes	Post-boxes in Italy are painted red.
Stamps	Stamps (*francobolli*) can be bought at tobacconists (identified by a sign with the letter T over the door) as well as in post offices.
Telephone	Coin operated call boxes accept tokens (*gettoni*, costing 200 lire), or 100, 200 or 500 lire coins. For most public telephones however a phonecard (*carta telefonica*) is necessary. Cards with values of 5000, 10,000 or 15,000 lire are obtainable from Telecom Italia (see below), also from motorway cafés, bars, newspaper kiosks and tobacconists. Most bars have public telephones (look for a circular yellow sign over the entrance).
Telecom Italia SpA	Long-distance and international calls can made from offices of the Italian state telephone company, Telecom Italia SpA.
Tariffs	The Italian telephone tariff system is complex; the most favourable rates are for calls between 10pm and 8am
International dialling codes	From Italy to the United Kingdom: 0044 From Italy to the United States or Canada: 001 (In calls to the United Kingdom the initial zero of the local dialling code should be omitted.)
N.B.	Since 1998 dialling codes have been used even for local calls. For calls to Italy from abroad the initial zero of the local dialling code must be included (previously omitted).

Public Holidays

Statutory public holidays	January 1st (New Year's Day: Capo d'anno) January 6th (Epiphany: Epifania) Easter Monday (Pasqua) April 25th (Liberation Day 1945: Festa nazionale) May 1st (Labour Day: Festa del primo maggio) August 15th (Ferragosto; Assumption; family celebrations; the climax of the Italian holiday season: Assunzione) November 1st (All Saints: Ognissanti) December 8th (Immaculate Conception: Immacolata Concezione) December 25th and 26th (Christmas: Natale)
Patron saints' days	Patron saints' days are marked with great celebrations in many Italian villages and towns, including: April 25th: San Marco (Venice) June 24th: San Giovanni (Florence, Genoa, Turin) June 29th: San Pietro (Rome) July 11th: Santa Rosalia (Palermo) September 19th: San Gennaro (Naples) October 4th: San Petronio (Bologna) December 7th: Sant'Ambrogio (Milan)

Radio

RAI (Radiotelevisione Italiana), the Italian radio and television corpora-   RAI
tion, puts out special English-language transmissions.
   Traffic and road reports in English, French and German are also included in the news programme "Onda Verde Europa", broadcast on all three
Italian radio channels.

Railways

The Italian railway system has a total length of some 16,000 km (10,000 mi.).   Ferrovie Italiane
Most of it is run by the Italian State Railways (Ferrovie Italiane dello Stato,   dello Stato (FS)
FS), but there are also a number of privately run lines, the timetables for
which are included in the published timetables of the State Railways. There
are two classes of travel on FS trains, First Class and Second Class.

The State Railways have information bureaux at most stations (open   Information
7/8am–8pm or in some cases 10.30pm; they also deal with matters such
as lost or stolen tickets). Timetables are obtainable at station ticket offices
or any newspaper kiosk.

The central telephone number for railway information throughout Italy is
14 78/88088 (open daily 7am–9pm).

Wasteels Travel   Offices in UK,
(adjacent to platform 2, Victoria Station)   USA and Canada
121 Wilton Road, London SW1 1JY
tel. (0171) 8347066

C.I.T.
Marco Polo House
3–5 Lansdowne Road, Croydon, Surrey CRO 2BX
tel. (0181) 6860677

C.I.T.
342 Madison Avenue
Suite 207,
New York NY 10173
tel. (1–800) 2237987

500 North Michigan Avenue
Chicago IL 60611
tel. (312) 6446651 or 6440996

630 Fifth Avenue
New York NY 10103
tel. (212) 2454822

12400 Wilshire Boulevard
Los Angeles CA 90025
tel. (213) 8201898

111 Avenue Road
Toronto, Ontario M5R 3J8
tel. (416) 9277712

2055 Peel Street
Montreal, Québec H3A 1V4
tel. (514) 845901

Restaurants

Tickets	International tickets are valid for two months and allow the journey to be broken as often as desired. Tickets purchased in Italy, however, are valid only for periods of one or three days (journeys up to 50 km (30 mi.) or over 50 km (30 mi.) respectively). Return tickets are issued for journeys of up to 250 km (155 mi.). Tickets *must* be validated in platform machines at time of travel.
Reduced fares	Tourist cards, valid for 8, 15, 21 or 30 days, allow unlimited travel on Italian State Railways (mainland Italy, Sicily, Sardinia). Kilometric tickets *(Biglietto Chilometrico)*, valid for two months, allow travel totalling 3000km/1865 miles on FS lines with reductions of 10 per cent on standard rates. There are special concessions for those under 26 ("Carta Verde") and the over 60s ("Carta d'Argento") as well as for group travel. Children under 4 accompanied by an adult and not occupying a seat travel free. Children between 4 and 12 pay half fare.
Trains	In addition to Eurostar, EuroCity (EC) and Intercity (IC) trains (on which passengers pay a supplementary fare), there are express trains *(espressi)* stopping only at larger stations, and local services *(locali)* stopping at every station. The Turin-Milan-Rome route is served by high-speed trains, (Pendolino and Eurostar). Sleepers and couchettes are available on longer journeys. Bicycles may only be transported on certain days, special carriages being provided. Motorail services only operate on some routes. It is essential to book in good time.
Rome Airport	Air-conditioned trains (First Class only) maintain an hourly non-stop service between Rome main railway station and Fiumicino Airport, the journey taking 30 minutes. Passengers with hand luggage only can check-in for their flight in the waiting room of the main railway station.
Treno + Auto	Treno + Auto (Train + Car) means cars can be rented at the stations.

Restaurants

General	Prices for à la carte dishes tend to be high; the "menù turistico" however is cheaper but can be a gamble and the portions are small. Among the alternatives to expensive "ristorante" are the rather more modest "tavola calda" or "rosticceria" and "fiaschetteria" where the food is generally excellent. "Trattorie" are inns, often furnished in the style of the region. An "osteria" will serve drinks not necessarily accompanied by food; the only drinks served at an "enoteca" are wines. In bars, drinks taken standing at the bar cost less than those served at tables. (For opening times of bars, cafés and restaurants, see Business Hours.)
NB	To prevent possible tax evasion restaurants are required by law to issue customers with a receipted bill, which the police may then ask to inspect (within 50m of the restaurant); failure to produce the receipt may lead to a fine.
No smoking	Smoking is banned in many restaurants, cafés, and bars, particularly those without air-conditioning.
Service and cover charges	There is no longer uniformity of practice with regard to service *(servizio)* and cover charges *(pane e coperto)*; some restaurants impose both, others neither. Where a charge is made, service can add between 10 and 15 per cent to the bill and the cover charge anything from 1,000 to 5,000 lire.
Reservations	The list below contains a selection of restaurants. Booking in advance by telephone is almost always advisable (the relevant area codes being given in the margin which must be used at all times).

Big-city coffee house – full of atmosphere

Il Dottore–Pizzeria, Via 1° Maggio 23, tel. 776410
Ill Gatto e la Voilpe, Via della Pace, tel. 778751
In I Prati: I Prati, tel. 777511

Abbadia San
Salvatore
(0577)

La Brocca d'u Cinc'oru (near the cathedral; good solid trattoria, traditional cuisine), Corso Savoia 49/a, tel. 607196

Acireale
(095)

Carlo Parisio (meat and fish), Via Mazzini 14, tel. 56650
Il Ciarlocco, Via Don Bosco 1, tel. 57720

Acqui Terme
(0144)

Le Caprice, Strada Panoramica dei Templi 51, tel. 26469

Agrigento
(0922)

Palma (Ligurian and Provençal cuisine), Via Cavour 5, tel. 640314

Alassio
(0182)

Osteria dell'Arco (informal atmosphere, traditional cuisine), Piazza Savona
5, tel. 363974

Alba
(0173)

Minisport da Luciano (speciality seafood), Viale Italia 35, tel. 53458

Albenga
(0182)

Il Poeta Contadino (creative as well as traditional cuisine), Via Indipendenza
21, tel. 721917

Alberobello
(080)

Caval Mari (on the seaside promenade; fish and meat dishes), ★ Alghero
Lungomare Dante, tel. 981570
La Lepanto (local cuisine, fish and shellfish), Via Carlo Albero 135, tel. 979116

Alghero
(079)

La Caravella, Via M. Camera 12, tel. 871029
Eolo, Via P. Comite 3, tel. 871241

Amalfi
(089)

Restaurants

Ancona (071)	Passeto (elegant; faultless cuisine) Piazzale IV Novembre, tel. 33214 La Moretta (in the Old Town; country-style; traditional cuisine), Piazza del Plebiscito 52, tel. 202317 In Portonovo: Fortino Napoleonico (★location, refined atmosphere; imaginative cooking), Via Poggio 166, tel. 801450
Anzio (06)	Pierino (fish dishes, etc.), Piazza C. Battisti 3, tel. 9845683
Aosta (0165)	Vecchio Ristoro, Via Tourneuve 4, tel. 33238
Arco (0464)	La Lanterna (Trentine cuisine), 2.5 km (1½ mi.) north, Prabi 30, Via L. Cecoslovacchi 30, tel. 517013
Arenzano (010)	Lazzaro e Gabriella, Via S. M. Rapallo 14, tel. 9124259
Arezzo (0575)	Buca di San Francesco (14th c. palazzo; plenty of atmosphere, Tuscan cuisine), Piazza di San Francesco 1, tel. 23271
Arzachena (0789)	Grazia Deledda (country atmosphere), on the road to Baia Sardinia, tel. 98988 Casablanca (touch of elegance; veranda with ★sea view), in Baia Sardinia, tel. 99006
Ascoli Piceno (0736)	Gallo d'Oro, Corso Vittorio Emanuele 13, tel. 253520
Assisi (75)	Buca di San Francesco (in a 14th c. palazzo; al fresco service in summer; traditional cuisine), Via Brizi 1, tel. 812204 San Francesco (local cuisine), Via San Francesco 52, tel. 812329 Medio Evo (very comfortable; local cuisine), Via Arco dei Priori 4/b, tel. 813068
Asti (0141)	Gener Neuv (★view of garden and the embankment; Piedmontese cuisine), Lungotanaro Pescatori 4, tel. 557270, fax 436723 L'Angolo del Beato (in a medieval house in the Old Town; informal atmosphere, local cuisine), Via Gattuari 12, tel. 531668 Il Cenacolo, Viale Pilone 59, tel. 531110 La Greppia (trattoria), Corso Alba 140, tel. 593262 In Castiglione: Da Aldo (local cuisine), Via San Defendente 22, tel. 206008
Barbaresco (0173)	Antica Torre (informal atmosphere, plain traditional cooking), Via Torino 8, tel. 635170
Bari (080)	La Pignata (local cuisine), Corso Vittoria Emanuele 173, tel. 5232481
Baschi (0744)	In Civitella del Lago, on the SS to Todi: ★Vissani (behind the rather ordinary-looking bar in Lago di Corbara; restaurant run by Umbrian master-chef Gianfranco Vissani, the Gault Millau Guide for Italy's "Chef of the Year". Top quality restaurant – the art of cooking at its very best but with prices to match), tel. 950396
Belluno (0437)	Delle Alpi, Via Jacopo Tasso 15, tel. 940302 Al Borgo (in a lovely park; pleasant atmosphere), Via Anconetta 8, tel. 926755
Bergamo (035)	Da Vittorio (outstandingly good cuisine; fish specialities), Viale Papa Giovanni XXIII 21, tel. and fax 218060 La Nicchia (pleasant, small restaurant; highly commended both for its food and its wine list), Piazza Mercato del Fieno (Old Town), tel. 220114 Lio Pellegrini (Tuscan dishes, etc.), Via San Tomaso 47, tel. 247813 Taverna Colleoni dell'Angelo (popular with the locals; mainly fish), Piazza Vecchia 7, tel. 232596

I Carracci (exclusive), Via Manzoni 2, tel. 222049 Bologna
(051)
Bitone (exclusive), Via Emilia Levante 111, tel. 546110
Franco Rossi (elegant restaurant, Bolognese cuisine, fish dishes), Via Goito 3, tel. 238818
Il Pescatore (seafood), Via Marco Emilio Lepido 193, tel. 400358
Panoramica, Via San Mamolo 31, tel. 580337
Pappagallo (exclusive – autographed photos of Arturo Toscanini, Alfred Hitchcock and many others; Bolognese cuisine), Piazza Mercanzia 3/c, tel. 232807
Torre de' Galluzzi (Baroque furnishings; Bolognese and vegetarian cuisine), Corte de' Galluzzi 5/a, tel. 267638
Rosteria Luciano (Bolognese cuisine, side-dishes according to season), Via Nazario Sauro 19, tel. 231249
Le Maschere (fish specialities), Via Zappoli 5, tel. 261035
Caffè Zamboni (much favoured by the locals), Via Zamboni 6, tel. 231835

Da Abramo (gourmet cuisine, fish dishes), Grieser Platz 16, tel. 280141 Bolzano
(0471)
Amandè, Vicolo Ca' de Bezzi 8, tel. 971278
Rastbichler (local Italian cuisine), Cadornastr. 1, tel. 261131
Zur Kaiserkron' (gourmet cuisine; also served al fresco), Mustergasse 1, tel. 970770
Bierlokal: Accademia della Birra, Kapuzinergasse 6/8
Cafés: Aida, Pfarrplatz 3, tel. 970155
Vienna (also bistro; hot and cold dishes, own confectionery, ice cream specialities), Waltherplatz 1, tel. 974900

Carletto, Via Vittorio Emanuele 339, tel. 261725 Bordighera
(0184)
Le Chaudron, Piazza Bengasi 2, tel. 263592
La Via Romana (plenty of atmosphere; outstanding Ligurian cuisine), Via Romana 57, tel. 266681

Taulà (in a converted 17th c. barn; traditional cuisine), Via Dante 6, tel. 901424 Bormio
(0342)

La Sosta, Via San Martino della Battaglia 20, tel. 295603 Brescia
(030)
Olimpo-il Torricino, Via Fura 131, tel. 347565
In Mompiano: Castello Malvezzi (imaginative Mediterranean cooking in a building dating from 1480; also open air café), Via Colle San Giuseppe 1, tel. 2004224
In Sant'Eufernia: La Piazzetta (choice fish dishes), Via Indipendenza 87/c, tel. 362668

Fink (Tyrolean and international cuisine; caféteria on the ground floor), Via Portici Minori 4, tel. 834883 Bressanone
(0472)

Ai Pescatori (first-class trattoria; good local cuisine, fish), Via Galuppi 371, tel. 730650 Burano
(041)

In Samboseto, 8 km (5 mi.) east:
Palazzo Calvi (in a 17th c. palazzo, seat at one time of the Calvi family, Parmesan-Bolognese aristocrats; Parmesan cuisine with anolini – meat-filled pasta – a particular speciality), tel. 90211, fax 90213 Busseto
(0524)

Dal Corsaro (local cuisine), Viale Regina Margherita 28, tel. 664318 Cagliari
(070)
Saint Remy (in the former cellar of a 17th c. palazzo: seafood a speciality), Via Torino 16, tel. 657377

In Fiumara, 10 km (6 mi.) south-east: Bontempo, tel. 961188 Capo d'Orlando
(0941)

Quisi (in the Hotel Quisisana; international cuisine), Via Camerelle 2, tel. 8370788 Capri
(081)
La Capannina (traditional cuisine, fish dishes), Via delle Botteghe 14, tel. 8370732, fax 8376990

Restaurants

Da Luigi ai Faraglioni (★location; fish dishes, etc.), Strada dei Faraglioni, tel. 8370591

Casale Monferrato (0142)
La Torre (Piedmontese cuisine), Via Garoglio 3, tel. 70295

Castelsardo (079)
La Guardiola (country-style; al fresco service on the terrace in summer; fish dishes), Piazza Bastione 4, tel. 470755

Catania (095)
La Siciliana (traditional cuisine, fish dishes, etc.), Viale Marco Polo 52/a, tel. 376400

Cattolica (0541)
La Lampara di Mario (traditional cuisine, fish dishes), Piazzale Darsena 3, tel. 963296
Protti, Via Emilia Romagna 185, tel. 954457

Cefalù (0921)
Ostaria del Duomo (service outdoors in the summer), Via Seminario 5, tel. 421838

Celle Ligure (019)
Mosè, Via Colla 30, tel. 991560

Cesenático (0547)
La Buca (terrace overlooking the harbour; fish dishes), Corso Garibaldi 41, tel. 82474
Bistrot Claridge (excellent Romagna cuisine), Viale dei Mille 55, tel. 82055
Pino, Via Anita Garibaldi 7, tel. 80645, 75350
Vittorio, Via Andrea Doria 3, tel. 672588

Chiavari (0185)
Luchin (authentic osteria with bar, long tables and wooden stools; Ligurian cuisine), Via Brighenti 53, tel. 301063

Chieti (0871)
Venturini, Via De Lollis 10, tel. 330663
Nino (trattoria in the centre of the Old Town; plain wholesome cooking), Via Principe di Piemonte 7, tel. 65396, 63781

Città di Castello (075)
Amici Miei (in the centre of the Old Town), Via del Monte 2, tel. 8559904
Il Bersaglio (specialities: mushrooms, game, truffles), Via V. E. Orlando 14, tel. 8555534

Cividale del Friuli (0432)
Locanda Al Castello (in a former Jesuit monastery in gardens on a hill; local Friuli and Italian cuisine), Via del Castello 18, tel. 733242

Como (031)
Catene, Via Borsieri 18, tel. 263775
Imbarcadero (pleasant atmosphere, traditional cuisine), Piazza Cavour 20, tel. 277341
Sant'Anna '1907 (comfortable; international cuisine), Via Turati 1/3, tel. 505266

Cortina d'Ampezzo (0436)
Beppe Sello, Via Rovico 68, tel. 3236
Tivoli (★panoramic view from the terrace; creative as well as traditional cuisine), Via Lacedel 34 (in the direction of Pocol), tel. 866400

Cosenza (0984)
In Rende, 11 km (6³/4 mi.) outside Cosenza: Il Pozzo dei Desideri, Via Antonio Gramsci, tel. 443618
Il Setaccio (country cooking in a former stables; local wines), Corso da Santa Rosa 62, tel. 837211

Cremona (0372)
Aquila Nera (by the cathedral; wooden beams, antique furnishings), Via Sicardo 3, tel. 25646
Ceresole (elegant), Via Ceresole 4, tel. 30990
Il Ceppo, Via Casalmaggiore 222, tel. 496363
La Locanda (high-class restaurant in a small cross-vaulted hall; Cremonese specialities) Via Pallavicino 4, tel. 457834
La Sosta (decorated with items from the worlds of music and theatre and hence a popular meeting place after visits to the theatre; Cremonese specialities, etc.), Via Sicardo 9, tel. 456656

Mellini (small restaurant, plainly furnished; excellent cuisine), Via Bissolati 105, tel. 30535

La Sosta, Via Corrado Alvaro, tel. 23831

Crotone (0962)

Della Chiocciola (osteria in basement, restaurant with coffered ceiling above; Piedmontese cuisine), Via Fossano 1, tel. 66277
Le Plait d'Etain (French cuisine), Corso Giolitti 18/a, tel. 681918
Lo Zuavo, Via Roma 23, tel. 602020

Cuneo (0171)

Cavallino (one of the best places to eat in Brescia province; al fresco service in summer), Via Gherla 30, corner of Via Murachette, tel. 9120217
Esplanade (elegant restaurant; meals outdoors in summer, ★view; seafood), Via Lario 10, tel. 9143361

Desenzano del Garda (030)

Le Volte (near the Pinakothek and Teatro Masini), Corso Mazzini 54, tel. 661600
Turandot, Corso Mazzini 195, tel. 24750

Faenza (0763)

Il Restorantino-da Giulio (fish specialities), Viale Adriatico 100, tel. 805680

Fano (0721)

Centrale, Via Boccaleone 8, tel. 206735
La Provvidenza, Corso Ercole I d'Este 92, tel. 2051 7
Quel Fantastico Giovedì (usually crowded; good food and reasonable prices; advance booking essential), Via Castelnuovo 9, tel. 760570

Ferrara (0532)

Harmony, Corso Europa 67, tel. 601728

Finale Ligure (019)

★Enoteca Pinchiorri (the best restaurant in Italy), Via Ghibellina 87, tel. 242777, fax 244983
Sabatini (a restaurant with a great tradition), Via de'Panzani 9/a, tel. 211559
Harry's Bar, Lungarno Vespucci 22r, tel. 2 396700
Don Chisciotte, Via Cosima Ridolfi 4r, tel. 475430
Al Lume di Candela, Via delle Terme 23r, tel. 294566
Cantinetta Antinori (Tuscan specialities), Piazza Antinori 3, tel. 292234
La Posta, Via de' Lamberti 20r, tel. 212701
Oliviero, Via delle Terme 51r, tel. 2302407
Cibreo, Via dei Macci 118, tel. 2341100
Del Carmine, Piazza del Carmine 18, tel. 218601
Il Latini (typical trattoria), Via dei Palchetti 6, tel. 210916
Quattro Stugioni, Via Maggio 61r, tel. 218906
Café-bar: Bar Pasticceria Gilli (famous café in the heart of Florence; specialities: home-made pies, chocolate, elaborate ice-cream sundaes, coffee and liqueurs), Piazza della Repubblica 39/R, tel. 2396310

Florence (055)

Il Ventaglio (seafood, etc.), Via Postiglione 6, tel. 661500

Foggia (0881)

Villa Roncalli (elegant country villa; excellent simple dishes), Viale Roma 25, tel. 391091

Foligno (0742)

Vicolo di'Mblò (local dishes, fish), Corso Italia 126, tel. 502385

Fondi (0771)

La Barca (sophisticated cuisine, fish and seafood), Viale Italico 3 (town centre), tel. 89323
Lorenzo (sophisticated cuisine), Viale Carducci 61 (town centre), tel. 84030

Forte dei Marmi (0584)

Cacciani (meals served on the magnificent terrace in summer; Roman specialities, lamb, seafood), Via A. Diaz 13, tel. 9420378
Zarazà (traditional Roman specialities, lamb, tripe), Viale Regina Margherita 21, tel. 9422053

Frascati (06)

Restaurants

Frosinone
(0775)
La Palombella, Via Maria 234, tel. 873549
Stella (in the town centre; meat and fish dishes, home-made cakes), Via Garibaldi 90, tel. 250085

Gaeta
(0771)
Antico Vito, Vico del Cavallo 2–4, tel. 465116

Gardone
(0365)
Villa Fiordaliso (first-class restaurant, beautiful art nouveau villa in small park; terrace restaurant also), Via Zanardello 132, tel. 20158

Genoa
(010)
Gran Gotto (stylish restaurant, Ligurian cuisine), Viale Brigata Bisagno 69 R, tel. 564344
Vittorio al Mare e la Sua Cambusetta (restaurant-pizzeria; Ligurian cuisine), Belvedere Edoardo Firpo 1, tel. 3760141
Zeffirino (rustic; Genoese, also Ligurian, Italian and international cuisine), Via XX Settembre 20, tel. 591990
Il Cucciolo (Tuscan specialities), Viale Sauli 33, tel. 561321
Saint Cyr (elegant, modern restaurant; Piedmontese, Ligurian and international cusine), Piazza Marsala 4 R, tel. 886897

Grado
(0431)
Al Balaor, Calle Zanini 3, tel. 80150
All'Androna (al fresco service in summer; international cuisine, fish and shellfish), Calle Porta Piccola 4, tel. 80950

Grosseto
(0564)
Buca San Lorenzo, Viale Manetti 1, tel. 25142

Gubbio
(075)
In the historic town centre:
Alla Fornace di Mastro Giorgio (in a medieval palazzo, very dignified; fish and regional cuisine, etc.), Via Mastro Giorgio 2, tel. 9221836
Fabiani (open air café also), Piazza 40 Martiri 26/B, tel. 9274639
Taverna del Lupo (meals in comfort beneath a medieval vault; Umbrian specialities, etc.), Via G. Ansidei 21, tel. 9274368

Imola
(0542)
★San Domenico (the perfect combination: exceptional comfort and outstanding cuisine), Via Sacchi 1, tel. 29000

Imperia
(0183)
In Porto Maurizio: Lanterna Blu da Tonino (elegant restaurant on the promenade; Mediterranean cuisine, fish), Via Scarincio 32, tel. 63859

Isernia
(0865)
La Tequila, Via San Lazzaro 85, tel. 412345
Taverna Maresca (country-style; specialities drawn from traditional gypsy cooking), Corso Marcelli 186, tel. 3976

Jesolo
(0421)
La Vecchia Marina (elegant atmosphere; fish specialities), Lido di Jesolo, Via Roma Destra 120/c, tel. 370645

L'Aquila
(0862)
Ernesto (best in the town; fungi, truffles, etc), Piazza Palazzo 1, tel. 21094
Tre Marie, Via Tre Marie 3, tel. 413191, 21904

La Spezia
(0187)
La Pettegola (seafood specialities, etc.), Canaletto, Via del Popolo 39, tel. 514041
Parodi-Peyton Place (seafood specialities, etc.), Viale Amendola 212, tel. 715777

Latina
(0773)
Abaco, Via V. Rossetti 24, tel. 661923
La Risacca, Via Lungomare 93, Lido di Latina (12 km (7¹/₂ m.)), tel. 273223

Lavagna
(0185)
Il Gabbiano (★ panoramic view from the terrace), Via San Benedetto 26, tel. 390228

Lecco
(0341)
Al Porticciolo 84 (seafood specialities), Via Valsecchi 5/7, tel. 498103

Lipari
(090)
E Pulera (typical Lipari Islands cuisine), Via Diana, tel. 9 811158
Filippino (fish soups a speciality), Piazza Municipio, tel. 9811002

Ciglieri, Via O. Franchini 38, tel. 508194
Gennarino, Via Santa Fortunata 11, tel. 888093

Livorno
(0586)

Antica Locanda dell'Angelo (very nice, in the centre of Lucca; extensive menu, Tuscan cuisine), Via Pescheria 21, tel. 47711
La Buca di Sant'Antonio (traditional, local cuisine), Via della Cervia 3, tel. 55881
Antico Caffè delle Mura, Via Vittorio Emanuele 2, tel. 47962
In Ponte a Moriano (9 km (5 mi.)): La Mora (local Lucca cuisine), Via Sesto di Moriano 1748, tel. 406402

Lucca
(0583)

Da Secondo (many distinguished patrons; terrace; advance booking essential), Via Pescheria Vecchia 28, tel. 260912

Macerata
(0733)

Aquila Nigra (pleasant atmosphere, wholesome home cooking), Vicolo Bonacolsi 4, tel. 327180
Ochina Bianca, Via Finzi 2, tel. 323700
Campana, Vic. Santa Maria-Cittadella 10, tel. 391885
Rigoletto, Strada Cipata 10, tel. 370500

Mantua
(0376)

Delfino, by the Mediterranean, Lungomare Mediterraneo 672, tel. 998188

Marsala
(0923)

Francolino-Casino del Diavolo (Materan cooking, pasta from the basilicata), Via La Martella 48, tel. 261986

Matera
(0835)

Grillstube Schloss Maur, Via Cavour 2–4, tel. 211300
Sissi (small restaurant serving national cuisine), Via Plankestein 5, tel. 231062
Terlaner Weinstube, Via Portici 231, tel. 235571

Merano
(0473)

Savoua, Via XXXVII Luglio 36–38, tel. 2934865
Piero, Via Ghibellina 121, tel. 718365
Pranpou, Via Ugo Bassi 157, tel. 2938584

Messina
(090)

Marco Polo, Via Forte Marghera 67, tel. 989855
Dall'Amelia (Venetian specialities, fish dishes), Via Miranese 113, tel. 913955

Mestre
(041)

★Savini (famous restaurant with a great tradition), Galleria Vittorio Emanuele II, tel. 72003433
★Giannino (another restaurant with a great tradition; conservatory), Via Amatore Sciesa 8, tel. 55195582
Aimo e Nadia (Italian and French cuisine), Via Montecuccoli 6, tel. 416886
Sadler Osteria di Porta Cicca (sophisticated, elegant atmosphere, traditional cuisine), Ripa di Porta Ticinese 51, Via Conchetta, tel. 58104451
L'Ulmet, Via Olmetto 2, tel. 86452718
Olivia, Via G. D'Annunzio 7–9, tel. 89406052
Peck, Via Victor Hugo 4, tel. 876774
Royal Dynasty (oriental), Via Bocchetto 15/a, tel. 86450905
Alfredo-Gran San Bernardino (Milanese cuisine), Via Borghese 14, tel. 3319000
Biffi Scala, Piazza della Scala, tel. 866651
Boeucc, Piazza Belgioioso 2, tel. 76020224
Nino Arnaldo, near the main railway station, Via Poerio 3, tel. 76005981
Innocenti Evasioni, Via della Bindellina, tel. 33001882
Suntory (Japanese), Via Verdi 6, tel. 8693022
Yar (Russian), Via Mercalli 22, tel. 58305234
Joia (vegetarian restaurant), near the main railway station, Via Panfilo Castaldi 18, tel. 29522124
Bagutta (artists' rendezvous), Via Bagutta 14, tel. 76002767
Vecchia Viscontea, Via Giannone 10, tel. 0338/8769032
Antica Trattoria San Bernardo, Via San Bernardo 36, in Chiaravalle, tel. 57409831

Milan
(02)

Restaurants

Modena (059)	Borso d'Este, Piazza Roma 5, tel. 214114 Fini (elegant restaurant; regional and Italian cuisine), Rua Frati Minori 54, tel. 223314 Aurora, Via Coltellina 24, tel. 225191
Montecatini Terme (0572)	Gourmet, Viale Amendola 6, tel. 771012 San Francesco, Corso Roma 112, tel. 79632
Montegrotto Terme (049)	Da Mario, Viale delle Terme 4, tel. 794090
Monterosso al Mare (0187)	Miki, Via Fegina 104, tel. 817546
Naples (081)	La Sacrestia (elegant atmosphere, garden terrace with ★view), Via Orazio 116, tel. 664186 La Cantinella (in the Old Town; ★fine view from the veranda; Neapolitan specialities and Italian cuisine), Via Cuma 42, tel. 7648684 ★A Fenestella (terrace by the sea), Via Marechiaro 23, tel. 7690020 Don Salvatore (restaurant and pizzeria), Via Mergellina 5, tel. 681817 Dante e Beatrice (excellent fish hors d'œuvres), Piazza Dante 44/45, tel. 5499438
Nervi (010)	Dai Pescatori, Via Casotti 6/r, tel. 3726168 La Ruota, Via Oberdan 215r, tel. 3726027
Noli (019)	Lilliput, Via Zuglieno 49 (at Voze, 4 km (2½ mi.)), tel. 748009 Ines (seafood specialities), Via Vignolo 1, tel. 748086
Novara (0321)	Moroni, Via Solaroli 6, tel. 62 92 78
Nuoro (0784)	Canne al Vento, Viale della Repubblica, tel. 201762
Olbia (0789)	Leone e Anna, Via Barcellona 90, tel. 26333 Gallura (regional cuisine, seafood dishes), Corso Umberto I 145, tel. 24648
Oristano (0783)	Il Faro (stylish restaurant; seafood dishes, traditional Italian cuisine), Via Bellini 25, tel. 70002 La Forchetta d'Oro, Via Giovanni XXIII 8, tel. 302731
Orvieto (0763)	Giglio d'Oro, Piazza Duomo 8, tel. 41903 La Volpe e l'Uva (country-style; traditional cuisine), Via Ripa Corsica 1, tel. 41612 Le Grotte del Funaro (restaurant, pizzeria and piano bar, all in tufa caves), tel. 43276
Padua (049)	Antico Brolo (regional cuisine), Corso Milano 22, tel. 664555 Belle Parti-Toulà (regional cuisine), Via Belle Parti 11, tel. 8751822 Bastioni del Moro, Via P. Bronzetti 18, tel. 8710006
Palermo (091)	Charleston (popular with the locals; regional cuisine), Piazzale Ungheria 30, tel. 321366 L'Approdo Ristorante Renato (★sea view, Sicilian cuisine), Via Messina Marine 242, tel. 6302881 Gourmand's, Via della Libertà 37/e, tel. 323431 La Scuderia, Viale del Fante 9, tel. 520323 Il Ristorantino, Piazzale de'Gasperi 19, tel. 512861
Parma (0521)	Angiol d'Oro (opposite the cathedral square; terrace; Parmesan cuisine), Vicolo Scutellari 1, tel. 282632 Parizzi, Strada della Repubblica 71, tel. 285952 Santa Croce, Via Pasini 20, tel. 293529

La Greppia, Strada Garibaldi 39/a, tel. 233686
Il Cortile, Borgo Paglia 3, tel. 285779

Vecchia Pavia (small restaurant near the cathedral; Italian cuisine), Via Cardinal Riboldi 2, tel. 304132
Al Cassinino (elegant restaurant, international cuisine, extensive wine list), Via C. Conca 1 (at Cassinino, 4 km (2½ mi.)), tel. 422097
Della Madonna (classic regional cuisine), Via dei Liguri 28, tel. 302833

Pavia
(0382)

Osteria del Bartolo (extensive menu), Via Bartolo 30, tel. 5731561
La Taverna (Umbrian cuisine), Via delle Streghe 8, tel. 5724128
Fulchetto, Via Bartolo 20, tel. 5731775
Da Giancarlo (Umbrian cuisine), Via dei Priori 36, tel. 5724314
Dal Mi'Cocco (Perugian cuisine, especially fine pasta and risotto; popular with students), Corso Garibaldi 12, tel. 5732511
Café: Sandri (Perugia's oldest, with wood panelling; confectionery, Umbrian specialities), Corso Vannucci 32, tel. 5724112

Perugia
(075)

Lo Scudiero, Via Baldassini 2, tel. 64107
Da Teresa, Viale Trieste 180, tel. 30096
Da Carlo (seafood specialities, conservatory), Viale Zara 54, tel. 65355
Il Castiglione (pleasantly-shaded garden), Viale Trento 148, tel. 64934

Pesaro
(0721)

Guerino, Viale della Riviera 4, tel. 4212065
La Regina del Porto, Via Paolucci 65, tel. 389141

Pescara
(085)

Antica Osteria del Teatro (international and regional cuisine), Via Verdi 16, tel. 323777

Piacenza
(0523)

Osteria dei Cavalieri, Via San Frediano 16, tel. 580858
Ristoro dei Vecchi Macelli (cosy atmosphere; fish and game specialities, seafood), Via Volturno 49, tel. 20424
La Mescita (varied cuisine), Via Cavalca 2, tel. 544294
Schiaccianoci, Via Vespucci 108, tel. 21024

Pisa
(050)

S. Jacopo (Tuscan specialities and fish), Via Crispi 15, tel. 27786
Manzoni (fish dishes), Corso Gramsci 112, tel. 28101
Casa degli Ancici, Via Bonellina 111, tel. 380305

Pistoia
(0573)

Il Principe, Piazza Bartolo Longo 8, tel. 8505566

Pompei
(081)

Da Zelina, Piazza San Marco 13, tel. 27290

Pordenone
(0434)

La Ferrigna, Piazza della Repubblica 22, tel. 914129

Portoferraio
(0565)

Il Pitosforo (★view, fish dishes), Molo Umberto I 9, tel. 269020
Puny (★view), Piazza Martiri dell'Olivetta 5, tel. 269037

Portofino
(0185)

La Fattoria, Via Verderuolo Inferiore 4, tel. 34501

Potenza
(0971)

Il Piraña (fish dishes), Via G. Valentini 110/corner of Via Valentini, tel. 25746
Osvaldo Baroncelli, Via Fra Bartolomero 13, tel. 23810

Prato
(0574)

Il Barocco, Via Orfanatrofio 29, tel. 652397
On the Marina di Ragusa road, 5 km (3 mi.) south-west: Villa Fortugno (historic, elegant building), tel. 667134
In Marina di Ragusa: Alberto (seafood specialities), by the sea, Doria 48, tel. 239023

Ragusa
(0932)

Monique, by the sea, Lungomare Vittorio Veneto 6, tel. 50541
Hostaria Vecchia Rapallo, Via Cairoli 20, tel. 50053

Rapallo
(0185)

Restaurants

In San Massimo: U Giancu (with garden restaurant), Via San Massimo 78, tel. 260505
In Savagna: Roccabruna (lovely veranda), Via Sotto la Croce 6, tel. 261400

Ravenna
(0544)
Al Gallo (elegant, with garden restaurant also; fish, etc.), Via Maggiore 87, tel. 213775
Capannetti, Vicolo Capannetti 2, tel. 66681
Tre Spade, Via Faentina 136, tel. 500522
Bella Venezia, Via 4 Novembre 16, tel. 212746
La Gardela, Via Ponte Marino 3, tel. 217147
Wine bar: Ca'de Ven, Via C. Ricci 24, tel. 30163
Enoteca Bastione, Via Bastione 29, tel. 218147

Reggio Calabria
(0965)
Baylik (seafood specialities), Via Leone 1, tel. 48624
Bonaccorso, Via Nino Bixio 5, tel. 896048
Rodrigo (simple but tasty food), Via XXIV Maggio 25, tel. 20170

Rieti
(0746)
Bistrot (small restaurant serving wholesome plain food), Piazza San Rufo 25, tel. 498798
Checco al Calice d'Oro, Via Marchetti 10, tel. 204271

Rimini
(0541)
Piero e Gilberto Ristorante Europa (good Italian cuisine), Via Roma 51, tel. 28761
Lo Squero (fish specialities), Lungomare Tintori 7, tel. 27676

Riva del Garda
(0464)
Vecchia Riva (al fresco meals in summer; fish dishes, etc.), Via Bastione 3, tel. 555061
Al Volt, Via Fiume 73, tel. 552570
Bastione, Via Bastione 19, tel. 552652

Rome
(06)
West city (Vatican City, Gianicolo, etc.):
Antica Enoteca Capranica, Piazza Capranica 100, tel. 69940992
El Toulà (elegant restaurant), Via della Lupa 29, tel. 6873750
Les Etoiles, Via dei Bastioni 1, tel. 6893434, 6873233
Il Drappo (Sardinian cuisine), Vicolo del Malpasso 9, tel. 6877365
Ranieri, Via Mario de'Fiori 26, tel. 6786505
Hostaria Costanza (romantic setting in the ruins of the Pompei Theatre; al fresco meals at vine-shaded tables; fish and offal specialities), Piazza Paradiso 63/65, tel. 6861717 and 68801002

East city (Via Vittorio Veneto, Coliseum, etc.):
Sans Souci (elegant restaurant), Via Sicilia 20/24, tel. 4821814
Harry's Bar, Via Vittorio Veneto 150, tel. 4745832, 484643
Il Pavone (Art Déco style), Via Palestro 19/B, tel. 4465433
Coriolano (elegant restaurant), Via Ancona 14, tel. 44249863
Charly's Saucière (French and Swiss cuisine), Via di San Giovanni in Laterano, tel. 70495666

South city (Via Appia Nuova, Terme di Caracalla, etc.):
Checchino dal 1887 (famous restaurant, one of the finest in Rome; Roman cuisine), Via Monte Testaccio 30, tel. 5746318

Trastevere:
Alberto Ciarla (one of the best-known fish restaurants in Rome), Piazza San Cosimato 40, tel. 5818668
Taverna Trilussa (Roman specialities), Via del Politeama, tel. 5818918
Da Lucia (osteria serving Roman cuisine; highly regarded by local people and visitors alike), Vicolo del Mattonato 2/b, tel. 5803601

In San Lorenzo:
Pommidoro (rendezvous for students, artists, writers, etc; traditional dishes, grilled specialities, fish), Piazza dei Sanniti 44, tel. 4452692

Cafés:
Greco, Via Condotti 86, tel. 6782554
Morganti, Via Tor Cervara 236, tel. 2294990
Tomeucci, Viale Europa 52–56, tel. 5923091

A favourite among the city's ice-cream parlours: Giolitti (bar, pasticceria, gelateria), Via Uffici del Vicario 40, tel. 6991243

Al Borgo (elegant surroundings, excellent cuisine), Via Garibaldi 13, tel. 436300
Novecento, Corso Rosinini 82/d, tel. 435222

Rovereto
(0464)

Alla Campagnola, Via Brunati 11, tel. 22153
Lepanto, Lungolago Zanardelli 67, tel. 20428

Salò
(0365)

Vecchio Parco, Via Parma 95, tel. 573492

Salsomaggiore
Terme
(0524)

Righi la Taverna, Piazza della Libertà 10, tel. 991196
La Fratta, Via Salita alla Rocca 14, tel. 991594

San Marino
(0549)

Da Giannino, Corso Trento e Trieste 23, tel. 504014
Paolo e Barbara (sophisticated cuisine), Via Roma 47, tel. 531653
Il Bagatto (opposite the Teatro Ariston; fish specialities), Via Matteotti 145, tel. 531925
Angolo di Beppe, Corso Inglesi 31, tel. 531748

San Remo
(0184)

Don Alfonso 1890 (Sorrentine specialities), Corso Sant'Agata 11, tel. 8780026

Sant'Agata sui
due Golfi
(081)

★Gambero Rosso (one of Italy's best restaurants; San Vincenzo harbour; fish specialities but roasts above all), Piazza della Vittoria 13, tel. 701021

San Vincenzo
(0565)

Castello, Piazza Castello 6/7, tel. 232041
Senato, Via Alghero 36, tel. 277788

Sassari
(070)

Last Tango, Via La Glesia 5/a, tel. 76337

Sestriere
(0122)

Angiolina, Viale Rimembranza 49, tel. 41198
El Pescador, on the harbour, Via Pilade Queirolo 1, tel. 42888
Santi's, Viale Rimembranza 46, tel. 485019
In Riva Trigoso: Fiammanghilla dei Fieschi (★view from the villa; Genoese specialities, nouvelle cuisine, Ligurian produce), Via Pestella 6, tel. 481041

Sestri Levante
(0185)

Al Marsili (historic building), Via del Castoro 3, tel. 47154
Bottega Nova, Via Chiantigiana 29, tel. 284230
Al Mangia, Piazza del Campo 42, tel. 281121
Le Logge, Via del Porrione 33, tel. 48013

Siena
(0577)

Caruso (walls adorned with pictures of Enrico Caruso, the famous tenor; local cooking, seafood), Via Sant'Antonino 12, tel. 8073156
L'Antica Trattoria, Via Padre R. Giuliani 33, tel. 8071082
Correale, Via Correale 11/a, tel. 8785809
La Lanterna Mare, Via Marina Grande 180, tel. 8073033
Roxy Pub Cafè, Via degli Aranci 73, tel. 8782392

Sorrento
(081)

Emiliano (elegant), Corso Italia 50, tel. 31396
Piemontese (stylish surroundings, fish specialities), Via Mazzini 25, tel. 30235

Stresa
(0323)

Restaurants

Subiaco (0774)	Pub dell'Arco, Via V. Veneto, tel. 83538
Syracuse (0931)	Ionico-A Rutta e Ciauli (★view; Sicilian cuisine), Riviera Dionisio il Grande 194, tel. 65540 Don Camillo, Via Maestranza 92–100, tel. 67133
Taormina (0942)	La Giara (restaurant and piano bar), Via La Floresta 1, tel. 23360 Al Duomo, Vico Ebrei 11, tel. 625656 La Griglia (traditional cuisine, fish), Corso Umberto 54, tel. 23980 In Mazzarò: Il Pescatore (opposite the Isola Bella; ★view, fish dishes), Via Nazionale 107, tel. 23460
Taranto (099)	Monsieur Mimmo, Viale Virgilio 101, tel. 372691 Al Gambero, Vico del Ponte 4, tel. 4711190
Terni (0744)	Alfio, Via Galileo Galilei 4, tel. 420120
Tivoli (0774)	Cinque Statue (pleasant atmosphere, garden restaurant, large selection of hors d'œuvres), Largo Sant'Angleo 1, tel. 335366
Torre Pellice (0121)	Flipot, Corso Gramsci 17, tel. 953465
Trapani (0923)	P e G, Via Spalti 1, tel. 547701 Da Peppe, Via Spalti 50–52, tel. 28246 Del Porto, Via A. Staiti 45, tel. 547822
Trento (0461)	Chiesa (Trentine specialities among others) Parco San Marco, Via Marchetti 9, tel. 238766 Cantinota (old 16th-century wine cellar with garden), Via San Marco 22–24, tel. 238527 A La Due Spade, Via Don Rizzi 11, tel. 234343
Treviso (0422)	All'Antica Torre (fish), Via Inferiore 55, tel. 53694 Beccherie, Piazza Ancillotto 10, tel. 540871
Trieste (040)	Antica Trattoria Suban (in summer meals served in the shade of a leafy arcade), Via Comici 2, tel. 54368 L'Ambasciata d'Abbruzzo (specialities from the Abruzzi), Via Furlani 6, tel. 395050 Caffè San Marco (Art Déco coffee-house atmosphere, several floors; popular meeting place for intellectuals and others), Via Cesare Battisti, tel. 371373 and 371173
Turin (011)	Villa Sassi-El Toulà (historic building in a large park; Piedmontese and international cuisine), Strada al Traforo del Pino 47, tel. 8980556 Vecchia Lanterna (regional and international cuisine), Corso Re Umberto 21, tel. 537047 Cambio (historic building, long and rich tradition; Piedmontese and international cuisine), Piazza Carignano 2, tel. 546690 Due Lampioni (Piedmontese and international cuisine), Via Carlo Alberto 45, tel. 8179380 Tiffany (Piedmontese and international cuisine), Piazza Solferino 16, tel. 535948 In Mirafiori: Al Gatto Nero (Tuscan cuisine and fish), Corso Filippo Turati 14, tel. 590414 Il Porticciolo (national cuisine, fish dishes), Via Barletta 58, tel. 321601
Udine (0432)	Astoria Italia (fish dishes among others), Piazza XX Settembre 24, tel. 505091 Passeggio, Viale Volontari della Libertà 49, tel. 46216

Alla Vedova, Via Tavagnaccio 9, tel. 470291
Al Vitello d'Oro (fish dishes among others), Via Valvason 4, tel. 508982

Lago Maggiore (creatively prepared as well as traditional dishes, excellent   Varese
    wines), Via Carrobbio 19, tel. 231183   (0332)
Da Vittorio, Piazza Beccaria 1, tel. 234312

Caffè Quadri (elegant), Piazza San Marco 120, tel. 5222105   Venice
Antico Martini (elegant restaurant; international and Venetian cuisine),   (041)
    Campo San Fantin 1983, tel. 5224121
Harry's Bar (two-storeyed; immortalised by Hemingway; Picasso and
    Braque were among the artists who paid their bills with pictures; once
    popular with writers and film stars including Patricia Highsmith,
    Somerset Maugham, Humphrey Bogart, Richard Burton and Orson
    Welles; still boasts a distinguished list of patrons), Calle Vallaresso 1323,
    tel. 5285777
La Caravella (international and Venetian cuisine), Calle Larga XXII Marzo
    2397, tel. 5208901
Taverne La Fenice, Campiello de la Fenice 1938, tel. 5223856
Do Forni, Calle dei Specchieri 457/468, tel. 5237729, 5230663
Harry's Dolci (international and Venetian cuisine), Giudecca 773, tel.
    5224844
Da Fiore (Venetian cuisine, also fish specialities), Calle del Scaleter 2202/A,
    San Polo, tel. 721308
Al Covo (wine restaurant; light meals, large wine list), Campiello della
    Pescaria 3968, Castello, tel. 5223812
Da Ivo (behind the Teatro La Fenice; regional dishes), Ramo dei Fuseri
    1809, San Marco, tel. 5285004
Corte Sconta (regional cuisine; meals served in the garden in summer),
    Calle del Pestrin 3886, Castello, tel. 5227024
Poste Vecchie (in summer, meals served in the vine-shaded courtyard; fish
    specialities, etc.), Calle de la Poste Vecchie 1608, San Polo, tel. 721822
Vino Vino (comprehensive wine list; light meals), Calle del Cafetier 2007,
    San Marco, tel. 5237027
Cantina dei Do Mori (a bàcaro, i.e. a wine bar serving reasonably-priced
    meals; near the fish market), Calle dei Do Mori 429, San Polo, tel. 5225401
Do Spade (wine bar; can boast Casanova among its patrons; serves
    tramezzini i.e. sandwiches, among other things), Sottoportego de la Do
    Spade 860, San Polo, tel. 5210574

Marco Polo, Passeggiata Felice Cavallotti, tel. 352678   Ventimiglia
Nanni, Via Milite Ignoto 3/d, tel. 33230   (0184)
On the Franco-Italian border (8 km (5 mi.)): Balzi Rossi, Ponte San Ludovico,
    tel. 38132

Paiolo (peasant-style, good plain food), Viale Garibaldi 72, tel. 250577   Vercelli
                                                              (0161)

Il Desco (nicest restaurant in the town; outstanding Italian cooking, good   Verona
    wines), Via Dietro San Sebastiano 3/5, tel. 595358   (045)
12 Apostoli, Vicolo Corticella San Marco 3, tel. 596999
Arche (seafood specialities), Via Arche Scaligere 6, tel. 8007415
Baracca (seafood specialities), Via Legnago 120, tel. 500013
Re Teodorico (with terrace restaurant), Piazzale Castel San Pietro 1, tel.
    8349990

L'Oca Bianca, Via Coppino 409, tel. 388477   Viareggio
Pino, Via Matteotti 18, tel. 916356   (0584)
Tito del Molo, Lungomolo Corrado del Greco 3, tel. 962016
Da Romano, Via Mazzini 122, tel. 31382
Montecatini, Viale Manin 8, tel. 962129

Shopping

Vicenza (0444)	Cinzia e Valerio (seafood specialities), Piazzetta Porta Padova 65/67, tel. 505213
	Storione (seafood specialities), Via Pasubio 62/64, tel. 566244
	Tre Visi, Corsa Palladio 25, tel. 324868
	Coffé Garibaldi, Piazza dei Signori 5, tel. 542455
Viterbo (0761)	Aquila Nera, Via della Fortezza, tel. 344220
	Il Richiastro (with garden restaurant), Via della Marrocca 16–18, tel. 228009
	Grottino, Via della Cava 7, tel. 308188
Volterra (0588)	Il Sacco Fiorentino (Tuscan cuisine; truffles), Piazza XX Settembre 18, tel. 88537
	Osteria dei Poeti, Via Matteotti 55, tel. 86029

Shopping

NB	Many items including decorated terracotta ware, marble (e.g. slabs), genuine espresso coffee machines and small pieces of furniture (such as swing chairs) are cheaper in Italy than elsewhere. Prices, place of manufacture and import duty if any should be investigated prior to leaving home. Once in Italy it is always best to buy direct from the manufacturer or from a specialist shop.
Weekly markets	Household goods, foodstuffs and, for example, clothes, are sold not only in shops but also at the colourful weekly markets (*mercato settimanale*) which are such an important element in Italian life.
Antique markets	Arezzo (1st Sat. and Sun. in the month), Lucca (3rd Sat. and Sun. in the month), Milan (last Sun. in the month), Modena (last Sat. and Sun. in the month), Ravenna (3rd Sat. and Sun. in the month), Sarzana (August), Taggia (last weekend in the month) and Turin (2nd in the month) are renowned among others for their antique markets.
Famous shopping streets	Italy boasts some celebrated shopping streets including Milan's Via Montenapoleone, Via Spiga and world-famous covered arcade, the Galleria Vittorio Emanuele II, Rome's Via Condotti and Via del Corso, Florence's Ponte Vecchio and Naples's Via Toledo.
Arts and crafts	In Italy it is still possible to find an amazingly wide range of traditional arts and crafts. As well as delightful woodcarving from Val Gardena, the Alto Adige is noted for its traditional costumes, jewellery and dolls. Piedmont too produces some fine woodcarving, also gold- and silver-work, brocades and embroideries, and elegant clothes. Liguria is the place for damask, bobbin lace and articles of olive wood, while Lombardy is known for its shoes, furniture, silk, ceramics and porcelain, and Cremona, of course, for its violins. Though Venetian glass and crystal are legendary, Venice produces much much more: gold- and silver-work, embroidery, and clothes from a celebrated design studio. From Tuscany come gold-, wood- and alabaster-work, ceramics, leather and straw goods and fabrics including fine linen. Straw and wickerwork, ceramics, carpets and musical instruments are typical of the Marches; Umbria's specialities are painting on glass and fine majolica ware. Southern Italy is famous for its iron- and copperware, coral jewellery (mainly Sardinia and Campania), porcelain, small items of furniture, ceramics, terracottas, fabrics, embroideries and carpets.
Culinary favourites	To this already impressive list of popular Italian products must be added culinary favourites such as confectionery (*panettone*, candied fruit), wine, spirits, olive oil, pasta and prepared sauces (*salse*, see Food and Drink).
NB	If you buy any valuable articles or have to pay a large garage bill, etc., you should take care to keep the receipt, since you may be required to produce it to a police officer checking on tax evasion.

Colourful Neapolitan street market

Ceramics are one of the most popular souvenirs of Italy

Time

Recovery of VAT   Value-added taxes in Italy are high, but can be recovered by foreign visitors. If you have bought any expensive item in Italy you should present the receipted bill to a customs officer on leaving the country and ask for a certificate confirming that it has been exported. This certificate should then be sent to the shop where you bought the article, and they should then refund the VAT paid on it.

Time

Italy is on Central European Time (one hour ahead of Greenwich Mean Time, six hours ahead of New York time).

From the end of March to the end of September summer time (two hours ahead of GMT, seven hours ahead of New York time) is in force.

Tipping

Tipping is normal practice in Italy. Generally speaking tips (*mancia*) are given only for services rendered on specific request. Also, the usherette who shows you to your seat in the cinema or theatre is normally given a tip. In the case of taxis it is customary to round up the fare, giving the driver the change from e.g. a 1000 lire note.

Travel Documents

Officially there are no passport controls for citizens of member countries travelling within the EU. Since spot checks may nevertheless be carried out, and proof of identity be required at airports and ports, a passport must still be carried when visiting Italy. Children under 16 should either possess their own passport or be entered on that of a parent. Citizens of the United States, Canada and many other countries likewise require only a passport; no visa is necessary.

Vehicle
documentation   British, US and other national driving licences and registration documents are accepted in Italy and should be carried, as should a "Green Card" international insurance certificate. This latter must be produced at traffic checks or in the event of an accident (failure to do so at the frontier if and when required can lead to a large fine).

Foreign cars must bear an oval nationality plate.

When to Go

Spring and
autumn   The best times of year for travelling in Italy are spring (end of March to mid June) and autumn (mid September to mid November). Of these, autumn is the season most favoured by tourists intent on visiting the cities with their world-famous art treasures.

The macchia blooms on Sardinia from the beginning of March to early summer, carpeting this generally rather bare island with flowers; the air is heavy with the scent of myrtle, thyme, rosemary and other herbs.

In late September the sirocco, a hot, moist south-easterly wind, can bring oppressive conditions, particularly on the coast and in Tuscany.

Autumnal fogs are something of a hazard in northern Italy, disrupting road and air traffic.

Summer   At the height of summer the most popular places are the coastal and hill resorts. In the south of the country, particularly in the towns, it can become unbearably hot. It should be borne in mind too that, over the mid-August Ferragosto (Assumption) holiday (see Public Holidays), many museums and other institutions in larger towns remain closed.

During the winter season the most popular resorts are the ski areas in the Italian Alps (see Winter Sports). Winter

Winter Sports

The winter sports areas in the Italian Alps have long enjoyed an international reputation. In the Western Alps the principal area is the Aosta valley, to the south-east of the Mont Blanc massif, which can be conveniently reached from Turin. The best known resorts are Courmayeur and Breuil-Cervinia. `Alps`

Another popular winter sports region lies east of Lake Como and north of Bergamo. Livigno, on the west side of the Ortles group, attracts many skiing enthusiasts with its dependable covering of good snow.

Particularly well equipped with winter sports facilities and other amenities is the area known as Dolomiti Superski (it celebrated 20 years in existence in 1995), to which such old-established resorts as Cortina d'Ampezzo and San Martino di Castrozza belong, as well as the Alpi di Siusi, the Val Gardena, the Val di Fassa and the Val d'Ega; recently added is the Civetta area at the foot of the Marmolada. The most striking peak is Marmolada (3342 m (10,965 ft)), which offers the possibility of summer skiing. A well coordinated system of lifts and cableways brings the pistes within easy reach. `Dolomiti Superski`

Perhaps the best known "round trip" (depending on snow conditions) is the Sella Ronda, a circuit of the Sella massif. `Sella Ronda`

The ski pass for Dolomiti Superski is valid for the whole of the Dolomites apart from Marmolada and for some adjoining areas and gives access to more than 400 facilities (cableways, ski-lifts, etc.) and more than 1000 km (600 mi.) of pistes. It is, however, not cheap.

There are popular skiing areas, almost exclusively frequented by Italians, in the Apennines to the west of Bologna, in the Ancona area, and north and south of Pescara. `Apennines`

Federazione Italiana Sport Invernali (FISI)
Via Piranesi 44, 1-20137
Milano (Milan)
Tel. (02) 719518 `Information`

Youth Hostels

Youth hostels (*ostelli per la gioventù*) provide accommodation at very reasonable rates. Priority is given to young people under 30 travelling on foot. If the hostel is full the period of stay is limited to three nights. Advance booking is advisable during the main holiday season and for groups of more than five. Hostellers are not allowed to use their own sleeping bags: the hire of a sleeping bag is included in the overnight charge. Foreign visitors must produce a membership card of their national youth hostel association.

Associazione Italiana Alberghi per la Gioventù (AIG)
Via Cavour 44
I-00184 Roma (Rome)
Tel. (06) 4871152 `Information`

International Youth Hostel Federation (UK headquarters)
Fountain House, Parkway
Welwyn Garden City
Hertfordshire AL8 6JH
Tel. (01707) 324170

Index

Index

Index

Principal Places of Tourist Interest

The places listed above are merely a selection of the principal sights – places of interest in themselves or for attractions in the surrounding area. There are of course innumerable other sights throughout Italy, to which attention is drawn by one or two stars.

297 colour photographs, 89 maps, plans and drawings

German text: Rosemarie Arnold, Walter R. Arnold, Eva Bakos, Monika I. Baumgarten, Vera Beck, Gisela Bockamp, Prof. Dr Wolfgang Hassenpflug, Reinhard Komar, Andreas März, Peter M. Nahm, Reinhard Paesler, Manfred Strobel, Moritz Wullen, Andrea Wurth

Editorial work: Baedeker-Redaktion (Gisela Bockamp, Peter M. Nahm, Andrea Wurth)

General direction: Reiner Eisenschmid, Baedeker Stuttgart

Cartography: Waldemar Aniol, Neusorg; Christoph Gallus, Hohberg; Ingenieurbüro für Kartographie Harms, Erlenbach bei Kandel/Pfalz; Franz Huber, München; Franz Kaiser, Sindelfingen; Archiv für Flaggenkunde Ralf Stelter, Hattingen; Mairs Geographischer Verlag, Ostfildern

Source of illustrations: Abend (2), Agostini (6), Anthony (1), APT Chianciano Terme (1), APT Lucca (2), APT Trentino (2), Archiv für Kunst und Geschichte (10), Atelier Mendini (1), Baedeker-Archiv (6), Bahnacker (18), Borowski (2), Focus (1), Fuchs-Hauffen (1), Galleria d'Arte Moderna, Undine (1), Gärtner (1), Griesinger (1), Hackenberg (15), HB-Verlag Hamburg (23), Historia-Photo (12), IFA (32), Jung (2), Lade (23), Messina (4), Nahm (9), Neumeister (1), Regione Autonoma Valle d'Aosta (3), Regione Liguria (2), Regione Lombarda (6), Reincke (4), Roli (1), Schleicher (1), Schliebitz (1), Smettan (6), Stetter (2), Strasser (2), Strobel (11), Tanasi (1), Thomas (65), Zefa (13)

Front cover: AA Photo Library (C. Sawyer). Back cover: AA Phot Library (K. Paterson)

Original English Translation: James Hogarth, Alec Court

Revised text: David Cocking, Wendy Bell

Editorial work: Margaret Court

4th English edition 1999

© Baedeker Stuttgart
Original German edition 1999

© 1999 The Automobile Association
English language edition worldwide

Published by AA Publishing (a trading name of Automobile Association Developments Limited, whose registered office is Norfolk House, Priestley Road, Basingstoke, Hampshire RG24 9NY.
Registered number 1878835).

Distributed in the United States and Canada by:
Fodor's Travel Publications, Inc.
201 East 50th Street
New York, NY 10022

All rights reserved. No part of this publication may be reproduced, stored in a retrieval system or transmitted in any form by any means – electronic, photocopying, recording or otherwise – unless the written permission of the publisher has been obtained

The name *Baedeker* is a registered trade mark

A CIP catalogue record of this book is available from the British Library

Licensed user:
Mairs Geographischer Verlag GmbH & Co.
Ostfildern-Kemnat bei Stuttgart

Printed in Italy by G. Canale & C. S.p.A Turin

ISBN 0 7495 2050 7